應天平

TIEN-PING YING

Programming in Ada

INTERNATIONAL COMPUTER SCIENCE SERIES

Cover A portrait of Ada, Countess of Lovelace, acknowledged to be the world's first programmer. Adapted and reproduced by permission of John Murray.

Programming in Ada

J G P BARNES (SPL International)

To Barbara

Foreword

In May 1979 came the eagerly awaited announcement by the United States High Order Language Working Group, that 'Green is Ada'.

We were all expecting it in our team and were thus not surprised, but the announcement was certainly an enormous pleasure for all of us. At that time we all considered the preliminary version of Ada to be perfect. It may sound strange, considering the amount of revision that was done in the next fifteen months leading to the July 1980 Ada definition. But there is an easy explanation. In order to design anything you must believe in what you design, you must be continually examining the interweaving of all the features. Certainly, many decisions are the result of compromises between conflicting goals, but after rehearsing time and time again the arguments leading to these compromises you end up by integrating them into the basic assumptions of your design. And so it is not surprising that the result should appear to be the perfect answer.

Clearly, further progress can only come by a reappraisal of implicit assumptions underlying certain compromises. Here is the major contradiction in any design work. On the one hand, one can only reach an harmonious integration of several features by immersing oneself into the logic of the existing parts; it is only in this way that one can achieve a perfect combination. On the other hand, this perception of perfection, and the implied acceptance of certain unconscious assumptions, will prevent further progress.

In the design of Ada, John Barnes has certainly shown a unique ability to switch appropriately between acceptance and reappraisal. In May 1979, John was as proud as anyone else in the design team about our achievement. But, even by the early days of June, John was already reflective, giving a sharp, even severe look to the Ada tasking model as if he had had nothing to do with its design. He authored the first Language study note, of a series of two hundred, called 'Problems with tasking'. The note outlined ten major problems perceived in the preliminary Ada tasking facilities. These problems occupied our team for several months in the Ada revision, and satisfactory solutions could then be given to these ten issues in the final Ada version. In my own case it undoubtedly took me much more time to become objective about preliminary Ada and I certainly was initially upset by John's sacrilege. But with time I have learned to value enormously this kind of interaction with John.

Programming in Ada is thus written by one of the key members of the Ada language design team, by someone who understands all facets of the design of the language, both in a constructive and in a critical manner. I am confident that – with humour as usual – John's enthusiasms and understanding of the spirit of the language will be passed on to readers of this book.

Versailles
May 1981

Jean D. Ichbiah

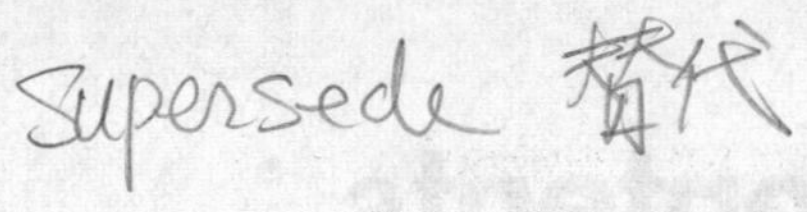

Preface

This book is about Ada, the new and powerful programming language originally developed on behalf of the US Department of Defense for use in embedded systems. Typical of such systems are those for process control, missile guidance or even the sequencing of a dishwasher. Historically these systems have been programmed in languages such as JOVIAL, CORAL 66 and RTL/2.

Based on Pascal, Ada is the first practical language to bring together important features such as data abstraction, multitasking, exception handling, encapsulation and generics. Although originally intended for embedded systems, it is a general purpose language and could, in time, supersede FORTRAN and even COBOL. The political and technical forces behind Ada suggest it will become an important language in the 1980s.

My purpose in writing this book is to present an overall description of Ada. Some knowledge of the principles of programming is assumed and an acquaintance with Pascal would be helpful but is not strictly necessary. The book is written in a tutorial style with numerous examples and exercises. I have also tried to explain the rationale behind many of the features of the language because this not only makes the discussion of more interest but also makes the facts easier to remember. Wherever possible I have tried to use examples which do not assume a particular application background; they are mostly drawn from parallels with normal human life or from mathematics which, after all, is the cornerstone of science and engineering. I hope the reader does not find the occasional attempt at humour misplaced; learning a programming language can be dull and any means of easing the burden seems worthwhile.

I would like to take this opportunity to thank those who directly or indirectly have helped me to write this book. First, I must acknowledge the US Department of Defense for permission to use material from the Ada Language Reference Manual. Then, I must acknowledge Jean Ichbiah and Robert Firth with whom I have had the pleasure of giving Ada courses in various parts of the world. These courses not only helped me to gain a useful perspective of the language as a whole but also provided the origins of some of the examples. Next, I must thank Andrew McGettrick for a great number of useful comments on the original draft and for spurring me on to completion with many helpful suggestions. I must also thank my colleagues on the UK Ada Study for their valued comments. Finally, I am deeply grateful to my wife for her untiring efforts in typing the manuscript; without her assistance the labour would have been much prolonged.

Reading
April 1981

J. G. P. Barnes

Contents

Foreword v

Preface vii

Chapter 1 : Introduction 1
- 1.1 History 1
- 1.2 Technical background 3
- 1.3 Structure and objectives of this book 5
- 1.4 References 6

Chapter 2 : Ada Concepts 7
- 2.1 Key goals 7
- 2.2 Overview 8
- 2.3 Errors 12
- 2.4 Input-output 13
- 2.5 Terminology 13

Chapter 3 : Lexical Style 15
- 3.1 Syntax notation 15
- 3.2 Lexical units 16
- 3.3 Identifiers 17
- 3.4 Numbers 18
- 3.5 Comments 20

Chapter 4 : Scalar Types 22
- 4.1 Object declarations and assignments 22
- 4.2 Blocks and scopes 24
- 4.3 Types 26
- 4.4 Subtypes 28
- 4.5 Simple numeric types 29
- 4.6 Enumeration types 34
- 4.7 The Boolean type 37
- 4.8 Type classification 40
- 4.9 Expression summary 42

Chapter 5 : Control Structures 47
- 5.1 If statements 47
- 5.2 Case statements 51
- 5.3 Loop statements 55
- 5.4 Goto statements and labels 60
- 5.5 Statement classification 61

Chapter 6 : Composite Types 63
6.1 Arrays 63
6.2 Array types 67
6.3 Characters and strings 74
6.4 One dimensional array operations 77
6.5 Records 82

Chapter 7 : Subprograms 87
7.1 Functions 87
7.2 Operators 93
7.3 Procedures 95
7.4 Named and default parameters 99
7.5 Overloading 101
7.6 Declarations, scopes and visibility 102

Chapter 8 : Overall Structure 106
8.1 Packages 106
8.2 Library units 110
8.3 Subunits 113
8.4 Scope and visibility 114
8.5 Renaming 116

Chapter 9 : Private Types 119
9.1 Normal private types 119
9.2 Limited private types 123
9.3 Resource management 126

Chapter 10 : Exceptions 131
10.1 Handling exceptions 131
10.2 Declaring and raising exceptions 134
10.3 Scope of exceptions 138

Chapter 11 : Advanced Types 143
11.1 Discriminated record types 143
11.2 Variant parts 150
11.3 Access types 154
11.4 Access types and private types 161
11.5 Access types and constraints 164
11.6 Derived types 169

Chapter 12 : Numeric Types 176
12.1 Integer types 176
12.2 Real types 180
12.3 Floating point types 182
12.4 Fixed point types 186

Chapter 13 : Generics 189
13.1 Declarations and instantiations 189
13.2 Type parameters 193
13.3 Subprogram parameters 197

Chapter 14 : Tasking 201
- 14.1 Parallelism 201
- 14.2 The rendezvous 203
- 14.3 Timing and scheduling 207
- 14.4 Select statements 211
- 14.5 Task types 222
- 14.6 Termination and exceptions 227
- 14.7 Resource scheduling 233
- 14.8 Comparison with packages 236

Chapter 15 : External Interfaces 240
- 15.1 Input and output 240
- 15.2 Text input-output 243
- 15.3 Interrupts 249
- 15.4 Representation specifications 249
- 15.5 Implementation considerations 251
- 15.6 Unchecked programming 252
- 15.7 Other languages 254

Chapter 16 : Finale 255
- 16.1 Names and expressions 255
- 16.2 Type equivalence 259
- 16.3 Structure summary 261
- 16.4 Portability 263
- 16.5 Program design 265

Appendix 1 : Reserved Words, Attributes and Pragmas 273
- A1.1 Reserved words 273
- A1.2 Predefined attributes 275
- A1.3 Predefined pragmas 279

Appendix 2 : Predefined Language Environment 280

Appendix 3 : Glossary 284

Appendix 4 : Syntax 288
- A4.1 Syntax rules 288
- A4.2 Syntax index 297

Answers to Exercises 301

Index 336

1 Introduction

Ada is a high level programming language originally sponsored by the US Department of Defense for use in the so-called embedded system application area. (An embedded system is one in which the computer is an integral part of a larger system such as a chemical plant, missile or dishwasher.) In this introductory chapter we briefly trace the development of Ada, its place in the overall language scene and the general structure of the remainder of this book.

1.1 History

The story of Ada goes back to about 1974 when the United States Department of Defense realised that it was spending far too much on software. It carried out a detailed analysis of how its costs were distributed over the various application areas and discovered that over half of them were directly attributed to embedded systems.

Further analysis was directed towards the programming languages in use in the various areas. It was discovered that COBOL was the universal standard for data processing and FORTRAN was a similar standard for scientific and engineering computation. Although these languages were not modern, the fact that they were uniformly applied in their respective areas meant that unnecessary and expensive duplication was avoided.

The situation with regard to embedded systems was however quite different. The number of languages in use was enormous. Not only did each of the three Armed Services have their own favourite high level languages, but they also used many assembly languages as well. Moreover, the high level languages had spawned variants. It seemed that successive contracts had encouraged the development of special versions aimed at different applications. The net result was that a lot of money was being spent on an unnecessary number of compilers. There were also all the additional costs of training and maintenance associated with a lack of standardisation.

It was therefore realised that standardisation had to be established in the embedded system area if the costs were to be contained. The ultimate goal was, of course, a single language. In the short term a list of interim approved languages was introduced. This consisted of CMS-2Y, CMS-2M, SPL/1, TACPOL, JOVIAL J3, JOVIAL J73 and of course COBOL and FORTRAN for the other areas.

The first step in moving towards the development of a single standard was the writing of a document outlining the requirements. The first version was known as Strawman and was published in early 1975. After receiving comments from various sources it was refined and became Woodenman. A further iteration produced Tinman in June 1976. This was quite a specific document and identified the functionality required of the language.

At this stage many existing languages were evaluated against Tinman partly to see whether one of them could be used as the ultimate standard and partly to invoke detailed evaluation of the requirements themselves. As one might expect, none of the existing languages proved satisfactory; on the other hand the general impression was gained that a single language based on state-of-the-art concepts could be developed to meet the requirements.

The evaluation classified the existing languages into three categories which can be paraphrased as

'not appropriate' — These languages were obsolete or addressed the wrong area and were not to be considered further. This category included FORTRAN and CORAL 66.

'not inappropriate' — These languages were also unsatisfactory as they stood but had some interesting features which could be looked at for inspiration. This category included RTL/2 and LIS.

'recommended bases' — These were the three languages Pascal, PL/I and Algol 68 and were seen as possible starting points for the design of the final language.

At this point the requirements document was revised and reorganised to give Ironman. Proposals were then invited from contractors to design a new language starting from one of the recommended bases. Seventeen proposals were received and four were chosen to go ahead in parallel and in competition. The four contractors with their colour codings were CII Honeywell Bull (Green), Intermetrics (Red), Softech (Blue) and SRI International (Yellow). The colour codings were introduced so that the resulting initial designs could be compared anonymously and hopefully therefore without bias.

The initial designs were delivered in early 1978 and many groups all over the world considered their relative merit. It was concluded that the Green and Red designs were significantly better than Blue and Yellow and so the latter were eliminated.

The development then entered its second phase and the two remaining contractors were given a further year in which to refine their designs. The requirements were also revised in the light of feedback from the initial designs and became the final document Steelman.[1]

The final choice of language was made in May 1979 when the Green language developed at CII Honeywell Bull by an international team led by Jean Ichbiah was declared the winner.

The DoD then announced that the new language would be known as Ada in honour of Augusta Ada Byron, Countess of Lovelace (1816–1851). Ada, the daughter of Lord Byron was the assistant and patron of Charles Babbage and worked on his mechanical analytical engine. In a very real sense she was therefore the world's first programmer.

The development of Ada then entered a third phase. The purpose of this was to expose the language to a significant cross section of eventual users in order to allow them to comment on its suitability for their needs. Various courses were given in the USA and Europe and many teams then settled down to carry out their evaluations. Some 80 general reports were written and presented at a conference in Boston in October 1979. The general conclusion was that Ada was good but a few areas needed further refinement. In addition nearly a thousand shorter technical language issue reports were received. After considering all these reports the preliminary Ada design was revised and this resulted in the publication in July 1980 of the Ada language which is the subject of this book. A reprint of the Language Reference Manual (LRM) in November 1980 removed various typographical errors. It is this edition that we will refer to from time to time.[2]

However, it should not be thought that Ada is just another programming language. It was also recognised that the language is just one component, although an important one, of the toolkit that every programmer should have available. It was therefore felt that additional benefit would be achieved if a uniform programming environment could also be established. And so, in parallel with the language design, a series of requirements documents for an Ada Programming Support Environment (APSE) were developed. These were entitled Sandman, Pebbleman and finally Stoneman.[3] These documents are less detailed than the corresponding language documents because the state-of-the-art in this area is still in its infancy. Nevertheless, it is hoped that the exercise will prevent unnecessary diversification and result in the development of one or more high quality APSEs. But that is another story outside the scope of this book.

1.2 Technical background

The evolution of programming languages has apparently occurred in a rather *ad hoc* fashion but with hindsight it is now possible to see three major advances. Each advance seems to be associated with the introduction of a level of abstraction which removes unnecessary and harmful detail from the program.

The first advance occurred in the early 1950s with high level languages such as FORTRAN and Autocode which introduced 'expression abstraction'. It thus became possible to write statements such as

```
X=A+B(I)
```

so that the use of the machine registers to evaluate the expression was completely hidden from the programmer. In these early languages the expression abstraction was not perfect since there were somewhat arbitrary constraints on the complexity of expressions; subscripts had to take a particularly simple form for instance. Later languages such as Algol 60 removed such constraints and completed the abstraction.

The second advance concerned 'control abstraction'. The prime example was Algol 60 which took a remarkable step forward; no language since then has made such an impact on later developments. The point about control abstraction is that the flow of control is structured and individual control points do not have to be named or numbered. Thus we write

```
if X=Y then P:=Q else A:=B
```

and the compiler generates the gotos and labels which would have to be explicitly used in languages such as FORTRAN. The imperfection of early expression abstraction was repeated with control abstraction. In this case the obvious flaw was the horrid Algol 60 switch which has now been replaced by the case statement of languages such as Pascal. (The earlier case clause of Algol 68 had its own problems.)

The third advance which is now occurring is 'data abstraction'. This means separating the details of the representation of data from the abstract operations defined upon the data.

Most existing languages take a very simple view of data types. In all cases the data is directly described in numerical terms. Thus if the data to be manipulated is not really numerical (it could be traffic light colours) then some mapping of the abstract type must be made by the programmer into a numerical type (usually integer). This mapping is purely in the mind of the programmer and does not appear in the written program except perhaps as a comment. It is probably a consequence of this fact that software libraries have not emerged except in numerical analysis. Numerical algorithms, such as those for finding eigenvalues of a matrix, are directly concerned with manipulating numbers and so these languages, whose data values are numbers, have proved appropriate. The point is that the languages provide the correct abstract values in this case only. In other cases, libraries are not successful because there is unlikely to be agreement on the required mappings. Indeed different situations may best be served by different mappings and these mappings pervade the whole program. A change in mapping usually requires a complete rewrite of the program.

Pascal introduced a certain amount of data abstraction as instanced by the enumeration type. Enumeration types allow us to talk about the traffic light colours in their own terms without our having to know how they are represented in the computer. Moreover, they prevent us from making an important class of programming errors – accidently mixing traffic lights with other abstract types such as the names of fish. When all such types are described in the program as numerical types, such errors can occur.

Another form of data abstraction concerns visibility. It has long been recognised that the traditional block structure of Algol 60 is not adequate. For example, it is not possible in Algol 60 to write two procedures to operate on some common data and make the procedures accessible without also making the data directly accessible. Many languages have provided control of visibility through separate compilation; this technique is adequate for medium sized systems but since the separate compilation facility usually depends upon some external system, total control of visibility is not gained. The module of Modula is an example of an appropriate construction.

Another language which made an important contribution to the development of data abstraction is Simula 67 with its concept of class. Many other experimental languages too numerous to mention have also made detailed contributions.

Ada seems to be the first practical language to bring together the various categories of data abstraction. We are probably too close to the current scene to achieve a proper perspective. There are no doubt several imperfections in Ada data abstraction just as FORTRAN expression abstraction and Algol 60 control abstraction were imperfect. However, Ada is an important advance and offers the possibility of writing significant reusable software libraries for areas other than numerical analysis. It should therefore encourage the creation of a software components industry.

1.3 Structure and objectives of this book

Learning a programming language is a bit like learning to drive a car. Certain key things have to be learnt before any real progress is possible. Although we need not know how to use the windscreen washer, nevertheless we must at least be able to start the engine, engage gears, steer and brake. So it is with programming languages. We do not need to know all about Ada before we can write useful programs but quite a lot must be learnt. Moreover many virtues of Ada become apparent only when writing large programs just as many virtues of a Rolls Royce are not apparent if we only use it to drive to the local shop.

This book is not an introduction to programming but an overall description of programming in Ada. It is assumed that the reader will have a significant knowledge of programming in some high level language. A knowledge of Pascal would be helpful but is not strictly necessary.

Chapter 2 gives a brief overview of some Ada concepts and is designed to give the reader a feel of the style and objectives of Ada. The rest of the book is in a tutorial style and introduces topics in a fairly straightforward sequence. By Chapter 7 we will have covered the traditional facilities of small languages such as Pascal. The remaining chapters cover modern and exciting material associated with data abstraction: programming in the large and parallel processing.

Most sections contain exercises. It is important that the reader does most, if not all, of these since they are an integral part of the discussion and later sections often use the results of earlier exercises. Solutions to all the exercises will be found at the end of the book; it is hoped that these are correct although at the time of writing they have not been submitted to an Ada compiler.

Most chapters conclude with a short checklist of key points to be remembered. Although incomplete, these checklists should help to consolidate understanding. Furthermore the reader is encouraged to refer to the syntax in Appendix 4 which is organised to correspond to the order in which the topics are introduced.

This book covers all aspects of Ada but does not explore every pathological situation. Its purpose is to teach the reader the effect of and intended use of the features of Ada. In a few areas the discussion is incomplete; these are fixed point arithmetic, machine dependent programming and input-output. Fixed point arithmetic is a highly specialised topic and will not be necessary for most programmers. Machine dependent programming (as its name implies) is so dependent upon the particular implementation that only a brief overview seems appropriate. Input-output, although important, does not introduce new concepts but is rather a mass of detail; again a simple overview is presented. Further details of these areas can be found in the Language Reference Manual (LRM) which is referred to from time to time.

Various appendices are provided in order to make this book reasonably self-contained; they are mostly based upon material drawn from the Language Reference Manual. Access to the LRM, which is the official definition of Ada, is recommended but should not be absolutely essential.

Finally it should be noted that the LRM has been proposed as an International Standard. It is inevitable that a few minor changes will prove necessary during the course of the standardisation process. Indeed, since the publication of the LRM in July 1980 a few such changes have been identified; these have been incorporated into this book at the time of going to press (September 1981). The most important are that **others** is no longer allowed in record aggregates (p.83) and the RANGE attribute is merely a shorthand for the corresponding range and not a subtype (p.65). Both of these changes have proved necessary in order to resolve obscure ambiguities in pathological situations. Further minor changes will no doubt occur. A particularly vulnerable area is input-output and the packages described in Chapter 15, although strictly outside the language itself, are likely to be slightly modified in the light of experience. However, future changes are likely to be small and it is probably safe to conclude that they will not alter the general principles explained in this book or the detail as seen by the practical programmer.

1.4 References

1 *Department of Defense Requirements for High Order Computer Programming Languages* – "STEELMAN", Defense Advanced Research Projects Agency, Arlington, Virginia, June 1978.

2 *Reference Manual for the Ada Programming Language*, United States Department of Defense, Washington D.C., November 1980.

3 *Department of Defense Requirements for Ada Programming Support Environments* – "STONEMAN", Defense Advanced Research Projects Agency, Arlington, Virginia, February 1980.

Ada Concepts

In this chapter we present a very brief overview of some of the goals, concepts and features of Ada.

2.1 Key goals

Ada is a large language since it addresses many important issues relevant to the programming of practical systems in the real world. It is, for instance, much larger than Pascal which, unless extended in some way, is really only suitable for training purposes (for which it was designed) and for small personal programs. Some of the key issues in Ada are

- Readability – it is recognised that professional programs are read much more often than they are written. It is important therefore to avoid an over terse notation such as in APL which although allowing a program to be written down quickly, makes it almost impossible to be read except perhaps by the original author soon after it was written.
- Strong typing – this ensures that each object has a clearly defined set of values and prevents confusion between logically distinct concepts. As a consequence many errors are detected by the compiler which in other languages would have led to an executable but incorrect program.
- Programming in the large – mechanisms for encapsulation, separate compilation and library management are necessary for the writing of portable and maintainable programs of any size.
- Exception handling – it is a fact of life that programs of consequence are rarely correct. It is necessary to provide a means whereby a program can be constructed in a layered and partitioned way so that the consequences of errors in one part can be contained.
- Data abstraction – as mentioned earlier, extra portability and maintainability can be obtained if the details of the representation of data can be kept separate from the specifications of the logical operations on the data.
- Tasking – for many applications it is important that the program be conceived as a series of parallel activities rather than just as a single sequence of actions. Building appropriate facilities into a language rather than adding them via calls to an operating system gives better portability and reliability.
- Generic units – in many cases the logic of part of a program is independent of the types of the values being manipulated. A mechanism is therefore necessary for the creation of related pieces of program from a single template. This is particularly useful for the creation of libraries.

2.2 Overview

A complete Ada program is written as a series of units. The outermost layer of units will include a main program and possible additional library units which can be thought of as providing services to the main program.

The main program takes the form of a procedure of an appropriate name. The service library units can be other subprograms (procedures or functions) but they are more likely to be packages. A package is a group of related items which may be other entities as well as subprograms.

Suppose we wish to write a program to print out the square root of some number such as 2.5. We can expect various library units to be available to provide us with a means of computing square roots and producing output. Our job is merely to write a main program to use these services as we wish.

For the sake of argument we will suppose that the square root can be obtained by calling a function in our library whose name is SQRT. In addition we will suppose that our library includes a package called SIMPLE_IO containing various simple input-output facilities. These facilities might include procedures for reading numbers, printing numbers, printing strings of characters and so on.

Our program might look like

```
with SQRT, SIMPLE_IO;
procedure PRINT_ROOT is
   use SIMPLE_IO;
begin
   PUT(SQRT(2.5));
end PRINT_ROOT;
```

The program is written as a procedure called PRINT_ROOT preceded by a with clause giving the names of the library units which it wishes to use. The body of the procedure contains the single statement

```
PUT(SQRT(2.5));
```

which calls the procedure PUT in the package SIMPLE_IO with a parameter which in turn is the result of calling the function SQRT with the parameter 2.5.

Writing

```
use SIMPLE_IO;
```

gives us immediate access to the facilities in the package SIMPLE_IO. If we had omitted this use clause we would have had to write

```
SIMPLE_IO.PUT(SQRT(2.5));
```

in order to indicate where PUT was to be found.

We can make our program more useful by making it read in the number whose square root we require. It might then become

```
with SQRT, SIMPLE_IO;
procedure PRINT_ROOT is
    use SIMPLE_IO;
    X: FLOAT;
begin
    GET(X);
    PUT(SQRT(X));
end PRINT_ROOT;
```

The overall structure of the procedure is now clearer. Between **is** and **begin** we can write declarations and between **begin** and **end** we write statements. Broadly speaking declarations introduce the entities we wish to manipulate and statements indicate the sequential actions to be performed.

We have now introduced a variable X of type FLOAT which is a predefined language type. Values of this type are a set of certain floating point numbers and the declaration of X indicates that X can have values only from this set. In our example a value is assigned to X by calling the procedure GET which is also in our package SIMPLE_IO.

Some small scale details should be noted. The various statements and declarations all terminate with a semicolon; this is unlike some other languages such as Algol and Pascal where semicolons are separators rather than terminators. The program contains various identifiers such as **procedure**, PUT and X. These fall into two categories. A few (62 in fact) such as **procedure** and **is** are used to indicate the structure of the program; they are reserved and can be used for no other purpose. All others, such as PUT and X, can be used for whatever purpose we desire. Some of these, notably FLOAT in our example, have a predefined meaning but we can nevertheless reuse them if we so wish although it might be confusing to do so. For clarity in this book we use lower case bold letters for the reserved identifiers and upper case letters for the others. This is purely a notational convenience; the language rules do not distinguish the two cases except when we consider the manipulation of characters themselves. Note also how the underscore character is used to break up long identifiers into meaningful parts.

Finally observe that the name of the procedure, PRINT_ROOT, is repeated between the final **end** and the terminating semicolon. This is optional but is recommended in order to clarify the overall structure although this is obvious in a small example such as this.

Our program is still very simple; it might be more useful to enable it to cater for a whole series of numbers and print out each answer on a separate line. We could stop the program somewhat arbitrarily by giving it a value of zero.

```
with SQRT, SIMPLE_IO;
procedure PRINT_ROOTS is
    use SIMPLE_IO;
    X: FLOAT;
begin
    PUT("Roots of various numbers");
    NEW_LINE(2);
    loop
        GET(X);
```

```
            exit when X = 0.0;
            PUT("Root of ");
            PUT(X);
            PUT(" is ");
            if X < 0.0 then
                PUT("not calculable");
            else
                PUT(SQRT(X));
            end if;
            NEW_LINE;
        end loop;
        NEW_LINE;
        PUT("Program finished");
        NEW_LINE;
    end PRINT_ROOTS;
```

The output has been enhanced by the calls of further procedures NEW_LINE and PUT in the package SIMPLE_IO. A call of NEW_LINE will output the number of new lines specified by the parameter; the procedure NEW_LINE has been written in such a way that if no parameter is supplied then a default value of one is assumed. There are also calls of PUT with a string as argument. This is in fact a different procedure from the one which prints the number X. The compiler knows which is which because of the different types of parameters. Having more than one procedure with the same name is known as overloading. Note also the form of the string; this is a situation where the case of the letters does matter.

Various new control structures are also introduced. The statements between **loop** and **end loop** are repeated until the condition X = 0.0 in the **exit** statement is found to be true; when this is so the loop is finished and we immediately carry on after **end loop**. We also check that X is not negative; if it is we output the message 'not calculable' rather than attempting to call SQRT. This is done by the if statement; if the condition between **if** and **then** is true, then the statements between **then** and **else** are executed, otherwise those between **else** and **end if** are executed.

The general bracketing structure should be observed; **loop** is matched by **end loop** and **if** by **end if**. All the control structures of Ada have this closed form rather than the open form of Pascal which can lead to poorly structured and incorrect programs.

We might well ask what would have happened if we had not tested for a negative value of X and consequently called SQRT with a negative argument. Assuming that SQRT has itself been written in an appropriate manner then it clearly cannot deliver a value to be used as the parameter of PUT. Instead an exception will be raised. The raising of an exception indicates that something unusual has happened and the normal sequence of execution is broken. In our case the exception might be NUMERIC_ERROR. If we did nothing to cope with this possibility then our program would be terminated and no doubt the Ada Programming Support Environment (APSE) will give us a rude message saying that our program has failed and why. We can, however, look out for an exception and take remedial action if it occurs. In fact we could replace our conditional statement by

```
begin
    PUT(SQRT(X));
exception
    when NUMERIC_ERROR =>
        PUT("not calculable");
end;
```

We will now consider in outline the possible general form of the function SQRT and the package SIMPLE_IO that we have been using.

The function SQRT will have a structure similar to that of our main program; the major difference will be the existence of parameters

```
function SQRT(F: FLOAT) return FLOAT is
    R: FLOAT;
begin
    -- compute value of SQRT(F) in R
    return R;
end SQRT;
```

We see here the description of the formal parameters (in this case only one) and the type of the result. The details of the calculation are represented by the comment which starts with a double hyphen. The return statement is the means by which the result of the function is indicated. Note the distinction between a function which returns a result and is called as part of an expression and a procedure which does not have a result and is called as a single statement.

The package SIMPLE_IO will be in two parts, the specification which describes its interface to the outside world and the body which contains the details of how it is implemented. If it just contained the procedures that we have used, its specification might be

```
package SIMPLE_IO is
    procedure GET(F: out FLOAT);
    procedure PUT(F: in FLOAT);
    procedure PUT(S: in STRING);
    procedure NEW_LINE(N: in INTEGER:=1);
end SIMPLE_IO;
```

The parameter of GET is an **out** parameter because the effect of calling GET as in

```
GET(X);
```

is to transmit a value out from the procedure to the actual parameter X. The other parameters are all **in** parameters because the value goes in to the procedures.

Only part of the procedures occurs in the package specification; this part is known as the procedure specification and just gives enough information to enable the procedures to be called.

We see also the two overloaded specifications of PUT, one with a parameter of type FLOAT and the other with a parameter of type STRING. Finally, note how the default value of 1 for the parameter of NEW_LINE is indicated.

The package body for SIMPLE_IO will contain the full procedure bodies plus any other supporting material needed for their implementation and which is naturally hidden from the outside user. In vague outline it might look like

```
with INPUT_OUTPUT;
package body SIMPLE_IO is
    ...
    procedure GET(F: out FLOAT) is
        ...
    begin
        ...
    end GET;
    --other procedures similarly
end SIMPLE_IO;
```

The with clause shows that the implementation of the procedures in SIMPLE_IO uses the more general package INPUT_OUTPUT. It should also be noticed how the full body of GET repeats the procedure specification which was given in the corresponding package specification. (The procedure specification is the bit up to but not including **is**.)

The example in this section has briefly revealed some of the overall structure and control statements of Ada. Details of data types will be discussed in due course. One purpose of this section has been to stress that the idea of packages is one of the most important concepts in Ada. A program should be conceived as a number of components which provide services to and receive services from each other. In the next few chapters we will of necessity be dealing with the small scale features of Ada but in doing so we should not lose sight of the overall structure which we will return to in Chapter 8.

Perhaps this is an appropriate point to mention the special package STANDARD. This is a package which exists in every implementation and contains the declarations of all the predefined identifiers such as FLOAT and NUMERIC_ERROR. We can assume access to STANDARD automatically and do not have to give its name in a with clause. It is discussed in detail in Appendix 2.

Exercise 2.2

1 In practice it is likely that the function SQRT will not be in the library on its own but in a package along with other mathematical functions. Suppose this package has the identifier SIMPLE_MATHS and other functions are LOG, EXP, SIN and COS. By analogy with the specification of SIMPLE_IO, write the specification of such a package. How would our program PRINT_ROOTS need to be changed?

2.3 Errors

An Ada program may be incorrect for various reasons. Three categories are recognised according to how they are detected.

Some errors will be detected by the compiler – these will include simple punctuation mistakes such as leaving out a semicolon or attempting to violate the type rules such as mixing up colours and fish. In these cases the program will not be executed.

Other errors are detected when the program is executed. An attempt to find the square root of a negative number or divide by zero are examples of such errors. In these cases an exception is raised as we saw in the last section and we have an opportunity to recover from the situation.

Finally there are certain situations where the program breaks the language rules but there is no simple way in which this violation can be detected. For example a program should not depend on the order in which parameters of a procedure call are evaluated. If it does then the behaviour may depend upon the implementation. Such a program is said to be erroneous. Care must be taken to avoid writing erroneous programs; in practice if we avoid clever tricks then all will be well.

2.4 Input-output

The Ada language is defined in such a way that all input and ouput is performed in terms of other language features. There are no special intrinsic features just for input and output. In fact input-output is just a service required by a program and so is provided by one or more Ada packages. This approach runs the attendant risk that different implementations will provide different packages and program portability will be compromised. In order to avoid this, the Language Reference Manual describes certain standard packages that can be expected to be available. Other, more elaborate, packages may be appropriate to special circumstances and the language does not prevent this. Indeed very simple packages such as our purely illustrative SIMPLE_IO may also be appropriate. Further consideration of input and output is deferred until Chapter 15 when we discuss interfaces between our program and the outside world in general.

2.5 Terminology

Every subject has its own terminology or jargon and Ada is no exception. (Indeed in Ada an exception is a kind of error as we have seen!) A glossary of terms will be found in Appendix 3.

Terminology will generally be introduced as required but before starting off with the detailed description of Ada it is convenient to mention a few concepts which will occur from time to time.

The term static refers to things that can be determined at compilation whereas dynamic refers to things determined during execution. Thus a static expression is one whose value can be determined by the compiler such as

```
2 + 3
```

and a static array is one whose bounds are known at compilation time.

Sometimes it is necessary to make a parenthetic remark to the compiler where the remark is not a part of the program as such but more a useful hint. This can be done by means of a construction known as a pragma. As an example we can indicate that only parts of our program are to be listed by writing

```
pragma LIST(ON);
```

and

```
pragma LIST(OFF);
```

at appropriate places. Generally a pragma can appear anywhere that a declaration or statement can appear, but sometimes there may be restrictions on the position of a particular pragma.

pragma

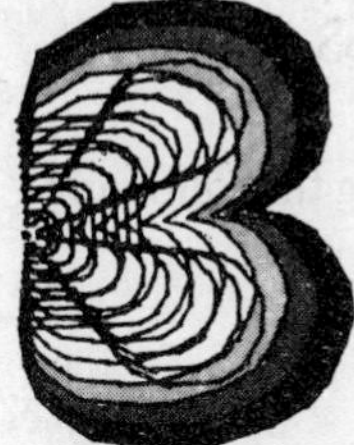

Lexical Style

In the previous chapter, we introduced some concepts of Ada and illustrated the general appearance of Ada programs with some simple examples. However, we have so far only talked around the subject. In this chapter we get down to serious detail.

Regrettably it seems best to start with some rather unexciting but essential material – the detailed construction of things such as identifiers and numbers which make up the text of a program. However, it is no good learning a human language without getting the spelling sorted out. And as far as programming languages are concerned compilers are usually very unforgiving regarding such corresponding and apparently trivial matters.

We also take the opportunity to introduce the notation used to describe the syntax of Ada language constructs. In general we will avoid using this syntax notation to introduce concepts but, in some cases, it is the easiest way to be precise. Moreover, if the reader wishes to consult the LRM then knowledge of the syntax notation is necessary. For completeness and easy reference the full syntax is given in Appendix 4.

3.1 Syntax notation

The syntax of Ada is described using a modified version of Backus-Naur Form or BNF. In this, syntactic categories are represented by lower case names; some of these contain embedded underscores to increase readability. A category is defined in terms of other categories by a sort of equation known as a production. Some categories are atomic and cannot be decomposed further – these are known as terminal symbols. A production consists of the name being defined followed by the special symbol ::= and its defining sequence.

Other symbols used are

- [ ] square brackets enclose optional items,
- { } braces enclose items which may be omitted, appear once or be repeated many times,
- | a vertical bar separates alternatives.

In some cases the name of a category is prefixed by a word in italics. In such cases the prefix is intended to convey some semantic information and can be treated as a form of comment as far as the context free syntax is concerned. Sometimes a production is presented in a form that shows the recommended layout.

3.2 Lexical units

An Ada program is written as a sequence of lines of text containing the following characters

- the alphabet A-Z
- the digits 0-9
- various other characters " # % & ' ( ) * + , – . / : ; < = > _ |
- the space character

The lower case alphabet may be used instead of or in addition to the upper case alphabet, but the two are generally considered the same. (The only exception is where the letters stand for themselves in character strings and character literals.)

It is possible to use certain other characters as alternatives to |, # and " if these are not available. We will not bother with the alternatives and the extra rules associated with them but will stick to the normal characters in this book.

The LRM also prescribes various rules about how one proceeds from one line of text to the next. This need not concern us. We can just imagine that we type our Ada program as a series of lines using whatever mechanism the keyboard provides for starting a new line.

A line of Ada text can be thought of as a sequence of groups of characters known as lexical units. We have already met several forms of lexical units in Chapter 2. Consider for example

```
AGE := 43;    -- John's age
```

This consists of five such units

- the identifier AGE
- the compound symbol :=
- the number 43
- the single symbol ;
- the comment -- John's age

Other classes of lexical unit are strings and character literals; they are dealt with in Chapter 6.

Individual lexical units may not be split by spaces but otherwise spaces may be inserted freely in order to improve the appearance of the program. A most important example of this is the use of indentation to reveal the overall structure. Naturally enough a lexical unit must fit on one line.

Particular care should be taken that the following compound symbols do not contain spaces

=>	used in aggregates, cases etc.
..	for ranges
**	exponentiation
:=	assignment
/=	not equals

>= greater than or equals
<= less than or equals
<< label bracket
>> the other label bracket
<> the 'box' for arrays and generics

However, spaces may occur in strings and character literals where they stand for themselves and also in comments.

Note that adjacent identifiers and numbers must be separated from each other by spaces otherwise they would be confused. Thus we must write **end loop** rather than **endloop**.

3.3 Identifiers

We met identifiers in the simple examples in Chapter 2. As an example of the use of the syntax notation we now consider the following definition of an identifier.

identifier ::= letter{[underscore] letter_or_digit}
letter_or_digit ::= letter | digit
letter ::= upper_case_letter | lower_case_letter

This states that an identifier consists of a letter followed by zero, one or more instances of letter_or_digit optionally preceded by a single underscore. A letter_or_digit is, as its name implies, either a letter or a digit. Finally a letter is either an upper_case_letter or a lower_case_letter. As far as this example is concerned the categories underscore, digit, upper_case_letter and lower_case_letter are not decomposed further and so are considered to be terminal symbols.

In plain English this merely says that an identifier consists of a letter possibly followed by one or more letters or digits with embedded isolated underscores. Either case of letter can be used. What the syntax does not convey is that the meaning attributed to an identifier does not depend upon the case of the letters. In fact identifiers which differ only in the case of corresponding letters are considered to be the same. But, on the other hand, the underscore characters are considered to be significant.

Ada does not impose any limit on the number of characters in an identifier. Moreover all are significant. There may however be a practical limit since an identifier must fit onto a single line and an implementation is likely to impose some maximum line length. Programmers are encouraged to use meaningful names such as TIME_OF_DAY rather than cryptic meaningless names such as T. Long names may seem tedious when first writing a program but in the course of its lifetime a program is read much more often than it is written and clarity aids subsequent understanding both by the original author and by others who may be called upon to maintain the program. Of course, in short mathematical or abstract subprograms, identifiers such as X and Y may be appropriate.

Identifiers are used to name all the various entities in a program. However, some identifiers are reserved for special syntactic significance and may not be reused. We encountered several of these in Chapter 2 such as **if**, **procedure** and **end**. There are 62 reserved words; they are listed in Appendix 1. For readability they are printed in boldface in this book but that is not important. In program text they could, like all identifiers, be in either case or indeed in a mixture of cases – procedure, PROCEDURE and Procedure are all acceptable. Nevertheless some discipline aids understanding and a useful convention is to use lower case for the reserved words and upper case for all others. But this is a matter of taste.

There are minor exceptions regarding the reserved words **delta**, **digits** and **range**. As will be seen later they are also used as attributes DELTA, DIGITS and RANGE. However, when so used they are always preceded by a prime or single quote character and so there is no confusion.

Some identifiers such as INTEGER and TRUE have a predefined meaning from the package STANDARD. These are not reserved and can be reused although to do so is usually unwise since the program could become very confusing.

Exercise 3.3

1 Which of the following are not legal identifiers and why?

a) Ada	d) UMO164G	g) X_
b) fish_&_chips	e) TIME_LAG	h) tax rate
c) RATE-OF-FLOW	f) 77E2	i) goto

3.4 Numbers

Numbers (or numeric literals to use the proper jargon) take two forms according to whether they denote an integer (an exact whole number) or a real (an approximate and not usually whole number). The important distinguishing feature is that real literals always contain a decimal point whereas integer literals never do. Ada is strict on mixing up types. It is illegal to use an integer literal where the context demands a real literal and vice versa. Thus

```
AGE: INTEGER:=43.0;
```

and

```
WEIGHT: REAL:=150;
```

are both illegal. (We are using type REAL rather than FLOAT for reasons which will become clear later.)

The simplest form of integer literal is simply a sequence of decimal digits. If the number is very long it may be convenient to split it up into groups of digits by inserting isolated underscores thus

```
123_456_789
```

In contrast to identifiers such underscores are, of course, of no significance other than to make the number easier to read.

The simplest form of real literal is a sequence of decimal digits containing a decimal point. Note that there must be at least one digit on either side of the decimal point. Again, isolated underscores may be inserted to improve legibility provided they are not adjacent to the decimal point; thus

3.14159_26536

Unlike most languages both integer and real literals can have an exponent. This takes the form of the letter E (either case) followed by a signed or unsigned decimal integer. This exponent indicates the power of ten by which the preceding simple number is to be multiplied. The exponent cannot be negative in the case of an integer literal – otherwise it might not be a whole number.

Thus the real literal 98.4 could be written with an exponent in any of the following ways.

9.84E1 98.4e0 984.0e−1 0.984E+2

Note that 984e−1 would not be allowed.

Similarly, the integer literal 1900 could also be written as

19E2 190e+1 1900E+0

but not as 19000e−1.

The exponent may itself contain underscores if it consists of two or more digits but it is unlikely that the exponent would be so large as to make this necessary. However, the exponent may not itself contain an exponent!

A final facility is the ability to express a number in a base other than 10. This is done by enclosing the digits between # characters and preceding the result by the base.

Thus 2#111#

is an integer literal of value $4 + 2 + 1 = 7$.

Any base from 2 to 16 inclusive can be used and, of course, base 10 can always be expressed explicitly. For bases above 10 the letters A to F are used to represent the superdigits 10 to 15.

Thus 14#ABC#
equals $10 \times 14^2 + 11 \times 14 + 12 = 2126$

A based number can also have an exponent. But note carefully that the exponent gives the power of the base by which the simple number is to be multiplied and not a power of ten – unless, of course, the base happens to be ten. The exponent itself, like the base, is always expressed in normal decimal notation.

Thus 16#A#E2
equals $10 \times 16^2 = 2560$

and 2#11#E11
equals $3 \times 2^{11} = 6144$

A based number can be real. The distinguishing mark is again the point. (We can hardly say 'decimal point' if we are not using a decimal base! A better term is radix point.)

So 2#101.11#

equals $4 + 1 + \frac{1}{2} + \frac{1}{4} = 5.75$

and 7#3.0#e−1

equals $\frac{3}{7} = 0.\dot{4}2857\dot{1}$

The reader may have felt that the possible forms of based number are unduly elaborate. This is not really so. Based numbers are useful – especially for fixed point types since they enable the programmer to represent values in the form in which he thinks about them. Obviously bases 2, 8 and 16 will be the most useful. But the notation is applicable to any base and the compiler can compute to any base so why not?

Finally note that a numeric literal cannot be negative. A form such as −3 consists of a literal preceded by the unary minus operator.

Exercise 3.4

1 Which of the following are not legal literals and why? For those that are legal, state whether they are integer or real literals.

a) 38.6	e) 2#1011	i) 16#FfF#
b) .5	f) 2.71828_18285	j) 1_0#1_0#E1_0
c) 32e2	g) 12#ABC#	k) 27.4e_2
d) 32e−2	h) E+6	l) 2#11#e−1

2 What is the value of the following?

a) 16#E#E1	c) 16#F.FF#E+2
b) 2#11#E11	d) 2#1.1111_1111_111#E11

3 How many different ways can you express the following as a numeric literal?

a) the integer 41 b) the integer 150

(Forget underscores, distinction between E and e and optional + in an exponent.)

3.5 Comments

It is important to add appropriate comments to a program to aid its understanding by someone else or yourself at a later date. We met some comments in Chapter 2.

A comment in Ada is written as an arbitrary piece of text following two hyphens (or minus signs – the same thing). Thus

```
-- this is a comment
```

The comment extends to the end of the line. There is no facility in Ada to insert a comment into the middle of a line. Of course, the comment may be the only thing on the line or it may follow some other Ada text. A long comment that needs several lines is merely written as successive comments.

```
-- this comment is spread
-- over
-- several
-- lines.
```

It is important that the leading hyphens are adjacent and are not separated by spaces.

Exercise 3.5

1 How many lexical units are there in each of the following lines of text?

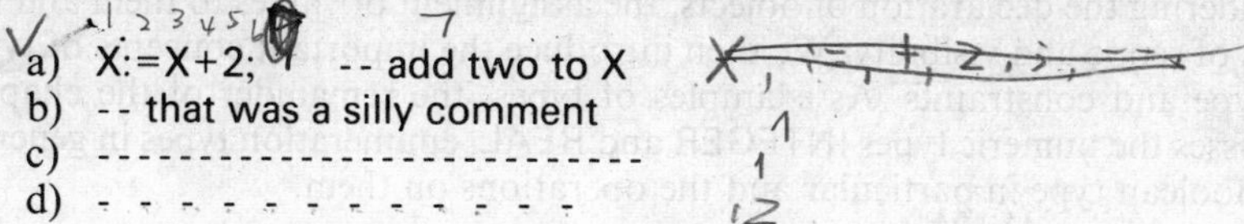

```
a) X:=X+2;   -- add two to X
b) -- that was a silly comment
c) ----------------------------
d) - - - - - - - - - - - - -
```

2 Distinguish

a) **delay** 2.0;
b) **delay**2.0;

Checklist 3

The case of a letter is immaterial in all contexts except strings and character literals.

Underscores are significant in identifiers but not in numeric literals.

Spaces are not allowed in lexical units, except in strings, character literals and comments.

The presence or absence of a point distinguishes real and integer literals.

An integer may not have a negative exponent.

Numeric literals cannot be signed.

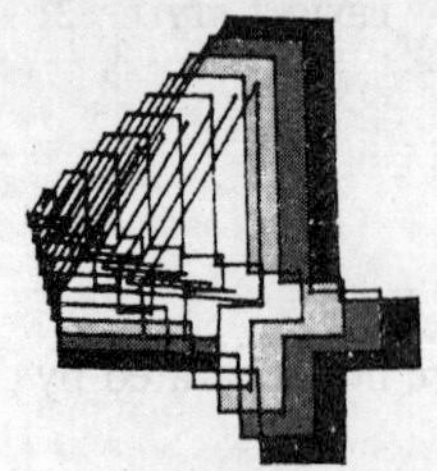

Scalar Types

This chapter lays the foundations for the small scale aspects of Ada. We start by considering the declaration of objects, the assignment of values to them and the ideas of scope and visibility. We then introduce the important concepts of type, subtype and constraints. As examples of types, the remainder of the chapter discusses the numeric types INTEGER and REAL, enumeration types in general, the Boolean type in particular and the operations on them.

4.1 Object declarations and assignments

Values can be stored in objects which are declared to be of a specific type. Objects are either variables, in which case their value may change (or vary) as the program executes, or they may be constants, in which case they keep their same initial value throughout their life.

A variable is introduced into the program by a declaration which consists of the name (that is, the identifier) of the variable followed by a colon and then the name of the type. This can then optionally be followed by the := symbol and an initial value. The declaration terminates with a semicolon. Thus we might write

```
I: INTEGER;
P: INTEGER:=38;
```

This introduces the variable I of type INTEGER but gives it no particular initial value and then the variable P and gives it the specific initial value of 38.

We can introduce several variables at the same time in one declaration by separating them by commas thus

```
I,J,K: INTEGER;
P,Q,R: INTEGER:=38;
```

In the second case all of P,Q and R are given the same initial value of 38.

If a variable is declared and not given an initial value then great care must be taken not to use the undefined value of the variable until one has been properly given to it. If a program does use the undefined value in an uninitialised variable, its behaviour will be unpredictable; the program is said to be erroneous. As mentioned in Chapter 2, this means that the program is strictly illegal but the compiler and run time system may not be able to tell us.

A common way to give a value to a variable is by using an assignment statement. In this, the identifier of the variable is followed by := and then some expression giving the new value. The statement terminates with a semicolon. Thus

```
I:=36;
```

and

```
P:=Q+R;
```

are both valid assignment statements and place new values in I and P thereby overwriting their previous values.

Note that := can be followed by any expression provided that it produces a value of the type of the variable being assigned to. We will discuss all the rules about expressions later but it suffices to say at this point that they can consist of variables and constants with operations such as + and brackets and so on just like an ordinary mathematical expression.

There is a lot of similarity between a declaration containing an initial value and an assignment statement. Both use := before the expression and the expression can be of arbitrary complexity.

An important difference, however, is that although several variables can be declared and given the same initial value together, it is not possible for an assignment statement to give the same value to several variables. This may seem odd but in practice the need to give the same value to several variables usually only arises with initial values anyway.

A constant is declared in a similar way to a variable by inserting the reserved word **constant** after the colon. Of course, a constant must normally be initialised in its declaration otherwise it would be useless. Why? (An exception is mentioned later.) An example might be

```
PI: constant REAL:=3.14159_26536;
```

In the case of numeric types, and only numeric types, it is possible to omit the type from the declaration of a constant thus

```
PI: constant :=3.14159_26536;
```

It is then technically known as a number declaration. The distinction between integer and real constants is made by the form of the initial value. In this case it is real because of the presence of the decimal point. It is usually good practice to omit the type when declaring numeric constants for reasons which will appear later. We will therefore do so in future examples. But note that the type cannot be omitted in numeric variable declarations even when an initial value is provided.

There is an important distinction between the allowed forms of initial values in constant declarations (with a type) and number declarations (without a type). In the former case the initial value may be any expression and is evaluated when the declaration is encountered at run time whereas in the latter case it must be of a special form which is evaluated at compilation time. Full details are deferred until Chapter 12

Exercise 4.1

1 Write a declaration of a real variable R giving it an initial value of one.

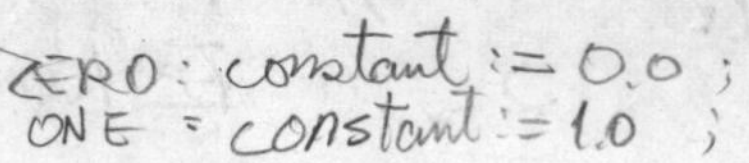

2 Write appropriate declarations of real constants ZERO and ONE.

3 What is wrong with the following declarations and statements?

a) **var** I: INTEGER;
b) G: **constant** :=981
c) P,Q: **constant** INTEGER;
d) P:=Q:=7;
e) MN: **constant** INTEGER:=M*N;
f) 2PI: **constant** :=2.0*PI;

4.2 Blocks and scopes

Ada carefully distinguishes between declarations which introduce new identifiers and statements which do not. It is clearly only sensible that the declarations which introduce new identifiers should precede the statements which manipulate them. Accordingly, declarations and statements occur in separate places in the program text. The simplest fragment of text which includes declarations and statements is a block.

A block commences with the reserved word **declare**, some declarations, **begin**, some statements and concludes with the reserved word **end** and the terminating semicolon. A trivial example is

```
declare
    I: INTEGER:=0;          -- declarations here
begin
    I:=I+1;                 -- statements here
end;
```

A block is itself an example of a statement and so one of the statements in its body could be another block. This textual nesting of blocks can continue indefinitely.

Since a block is a statement it can be executed like any other statement. When this happens the declarations in its declarative part (the bit between **declare** and **begin**) are elaborated in order and then the statements in the body (between **begin** and **end**) are executed in the usual way. Note the terminology: we elaborate declarations and execute statements. All that the elaboration of a declaration does is make the thing being declared come into existence and then evaluate and assign any initial value to it. When we come to the **end** of the block all the things which were declared in the block automatically cease to exist.

We can now see that the above simple example of a block is rather foolish; it introduces I, adds 1 to it but then loses it before use is made of the resulting value.

Another point to note is that the objects used in an initial value must, of course, exist. They could be declared in the same declarative part but the declarations must precede their use.
For example

```
declare
    I: INTEGER:=0;
    K: INTEGER:=I;
begin
```

is allowed, but

```
declare
    K: INTEGER:=I;
    I: INTEGER:=0;
begin
```

is generally not. (We will see in a moment that this could have a valid but different meaning.)

This idea of elaborating declarations in order is important: the jargon is 'linear elaboration of declarations'.

Like other block structured languages Ada also has the idea of hiding. Consider

```
declare
    I,J: INTEGER;
begin
    ...                             -- here I is the outer one
    declare
        I: INTEGER;
    begin
        ...                         -- here I is the inner one
    end;
    ...                             -- here I is the outer one
end;
```

In this, a variable I is declared in an outer block and then redeclared in an inner block. This redeclaration does not cause the outer I to cease to exist but merely makes it temporarily invisible. In the inner block I refers to the new I, but as soon as we leave the inner block, this new I ceases to exist and the outer one again becomes visible.

We distinguish the terms 'scope' and 'visibility'. The scope is the region of text where the identifier is potentially visible – we will now illustrate these terms but a fuller discussion has to be left until Chapter 8.

In the case of a block the scope of a variable (or constant) extends from the point where its name is introduced in its declaration until the end of the block. However, it is not visible in any inner block after the redeclaration of the same identifier. The regions of scope and visibility are illustrated by the following

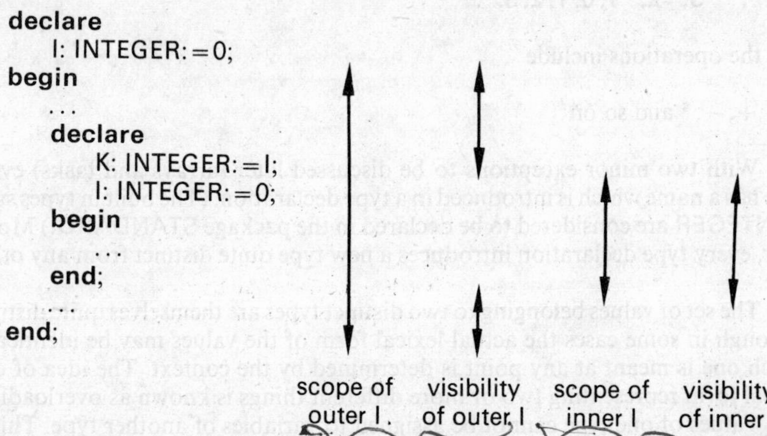
declare
I: INTEGER:=0;
begin
...
declare
K: INTEGER:=I;
I: INTEGER:=0;
begin
end;
end;
scope of outer I
visibility of outer I
scope of inner I
visibility of inner I

The initial value of K refers to the outer I because it precedes the introduction of the inner I.

Thus

```
K: INTEGER:=I;
I: INTEGER:=0;
```

may or may not be legal – it depends upon its environment.

Exercise 4.2

1 How many errors can you see in the following?

```
declare
    I: INTEGER:=7;
    J,K: INTEGER
begin
    J:=I+K;
    declare
        P: INTEGER=I;
        I, J: INTEGER;
    begin
        I:=P+Q;
        J:=P-Q;
        K:=I*J;
    end;
    PUT(K);    -- output value of K
end;
```

4.3 Types

'A type characterizes a set of values and a set of operations applicable to those values' (LRM 3.3).

In the case of the built in type INTEGER, the set of values is represented by

... −3, −2, −1, 0, 1, 2, 3, ...

and the operations include

+, −, * and so on

With two minor exceptions to be discussed later (arrays and tasks) every type has a name which is introduced in a type declaration. (The built in types such as INTEGER are considered to be declared in the package STANDARD.) Moreover, every type declaration introduces a new type quite distinct from any other type.

The set of values belonging to two distinct types are themselves quite distinct although in some cases the actual lexical form of the values may be identical – which one is meant at any point is determined by the context. The idea of one lexical form representing two or more different things is known as overloading.

Values of one type cannot be assigned to variables of another type. This is the fundamental rule of strong typing. It is an enormous aid to the rapid development of correct programs since it ensures that many errors are detected at compilation time.

A type declaration uses a somewhat different syntax to an object declaration in order to emphasise the conceptual difference. It consists of the reserved word **type**, the identifier to be associated with the type, the reserved word **is** and then the definition of the type followed by the terminating semicolon. We can imagine that the package STANDARD contains type declarations such as

```
type INTEGER is ...;
```

The type definition between **is** and ; gives in some way the set of values belonging to the type. As a concrete example consider the following

```
type COLOUR is (RED, AMBER, GREEN);
```

(This is an example of an enumeration type and will be dealt with in more detail in a later section in this chapter.)

This introduces a new type called COLOUR. Moreover, it states that there are only 3 values of this type and they are denoted by the identifiers RED, AMBER and GREEN.

Objects of this type can then be declared in the usual way

```
C: COLOUR;
```

An initial value can be supplied

```
C: COLOUR:=RED;
```

or a constant can be declared

```
DEFAULT: constant COLOUR:=RED;
```

We have stated that values of one type cannot be assigned to variables of another type. Therefore one cannot mix colours and integers and so

```
I: INTEGER;
C: COLOUR;
...
I:=C;
```

is illegal. In older languages it is often necessary to implement concepts such as enumeration types by more primitive types such as integers and give values such as 0,1 and 2 to variables named RED, AMBER and GREEN. Thus in Algol 60 one could write

```
integer RED, AMBER, GREEN;
RED:=0; AMBER:=1; GREEN:=2;
```

and then use RED, AMBER and GREEN as if they were literal values. Obviously the program would be easier to understand than if the code values 0,1 and 2 had been used directly. But on the other hand the compiler could not detect the accidental assignment of a notional colour to a variable which was, in the mind of the programmer, just an ordinary integer. In Ada, as we have seen, this is detected during compilation.

4.4 Subtypes

We now introduce subtypes and constraints. A subtype, as its name suggests, characterises a set of values which is just a subset of the values of some other type known as the base type. The subset is defined by means of a constraint. Constraints take various forms according to the category of the base type. As is usual with subsets, the subset may be the complete set. There is, however, no way of restricting the set of operations of the base type. The subtype takes all the operations; subsetting applies only to the values.

As an example suppose we wish to manipulate dates; we know that the day of the month must lie in the range 1 .. 31 so we declare a subtype thus

```
subtype DAY_NUMBER is INTEGER range 1 .. 31;
```

We can then declare variables and constants using the subtype identifier in exactly the same way as a type identifier

```
D: DAY_NUMBER;
```

We are then assured that the variable D can take only integer values from 1 to 31 inclusive. The compiler will insert run time checks if necessary to ensure that this is so; if a check fails then the CONSTRAINT_ERROR exception is raised.

It is important to realise that a subtype declaration does not introduce a new distinct type. An object such as D is of type INTEGER and so the following is perfectly legal from the syntactic point of view

```
D: DAY_NUMBER;
I: INTEGER;
...
D:=I;
```

Of course, on execution, the value of I may or may not lie in the range 1 .. 31. If it does, then all is well; if not then CONSTRAINT_ERROR will be raised. Assignment in the other direction

```
I:=D;
```

will, of course, always work.

It is not necessary to introduce a subtype explicitly in order to impose a constraint. We could equally have written

```
D: INTEGER range 1 .. 31;
```

Furthermore a subtype need not impose a constraint. It is perfectly legal to write

```
subtype DAY_NUMBER is INTEGER;
```

although in this instance it is not of much value.

A subtype (explicit or not) may be defined in terms of a previous subtype

```
subtype FEB_DAY is DAY_NUMBER range 1 .. 29;
```

Any additional constraint must of course satisfy existing constraints

```
DAY_NUMBER range 0 .. 10;
```

would be incorrect and cause CONSTRAINT_ERROR to be raised.

In conclusion then a subtype does not introduce a new type but is merely a shorthand for an existing type with an optional constraint.

The sensible use of subtypes has two advantages. It can ensure that programming errors are detected earlier by preventing variables from being assigned inappropriate values. It can also increase the execution efficiency of a program. This particularly applies to array subscripts as we shall see later.

We have now introduced the basic concepts of types and subtypes. The remaining sections of this chapter illustrate these concepts further by considering in more detail the properties of the simple types of Ada.

4.5 Simple numeric types

Perhaps surprisingly a full description of the numeric types of Ada is deferred until much later in this book. The problems of numerical analysis (error estimates and so on) are complex and Ada is correspondingly complex in this area so that it can cope in a reasonably complete way with the needs of the numerical specialist. For our immediate purposes such complexity can be ignored. Accordingly, in this section, we merely consolidate a simple understanding of the two numeric types INTEGER and REAL which we have been using as background for elementary examples. For the everyday programmer these two numeric types will probably suffice.

First a confession. The type INTEGER is a genuine built-in Ada type. But the type REAL is not. It has to be declared somewhere in terms of one of the built-in floating point types. The reason for supposing that this has been done concerns portability and will be discussed when the truth about numeric types is revealed in more detail. For the moment, however, we will suppose that REAL is the floating point type. (The author is not deceiving you but in fact encouraging good Ada programming practice.)

As we have seen, a constraint may be imposed on the type INTEGER by using the reserved word **range**. This is then followed by two expressions separated by two dots which, of course, must produce values of integer type. These expressions need not be literal constants. One could have

```
P: INTEGER range 1 .. I+J;
```

A range can be null as would happen in the above case if I+J turned out to be zero. Null ranges may seem pretty useless but they often automatically occur in limiting cases, and to exclude them would mean taking special action in such cases.

The minimum value of the type INTEGER is given by INTEGER'FIRST and the maximum value by INTEGER'LAST. These are our first examples of attributes. Ada contains various attributes denoted by a single quote followed by an identifier.

The value of INTEGER'FIRST will depend on the implementation but will always be negative. On a twos complement machine it will be -INTEGER'LAST-1 whereas on a ones complement machine it will be -INTEGER'LAST. So on a typical 16 bit twos complement implementation we will have

```
INTEGER'FIRST = -32768
INTEGER'LAST  = +32767
```

Of course, we should always write INTEGER'LAST rather than +32767 if that is what we logically want. Otherwise program portability could suffer.

A useful subtype is

```
subtype NATURAL is INTEGER range 1 .. INTEGER'LAST;
```

This is so useful that it is declared for us in the package STANDARD.

The attributes FIRST and LAST also apply to subtypes so

```
NATURAL'FIRST = 1
NATURAL'LAST = INTEGER'LAST
```

We turn now to a brief consideration of the type REAL. It is possible to apply constraints to the type REAL in order to reduce the range and precision but this takes us into the detail which has been deferred until later. There are also attributes REAL'FIRST and REAL'LAST. It is not really necessary to say any more at this point.

The other predefined operations that can be performed on the types INTEGER and REAL are much as one would expect in a modern programming language. They are summarised below.

+, − These are either unary operators (that is, taking a single operand) or binary operators taking two operands.

In the case of a unary operator, the operand can be either integer or real; the result will be of the same type. Unary + effectively does nothing. Unary − changes the sign.

In the case of a binary operator, both operands must be integer or both operands must be real; the result will be of the type of the operands. Normal addition or subtraction is performed.

* Multiplication; both operands must be integer or both operands must be real; again the result is of the same type.

/ Division; both operands must be integer or both operands must be real; again the result is of the same type. Integer division truncates towards zero.

rem Remainder; in this case both operands must be integer and the result is an integer. It is the remainder on division.

mod Modulo; again both operands must be integer and the result is an integer. This is the mathematical modulo operation.

ABS Absolute value; ABS is a built-in function and the single operand which may be integer or real is placed in brackets after the function name. The result is again of the same type and is the absolute value. That is, if the operand is positive, the result is the same but if it is negative, the result is the corresponding positive value.

** Exponentiation; this raises the first operand to the power of the second. If the first operand is of integer type, the second must be a positive integer or zero. If the first operand is of real type, the second can be any integer. The result is of the same type as the first operand.

In addition, we can perform the operations =, /=, <, <=, >, and >= in order to return a Boolean result TRUE or FALSE. Again both operands must be of the same type. Note the form of the not equals operator /=.

Although the above operations are mostly straightforward a few points are worth noting.

It is a general rule that mixed mode arithmetic is not allowed. One cannot, for example, add an integer value to a real value; both must be of the same type. A change of type from INTEGER to REAL or vice versa can be done by using the desired type name (or indeed subtype name) followed by the expression to be converted in brackets.

So given

```
I: INTEGER:=3;
R: REAL:=5.6;
```

we cannot write

```
I+R
```

but must write

```
REAL(I)+R
```

which uses real addition to give the real value 8.6, or

```
I+INTEGER(R)
```

which uses integer addition to give the integer value 9.

Conversion from real to integer always rounds rather than truncates, thus

```
1.4 becomes 1
1.6 becomes 2
```

There is a subtle distinction between **rem** and **mod**. The **rem** operation produces the remainder corresponding to the integer division operation /. Integer division truncates towards zero; this means that the absolute value of the result is always the same as that obtained by dividing the absolute values of the operands. So

```
 7/3  =  2
-7/3  = -2
 7/-3 = -2
-7/-3 =  2
```

and the corresponding remainders are

```
 7 rem  3 =  1
-7 rem  3 = -1
 7 rem -3 =  1
-7 rem -3 = -1
```

The remainder and quotient are always related by

```
(I/J)*J + I rem J = I
```

and it will also be noted that the sign of the remainder is always equal to the sign of the first operand I (the dividend).

However, **rem** is not always satisfactory. If we plot the values of I **rem** J for a fixed value of J (say 5) for both positive and negative values of I we get the pattern shown in Fig. 4.1.

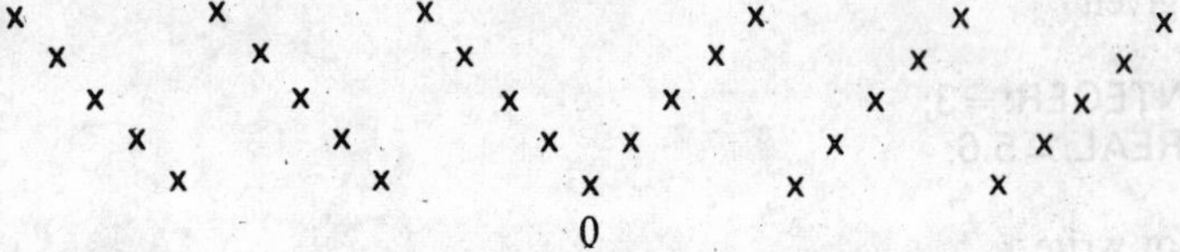

Fig. 4.1 Behaviour of I **rem** 5 around zero

As we can see the pattern is symmetric about zero and consequently changes its incremental behaviour as we pass through zero.

The **mod** operation, on the other hand does have uniform incremental behaviour as shown in Fig. 4.2.

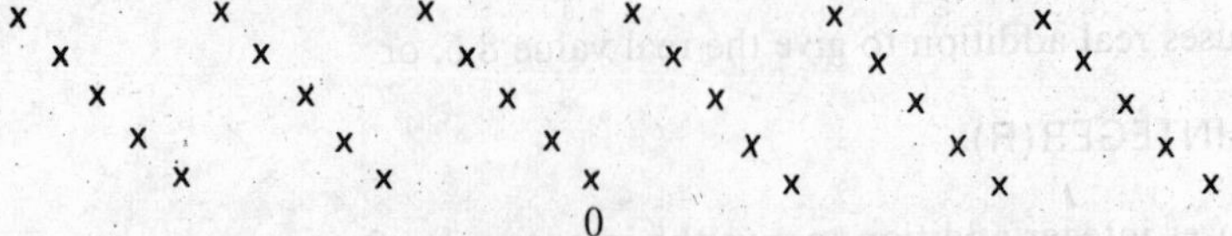

Fig. 4.2 Behaviour of I **mod** 5 around zero

The **mod** operation enables us to do normal modulo arithmetic. For example

```
(A+B) mod n = (A mod n + B mod n) mod n
```

for all values of A and B both positive and negative. For positive n, A **mod** n is always in the range 0 .. n−1; for negative n, A **mod** n is always in the range n+1 .. 0. Of course, modulo arithmetic is only usually performed with a positive value for n. But the **mod** operator gives consistent and sensible behaviour for negative values of n also.

We can look upon **mod** as giving the remainder corresponding to division with truncation towards minus infinity. So

```
 7 mod  3 =  1
-7 mod  3 =  2
 7 mod -3 = -2
-7 mod -3 = -1
```

In the case of **mod** the sign of the result is always equal to the sign of the second operand whereas with **rem** it is the sign of the first operand.

The reader may have felt that this discussion has been somewhat protracted. In summary, it is perhaps worth saying that integer division with negative operands is rare. The operators **rem** and **mod** only differ when one or both operands is negative. It will be found that in such cases it is almost always **mod** that is wanted.

Finally some notes on the exponentiation operator **. For a positive second operand, the operation corresponds to repeated multiplication. So

```
  3**4 = 3*3*3*3 = 81
3.0**4 = 3.0*3.0*3.0*3.0 = 81.0
```

The second operand can be 0 and, of course, the result is then always the value one

```
  3**0 = 1
3.0**0 = 1.0
  0**0 = 1
0.0**0 = 1.0
```

The second operand cannot be negative if the first operand is an integer, as the result might not be a whole number. In fact, the exception CONSTRAINT_ERROR would be raised in such a case. But it is allowed for a real first operand and produces the corresponding reciprocal

```
3.0**(-4) = 1.0/81.0 = 0.0123456780123...
```

We conclude this section with a brief discussion on combining operators in an expression. As is usual the operators have different precedence levels and the natural precedence can be over-ruled by the use of brackets. Operators of the same precedence are applied in order from left to right. A subexpression in brackets obviously has to be evaluated before it can be used. But note that the order of evaluation of the two operands of a binary operator is not specified. The precedence levels of the operators we have met so far are shown below in increasing order of precedence

= /= < <= > >=
+ − (binary)
+ − (unary)
* / **mod rem**
**

Thus

```
A/B*C        means   (A/B)*C
A+B*C+D      means   A+(B*C)+D
A*B+C*D      means   (A*B)+(C*D)
A*B**C       means   A*(B**C)
```

The precedence of unary minus needs care

```
-A**B    means   -(A**B)    rather than    (-A)**B
```

as in Algol 68.

Also

```
A**-B    and    A*-B
```

are illegal. Brackets are necessary.

Exercise 4.5

1 Evaluate the expressions below given the following

```
I: INTEGER:=7;
J: INTEGER:=-5;
K: INTEGER:=3;
```

a) I*J*K
b) I/J*K
c) I/J/K
d) J + 2 **mod** I
e) J + 2 **rem** I
f) K**K**K
g) −J **mod** 3
h) −J **rem** 3

2 Rewrite the following mathematical expressions in Ada. Use suitable identifiers of appropriate type.

a) $b^2 - 4ac$ – discriminant of quadratic
b) $\frac{4}{3}\pi r^3$ – volume of sphere
c) $\dfrac{p\pi \quad a^4}{8\,l\eta}$ – viscous flowrate through tube

4.6 Enumeration types

Here are some examples of declarations of enumeration types starting with COLOUR which we introduced when discussing types in general.

```
type COLOUR is (RED, AMBER, GREEN);
type DAY is (MON, TUE, WED, THU, FRI, SAT, SUN);
```

```
type STONE is (AMBER, BERYL, QUARTZ);
type GROOM is (TINKER, TAILOR, SOLDIER, SAILOR,
               RICH_MAN, POOR_MAN, BEGGAR_MAN, THIEF);
type SOLO is (ALONE);
```

This introduces an example of overloading. The literal AMBER can represent a COLOUR or a STONE. Both meanings of the same name are visible together and the second declaration does not hide the first whether they are declared in the same declarative part or one is in an inner declarative part. We can usually tell which is meant from the context but in those odd cases when we cannot we can always qualify the literal by placing it in brackets and preceding it by its type name (or indeed subtype name) and a single quote. Thus

```
COLOUR'(AMBER)
STONE'(AMBER)
```

Examples where this is necessary will occur later.

Although we can use AMBER as an enumeration literal in two distinct enumeration types, we cannot use it as an enumeration literal and the identifier of a variable at the same time. The declaration of one would hide the other and they could not both be declared in the same declarative part. Later we will see that an enumeration literal can be overloaded with a subprogram.

There is no upper limit on the number of values in an enumeration type but there must be at least one. An empty enumeration type is not allowed.

Constraints on enumeration types and subtypes are much as for integers. The constraint has the form

```
range lower_bound_expression .. upper_bound_expression
```

and this indicates the set of values from the lower bound to the upper bound inclusive. So we can write

```
subtype WEEKDAY is DAY range MON .. FRI;
D: WEEKDAY;
```

or

```
D: DAY range MON .. FRI;
```

and then we know that D cannot be SAT or SUN.

If the lower bound is above the upper bound then we get a null range, thus

```
subtype COLOURLESS is COLOUR range AMBER .. RED;
```

Note the curious anomaly that we cannot have a null subtype of a type such as SOLO.

The attributes FIRST and LAST also apply to enumeration types and subtypes, so

```
COLOUR'FIRST = RED
WEEKDAY'LAST = FRI
```

There are built in functional attributes to give the successor or predecessor of an enumeration value. These consist of SUCC or PRED following the type name and a single quote. Thus

```
COLOUR'SUCC(AMBER) = GREEN
STONE'SUCC(AMBER) = BERYL
DAY'PRED(FRI) = THU
```

Of course, the thing in brackets can be an arbitrary expression of the appropriate type. If we try to take the predecessor of the first value or the successor of the last then the exception CONSTRAINT_ERROR is raised. In the absence of this exception we have, for any type T and any value X,

```
T'SUCC(T'PRED(X)) = X
```

and vice versa.

Another functional attribute is POS. This gives the position number of the enumeration value, that is the position in the declaration with the first one having a position number of zero. So

```
COLOUR'POS(RED) = 0
COLOUR'POS(AMBER) = 1
COLOUR'POS(GREEN) = 2
```

The opposite to POS is VAL. This takes the position number and returns the corresponding enumeration value. So

```
COLOUR'VAL(0) = RED
DAY'VAL(6) = SUN
```

If we give a position value outside the range, as for example

```
SOLO'VAL(1)
```

then CONSTRAINT_ERROR is raised.

Clearly we always have

```
T'VAL(T'POS(X)) = X
```

and vice versa.

We also note that

```
T'SUCC(X) = T'VAL(T'POS(X)+1)
```

they either both give the same value or both raise an exception.

It should be noted that these four attributes SUCC, PRED, POS and VAL may also be applied to subtypes but are then identical to the same attributes of the corresponding base type.

It is probably rather bad practice to mess about with POS and VAL when it can be avoided. To do so encourages the programmer to think in terms of numbers rather than the enumeration values and hence destroys the abstraction. Finally the operators =, /=, <, <=, > and >= also apply to enumeration types. The result is defined by the order of the values in the type declaration. So

```
RED < GREEN        is TRUE
WED >= THU         is FALSE
```

The same result would be obtained by comparing the position values. So

T'POS(X) < T'POS(Y) and X < Y

are always equivalent (except that X < Y might be ambiguous).

Exercise 4.6

1 Evaluate

a) DAY'SUCC(WEEKDAY'LAST)
b) WEEKDAY'SUCC(WEEKDAY'LAST)
c) STONE'POS(QUARTZ)

2 Write suitable declarations of enumeration types for

a) the colours of the rainbow,
b) typical fruits.

3 Write an expression that delivers one's predicted bridegroom after eating a portion of pie containing N stones. Use the type GROOM declared at the beginning of this section.

4 If the first of the month is in D where D is of type DAY, then write an assignment replacing D by the day of the week of the Nth day of the month.

5 Why might X < Y be ambiguous?

4.7 The Boolean type

The Boolean type is a predefined enumeration type whose declaration can be considered to be

```
type BOOLEAN is (FALSE,TRUE);
```

Boolean values are used in constructions such as the if statement which we briefly met in Chapter 2. Boolean values are produced by the operators =, /=, <, <=, > and >= which have their expected meaning and apply to many types. So we can write constructions such as

```
if TODAY = SUN then
    TOMORROW:=MON;
else
    TOMORROW:=DAY'SUCC(TODAY);
end if;
```

The Boolean type (we capitalise the name in memory of the mathematician Boole) has all the normal properties of an enumeration type, so, for instance

```
FALSE < TRUE = TRUE!
BOOLEAN'POS(TRUE) = 1
```

We could even write

```
subtype ALWAYS is BOOLEAN range TRUE .. TRUE;
```

although it would not seem very useful.

The Boolean type also has other operators which are as follows

not This is a unary operator and changes TRUE to FALSE and vice versa. It has the same precedence as the other unary operators.

and This is a binary operator. The result is TRUE if both operands are TRUE, and FALSE otherwise.

or This is a binary operator. The result is TRUE if one or other or both operands are TRUE, and FALSE only if they are both FALSE.

xor This is also a binary operator. The result is TRUE if one or other operand but not both are TRUE. (Hence the name – eXclusive OR.) Another way of looking at it is to note that the result is TRUE if and only if the operands are different. (This operator is known as 'not equivalent' in some languages.)

The effects of **and**, **or** and **xor** are summarised in the usual truth tables shown in Fig. 4.3.

and	F	T
F	F	F
T	F	T

or	F	T
F	F	T
T	T	T

xor	F	T
F	F	T
T	T	F

Fig. 4.3 Truth tables for **and**, **or** and **xor**

The precedences of **and**, **or** and **xor** are equal to each other but lower than that of any other operator. In particular they are of lower precedence than the relational operators =, /=, <, <=, > and >=. This is unlike Pascal and as a consequence brackets are not needed in expressions such as

```
P < Q and I = J
```

However, although the precedences are equal, **and**, **or** and **xor** cannot be mixed up in an expression without using brackets (unlike + and − for instance). So

```
B and C or D                    is illegal
```

whereas

```
I + J - K                         is OK
```

We have to write

```
B and (C or D)      or      (B and C) or D
```

in order to emphasise which meaning is required.

The reader familiar with other programming languages will remember that **and** and **or** usually have a different precedence. The problem with this is that the programmer often gets confused and writes the wrong thing. It is to prevent this that Ada makes them the same precedence and insists on brackets. Of course, successive applications of the same operator are permitted so

```
B and C and D                     is legal
```

and as usual evaluation goes from left to right although, of course, it does not matter in this case since the operator **and** is associative.

Take care with **not**. Its precedence is higher than **and**, **or** and **xor** as in other languages and so

```
not A or B
```

means

```
(not A) or B
```

rather than

```
not (A or B)
```

which those familiar with logic will remember is the same as

```
(not A) and (not B)
```

Boolean variables and constants can be declared and manipulated in the usual way.

```
DANGER:  BOOLEAN;
SIGNAL :  COLOUR;
...
DANGER:=SIGNAL=RED;
```

The variable DANGER is then TRUE if the signal is RED. We can then write

```
if DANGER then
   STOP_TRAIN;
end if;
```

Note that we do not have to write

```
if DANGER=TRUE then
```

although this is perfectly acceptable; it just misses the point that DANGER is already a Boolean and so can be used directly as the condition.

A worse sin is to write

```
if SIGNAL=RED then
   DANGER:=TRUE;
else
   DANGER:=FALSE;
end if;
```

rather than

```
DANGER:=SIGNAL=RED;
```

The literals TRUE and FALSE could be overloaded by declaring for example

```
type ANSWER is (FALSE, DONT_KNOW, TRUE);
```

but to do so might make the program rather confusing.

Exercise 4.7

1 Write declarations of constants T and F having the values TRUE and FALSE.

2 Using T and F from the previous exercise, evaluate

a) T **and** F **and** T
b) **not** T **or** T
c) F = F = F = F
d) (F = F) = (F = F)
e) T < T < T < T

3 Evaluate

(A /= B) = (A **xor** B)

for all combinations of values of Boolean variables A and B.

4.8 Type classification

At this point we pause to consolidate the material presented in this chapter so far.

The types in Ada can be classified as shown in Fig. 4.4.

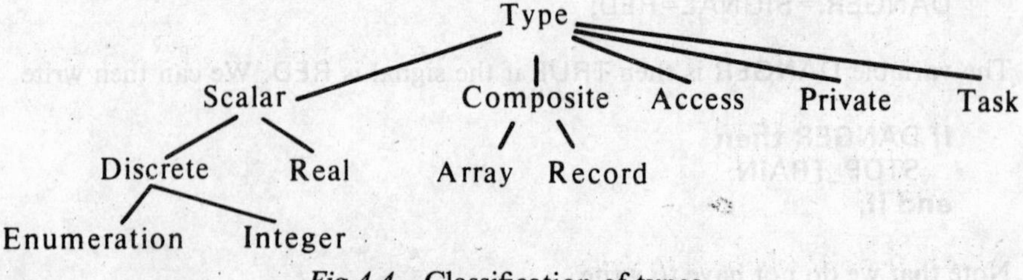

Fig 4.4 Classification of types

This chapter has discussed scalar types. In Chapter 6 we will deal with the composite types but access, private and task types will be dealt with much later.

The scalar types themselves are subdivided into real types and discrete types. Our sole example of a real type has been the type REAL – other real types are discussed in Chapter 12. The other types, INTEGER, BOOLEAN and enumeration types in general are discrete types – the only other kinds of discrete types to be introduced are other integer types, again dealt with in Chapter 12, and character types which are in fact a form of enumeration type and are dealt with in Chapter 6.

The key abstract distinction between the discrete types and the real types is that the former have a clear cut set of distinct separate (i.e. discrete) values. The type REAL, on the other hand, should be thought of as having a continuous set of values – we know in practice that a finite digital computer must implement a real type as actually a set of distinct values but this is an implementation detail, the abstract concept is of a continuous set of values.

The attributes POS, VAL, SUCC and PRED apply to all discrete types (and subtypes) because the operations reflect the discrete nature of the values. We explained their meaning with enumeration types in Section 4.6. In the case of type INTEGER the position number is simply the number itself so

```
INTEGER'POS(N)=N
INTEGER'VAL(N)=N
INTEGER'SUCC(N)=N+1
INTEGER'PRED(N)=N-1
```

The application of these attributes to integers does at first sight seem pretty futile but when we come to the concept of generic units in Chapter 13 we will see that it is convenient to allow them to apply to all discrete types.

The attributes FIRST and LAST however apply to all scalar types and subtypes including real types.

Again we emphasise that POS, VAL, SUCC and PRED for a subtype are identical to the corresponding operations on the base type, whereas in the case of FIRST and LAST this is not so.

Finally we note the difference between a type conversion and a type qualification

```
REAL(I)             -- conversion
INTEGER'(I)         -- qualification
```

In the case of a conversion we are changing the type, in the second we are just stating it (usually to overcome an ambiguity). As a mnemonic aid *qu*alification uses a *qu*ote.

In both cases we can use a subtype name and CONSTRAINT_ERROR could consequently arise.

Thus

```
NATURAL(R)
```

would convert the value of the real variable R to integer and then check that it was positive, whereas

```
NATURAL'(I)
```

would just check that the value of I was positive. In both cases, of course, the result is the checked value and is then used in an overall expression; these checks cannot just stand alone.

4.9 Expression summary

All the operators introduced so far are shown in Fig. 4.5, grouped by precedence level.

Operator	*Operation*	*Operand(s)*	*Result*
and	conjunction	BOOLEAN	BOOLEAN
or	inclusive or	BOOLEAN	BOOLEAN
xor	exclusive or	BOOLEAN	BOOLEAN
=	equality	any	BOOLEAN
/=	inequality	any	BOOLEAN
<	less than	scalar	BOOLEAN
<=	less than or equals	scalar	BOOLEAN
>	greater than	scalar	BOOLEAN
>=	greater than or equals	scalar	BOOLEAN
+	addition	numeric	same
−	subtraction	numeric	same
+	identity	numeric	same
−	negation	numeric	same
not	negation	BOOLEAN	BOOLEAN
*	multiplication	INTEGER	INTEGER
		REAL	REAL
/	division	INTEGER	INTEGER
		REAL	REAL
mod	modulo	INTEGER	INTEGER
rem	remainder	INTEGER	INTEGER
**	exponentiation	INTEGER: nonnegative INTEGER	INTEGER
		REAL : INTEGER	REAL

Fig. 4.5 Scalar operators

In all the cases of binary operators except for **, the two operands must be of the same type.

We have actually now introduced all the operators of Ada except for one (&) although as we shall see in Chapter 6 there are further possible meanings to be added.

There are also two membership tests which apply to all scalar types. These are **in** and **not in**. They are technically not operators although their precedence is the same as that of the relational operators =, /= and so on. They enable us to test whether a value lies within a specified range (including the end values) or satisfies a constraint implied by a subtype. The first operand is therefore a scalar expression, the second is a range or subtype and the result is, of course, of type Boolean. Examples are

```
I not in range 1..10
I in NATURAL
TODAY in DAY range MON..WED
```

The test **not in** is equivalent to using **in** and then applying **not** to the result, but **not in** is usually more readable. So the first expression above could be written as

```
not (I in range 1..10)
```

where the brackets are necessary.

The reason that **in** and **not in** are not technically operators is explained in Chapter 7 when we deal with subprograms.

There are also two short circuit control forms **and then** and **or else** which like **in** and **not in** are also not technically classed as operators.

The form **and then** is closely related to the operator **and** whereas **or else** is closely related to the operator **or**. They may occur in expressions and have the same precedence as **and, or** and **xor**. The difference lies in the rules regarding the evaluation of their operands.

In the case of **and** and **or,** both operands are always evaluated but the order is not specified. In the case of **and then** and **or else** the left hand operand is always evaluated first and the right hand operand is only evaluated if it is necessary in order to determine the result.

So in

```
X and then Y
```

X is evaluated first. If X is false, the answer is false whatever the value of Y so Y is not evaluated. If X is true, Y has to be evaluated and the value of Y is the answer.

Similarly in

```
X or else Y
```

X is evaluated first. If X is true, the answer is true whatever the value of Y so Y is not evaluated. If X is false, Y has to be evaluated and the value of Y is the answer.

The forms **and then** and **or else** should be used in cases where the order of evaluation matters. A common circumstance is where the first condition protects against the evaluation of the second condition in circumstances that could raise an exception.

Suppose we need to test

```
I/J > K
```

and we wish to avoid the risk that J is zero. In such a case we could write

J /= 0 **and then** I/J > K

and we would then know that if J is zero there is no risk of an attempt to divide by zero. The observant reader will realise that this is not a very good example because one could usually write I > K*J (assuming J positive) – but even here we could get overflow. Better examples occur with arrays and access types and will be mentioned in due course.

Like **and** and **or**, the forms **and then** and **or else** cannot be mixed without using brackets.

We now summarise the primary components of an expression (that is the things upon which the operators operate) that we have met so far. They are

- identifiers — used for variables, constants, numbers and enumeration literals
- literals — such as 4.6, 2#101#
- type conversions — such as INTEGER(R)
- qualified expressions — such as COLOUR'(AMBER)
- function calls — such as ABS(I+J)
- attributes — such as INTEGER'LAST

A full consideration of functions and how they are declared and called has to be deferred until later. However, it is worth noting at this point that a function with one parameter is called by following its name by the parameter in brackets. The parameter can be any expression and could include further function calls. As well as the built in function ABS we can assume that we have available a mathematical library containing familiar functions such as

SQRT	square root
SIN	sine
COS	cosine
LOG	logarithm to base 10
LN	natural logarithm
EXP	exponential function

In each case they take a REAL argument and deliver a REAL result.

We are now in a position to write statements such as

```
ROOT:=(-B+SQRT(B**2 - 4.0*A*C))/(2.0*A);
SIN2X:=2.0*SIN(X)*COS(X);
```

Finally a note on errors although this is not the place to deal with them in depth. The reader will have noticed that whenever anything could go wrong we have usually stated that the exception CONSTRAINT_ERROR will be raised. This is a general exception which applies to all sorts of violations of ranges. The only other exception which needs to be mentioned at this point is NUMERIC_ERROR. This will usually be raised if something goes wrong with the evaluation of an arithmetic expression itself before an attempt is made to store the result. An obvious example is an attempt to divide by zero. There are subtle distinctions which need not concern the normal user, for example

```
INTEGER'SUCC(INTEGER'LAST)
```

will raise CONSTRAINT_ERROR, whereas

```
INTEGER'LAST+1
```

should raise NUMERIC_ERROR. (We say should because an implementation is not obliged to raise NUMERIC_ERROR if the hardware is not cooperative.)

As well as exceptions there are erroneous programs, as mentioned in Chapter 2. These are where programs depend upon implementation details which are stated to be undefined. The important things encountered so far which are undefined are

- The destination variable in an assignment statement may be evaluated before or after or in parallel with the expression to be assigned.
- The order of evaluation of the two operands of a binary operator is not defined.

Examples where these orders matter cannot be given until we deal with functions in Chapter 7.

Exercise 4.9

1 Rewrite the following mathematical expressions in Ada.

a) $2\pi\sqrt{l/g}$ – period of a pendulum

b) $\dfrac{m_0}{\sqrt{1 - v^2/c^2}}$ – mass of relativistic particle

c) $\sqrt{2\pi n}\ .\ n^n\ .\ e^{-n}$ – Stirling's formula for $n!$ (integral n)

2 Rewrite **1**(c) replacing n by the real value x.

Checklist 4

Declarations and statements are terminated by a semicolon.

Initialisation, like assignment uses :=.

Use number declarations rather than constants.

Elaboration of declarations is linear.

Each type definition introduces a quite distinct type.

A subtype is not a new type but merely a shorthand for a type with a possible constraint.

No mixed mode arithmetic.

Distinguish **rem** and **mod** for negative operands.

Exponentiation with a negative exponent only applies to real types.

Take care with the precedence of the unary operators.

A type cannot be empty, a subtype can.

POS, VAL, SUCC and PRED on subtypes are the same as on the base type.

FIRST and LAST are different for subtypes.

Qualification uses a quote.

Order of evaluation of binary operands is not defined.

Distinguish **and, or** and **and then, or else.**

5 Control Structures

This chapter describes the three bracketed sequential control structures of Ada. These are the if statement which we have briefly met before, the case statement and the loop statement. It is now recognised that these three control structures are not only necessary but also sufficient to be able to write programs with a clearly discernible flow of control without recourse to goto statements and labels. However, for pragmatic reasons, Ada does actually contain a goto statement and this is also described in this chapter.

The three control structures exhibit a similar bracketing style. There is an opening reserved word **if**, **case** or **loop** and this is matched at the end of the structure by the same reserved word preceded by **end**. The whole is, as usual, terminated by a semicolon. So we have

```
if              case             loop
...             ...              ...
end if;         end case;        end loop;
```

In the case of the loop statement the word **loop** can be preceded by an iteration clause commencing with **for** or **while**.

5.1 If statements

The simplest form of if statement starts with the reserved word **if** followed by a Boolean expression and the reserved word **then**. This is then followed by a sequence of statements which will be executed if the Boolean expression turns out to be TRUE. The end of the sequence is indicated by the closing **end if**. The Boolean expression can, of course, be of arbitrary complexity and the sequence of statements can be of arbitrary length.

A simple example is

```
if HUNGRY then
   EAT;
end if;
```

In this, HUNGRY is a Boolean variable and EAT is a subprogram describing the details of the eating activity. The statement EAT; merely calls the subprogram (subprograms are dealt with in detail in Chapter 7).

The effect of this if statement is that if variable HUNGRY is TRUE then we call the subprogram EAT and otherwise we do nothing. In either case we then obey the statement following the if statement.

As we have said there could be a long sequence between **then** and **end if**. Thus we might break down the process into more detail

```
if HUNGRY then
    COOK;
    EAT;
    WASH_UP;
end if;
```

Note how we indent the statements to show the flow structure of the program. This is most important since it enables the program to be understood so much more easily. The **end if** should be underneath the corresponding **if** and **then** is best placed on the same line as the **if**.

Sometimes, if the whole statement is very short it can all go on one line.

```
if X < 0.0 then X:=-X; end if;
```

Note that **end if** will always be preceded by a semicolon. This is because the semicolons terminate statements rather than separate them as in Algol and Pascal. Readers familiar with those languages will probably feel initially that the Ada style is irksome. However, it is consistent and makes line by line program editing so much easier.

Often we will want to do alternative actions according to the value of the condition. In this case we add **else** followed by the alternative sequence to be obeyed if the condition is FALSE. We saw an example of this in the last chapter

```
if TODAY = SUN then
    TOMORROW:=MON;
else
    TOMORROW:=DAY'SUCC(TODAY);
end if;
```

Algol 60 and Algol 68 users should note that Ada is not an expression language and so conditional expressions are not allowed. We cannot write something like

```
TOMORROW:=
  if TODAY = SUN then MON else DAY'SUCC(TODAY) end if;
```

The statements in the sequence can be quite arbitrary and so could be further nested if statements. Suppose we have to solve the quadratic equation

$$ax^2 + bx + c = 0$$

The first thing to check is *a*. If $a = 0$ then the equation degenerates into a linear equation with a single root $-c/b$. (Mathematicians will understand that the other root has slipped off to infinity.) If *a* is not zero then we test the discriminant $b^2 - 4ac$ to see whether the roots are real or complex. We could program this as

```
if A = 0.0 then
        -- linear case
else
    if B**2-4.0*A*C >= 0.0 then
        -- real roots
    else
        -- complex roots
    end if;
end if;
```

Observe the repetition of **end if**. This is rather ugly and occurs sufficiently frequently to justify an additional construction. This uses the reserved word **elsif** as follows

```
if A = 0.0 then
    -- linear case
elsif B**2-4.0*A*C >= 0.0 then
    -- real roots
else
    -- complex roots
end if;
```

This construction emphasises the essentially equal status of the three cases and also the sequential nature of the tests.

The **elsif** part can be repeated an arbitrary number of times and the final **else** part is optional. The behaviour is simply that each condition is evaluated in turn until one that is TRUE is encountered; the corresponding sequence is then obeyed. If none of the conditions turns out to be TRUE then the else part, if any, is taken; if there is no else part then none of the sequences is obeyed.

Note the spelling of **elsif**. It is the only reserved word of Ada that is not an English word. Note also the layout – we align **elsif** and **else** with the **if** and **end if** and all the sequences are indented equally.

As a further example, suppose we are drilling soldiers and they can obey four different orders described by

```
type MOVE is (LEFT, RIGHT, BACK, ON);
```

and that their response to these orders is described by calling subprograms TURN_LEFT, TURN_RIGHT and TURN_BACK or by doing nothing at all respectively. Suppose that the variable ORDER of type MOVE contains the order to be obeyed. We could then write the following

```
if ORDER = LEFT then
    TURN_LEFT;
else
    if ORDER = RIGHT then
        TURN_RIGHT;
    else
        if ORDER = BACK then
            TURN_BACK;
        end if;
    end if;
end if;
```

But it is far clearer and neater to write

```
if ORDER = LEFT then
    TURN_LEFT;
elsif ORDER = RIGHT then
    TURN_RIGHT;
elsif ORDER = BACK then
    TURN_BACK;
end if;
```

This illustrates a situation where there is no **else** part. However, although better than using nested if statements, this is still a bad solution because it obscures the symmetry and mutual exclusion of the four cases ('mutual exclusion' means that by their very nature only one can apply). We have been forced to impose an ordering on the tests which is quite arbitrary and not the essence of the problem. The proper solution is to use the case statement as we shall see in the next section.

Contrast this with the quadratic equation. In that example, the cases were not mutually exclusive and the tests had to be performed in order. If we had tested $b^2 - 4ac$ first then we would have been forced to test a against zero in each alternative.

There is no directly corresponding contraction for **then if** as in Algol 68. Instead the short circuit control form **and then** can often be used.

So, rather than

```
if J > 0 then
    if I/J > K then
        ACTION;
    end if;
end if;
```

we can, as we have seen, write

```
if J > 0 and then I/J > K then
    ACTION;
end if;
```

Exercise 5.1

1 The variables DAY, MONTH and YEAR contain today's date. They are declared as

```
DAY: INTEGER range 1 .. 31;
MONTH: MONTH_NAME;
YEAR: INTEGER range 1901 .. 2099;
```

where

```
type MONTH_NAME is (JAN, FEB, MAR, APR, MAY, JUN, JUL,
                    AUG, SEP, OCT, NOV, DEC);
```

Write statements to update the variables to contain tomorrow's date. What happens if today is 31 DEC 2099?

2 X and Y are two real variables. Write statements to swap their values, if necessary, to ensure that the larger value is in X. Use a block to declare a temporary variable T.

5.2 Case statements

A case statement allows us to choose one of several sequences of statements according to the value of an expression. For instance, the example of the drilling soldiers should be written as

```
case ORDER is
    when LEFT => TURN_LEFT;
    when RIGHT => TURN_RIGHT;
    when BACK => TURN_BACK;
    when ON => null;
end case;
```

All possible values of the expression must be provided for in order to guard against accidental omissions. If, as in this example, no action is required for one or more values then the null statement has to be used.

The null statement, written

```
null;
```

does absolutely nothing but its presence indicates that we truly want to do nothing. The sequence of statements here, as in the if statement, must contain at least one statement. (There is no empty statement as in Algol 60.)

It often happens that the same action is desired for several values of the expression. Consider the following

```
case TODAY is
    when MON|TUE|WED|THU => WORK;
    when FRI             => WORK;
                            PARTY;
    when SAT|SUN         => null;
end case;
```

This expresses the idea that on Monday to Thursday we go to work. On Friday we also go to work but then go to a party. At the weekend we do nothing. The alternative values are separated by the vertical bar character. Note again the use of a null statement.

If several successive values have the same action then it is more convenient to use a range

```
when MON .. THU => WORK;
```

Sometimes we wish to express the idea of a default action to be taken by all values not explicitly stated; this is provided for by the reserved word **others**. The above example could be rewritten

```
case TODAY is
    when MON .. THU => WORK;
    when FRI        => WORK;
                       PARTY;
    when others     => null;
end case;
```

It is possible to have ranges as alternatives. In fact this is probably a situation where the clearest explanation of what is allowed is given by the formal syntax[†].

```
case_statement ::=
    case expression is
        {when choice} |choice {=> sequence_of_statements}
    end case;

choice ::= simple_expression | discrete_range | others

discrete_range ::= type_mark[range_constraint] | range

range_constraint ::= range range

range ::= simple_expression .. simple_expression

type_mark ::= type_name | subtype_name
```

We see that **when** is followed by one or more choices separated by vertical bars and that a choice is either a simple expression or a discrete range or **others**. A simple expression, of course, just gives a single value – FRI being a trivial example. A discrete range offers several possibilities. The usual case will be when it has the form range which the syntax tells us is two simple expressions separated by

[†]In the production for case_statement, the vertical bar stands for itself and is not a metasymbol.

two dots – MON . . THU is a simple case. However, the syntax also tells us that a discrete range can be a type mark (which is a type name or subtype name) followed optionally by a range constraint which is merely the reserved word **range** followed by the syntactic form range. Examples of discrete ranges are

```
DAY range MON . . THU
WEEKDAY
WEEKDAY range MON . . THU
```

All these possibilities may seem unnecessary but as we shall see later the form, discrete range, is used in other contexts as well as the case statement. In the case statement there is not usually much point in using the type name since this is known from the context anyway. Similarly there is not much point in using the subtype name followed by a constraint since the constraint alone will do. However, it might be useful to use a subtype name alone when that exactly corresponds to the range required. So we could rewrite the example as

```
case TODAY is
    when WEEKDAY => WORK;
                    if TODAY = FRI then
                      PARTY;
                    end if;
    when others   => null;
end case;
```

although this solution feels untidy.

There are various other restrictions that the syntax does not tell us. One is that if we use **others** then it must appear alone and as the last alternative. As stated earlier it covers all values not explicitly covered by the previous alternatives (one is still allowed to write **others** even if there are no other cases to be considered!).

Another very important restriction is that the expressions in the choices must be such that they can be evaluated at compilation time. In practice they will usually be literals as in our examples.

Finally we return to the point made at the beginning of this section that all possible values of the expression must be provided for. This usually means all values of the type of the expression. This is certainly the case of a variable declared as of a type without any constraints (as in the case of TODAY). However, if the expression is such that the value must belong to a subtype and moreover that subtype has compilation time determinable constraints then only values of that subtype need be provided for. In other words if the compiler can tell that only a subset of values is possible then only that subset need and must be covered.

In the case of our example, if TODAY had been of subtype WEEKDAY then we would know that only the values MON . . FRI are possible and so only these can and need be covered. Even if TODAY is not constrained we can still write our expression as a qualified expression WEEKDAY'(TODAY) and then again only MON . . FRI is possible. So we could write

```
case WEEKDAY'(TODAY) is
    when MON..THU=> WORK;
    when FRI      => WORK;
                     PARTY;
end case;
```

but, of course, if TODAY happens to take a value not in the subtype WEEKDAY (i.e. is SAT or SUN) then CONSTRAINT_ERROR will be raised. Mere qualification cannot prevent TODAY from being SAT or SUN. So this is not really a solution to our original problem.

As further examples, suppose we had variables

```
I: INTEGER range 1..10;
J: INTEGER range 1..N;
```

where N is not static. Then we know that I belongs to a static subtype (albeit anonymous) whereas we cannot say the same about J. If I is used as an expression in a case statement then only the values 1..10 have to be catered for, whereas if J is so used then the full range of values of type INTEGER (INTEGER'FIRST.. INTEGER'LAST) have to be catered for.

The above discussion on the case statement has no doubt given the reader the impression of considerable complexity. It therefore seems wise to summarise the key points which will in practice need to be remembered.

- Every possible value of the expression must be covered once and once only.
- All values and ranges must be static.
- If **others** is used it must be last and on its own.

Exercise 5.2

1 Rewrite Exercise 5.1(**1**) to use a case statement to set the correct value in END_OF_MONTH.

2 A vegetable gardener digs in winter, sows seed in spring, tends the growing plants in summer and harvests the crop in the autumn or fall. Write a case statement to call the appropriate subprogram DIG, SOW, TEND or HARVEST according to the month M. Declare appropriate subtypes if desired.

3 An improvident man is paid on the first of each month. For the first ten days he gorges himself, for the next ten he subsists and for the remainder he starves. Call subprograms GORGE, SUBSIST and STARVE according to the day D. Assume END_OF_MONTH has been set and that D is declared as

```
D: INTEGER range 1..END_OF_MONTH;
```

5.3 Loop statements

The simplest form of loop statement is

```
loop
    sequence_of_statements
end loop;
```

The statements of the sequence are then repeated indefinitely unless one of them terminates the loop by some means. So immortality could be represented by

```
loop
    WORK;
    EAT;
    SLEEP;
end loop;
```

As a more concrete example consider the problem of computing the base e of natural logarithms from the infinite series

$$e = 1 + \frac{1}{1!} + \frac{1}{2!} + \frac{1}{3!} + \frac{1}{4!} + \dots$$

where

$$n! = n \times (n-1) \times (n-2) \dots 3 \times 2 \times 1$$

A possible solution is

```
declare
    E: REAL:=1.0;
    I: INTEGER:=0;
    TERM: REAL:=1.0;
begin
    loop
        I:=I+1;
        TERM:=TERM/REAL(I);
        E:=E+TERM;
    end loop;
    ...
```

Each time around the loop a new term is computed by dividing the previous term by I. The new term is then added to the sum so far which is accumulated in E. The term number I is an integer because it is logically a counter and so we have to write REAL(I) as the divisor. The series is started by setting values in E, I and TERM which correspond to the first term (that for which I = 0).

The computation then goes on for ever with E becoming a closer and closer approximation to e. In practice, because of the finite accuracy of the computer, TERM will become zero and continued computation will be pointless. But in any event we presumably want to stop at some point so that we can do something with our computed result. We can do this with the statement

```
exit;
```

If this is obeyed inside a loop then the loop terminates at once and control passes to the point immediately after **end loop**.

Suppose we decide to stop after N terms of the series – that is when I = N. We can do this by writing the loop as

```
loop
   if I = N then exit; end if;
   I:=I+1;
   TERM:=TERM/REAL(I);
   E:=E+TERM;
end loop;
```

The construction

```
if condition then exit; end if;
```

is so common that a special shorthand is provided

```
exit when condition;
```

So we now have

```
loop
   exit when I = N;
   I:=I+1;
   TERM:=TERM/REAL(I);
   E:=E+TERM;
end loop;
```

Although an exit statement can appear anywhere inside a loop – it could be in the middle or near the end – a special form is provided for the frequent case where we want to test a condition at the start of each iteration. This uses the reserved word **while** and gives the condition for the loop to be continued. So we could write

```
while I /= N loop
   I:=I+1;
   TERM:=TERM/REAL(I);
   E:=E+TERM;
end loop;
```

The condition is naturally evaluated each time around the loop.

The final form of loop allows for a specific number of iterations with a loop parameter taking in turn all the values of a discrete range. Our example could be recast as

```
for I in 1 .. N loop
    TERM:=TERM/REAL(I);
    E:=E+TERM;
end loop;
```

where I takes the values 1, 2, 3 ... N.

The parameter I is implicitly declared by its appearance in the iteration clause and does not have to be declared outside. It takes its type from the discrete range and within the loop it behaves as a constant so that it cannot be changed except by the loop mechanism itself. When we leave the loop (by whatever means) I ceases to exist (because it was implicitly declared by the loop) and so we cannot read its final value from outside.

We could leave the loop by an exit statement – if we wanted to know the final value we could copy the value of I into a variable declared outside the loop thus

```
if condition_to_exit then
    LAST_I:=I;
    exit;
end if;
```

The values of the discrete range are normally taken in ascending order. Descending order can be specified by writing

```
for I in reverse 1 .. N loop
```

but the range itself is always written in ascending order.

It is not possible to specify a numeric step size of other than 1. This should not be a problem since the vast majority of loops go up by steps of 1 and almost all the rest go down by steps of 1. The very few which do behave otherwise can be explicitly programmed using the while form of loop.

The range can be empty (as for instance if N happened to be zero or negative in our example) in which case the sequence of statements will not be obeyed at all. Of course, the range itself is evaluated only once and cannot be changed inside the loop itself.

Thus

```
N:=4;
for I in 1 .. N loop
    ...
    N:=10;
end loop;
```

results in the loop being executed just four times despite the fact that N is changed to ten.

Our examples have all shown the lower bound of the range being 1. This, of course, need not be the case. Both bounds can be arbitrary dynamically evaluated expressions. Furthermore the loop parameter need not be of integer type. It can be of any discrete type, as determined by the discrete range.

We could, for instance, simulate a week's activity by

```
for TODAY in MON .. SUN loop
    case TODAY is
        ...
    end case;
end loop;
```

This implicitly declares TODAY to be of type DAY and obeys the loop with the values MON, TUE, ... SUN in turn.

The other forms of discrete range (using a type or subtype name) are of advantage here. The essence of MON .. SUN is that it embraces all the values of the type DAY. It is therefore better to write the loop using a form of discrete range that conveys the idea of completeness

```
for TODAY in DAY loop
    ...
end loop;
```

And again since we know that we do nothing at weekends anyway we could write

```
for TODAY in DAY range MON .. FRI loop
```

or better

```
for TODAY in WEEKDAY loop
```

It is interesting to note a difference regarding the determination of types in the case statement and for statement. In the case statement, the type of the discrete range is determined from the type of the expression after **case**. In the for statement, the type of the loop parameter is determined from the type of the discrete range. The dependency is the other way round.

It is therefore necessary for the type of the discrete range to be unambiguous in the for statement. This is usually the case but if we had two enumeration types with two overloaded literals such as

```
type PLANET is (MERCURY, VENUS, EARTH, MARS, JUPITER,
                   SATURN, URANUS, NEPTUNE, PLUTO);
type ROMAN_GOD is (JANUS, MARS, JUPITER, JUNO, VESTA,
                      VULCAN, SATURN, MERCURY, MINERVA);
```

then

```
for X in MARS..SATURN loop
```

would be ambiguous and the compiler would not compile our program. We could resolve the problem by qualifying one of the expressions

```
for X in PLANET'(MARS)..SATURN loop
```

or (probably better) by using a form of discrete range giving the type explicitly

```
for X in PLANET range MARS..SATURN loop
```

When we have dealt with numerics in more detail we will realise that the range 1..10 is not necessarily of type INTEGER. A general application of our rule that the type must not be ambiguous in a for statement would lead us to have to write

```
for I in INTEGER range 1..10 loop
```

However, this would be so tedious in such a common case that there is a special rule which applies to discrete ranges in for statements which merely says that integer literal ranges imply type INTEGER.

Finally we reconsider the exit statement. The simple form encountered earlier always transfers control to immediately after the innermost embracing loop. But of course loops may be nested and sometimes we may wish to exit from a nested construction. As an example suppose we are searching in two dimensions

```
for I in 1..N loop
    for J in 1..M loop
        -- if values of I and J satisfy
        -- some condition then leave nested loop
    end loop;
end loop;
```

A simple exit statement in the inner loop would merely take us to the end of that loop and we would then have to recheck the condition and exit again. This can be avoided by naming the outer loop and using the name in the exit statement thus

```
SEARCH:
for I in 1..N loop
    for J in 1..M loop
        if condition_O_K then
            I_VALUE:=I;
            J_VALUE:=J;
            exit SEARCH;
        end if;
    end loop;
end loop SEARCH;
-- control passes here
```

A loop is named by preceding it with an identifier and colon. (It looks remarkably like a label in other languages but it is not and cannot be 'gone to'.) The identifier must be repeated between the corresponding **end loop** and the semicolon.

The conditional form of exit can also refer to a loop by name

```
exit SEARCH when condition;
```

Exercise 5.3

1 The statement GET(I); reads the next value from the input file into the integer variable I. Write statements to read and add together a series of numbers. The end of the series is indicated by a dummy negative value.

2 Write statements to determine the power of 2 in the factorisation of N. Compute the result in COUNT but do not alter N.

3 Compute

$$g = \sum_{p=1}^{n} \frac{1}{p} - \log n$$

(As $n \to \infty$, $g \to \gamma = 0.577215665\ldots$)

5.4 Goto statements and labels

Many will be surprised that a modern programming language should contain a goto statement at all. It has become considered to be extremely bad practice to use goto statements because of the resulting difficulty in proving correctness of the program, maintenance and so on. And indeed Ada contains adequate control structures so that it should not normally be necessary to use a goto at all.

So why provide a goto statement? The main reason concerns automatically generated programs. If we try to transliterate (by hand or machine) a program from some other language into Ada then the goto will probably be useful. Another example might be where the program is generated automatically from some high level specification. Finally there may be cases where the goto is the neatest way – perhaps as a way out of some deeply nested structure – but the alternative of raising an exception (see Chapter 10) could also be considered.

In order to put us off using gotos and labels (and perhaps so that our manager can spot them if we do) the notation for a label is unusual and stands out like a sore thumb. A label is an identifier enclosed in double angled brackets thus

```
<<THE_DEVIL>>
```

and a goto statement takes the expected form of the reserved word **goto** followed by the label identifier and semicolon

```
goto THE_DEVIL;
```

A goto statement cannot be used to transfer control into an if, case or loop statement nor between the arms of an if or case statement.

Exercise 5.4

1 Rewrite the nested loop of Section 5.3 using a label <<SEARCH>> rather than naming the outer loop. Why is this not such a good solution?

5.5 Statement classification

The statements in Ada can be classified as shown in Fig. 5.1

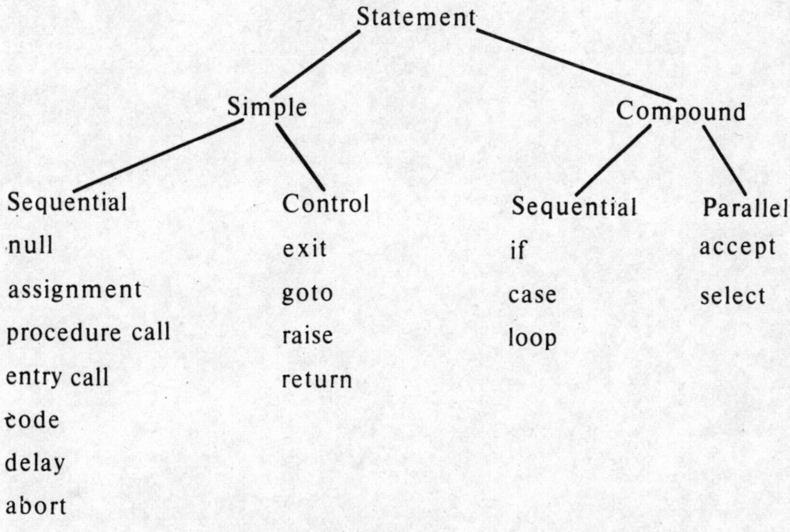

Fig. 5.1 Classification of statements

Further detail on the assignment statement is in the next chapter when we discuss composite types. Procedure calls and return statements are discussed in Chapter 7 and the raise statement which is concerned with exceptions is discussed in Chapter 10. The code statement is mentioned in Chapter 15. The remaining statements (entry call, delay, abort, accept and select) concern tasking and are dealt with in Chapter 14.

All statements can have one or more labels. The simple statements cannot be decomposed lexically into other statements whereas the compound statements can be so decomposed and can therefore be nested. Statements are obeyed sequentially unless one of them is a control statement (or an exception is implicitly raised).

Checklist 5

Statement brackets must match correctly.

Use **elsif** where appropriate.

All possibilities in a case statement must be catered for.

If **others** is used it must be last and on its own.

The expression after **case** can be qualified in order to reduce the alternatives.

A loop parameter behaves as a constant.

A named loop must have the name at both ends.

Avoid gotos.

6 Composite Types

In this chapter we describe the composite types which are arrays and records. We also complete our discussion of enumeration types by introducing characters and strings. At this stage we discuss arrays fairly completely but consider only simple forms of records. The more elaborate discriminated records which include variant records are deferred until Chapter 11.

6.1 Arrays

An array is a composite object consisting of a number of components all of the same type. An array can be of one, two or more dimensions. A typical array declaration might be

```
A: array (INTEGER range 1..6) of REAL;
```

This declares A to be a variable object which has 6 components, each of which is of type REAL. The individual components are referred to by following the array name with an expression in brackets giving an integer value in the discrete range 1 .. 6. If this expression, known as the index value, has a value outside the range, then the exception CONSTRAINT_ERROR will be raised. We could set zero in each component of A by writing

```
for I in 1..6 loop
   A(I):=0.0;
end loop;
```

An array can be of several dimensions, in which case a separate range is given for each dimension. So

```
AA: array (INTEGER range 0..2, INTEGER range 0..3) of REAL;
```

is an array of 12 components in total, each of which is referred to by two integer index values, the first in the range 0 .. 2 and the second in the range 0 .. 3. Each element of this two dimensional array could be set to zero by a nested loop thus

```
for I in 0..2 loop
   for J in 0..3 loop
      AA(I, J):=0.0;
   end loop;
end loop;
```

The discrete ranges do not have to be static: one could have

```
N: INTEGER:= ... ;
B: array (INTEGER range 1 .. N) of BOOLEAN;
```

and the value of N at the point when the declaration of B is elaborated would determine the number of elements in B. Of course, the declaration of B might be elaborated many times during the course of a program – it might be inside a loop for example – and each elaboration will give rise to a new life of a new array and the value of N could be different each time. Like other declared objects, the array B ceases to exist once we pass the end of the block containing its declaration. Because of 'linear elaboration of declarations' both N and B could be declared in the same declarative part but the declaration of N would have to precede that of B.

The discrete range in an array index follows similar rules to that in a for statement. An important one is that a range such as 1 .. 6 implies type INTEGER so we could have written

```
A: array (1 .. 6) of REAL;
```

However, an array index could be of any discrete type. We could for example have

```
HOURS_WORKED: array (DAY) of REAL;
```

This array has seven components referred to as HOURS_WORKED(MON), .. HOURS_WORKED(SUN). We could set suitable values in these variables by

```
for D in WEEKDAY loop
    HOURS_WORKED(D):=8.0;
end loop;
HOURS_WORKED(SAT):=0.0;
HOURS_WORKED(SUN):=0.0;
```

If we only wanted to declare the array HOURS_WORKED to have components corresponding to MON .. FRI then we could write

```
HOURS_WORKED: array (DAY range MON .. FRI) of REAL;
```

or (better)

```
HOURS_WORKED array (WEEKDAY) of REAL;
```

Arrays have various attributes relating to their indexes. A'FIRST and A'LAST give the lower and upper bound of the first (or only) index of A. So using our last declaration of HOURS_WORKED

```
HOURS_WORKED'FIRST = MON
HOURS_WORKED'LAST  = FRI
```

A'LENGTH gives the number of values of the first (or only) index.

So

```
HOURS_WORKED'LENGTH = 5
```

A'RANGE is short for A'FIRST .. A'LAST. So

```
HOURS_WORKED'RANGE is MON .. FRI
```

The same attributes can be applied to the various dimensions of a multi-dimensional array by adding the dimension number in brackets. It has to be a static expression. So, in the case of our two dimensional array AA we have

```
AA'FIRST(1)    = 0
AA'FIRST(2)    = 0
AA'LAST(1)     = 2
AA'LAST(2)     = 3
AA'LENGTH(1) = 3
AA'LENGTH(2) = 4
```

and

```
AA'RANGE(1) is 0..2
AA'RANGE(2) is 0..3
```

The first dimension is assumed if (1) is omitted. It is perhaps better practice to specifically state (1) for multidimensional arrays and omit it for one dimensional arrays.

It is always best to use the attributes where possible in order to reflect relationships among entities in a program because it generally means that if the program is modified, the modifications are localised.

The RANGE attribute is particularly useful with loops. Our earlier examples are better written as

```
for I in A'RANGE loop
   A(I):=0.0;
end loop;

for I in AA'RANGE(1) loop
   for J in AA'RANGE(2) loop
      AA(I,J):=0.0;
   end loop;
end loop;
```

The RANGE attribute can also be used in a declaration. Thus

```
J: INTEGER range A'RANGE;
```

is equivalent to

```
J: INTEGER range 1 .. 6;
```

If a variable is to be used to index an array as in A(J) it is usually best if the variable has the same constraints as the discrete range in the array declaration. This will usually minimise the run time checks necessary. It has been found that in such circumstances it is usually the case that the index variable J is assigned less frequently than the array component A(J) is accessed.

The array components we have seen are just variables in the ordinary way. They can therefore be assigned to and used in expressions.

Like other variable objects, arrays can be given an initial value. This will often be denoted by an aggregate which is the literal form for an array value. The simplest form of aggregate consists of a list of expressions giving the values of the components in order, separated by commas and enclosed in brackets. So we could initialise the array A by

```
A: array (1..6) of REAL:=(0.0,0.0,0.0,0.0,0.0,0.0,);
```

In the case of a multidimensional array the aggregate is written in a nested form.

```
AA: array (0..2, 0..3) of REAL:=((0.0,0.0,0.0,0 0),
                                 (0.0,0.0,0.0,0.0),
                                 (0.0,0.0,0.0,0.0));
```

An aggregate must be complete. If we initialise any component of an array, we must initialise them all.

The initial values for the indvidual components need not be literals, they can be any expressions. These expressions are evaluated when the declaration is elaborated but the order of evaluation of the expressions in the aggregate is not specified.

An array can be declared as constant in which case an initial value is mandatory. Constant arrays are of frequent value as look-up tables. The following array can be used to determine whether a particular day is a working day or not

```
WORK_DAY: constant array (DAY) of BOOLEAN
          :=(TRUE,TRUE,TRUE,TRUE,TRUE,FALSE,FALSE);
```

An interesting example would be an array enabling tomorrow to be determined without worrying about the end of the week.

```
TOMORROW: constant array (DAY) of DAY
          :=(TUE,WED,THU,FRI,SAT,SUN,MON);
```

For any day D, TOMORROW(D) is the following day.

Finally, it should be noted that the array components can be of any type or subtype. Also the dimensions of a multidimensional array can be of different discrete types. An extreme example would be

```
STRANGE: array (COLOUR,2..7,WEEKDAY range TUE..THU)
         of PLANET range MARS..SATURN;
```

Exercise 6.1

1 Declare an array F of integers with index running from 0 to N. Write statements to set the components of F equal to the Fibonacci numbers given by

$$F_0 = 0, \quad F_1 = 1, \quad F_i = F_{i-1} + F_{i-2}$$

2 Write statements to find the index values I, J of the maximum component of

```
A: array (1 .. N, 1 .. M) of REAL;
```

3 Declare an array DAYS_IN_MONTH giving the number of days in each month. See Exercise 5.1(**1**). Use it to rewrite that example. See also Exercise 5.2(**1**).

4 Declare an array YESTERDAY analagous to the example TOMORROW above.

5 Declare a constant array BOR such that

```
BOR(P, Q) = P or Q
```

6 Declare a constant unit matrix UNIT of order 3. A unit matrix is one for which all components are zero except those whose indexes are equal which have value one.

6.2 Array types

The arrays we introduced in the last section did not have an explicit type name. They were in fact of anonymous type. This is one of the few cases in Ada where an object can be declared without naming the type – another case is with tasks.

Reconsidering the first example in the previous section, we could write

```
type VECTOR_6 is array (1 .. 6) of REAL;
```

and then declare A using the type name in the usual way

```
A: VECTOR_6;
```

An advantage of using a type name is that it enables us to assign whole arrays that have been declared separately. If we also have

```
B: VECTOR_6;
```

then we can write

```
B:=A;
```

which has the effect of

```
B(1):=A(1); B(2):=A(2); ... B(6):=A(6);
```

although the order of assigning the components is not relevant.

On the other hand if we had written

```
C: array (1 .. 6) of REAL;
D: array (1 .. 6) of REAL;
```

then D:=C; is illegal because C and D are not of the same type. They are of different types both of which are anonymous. However, if we had written

```
E, F: array (1 .. 6) of REAL;
```

then F:=E; would be allowed because E and F are of the same type even though it is anonymous. The underlying rule is that every type definition introduces a new type and in this case the syntax tells us that an array type definition is the piece of text from **array** up to (but not including) the semicolon.

Whether we introduce a type name for particular arrays depends very much on the abstract view of each situation. If we are thinking of the array as a complete object in its own right then we should use a type name. If on the other hand we are thinking of the array as merely an indexable conglomerate not related as a whole to other arrays then it should probably be of an anonymous type.

Arrays like TOMORROW and WORK_DAY of the last section are good examples of arrays which are of the anonymous category. To be forced to introduce a type name for such arrays would introduce unnecessary clutter and a possibly false sense of abstraction.

On the other hand if we are manipulating lots of arrays of reals of length 6 then there is a common underlying abstract type and so it should be named.

The model for array types introduced so far is still not satisfactory. It does not allow us to represent an abstract view that embraces the commonality between arrays which have different bounds but are otherwise of the same type. In particular, it would not allow the writing of subprograms which could take an array of arbitrary bounds as an actual parameter. This is generally recognised as a major difficulty with Pascal. So the concept of an unconstrained array type is introduced in which the range constraints for the indexes are not given. Consider

```
type VECTOR is array (INTEGER range <>) of REAL;
```

(The compound symbol <> is read as 'box'.)

This says that VECTOR is the name of a type which is a one dimensional array of REAL components with an INTEGER index. But the lower and upper bounds are not given; **range** <> is meant to convey the notion of information to be added later.

When we declare objects of type VECTOR we must supply the bounds. We can do this in various ways. We can introduce an intermediate subtype and then declare the objects

```
subtype VECTOR_5 is VECTOR(1 .. 5);
V: VECTOR_5;
```

Or we can declare the objects directly

```
V: VECTOR(1 .. 5);
```

In either case the bounds are given by a discrete range in brackets. All the usual forms of discrete range can be used.

We can now see that when we wrote

```
type VECTOR_6 is array (1 .. 6) of REAL;
```

this was really a shorthand for

```
type anon is array (INTEGER range <>) of REAL;
subtype VECTOR_6 is anon(1 .. 6);
```

Another useful array type declaration is

```
type MATRIX is array (INTEGER range <>, INTEGER range <>)
                                 of REAL;
```

And again we could introduce subtypes thus

```
subtype MATRIX_3 is MATRIX(1 .. 3, 1 .. 3);
M: MATRIX_3;
```

or the objects directly

```
M: MATRIX(1 .. 3, 1 .. 3);
```

An important point to notice is that an array type or subtype must give all the bounds or none at all. It would be perfectly legal to introduce an alternative name for MATRIX by

```
subtype MAT is MATRIX;
```

in which no bounds are given, but we could not have a type or subtype that just gave the bounds for one dimension but not the other.

In all of the cases we have been discussing, the discrete range need not have static bounds. The bounds could be any expressions and are evaluated when the discrete range is encountered. We could have

```
M: MATRIX(1 .. N, 1 .. N);
```

and then the upper bounds of M would be the value of N when M is declared. A range could even be null as would happen in the above case if N turned out to be zero. In this case the matrix M would have no components at all.

There is a further way in which the bounds of an array can be supplied but this only applies to constant arrays which like other constants have to be given an initial value. In the previous section we showed how an initial value can be given in the form of a simple aggregate. This consists of a list of expressions in brackets. Such an aggregate is known as a positional aggregate since the values are given in position order. In the case of such an aggregate, the lower bound is S'FIRST where S is the subtype of the index. The upper bound is deduced from the number of components.

Suppose we had

```
type W is array (WEEKDAY range <>) of DAY;
NEXT_WORK_DAY: constant W:= (TUE, WED, THU, FRI, MON);
```

then the lower bound of the array is WEEKDAY'FIRST = MON and the upper bound is FRI. It would not have mattered whether we had written DAY or WEEKDAY in the declaration of W because DAY'FIRST and WEEKDAY'FIRST are the same

Using initial values to supply the bounds needs care. Consider

```
UNIT_2: constant MATRIX:=((1.0,0.0), (0.0,1.0));
```

intended to declare a 2 × 2 unit matrix with UNIT_2(1,1) = UNIT_2(2,2) = 1.0 and UNIT_2(1,2) = UNIT_2(2,1) = 0.0.

But disaster! We have actually declared an array whose lower bounds are INTEGER'FIRST which is probably −32768 or some such number but is certainly not 1.

If we declared the type MATRIX as

```
type MATRIX is array (NATURAL range <>, NATURAL range <>)
                                    of REAL;
```

then all would have been well since NATURAL' FIRST = 1.

So array bounds deduced from an initial value may lead to surprises.

There is another form of aggregate known as a named aggregate in which the component values are preceded by the corresponding index value and =>. A simple example would be

```
(1 => 0.0, 2=> 0.0, 3=> 0.0, 4=> 0.0, 5=> 0.0, 6 => 0.0)
```

with the expected extension to several dimensions. Our problem with the unit 2 × 2 matrix could be overcome by writing

```
UNIT_2: constant MATRIX:=(1 => (1 => 1.0, 2 => 0.0),
                          2 => (1 => 0.0, 2 => 1.0));
```

in which the bounds can obviously be deduced explicitly.

The rules for named aggregates are very similar to the rules for the alternatives in a case statement.

Each choice can be given as a series of alternatives each of which can be a single value or a discrete range. We could therefore rewrite some previous examples as follows

```
A: array (1 ..6) of REAL:=(1 ..6 => 0.0);

WORK_DAY: constant array (DAY) of BOOLEAN
            :=(MON..FRI => TRUE, SAT|SUN => FALSE);
```

In contrast to a positional aggregate, the index values need not appear in order. We could equally have written

```
(SAT|SUN => FALSE, MON .. FRI => TRUE)
```

We can also use **others** but then as for the case statement it must be last and on its own.

The use of **others** raises some problems since it must be clear what the totality of values is. It should also be realised that although we have been showing aggregates as initial values, they can be used quite generally in any place where an expression of an array type is required. It is therefore necessary that the context supplies the bounds if **others** is used. One way of supplying the context is by qualifying the aggregate as we did to distinguish between overloaded enumeration literals. In order to do this we must have an appropriate type or subtype name.

So
```
WEEKDAY'(others => TRUE)
```

is equivalent to

```
(MON .. FRI => TRUE)
```

(Note that when qualifying an aggregate we do not, as for an expression, need to put it in brackets because it already has brackets.)

Perhaps surprisingly, the context of an initial value, even when the bounds are known from the type is not enough. We cannot write

```
WORK_DAY: constant array (DAY) of BOOLEAN
          :=(MON .. FRI => TRUE, others => FALSE);
```

but must instead write

```
WORK_DAY: constant array (DAY) of BOOLEAN
          :=DAY'(MON .. FRI => TRUE, others => FALSE);
```

Remember that the other forms of discrete range can be used thus

```
DAY'(WEEKDAY => TRUE, others => FALSE);
```

Array aggregates are rather complicated and we still have a few points to make. The first is that in a named aggregate all the ranges and values before => must be static (as in a case statement) except for one special situation. This is where there is only one alternative consisting of a single choice – it could then be a dynamic range or (unlikely) a single dynamic value. An example might be

```
A: array (1 .. N) of REAL:=(1 .. N => 0.0);
```

This is valid even if N is zero giving a null array and null aggregate. But N cannot be less than zero. A null array must not be 'overdone'.

Another point is that array aggregates may not mix positional and named notation except that **others** may be used at the end of a positional aggregate. The use of **others** in a positional aggregate, of course, means that although the lower bound can be determined from the index subtype, the upper bound cannot be determined because the number of components is not known. The same rules then apply as for a named aggregate with **others** – the bounds must be supplied by the context. As mentioned above a suitable context is provided by qualifying the aggregate; other acceptable contexts will be met in due course when we discuss subprogram parameters and results in Chapter 7, and allocators for access types in Chapter 11.

Although we cannot mix named and positional notation within an aggregate, we can, however, use different forms for the different components and levels of a multidimensional aggregate. So the initial value of our matrix UNIT_2 could also be written as

```
(1 => (1.0,0.0),        or     ((1 => 1.0,2 => 0.0),
 2 => (0.0,1.0))                (1 => 0.0,2 => 1.0))
```

or even as

```
(1 => (1 => 1.0,2 => 0.0),
 2 => (       0.0,       1.0))
```

and so on.

Note also that the RANGE attribute stands for a range and therefore can be used as one of the choices in a named aggregate. We can even use the range attribute of an object in its own initial value. Thus

```
A: array (1..N) of REAL:=(A'RANGE => 0.0);
```

– this is better than repeating 1..N because it localises the dependency on N. The reader might feel that we are cheating by using A in its own declaration. However, there is a general principle that a declaration with initial value

```
A: T:=I;
```

is essentially equivalent to

```
A: T;
...
A:=I;
```

in which the declaration is given without the initial value and is then followed by an assignment statement.

A final point is that a positional aggregate cannot contain just one component because otherwise it would be ambiguous. We could not distinguish an aggregate of one component from a scalar value which happened to be in brackets. An aggregate of one component must therefore use the named notation.

We continue by returning to the topic of whole array assignment. In order to perform such assignment it is necessary that the array value and the array being assigned to have the same type and that the components can be matched. This does not mean that the bounds have to be equal but merely that the number of components in corresponding dimensions is the same. So we can write

```
V: VECTOR(1..5);
W: VECTOR(0..4);
...
V:=W;
```

Both V and W are of type VECTOR and both have 5 components.

We could also use an aggregate to give an array value as in

```
V:=(1.0, 2.0, 3.0, 4.0, 5.0);
```

Our rules tell us that the bounds of the aggregate are INTEGER'FIRST .. INTEGER'FIRST+4. However, there are five components and that is all that matters. So the problems with aggregate bounds are not so dramatic in practice as we might have feared.

It is also valid to have

```
P: MATRIX(0..1, 0..1);
Q: MATRIX(6..7, N..N+1);
...
P:=Q;
```

Equality and inequality of arrays follow similar rules to assignment. Two arrays may only be compared if they are of the same type. They are equal if corresponding dimensions have the same number of components and the corresponding components are themselves equal.

Although assignment and equality can only occur if the arrays are of the same type, nevertheless an array value of one type can be converted to another type if the component types and index types are the same. The usual notation for type conversion is used. So if we have

```
type VECTOR is array (INTEGER range<>) of REAL;
type ROW    is array (INTEGER range<>) of REAL;

V: VECTOR(1..5);
R: ROW(0..4);
```

then

```
R:=ROW(V);
```

is valid. In fact, since ROW is an unconstrained type, the bounds of ROW(V) are those of V. The normal assignment rules then apply. However, if the conversion uses a constrained type or subtype then the bounds are those of the type or subtype and the number of components in corresponding dimensions must be the same. Array type conversion is of particular value when subprograms from different libraries are used together as we shall see later.

The reader will by now have concluded that arrays in Ada are somewhat complicated. That is a fair judgement, but in practice there should be few difficulties. There is always the safeguard that if we do something wrong, the compiler will inevitably tell us. In cases of ambiguity, qualification solves the problems provided we have an appropriate type or subtype name to use. Much of the complexity with aggregates is similar to that in the case statement.

We conclude this section by observing that the attributes FIRST, LAST, LENGTH and RANGE, as well as applying to array objects, may also be applied to array types and subtypes provided they are constrained (i.e. have their bounds given). So

```
VECTOR_6'LENGTH = 6
```

but

```
VECTOR'LENGTH        is illegal
```

Exercise 6.2

1 Rewrite the declaration of the array DAYS_IN_MONTH in Exercise 6.1(3) using a named aggregate for an initial value.

2 Declare a constant MATRIX whose bounds are both 1 . . N where N is dynamic and whose components are all zero.

3 Declare a constant MATRIX as in **2** but make it a unit matrix.

4 Declare an array type BBB corresponding to the array BOR of Exercise 6.1(5).

6.3 Characters and strings

We now complete our discussion of enumeration types by introducing character types. In the enumeration types seen so far such as

```
type COLOUR is (RED, AMBER, GREEN);
```

the values have been represented by identifiers. It is also possible to have an enumeration type in which some or all of the values are represented by character literals.

A character literal is a further form of lexical unit. It consists of a single character within a pair of single quotes. The character must be one of the printable characters or it could be a single space. It must not be a control character such as horizontal tabulate or new line.

This is a situation where there is a distinction between upper and lower case letters. The character literals

```
'A',      'a'
```

are different.

So we could declare an enumeration type

```
type ROMAN_DIGIT is ('I', 'V', 'X', 'L', 'C', 'D', 'M');
```

and then

```
DIG: ROMAN_DIGIT:='D';
```

All the usual properties of enumeration types apply.

```
ROMAN_DIGIT'FIRST = 'I'
ROMAN_DIGIT'SUCC('X') = 'L'
ROMAN_DIGIT'POS('M') = 6
DIG < 'L' = FALSE
```

There is a predefined enumeration type CHARACTER which is (naturally) a character type. We can think of its declaration as being of the form

```
type CHARACTER is (nul, ..., 'A', 'B', 'C', ..., del);
```

but for technical reasons which cannot be explained here the literals which are not actual character literals (such as *nul*) are not really identifiers either (which is why they are represented here in italics). It is however possible to refer to them as ASCII.NUL and so on (or under suitable circumstances to be discussed later as simply NUL). This predefined type CHARACTER represents the standard ASCII character set and describes the set of characters normally used for input and output. It is unfortunate that the type CHARACTER is hedged around with subtleties but in practice these do not matter. For details the reader is referred to the LRM.

It should be noted that the introduction of both the type ROMAN_DIGIT and the predefined type CHARACTER results in overloading of some of the literals. An expression such as

```
'X' < 'L'
```

is ambiguous. We do not know whether we are comparing characters of the type ROMAN_DIGIT or CHARACTER. In order to resolve the ambiguity we must qualify one or both literals

```
CHARACTER'('X') < 'L' = FALSE
ROMAN_DIGIT'('X') < 'L' = TRUE
```

As well as the predefined type CHARACTER there is also the predefined type STRING

```
type STRING is array (NATURAL range <>) of CHARACTER;
```

This is a perfectly normal array type and obeys all the rules of the previous section. So we can write

```
S: STRING(1 .. 7);
```

to declare an array of range 1 .. 7. In the case of a constant array the bounds can be deduced from the initial value thus

```
G: constant STRING:=('P','I','G');
```

where the initial value takes the form of a normal positional aggregate. The lower bound of G (i.e. G'FIRST) is 1 since the index type of STRING is NATURAL and NATURAL'FIRST is 1.

An alternative notation is provided for a positional aggregate each of whose components is a character literal. This is the string. So we could more conveniently write

```
G: constant STRING:="PIG";
```

The string is the last lexical unit to be introduced. It consists of a sequence of printable characters and spaces enclosed in double quotes. A double quote may be represented in a string by two double quotes so that

```
('A','"','B') = "A""B"
```

The string may also have just one character or may be null. The equivalent aggregates using character literals have to be written in named notation.

```
(1 => 'A') = "A"
(1 .. 0 => 'A') = ""
```

Note how we have to introduce an arbitrary character in the null named form. Ada has some strange quirks!

Another rule about a lexical string is that it must fit onto a single line. Moreover it cannot contain control characters such as SOH. And, of course, as for character literals, the two cases of alphabet are distinct in strings

```
"PIG" /= "pig"
```

In the next section we will see how to overcome the limitations that a string must fit onto a single line and cannot contain control characters.

A major use for strings is, of course, for creating text to be output. A simple sequence of characters can be output by a call of the (overloaded) subprogram PUT. Thus

```
PUT("The Countess of Lovelace");
```

will output the text

```
The Countess of Lovelace
```

onto some appropriate file.

However, the lexical string is not reserved just for use with the built-in type

STRING. It can be used to represent an array of any character type. We can write

```
type ROMAN_NUMBER is array (NATURAL range <>) of
                                        ROMAN_DIGIT;
```

and then

```
NINETEEN_EIGHTY_FOUR: constant ROMAN_NUMBER
                              :="MCMLXXXIV";
```

or indeed

```
FOUR: array (1 .. 2) of ROMAN_DIGIT:="IV";
```

Exercise 6.3

1 Declare a constant array ROMAN_TO_INTEGER which can be used for table look-up to convert a ROMAN_DIGIT to its normal integer equivalent (e.g. converts 'C' to 100).

2 Given an object R of type ROMAN_NUMBER write statements to compute the equivalent integer value V. It may be assumed that R obeys the normal rules of construction of Roman numbers.

6.4 One dimensional array operations

Many of the operators that we met in Chapter 4 may also be applied to one dimensional arrays.

The Boolean operators **and**, **or**, **xor** and **not** may be applied to one dimensional Boolean arrays. In the case of the binary operators, the two operands must have the same number of components and be of the same type. The underlying scalar operation is applied component by component and the resulting array is again of the same type. The lower bound of the index of the result is equal to the lower bound of the subtype of the array index.

Consider

```
A, B: array (1 .. 4) of BOOLEAN;
C: array (1 .. 4) of BOOLEAN;
T: constant BOOLEAN:=TRUE;
F: constant BOOLEAN:=FALSE;
```

then we can write

```
A:=(T, T, F, F);
B:=(T, F, T, F);

A:=A and B;
B:=not B;
```

and A now equals (T, F, F, F), and B equals (F, T, F, T). Similarly for **or** and **xor**.

But note that A **and** C would not be allowed because they are of different types. This is clearly a case where it is appropriate to give a name to the array type because we are manipulating the arrays as complete objects.

Note that the lower bound of A **and** B is actually INTEGER'FIRST. This does not matter since as pointed out in Section 6.2 assignment only demands the same type and same number of components. The bounds themselves do not have to be equal.

Boolean arrays can be used to represent sets. Consider

```
type PRIMARY is (R,Y,B);
type COLOUR is array (PRIMARY) of BOOLEAN;
C: COLOUR;
```

then there are 8 = 2 × 2 × 2 values that C can take. C is, of course, an array with three components and each of these has value TRUE or FALSE; the three components are

```
C(R),   C(Y)   and   C(B)
```

The 8 possible values of the type COLOUR can be represented by suitably named constants as follows

```
WHITE  : constant COLOUR:=(F,F,F);
RED    : constant COLOUR:=(T,F,F);
YELLOW: constant COLOUR:=(F,T,F);
BLUE   : constant COLOUR:=(F,F,T);
GREEN  : constant COLOUR:=(F,T,T);
PURPLE : constant COLOUR:=(T,F,T);
ORANGE: constant COLOUR:=(T,T,F);
BLACK  : constant COLOUR:=(T,T,T);
```

and then we can write expressions such as

```
RED or YELLOW
```

which is equal to ORANGE and

```
not BLACK
```

which is WHITE.

So the values of our type COLOUR are effectively the set of colours obtained by taking all combinations of the primary colours represented by R, Y, B. The empty set is the value of WHITE and the full set is the value of BLACK.

The operations **or**, **and** and **xor** may be interpreted as set union, set intersection and symmetric difference. A test for set membership can be made by inspecting the value of the appropriate component of the set. Thus

```
C(R)
```

is TRUE if R is in the set represented by C. We cannot use the predefined operation **in** for this. A literal value can be represented using the named aggregate notation, so

```
(R|Y => T, others F)
```

has the same value as ORANGE. A more elegant way of doing this will appear in the next chapter.

We now consider the equality and relational operators. The operators = and /= apply to all types anyway and we gave the rules for arrays when we discussed assignment in Section 6.2.

The relational operators <, <=, > and >= may be applied to one dimensional arrays of a discrete type. (Note discrete.) The result of the comparison is based upon the lexicographic (i.e. dictionary) order using the defined order relation for the components. This is best illustrated with strings which we assume for the moment are unambiguously values of the type STRING. The following are all TRUE

```
"CAT" < "DOG"
"CAT" < "CATERPILLAR"
"AZZ" < "B"
""    < "A"
```

The strings are compared component by component until they differ in some position. The string with the lower component is then lower. If one string runs out of components as in CAT *versus* CATERPILLAR then the shorter one is lower. The null string is lowest of all.

If we assume that we have declared our **type** ROMAN_NUMBER then

```
"CCL" < "CCXC"
```

is ambiguous since we do not know whether we are comparing type STRING or type ROMAN_NUMBER. We must qualify one or both of the strings. This is done in the usual way but a string, unlike the bracketed form of aggregates, has to be placed in brackets otherwise we would get an ugly juxtaposition of a single and double quote. So

```
STRING'("CCL") < "CCXC"                    is TRUE
ROMAN_NUMBER'("CCL") < "CCXC"              is FALSE
```

Note that our compiler is too stupid to know about the interpretation of Roman numbers in our minds and has said that 250 < 290 is false. The only thing that matters is the order relation of the characters 'L' and 'X' in the type definition. In the next chapter we will show how we can redefine < so that it works 'properly' for Roman numbers.

Of course, the relational operators also apply to values and not just to literal strings.

```
NINETEEN_EIGHTY_FOUR < "MM"          is TRUE
```

The relational operators can be applied to arrays of any discrete types. So

```
(1,2,3) < (2,3)
(JAN,JAN) < (1 => FEB)
```

The predefined operators < =, > and > = are defined by analogy with <.

We now introduce a new binary operator & which denotes catenation (or concatenation) of one dimensional arrays. It has the same precedence as binary plus and minus. The two operands must be of the same type and the result is an array of the same type whose value is obtained by juxtaposing the two operands. The lower bound of the result is, as usual, the lower bound of the index subtype.

So

```
"CAT" & "ERPILLAR" = "CATERPILLAR"
```

String catenation can be used to construct a string which is too long to fit on one line

```
"This string goes" &
"on and on"
```

The & operator is also defined to take a one dimensional array as one operand and a value of the component type as the other operand. But both operands may not be scalars

```
"CAT" & 'S' = "CATS"
'S' & "CAT"= "SCAT"
```

but 'S' & 'S' is illegal.

This is useful for representing the control characters such as CR and LF in strings.

```
"First line" & ASCII.CR & ASCII.LF & "Next line"
```

Of course, it might be neater to declare

```
CRLF: constant STRING:=(ASCII.CR, ASCII.LF);
```

and then write

```
"First line" & CRLF & "Next line"
```

The operation & can be applied to any one dimensional array type and so we can apply it to our Roman numbers. Consider

```
R:  ROMAN_NUMBER(1 .. 5);
S:  STRING(1 .. 5);

R:="CCL" & "IV";
S:="CCL" & "IV";
```

This is valid. The context tells us that in the first case we apply & to two Roman numbers whereas in the second we apply it to two values of type STRING. There is no ambiguity as in

```
B: BOOLEAN:="CCL" < "IV";
```

The final special feature of one dimensional arrays is the ability to denote a slice of an array object. A slice is written as the name of the object (variable or constant) followed by a discrete range in brackets. Note carefully that slicing applies to objects and not to values.

So given

```
S: STRING(1..10);
```

then we can write S(3..8) to denote the middle six characters of S. The bounds of the slice are the bounds of the range and not those of the index subtype. We could write

```
T: constant STRING:=S(3..8);
```

and then T'FIRST = 3, T'LAST = 8.

But on the other hand if we wrote

```
T: constant STRING:=S(3..8) & S(9..10);
```

then the bounds of T would be NATURAL'FIRST=1 and 8.

The bounds of the slice need not be static but can be any expressions. A slice would be null if the range turned out to be null.

The use of slices emphasises the nature of array assignment. The value of the expression to be assigned is completely evaluated before any components are assigned. No problems arise with overlapping slices. So

```
S(1..4):="BARA";
S(4..7):=S(1..4);
```

results in S(1..7) = "BARBARA". S(4) is only updated after the expression S(1..4) is safely evaluated. There is no risk of setting S(4) to 'B' and then consequently making the expression "BARB" with the final result of "BARBARB".

Exercise 6.4

1 Write the 8 possible constants WHITE . . . BLACK of the type COLOUR in ascending order as determined by the operator < applied to one dimensional arrays.

2 Evaluate

a) RED **or** GREEN
b) BLACK **xor** RED
c) **not** GREEN

3 Show that **not** (BLACK **xor** C) = C is true for all values of C.

4 Why did we not write

```
(JAN, JAN) < (FEB)
```

5 Assume that R contains a Roman number. Write statements to see if the last digit of the corresponding decimal arabic value is a 4 and change it to a 6 if it is.

6 In

```
T: constant STRING:=S(3..8) & S(9..10);
```

why is T'FIRST = 1 and not 3?

6.5 Records

As stated at the beginning of this chapter we are only going to consider the simplest form of record at this point. A fuller treatment covering variant records and so on is left until Chapter 11.

A record is a composite object consisting of named components which may be of different types. In contrast to arrays, we cannot have anonymous record types – they all have to be named. Consider

```
type MONTH_NAME is (JAN, FEB, MAR, APR, MAY, JUN, JUL,
                    AUG, SEP, OCT, NOV, DEC);

type DATE is
   record
      DAY: INTEGER range 1..31;
      MONTH: MONTH_NAME;
      YEAR: INTEGER;
   end record;
```

This declares the type DATE to be a record containing three named components, DAY, MONTH and YEAR.

We can declare variables and constants of record types in the usual way.

```
D: DATE;
```

declares an object D which is a date. The individual components of D can be denoted by following D with a dot and the component name. Thus we could write

```
D.DAY:=4;
D.MONTH:=JUL;
D.YEAR:=1776;
```

in order to assign new values to the individual components.

Records can be manipulated as whole objects. Literal values can be written as aggregates much like arrays; both positional and named forms can be used. So we could write

```
D: DATE:=(4, JUL, 1776);
E: DATE;
```

and then

```
E:=D;
```

or

```
E:=(MONTH => JUL, DAY=> 4, YEAR=> 1776);
```

The reader will be relieved to know that much of the complexity of array aggregates does not apply to records. This is because the number of components is always known.

In a positional aggregate the components come in order. In a named aggregate they may be in any order. In the particular example shown the use of a named aggregate avoids the necessity to know on which side of the Atlantic the record type was declared.

A named aggregate cannot use a range because the components are not considered to be closley related and the vertical bar can only be used with components which do have the same type.

There is one extra possibility for records and that is that the positional and named notations can be mixed in one aggregate. But if this is done then the positional components must come first and in order (without holes) as usual. So in other words we can change to the named notation at any point in the aggregate but must then stick to it. The above date could therefore also be expressed as

```
(4, JUL, YEAR=>1776)
(4, YEAR=> 1776, MONTH=> JUL)
```

and so on.

It is possible to give default values for some or all of the components in the type declaration. Thus

```
type COMPLEX is
    record
        RL: REAL:=0.0;
        IM: REAL:=0.0;
    end record;
```

or more succinctly

```
type COMPLEX is
    record
        RL, IM: REAL:=0.0;
    end record;
```

declares a record type containing two components of type REAL and gives a default value of 0.0 for each. We can now declare

```
C1: COMPLEX;
C2: COMPLEX:=(1.0,0.0);
```

The object C1 will now have the values 0.0 for its components by default. In the case of C2 we have overridden the default values. Note that, irritatingly, even if there are default values, an aggregate must be complete even if it supplies the same values as the default values for some of the components.

In this case both components are the same type and so we can write

```
(RL|IM => 1.0)
```

The only operations predefined on record types are = and /= as well as assignment of course. Other operations must be performed at the component level or be explicitly defined by a subprogram as we shall see in the next chapter.

A record type may have any number of components. It may pathologically have none in which case its declaration takes the form

```
type HOLE is
    record
        null;
    end record;
```

The reserved word **null** confirms that we meant to declare a null record type. Null records have their uses but they will not be apparent yet.

The components of a record type can be of any type; they can be other records or arrays. However, if a component is in array then it must be fully constrained (i.e. its index must not contain < >). And obviously a record cannot contain an instance of itself.

The components cannot be constants but the record as a whole can be. Thus

```
I: constant COMPLEX:=(0.0,1.0);
```

is allowed and represents the square root of −1.

A more elaborate example of a record is

```
type PERSON is
    record
        BIRTH: DATE;
        NAME: STRING (1..20):=(NAME'RANGE => ' ');
    end record;
```

The record PERSON has two components, the first is another record, a DATE, the second an array. The array which is a string of length 20 has a default value of all spaces.

We can now write

```
JOHN: PERSON;
JOHN.BIRTH:=(19,AUG,1937);
JOHN.NAME(1..4):="JOHN";
```

and we would then have

```
JOHN = ((19, AUG, 1937), "JOHN ");
```

The notation is as expected. The aggregates nest and for objects we proceed from left to right using the dot notation to select components of a record and indexes in brackets to select components of an array and ranges in brackets to slice arrays. There is no limit. We could have an array of persons

```
PEOPLE: array (1 .. N) of PERSON;
```

and then have

```
PEOPLE(6).BIRTH.DAY:=19;
PEOPLE(8).NAME(3):='H';
```

and so on.

A final point worth making about records is that any expressions occurring in the type declaration are evaluated when the declaration is elaborated and not when objects of the type are declared. However, a component which is an array must have static bounds. So our type PERSON could not have

```
NAME: STRING(1 .. N) :=(NAME'RANGE => ' ');
```

unless N is static. One exception to this rule will be met in Chapter 11 when we discuss discriminated records.

Exercise 6.5

1 Rewrite the solution to Exercise 6.1(**3**) using a variable D of type DATE rather than three individual variables.

2 Declare three variables C1, C2 and C3 of type COMPLEX. Write one or more statements to assign a) the sum, b) the product, of C1 and C2 to C3.

3 Write statements to find the index of the first person of the array PEOPLE born on or after January 1st, 1950.

Checklist 6

Array types can be anonymous, but records cannot.

Aggregates must always be complete.

Distinguish constrained array types from unconstrained array types (those with < >).

Named and positional notations cannot be mixed for array aggregates – they can for records.

A positional array aggregate with **others** must have a context giving its bounds.

A null array cannot be 'overnull'.

The attributes FIRST, LAST, LENGTH and RANGE apply to array objects and constrained array types and subtypes but not to unconstrained types and subtypes.

For array assignment to be valid, the number of components must be equal for each dimension – not the bounds.

The cases of alphabet are distinct in character literals and strings.

An aggregate with one component must use the named notation. This applies to records as well as to arrays.

7 Subprograms

Subprograms are the conventional parameterised unit of programming. In Ada, subprograms fall into two categories: functions and procedures. Functions are called as components of expressions and return a result, whereas procedures are called as statements and do not return a result.

As we shall see, the actions to be performed when a subprogram is called are described by a subprogram body. Subprogram bodies are declared in the usual way in a declarative part which may for instance be in a block or indeed in another subprogram.

7.1 Functions

A function is a form of subprogram that can be called as part of an expression. In Chapter 4 we met examples of calls of functions such as ABS, SQRT and so on.

We now consider the form of a function body which describes the statements to be executed when the function is called. For example the body of the function SQRT might have the form

```
function SQRT(X: REAL) return REAL is
   R: REAL;
begin
   -- compute value of SQRT(X) in R
   return R;
end SQRT;
```

All function bodies start with the reserved word **function** and the designator of the function being defined. If the function has parameters the designator is followed by a list of parameter declarations in brackets. If there are several declarations then they are separated by semicolons. Each declaration gives the identifiers of one or more parameters followed by a colon and its type or subtype. The parameter list, if any, is then followed by the reserved word **return** and the type or subtype of the result of the function.

The part of the body we have described so far is called the function specification. It specifies the function to the outside world in the sense of providing all the information needed to call the function.

After the specification comes **is** and then the body proper which is just like a block – it has a declarative part, **begin**, a sequence of statements, and then **end**. As for a block the declarative part can be empty but there must be at least one statement in the sequence of statements. Between **end** and the terminating semicolon we may repeat the designator of the function. This is optional but, if present, must correctly match the designator after **function**.

It is often necessary or just convenient to give the specification on its own but without the rest of the body. In such a case it is immediately followed by a semicolon and is then known as a function declaration. The uses of such declarations will be discussed later.

The formal parameters of a function act as local constants whose values are provided by the corresponding actual parameters. When the function is called the declarative part is elaborated in the usual way and then the statements are executed. A return statement is used to indicate the value of the function call and to return control back to the calling expression.

Thus considering our example suppose we had

```
S:=SQRT(T +0.5);
```

then first T + 0.5 is evaluated and then SQRT is called. Within the body the parameter X behaves as a constant with the initial value given by T + 0.5. It is rather as if we had

```
X: constant REAL :=T + 0.5;
```

The declaration of R is then elaborated. We then obey the sequence of statements and assume they compute the square root of X and assign it to R. The last statement is **return** R; this passes control back to the calling expression with the result of the function being the value of R. This value is then assigned to S.

The expression in a return statement can be of arbitrary complexity and must be of the same type and satisfy the constraints (if any) given in the function specification. If the constraints are violated then, of course, the exception CONSTRAINT_ERROR is raised.

A function body may have several return statements. The execution of any of them will terminate the function. Thus the function SIGN which takes an integer value and returns +1, 0 or −1 according to whether the parameter is positive, zero or negative could be written as

```
function SIGN(X: INTEGER) return INTEGER is
begin
   if X > 0 then
      return +1;
   elsif X < 0 then
      return -1;
   else
      return 0;
   end if;
end SIGN;
```

So we see that the last lexical statement of the body need not be a return statement since there is one in each branch of the if statement. But take care not to 'run' into the final **end** since this would result in the function returning an undefined value and the program is likely to be erroneous.

It should be noted that each call of a function produces a new instance of any objects declared within it (including parameters of course) and these disappear when we leave the function. It is therefore possible for a function to be called recursively without any problems. So the factorial function could be declared as

```
function FACTORIAL(N: NATURAL) return NATURAL is
begin
    if N = 1 then
        return 1;
    else
        return N * FACTORIAL(N-1);
    end if;
end FACTORIAL;
```

If we write

```
F:=FACTORIAL(4);
```

then the function calls itself until, on the fourth call (with the other three calls all partly executed and waiting for the result of the call they did before doing the multiply) we find that N is 1 and the calls then all unwind and all the multiplications are performed.

Note that there is no need to check that the parameter N is positive since the parameter is of subtype NATURAL. So calling FACTORIAL(−2) will result in CONSTRAINT_ERROR. Of course, FACTORIAL(10000) could result in the computer running out of space in which case STORAGE_ERROR would be raised. The more moderate call FACTORIAL(20) would probably raise NUMERIC_ERROR.

A formal parameter may be of any type but the type must have a name. It cannot be an anonymous type such as

```
array (1..6) of REAL
```

In any event no actual parameter could match such a formal parameter even if it were allowed since the actual and formal parameters must have the same type.

A formal parameter can, however, be an unconstrained array type such as

```
type VECTOR is array (INTEGER range <>) of REAL;
```

In such a case the bounds of the formal parameter are taken from those of the actual parameter.

Consider

```
function SUM(A: VECTOR) return REAL is
    RESULT: REAL:=0.0;
begin
    for I in A'RANGE loop
        RESULT:=RESULT+A(I);
    end loop;
    return RESULT;
end SUM;
```

then we can write

```
V: VECTOR(1..4):=(1.0,2.0,3.0,4.0);
S: REAL;
...
S:=SUM(V);
```

The formal parameter A then takes the bounds of the actual parameter V. So for this call we have

```
A'RANGE  is  1..4
```

and the effect of the loop is to compute the sum of A(1), A(2), A(3) and A(4). The final value of RESULT which is returned and assigned to S is therefore 10.0.

The function SUM can be used to sum the components of a vector with any bounds. Ada overcomes one of the problems of Pascal which insists that array parameters have static bounds. Of course, an Ada function could have a constrained array type as a formal parameter either by applying the constraint in the parameter list as in

```
function SUM_6(A: VECTOR(1..6)) return REAL
```

or by using the name of a constrained array type such as

```
type VECTOR_6 is array (1..6) of REAL;
```

as in

```
function SUM_6(A: VECTOR_6) return REAL
```

As another example consider

```
function INNER(A,B: VECTOR) return REAL is
    RESULT: REAL:=0.0;
begin
    for I in A'RANGE loop
        RESULT:=RESULT+A(I)*B(I);
    end loop;
    return RESULT;
end INNER;
```

This computes the inner product of the two vectors A and B by adding together the sum of the products of corresponding components. This is our first example of a function with more than one parameter. Such a function is called by following the function name by a list of the expressions giving the values of the actual parameters separated by commas and in brackets. The order of evaluation of the actual parameters is not defined.

So

```
V : VECTOR(1 .. 3):=(1.0,2.0,3.0);
W: VECTOR(1 .. 3):=(2.0,3.0,4.0);
R : REAL;
. . .
R :=INNER(V,W);
```

results in R being assigned the value

```
1.0 * 2.0 + 2.0 * 3.0 + 3.0 * 4.0 = 20.0
```

Note that the function INNER is not written well since it does not check that the bounds of A and B are the same. It is not symmetric with respect to A and B since I takes (or tries to take) the values of the range A'RANGE irrespective of B'RANGE. So if the array W had bounds of 2 and 4, CONSTRAINT_ERROR would be raised on the third time round the loop. If the array W had bounds of 1 and 4 then no exception would be raised but the result might not be what we expected.

It is tempting to ensure the equality of the bounds by placing a constraint on B at the time of call by, for example, writing the formal parameter list as

```
(A: VECTOR; B: VECTOR(A'RANGE))
```

but this is not allowed. For one thing the order of the association of actual and formal parameters is not defined; secondly, no dependency is allowed between the formal parameters; thirdly, any constraints in the formal parameter list are evaluated when the function is declared and not when it is called.

The best we can do is simply check the bounds for equality inside the function body and perhaps explicitly raise CONSTRAINT_ERROR if they are not equal.

```
if A'FIRST /= B'FIRST or A'LAST /= B'LAST then
    raise CONSTRAINT_ERROR;
end if;
```

(The use of the raise statement is described in detail in Chapter 10).

We noted above that any constraints in the formal parameter list are evaluated when the function is declared and not when it is called. The same applies to constraints on the result. However, this does not prevent the result from being an array whose bounds are not known until the function is called. The result type can be an unconstrained array and the bounds are then obtained from the expression in the appropriate return statement.

As an example the following function returns a vector which has the same bounds as the parameter but whose component values are in the reverse order

```
function REVERSE(X: VECTOR) return VECTOR is
    R: VECTOR(X'RANGE);
begin
    for I in X'RANGE loop
        R(I):= X(X'FIRST+X'LAST-I);
    end loop;
    return R;
end REVERSE;
```

The variable R is declared to be of type VECTOR with the same bounds as X. Note how the loop reverses the value. The result takes the bounds of the expression R.

If a function returns a record or array value then a component can be immediately selected, indexed or sliced as appropriate without assigning the value to a variable. So we could write

```
REVERSE(Y) (I)
```

which denotes the component indexed by I of the array returned by the call of REVERSE.

It should be noted that a parameterless function call, unlike a parameterless procedure call, has empty brackets. This avoids confusion between calling a function with one parameter and indexing the result of a parameterless call.

Exercise 7.1

1 Write a suitable body for the predefined function ABS with an INTEGER parameter.

2 Rewrite the factorial function so that the parameter may be positive or zero but not negative. Remember that the value of FACTORIAL(0) is to be 1.

3 Write a function OUTER that forms the outer product of two vectors. The outer product $\boldsymbol{C}$ of two vectors $\boldsymbol{A}$ and $\boldsymbol{B}$ is a matrix such that $C_{ij} = A_i \,.\, B_j$.

4 Write a function MAKE_COLOUR which takes an array of values of type PRIMARY and returns the corresponding value of type COLOUR. See Section 6.4. Check that MAKE_COLOUR ((R, Y)) = ORANGE.

5 Write a function VALUE which takes a parameter of type ROMAN_NUMBER and returns the equivalent integer value. See Exercise 6.3(2).

6 Write a function MAKE_UNIT that takes a single parameter N and returns a unit $N \times N$ real matrix. Use the function to declare a constant unit $N \times N$ matrix. See Exercise 6.2(3).

7 Write a function GCD to return the greatest common divisor of two non-negative integers. Use Euclid's algorithm that

$$\begin{aligned} \gcd(x, y) &= \gcd(y, x \bmod y) \qquad y \neq 0 \\ \gcd(x, 0) &= x \end{aligned}$$

Write the function using recursion and then rewrite it using a loop statement.

7.2 Operators

In the last section we carefully stated that a function body commenced with the reversed word **function** followed by the designator of the function. In all the examples of the last section the designator was in fact an identifier. However, it can also be a character string provided that the string is one of the following language operators in double quotes.

and	**or**	**xor**		
=	<	<=	>	>=
+	–	&	**not**	
*	/	mod	rem	**

In such a case the function defines a new meaning of the operator concerned. As an example we can rewrite the function INNER of the last section as an operator.

```
function "*" (A,B: VECTOR) return REAL is
    RESULT: REAL:=0.0;
begin
    for I in A'RANGE loop
        RESULT:=RESULT+A(I)*B(I);
    end loop;
    return RESULT;
end "*";
```

We call this new function by the normal syntax of uses of the operator * Thus instead of

```
R:=INNER(V,W);
```

we now write

```
R:=V*W;
```

This meaning of * is distinguished from the existing meanings of integer and real multiplication by the context provided by the types of the actual parameters V and W and the type required by R.

The giving of several meanings to an operator is another instance of overloading which we have already met with enumeration literals. The rules for the overloading of subprograms in general are discussed later in this chapter. It suffices to say at this point that any ambiguity can always be resolved by qualification. Overloading of predefined operators is not new. It has existed in most programming languages for the past quarter century. What is new is the ability to define additional overloadings and indeed the use of the term 'overloading' is itself relatively new.

We can now see that the predefined meanings of all operators are as if there were a series of functions with declarations such as

```
function "+"(X,Y: INTEGER) return INTEGER;
function "<"(X,Y: INTEGER) return BOOLEAN;
function "<"(X,Y: BOOLEAN) return BOOLEAN;
```

Moreover, every time we declare a new type, new overloadings of some operators such as = and < may be created.

Although we can add new meanings to operators we cannot change the syntax of the call. Thus the number of parameters of "*" must always be two and the precedence cannot be changed and so on. The operators + and − are unusual in that a new definition can have either one parameter or two parameters according to whether it is to be called as a unary or binary operator. Thus the function SUM could be rewritten as

```
function "+"(A: VECTOR) return REAL is
    RESULT: REAL:=0.0;
begin
    for I in A'RANGE loop
        RESULT:=RESULT+A(I);
    end loop;
    return RESULT;
end "+";
```

and we would then write

```
S:=+V;
```

rather than

```
S:=SUM(V);
```

Function bodies whose designators are operators often contain interesting examples of uses of the operator being overloaded. Thus the body of "*" contains a use of * in A(I)*B(I). There is, of course, no ambiguity since the expressions A(I) and B(I) are of type REAL whereas our new overloading is for type VECTOR. Sometimes there is the risk of accidental recursion. This particularly applies if we try to replace an existing meaning rather than add a new one.

Apart from the operator "=" there are no special rules regarding the types of the operands and results of new overloadings. Thus a new overloading of "<" need not return a BOOLEAN result. The rules for "=" will be given in Chapter 9. Note that /= may not be overloaded – it always takes its meaning from =.

The membership tests **in** and **not in** and the short circuit forms **and then** and **or else** cannot be given new meanings. That is why we said in Section 4.9 that they were not technically classed as operators.

Finally note that in the case of operators represented by reserved words, the characters in the string can be in either case. Thus a new overloading of **or** can be declared as "or" or "OR" or even "Or".

Exercise 7.2

1 Write a function "<" that operates on two Roman numbers and compares them according to their corresponding numeric values. That is, so that "CCL" < "CCXC". Use the function VALUE of Exercise 7.1(**5**).

2 Write functions "+"and "*" to add and multiply two values of type COMPLEX. See Exercise 6.5(**2**).

3 Write a function "<" to test whether a value of type PRIMARY is in a set represented by a value of type COLOUR. See Section 6.4.

4 Write a function "<=" to test whether one value of type COLOUR is a subset of another.

7.3 Procedures

The other form of subprogram is a procedure; a procedure is called as a statement. We have seen many examples of procedure calls where there are no parameters such as WORK; PARTY; ACTION; and so on.

The body of a procedure is very similiar to that of a function. The differences are

- a procedure starts with **procedure**,
- its name must be an identifier,
- it does not return a result,
- the parameters may be of three different modes **in**, **out** or **in out**.

The mode of a parameter is indicated by following the colon in the parameter declaration by **in** or by **out** or by **in out**. If the mode is omitted then it is taken to be **in**. In the case of functions the only allowed mode is **in**; the examples earlier in this chapter omitted **in** but could have been written for instance, as

```
function SQRT(X: in REAL) return REAL;
function "*"(A, B: in VECTOR) return REAL;
```

The effect of the three modes is best summarised by quoting the LRM (section 6.2).

in	The parameter acts as a local constant whose value is provided by the corresponding actual parameter.
out	The parameter acts as a local variable whose value is assigned to the corresponding actual parameter as a result of the execution of the subprogram.
in out	The parameter acts as a local variable and permits access and assignment to the corresponding actual parameter.

As a simple example of the modes **in** and **out** consider

```
procedure ADD(A, B: in INTEGER; C: out INTEGER) is
begin
      C:=A+B;
end ADD;
```

with

```
P, Q: INTEGER;
. . .
ADD(2+P, 37, Q);
```

On calling ADD, the expressions 2+P and 37 are evaluated (in any order) and assigned to the formals A and B which behave as constants. The value of A+B is then assigned to the formal variable C. On return the value of C is assigned to the variable Q. Thus it is (more or less) as if we had written

```
declare
      A: constant INTEGER:=2+P;          -- in
      B: constant INTEGER:=37;           -- in
      C: INTEGER;                        -- out
begin
      C:=A+B;                            -- body
      Q:=C;                              -- out
end;
```

As an example of the mode **in out** consider

```
procedure INCREMENT(X: in out INTEGER) is
begin
      X:=X+1;
end;
```

with

```
I: INTEGER;
. . .
INCREMENT(I);
```

On calling INCREMENT, the value of I is assigned to the formal variable X. The value of X is then incremented. On return, the final value of X is assigned to the actual parameter I. So it is rather as if we had written

```
declare
      X: INTEGER:=I;
```

```
begin
    X:=X+1;
    I:=X;
end;
```

For any scalar type (such as INTEGER) the modes correspond simply to copying the value **in** at the call or **out** upon return or both in the case of **in out**.

If the mode is **in** then the actual parameter may be any expression of the appropriate type or subtype. If the mode is **out** or **in out** then the actual parameter must be a variable. The identity of such a variable is determined when the procedure is called and cannot change during the call.

Suppose we had

```
I: INTEGER;
A: array (1..10) of INTEGER;
procedure SILLY (X: in out INTEGER) is
begin
    I:=I+1;
    X:=X+1;
end;
```

then the statements

```
A(5):=1;
I:=5;
SILLY(A(I));
```

result in A(5) becoming 2, I becoming 6, but A(6) is not affected.

If a parameter is a composite type (such as an array or record) then the mechanism of copying, described above, may be used but alternatively an implementation may use a mechanism in which the formal parameter provides direct access to the actual parameter. A program which depends on the particular mechanism is erroneous. An example of such a program is given in the exercises at the end of this section.

We now discuss the question of constraints on parameters.

In the case of scalar parameters the situation is as expected from the copying model. For an **in** or **in out** parameter any range constraint on the formal must be satisfied by the actual at the beginning of the call. Conversely for an **in out** or **out** parameter any range constraint on the variable which is the actual parameter must be satisfied by the value of the formal parameter upon return from the subprogram.

In the case of arrays the situation is somewhat different. If the formal parameter is a constrained array type, the bounds of the actual must be identical; it is not enough for the number of components in each dimension to be the same; the parameter mechanism is more rigorous than assignment. If, on the other hand, the formal parameter is an unconstrained array type, then, as we have seen, it takes its bounds from those of the formal. The foregoing applies irrespective of the mode of the array parameter. Similar rules apply to function results; if the result is a constrained array type then the expression in a return statement must have the same bounds. As an aside, one consequence of the parameter and result mechanism being more rigorous than assignment is that array aggregates with **others** are allowed as actual parameters and in return statements. On the other hand, as we saw in Section 6.2, they are not allowed in an assignment statement unless qualified.

In the case of the simple records we have discussed so far there are no constraints and so there is nothing to say. The parameter mechanism for other types will be discussed when they are introduced.

We stated above that an actual parameter corresponding to a formal **out** or **in out** parameter must be a variable. However, it can also be a type conversion of a variable provided, of course, that the conversion is allowed. As an example, since conversion is allowed between any numeric types, we can write

```
R: REAL;
...
INCREMENT(INTEGER(R));
```

If R initially had the value 2.3, it would be converted to the integer value 2 incremented to give 3 and then on return converted back to 3.0 and assigned to R.

This conversion of **in out** or **out** parameters is particularly useful with arrays. Suppose we write a library of subprograms applying to our type VECTOR and then acquire from someone else some subprograms written to apply to the type ROW of Section 6.2. The types ROW and VECTOR are essentially the same; it just so happened that the authors used different names. Array type conversion allows us to use both sets of subprograms without having to change the type names systematically.

As a final example consider the following

```
procedure QUADRATIC(A, B, C: in REAL; ROOT_1, ROOT_2:
                        out REAL;  OK: out BOOLEAN) is
   D: constant REAL:=B**2-4.0*A*C;
begin
   OK:=D >= 0.0 and A /=0.0;
   if not OK then
         return;
   end if;
   ROOT_1:=(-B+SQRT(D))/(2.0*A);
   ROOT_2:=(-B-SQRT(D))/(2.0*A);
end QUADRATIC;
```

The procedure QUADRATIC attempts to solve the equation

$$ax^2 + bx + c = 0$$

If the roots are real they are returned via the parameters ROOT_1 and ROOT_2 and OK is set to TRUE. If the roots are complex (D< 0.0) or the equation degenerates (A = 0.0) then OK is set to FALSE.

Note the use of the return statement. Since this is a procedure there is no result to be returned and so the word **return** is not followed by an expression.

It just updates **out** or **in out** parameters as necessary and returns control back to where the procedure was called. Note also that unlike a function we can 'run' into the **end**; this is equivalent to obeying **return**.

The reader will note that if OK is set to FALSE then no value is assigned to the **out** parameters ROOT_1 and ROOT_2. Presumably, a junk value is therefore assigned to the corresponding actual parameters which could possibly raise CONSTRAINT_ERROR if the actual parameter were constrained. This is probably bad practice and so it might be better to assign safe values such as 0.0 to the roots just in case. (In examples like this, the **out** mechanism does not seem so satisfactory as the simple reference mechanism of Algol 68 or Pascal.)

The procedure could be used in a sequence such as

```
declare
    L, M, N: REAL;
    P, Q: REAL;
    STATUS: BOOLEAN;
begin
    -- sets values into L, M and N
    QUADRATIC(L, M, N, P, Q, STATUS);
    if STATUS then
        -- roots are in P and Q
    else
        -- fails
    end if;
end;
```

Exercise 7.3

1 Write a procedure SWAP to interchange the values of the two real parameters.

2 Rewrite the function REVERSE of Section 7.1 as a procedure with a single parameter. Use it to reverse an array R of type ROW.

3 Why is the following erroneous?

```
A: VECTOR(1 .. 1);

procedure P(V: VECTOR) is
begin
    A(1):=V(1)+V(1);
    A(1):=V(1)+V(1);
end;

...
A(1):=1.0;
P(A);
```

7.4 Named and default parameters

The forms of subprogram call we have been using so far have given the actual parameters in positional order. As with aggregates we can also use the named notation in which the formal parameter name is also supplied; the parameters do not then have to be in order.

So we could write

```
QUADRATIC(A => L, B => M, C => N, ROOT_1 => P,
                    ROOT_2 => Q, OK => STATUS);
INCREMENT(X => I);
ADD(C => Q, A => 2+P, B => 37);
```

We could even write

```
INCREMENT(X => X);
```

the scopes do not interfere.

This notation can also be used with functions

```
F:=FACTORIAL(N => 4);
S:=SQRT(X => T+0.5);
R:=INNER(B => W, A => V);
```

The named notation cannot, however, be used with operators called with the infixed syntax.

As with record aggregates, the named and positional notations can be mixed and any positional parameters must come first and in their correct order. However, unlike record aggregates, each parameter must be given individually and again **others** may not be used. So we could write

```
QUADRATIC(L, M, N, ROOT_1 => P, ROOT_2 => Q,
                 OK => STATUS);
```

The named notation leads into the topic of default parameters. It sometimes happens that one or more **in** parameters usually take the same value on each call; we can give a default value in the subprogram specification and then omit it from the call.

Consider the problem of ordering a dry martini in the USA. One is faced with choices described by the following enumeration types

```
type SPIRIT is (GIN, VODKA);
type STYLE is (ON_THE_ROCKS, STRAIGHT_UP);
type TRIMMING is (OLIVE, TWIST);
```

The standard default values can then be given in a procedure specification thus

```
procedure DRY_MARTINI(BASE: SPIRIT:=GIN;
                      HOW: STYLE:=ON_THE_ROCKS;
                      PLUS: TRIMMING:=OLIVE);
```

Typical calls might be

```
DRY_MARTINI(HOW => STRAIGHT_UP);
DRY_MARTINI(VODKA, PLUS => TWIST);
```

```
DRY_MARTINI;
DRY_MARTINI(GIN,STRAIGHT_UP);
```

The first call uses the named notation; we get gin, straight up plus olive. The second call mixes the positional and named notations; as soon as a parameter is omitted the named notation must be used. The third call illustrates that all parameters can be omitted. The final call shows that a parameter can, of course, be supplied even if it happens to take the default value; in this case it avoids using the named form for the second parameter.

Note that default parameters can only be given for **in** parameters. They cannot be given for operators but they can be given for functions designated by identifiers. The default values, like constraints on the formal parameters, are evaluated when the subprogram is declared. Thus each call has the same default value. Default values are widely used in the standard input output package to provide default formats.

Exercise 7.4

1 Write a function ADD which returns the sum of the two integer parameters and takes a default value of 1 for the second parameter. How many different ways can it be called to return N+1 where N is the first actual parameter?

7.5 Overloading

We saw in Section 7.2 how new meanings could be given to existing language operators. This overloading applies to subprograms in general.

A subprogram will overload an existing meaning rather than hide it, provided that its specification is sufficiently different. Hiding will occur if

for a procedure
: The order, names and base types of the parameters are the same and the same parameters have default values. The default values themselves, the values of any constraints and the modes of the parameters do not matter.

for a function
: As for a procedure plus the result base type must also be the same. Any constraints on the result do not matter.

for an operator
: As for a function but the parameter names do not matter.

A procedure cannot hide a function and vice versa.

Two or more overloaded subprograms may be declared in the same declarative part but there is an additional rule that they must then differ by more than just the parameter names. Indeed in view of the fact that the names do not count for operators, it seems wiser to forget about the parameter names in all cases and only rely upon the base types of the parameters and any result.

Subprograms and enumeration literals can overload each other. There are two classes of uses of identifiers – the overloadable ones and the non overloadable ones. At any point an identifier either refers to a single entity of the non overloadable class or to one or many of the overloadable class. A declaration of one class hides the other class and cannot occur in the same declaration list.

As we have seen, ambiguities arising from overloading can be resolved by qualification. This was necessary when the operator "<" was used with the strings in Section 6.3. As a further example consider the British Channel Islands; the larger three are Guernsey, Jersey and Alderney. There are woollen garments named after each island

```
type GARMENT is (GUERNSEY, JERSEY, ALDERNEY);
```

and breeds of cattle named after two of them (the Alderney breed became extinct as a consequence of the Second World War)

```
type COW is (GUERNSEY, JERSEY);
```

and we can imagine (just) shops that sell both garments and cows according to

```
procedure SELL(G: GARMENT);
procedure SELL(C: COW);
```

Although

```
SELL(ALDERNEY);
```

is not ambiguous

```
SELL(JERSEY);
```

is, since we cannot tell which subprogram is being called. We must write for example

```
SELL(COW'(JERSEY));
```

Exercise 7.5

1 How else could SELL(JERSEY); be made unambiguous?

7.6 Declarations, scopes and visibility

We said earlier that it is sometimes necessary or just convenient to give a subprogram specification on its own without the body. The specification is then followed by a semicolon and is known as a subprogram declaration. A complete subprogram, which always includes the full specification, is known as a subprogram body.

Subprogram declarations and bodies must, like other declarations, occur in a declarative part and a subprogram declaration must be followed by the corresponding body in the same declarative part.

An example of where it is necessary to use a subprogram declaration occurs with mutually recursive procedures. Suppose we wish to declare two procedures F and G which call each other. Because of the rule regarding linear elaboration of declarations we cannot write the call of F in the body of G until after F has been declared and vice versa. Clearly this is impossible if we just write the bodies because one must come second. However, we can write

```
procedure F(...);      -- declaration of F

procedure G(...) is    -- body of G
begin
   F(...);
end G;

procedure F(...) is    -- body of F repeats
begin                  -- its specification
   G(...);
end F;
```

and then all is well.

If the specification is repeated then it must be given in full and the two must be the same. Even default values and constraints must be repeated although they are only evaluated in the first specification. However, there are restrictions on the expressions allowed as default values and constraints to ensure that if they were evaluated again then the same values would be obtained. For details the reader is referred to the LRM. But expressions containing just constants, literals and the predefined operators are clearly acceptable.

Another important case, where we have to write a subprogram declaration as well as a body, occurs in the next chapter when we discuss packages. Even if not always necessary, it is sometimes clearer to write subprogram declarations as well as bodies. An example might be in the case where many subprogram bodies occur together. The subprogram declarations then act as a summary.

Subprogram bodies and other declarations must not be mixed up in an arbitrary way. The bodies must follow other declarations. This ensures that small declarations are not 'lost' in between large bodies. In fact a subprogram body is classed as a 'program component'. Other forms of program component, which we have not yet met, are packages and tasks.

Since subprograms occur in declarative parts and themselves contain declarative parts they may be textually nested without limit. The normal hiding rules applicable to blocks described in Section 4.2 also apply to declarations in subprograms. (The only complication concerns overloading as discussed in the previous section.) Consider

```
procedure P is
   I: INTEGER:=0;

   procedure Q is
      K: INTEGER:=I;
      I: INTEGER;
      J: INTEGER;
   begin
      ...
   end Q;
   ...
end P;
```

Just as for the example in Section 4.2, the inner I hides the outer one and so the outer I is not visible inside the procedure Q after the declaration of the inner I.

However, we can always refer to the outer I by the so-called dotted notation, in which it is prefixed by the name of the unit immediately containing its declaration followed by a dot. So within Q we can refer to the outer I as P.I and so, for example, we could initialise J by writing

```
J: INTEGER:=P.I;
```

If the prefix is itself hidden then it can always be written the same way. Thus the inner I could be referred to as P.Q.I.

An object declared in a block cannot usually be referred to in this way since a block does not normally have a name. However, a block can be named in a similar way to a loop as shown in the following

```
OUTER:
declare
    I: INTEGER:=0;
begin
    ...
    declare
        K: INTEGER:=I;
        I: INTEGER;
        J: INTEGER:=OUTER.I;
    begin
        ...
    end;
end OUTER;
```

Here the outer block has the identifier OUTER. Unlike subprograms, the identifier has to be repeated after the matching **end**. Naming the block enables us to initialise the inner declaration of J with the value of the outer I.

Within a loop it is possible to refer to a hidden loop parameter in the same way. We could even rewrite the example in Section 6.1 of assigning zero to the elements of AA as

```
L:
for I in AA'RANGE(1) loop
    for I in AA'RANGE(2) loop
        AA(L.I, I):= 0.0;
    end loop;
end loop L;
```

although one would be a little crazy to do so!

It should be noted that the dotted form can always be used even if it is not necessary.

This notation can also be applied to operators and character literals. Thus the variable RESULT declared inside "*" can be referred to as "*". RESULT. And equally if "*" were declared inside a block B then it could be referred to as B."*". If it is called with this form of name then the normal function call must be used.

```
R:=B."*"(V,W);
```

Indeed, the functional form can always be used as in

```
R:="*"(V,W);
```

As we have seen, subprograms can alter global variables and therefore have side effects. (A side effect is one brought about other than via the parameter mechanism.) It is generally considered rather undesirable to write subprograms, especially functions, which have side effects. However, some side effects are beneficial. Any subprogram which performs input-output has a side effect on the file; a function delivering successive members of a sequence of random numbers only works because of its side effects; if we need to count how many times a function is called then we use a side effect; and so on. However, care must be taken when using functions with side effects that the program is not erroneous since there are various circumstances in which the order of evaluation is not defined.

We conclude this section with a brief discussion of the hierarchy of **exit**, **return** and **goto** and the scopes of block and loop identifiers and labels.

A **return** statement terminates the execution of the immediately embracing subprogram. It can occur inside an inner block or inside a loop in the subprogram and therefore also terminates the loop. On the other hand an **exit** statement terminates the named or immediately embracing loop. It can also occur inside an inner block but cannot occur inside a subprogram declared in the loop and thereby also terminates the subprogram. A **goto** statement can transfer control out of a loop or block but not out of a subprogram.

As far as scope is concerned, block and loop identifiers behave as if they are declared at the end of the declarative part of the immediately embracing subprogram or block (or package or task body). Thus two loops in the same block cannot have the same identifier. For labels, however, embracing blocks are discounted, so that two labels in the same subprogram cannot have the same identifier even if they are inside different inner blocks. This rule reduces the risk of goto statements going to the wrong label particularly when a program is amended.

Checklist 7

A function must return a result and so should not run into its final **end** although a procedure can.

The order of evaluation of parameters is not defined.

Constraints and default initial values are evaluated when a subprogram is declared and not when it is called.

Parameters of a constrained array type must have equal bounds.

A parameterless function call has empty brackets whereas a parameterless procedure call does not.

Scalar parameters are copied. The mechanism for arrays and records is not defined.

Formal parameter declarations are separated by semicolons not commas.

8 Overall Structure

The previous chapters have described the small scale features of Ada in considerable detail. The language presented so far corresponds to the areas addressed by languages of the sixties and early seventies, although Ada provides more functionality in those areas. However, we now come to the new areas which broadly speaking correspond to the concepts of data abstraction and programming in the large which were discussed in Chapter 1.

In this chapter we discuss packages (which is what Ada is all about) and the mechanisms for separate compilation. We also say a little more about scope and visibility.

8.1 Packages

One of the major problems with the traditional block structured languages, such as Algol and Pascal, is that they do not offer enough control of visibility. For example, suppose we have a stack represented by an array and a variable which indexes the current top element, a procedure PUSH to add an item and a function POP to remove an item. We might write

```
MAX: constant:=100;
S: array (1 .. MAX) of INTEGER;
TOP: INTEGER range 0 .. MAX;
```

to represent the stack and then declare

```
procedure PUSH(X: INTEGER) is
begin
    TOP:=TOP+1;
    S(TOP):=X;
end PUSH;

function POP return INTEGER is
begin
    TOP:=TOP-1;
    return S(TOP+1);
end POP;
```

In a simple block structured language there is no way in which we can be given access to the subprograms PUSH and POP without also being given direct access to the variables S and TOP. As a consequence we cannot be forced to use the correct protocol and so be prevented from making use of knowledge of how the stack is implemented.

The Ada package overcomes this by allowing us to place a wall around a group of declarations and only permit access to those which we intend to be visible. A package actually comes in two parts: the specification which gives the interface to the outside world, and the body which gives the hidden details.

The above example should be written as

```
package STACK is                              -- specification
   procedure PUSH(X: INTEGER);
   function POP return INTEGER;
end STACK;

package body STACK is                         -- body
   MAX: constant:=100;
   S: array (1 .. MAX) of INTEGER;
   TOP: INTEGER range 0 .. MAX;

   procedure PUSH(X: INTEGER) is
   begin
      TOP:=TOP+1;
      S(TOP):=X;
   end PUSH;

   function POP return INTEGER is
   begin
      TOP:=TOP-1;
      return S(TOP+1);
   end POP;

begin                                         -- initialisation
   TOP:=0;
end STACK;
```

The package specification starts with the reserved word **package**, the identifier of the package and **is**. This is then followed by declarations of the entities which are to be visible. It finishes with **end**, the identifier (optionally) and the terminating semicolon. In the example we just have the declarations of the two subprograms PUSH and POP.

The package body also starts with **package** but this is then followed by **body**, the identifier and **is**. We then have a normal declarative part, **begin**, sequence of statements, **end**, optional identifier and semicolon just as in a block or subprogram body.

In the example the declarative part contains the variables which represent the stack and the bodies of PUSH and POP. The sequence of statements between **begin** and **end** is executed when the package is declared and can be used for initialisation. If there is no need for an initialisation sequence, the **begin** can be omitted. Indeed in this example we could equally and perhaps more naturally have performed the initialisation by writing

```
TOP: INTEGER range 0 .. MAX:=0;
```

Note that a package is itself declared and so is just one of the items in an outer declarative part (unless it is a library unit which is the outermost layer anyway).

The package illustrates another case where we need distinct subprogram declarations and bodies. Indeed we cannot put a body into a package specification. And moreover, if a package specification contains the specification of a subprogram, then the package body must contain the corresponding subprogram body. We can think of the package specification and body as being just one large declarative part with only some items visible. But, of course, a subprogram body can be declared in a package body without its specification having to be given in the package specification. Such a subprogram would be internal to the package and could only be called from within, either from other subprograms, some of which would presumably be visible, or perhaps from the initialisation sequence.

The elaboration of a package body consists simply of the elaboration of the declarations inside it followed by the execution of the initialisation sequence if there is one. The package continues to exist until the end of the scope in which it is declared. Entities declared inside the package have the same lifetime as the package itself. Thus the variables S and TOP can be thought of as 'own' variables in the Algol 60 sense; their values are retained between successive calls of PUSH and POP.

Packages may be declared in any declarative part such as that in a block, subprogram or indeed another package. If a package specification is declared inside another package specification then, as for subprograms, the body of one must be declared in the body of the other. But again both specification and body could be in a package body.

Apart from the rule that a package specification cannot contain bodies, it can contain any of the other kinds of declarations we have met.

Now to return to the use of our package. The package itself has a name and the entities in its visible part can be thought of as components of the package in some sense. It is entirely natural therefore that, in order to call PUSH, we must also mention STACK. In fact the dotted notation is used. So we could write

```
declare
    package STACK is          -- specification
      ...                     -- and
      ...                     -- body
    end STACK;
begin
    ...
    STACK.PUSH(M);
    ...
    N:=STACK.POP();
    ...
end;
```

Inside the package we would call PUSH as just PUSH, but we could still write STACK.PUSH just as in the last chapter we saw how we could refer to a local variable X of procedure P as P.X. Inside the package we can refer to S or STACK.S, but outside the package MAX, S and POP are not accessible in any way.

It would in general be painful always to have to write STACK.PUSH to call PUSH from outside. Instead we can write

```
use STACK;
```

as a sort of declaration and we may then refer to PUSH and POP directly. The use clause could follow the declaration of STACK in the same declarative part or in another declarative part where it is visible. So we could write

```
declare
    use STACK;
begin
    ...
    PUSH(M);
    ...
    N:=POP();
    ...
end;
```

The use clause is like a declaration and similarly has a scope to the end of the block. Outside we would have to revert to the dotted notation. We could have an inner use clause referring to the same package – it would do no harm.

Two or more packages could be declared in the same declarative part. Generally, we could arrange all the specifications together and then all the bodies, or alternatively the corresponding specifications and bodies, could be together. Thus we could have spec A, spec B, body A, body B, or spec A, body A, spec B, body B.

The rules governing the order are simply

- linear elaboration of declarations,
- specification must precede body for same package (or subprogram),
- small items must precede large ones.

More precisely the last rule is that program components must be last. These are subprogram bodies and package (and task) specifications and bodies. Other declarations must precede program components but package specifications can be treated as large or small.

Of course, the visible part of a package may contain things other than subprograms. Indeed an important case is where it does not contain subprograms at all but merely a group of related variables, constants and types. In such a case the package needs no body. It does not provide any hiding properties but merely gives commonality of naming. (A body could be provided; its only purpose would be for initialisation.)

As an example we could provide a package containing our type DAY and some useful related constants.

```
package DIURNAL is
    type DAY is (MON, TUE, WED, THU, FRI, SAT, SUN);
    subtype WEEKDAY is DAY range MON . . FRI;
    TOMORROW: constant array (DAY) of DAY:=
                (TUE, WED, THU, FRI, SAT, SUN, MON);
```

```
    NEXT_WORK_DAY: constant array (WEEKDAY) of
                        WEEKDAY:=(TUE, WED, THU, FRI, MON);
end DIURNAL;
```

A final point. A subprogram cannot be called during the elaboration of a declarative part if its body appears later. This does not prevent mutual recursion because in that case the call actually only occurs when we execute the sequence of statements. But it does prevent its use as an initial value. So

```
function A return INTEGER;
I: INTEGER:=A();
```

is illegal.

This rule also applies to subprograms in packages. We cannot call a subprogram from outside the package until after the package body.

Exercise 8.1

1 The sequence defined by

$$X_{n+} = X_n.5^5 \bmod 2^{13}$$

provides a crude source of pseudo random numbers. The initial value X_0 should be an odd integer in the range $0 \ldots 2^{13}$.

Write a package RANDOM containing a procedure INIT to initialise the sequence and a function NEXT to deliver the next value in the sequence.

2 Write a package COMPLEX_NUMBERS which makes visible

- the type COMPLEX,
- a constant I =
- functions +, −, *, / acting on values of type COMPLEX.

See Exercise 7.2 (**2**).

8.2 Library units

Many languages in the past have ignored the simple fact that programs are written in pieces, compiled separately and then joined together. Ada recognises the need for separate compilation and provides two mechanisms – one top down and one bottom up.

The top down mechanism is appropriate for the development of a large coherent program which nevertheless, for various reasons, is broken down into subunits which can be compiled separately. The subunits are compiled after the unit from which they are taken. This mechanism is described in the next section.

The bottom up mechanism is appropriate for the creation of a program library where units are written for general use and consequently are written before the programs that use them. This mechanism will now be discussed in detail.

A library unit may be a subprogram specification, a subprogram body, a package specification or a package body. These units may be compiled individually or for convenience several could be submitted to the compiler together. Thus we could compile the specification and body of a package together but as we shall see it may be more convenient to compile them individually. As usual a subprogram body alone is sufficient to define the subprogram fully.

When a library unit is compiled it goes into a program library. There will obviously be several such libraries according to user and project, etc. The creation and manipulation of libraries is outside the scope of this book. Once in the library, a unit can be used by any subsequently compiled unit but the using unit must indicate the dependency by a with clause.

As a simple example suppose we compile the package STACK. This package depends on no other unit and so it needs no with clause. We will compile both specification and body together so the text submitted will be

```
package STACK is
   ...
end STACK;
package body STACK is
   ...
end STACK;
```

We now suppose that we write a procedure MAIN which will use the package STACK. Our procedure MAIN is going to be the main program in the usual sense. It will have no parameters and we can imagine that it is called by some magic outside the language itself. The Ada definition does not prescribe that the main program should have the identifier MAIN; it is merely a convention which we are adopting here because it has to be called something.

The text we submit to the compiler could be

```
with STACK;
procedure MAIN is
   use STACK;
   M, N: INTEGER;
begin
   ...
   PUSH(M);
   ...
   N:=POP();
   ...
end MAIN;
```

The with clause goes before the unit so that the dependency of the unit on other units is clear at a glance. A with clause may not be embedded in an inner scope.

If the unit is dependent on several other units then they can go in the one with clause, or it might be a convenience to use distinct with clauses. Thus we could write

```
with STACK, DIURNAL;
procedure MAIN is
   ...
```

or equally

```
with STACK;
with DIURNAL;
procedure MAIN is
    ...
```

For convenience we can place a use clause after a with clause. Thus

```
with STACK; use STACK;
procedure MAIN is
    ...
```

and then PUSH and POP are directly visible without more ado.

Only direct dependencies need be given in a with clause. Thus if package P uses the facilities of package Q which in turn uses the facilities of package R, then, unless P also directly uses R, the with clause for P should mention only Q. The user of Q does not care about R and must not need to know since otherwise the hierarchy of development would be made more complicated.

Another point is that the with clause in front of a package or subprogram declaration will also apply to the body. It can but need not be repeated. Of course, the body may have additional dependencies which will need indicating with a clause anyway. Dependencies which apply only to the body should not be given with the specification since otherwise the independence of the body and the specification would be reduced.

If a package specification and body are compiled separately then the body must be compiled after the specification. We say that the body is dependent on the specification. However, any unit using the package is dependent only on the specification and not the body. If the body is changed in a manner consistent with not changing the specification, any unit using the package will not need recompiling. The ability to compile specification and body separately should simplify program maintenance.

The general rule regarding the order of compilation is simply that a unit must be compiled after any units on which it depends. Consequently, if a unit is changed and recompiled then all dependent units must also be recompiled. Any order of compilation consistent with the dependency rule is acceptable.

There is one package that need not be mentioned in a with clause. This is the package STANDARD which effectively contains the declarations of all the predefined types such as INTEGER and BOOLEAN. It also contains an internal package ASCII containing constants defining the control characters such as CR and LF. We now see why the control characters were represented as ASCII.CR etc. in Chapter 6. By writing **use** ASCII; they can, of course, just be referred to as CR. The package STANDARD is described in more detail in Appendix 2..

There is a final very important rule regarding library units. They must have distinct identifiers; they cannot be overloaded. Moreover they cannot be operators.

Exercise 8.2

1 The package D and subprograms P and Q and MAIN have correct with clauses as follows

specification of D   no with clause

body of D	**with** P, Q;
subprogram P	no with clause
subprogram Q	no with clause
subprogram MAIN	**with** D;

Draw a graph showing the dependencies between the units. How many different orders of compilation are possible?

8.3 Subunits

The body of a package, subprogram (or task, see Chapter 14) can be 'taken out' of an immediately embracing unit and compiled separately. The body in the embracing unit is then replaced by a body stub. As an example suppose we remove the bodies of the subprograms PUSH and POP from the package STACK. The body of STACK would then become

```
package body STACK is
    MAX: constant:=100;
    S: array (1 .. MAX) of INTEGER;
    TOP: INTEGER range 0 .. MAX;
    procedure PUSH(X: INTEGER) is separate;        -- stub
    function POP return INTEGER is separate;       -- stub
begin
    TOP:=0;
end STACK;
```

The removed units are termed subunits; they may then be compiled separately. They have to be preceded by **separate** followed by the name of the parent unit in brackets. Thus the subunit PUSH becomes

```
separate (STACK)
procedure PUSH(X: INTEGER) is
begin
    TOP:=TOP+1;
    S(TOP):=X;
end PUSH;
```

and similarly for POP.

In the above example the parent unit is a library unit. The parent unit could itself be a subunit; in such a case its name must be given in full using the dotted notation starting with the ancestor library unit. Thus if R is a subunit of Q which is a subunit of P which is a library unit, then the text of R must start

```
separate (P.Q)
```

As with library units, the subunits of a unit must have distinct identifiers. But, of course, this does not prevent subunits of different units having the same identifier. And again subunits cannot be operators.

A subunit is dependent on its parent (and any library units explicitly mentioned) and so must be compiled after them.

Visibility within a subunit is as at the corresponding body stub – it is exactly as if the subunit were plucked out with its environment intact. As a consequence any with clause applying to the parent need not be repeated just because the subunit is compiled separately. However, it is possible to give the subunit access to additional library units by preceding it with its own with clauses (and possible use clauses). Such clauses precede **separate**. So the text of R might commence

```
with X; use X;
separate (P.Q)
...
```

A possible reason for doing this might be if we can then remove any reference to library unit X from the parent P.Q and so reduce the dependencies. This would give us greater freedom with the order of compilation; if X were recompiled for some reason then only R would need recompiling as a consequence and not also Q.

Note that a with clause only refers to library units and never to subunits. Finally observe that several subunits or a mixture of library units and subunits can be compiled together.

Exercise 8.3

1 Suppose that the package STACK is written with separate subunits PUSH and POP. Draw a graph showing the dependencies between the five units: procedure MAIN, procedure PUSH, function POP, package specification STACK, package body STACK. How many different orders of compilation are possible?

8.4 Scope and visibility

We return once more to the topic of scope and visibility. In this section we summarise the major points which will be relevant to the everyday use of Ada. For some of the fine detail, the reader is referred to the LRM. The normal scope rules associated with the block structure were described in Section 4.2. We now have to consider the effect of the introduction of packages.

In the case of a declaration in the visible part of a package, its scope extends from the declaration to the end of the scope of the package itself. Note that if the package is inside the visible part of another package then this means that, applying the rule again, the scope extends to the end of that of the outer package and so on.

In the case of a declaration in a package body (or in the private part of a package – to be described in the next chapter), its scope extends to the end of the package body.

In the case of the simple nesting of blocks and subprograms an entity is visible throughout its scope unless hidden by another declaration. We saw in Section 7.6 how even if it was hidden it could nevertheless in general be referred to by using the dotted notation where the prefixed name is that of the unit embracing the declaration. In essence, writing the name of the embracing unit makes the entity visible.

In the case of an entity declared in a package the same rules apply inside the package. But outside the package it is not visible unless we write the package name or alternatively write a use clause.

The identifiers visible at a given point are those visible before considering any use clauses plus those made visible by use clauses.

The basic rule is that an identifier in a package is made visible by a use clause provided the same identifier is not also in another package with a use clause and also provided that the identifier is not already visible anyway. If these conditions are not met then the identifier is not made visible and we have to continue to use the dotted notation.

There are additional rules concerning the overloading of enumeration literals and subprograms. The general intent is that an identifier made visible by a use clause can never hide another identifier although it may overload it.

When we consider the analysis of an assignment statement, subprogram call or expression in which there may be overloading and therefore ambiguity, we first try to identify a unique meaning ignoring all use clauses. If we can, that meaning is taken; if not, we try again but taking the use clauses into account.

The general purpose of these rules is to ensure that adding a use clause cannot invalidate an existing piece of text. We have only given a brief sketch here and the reader is probably confused. In practice there should be no problems since the Ada compiler will, we hope, indicate any ambiguities or other difficulties and things can always be put right by adding a qualifier or using a dotted name.

There are other rules regarding record components names, subprogram parameters and so on which are as expected. For example there is no conflict between an identifier of a record component and another use of the identifier outside the type definition itself. The reason is that although the scopes may overlap, the regions of visibility do not. Consider

```
declare
    type R is
        record
            I: INTEGER;
        end record;
    type S is
        record
            I: INTEGER;
        end record;
    AR: R;
    AS: S;
    I: INTEGER;
begin
    ...
    I:=AR.I+AS.I;               -- legal
    ...
end;
```

The scope of the I in the type R extends from the component declaration until the end of the block. However, its visibility is confined to within the declaration of R except that it is made visible by the use of AR in the selected component. Hence no conflict.

Similar considerations prevent conflict in named aggregates and in named parameters in subprogram calls

Observe that a use clause can mention several packages and that it may be necessary for a package name to be given as a selected component itself. A use clause does not take effect until the semicolon. Suppose we have nested packages

```
package P1 is
    package P2 is
        ...
    end P2;
    ...
end P1;
```

then outside P1 we could write

```
use P1; use P2;
```

or

```
use P1, P1.P2;
```

but not

```
use P1, P2;
```

We could even write **use** P1.P2; to gain visibility of the entities in P2 but not those in P1 – however, this seems an odd thing to do.

Earlier we mentioned the existence of the package STANDARD. This contains all the predefined entities but moreover every library unit should be thought of as being declared inside and at the end of STANDARD. This explains why an explicit use clause for STANDARD is not required. Another important consequence is that, provided we do not hide the name STANDARD by redefining it, a library unit P can always be referred to as STANDARD.P. Hence, in the absence of anonymous blocks, loops and overloading every identifier in the program has a unique name commencing with STANDARD. It is probably good advice not to redefine STANDARD.

8.5 Renaming

Certain entities can be renamed. As an example we can write

```
declare
    procedure SPUSH(X: INTEGER) renames STACK.PUSH;
    function SPOP return INTEGER renames STACK.POP;
begin
    ...
    SPUSH(M);
    ...
    N:=SPOP();
    ...
end;
```

A possible reason for doing this is to resolve ambiguities and yet avoid the use of the full dotted notation. Thus if we had two packages with a procedure PUSH(with an INTEGER parameter) then the use clause would be of no benefit since the full name would still be needed to resolve the ambiguity.

As another example suppose we wish to use both the function INNER and the equivalent operator "*" of Chapter 7 without declaring two distinct subprograms. We can write

```
function "*" (X, Y: VECTOR) return REAL renames INNER;
```

or

```
function INNER(X, Y: VECTOR) return REAL renames "*";
```

according to which we declare first.

If a subprogram is renamed, the number, base types and modes of the parameters (and result if a function) must be the same. This information can be used to resolve overloadings (as in the example of "*") and, of course, this matching occurs during compilation. At the time of elaboration of the renaming declaration any constraints must also match.

On the other hand, the presence, absence or value of default parameters do not have to match. Renaming can be used to introduce, change or delete default values; the default parameters associated with the new name are those shown in the renaming declaration. Hence renaming cannot be used as a trick to give an operator default values. Similarly, parameter names do not have to match.

Renaming can also be used to partially evaluate the name of an object. Suppose we have an array of records such as the array PEOPLE in Section 6.5 and that we wish to scan the array and print out the dates of birth in numerical form. We could write

```
for I in PEOPLE'RANGE loop
     PUT(PEOPLE(I).BIRTH.DAY); PUT(" : ");
     PUT(MONTH_NAME'POS(PEOPLE(I).BIRTH.MONTH)+1;
     PUT(" : ");
     PUT(PEOPLE(I).BIRTH.YEAR);
end loop;
```

It is clearly painful to repeat PEOPLE(I) each time. We could declare a variable D of type DATE and copy PEOPLE(I).BIRTH into it, but this would be very wasteful if the record were at all large. A better technique is to use renaming thus

```
for I in PEOPLE'RANGE loop
     declare
          D: DATE renames PEOPLE(I).BIRTH;
```

```
    begin
        PUT(D.DAY); PUT(" : ");
        PUT(MONTH_NAME'POS(D.MONTH)+1);
        PUT(" : ");
        PUT(D.YEAR);
    end;
end loop;
```

Beware that renaming does not correspond to text substitution – the identity of the object is determined when the renaming occurs. If any variable in the name subsequently changes then the identity of the object does not change. Because renaming corresponds to identification it is necessary that the type or subtype name (DATE in this example) must express the same constraints (if any) as those of the renamed object. Explicit constraints are not allowed after the type or subtype name in renaming declarations.

Renaming can be applied to objects (variables and constants), exceptions (see Chapter 10), subprograms and packages. In the case of a package it takes the simple form

```
package P renames STACK;
```

Although renaming does not directly apply to types an identical effect can be achieved by the use of a subtype

```
subtype S is T;
```

Finally note that renaming does not hide the old name. The indiscriminate use of renaming should be avoided since the aliases introduced make program proving much more difficult.

Checklist 8

Variables inside a package exist between calls of subprograms of the package.

A library unit must be compiled after other library units mentioned in its with clause.

A subunit must be compiled after its parent.

A body must be compiled after the corresponding specification.

Do not redefine STANDARD.

Renaming is not text substitution.

Private Types

We have seen how packages enable us to hide internal objects from the user of a package. Private types enable us to hide the details of the construction of a type from a user.

9.1 Normal private types

In Exercise 8.1(**2**) we wrote a package COMPLEX_NUMBERS providing a type COMPLEX, a constant I and some operations on the type. The specification of the package was

```
package COMPLEX_NUMBERS is
   type COMPLEX is
      record
         RL, IM: REAL;
      end record;
   I: constant COMPLEX:= (0.0, 1.0);

   function "+" (X, Y: COMPLEX) return COMPLEX;
   function "-" (X, Y: COMPLEX) return COMPLEX;
   function "*" (X, Y: COMPLEX) return COMPLEX;
   function "/" (X, Y: COMPLEX) return COMPLEX;
end;
```

The trouble with this formulation is that the user can make use of the fact that the complex numbers are held in cartesian representation. Rather than always using the complex operator +, the user could also write things like

```
C.IM:= C.IM+1.0;
```

rather than the more abstract

```
C:= C+I;
```

In fact, with the above package, the user has to make use of the representation in order to construct values of the type.

We might wish to prevent use of knowledge of the representation so that we could change the representation to perhaps polar form at a later date and know that the user's program would still be correct. We can do this with a private type.

Consider

```
package COMPLEX_NUMBERS is
    type COMPLEX is private;
    I: constant COMPLEX;
    function "+" (X, Y: COMPLEX) return COMPLEX;
    function "-" (X, Y: COMPLEX) return COMPLEX;
    function "*" (X, Y: COMPLEX) return COMPLEX;
    function "/" (X, Y: COMPLEX) return COMPLEX;
    function CONS(R, I: REAL) return COMPLEX;
    function RL_PART(X: COMPLEX) return REAL;
    function IM_PART(X: COMPLEX) return REAL;
private
    type COMPLEX is
        record
            RL, IM: REAL;
        end record;
    I: constant COMPLEX:= (0.0, 1.0);
end;
```

The part of the package specification before the reserved word **private** is the visible part and gives the information available externally to the package. The type COMPLEX is declared to be private. This means that outside the package nothing is known of the details of the type. The only operations available are assignment, =, and /= plus those added by the writer of the package as subprograms specified in the visible part.

We may also declare constants of a private type such as I, in the visible part. The initial value cannot be given in the visible part because the details of the type are not yet known. Hence we just state that I is a constant.

After **private** we have to give the details of types declared as private and give the initial values of corresponding constants.

A private type can be implemented in any way consistent with the operations visible to the user. It can be a record as we have shown; equally it could be an array, an enumeration type and so on. In our case it is fairly obvious that the type COMPLEX is naturally implemented as a record; but we could equally have used an array of two components such as

```
type COMPLEX is array (1 .. 2) of REAL;
```

Having declared the details of the private type we can use them and so declare the constants properly and give their initial values..

It should be noted that as well as the functions +, −, * and / we have also provided CONS to create a complex number from its real and imaginary components and RL_PART and IM_PART to return the components. These functions are necessary because the user no longer has direct access to the structure of the type. Of course, the fact that CONS, RL_PART and IM_PART correspond to our thinking of the complex numbers in cartesian form does not prevent us from implementing them in polar form.

The body of the package is as shown in the answer to Exercise 8.1(**2**) plus the additional functions which are trivial. It is therefore

```
package body COMPLEX is
    function "+" (X, Y: COMPLEX) return COMPLEX is
    begin
        return (X.RL+Y.RL, X.IM+Y.IM);
    end "+";

    -- - * / similarly

    function CONS(R, I: REAL) return COMPLEX is
    begin
        return (R, I);
    end CONS;
    function RL_PART(X: COMPLEX) return REAL is
    begin
        return X.RL;
    end RL_PART;
    -- IM_PART similarly
end COMPLEX_NUMBERS;
```

The package COMPLEX_NUMBERS could be used in a fragment such as

```
declare
    use COMPLEX_NUMBERS;
    C, D: COMPLEX;
    R, S: REAL;
begin
    C:=CONS(1.5, -6.0);
    D:=C+I;                      -- COMPLEX +
    R:=RL_PART(D)+6.0;           -- REAL +
    ...
end;
```

Outside the package we can declare variables and constants of type COMPLEX in the usual way. Note the use of CONS to create a complex literal. We cannot, of course, do mixed operations between our complex and real numbers. Thus we cannot write

```
    C:=2.0*C;
```

but instead must write

```
    C:=CONS(2.0, 0.0)*C;
```

If this is felt to be tedious we could add further overloadings of the operators to allow mixed operations.

Let us suppose that for some reason we now decide to represent the complex numbers in polar form. The visible part of the package will be unchanged but the private part could now become

```
private
    PI: constant:=3.14159_26536;
    type COMPLEX is
        record
            R: REAL;
            THETA: REAL range 0.0..2.0*PI;
        end record;
    I: constant COMPLEX:=(1.0,0.5*PI);
end;
```

Note how the constant PI is for convenience declared in the private part; anything other than a body can be declared in a private part if it suits us – we are not restricted to just declaring the types and constants in full. Things declared in the private part are also available in the body.

The body of our package COMPLEX_NUMBERS will now need completely rewriting. Some functions will become simpler and others will be more intricate. In particular it will be convenient to provide a function to normalise the angle θ so that it lies in the range 0 to 2π. The details are left for the reader.

However, since the visible part has not been changed the user's program will not need changing; we are assured of this since there is no way in which the user could have written anything depending on the details of the private type. Nevertheless, the user's program will need recompiling because of the general dependency rules explained in Section 8.2. This may seem slightly contradictory but remember that the compiler needs the information in the private part in order to be able to allocate storage for objects of the private type declared in the user's program. If we change the private part the size of the objects could change.

Exercise 9.1

1 Write additional functions "*" to enable mixed multiplication of real and complex numbers.

2 Complete the package RATIONAL_NUMBERS whose visible part is

```
package RATIONAL_NUMBERS is
    type RATIONAL is private;
    function "+"(X: RATIONAL) return RATIONAL;       -- unary +
    function "-"(X: RATIONAL) return RATIONAL;       -- unary -
    function "+"(X, Y: RATIONAL) return RATIONAL;
    function "-"(X, Y: RATIONAL) return RATIONAL;
    function "*"(X, Y: RATIONAL) return RATIONAL;
    function "/"(X, Y: RATIONAL) return RATIONAL;

    function "/"(X: INTEGER; Y: NATURAL) return RATIONAL;
    function NUMERATOR(R: RATIONAL) return INTEGER;
    function DENOMINATOR(R: RATIONAL) return NATURAL;
private
    ...
end;
```

A rational number is a number of the form N/D where N is an integer and D is a positive integer. For predefined equality to work it is essential that rational numbers are always reduced by cancelling out common factors. This may be done using the function GCD of Exercise 7.1(7).

3 Why does

function "/"(X: INTEGER; Y: NATURAL) **return** RATIONAL;

not hide the predefined integer division?

9.2 Limited private types

The operations available on a private type can be completely restricted to those specified in the visible part of the package. This is done by declaring the type as limited private thus

```
type T is limited private;
```

In such a case assignment and predefined = and /= are not available outside the package. However, the package may define a function "=" if the two parameters are of the same limited private type; it must return a value of type BOOLEAN. The operator /= always takes its meaning from = and so cannot be explicitly defined.

There are various natural consequences of the absence of assignment for limited private types: the declaration of a variable cannot include an initialisation, constants cannot be declared outside the defining package, and parameters cannot have default values. However, we can nevertheless declare our own subprograms with limited private types as parameters.

The advantage of making a private type limited is that the package writer has complete control over the objects of the type – the copying of resources can be monitored and so on.

As a simple example consider the following

```
package STACKS is
    type STACK is limited private;
    procedure PUSH(S: in out STACK; X: in INTEGER);
    procedure POP(S: in out STACK; out INTEGER);
    function "="(S,T: STACK) return BOOLEAN;
private
    MAX: constant:=100;
    type STACK is
        record
            S: array (1 .. MAX) of INTEGER;
            TOP: INTEGER range 0 .. MAX:=0;
        end record;
end;
```

Each object of type STACK is a record containing an array S and integer TOP. Note that TOP has a default initial value of zero. This ensures that when we declare a stack object, it is correctly initialised to be empty.

The body of the package could be

```
package body STACKS is
    procedure PUSH(S: in out STACK; X: in INTEGER) is
    begin
        S.TOP:=S.TOP+1;
        S.S(TOP):=X:
    end PUSH;
    procedure POP(S: in out STACK; X: out INTEGER) is
    begin
        X: =S.S(TOP);
        S.TOP:=S.TOP-1;
    end POP;
    function "="(S,T: STACK) return BOOLEAN is
    begin
        if S.TOP /= T.TOP then
            return FALSE;
        end if;
        for I in 1..S.TOP loop
            if S.S(I) /= T.S(I) then
                return FALSE;
            end if;
        end loop;
        return TRUE;
    end "=";
end STACKS;
```

This example illustrates many points. The parameter S of PUSH has mode **in out** because we need both to read from and to write to the stack. Further note that POP cannot be a function since S has to be **in out** and functions can only have **in** parameters. However, "=" can be a function because we only need to read the values of the two stacks and not to update them.

The function "=" has the interpretation that two stacks are equal only if they have the same number of items and the corresponding items have the same value. It would obviously be quite wrong to compare the whole records because the unused components of the arrays would also be compared. It is because of this that the type STACK has been made limited private rather than just private. If it were just private then we could not redefine = to give the correct meaning.

This is a typical example of a data structure where the value of the whole is more than just the sum of the parts; the interpretation of the array S depends on the value of TOP. Cases where there is such a relationship usually need a limited private type.

A minor point is that we are using the identifier S in two ways: as the name of the formal parameter denoting the stack and as the array inside the record. There is no conflict because, although the scopes overlap, the regions of visibility do not as was explained in Section 8.4. Of course, it is rather confusing to the reader and not good practice but it illustrates the freedom of choice of record component names.

The package could be used in a fragment such as

```
declare
    use STACKS;
    ST: STACK;
    EMPTY: STACK;
    ...
begin
    PUSH(ST, N);
    ...
    POP(ST, M);
    ...
    if ST=EMPTY then
    ...
    end if;
    ...
end;
```

Here we have declared two stacks ST and EMPTY. Both are originally empty because their internal component TOP has an initial value of zero. Assuming that we do not manipulate EMPTY then it can be used to see whether the stack ST is empty or not by calling the function =. This seems a rather dubious way of testing for an empty stack since there is no guarantee that EMPTY has not been manipulated. It would be better if EMPTY were a constant but as mentioned earlier we cannot declare a constant of a limited private type outside the package. We could however declare a constant EMPTY in the visible part of the package. A much better technique for testing the state of a stack would, of course, be to provide a function EMPTY and a corresponding function FULL in the package.

We can write subprograms with limited private types as parameters outside the defining package despite the absence of assignment. As a simple example, the following procedure enables us to determine the top value on the stack without removing it.

```
procedure TOP_OF(S: in out STACK; X: out INTEGER) is
begin
    POP(S, X);
    PUSH(S, X);
end;
```

The declaration of a function "=" does not have to be confined to the package containing the declaration of the limited private type. The only point is that outside the package, we cannot see the structure of the type. The ability to define "=" extends to any composite type containing a component of a limited private type. Thus outside the package STACKS we could declare

```
type STACK_ARRAY is array (INTEGER range <>) of STACK;
function "="(A,B: STACK_ARRAY) return BOOLEAN;
```

where the definition of an appropriate body is left to the reader.

Observe that within the private part (after the full type declaration) and within the body, any private type (limited or not) is treated in terms of how it is represented. Thus within the body of STACKS the type STACK is just a record type and so assignment and the things consequential upon assignment (initialisation, constants and default parameters) are allowed. So we could declare a procedure ASSIGN (intended to be used outside the package) as

```
procedure ASSIGN(S: in STACK; T: out STACK) is
begin
    T:=S;
end;
```

Similar considerations apply to the parameter mechanism for private types. Outside the defining package we can make no assumptions about the private type and so either the copying mechanism used for scalars or some other direct access mechanism may be used as mentioned in Section 7.3. But inside the package the rule applicable to how the type is represented must be used. If the private type is in fact a scalar type such as an enumeration type then copying will be used; if it is a composite type then the mechanism is undefined.

It is unfortunate that Ada does not separate the ability to permit assignment and user defined equality. For instance, it would be reasonable to allow assignment of stacks, but, of course, predefined quality is of no value. Equally in the case of a type such as RATIONAL of Exercise 9.1(2), it would be quite reasonable to allow manipulation – including assignment – of values which were not reduced provided that equality was suitably redefined. We are therefore forced to use a procedural form such as ASSIGN or reduce all values to a canonical form in which component by component equality is satisfactory. In the case of type STACK a suitable form would be one in which all unused elements of the stack had a standard dummy value such as zero.

Exercise 9.2

1 Rewrite the specification of STACKS to include a constant EMPTY in the visible part.

2 Write functions EMPTY and FULL for STACKS.

3 Write a suitable body for the function "=" applying to the type STACK_ARRAY. Make it conform to the normal rules for array equality which we mentioned towards the end of Section 6.2.

4 Rewrite ASSIGN for STACKS so that only the meaningful part of the record is copied.

5 Rewrite STACKS so that STACK is a normal private type. Ensure that predefined equality is satisfactory.

9.3 Resource management

An important example of the use of a limited private type is in providing controlled resource management. Consider the simple human model where each resource has a corresponding unique key. The key is then issued to the user when the resource is allocated and then has to be shown whenever the resource is accessed. So long as there is only one key and copying and stealing are prevented we know that the system is foolproof. A mechanism for handing in keys and reissuing them is usually necessary if resources are not to be permanently locked up. Typical human examples are the use of metal keys with post office boxes, credit cards and so on.

Now consider the following

```
package KEY_MANAGER is
    type KEY is limited private;
    procedure GET_KEY(K: in out KEY);
    procedure RETURN_KEY(K: in out KEY);
    function VALID(K: KEY) return BOOLEAN;
    . . .
    procedure ACTION(K: in KEY; . . . );
    . . .
private
    MAX: constant:=100;                    -- no of keys
    subtype KEY_CODE is INTEGER range 0 .. MAX;
    type KEY is
        record
            CODE: KEY_CODE:=0;
        end record;
end;

package body KEY_MANAGER is
    FREE: array (KEY_CODE range 1 .. KEY_CODE'LAST) of
                BOOLEAN:=(FREE'RANGE => TRUE);

    function VALID(K: KEY) return BOOLEAN is
    begin
        return K.CODE /= 0;
    end;

    procedure GET_KEY(K: in out KEY) is
    begin
        if K.CODE = 0 then
            for I in FREE'RANGE loop
                if FREE(I) then
                    FREE(I):= FALSE;
                    K.CODE:= I;
                    return;
                end if;
            end loop;
                                        -- all keys in use
        end if;
    end;

    procedure RETURN_KEY(K: in out KEY) is
    begin
        if K.CODE /= 0 then
            FREE(K.CODE):= TRUE;
            K.CODE:= 0;
```

```
        end if;
    end;
    ...
    procedure ACTION(K: in KEY; ...) is
    begin
        if VALID(K) then
            ...
    end;
end KEY_MANAGER;
```

The type KEY is represented by a record with a single component CODE. This has a default value of 0 which represents an illegal key. Values from 1 .. MAX represent the allocation of the corresponding resource. When we declare a variable of type KEY it automatically takes an internal code value of zero. In order to use the key we must first call the procedure GET_KEY; this allocates the first free key number to the variable. The key may then be used with various procedures such as ACTION which represents a typical request for some access to the resource guarded by the key.

Finally, the key may be relinquished by calling RETURN_KEY. So a typical fragment of user program might be

```
declare
    use KEY_MANAGER;
    MY_KEY: KEY;
begin
    ...
    GET_KEY(MY_KEY);
    ...
    ACTION(MY_KEY, ...);
    ...
    RETURN_KEY(MY_KEY);
    ...
end;
```

A variable of type KEY can be thought of as a container for a key. When initially declared the default value can be thought of as representing that the container is empty; the type KEY has to be a record because only record components can take default initial values. Note how the various possible misuses of keys are overcome.

- If we call GET_KEY with a variable already containing a valid key then no new key is allocated. It is important not to overwrite an old valid key otherwise that key would be lost.
- A call of RETURN_KEY resets the variable to the default state so that the variable cannot be used as a key until a new one is issued by a call of GET_KEY. Note that the user is unable to retain a copy of the key because assignment is not valid since the type KEY is limited private.

The function VALID is provided so that the user can see whether a key variable contains the default value or an allocated value. It is obviously useful to call VALID after GET_KEY to ensure that the key manager was able to provide a new key value; note that once all keys are issued, a call of GET_KEY does nothing.

One apparent flaw is that there is no compunction to call RETURN_KEY before the scope containing the declaration of MY_KEY is left. The key would then be lost. This corresponds to the real life situation of losing a key (although in our model no one else can find it again – it is as if it were thrown into a black hole). To guard against this the key manager might assume (as in life) that a key not used for a certain period of time is no longer in use. Of course, the same key would not be reissued but the resource guarded might be considered reusable; this would involve keeping separate records of keys in use and resources in use and a cross reference from keys to resources.

Exercise 9.3

1 Complete the package whose visible part is

```
package BANK is
    subtype MONEY is INTEGER range 0..INTEGER'LAST;
    type KEY is limited private;
    procedure OPEN_ACCOUNT(K: in out KEY; M: in MONEY);
        -- open account with initial deposit M
    procedure CLOSE_ACCOUNT(K: in out KEY; M: out MONEY);
        -- close account and return balance
    procedure DEPOSIT(K: in KEY; M: in MONEY);
        -- deposit amount M
    procedure WITHDRAW(K: in out KEY; M: in out MONEY);
        -- withdraw amount M; if account does not contain M
        -- then return what is there and close account
    function STATEMENT(K: KEY) return MONEY;
        -- returns a statement of current balance
    function VALID(K: KEY) return BOOLEAN;
        -- checks the key is valid
private
    ...
```

2 Assuming that your solution to the previous question allowed the bank the use of the deposited money, reformulate the private type to represent a home savings box where the money is in a box kept by the user.

3 A thief writes the following

```
declare
    use KEY_MANAGER;
    MY_KEY: KEY;
    procedure CHEAT(COPY: in KEY) is
    begin
        RETURN_KEY(MY_KEY);
        ACTION(COPY, ... );
        ...
    end;
```

```
begin
    GET_KEY(MY_KEY);
    CHEAT(MY_KEY);
    ...
end;
```

He attempts to return his key and then use the copy. Why is he thwarted?

Checklist 9

For predefined equality to be sensible, the values should be in a canonical form.

An unlimited private type can be implemented in terms of another private type provided it is also unlimited.

A limited private type can be implemented in terms of any private type limited or not.

/= can never be defined – it always follows from =.

= can be defined outside the package defining the limited private type concerned.

The rules apply transitively to composite types.

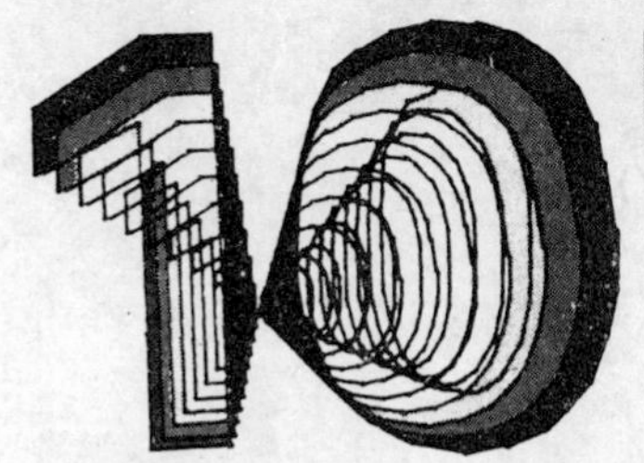

Exceptions

At various times in the preceding chapters we have said that if something goes wrong when the program is executed, then an exception, usually CONSTRAINT_ERROR, will be raised. In this chapter we describe the exception mechanism and show how remedial action can be taken when an exception occurs. We also show how we may define and use our own exceptions. Exceptions concerned with interacting tasks are dealt with when we come to Chapter 14.

10.1 Handling exceptions

We have seen that if we break various language rules then an exception may be raised when we execute the program.

There are five predefined exceptions of which we have met three so far

CONSTRAINT_ERROR	this generally corresponds to something going out of range,
NUMERIC_ERROR	this can occur when something goes wrong with arithmetic such as an attempt to divide by zero – see Section 4.9,
STORAGE_ERROR	this will occur if we run out of storage space as for example if we called our recursive function FACTORIAL with a large parameter – see Section 7.1

The other two predefined exceptions are SELECT_ERROR and TASKING_ERROR. These are concerned with tasking and so are dealt with in Chapter 14.

If we anticipate that an exception may occur in a part of our program then we can write an exception handler to deal with it. For example, suppose we write

```
begin
    -- sequence of statements
exception
    when CONSTRAINT_ERROR =>
    -- do something
end;
```

If CONSTRAINT_ERROR is raised while we are executing the sequence of statements between **begin** and **exception** then the flow of control is interrupted and immediately transferred to the sequence of statements following the =>. The clause starting **when** is known as an exception handler.

As a trivial example we could compute TOMORROW from TODAY by writing

```
begin
    TOMORROW:=DAY'SUCC(TODAY);
exception
    when CONSTRAINT_ERROR =>
        TOMORROW:=DAY'FIRST;
end;
```

If TODAY is DAY'LAST (i.e. SUN) then when we attempt to evaluate DAY'SUCC(TODAY), the exception CONSTRAINT_ERROR is raised. Control is then transferred to the handler for CONSTRAINT_ERROR and the statement TOMORROW:=DAY'FIRST; is executed. Control then passes to the end of the block.

This is really a bad example. Exceptions should be used for rarely occurring cases or those which are inconvenient to test for at their point of occurrence. By no stretch of the imagination is Sunday a rare day. Over 14% of all days are Sundays. Nor is it difficult to test for the condition at the point of occurrence. So we should really have written

```
if TODAY = DAY'LAST then
    TOMORROW:=DAY'FIRST;
else
    TOMORROW:=DAY'SUCC(TODAY);
end if;
```

However, it is a simple example with which to illustrate the mechanism involved.

Several handlers can be written between **exception** and **end**. Consider

```
begin
    -- sequence of statements
exception
    when NUMERIC_ERROR|CONSTRAINT_ERROR =>
        PUT ("Numeric or Constraint error occurred");

    when STORAGE_ERROR =>
        PUT("Ran out of space");
        ...
    when others =>
        PUT("Something else went wrong");
        ...
end;
```

In this example a message is output according to the exception. Note the similarity to the case statement. Each **when** is followed by one or more exception names separated by vertical bars. As usual we can write **others** but it must be last and on its own; it handles any exception not listed in the previous handlers.

Exception handlers can appear at the end of a block, subprogram body, package body (or task body) and have access to all entities declared in the unit. The examples above have shown a degenerate block in which there is no **declare** and declarative part; the block was introduced just for the purpose of providing somewhere to hang the handlers. We could rewrite our bad example to determine tomorrow as a function thus

```
function TOMORROW(TODAY: DAY) return DAY is
begin
    return DAY'SUCC(TODAY);
exception
    when CONSTRAINT_ERROR =>
        return DAY'FIRST;
end TOMORROW;
```

It is important to realise that control can never be returned to the unit where the exception was raised. The sequence of statements following => replaces the remainder of the unit containing the handler and thereby completes execution of the unit. Hence a handler for a function must generally contain a return statement in order to provide the 'emergency' result.

In particular, a goto statement cannot transfer control from a unit into one of its handlers or vice versa or from one handler to another. However, the statements of a handler can otherwise be of arbitrary complexity. They can include blocks, calls of subprograms and so on. A handler of a block could contain a goto statement which transferred control to a label outside the block and it could contain an exit statement if the block were inside a loop.

A handler at the end of a package body applies only to the initialisation sequence of the package and not to subprograms in the package. Such subprograms must have individual handlers if they are to deal with exceptions.

We now consider the question of what happens if a unit does not provide a handler for a particular exception. The answer is that the exception is propagated dynamically. This simply means that the unit is terminated and the exception is raised at the point where the unit was invoked. In the case of a block we therefore look for a handler in the unit containing the block.

In the case of a subprogram, the call is terminated and we look for a handler in the unit which called the subprogram. This unwinding process is repeated until either we reach a unit containing a handler for the particular exception or come to the top level. If we find a unit containing a relevant handler then the exception is handled at that point. Alternatively we have reached the main program and have still found no handler – the main program is then abandoned and we can expect the run time environment to provide us with a suitable diagnostic message. (Unhandled exceptions in tasks are dealt with in Chapter 14.)

It is most important to understand that exceptions are propagated dynamically and not statically. That is, an exception not handled by a subprogram is propagated to the unit calling the subprogram and not to the unit containing the declaration of the subprogram – these may or may not be the same.

If the statements in a handler themselves raise an exception then the unit is terminated and the exception propagated to the calling unit; the handler does not loop.

Exercise 10.1

Note: these are exercises to check your understanding of exceptions. They do not necessarily reflect good Ada programming techniques.

1 Assuming that calling SQRT with a negative parameter or attempting to divide by zero raise NUMERIC_ERROR, rewrite the procedure QUADRATIC of Section 7.3 without explicitly testing D and A.

2 Rewrite the function FACTORIAL of Section 7.1 so that if it is called with a negative parameter (which would normally raise CONSTRAINT_ERROR) or a large parameter (which would normally raise STORAGE_ERROR or NUMERIC_ERROR) then a standard result of say −1 is returned. Hint: declare an inner function SLAVE which actually does the work.

10.2 Declaring and raising exceptions

Relying on the predefined exceptions to detect unusual but anticipated situations is usually bad practice because they do not provide a guarantee that the exception has in fact been raised because of the anticipated situation. Something else may have gone wrong instead.

As an illustration consider the package STACK of Section 8.1. If we call PUSH when the stack is full then the statement TOP:=TOP+1; will raise CONSTRAINT_ERROR and similarly if we call POP when the stack is empty then TOP:=TOP−1; will also raise CONSTRAINT_ERROR. Since PUSH and POP do not themselves have exception handlers, the exception will be propagated to the unit calling them. So we could write

```
declare
    use STACK;
begin
    ...
    PUSH(M);
    ...
    N:=POP();
    ...
exception
    when CONSTRAINT_ERROR =>
        --stack manipulation incorrect?
end;
```

and misuse of the stack would then result in control being transferred to the handler for CONSTRAINT_ERROR. However, there would be no guarantee that the exception had arisen because of misuse of the stack; something else in the block could have gone wrong.

A better solution is to raise an exception specifically declared to indicate misuse of the stack. Thus the package could be rewritten

```
package STACK is
    ERROR: exception;
    procedure PUSH(X: INTEGER);
    function POP return INTEGER;
end STACK;
```

```
package body STACK is
    MAX: constant:=100;
    S: array (1..MAX) of INTEGER;
    TOP: INTEGER range 0..MAX;

    procedure PUSH(X: INTEGER) is
    begin
        if TOP = MAX then
            raise ERROR;
        end if;
        TOP:=TOP+1;
        S(TOP):=X;
    end PUSH;

    function POP return INTEGER is
    begin
        if TOP = 0 then
            raise ERROR;
        end if;
        TOP:=TOP-1;
        return S(TOP+1);
    end POP;
begin
    TOP:=0;
end STACK;
```

An exception is declared in a similar way to a variable and is raised by an explicit raise statement naming the exception. The handling and propagation rules are just as for the predefined exceptions. We can now write

```
declare
    use STACK;
begin
    ...
    PUSH(M);
    ...
    N:=POP();
    ...
exception
    when ERROR =>
        -- stack manipulation incorrect
    when others =>
        -- something else wrong
end;
```

We have now successfully separated the handler for misusing the stack from the handler for other exceptions.

Note that if we had not provided a use clause then we would have had to refer to the exception in the handler as STACK.ERROR; the usual dotted notation applies.

What could we expect to do in the handler in the above case? Apart from reporting that the stack manipulation has gone wrong, we might also expect to reset the stack to an acceptable state although we have not provided a convenient means of doing so. A procedure RESET in the package STACK would be useful. A further thing we might do is relinquish any resources that were acquired in the block and might otherwise be inadvertently retained. Suppose for instance that we had also been using the package KEY_MANAGER of Section 9.3. We might then call RETURN_KEY to ensure that a key declared and acquired in the block had been returned. Remember that RETURN_KEY does no harm if called unnecessarily.

We would probably also want to reset the stack and return the key in the case of any other exception as well; so it would be as well to declare a procedure CLEAN_UP to do all the actions required. So our block might look like

```
declare
   use STACK, KEY_MANAGER;
   MY_KEY: KEY;

   procedure CLEAN_UP is
   begin
      RESET;
      RETURN_KEY (MY_KEY);
   end;
begin
   GET_KEY (MY_KEY);
   ...
   PUSH(M);
   ...
   ACTION(MY_KEY, ...);
   ...
   N:=POP();
   ...
   RETURN_KEY(MY_KEY);
exception
   when ERROR =>
      PUT("Stack used incorrectly");
      CLEAN_UP;
   when others =>
      PUT("Something else went wrong");
      CLEAN_UP:
end;
```

We have rather assumed that RESET is a further procedure declared in the package STACK but note that we could write our own procedure externally as follows

```
procedure RESET is
   JUNK: INTEGER;
   use STACK;
```

```
begin
    loop
        JUNK:=POP();
    end loop;
exception
    when ERROR =>
        null;
end RESET;
```

This works by repeatedly calling POP until ERROR is raised. We then know that the stack is empty. The handler needs to do nothing other than prevent the exception from being propagated; so we merely write **null**. This procedure seems a bit like trickery; it would be far better to have a reset procedure in the package.

Sometimes the actions that require to be taken as a consequence of an exception need to be performed on a layered basis. In the above example we returned the key and then reset the stack but it is probably the case that the block as a whole cannot be assumed to have done its job correctly. We can indicate this by raising an exception as the last action of the handler.

```
exception
    when ERROR =>
        PUT("Stack used incorrectly");
        CLEAN_UP;
        raise ANOTHER_ERROR;
    when others =>
        ...
end;
```

The exception ANOTHER_ERROR will then be propagated to the unit containing the block. We could, of course, put the statement **raise** ANOTHER_ERROR; in the procedure CLEAN_UP.

Sometimes it is convenient to handle an exception and then propagate the same exception. This can be done by just writing

```
raise;
```

This is particularly useful when we handle several exceptions with the one handler since there is no way in which we can explicitly name the exception which occurred.

So we might have

```
    when others =>
        PUT("Something else went wrong");
        CLEAN_UP;
        raise;
end;
```

The current exception will be remembered even if the action of the handler raises and handles its own exceptions such as occurred in our trick procedure RESET. However, note that there is a rule that we can only write **raise**; directly in a handler and not for instance in a procedure called by the handler such as CLEAN_UP.

The stack example illustrates a legitimate use of exceptions. The exception ERROR should rarely, if ever, occur and it would also be inconvenient to test for the condition at each possible point of occurence. To do that we would presumably have to provide an additional parameter to PUSH of type BOOLEAN and mode **out** to indicate that all was not well, and then test it after each call. In the case of POP we would also have to recast it as a procedure since a function cannot take a parameter of mode **out**.

The package specification would then become

```
package STACK is
    procedure PUSH(X: in INTEGER; B: out BOOLEAN);
    procedure POP(X: out INTEGER; B: out BOOLEAN);
end;
```

and we would have to write

```
declare
    use STACK;
    OK: BOOLEAN;
begin
    ...
    PUSH(M,OK);
    if not OK then ....          end if;
    ...
  POP(N,OK);
    if not  OK then ....         end if;
    ...
end;
```

It is clear that the use of an exception provides a better structured program.

Note finally that nothing prevents us from explicitly raising one of the predefined exceptions. We recall that in Section 7.1 when discussing the function INNER we stated that probably the best way of coping with parameters whose bounds were unequal was to explicitly raise CONSTRAINT_ERROR.

Exercise 10.2

1 Rewrite the package RANDOM of Exercise 8.1(**1**) so that it declares and raises an exception BAD if the initial value is not odd.

2 Rewrite your answer to Exercise 10.1(**2**) so that the function FACTORIAL always raises NUMERIC_ERROR if the parameter is negative or too large.

10.3 Scope of exceptions

To a large extent exceptions follow the same scope rules as other entities. An exception can hide and be hidden by another declaration; it can be made visible by the dotted notation and so on. An exception can be renamed

```
HELP: exception renames BANK.ALARM;
```

Exceptions are, however, different in many ways. We cannot declare arrays of exceptions, and they cannot be components of records, parameters of subprograms and so on. In short, exceptions are not objects and so cannot be manipulated. They are merely tags.

A very important characteristic of exceptions is that they are not created dynamically as a program executes but should be thought of as existing throughout the life of the program. This relates to the way in which exceptions are propagated dynamically up the chain of execution rather than statically up the chain of scope. An exception can be propagated outside its scope although of course it can then only be handled anonymously by **others**. This is illustrated by the following

```
declare
    procedure P is
        X: exception;
    begin
        raise X;
    end P;
begin
    P;
exception
    when others =>
                        -- X handled here
end;
```

The procedure P declares and raises the exception X but does not handle it. When we call P, the exception X is propagated to the block calling P where it is handled anonymously.

It is even possible to propagate an exception out of its scope, where it becomes anonymous, and then back in again where it can once more be handled by its proper name. Consider

```
declare
    package P is
        procedure F;
        procedure H;
    end P;

    procedure G is
    begin
        P.H;
    exception
        when others =>
            raise;
    end G;

    package body P is
        X: exception;
        procedure F is
```

```
            begin
                G;
            exception
                when X =>
                    PUT("Got it!");
            end F;
            procedure H is
            begin
                raise X;
            end H;
        end P;
    begin
        P.F;
    end;
```

The block declares a package P containing procedures F and H and also a procedure G. The block calls F in P which calls G outside P which in turn calls H back in P. The procedure H raises the exception X whose scope is the body of P. The procedure H does not handle X, so it is propagated to G which called H. The procedure G is outside the package P, so the exception X is now outside its scope; nevertheless G handles the exception anonymously and propagates it further by reraising it. G was called by F so X is now propagated back into the package and so can be handled by F by its proper name.

A further illustration of the nature of exceptions is afforded by a recursive procedure containing an exception declaration. Unlike variables declared in a procedure we do not get a new exception for each recursive call. Each recursive activation refers to the same exception. Consider the following artificial example

```
    procedure F(N: INTEGER) is
        X: exception;
    begin
        if N = 0 then
            raise X;
        else
            F(N-1);
        end if;
    exception
        when X =>
            PUT("Got it");
            raise;
        when others =>
            null;
    end F;
```

Suppose we execute F(4); we get recursive calls F(3), F(2), F(1) and finally F(0). When F is called with parameter zero, it raises the exception X, handles it, prints out a confirmatory message and then reraises it. The calling instance of F (which itself had N = 1) receives the exception and again handles it as X and so on. The message is therefore printed out five times in all and the exception is finally propagated anonymously. Observe that if each recursive activation had created a different exception then the message would only be printed out once.

In all the examples we have seen so far exceptions have been raised in statements. An exception can however also be raised in a declaration. Thus

```
N: NATURAL:=0;
```

would raise CONSTRAINT_ERROR because the initial value of N does not satisfy the range constraint 1..INTEGER'LAST of the subtype NATURAL. An exception raised in a declaration is not handled by a handler (if any) of the unit containing the declaration but is immediately propagated up a level. This means that in any handler we are assured that all declarations of the unit were successfully elaborated and so there is no risk of referring to something that does not exist.

Finally a warning regarding parameters of mode **out** or **in out**. If a subprogram is terminated by an exception then any actual parameter of a scalar type will not have been updated since such updating occurs on a normal return. For an array, record or private type the parameter mechanism is not so closely specified and the actual parameter may or may not have its original value. A program assuming a particular mechanism is of course erroneous. As an example consider the procedure WITHDRAW of the package BANK in Exercise 9.3(**1**). It would be incorrect to attempt to take the key away and raise an alarm as in

```
procedure WITHDRAW(K: in out KEY; M: in out MONEY) is
begin
   if VALID(K) then
      if M > amount remaining then
         M:=amount remaining;
         FREE (K.CODE):=TRUE;
         K.CODE:=0;
         raise ALARM;
      else
         ...
      end if;
   end if;
end;
```

If the parameter mechanism were implemented by copy then the bank would think that the key were now free but would have left the greedy customer with a copy.

Exercise 10.3

1 Rewrite the package BANK of Exercise 9.3(**1**) to declare an exception ALARM and raise it when any illegal banking activity is attempted. Avoid problems with the parameters.

Checklist 10

Do not use exceptions unnecessarily.

Use specific user declared exceptions rather than predefined exceptions where relevant.

Ensure that handlers return resources correctly.

Out and in out parameters may not be updated correctly if a procedure is terminated by an exception.

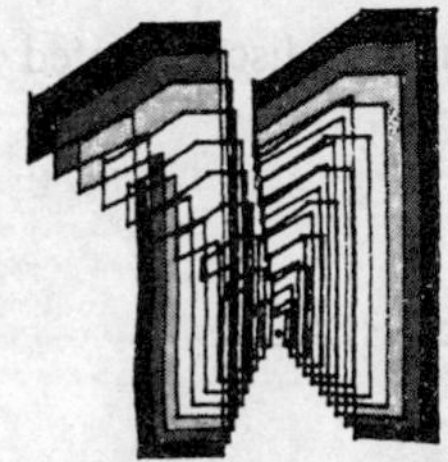

11 Advanced Types

In this chapter we describe most of the remaining classes of types. These are discriminated record types, access types and derived types. Numeric types, which are explained in terms of derived types, are described in the next chapter and task types are described in Chapter 14.

11.1 Discriminated record types

In the record types we have seen so far there was no formal language dependency between the components. Any dependency was purely in the mind of the programmer as for example in the case of the limited private type STACK in Section 9.2 where the interpretation of the array S depended on the value of the integer TOP.

In the case of a discriminated record type, some of the components are known as discriminants and the remaining components can depend upon these. The discriminants, which have to be of a discrete type, can be thought of as parameterising the type and the syntax reveals this analogy.

As a simple example suppose we wish to write a package providing various operations on square matrices and that in particular we wish to write a function TRACE which sums the diagonal elements of a square matrix. We could contemplate using the type MATRIX of Section 6.2.

```
type MATRIX is array (INTEGER range <>, INTEGER range <>)
                                    of REAL;
```

but our function would then have to check that the matrix passed as an actual parameter was indeed square. We would have to write something like

```
function TRACE(M: MATRIX) return REAL is
     SUM: REAL:=0.0;
begin
     if M'FIRST(1) /=M'FIRST(2) or M'LAST(1) /=M'LAST(2) then
          raise NON_SQUARE;
     end if;
     for I in M'RANGE loop
          SUM:=SUM+M(I, I);
     end loop;
     return SUM;
end TRACE;
```

This is somewhat unsatisfactory; we would prefer to use a formulation which ensured that the matrix was always square. We can do this using a discriminated type. Consider

```
type SQUARE(ORDER: NATURAL) is
    record
        MATRIX: array (1 .. ORDER,1 .. ORDER) of REAL;
    end record;
```

This is a record type having two components: the first, ORDER, is a discriminant of the discrete type NATURAL and the second, MATRIX, is an array whose bounds depend upon the value of ORDER.

Variables of type SQUARE can be declared in the usual way but a value of the discriminant must be given as a constraint thus

```
M: SQUARE(3);
```

The named form can also be used

```
M: SQUARE(ORDER=> 3);
```

The value provided as the constraint could be any dynamic expression but once the variable is declared its constraint cannot be changed. An initial value for M could be provided by an aggregate, but, perhaps surprisingly, this must be complete and repeat the constraint which must match, thus

```
M: SQUARE(3):=(3,(1 .. 3 => (1 .. 3 => 0.0)));
```

We could even write

```
M: SQUARE(N):=(M.ORDER,(M.MATRIX'RANGE(1) =>
                       (M.MATRIX'RANGE(2) => 0.0)));
```

in order to avoid repeating N. This is legal because of the rule that a declaration with initialisation is essentially equivalent to a declaration without initialisation followed by a corresponding assignment statement. Since

```
declare
    M: SQUARE(N);
begin
    M:=(M.ORDER,(M.MATRIX'RANGE(1) =>
              (M.MATRIX'RANGE(2) => 0.0)));
```

is clearly valid, the legality of the aggregate as an initial value then follows. If we attempt to assign a value to M which does not have the correct discriminant value then CONSTRAINT_ERROR will be raised.

Constants can be declared as usual but, unlike arrays as such, the constraint cannot be deduced from the initial value but must be given explicitly.

We can, of course introduce subtypes

```
subtype SQUARE_3 is SQUARE(3);
M: SQUARE_3;
```

We can now rewrite our function TRACE as follows

```
function TRACE(M: SQUARE) return REAL is
    SUM: REAL:=0.0;
begin
    for I in M.MATRIX'RANGE loop
        SUM:=SUM+M.MATRIX(I,I);
    end loop;
    return SUM;
end TRACE;
```

There is now no way in which a call of TRACE can be supplied with a non square matrix. Note that the discriminant of the formal parameter is taken from that of the actual parameter in a similar way to the bounds of an array. Again like arrays, the formal parameter could have an explicit constraint as in

```
function TRACE_3(M: SQUARE(3)) return REAL;
```

but then the actual parameter would have to have a discriminant value of 3; otherwise CONSTRAINT_ERROR would be raised.

The result of a function could be of a discriminated type and, like arrays, the result could be a value whose discriminant is not known until the function is called. Thus we could write a function to return the transpose of a square matrix

```
function TRANSPOSE(M: SQUARE) return SQUARE is
    R: SQUARE(M.ORDER);
begin
    for I in 1 .. M.ORDER loop
        for J in 1 .. M.ORDER loop
            R.MATRIX(I,J):=M.MATRIX(J,I);
        end loop;
    end loop;
    return R;
end TRANSPOSE;
```

A private type can also have discriminants and it must then be implemented in terms of a record type with corresponding discriminants. A good example is provided by considering the type STACK in Section 9.2. We can overcome the problem that all the stacks had the same maximum length of 100 by making MAX a discriminant. Thus we can write

```
package STACKS is
    type STACK(MAX: INTEGER range 0 .. INTEGER'LAST) is
                    limited private;
    procedure PUSH(S: in out STACK; X: in INTEGER);
    procedure POP(S: in out STACK; X: out INTEGER);
    function "="(S,T: STACK) return BOOLEAN;
```

```
private
    type STACK(MAX: INTEGER range 0..INTEGER'LAST) is
        record
            S: array (1..MAX) of INTEGER;
            TOP: INTEGER:=0;
        end record;
end;
```

Each variable of type STACK now includes a discriminant component giving the maximum stack size. When we declare a stack we must supply the value thus

```
ST: STACK(100);
```

and as for the type SQUARE the value of the discriminant cannot later be changed. Of course, the discriminant is visible and can be referred to as ST.MAX although the remaining components are private.

The body of the package STACKS remains as before (see Section 9.2). Observe in particular that the function "=" can be used to compare stacks with different values of MAX since it only compares those components of the internal array which are in use.

Although constants of the type STACK cannot be declared outside the defining package (because the type is limited private) we can declare a constant in the visible part. Such a declaration would need to supply a value for the discriminant although it will be repeated in the private part.

The discriminated types we have encountered so far have been such that once a variable is declared, its discriminant cannot be changed. It is possible, however, to provide a default value for a discriminant and the situation is then different. A variable can then be declared with or without a discriminant constraint. If one is supplied then that value overrides the default value and as before the discriminant cannot be changed. If, on the other hand, a variable is declared without a value for the discriminant, then the default value is taken but it can then be changed by a complete record assignment.

Suppose we wish to manipulate polynomials of the form

$$P(x) = a_0 + a_1x + a_2x^2 + \ldots a_nx^n$$

where $a_n \neq 0$ if $n \neq 0$.

Such a polynomial could be represented by

```
type POLY(N: INTEGER range 0..MAX) is
    record
        A: array (0..N) of INTEGER;
    end record;
```

but then a variable of type POLY would have to be declared with a constraint and would thereafter be a polynomial of that fixed size. This would be most inconvenient because the sizes of the polynomials may be determined as the consequences of elaborate calculations. For example if we subtract two polynomials which have $n = 3$, then the result will only have $n = 3$ if the coefficients of x^3 are different.

However, if we declare

```
type POLYNOMIAL(N: INTEGER range 0..MAX:=0) is
    record
        A: array (0..N) of INTEGER;
    end record;
```

then we can declare variables

```
P, Q: POLYNOMIAL;
```

which do not have constraints. The initial value of their discriminants would be zero because the default value of N is zero but the discriminants could later be changed by assignment. Note however that a discriminant can only be changed by a complete record assignment. So

```
P.N:=6;
```

would be illegal. This is quite natural since we cannot expect the array P.A to adjust its bounds by magic.

Variables of the type POLYNOMIAL could be declared with constraints

```
R: POLYNOMIAL(5);
```

but R would thereafter be constrained forever to be a polynomial with $n = 5$.

Initial values can be given in declarations in the usual way.

```
P: POLYNOMIAL:=(3, (5, 0, 4, 2));
```

which represents $5 + 4x^2 + 2x^3$. Note that despite the initial value, P is not constrained.

In practice we would make the type POLYNOMIAL a private type so that we could enforce the rule that $a_n \neq 0$. Observe that predefined equality is satisfactory and so we do not have to make it a limited private type. Both the private type declaration and the full type declaration must give the default value for N.

If we declare functions such as

```
function "-" (P, Q: POLYNOMIAL) return POLYNOMIAL;
```

then it will be necessary to ensure that the result is normalised so that a_n is not zero. This could be done by the following function.

```
function NORMAL(P: POLYNOMIAL) return POLYNOMIAL is
    SIZE: INTEGER:=P.N;
begin
    while SIZE > 0 and P.A(SIZE) = 0 loop
        SIZE:=SIZE-1;
    end loop;
    return (SIZE, P.A(0..SIZE));
end NORMAL;
```

This is a further illustration of a function returning a value whose discriminant is not known until it is called. Note the use of the array slice.

It is possible to declare a type with several discriminants. We may for instance wish to manipulate matrices which although not constrained to be square nevertheless have both lower bounds of 1. This could be done by

```
type RECTANGLE(ROWS, COLUMNS: NATURAL) is
    record
        MATRIX: array (1 .. ROWS, 1 .. COLUMNS) of REAL;
    end record;
```

and we could then declare

```
R: RECTANGLE(2, 3);
```

or

```
R: RECTANGLE(ROWS => 2, COLUMNS => 3);
```

The usual rules apply: positional values must be given in order, named ones may be in any order, mixed notation can be used but the positional ones must come first.

If default initial values are supplied then they must be supplied for all discriminants of the type. This rule is similar to that for multidimensional array types – all bounds must be constrained. And again, if default initial values are supplied then objects must be fully constrained or not at all. Similarly, a subtype must supply all the constraints or none at all. We could not declare

```
subtype ROW_3 is RECTANGLE(ROWS => 3);
```

in order to get the equivalent of

```
type ROW_3(COLUMNS: NATURAL) is
    record
        MATRIX: array (1 .. 3, 1 .. COLUMNS) of REAL;
    end record;
```

The attribute CONSTRAINED can be applied to an object of a discriminated type and gives a Boolean value indicating whether the object is constrained or not. For any object of types such as SQUARE and STACK which do not have default values for the discriminants this attribute will, of course, be TRUE. But in the case of objects of a type such as POLYNOMIAL which does have a default value, the attribute may be TRUE or FALSE.

```
P'CONSTRAINED = FALSE
R'CONSTRAINED = TRUE
```

We mentioned above that an unconstrained formal parameter will take the value of the discriminant of the actual parameter. In the case of an **out** or **in out** parameter, the formal parameter will be constrained if the actual parameter is constrained (an **in** parameter is constant anyway). Suppose we declare a procedure to truncate a polynomial by removing its highest order term.

```
procedure TRUNCATE(P: in out POLYNOMIAL) is
begin
    P:=(P.N-1, P.A(0..P.N-1));
end;
```

Then given

```
Q: POLYNOMIAL;
R: POLYNOMIAL(5);
```

the statement

```
TRUNCATE(Q);
```

will be successful, but

```
TRUNCATE(R);
```

will result in CONSTRAINT_ERROR being raised.

In the examples we have shown, discriminants have been used as the upper bounds of arrays; they can also be used as the lower bounds of arrays. In the next section we describe how a discriminant can also be used to introduce a variant part. In all cases a discriminant must be used directly and not as part of a larger expression. So we could not declare

```
type SYMMETRIC_ARRAY(N: NATURAL) is
    record
        A: array (-N..N) of REAL;
    end record;
```

or

```
type TWO_BY_ONE(N: NATURAL) is
    record
        A: array (1..N,1..2*N) of REAL;
    end record;
```

Finally, it is worth emphasising that the only dynamic arrays allowed in records are those whose bounds are discriminants.

Exercise 11.1

1 Suppose that M is an object of the type MATRIX. Write a call of the function TRACE whose parameter is an aggregate of type SQUARE in order to determine the trace of M. What would happen if the two dimensions of M were not equal?

2 Rewrite the specification of STACKS to include a constant EMPTY in the visible part. See also Exercise 9.2(**1**).

3 Write a function FULL for STACKS. See also Exercise 9.2(**2**).

4 Declare a POLYNOMIAL representing zero (i.e. $0x^0$).

5 Write a function "*" to multiply two polynomials.

6 Write a function "−" to subtract two polynomials. Use the function NORMAL.

7 Rewrite the procedure TRUNCATE to raise TRUNCATE_ERROR if we attempt to truncate a constrained polynomial.

11.2 Variant parts

It is sometimes convenient to have a record type in which part of the structure is fixed for all objects of the type but the remainder can take one of several different forms. This can be done using a variant part and the choice between the alternatives is governed by the value of a discriminant.

Consider the following

```
type GENDER is (MALE, FEMALE);

type PERSON(SEX: GENDER) is
    record
        BIRTH: DATE;
        case SEX is
            when MALE =>
                BEARDED: BOOLEAN;
            when FEMALE =>
                CHILDREN: INTEGER;
        end case;
    end record;
```

This declares a record type PERSON with a discriminant SEX. The component BIRTH of type DATE (see Section 6.5) is common to all objects of the type. However, the remaining components depend upon SEX and are declared as a variant part. If the value of SEX is MALE then there is a further component BEARDED whereas if SEX is FEMALE then there is a component CHILDREN. Only men can have beards and only women (directly) have children.

Since no default value is given for the discriminant all objects of the type must be constrained. We can therefore declare

```
JOHN: PERSON(MALE);
BARBARA: PERSON(FEMALE);
```

or we can introduce subtypes and so write

```
subtype MAN is PERSON(SEX => MALE);
subtype WOMAN is PERSON(SEX => FEMALE);
JOHN: MAN;
BARBARA: WOMAN;
```

Aggregates take the usual form but, of course, give only the components for the corresponding alternative in the variant. The value for a discriminant governing a variant must be static so that the compiler can check the consistency of the aggregate. We can therefore write

```
JOHN:=(MALE, (19,AUG,1937), FALSE);
BARBARA:=(FEMALE, (13,MAY,1943), 2);
```

but not

```
S: GENDER:=FEMALE;
BARBARA:=(S, (13,MAY,1943), 2);
```

because S is not static but a variable.

The components of a variant can be accessed and changed in the usual way. We could write

```
JOHN.BEARDED:=TRUE;
BARBARA.CHILDREN:=BARBARA.CHILDREN+1;
```

but an attempt to access a component of the wrong alternative such as JOHN. CHILDREN would raise CONSTRAINT_ERROR. Note that although the sex of objects of type PERSON cannot be changed, it need not be known at compilation time. We could have

```
S: GENDER:= ...;
CHRIS: PERSON(S);
```

where the sex of CHRIS is not determined until he or she is declared. The rule that a discriminant must be static applies only to aggregates.

The variables of type PERSON are necessarily constrained because the type had no default value for the discriminant. It is therefore not possible to assign a value which would change the sex; an attempt to do so would raise CONSTRAINT_ERROR. However, as with the type POLYNOMIAL, we could declare a default initial value for the discriminant and consequently declare unconstrained variables. Such unconstrained variables could then be assigned values with different discriminants but only by a complete record assignment.

We could therefore have

```
type GENDER is (MALE, FEMALE, NEUTER);

type MUTANT (SEX: GENDER:=NEUTER) is
   record
      BIRTH: DATE;
      case SEX is
```

```
        when MALE =>
            BEARDED: BOOLEAN;
        when FEMALE =>
            CHILDREN: INTEGER;
        when NEUTER =>
            null;
    end case;
end record;
```

Note that we have to write **null** as the alternative in the case of NEUTER where we did not want any components. In a similar way to the use of a null statement in a case statement this indicates that we really meant to have no components and did not omit them by accident.

We can now declare

```
M: MUTANT;
```

The sex of this unconstrained mutant is neuter by default but can be changed by a whole record assignment.

Note the difference between

```
M: MUTANT:=(NEUTER, (1, JAN, 1984));
```

and

```
N: MUTANT(NEUTER):=(NEUTER, (1, JAN, 1984));
```

In the first case the mutant is not constrained but just happens to be initially neuter. In the second case the mutant is permanently neuter. This example also illustrates the form of the aggregate when there are no components in the alternative; there are none so we write none – we do not write **null**.

The rules regarding the alternatives closely follow those regarding the case statement described in Section 5.2. Each **when** is followed by one or more choices separated by vertical bars and each choice is either a simple expression or a discrete range. The choice **others** can also be used but must be last and on its own. All values and ranges must be static and all possible values of the discriminant must be covered once and once only. The possible values of the discriminant are those of its static subtype (if there is one) or type. Each alternative can contain several component declarations and as we have seen could also be null.

A record can only contain one variant part and it must follow other components. However, variants can be nested; the component lists in a variant part could themselves contain one variant part but again it must follow other components.

Also observe that it is not possible to use the same identifier for components in different alternatives of a variant – all components of a record must have distinct identifiers.

It is perhaps worth emphasising the rules regarding the changing of discriminants. If an object is declared with a discriminant constraint then it cannot be changed – after all it is a constraint just like a range constraint and so the discriminant must always satisfy the constraint. Because the constraint allows only a single value this naturally means that the discriminant can only take that single value and so cannot be changed.

The other basic consideration is that, for implementation reasons, all objects must have values for discriminant components. Hence if the type does not provide a default initial value, the object declaration must and since it is expressed as a constraint, the object is then consequently constrained.

There is a restriction on renaming components of an object of a discriminated type. If the existence of the component depends upon the value of a discriminant then it cannot be renamed if the object is unconstrained. So we cannot write

```
C: INTEGER renames M.CHILDREN;
```

because there is no guarantee that the component M.CHILDREN of the mutant M will continue to exist after the renaming even if it does exist at the moment of renaming. However,

```
C: INTEGER renames BARBARA.CHILDREN;
```

is valid because BARBARA is a person and cannot change sex.

We have seen that a discriminant can be used as the bound of an array and also as the expression governing a variant. There is one other possibility – it can also be used as the discriminant constraint of an inner component. We could declare a type comprising two polynomials of the same size

```
type TWO_POLYNOMIALS(N: INTEGER range 1 .. MAX:=0) is
   record
      X: POLYNOMIAL(N);
      Y: POLYNOMIAL(N);
   end record;
```

However, we cannot use the discriminant for any other purpose. This unfortunately meant that when we declared the type STACK in the previous section we could not continue to apply the constraint to TOP by writing

```
type STACK(MAX: INTEGER range 0 .. INTEGER'LAST) is
   record
      S: array (1 .. MAX) of INTEGER;
      TOP: INTEGER range 0 .. MAX:=0;
   end record;
```

since the use of MAX in the constraint is not allowed.

Finally, a discriminant need not be used at all. It could just be treated as one component of a record. This might be particularly relevant when we wish to have a type where some components are private and others are visible. As an interesting and extreme example we can reconsider the type KEY of Section 9.3. We could change this to

```
type KEY(CODE: INTEGER:=0) is limited private;
```

with

```
type KEY(CODE: INTEGER:=0) is
    record
        null;
    end record;
```

With this formulation the user can read the code number of his key, but cannot change it.

Exercise 11.2

1 Write a procedure SHAVE which takes an object of type PERSON and removes any beard if the object is male and raises the exception SHAVING_ERROR if the object is female.

2 Write a procedure STERILISE which takes an object of type MUTANT and ensures that its sex is NEUTER by changing it if necessary and possible and otherwise raises an appropriate exception.

3 Declare a type OBJECT which describes geometrical objects which are either a circle, a square or a rectangle. A circle is characterised by its radius, a square by its side and a rectangle by its length and breadth.

4 Write a function AREA which returns the area of an OBJECT.

11.3 Access types

In the case of the types we have met so far, the name of an object has been bound irretrievably to the object itself, and the life time of an object has been from its declaration until control leaves the unit containing the declaration. This is too restrictive for many applications where a more fluid control of the allocation of objects is desired. In Ada this can be done by access types. Objects of an access type, as the name implies, provide access to other objects and these other objects can be allocated in a manner independent of the block structure.

For those familiar with other languages, an access object can be thought of as a reference or pointer. The term reference has been brought into disrepute because of dangling references in Algol 68 and pointer has been brought into disrepute because of anonymous pointers in PL/I. Thus the new term access can be thought of as a polite term for reference or pointer. However, Ada access objects are strongly typed and, as we shall see, there are no dangling reference problems.

One of the simplest uses of an access type is for list processing. Consider

```
type CELL;

type LINK is access CELL;
```

```
type CELL is
    record
        VALUE: INTEGER;
        NEXT: LINK;
    end record;

L: LINK;
```

These declarations introduce type LINK which accesses CELL. The variable L can be thought of as a reference variable which can only point at objects of type CELL; these are records with two components, VALUE of type INTEGER and NEXT which is also a LINK and can therefore access (point to or reference) other objects of type CELL. The records can therefore be formed into a linked list. Initially there are no record objects, only the single pointer L which by default takes the value **null** which points nowhere. We could have explicitly given L this default value thus

```
L: LINK:=null;
```

Note the circularity in the definitions of LINK and CELL. Because of this circularity and the rule of linear elaboration it is necessary first to give an incomplete declaration of CELL. Having done this we can declare LINK and then complete the declaration of CELL. Between the incomplete and complete declarations, which must be in the same list of declarations, the type name can only be used in the definition of an access type.

The accessed objects are created by the execution of an allocator which can (but need not) provide an initial value. An allocator consists of the reserved word **new** followed by the type of the new object and then possibly the initial value of the object. The result of an allocator is an access value which can then be assigned to a variable of the access type.

So

```
L:=new CELL;
```

creates a record of type CELL and then assigns to L a designation of (reference to or pointer to) the object. We can picture the result as in Fig. 11.1.

Fig. 11.1 An access object

Note that the NEXT component of the record takes the default value **null** whereas the VALUE component is undefined.

The components of the object referred to by L can be accessed using the normal dotted notation. So we could assign 37 to the VALUE component by

```
L.VALUE:=37;
```

Alternatively we could have provided an initial value with the allocator

```
L:=new CELL(37, null);
```

The initial value here takes the form of an aggregate and as usual has to provide values for all the components irrespective of whether some have default initial values.

Of course, the allocator could have been used to initialise L when it was declared

```
L: LINK:=new CELL(37, null);
```

Distinguish carefully the types LINK and CELL. L is of type LINK which accesses CELL and it is the accessed type which follows **new**.

Suppose we now want to create a further record and link it to our existing record. We can do this by declaring a further variable

```
N: LINK;
```

and then executing

```
N:=new CELL(10, L);
L:=N;
```

The effect of these three steps is illustrated in Fig. 11.2.

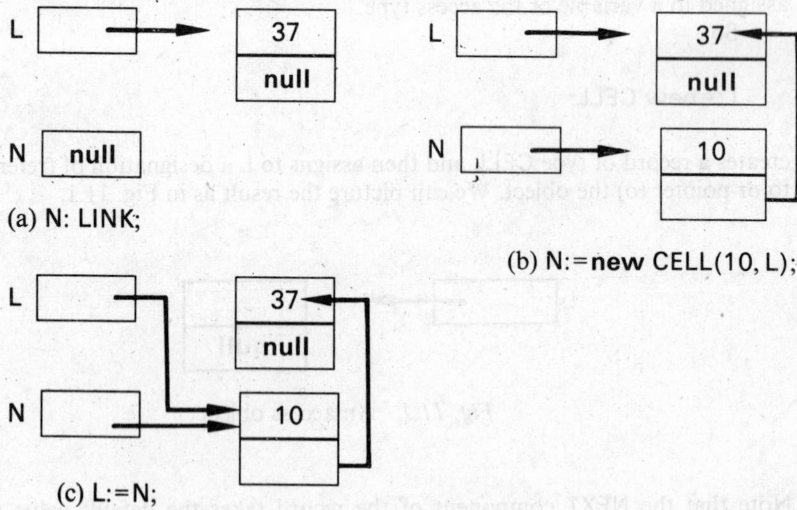

Fig. 11.2 Extending a list

Note how the assignment statement

```
L:=N;
```

copies the access values (i.e. the pointers) and not the objects. If we wanted to copy the objects we could do it component by component.

```
L.VALUE:=N.VALUE;
L.NEXT:=N.NEXT;
```

or by using **all**

```
L.all:=N.all;
```

L.**all** refers to the whole object accessed by L. In fact we can think of L.VALUE as short for L.**all**.VALUE. Unlike Pascal, dereferencing is automatic.

Similarly

```
L = N
```

will be true if L and N refer to the same object, whereas

```
L.all = N.all
```

will be true if the objects referred to happen to have the same value.

We could declare a constant of an access type but, of course, being a constant we must supply an initial value.

```
C: constant LINK:=new CELL(0, null);
```

The fact that C is constant means that it must always refer to the same object. However, the value of the object could itself be changed. So

```
C.all:=L.all;
```

is allowed but

```
C:=L;
```

is not.

We did not really need the variable N in order to extend the list since we could simply have written

```
L:=new CELL(V, L);
```

This statement can be made into a general procedure for creating a new record and adding it to the beginning of a list.

```
procedure ADD_TO_LIST(LIST: in out LINK; V: in INTEGER) is
begin
    LIST:=new CELL(V, LIST);
end;
```

The new record containing the value 10 can now be added to the list accessed by L by

```
ADD_TO_LIST(L, 10);
```

The parameter passing mechanism for access types is defined to be by copy like that for scalar types.

The value **null** is useful for determining when a list is empty. The following function returns the sum of the VALUE components of the records in a list.

```
function SUM(LIST: LINK) return INTEGER is
    L: LINK:=LIST;
    S: INTEGER:=0;
begin
    while L /= null loop
        S:=S+L.VALUE;
        L:=L.NEXT;
    end loop;
    return S;
end SUM;
```

Observe that we have to make a copy of LIST because formal parameters of mode **in** are constants. The variable L is then used to work down the list until we reach the end. The function works even if the list is empty.

A more elaborate data structure is the binary tree. This consists of nodes each of which has a value plus two subtrees one or both of which could be null. Appropriate declarations are

```
type NODE;
type TREE is access NODE;
type NODE is
    record
        VALUE: REAL;
        LEFT, RIGHT: TREE;
    end record;
```

As an interesting example of the use of trees consider the following procedure SORT which sorts the values in an array into ascending order.

```
procedure SORT(A: in out VECTOR) is
    I: INTEGER;
    BASE: TREE:=null;

    procedure INSERT(T: in out TREE; V: REAL) is
    begin
        if T = null then
            T:=new NODE(V, null, null);
        else
            if V < T.VALUE then
                INSERT(T.LEFT, V);
```

```
            else
                  INSERT(T.RIGHT,V);
            end if;
        end if;
    end INSERT;
    procedure OUTPUT(T: TREE) is
    begin
        if T /= null then
            OUTPUT(T.LEFT);
            A(I):=V;
            I:=I+1;
            OUTPUT(T.RIGHT);
        end if;
    end OUTPUT;
begin -- body of SORT
    for J in A'RANGE loop
        INSERT(BASE,A(J));
    end loop;
    I:=A'FIRST;
    OUTPUT(BASE);
end SORT;
```

The recursive procedure INSERT adds a new node containing the value V to the tree T in such a way that the values in the left subtree of a node are always less than the value at the node and the values in the right subtree are always greater than (or equal to) the value at the node.

The recursive procedure OUTPUT copies the values at all the nodes of the tree into the array A by first outputting the left subtree (which has the smaller values) and then copying the value at the node and finally outputting the right subtree.

The procedure SORT simply builds up the tree by calling INSERT with each of the components of the array in turn and then calls OUTPUT to copy the ordered values back into the array.

The access types we have met so far have referred to records. This will often be the case but an access type can refer to any type, even another access type. So we could have

```
type REF_INT is access INTEGER;
R: REF_INT:=new INTEGER(46);
```

Note that the value of the integer referred to by R is, perhaps inappropriately, denoted by R.**all**. So we can write

```
R.all:=13;
```

to change the value from 46 to 13.

It is most important to understand that all objects referred to by access types must be acquired through an allocator. We cannot write

```
I : INTEGER;
R: REF_INT:=I;        -- illegal
```

The accessed objects form a collection whose scope is that of the access type. The collection will cease to exist only when that scope is finally left but, of course, by then all the access variables will also have ceased to exist; so no dangling reference problems can arise.

If an object becomes inaccessible because no variables refer to it directly or indirectly then the storage it occupies may be reclaimed so that it can be reused by other objects. An implementation may (but need not) provide a garbage collector to do this.

Alternatively there is a mechanism whereby a program can indicate that an object is no longer required; if, mistakenly, there are still references to such objects then the program is erroneous. For fuller details the reader is referred to Section 15.6. In this chapter we will assume that a garbage collector tidies up for us when necessary.

A few final points of detail. An allocator in an aggregate is only executed once even if the value is assigned to several components. Thus

```
A: array (1 .. 10) of LINK:=(1 .. 10 => new CELL);
```

creates an array of ten components and initialises them so that they all access the same cell. To get ten different cells we would need to write

```
for I in A'RANGE loop
    A(I):=new CELL;
end loop;
```

If an allocator provides an initial value then this can take the form of any expression in brackets or an aggregate. So we could have

```
L: LINK:=new CELL(N.all);
```

in which case the new object is given the same value as the object referred to by N. We could have

```
I : INTEGER:=46;
R: REF_INT:=new INTEGER(I);
```

in which case the new object takes the value of I; it does not matter that I is not an access object since only its value concerns us.

The type accessed could be constrained, so we could have

```
type REF_NAT is access NATURAL;
```

or equivalently

```
type REF_NAT is access INTEGER range 1 .. INTEGER'LAST;
```

The values of the objects referred to are all constrained to be non negative. We can write

```
RN: REF_NAT:=new NATURAL(10);
```

or even

```
RN: REF_NAT:=new INTEGER(10);
```

Note that if we wrote **new** NATURAL(0) then CONSTRAINT_ERROR would be raised because 0 is not of subtype NATURAL. However, if we wrote **new** INTEGER(0) then CONSTRAINT_ERROR is only raised because of the context of the allocator. The syntax does not permit

```
new INTEGER range 1 .. INTEGER'LAST(0)
```

It is important to realise that each declaration of an access type introduces a new collection. Two collections can be of objects of the same type but the access objects must not refer to objects in the wrong collection. So we could have

```
type REF_INT_A is access INTEGER;
type REF_INT_B is access INTEGER;
RA: REF_INT_A:=new INTEGER(10);
RB: REF_INT_B:=new INTEGER(20);
```

The objects created by the two allocators are both of the same type but the access values are of different types determined by the context of the allocator and the objects are in different collections.

So, although we can write

```
RA.all:=RB.all;
```

we cannot write

```
RA:=RB;        -- illegal
```

Exercise 11.3

1 Write a

```
procedure APPEND(FIRST: in out LINK; SECOND: in LINK);
```

which appends the list SECOND (without copying) to the end of the list FIRST. Take care of any special cases.

2 Write a function SIZE which returns the number of nodes in a tree.

3 Write a function COPY which makes a complete copy of a tree.

11.4 Access types and private types

A private type can be implemented as an access type. Consider once more the type STACK and suppose that we wish to impose no maximum stack size other than that imposed by the overall size of the computer. This can be done by representing the stack as a list.

```
package STACKS is
    type STACK is limited private;
    procedure PUSH(S: in out STACK; X: in INTEGER);
    procedure POP(S: in out STACK; X: out INTEGER);
private
    type CELL;
    type STACK is access CELL;
    type CELL is
        record
            VALUE: INTEGER;
            NEXT: STACK;
        end record;
end;

package body STACKS is

    procedure PUSH(S: in out STACK; in INTEGER) is
    begin
        S:=new CELL(X, S);
    end;

    procedure POP(S: in out STACK; X: out INTEGER) is
    begin
        X:=S.VALUE;
        S:=S.NEXT;
    end;

end STACKS;
```

When the user declares a stack

```
S: STACK;
```

it automatically takes the default initial value **null** which denotes that the stack is empty. If we call POP when the stack is empty then this will result in attempting to evaluate

```
null.VALUE
```

and this will raise CONSTRAINT_ERROR. The only way in which PUSH can fail is by running out of storage; an attempt to evaluate

```
new CELL(X, S)
```

could raise STORAGE_ERROR.

This formulation of stacks is one in which we have made the type limited private. Predefined equality would merely have tested two stacks to see if they were the same stack rather than if they had the same values, and assignment would, of course, copy only the pointer to the stack rather than the stack itself. The writing of an appropriate function "=" needs some care. We could attempt

```
function "="(S, T: STACK) return BOOLEAN is
    SS: STACK:=S;
    TT: STACK:=T;
begin
    while SS /= null and TT /= null loop
        SS:=SS.NEXT;
        TT:=TT.NEXT;
        if SS.VALUE /= TT.VALUE then
            return FALSE;
        end if;
    end loop;
    return SS = TT;    --TRUE if both null
end;
```

but this does not work because we have hidden the predefined equality which we wish to use inside the body of = by the new definition itself. So this function will recurse indefinitely. The solution is to distinguish between the type STACK and its representation in some way. One possibility would be to make the type STACK a record of one component thus

```
type CELL;
type LINK is access CELL;
type CELL is
    record
        VALUE: INTEGER;
        NEXT: LINK;
    end record;
type STACK is
    record
        LIST: LINK;
    end record;
```

so that we can then distinguish between S, the STACK, and S.LIST, its internal representation.

An access type could conversely refer to a private type. So we could have

```
type REF_STACK is access STACK;
```

The only special point of interest is that if the accessed type is limited private then an allocator cannot provide an initial value since this would be equivalent to assignment and assignment is not allowed for limited private types.

Exercise 11.4

1 Assuming that the exception ERROR is declared in the specification of STACKS, rewrite procedures PUSH and POP so that they raise ERROR rather than STORAGE_ERROR and CONSTRAINT_ERROR.

2 Rewrite PUSH, POP and "=" to use the formulation

```
type STACK is
    record
        LIST: LINK;
    end record;
```

Ignore the possibility of exceptions.

3 Complete the package whose visible part is

```
package QUEUES is
    EMPTY: exception;
    type QUEUE is limited private;
    procedure JOIN(Q: in out QUEUE; X: in ITEM);
    procedure REMOVE(Q: in out QUEUE; X: out ITEM);
    function LENGTH(Q: QUEUE) return INTEGER;
private
```

Items join a queue at one end and are removed from the other so that a normal first come first served protocol is enforced. An attempt to remove an item from an empty queue raises the exception EMPTY. Implement the queue as a singly linked list but maintain pointers to both ends of the list so that scanning of the list is avoided. The function LENGTH returns the number of items in the queue; again, avoid scanning the list.

11.5 Access types and constraints

Access types can also refer to arrays and discriminated record types. In both cases they can be constrained or not.

Consider the problem of representing a family tree. We could declare

```
type PERSON;
type PERSON_NAME is access PERSON;

type PERSON is
    record
        SEX: GENDER;
        BIRTH: DATE;
        SPOUSE: PERSON_NAME;
        FATHER: PERSON_NAME;
        FIRST_CHILD: PERSON_NAME;
        NEXT_SIBLING: PERSON_NAME;
    end record;
```

This model assumes a monogamous and legitimate system. The children are linked together through the component NEXT_SIBLING and a person's mother is identified as the spouse of the father.

It might however be more useful to use a discriminated type for a person so that different components could exist for the different sexes and more particularly so that appropriate constraints could be applied. Consider

```
type PERSON(SEX: GENDER);
type PERSON_NAME is access PERSON;

type PERSON(SEX: GENDER) is
    record
        BIRTH: DATE;
        FATHER: PERSON_NAME(MALE);
        NEXT_SIBLING: PERSON_NAME;

        case SEX is
            when MALE =>
                WIFE: PERSON_NAME(FEMALE);
            when FEMALE =>
                HUSBAND: PERSON_NAME(MALE);
                FIRST_CHILD: PERSON_NAME;
        end case;
    end record;
```

The incomplete declaration of PERSON also gives the discriminants (and any initial values); these must, of course, match those in the subsequent complete declaration. The component FATHER is now constrained always to access a person whose sex is male (or **null** of course). Similarly the components WIFE and HUSBAND are constrained; note that these had to have distinct identifiers and so could not both be SPOUSE. However, the components FIRST_CHILD and NEXT_SIBLING are not constrained and so could access a person of either sex. We have also taken the opportunity to save on storage by making the children belong to the mother only.

When an object of type PERSON is created by an allocator a value must be provided for the discriminant. So we could write

```
JANET:=new PERSON(FEMALE, (22, FEB, 1967), JOHN, null,
                              null, null);
```

or

```
JANET:=new PERSON(FEMALE);
```

but not just

```
JANET:=new PERSON;
```

However we could declare

```
subtype WOMAN is PERSON(FEMALE);
```

and then

```
JANET: =new WOMAN;
```

Such an object cannot later have its discriminant changed. These rules apply ven if the discriminant has a default initial value; objects created by an allocator are in this respect different to objects created by a normal object declaration where , the reader will recall, a default initial value allows unconstrained objects to be declared and later to have their discriminant changed.

On the other hand, we see that despite the absence of a default initial value for the discriminant, we can nevertheless declare unconstrained objects of type PERSON_NAME; such objects, of course, take the default initial value **null** and so no problem arises. Thus although an allocated object cannot have its discriminant changed, nevertheless an unconstrained access object could refer from time to time to objects with different discriminants.

The reason for not allowing an allocated object to have its discriminant changed is that it could be accessed from several constrained objects such as the components FATHER and it would be difficult to ensure that such constraints were not violated.

For convenience we can define subtypes

```
subtype MANS_NAME is PERSON_NAME(MALE);
subtype WOMANS_NAME is PERSON_NAME(FEMALE);
```

We can now write a procedure to marry two people.

```
procedure MARRY(BRIDE: WOMANS_NAME; GROOM:
                        MANS_NAME) is
begin
   if BRIDE.HUSBAND /= null or GROOM.WIFE /= null then
      raise BIGAMY;
   end if;
   BRIDE.HUSBAND:=GROOM;
   GROOM.WIFE:=BRIDE;
end MARRY;
```

The constraints on the parameters are checked when the parameters are passed (remember that access parameters are always implemented by copy). An attempt to marry people of the wrong sex will raise CONSTRAINT_ERROR at the point of call. On the other hand an attempt to marry a non existent person will result in CONSTRAINT_ERROR being raised inside the body of the procedure. Remember that although **in** parameters are constants we can change the components of the accessed objects – we are not changing the values of BRIDE and GROOM to access different objects.

A function could return an access value as for example

```
function SPOUSE(P: PERSON_NAME) return PERSON_NAME is
begin
   case P.SEX is
      when MALE =>
         return P.WIFE;
      when FEMALE =>
         return P.HUSBAND;
   end case;
end SPOUSE;
```

The result of such a function call can be directly used as part of a name so we can write

```
SPOUSE(P).BIRTH
```

to give the birthday of the spouse of P. (See the end of Section 7.1.) We could even write

```
SPOUSE(P).BIRTH:=NEWDATE;
```

but this is only possible because the function delivers an access value. It could not be done if the function actually delivered a value of type PERSON rather than PERSON_NAME. However, we cannot write

```
SPOUSE(P):=Q;
```

in an attempt to replace our spouse by someone else, whereas

```
SPOUSE(P).all:=Q.all;
```

is valid and would change all the components of our spouse to be the same of those of Q.

The following function gives birth to a new child. We need the mother, the sex of the child and the date as parameters.

```
function NEW_CHILD(MOTHER: WOMANS_NAME;
                   BOY_OR_GIRL: GENDER; BIRTHDAY: DATE)
                   return PERSON_NAME is
   CHILD: PERSON_NAME;
begin
   if MOTHER.HUSBAND = null then
      raise ILLEGITIMATE;
   end if;
   CHILD:=new PERSON(BOY_OR_GIRL);
   CHILD.BIRTH:=BIRTHDAY;
   CHILD.FATHER:=MOTHER.HUSBAND;
   declare
      LAST: PERSON_NAME:=MOTHER.FIRST_CHILD;
   begin
      if LAST = null then
         MOTHER.FIRST_CHILD:=CHILD;
      else
         while LAST.NEXT_SIBLING /= null loop
            LAST:=LAST.NEXT_SIBLING;
         end loop;
         LAST.NEXT_SIBLING:=CHILD;
      end if;
   end;
   return CHILD;
end NEW_CHILD;
```

Observe that a discriminant constraint need not be static – the value of BOY_OR_GIRL is not known until the function is called. As a consequence we cannot give the complete initial value with the allocator because we do not know which components to provide. Hence we allocate the child with just the value of the discriminant and then separately assign the date of birth and the father. The remaining components take the default value **null**. We can now write

```
HELEN: PERSON_NAME:=NEW_CHILD(BARBARA,
                              FEMALE, (28, SEP, 1969));
```

Access types can also refer to constrained and unconstrained arrays. We could have

```
type REF_MATRIX is access MATRIX;
R: REF_MATRIX;
```

and then obtain new matrices with an allocator thus

```
R:=new MATRIX(1 .. 10, 1 .. 10);
```

Alternatively, the matrix could be initialised

```
R:=new MATRIX(1 .. 10 => (1 .. 10 => 0.0));
```

but as for discriminated records we could not write just

```
R:=new MATRIX;
```

because all array objects must have bounds. Moreover the bounds cannot be changed. However, R can refer to matrices of different bounds from time to time.

As expected we can create subtypes

```
subtype REF_MATRIX_3 is REF_MATRIX(1 .. 3,1 .. 3);
R_3: REF_MATRIX_3;
```

and R_3 can then only reference matrices with corresponding bounds. Alternatively we could have written

```
R_3:REF_MATRIX(1 .. 3,1 .. 3);
```

Using

```
subtype MATRIX_3 is MATRIX(1 .. 3 ,1 .. 3);
```

we can then write

```
R_3:=new MATRIX_3;
```

This is allowed because the subtype supplies the array bounds just as we were allowed to write

```
JANET:=new WOMAN;
```

because the subtype WOMAN supplied the discriminant SEX.

This introduces the last situation where we can use an array aggregate with **others**. Because the subtype MATRIX_3 supplies the array bounds, we could initialise the new object as follows

```
R_3:=new MATRIX_3(others => (others => 0.0));
```

The components of an accessed array can be referred to by the usual mechanism, so

```
R(1,1):=0.0;
```

would set component (1,1) of the matrix accessed by R to zero. The whole matrix can be referred to by **all**. So

```
R_3.all:=(1..3 => (1..3 => 0.0));
```

would set all the components of the matrix accessed by R_3 to zero. We can therefore think of R(1,1) as an abbreviation for R.**all**(1,1). As with records, dereferencing is automatic. We can also write attributes R'FIRST(1) or alternatively R.**all**'FIRST(1). In the case of a one dimensional array slicing is also allowed.

Exercise 11.5

1 Write a function to return a person's heir. Follow the normal rules of primogeniture – the heir is the eldest son if there is one and otherwise is the eldest daughter. Return **null** if there is no heir.

2 Write a procedure to divorce a woman. Divorce is only permitted if there are no children.

11.6 Derived types

Sometimes it is useful to introduce a new type which is similar in most respects to an existing type but which is nevertheless a distinct type. If T is a type we can write

```
type S is new T;
```

and then S is said to be a derived type and T is the parent type of S.

A derived type belongs to the same class of type as its parent. If T is a record type then S will be a record type and its components will have the same names and so on.

It will be remembered that the key things that distinguish a type are its set of values and its set of operations; we now consider these.

The set of values of a derived type is a copy of the set of values of the parent. An important instance of this is that if the parent type is an access type then the derived type is also an access type and they share the same collection. Note that we say that the set of values is a copy; this reflects that they are truly different types and values of one type cannot be assigned to objects of the other type; however, as we shall see in a moment, conversion between the two types is possible. The notation for literals and aggregates is the same and any default initial values for the type or its components are the same.

The operations applicable to a derived type are as follows. First it has the same attributes as the parent. Second, unless the parent type, and consequently the derived type, are limited private, assignment and predefined equality and inequality are also applicable. Third, a derived type will derive or inherit certain subprograms applicable to the parent type. (We say that a subprogram applies to a type if it has one or more parameters or a result of that type or one of its subtypes.) Such derived subprograms are implicitly declared at the place of the derived type definition but may be later redefined in the same declaration list. The subprograms which are derived are best illustrated with examples.

The simplest case is where the parent type is a predefined type. In this case the derived subprograms are just the predefined subprograms. So if we have

```
type INTEGER_A is new INTEGER;
```

then INTEGER_A will inherit all the predefined subprograms such as "+", "–" and ABS as well as the literals 0, 1, 2, and attributes such as FIRST and LAST.

If we derive a further type from INTEGER_A then these inherited subprograms are passed on again. However, suppose that INTEGER_A is declared in a package specification and that the specification includes further subprograms, thus

```
package P is
    type INTEGER_A is new INTEGER;
    procedure INCREMENT(I: in out INTEGER_A);
    function "&"(I, J: INTEGER_A) return INTEGER_A;
end;
```

If we now have

```
type INTEGER_B is new INTEGER_A;
```

declared after the end of the specification (either outside the package or in its body) then INTEGER_B will inherit the new subprograms INCREMENT and "&" as well as the predefined ones.

If we do not like one of the inherited subprograms then it can be redefined in the same declaration list. So we could write

```
package Q is
    type INTEGER_X is new INTEGER;
    function ABS(X: INTEGER_X) return INTEGER_X;
end;
```

in which for some reason we have chosen to replace the predefined function ABS by a new version.

If we now write

```
type INTEGER_Y is new INTEGER_X;
```

after the end of the package specification, the new version of ABS will be inherited rather than the original one. Note that if the declarations of INTEGER_B and INTEGER_Y had been inside the package specifications, the predefined programs would have been inherited and not the new or replaced ones.

If the original parent type is not a predefined type but just a user defined type then again there will be some predefined subprograms such as < and these will be inherited. If the parent type is declared in a package specification and the derived type is declared after the end of the package specification then again the applicable subprograms in the package will also be inherited. Thus the new subprograms only really 'belong' to the type in the sense that they can be derived with it when we reach the end of the specification; this is quite reasonable since it is at this point that the definition of the type and its operations can be considered to be complete in an abstract sense. We see, therefore, that the predefined types are not really a special case since they and the predefined subprograms are considered to be declared in the package STANDARD.

Although derived types are distinct, the values can be converted from one to another using the same notation as was used for converting between numeric types. So given

```
type S is new T;
TX: T;
SX: S;
```

we can write

```
TX:=T(SX);
```

or

```
SX:=S(TX);
```

but not

```
TX:=SX;       -- illegal
```

or

```
SX:=TX;       -- illegal
```

If multiple derivations are involved then each conversion must be given step by step; short cuts are not allowed. So if we have

```
type SS is new S;
type TT is new T;
SSX: SS;
TTX: TT;
```

then we can write

```
SSX:=SS(S(TX));
```

and

```
TTX:=TT(T(SX));
```

but not

```
SSX:=SS(TX);
```

or

```
TTX:=TT(SX);
```

However, numeric types are an exception to this rule. One numeric type can always be converted to another numeric type (the reason will be clear in the next chapter). So if we have

```
I: INTEGER;
IA: INTEGER_A;
IB: INTEGER_B;
IX: INTEGER_X;
IY: INTEGER_Y;
```

we can then write statements such as

```
IX:=INTEGER_X(IB);
```

The introduction of derived types extends the possibility of conversion between array types discussed in Section 6.2. In fact a value of one array type can be converted to another array type if the component types and index types are the same or one is derived from the other.

We can now rewrite the type STACK of Section 11.4 using a derived type as follows

```
type CELL;
type LINK is access CELL;
type CELL is
    record
        VALUE: INTEGER;
        NEXT: LINK;
    end record;
type STACK is new LINK;
```

It is now possible to write the function "=" thus

```
function "="(S,T: STACK) return BOOLEAN is
    SL: LINK:=LINK(S);
    TL: LINK:=LINK(T);
```

```
begin
    -- as the answer to Exercise 11.4(2)
end "=";
```

An advantage of using a derived type rather than making the type STACK into a record of one component is that the procedures PUSH and POP of Section 11.4 still work and do not have to be modified. This is because the type STACK is still an access type and shares its collection with the type LINK.

Derived types are often used for private types and in fact we have to use a derived type if we want to express the private type as an existing type such as INTEGER.

Another use for derived types is when we want to use the operations of existing types but wish to avoid the accidental mixing of objects of conceptually different types. Suppose we wish to count apples and oranges. Then we could declare

```
type APPLES is new INTEGER;
type ORANGES is new INTEGER;
NO_OF_APPLES: APPLES;
NO_OF_ORANGES: ORANGES;
```

Since APPLES and ORANGES are derived from the type INTEGER they have integer numbers as literals and both inherit "+". So we can write

```
NO_OF_APPLES:=NO_OF_APPLES+1;
```

and

```
NO_OF_ORANGES:=NO_ OF_ ORANGES+1;
```

but we cannot write

```
NO_OF_APPLES:=NO_OF_ORANGES;
```

If we did want to convert the oranges to apples we would have to write

```
NO_OF_APPLES:=APPLES(NO_OF_ORANGES);
```

Suppose also that we have overloaded procedures to sell apples and oranges

```
procedure SELL(N: APPLES);
procedure SELL(N: ORANGES);
```

Then we can write

```
SELL(NO_OF_APPLES);
```

but

```
SELL(6);
```

is ambiguous because we do not know which fruit we are selling. We can resolve the ambiguity by qualification thus

```
SELL(APPLES'(6));
```

When a subprogram is derived a new subprogram is not actually created. A call of the derived subprogram is really a call of the parent subprogram; **in** and **in out** parameters are implicitly converted just before the call; **in out** and **out** parameters or a function result are implicitly converted just after the call.

So

```
MY_APPLES + YOUR_APPLES
```

is effectively

```
APPLES(INTEGER(MY_APPLES)+INTEGER(YOUR_APPLES))
```

Derived types are in some ways an alternative to private types. Derived types have the advantage of inheriting literals but they often have the disadvantage of inheriting too much. For instance, we could derive types LENGTH and AREA from REAL.

```
type LENGTH is new REAL;
type AREA is new REAL;
```

We would then be prevented from mixing lengths and areas but we would also have inherited the ability to multiply two lengths to give a length and to multiply two areas to give an area as well as hosts of irrelevant operations such as exponentiation. Of course, it is possible to redefine these operations to be useful or to raise exceptions but it is often simpler to make them private types and just define the operations we need.

Finally we can derive from a subtype

```
type PEARS is new INTEGER range 0..INTEGER'LAST;
```

This is equivalent to introducing an intermediate anonymous type

```
type anon is new INTEGER;
subtype PEARS is anon range 0..anon'LAST;
```

So PEARS is not really a type at all but a subtype. The set of values of the new derived type is actually the full set of values of the type INTEGER. The derived operations "+", ">" and so on also work on the full set of values. So given

```
P: PEARS;
```

we can legally write

```
P > -2
```

even though −2 could never be assigned to P. The Boolean expression is, of course, always true.

The reader may have felt that derived types are not very useful because in the examples we have seen there is usually an alternative mechanism open to us – usually involving record types or private types. However, one importance of derived types is that they are fundamental to the mechanism for numeric types as we shall see in the next chapter.

Exercise 11.6

1 Declare a package containing types LENGTH and AREA with appropriate redeclarations of the incorrect operations "*".

Checklist 11

If a discriminant does not have a default value then all objects must be constrained.

Discriminants can only be used as array bounds or to govern variants or as nested discriminants.

A discriminant in an aggregate and governing a variant must be static.

Any variant must appear last in a component list.

An incomplete declaration can only be used in an access type.

The scope of an accessed object is that of the access type.

If an accessed object has a discriminant then it is always constrained.

Functions returning access values can be used in names.

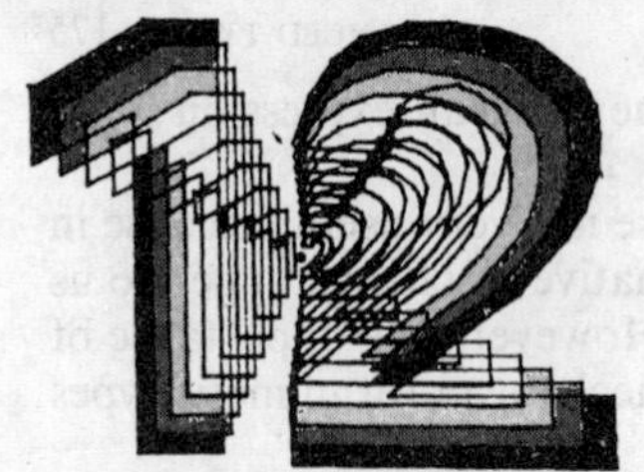

Numeric Types

We now come at last to a more detailed discussion of numeric types. There are two classes of numeric types in Ada: integer types and real types. The real types are further subdivided into floating point types and fixed point types.

There are two problems concerning the representation of numeric types in a computer. First, the range may be restricted and indeed many machines have hardware operations for various ranges so that we can choose our own compromise between range of values and space occupied by values. Second, it may not be possible to represent accurately all the possible values of a type. These difficulties cause problems with program portability because the constraints vary from machine to machine. Ada recognises these difficulties and provides numeric types in such a way that a recognised minimum set of properties is provided; this enables the programmer to keep portability problems to a minimum.

We start by discussing integer types because these suffer only from range problems but not from accuracy problems.

12.1 Integer types

All implementations of Ada have the predefined type INTEGER. In addition there may be other predefined types such as LONG_INTEGER, SHORT_INTEGER and so on. The range of values of these predefined types will be symmetric about zero except for an extra negative value in twos complement machines (which now seem to dominate over ones complement machines). All predefined types will have the same predefined operations.

Thus we might find that on machine A we have types INTEGER and LONG_INTEGER with

range of INTEGER:
−32768 .. +32767 (i.e. 16 bits)
range of LONG_INTEGER:
−21474_83648 .. +21474_83647 (i.e. 32 bits)

whereas on machine B we might have types SHORT_INTEGER, INTEGER and LONG_INTEGER with

range of SHORT_INTEGER:
−2048 .. +2047 (i.e. 12 bits)
range of INTEGER:
−83_88608 .. +83_88607 (i.e. 24 bits)
range of LONG_INTEGER:
−14073_74883_55328 .. +14073_74883_55327 (i.e. 48 bits)

For most purposes the type INTEGER will suffice on either machine and that is why we have simply used INTEGER in examples in this book so far. However, suppose we have an application where we need to manipulate signed values up to a million. The type INTEGER is inadequate on machine A and to use LONG_INTEGER on machine B would be extravagant. We can overcome our problem by using derived types and writing (for machine A)

```
type MY_INTEGER is new LONG_INTEGER;
```

and then using MY_INTEGER throughout the program. To move the program to machine B we just replace this one declaration by

```
type MY_INTEGER is new INTEGER;
```

However, Ada enables this choice to be made automatically; if we write

```
type MY_INTEGER is range -1E6..1E6;
```

then the implementation will implicitly choose the smallest appropriate type and it will be as if we had written either

```
type MY_INTEGER is new LONG_INTEGER range -1E6..1E6;
```

or

```
type MY_INTEGER is new INTEGER range -1E6..1E6;
```

So in fact MY_INTEGER will be a subtype of an anonymous type derived from one of the predefined types and so objects of type MY_INTEGER will be constrained to take only the values in the range -1E6..1E6 and not the full range of the anonymous type.

If, out of curiosity, we wanted to know the full range we could use MY_INTEGER'BASE'FIRST and MY_INTEGER'BASE'LAST.

The attribute BASE applies to any type or subtype and gives the corresponding base type. It can only be used to form other attributes as in this example. We could even go so far as to ensure that we could use the full range of the predefined type by writing

```
type X is range -1E6..1E6;
type MY_INTEGER is range X'BASE'FIRST..X'BASE'LAST;
```

This would have the dubious merit of avoiding the constraint checks when values are assigned to objects of type MY_INTEGER and would destroy the very portability we were seeking.

We can convert between one integer type and another by using the normal notation for type conversion. Given

```
type MY_INTEGER is range -1E6..1E6;
type INDEX is range 0..10000;
M: MY_INTEGER;
I: INDEX:
```

then we can write

```
M:=MY_INTEGER(I);
I:=INDEX(M);
```

On machine A a genuine hardware conversion is necessary but on machine B both types will be derived from INTEGER and the conversion will be null.

Note that, as mentioned in the last chapter, we can convert any numeric type directly to another, and do not have to convert via each derived type. If this were not so we would have to write

```
M:=MY_INTEGER(LONG_INTEGER(INTEGER(I)));
```

on machine A and

```
M:=MY_INTEGER(INTEGER(I));
```

on machine B and our portability would be lost.

The integer literals are considered to belong to a type known as universal integer. There are no bounds on this type and all operations on values of the type are performed at compilation time. Integer numbers declared in a number declaration (see Section 4.1) such as

```
TEN: constant:=10;
```

are also of type universal integer.

An expression involving only the operations +, −, *, /, **mod**, **rem**, ** and ABS on integer literals and integer numbers with the usual freedom to use brackets is known as a literal expression of type universal integer. (Such an expression could also include some attributes defined later in this chapter.) Literal expressions are always evaluated at compilation time. The initial value in a number declaration has to be a literal expression. So

```
M: constant:=10;
MM: constant:=M*M;
```

is allowed since M*M is a literal expression. However,

```
N: constant INTEGER:=10;
NN: constant:=N*N;
```

is not allowed since N*N is not a literal expression and so of type universal integer but merely a static expression of type INTEGER.

Conversion between integer literals and integer literal expressions to other integer types is automatic and is again performed at compilation time.

The use of integer type declarations which reflect the need of the program rather than the arbitrary use of INTEGER and LONG_INTEGER is good practice because it not only encourages portability but also enables us to distinguish between different classes of objects as for example when we were counting apples and oranges in the last chapter.

However, complete portability is not easily obtained. For example, assume

```
type MY_INTEGER is range -1E6 .. +1E6;
I, J: MY_INTEGER;
```

and consider

```
I := 100000;
J := I*I;
```

In order to understand the behaviour it is most important to remember that MY_INTEGER is really only a subtype of an anonymous type derived from LONG_INTEGER on machine A or INTEGER on machine B. The derived operations +, −, *, / and so on have the anonymous type as operands and results and the subtype constraint is only relevant when we attempt to assign to J. So J:=I*I; is effectively (on machine A)

```
J := anon(LONG_INTEGER(I)*LONG_INTEGER(I));
```

and the multiplication is performed with the operation of the type LONG_INTEGER. The result is 1E10 and this is well within the range of LONG_INTEGER. However, when we attempt to assign the result to J we get CONSTRAINT_ERROR.

On machine B on the other hand the type is derived from INTEGER and this time the result of the multiplication is outside the range of INTEGER. So NUMERIC_ERROR is raised by the multiplication itself.

Thus, although the program fails in both cases the actual exception raised could be different.

A worse case would be

```
I := 100000;
J := (I*I)/100000;
```

On machine A the intermediate product and final result are computed with no problem and moreover the final result lies within the range of J and so no exception is raised. But on machine B we again get NUMERIC_ERROR.

(The above analysis has assumed that an illegal predefined numeric operation raises NUMERIC_ERROR. However, we recall that an implementation is not obliged to do this if the underlying hardware is not cooperative and so the situation could be somewhat worse.)

Finally we note that the most negative and most positive values supported by the predefined integer types are given by SYSTEM.MIN_INT and SYSTEM.MAX_INT. These are, of course, implementation dependent and are numbers declared in the package SYSTEM which is itself in the package STANDARD.

Exercise 12.1

1 What types on machines A and B are used to represent

```
type P is range 1 .. 1000;
type Q is range 0 .. +32768;
type R is range -1E15 .. +1E15;
```

2 Would it make any difference if A and B were ones complement machines with the same number of bits in the representations?

3 Given

```
N: INTEGER:=6;
P: constant:=3;
R: MY_INTEGER:=4;
```

what is the type of

a) N+P　　d) N*N
b) N+R　　e) P*P
c) P+R　　f) R*R

4 Declare a type LONGEST_INTEGER which is the maximum supported by the implementation.

12.2 Real types

Integer types are exact types. Real types are however approximate and introduce problems of accuracy which have subtle effects. This book is not a specialised treatise on errors in numerical analysis and so we do not intend to give all the details of how the features of Ada can be used to minimise errors and maximise portability but will concentrate instead on outlining the basic principles.

Real types are subdivided into floating point types and fixed point types. Apart from the details of representation the key abstract difference is that floating point values have a relative error whereas fixed point values have an absolute error. Concepts common to both floating and fixed point types are dealt with in this section and further details of the individual types are in subsequent sections.

There is a type universal real having similar properties to the type universal integer. The real literals (see Section 3.4) are of type universal real. This type is notionally unbounded and infinitely accurate and all operations on its values are performed at compilation time. Real numbers declared in a number declaration such as

```
PI: constant:=3.14159_26536;
```

are also of type universal real. (The reader will recall that the difference between an integer literal and a real literal is that a real literal always has a point in it.)

A real literal expression is one which is evaluated at compilation time and delivers a universal real result. As well as the operations +, −, *, / and ABS on universal real operands delivering a universal real result, some mixing of universal real and universal integer operands is also allowed. Specifically, a universal real can be multiplied by a universal integer and vice versa and division and exponentiation are allowed with the first operand being universal real and the second operand being universal integer; in all cases the result is universal real.

So we can write either

```
TWO_PI: constant:=2*PI;
```

or

```
TWO_PI: constant:=2.0*PI;
```

but not

```
PI_PLUS_TWO: constant:=PI+2;
```

because mixed addition is not defined. Note that we cannot do an explicit type conversion between universal integer and universal real although we can always convert the former into the latter by multiplying by 1.0.

An important concept is the idea of a model number. When we declare a real type T we demand a certain accuracy. The implementation will, typically, use a greater accuracy just as an implementation of an integer type uses a base type which has a larger range than that requested. Corresponding to the accuracy requested will be a set of model numbers which are guaranteed to be exactly represented. Because the implemented accuracy will usually be higher, other values will also be exactly reprepresented. Associated with each implemented value will be a model interval. If a value is a model number then the model interval is simply the model number. Otherwise the model interval is simply the interval consisting of the two model numbers surrounding the value. Special cases arise if a value is greater than the largest model number T'LARGE.

When an operation is performed the bounds of the result are given by the smallest model interval that can arise as a consequence of operating upon any values in the model intervals of the operands.

The relational operators =, > and so on are also defined in terms of model intervals. If the result is the same, whatever values are chosen in the intervals, then its value is clearly not in dispute. If however the result depends upon which values in the intervals are chosen then the result is undefined.

Tł ɘhaviour of model numbers will be illustrated with examples in the next secı

Exercise 12.ɀ

1 Given

```
TWO: INTEGER:=2;
E: constant:=2.71828_18285;
MAX: constant:=100;
```

what is the type of

a) TWO*E
b) TWO*MAX
c) E*MAX
d) TWO*TWO
e) E*E
f) MAX*MAX

2 Given

```
N: constant:=100;
```

declare a real number R having the same value as N.

12.3 Floating point types

In a similar way to integers, all implementations have a predefined type FLOAT and may also have further predefined types SHORT_FLOAT, LONG_FLOAT and so on with respectively less and more precision. These types all have the predefined operations that were described in Chapter 4 as applicable to the type REAL.

We can derive our own type directly by

```
type REAL is new FLOAT;
```

or perhaps

```
type REAL is new LONG_FLOAT;
```

according to the implemented precision but as for the integer types it is better to state the precision required and allow the implementation to choose appropriately.

If we write

```
type REAL is digits 7;
```

then we are asking the implementation to derive REAL from a predefined type with at least 7 decimal digits of precision.

The precise behaviour is defined in terms of our model numbers. Suppose we consider the more general case

```
type REAL is digits D;
```

where D is a positive static integer expression. *D* is the number of decimal digits required and we first convert this to *B*, the corresponding number of binary digits of precision. *B* is taken to be the least integer greater than $D.\log_2 10$ or in other words

$$B-1 < 3.3219\ldots \times D < B$$

The binary precision *B* determines the model numbers; these are defined to be zero plus all numbers of the form

$$sign.mantissa.2^{exponent}$$

where

$sign$ is $+1$ or -1
$\frac{1}{2} \leqslant mantissa < 1,$
$-4B \leqslant exponent \leqslant +4B$

and the mantissa has exactly B digits after the binary point when expressed in base 2. The range of the exponent, which is an integer, has been chosen to be $\pm 4B$ somewhat arbitrarily after a survey of ranges provided by contemporary architectures.

When we say

type REAL **is digits** 7;

we are guaranteed that the model numbers of the predefined floating point type chosen will include the model numbers for decimal precision 7.

As an extreme example supppose we consider

type ROUGH **is digits** 1;

Then D is 1 and so B is 4. The model numbers are values where the mantissa can be one of

$\frac{8}{16}, \frac{9}{16}, \ldots, \frac{15}{16}$

and the binary exponent lies in $-16 .. 16$.

The model numbers around one are

$\ldots,\ \frac{14}{16},\ \frac{15}{16},\ 1,\ 1\frac{1}{8},\ 1\frac{2}{8},\ 1\frac{3}{8},\ \ldots$

and the model numbers around zero are

$\ldots,\ -\frac{9}{16}\cdot 2^{-16},\ -\frac{8}{16}\cdot 2^{-16},\ 0,\ +\frac{8}{16}\cdot 2^{-16},\ +\frac{9}{16}\cdot 2^{-16},\ \ldots$

Note the change of absolute accuracy at one and the hole around zero. By the latter we mean the gaps between zero and the smallest model numbers which in this case are 8 times the difference between them and the next model numbers. There is therefore a gross loss of accuracy at zero. These model numbers are illustrated in Fig. 12.1.

```
(a) around 1          ... x  x  x  x     x     x     x  ...
                                    1

(b) around 0 ... x x x x            x            x x x x ...
                                    0
```

Fig.12.1 Model numbers of type ROUGH

The largest model numbers are

$\ldots,\ \frac{13}{16}\cdot 2^{16},\ \frac{14}{16}\cdot 2^{16},\ \frac{15}{16}\cdot 2^{16}$

or

..., 425984, 458752, 491520

Suppose we write

```
R: ROUGH:=1.1;
```

then without considering the actual predefined floating point type chosen for R the literal 1.1 will be converted to 1 or $1\frac{1}{8}$ which are the model numbers surrounding 1.1 but we do not know which. So all we know is that the value of R lies in the model interval $[1, 1\frac{1}{8}]$.

If we compute

```
R:=R*R;
```

then the computed mathematical interval in which the result can lie is $[1, 1\frac{17}{64}]$ and this is then widened to the model interval $[1, 1\frac{3}{8}]$.

If we further write

```
R:=R+R;
```

then the computed mathematical interval is now $[1, 1\frac{3}{4}]$ which is also a model interval. So we now know that the result lies in this interval. And this is all we know! Type ROUGH indeed.

The result of

```
R>1.0
```

is not defined since $1>1$ is false but $1\frac{3}{4}>1$ is true.

Similarly

```
R=1.0
```

is not defined since $1=1$ is true but $1\frac{3}{4}=1$ is false.

However

```
R>=1.0
```

is well defined and is true. So, perhaps surprisingly, the operations =, > and >= do not always have their expected relationship when applied to floating point types.

The above example is extreme but illustrates the dangers of errors. The hole around zero is a particular danger – if a result falls in that hole then we say that underflow has occurred and all accuracy will be lost. Our value has gone down a black hole!

In practice we will do rather better because the type ROUGH will undoubtedly be derived from a predefined type with more precision. Suppose that on a particular machine we just have a predefined type FLOAT with D=7. Then writing

```
type ROUGH is digits 1;
```

is equivalent to

```
type anon is new FLOAT;
subtype ROUGH is anon digits 1;
```

The type ROUGH is therefore really a subtype of the derived type anon. The operations on values will be performed with the model numbers of the type FLOAT but storage in objects of type ROUGH will in principle be confined to the model numbers with D=1. But in practice we can expect an implementation to treat objects of type ROUGH as if they were of the type FLOAT.

We could also impose a range constraint on a floating point subtype or object by for example

```
R: ROUGH range 0.0 .. 100.0;
```

or

```
subtype POSITIVE is REAL range 0.0 .. REAL'LAST;
```

and so on. If a range is violated then CONSTRAINT_ERROR is raised.

Various attributes are available and they can be used to help in writing more portable programs. For any type (or subtype) F (predefined or not) they are

F'DIGITS	the number of decimal digits, D,
F'MANTISSA	the corresponding number of binary digits, B,
F'EMAX	the maximum mantissa, 4*F'MANTISSA,
F'SMALL	the smallest positive model number, 2.0**(−F'EMAX−1),
F'LARGE	the largest positive model number, 2.0**F'EMAX*(1.0−2.0**(−F'MANTISSA)),
F'EPSILON	the difference between one and the next model number, 2.0**(−F'MANTISSA+1).

There are also the usual attributes F'FIRST and F'LAST which need not be model numbers but are the extreme actually implemented values. Of course, F'LAST>=F'LARGE.

DIGITS, MANTISSA and EMAX are of type universal integer; SMALL, LARGE and EPSILON are of type universal real; FIRST and LAST are of type F.

The attribute BASE can again be used to enable us to find out about the implemented type. So ROUGH'DIGITS = 1 and ROUGH'BASE'DIGITS = 7.

We do not intend to say more about floating point but hope that the reader will have understood the principles involved. In general one can simply specify the precision required and all will work. But care is sometimes needed and the advice of a professional numerical analyst should be sought when in doubt. For further details the reader should consult the LRM.

Exercise 12.3

1 What is the value of ROUGH'EPSILON?

2 Compute the model interval in which the value of R must lie after

```
type REAL is digits 5;

P: REAL:=2.0;
Q: REAL:=3.0;
R: REAL:=(P/Q)*Q;
```

You may assume if necessary that REAL is derived from FLOAT which has digits 7.

3 What would be the effect of writing

```
P: constant:=2.0;
Q: constant:=3.0;
R: REAL:=(P/Q)*Q;
```

4 How many model numbers are there of type ROUGH?

5 The function

```
function HYPOTENUSE(X,Y: REAL) return REAL is
begin
    return SQRT(X**2+Y**2);
end;
```

suffers from underflow if X and Y are small. Rewrite it to avoid this by testing X and Y against a suitable value and then rescaling if necessary.

12.4 Fixed point types

Unlike floating point and integer types there are no predefined fixed point types. Fixed point is normally used only in specialised applications or for doing approximate arithmetic on machines without floating point hardware. We give only a cursory overview in this book.

A fixed point type declaration specifies an absolute error and also a mandatory range. It takes the form

```
type F is delta D range L .. R;
```

In effect this is asking for values in the range L to R with an accuracy of D which must be positive. D, L and R must be of a real type and D must be static.

The implementation will use an actual delta AD <= D and the model numbers will be the numbers K*AD where K is an integer in

```
-(2**N)+1 .. (2**N)-1
```

The integer N is chosen so that L and R are within D of a model number.

The various parameters are given by attributes

F'DELTA	the requested delta, D,
F'ACTUAL_DELTA	the actual delta, AD,
F'BITS	the integer, N,
F'LARGE	the largest model number, F'ACTUAL_DELTA*(2**F'BITS−1).

As a simple example on a 16 bit twos complement machine consider

```
DEL: constant:=2.0**(−15);
type FRAC is delta DEL range −1.0..1.0−DEL;
```

FRAC will undoubtedly be represented as a pure fraction with FRAC'ACTUAL_DELTA = FRAC'DELTA and F'BITS = 15.

The arithmetic operations +, −, *, / and ABS can be applied to fixed point values. Addition and subtraction can only be applied to values of the same type and, of course, return that type. Multiplication and division are allowed between different fixed types but always return values of an infinitely accurate type known as universal fixed. Such a value must be explicitly converted by a type conversion to a particular type before any further operation can be performed. Multiplication and division by integers are also allowed and these return a value of the fixed point type.

So given

```
F,G: FRAC;
```

we can write

```
F:=F+G;
```

but not

```
F:=F*G;
```

but must explicitly state

```
F:=FRAC(F*G);
```

The behaviour of fixed point arithmetic is, like floating point arithematic, defined in terms of the model numbers. Literals are converted to a value guaranteed to be in the appropriate model interval.

For further details the reader is referred to the LRM.

Exercise 12.4

1 Given F of type FRAC compute the model interval of F after

```
F:=0.1;
```

Checklist 12

Use implicitly derived types for increased portability.

Beware of overflow in intermediate expressions.

Use numbers rather than constants.

Beware of underflow into the hole around floating point zero.

Beware of the relational operations with real types.

If in doubt consult a numerical analyst.

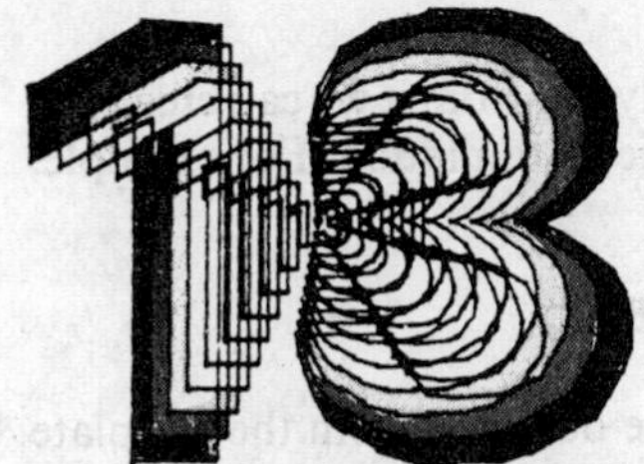

13 Generics

In this chapter we describe the generic mechanism which allows us to parameterise subprograms and packages with parameters which can be types and subprograms as well as values and objects.

13.1 Declarations and instantiations

One of the problems with a typed language such as Ada is that all types have to be determined at compilation time. This means naturally that we cannot pass types as run time parameters. However, we often get the situation that the logic of a piece of program is independent of the types involved and it therefore seems unnecessary to repeat it for all the different types to which we might wish it to apply. A simple example is provided by the procedure SWAP of Exercise 7.3(**1**)

```
procedure SWAP(X,Y: in out REAL) is
    T: REAL;
begin
    T:=X; X:=Y; Y:=T;
end;
```

It is clear that the logic is independent of the type of the values being swapped. If we also wanted to swap integers or Booleans we could of course write other procedures but this would be tedious. The generic mechanism allows us to overcome this. We can declare

```
generic
    type ITEM is private;
procedure EXCHANGE(X,Y: in out ITEM);

procedure EXCHANGE(X,Y: in out ITEM) is
    T: ITEM;
begin
    T:=X; X:=Y; Y:=T;
end;
```

The subprogram EXCHANGE is a generic subprogram and acts as a kind of template. The subprogram specification is preceded by the generic part consisting of the reserved word **generic** followed by a (possibly empty) list of generic formal parameters. The subprogram body is written exactly as normal but note that, in the case of a generic subprogram, we have to give both the body and the specification separately.

The generic procedure cannot be called directly but from it we can create an actual procedure by a mechanism known as generic instantiation. For example, we may write

```
procedure SWAP is new EXCHANGE(REAL);
```

This is a declaration and states that SWAP is to be obtained from the template described by EXCHANGE. Actual generic parameters are provided in a parameter list in the usual way. The actual parameter in this case is the type REAL which corresponds to the formal parameter ITEM. We could also use the named notation

```
procedure SWAP is new EXCHANGE(ITEM => REAL);
```

So we have now created the procedure SWAP acting on type REAL and can henceforth call it in the usual way. We can make further instantiations

```
procedure SWAP is new EXCHANGE(INTEGER);
procedure SWAP is new EXCHANGE(DATE);
```

and so on. We are here creating further overloadings of SWAP which can be distinguished by their parameter types just as if we had laboriously written them out in detail.

Superficially, it may look as if the generic mechanism is merely one of text substitution and indeed in this simple case the behaviour would be the same. However, the important difference relates to the meaning of identifiers in the generic body but which are neither parameters nor local to the body. Such non local identifiers have meanings appropriate to where the generic body is declared and not to where it is instantiated. If text substitution were used then non local identifiers would of course take their meaning at the point of instantiation and this could give very surprising results.

As well as generic subprograms we may also have generic packages. A simple example is provided by the package STACK in Section 8.2. The trouble with that package is that it only works on type INTEGER although of course the same logic applies irrespective of the type of the values manipulated. We can also take the opportunity to make MAX a parameter as well so that we are not tied to an arbitrary limit of 100. We write

```
generic
    MAX: NATURAL;
    type ITEM is private;
package STACK is
    procedure PUSH(X: ITEM);
    function POP return ITEM;
end STACK;

package body STACK is
    S: array (1 .. MAX) of ITEM;
    TOP: INTEGER range 0 .. MAX;
    -- etc as before but with INTEGER
    -- replaced by ITEM
end STACK;
```

We can now create and use a stack of a particular size and type by instantiating the generic package as in the following

```
declare
    package MY_STACK is new STACK(100, REAL);
    use MY_STACK;
begin
    ...
    PUSH(X);
    ...
    Y:=POP();
    ...
end;
```

The package MY_STACK which results from the instantiation behaves just as a normal directly written out package. The use clause allows us to refer to PUSH and POP directly. If we did a further instantiation

```
package ANOTHER_STACK is new STACK(50, INTEGER);
use ANOTHER_STACK;
```

then PUSH and POP are further overloadings and can be distinguished by the type provided by the context. Of course, if ANOTHER_STACK was also declared with the actual generic parameter being REAL, then we would have to use the dotted notation to distinguish the instances of PUSH and POP despite the use clauses.

If we added an exception ERROR to the package as in Section 10.2 so that the generic package declaration was

```
generic
    MAX: NATURAL;
    type ITEM is private;
package STACK is
    ERROR: exception;
    procedure PUSH(X: ITEM);
    function POP return ITEM;
end STACK;
```

then each instantiation would give rise to a distinct exception and because exceptions cannot be overloaded we would naturally have to use the dotted notation to distinguish them.

We could, of course, make the exception ERROR common to all instantiations by making it global to the generic package. It and the generic package could perhaps be declared inside a further package

```
package ALL_STACKS is
    exception ERROR;
    generic
        MAX: NATURAL;
        type ITEM is private;
```

```
    package STACK is
        procedure PUSH(X: ITEM);
        function POP return ITEM;
    end STACK;
end ALL_STACKS;

package body ALL_STACKS is
    package body STACK is
        ...
    end STACKS;
end ALL_STACKS;
```

This illustrates the binding of identifiers global to generic units. The meaning of ERROR is determined at the point of the generic declaration irrespective of the meaning at the point of instantiation.

The above examples have illustrated formal parameters which were types and also integers. In fact generic formal parameters can be any of the parameters applicable to subprograms; they can also be types and subprograms. As we shall see in the next sections, we can express the formal types and subprograms so that we can assume in the generic body that the actual parameters have the properties we require.

In the case of the familiar parameters which also apply to subprograms they can be of mode **in** or **in out** but not **out**. As with subprograms, **in** is taken by default as illustrated by MAX in the example above.

An **in** generic parameter acts as a constant whose value is provided by the corresponding actual parameter. An **in out** parameter, however, acts as a variable renaming the corresponding actual parameter. The actual parameter must therefore be the name of a variable and its identification occurs at the point of instantiation using the same rules as for renaming described in Section 8.5. So if any identifier in the name subsequently changes then the identity of the object referred to by the generic formal parameter does not change. Because of this there is a restriction that the actual parameter cannot be a component of an unconstrained discriminated record if the very existence of the component depends on the value of the discriminant. Thus if M is a MUTANT as in Section 11.2, M.CHILDREN could not be an actual generic parameter because M could have its SEX changed. However, M.BIRTH would be valid. This restriction also applies to renaming itself.

Inside the generic body, the formal generic parameters can be used quite freely except for one restriction. There are various places where an expression has to be static such as in the alternatives in a case statement or variant, and in the range in an integer type definition, or the number of digits in a floating point type definition and so on. In all these situations a generic formal parameter cannot be used because the expression would not then be static.

Our final example in this section illustrates the nesting of generics. The following generic procedure performs a cyclic interchange of three values and for amusement is written in terms of the generic procedure EXCHANGE.

```
generic
    type THING is private;
procedure CAB(A,B,C: in out THING);
```

```
procedure CAB(A,B,C: in out THING) is
    procedure SWAP is new EXCHANGE(ITEM => THING);
begin
    SWAP(A,B);
    SWAP(A,C);
end CAB;
```

Although nesting is allowed, it must not be recursive.

Exercise 13.1

1 Write a generic package declaration based on the package STACKS in Section 11.1 so that stacks of arbitrary type may be declared. Declare a stack S of length 30 and type BOOLEAN. Use named notation.

2 Write a generic package containing both SWAP and CAB.

13.2 Type parameters

In the previous section we introduced types as generic parameters. The examples showed the formal parameter taking the form

```
type T is private;
```

In this case, inside the generic subprogram or package, we may assume that assignment and equality are defined for T. We can assume nothing else unless we specifically provide other parameters as we shall see in a moment. Hence T behaves in the generic unit much as a private type outside the package defining it; this analogy explains the notation for the formal parameter. The corresponding actual parameter must, of course, provide assignment and equality and so it can be any type except one that is limited private.

A formal generic type parameter can take other forms. It can be

```
type T is limited private;
```

and in this case assignment and equality are not available automatically. The corresponding actual parameter can be any type.

Either of the above forms could have discriminants

```
type T( . . . ) is private;
```

and the actual type must then have discriminants with the same names, subtypes and default values.

The formal parameter could also be one of

```
type T is (<>);
type T is range <>;
type T is digits <>;
type T is delta <>;
```

In the first case the actual parameter must be a discrete type – an enumeration type or integer type. In the other cases the actual parameter must be an integer type, floating point type or fixed point type respectively. Within the generic unit the appropriate predefined operations and attributes are available.

As a simple example consider

```
generic
   type T is (<>);
function NEXT(X: T) return T;

function NEXT(X: T) return T is
begin
   if X=T'LAST then
      return T'FIRST;
   else
      return T'SUCC(X);
   end if;
end NEXT;
```

The formal parameter T requires that the actual parameter must be a discrete type. Since all discrete types have attributes FIRST, LAST and SUCC we can use these attributes in the body in the knowledge that the actual parameter will supply them.

We could now write

```
function TOMORROW is new NEXT(DAY);
```

so that TOMORROW(SUN)=MON.

An actual generic parameter could have a constraint or be a subtype. Thus

```
function NEXT_WORK_DAY is new NEXT(WEEKDAY);
```

and

```
function NEXT_WORK_DAY is new NEXT(DAY range MON..FRI);
```

are equivalent and NEXT_WORK_DAY(FRI)=MON.

The actual parameter could also be an integer type as in

```
function NEXT_DIGIT is new NEXT(INTEGER range 0..9);
```

Now consider the package COMPLEX_NUMBERS of Section 9.1; this could be made generic so that the particular floating point type upon which the type COMPLEX is based can be a parameter. It would then take the form

```
generic
   type REAL is digits <>;
package COMPLEX_NUMBERS is
   type COMPLEX is private;
   -- as before
   I: constant COMPLEX:=(0.0,1.0);
end;
```

Note that we can use the literals 0.0 and 1.0 because they are of the universal real type which can be converted to whichever type is passed as actual parameter. The package could then be instantiated by for instance

```
package MY_COMPLEX_NUMBERS is
                new COMPLEX_NUMBERS(MY_REAL);
```

A formal generic parameter can also be an array type. The actual parameter must then also be an array type with the same component type and constraints, if any, the same number of dimensions and same index subtypes. Either both must be unconstrained arrays or both must be constrained arrays. If they are constrained then the index ranges must be the same for corresponding indexes.

It is possible for one generic formal parameter to depend upon a previous formal parameter which is a type. This will often be the case with arrays. As an example consider the simple function SUM in Section 7.1. This added together the elements of a real array with integer index. We can generalise this to add together the elements of any floating point array with any index type.

```
generic
   type INDEX is (<>);
   type FLOATING is digits <>;
   type VEC is array (INDEX range <>) of FLOATING;
function SUM(A: VEC) return FLOATING;

function SUM(A: VEC) return FLOATING is
   RESULT: FLOATING:=0.0;
begin
   for I in A'RANGE loop
      RESULT:=RESULT+A(I);
   end loop;
   return RESULT;
end SUM;
```

Note that although INDEX is a formal parameter it does not explicitly appear in the generic body; nevertheless it is implicitly used since the loop parameter I is of type INDEX.

We could instantiate this by

```
function SUM_VECTOR is new SUM(INTEGER, REAL, VECTOR);
```

and this will give the function SUM of Section 7.1.

The matching of actual and formal arrays takes place after any formal types have been replaced in the formal array by the corresponding actual types. As an example of matching index subtypes note that if we had

```
type VECTOR is array (NATURAL range <>) of REAL;
```

then we would have to use NATURAL as the actual parameter for the INDEX (or alternatively the equivalent INTEGER range 1 .. INTEGER'LAST).

The final possibility for formal type parameters is the case of an access type.

The formal can be

```
type A is access T;
```

where T may but need not be a previous formal parameter. The actual parameter corresponding to A must then access T. Constraints on the accessed type must also be the same.

Observe that there is no concept of a formal record type. This is because the internal structure of records is somewhat arbitrary and the possibilities for matching would therefore be rare.

As a final example in this section we return to the question of sets. We saw in Section 6.4 how a Boolean array could be used to represent a set. Exercises 7.1 (**4**), 7.2(**3**) and 7.2(**4**) also showed how we could write suitable functions to operate upon sets of the type COLOUR. The generic mechanism enables us to write a package to enable the manipulation of sets of an arbitrary type.

Consider

```
generic
    type BASE is (<>);
package SET_OF is
    type SET is private;
    type LIST is array (NATURAL range <>) of BASE;

    EMPTY, FULL: constant SET;

    function MAKE_SET(X: LIST) return SET;
    function MAKE_SET(X: BASE) return SET;
    function DECOMPOSE(X: SET) return LIST;

    function "+"(X,Y: SET) return SET;    -- union
    function "*"(X,Y: SET) return SET;    -- intersection
    function "-"(X,Y: SET) return SET;    -- symmetric difference

    function "<"(X: BASE; Y: SET) return BOOLEAN;    -- inclusion
    function "<="(X,Y: SET) return BOOLEAN;    -- contains
    function SIZE(X: SET) return INTEGER;    -- no of elements
private
    type SET is array (BASE) of BOOLEAN;

    EMPTY: constant SET:=(SET'RANGE => FALSE);
    FULL: constant SET:=(SET'RANGE => TRUE);
end;
```

The single generic parameter is the base type which must, of course, be discrete. The type SET is made private so that the Boolean operations cannot be inadvertently applied. Aggregates of the type LIST are used to represent literal sets. The constants EMPTY and FULL denote the empty and full set respectively. The functions MAKE_SET enable the creation of a set from a list of the base values or a single base value. DECOMPOSE turns a set back into a list.

The operators +, * and − represent union, intersection and symmetric difference; they are chosen as more natural than the underlying **or, and** and **xor**.

The operator < tests to see whether a base value is in a set. The operator <= tests to see whether one set is a subset of another. Finally, the function SIZE returns the number of base values present in a particular set.

In the private part the type SET is of course declared as a Boolean array indexed by the base type. The constants EMPTY and FULL are declared as arrays whose elements are all FALSE and all TRUE respectively. The body of the package is left as an exercise.

Turning back to Section 6.4, we can instantiate the package to work on our type PRIMARY by

```
package PRIMARY_SETS is new SET_OF(PRIMARY);
use PRIMARY_SETS;
```

For comparison we could then write

```
subtype COLOUR is SET;
WHITE: COLOUR renames EMPTY;
BLACK: COLOUR renames FULL;
```

and so on.

Exercise 13.2

1 Instantiate NEXT to give a function behaving like **not**.

2 Rewrite the specification of the package RATIONAL_NUMBERS so that it is a generic package taking the integer type as a parameter. See Exercise 9.1(**2**).

3 Rewrite the function OUTER of Exercise 7.1(**3**) so that it is a generic function with appropriate parameters. Instantiate it to give the original function.

4 Write the body of the package SET_OF.

13.3 Subprogram parameters

Generic parameters can also be subprograms. In some languages, such as Algol and Pascal, parameters of subprograms can themselves be subprograms. This facility is useful for mathematical applications such as integration. In Ada, subprograms can only be parameters of generic units and so the generic mechanism is used for these applications.

We could have a generic function

```
generic
    with function F(X: REAL) return REAL;
function INTEGRATE(A, B: REAL) return REAL;
```

which evaluates $\int_a^b f(x)dx$.

In order to integrate a particular function we must instantiate INTEGRATE with our function as actual generic parameter. Thus suppose we needed

$$\int_o^p e^t \sin t \, dt$$

We would write

```
function G(T: REAL) return REAL is
begin
    return EXP(T)*SIN(T);
end;

function INTEGRATE_G is new INTEGRATE(G);
```

and then our result is given by the expression

```
INTEGRATE_G(0.0,P)
```

Note that a formal subprogram parameter is like a subprogram declaration preceded by **with**. (The leading **with** is necessary to avoid a syntactic ambiguity and has no other subtle purpose.) The corresponding subprogram supplied as actual parameter must have parameters and result (if any) of the same type, mode and with the same constraints. Parameter names and default values do not matter.

The specification of the formal subprogram could depend on preceding formal types. Thus we could extend our integration function to apply to any floating point type by writing

```
generic
    type FLOATING is digits <>;
    with function F(X: FLOATING) return FLOATING;
function INTEGRATE(A, B: FLOATING) return FLOATING;
```

and then

```
function INTEGRATE_G is new INTEGRATE(REAL, G);
```

In practice the function INTEGRATE would have other parameters indicating the accuracy required and so on.

Formal subprograms can also be used to supply other properties of type parameters. Consider the generic function SUM of the last section. We can generalise this even further by passing the adding operator itself as a generic parameter.

```
generic
    type INDEX is (<>);
    type ITEM is private;
    type VEC is array (INDEX range <>) of ITEM;
    with function "+"(X, Y: ITEM) return ITEM;
function APPLY(A: VEC) return ITEM;

function APPLY(A: VEC) return ITEM is
    RESULT: ITEM:=A(A'FIRST);
```

```
begin
    for I in INDEX'SUCC(A'FIRST)..A'LAST loop
        RESULT:=RESULT+A(I);
    end loop;
    return RESULT;
end APPLY;
```

The operator "+" has been added as a parameter and ITEM is now just private and no longer floating. This means that we can apply the generic function to any binary operation on any type. However, we no longer have a zero value and so have to initialise RESULT with the first component of the array A and then iterate through the remainder. In doing this, note that we cannot write

```
for I in A'FIRST+1..A'LAST loop
```

because we have not supplied the operator "+" applying to the type INDEX. Instead we use the attribute INDEX'SUCC which we know to be available since INDEX is guaranteed to be a discrete type.

Our original function SUM of Section 7.1 is now given by

```
function SUM is new APPLY(INTEGER, REAL, VECTOR, "+");
```

We could equally have

```
function PROD is new APPLY(INTEGER, REAL. VECTOR, "*");
```

Generic subprogram parameters (like generic object parameters) can have default values. These are given in the generic part and take two forms. In the above example we could write

```
with function "+"(X, Y: ITEM) return ITEM is <>;
```

This means that we can omit the corresponding actual parameter if there is visible at the point of instantiation a unique subprogram with the same designator and matching specification. With this alteration to APPLY we could have omitted the last parameter in the instantiation giving SUM.

The other form of default value is where we give an explicit default parameter. In this case identification occurs at the point of declaration of the generic unit and not at the point of instantiation. In our example

```
with function "+"(X, Y: ITEM) return ITEM is PLUS;
```

could never be valid because the specification of PLUS must match that of "+" and yet the parameter ITEM is not known until instantiation. The only valid possibilities are where the formal subprogram has no parameters depending on formal types or the default subprogram is an attribute. Thus we might have

```
with function NEXT(X: T) is T'SUCC;
```

The same rules for mixing named and positional notation apply to generic instantiation as to subprogram calls. Hence if a parameter is omitted, subsequent parameters must be given using named notation. Of course, a generic unit need have no parameters in which case the instantiation takes the same form as for a subprogram call – the brackets are omitted.

We conclude by emphasising the rules for evaluation. Any expressions occurring in the generic part (in a constraint or as a default value) are evaluated as far as possible at the time of declaration of the generic unit. However, an expression could contain references to a type that is itself a generic parameter (an attribute such as T'FIRST for instance) and in that case part of the evaluation has to be deferred until the point of instantiation. Expressions in the specification of the generic unit itself however are always evaluated at instantiation exactly as if the package or subprogram were declared directly.

Exercise 13.3

1 Given a function

```
generic
    with function F(X: REAL) return REAL;
function SOLVE return REAL;
```

that finds a root of the equation f(x) = 0, show how you would find the root of

$$e^x + x = 7$$

2 Instantiate APPLY to give a function to "and" together all the components of a Boolean array.

3 Rewrite APPLY so that a null array can be a parameter without raising an exception. Use this new version to redo the previous exercise.

4 Write a generic function EQUALS to define the equality of arrays of a limited private type. See Exercise 9.2(3). Instantiate it to give the function "=" applying to the type STACK_ARRAY.

5 Describe how to make a generic sort procedure based on the procedure SORT of Section 11.3. The parameters should supply the type of item being sorted, the corresponding array type and index and the comparison rule.

Checklist 13

The generic mechanism is not text replacement – non local name binding would be different.

Object **in out** parameters are bound by renaming.

Object **in** parameters are always copied unlike parameters of subprograms.

Generic subprograms may not overload – only the instantiations can.

Formal parameters may depend upon preceding type parameters.

Expressions in the generic part are evaluated as far as possible when the generic is declared.

14 Tasking

The final major topic to be introduced is tasking. This has been left to the end, not because it is unimportant, but because, apart from the interaction with exceptions, it is a fairly self contained part of the language.

14.1 Parallelism

So far we have only considered sequential programs in which statements are obeyed in order. In many applications it is convenient to write a program as several parallel activities which cooperate as necessary. This is particularly true of programs which interact in real time with physical processes in the real world.

In Ada, parallel activities are described by means of tasks. In simple cases a task is lexically described by a form very similar to a package. This consists of a specification describing the interface presented to other tasks and a body describing the dynamic behaviour of the task.

```
task T is              -- specification
   ...
end T;

task body T is         -- body
   ...
end T;
```

In some cases a task presents no interface to other tasks in which case the specification reduces to just

```
task T;
```

As a simple example of parallelism consider a family going shopping to buy ingredients for a meal. Suppose they need meat, salad and wine and that the purchase of these items can be done by calling procedures BUY_MEAT, BUY_SALAD and BUY_WINE respectively. The whole expedition could be represented by

```
procedure SHOPPING is
begin
     BUY_MEAT;
     BUY_SALAD;
     BUY_WINE;
end;
```

However, this solution corresponds to the family buying each item in sequence. It would be far more efficient for them to split up so that, for example, mother buys the meat, the children buy the salad and father buys the wine. They callsagree to meet again perhaps in the car park. This parallel solution can be represented by

```
procedure SHOPPING is
     task GET_SALAD;

     task body GET_SALAD is
     begin
          BUY_SALAD;
     end GET_SALAD;

     task GET_WINE;

     task body GET_WINE is
     begin
          BUY_WINE;
     end GET_WINE;

begin
     BUY_MEAT;
end SHOPPING;
```

In this formulation, mother is represented as the main processor and calls BUY_MEAT directly from the procedure SHOPPING. The children and father are considered as subservient processors and perform the locally declared tasks GET_SALAD and GET_WINE which respectively call the procedures BUY_SALAD and BUY_WINE.

The example illustrates the declaration, activation and termination of tasks. A task is a program component like a package and is declared in a similar way inside a subprogram, block, package or indeed another task body. A task specification can also be declared in a package specification in which case the task body must be declared in the corresponding package body. However, a task specification cannot be declared in the specification of another task but only in the body.

The activation of a task is automatic. In the above example the local tasks become active when the parent unit reaches the **begin** following the task declaration.

A task will terminate when it reaches its final **end**. Thus the task GET_SALAD calls the procedure BUY_SALAD and then promptly terminates.

A task declared in the declarative part of a subprogram, block or task body is said to depend on that unit. It is an important rule that a unit cannot be left until all dependent tasks have terminated. This termination rule ensures that objects declared in the unit and therefore potentially visible to local tasks cannot disappear while there exists a task which could access them. (Note that a task cannot depend on a package – we will return to this later.)

It is important to realise that the main program is itself considered to be called by a hypothetical main task. We can now trace the sequence of actions when this main task calls the procedure SHOPPING. First the tasks GET_SALAD and GET_WINE are declared and then when the main task reaches the **begin** these dependent tasks are set active in parallel with the main task. The dependent tasks call their respective procedures and terminate. Meanwhile the main task calls BUY_MEAT and then reaches the **end** of SHOPPING. The main task then waits until the dependent tasks have terminated if they have not already done so. This corresponds to mother waiting for father and children to return with their purchases.

Exercise 14.1

1 Rewrite procedure SHOPPING to contain three local tasks so that the symmetry of the situation is revealed.

14.2 The rendezvous

In the SHOPPING example the various tasks did not interact with each other once they had been set active except that their parent unit had to wait for them to terminate. Generally, however, tasks will interact with each other during their lifetime. In Ada this is done by a mechanism known as a rendezvous. This is similar to the human situation where two people meet, perform a transaction and then go on independently.

A rendezvous between two tasks occurs as a consequence of one task calling an entry declared in another. An entry is declared in a task specification in a similar way to a procedure in a package specification.

```
task T is
    entry E(...);
end;
```

An entry can have **in**, **out** and **in out** parameters in the same way as a procedure. It cannot however have a result like a function. An entry is called in a similar way to a procedure

```
T.E(...);
```

A task name cannot appear in a use clause and so the dotted notation is necessary to call the entry from outside the task. Of course, a local task could call an entry of its parent directly – the usual scope and visibility rules apply.

The statements to be obeyed during a rendezvous are described by corresponding accept statements in the body of the task containing the declaration of the entry. An accept statement usually takes the form

```
accept E(...) do
    -- sequence of statements
end E;
```

The formal parameters of the entry E are repeated in the same way that a procedure body repeats the formal parameters of a corresponding procedure declaration. The **end** is optionally followed by the name of the entry. A significant difference is that the body of the accept statement is just a sequence of statements. Any local declarations or exception handlers must be provided by writing a local block.

The most important difference between an entry call and a procedure call is that in the case of a procedure, the task that calls the procedure also immediately executes the procedure body whereas in the case of an entry, one task calls the entry but the corresponding accept statement is executed by the task owning the entry. Moreover, the accept statement cannot be executed until a task calls the entry and the task owning the entry reaches the accept statement. Naturally one of these will occur first and the task concerned will then be suspended until the other reaches its corresponding statement. When this occurs the sequence of statements of the accept statement is executed by the called task while the calling task remains suspended. This interaction is called a rendezvous. When the end of the accept statement is reached the rendezvous is completed and both tasks then proceed independently. The parameter mechanism is exactly as for a subprogram call; note that expressions in the actual parameter list are evaluated before the call is issued.

We can elaborate our shopping example by giving the task GET_SALAD two entries, one for mother to hand the children the money for the salad and one to collect the salad from them afterwards. We do the same for GET_WINE (although perhaps father has his own funds in which case he might keep the wine to himself anyway).

We can also replace the procedures BUY_SALAD, BUY_WINE and BUY_MEAT by functions which take money as a parameter and return the appropriate ingredient. Our shopping procedure might now become

```
procedure SHOPPING is

    task GET_SALAD is
        entry PAY(M: in MONEY);
        entry COLLECT(S: out SALAD);
    end GET_SALAD;

    task body GET_SALAD is
        CASH: MONEY;
        FOOD: SALAD;
    begin
        accept PAY(M: in MONEY) do
            CASH:=M;
        end PAY;

        FOOD:=BUY_SALAD(CASH);

        accept COLLECT(S: out SALAD) do
            S:=FOOD;
        end COLLECT;
    end GET_SALAD;

    -- GET_WINE similarly

begin
    GET_SALAD.PAY(50);
    GET_WINE.PAY(100);
    MM:=BUY_MEAT(200);
    GET_SALAD.COLLECT(SS);
    GET_WINE.COLLECT(WW);
end;
```

The final outcome is that the various ingredients end up in the variables MM, SS, and WW whose declarations are left to the imagination.

The logical behaviour should be noted. As soon as the tasks GET_SALAD and GET_WINE become active they encounter accept statements and wait until the main task calls the entries PAY in each of them. After calling the function BUY_MEAT, the main task calls the COLLECT entries. Curiously, mother is unable to collect the wine until after she has collected the salad from the children.

As a more abstract example consider the problem of providing a task to act as a single buffer between one or more tasks producing items and one or more tasks consuming them. Our intermediate task can hold just one item.

```
task BUFFERING is
    entry PUT(X: in ITEM):
    entry GET(X: out ITEM);
end;

task body BUFFERING is
    V: ITEM;
begin
    loop
        accept PUT(X: in ITEM) do
            V:=X;
        end PUT;
        accept GET(X: out ITEM) do
            X:=V;
        end GET;
    end loop;
end BUFFERING;
```

Other tasks may then dispose of or acquire items by calling

```
BUFFERING.PUT(...);
BUFFERING.GET(...);
```

Intermediate storage for the item is the variable V. The body of the task is an endless loop which contains an accept statement for PUT followed by one for GET. Thus the task alternately accepts calls of PUT and GET which fill and empty the variable V.

Several different tasks may call PUT and GET and consequently may have to be queued. Every entry has a queue of tasks waiting to call the entry – this queue is processed in a first in first out manner and may, of course, be empty at a particular moment. The number of tasks on the queue of entry E is given by E'COUNT but this attribute may only be used inside the body of the task owning the entry.

An entry may have several corresponding accept statements (usually only one). Each execution of an accept statement removes one task from the queue.

Note the asymmetric naming in a rendezvous. The calling task must name the called task but not vice versa. Moreover, several tasks may call an entry and be queued but a task can only be on one queue at a time.

Entries may be overloaded both with each other and with subprograms and obey the same rules. An entry may be renamed as a procedure

```
procedure WRITE(X: in ITEM) renames BUFFERING.PUT;
```

This mechanism may be useful in avoiding excessive use of the dotted notation. An entry, renamed or not, may be an actual or default generic parameter corresponding to a formal subprogram. An entry may have no parameters, such as

```
entry SIGNAL;
```

and it could then be called by

```
T.SIGNAL;
```

An accept statement need have no body as in

```
accept SIGNAL;
```

In such a case the purpose of the call is merely to effect a synchronisation and not to pass information. However, an entry without parameters can have an accept statement with a body and vice versa. There is nothing to prevent us writing

```
accept SIGNAL do
   FIRE;
end;
```

in which case the task calling SIGNAL is only allowed to continue after the call of FIRE is completed. We could also have

```
accept PUT(X: ITEM);
```

although clearly the parameter value is not used.

There are no particular constraints on the statements in an accept statement. They may include entry calls, subprogram calls, blocks and futher accept statements (possibly even for the same entry). On the other hand an accept statement may not appear in a subprogram body but must be in the sequence of statements of the task although it could be in a block or other accept statement. The execution of a return statement in an accept statement corresponds to reaching the final end and therefore terminates the rendezvous.

A task may call one of its own entries but, of course, will promptly deadlock. This may seem foolish but programming languages allow lots of silly things such as endless loops and so on. We could expect a good compiler to warn us of obvious potential deadlocks.

Exercise 14.2

1 Write the body of a task whose specification is

```
task BUILD_COMPLEX is
   entry PUT_RL(X: REAL);
   entry PUT_IM(X: REAL);
   entry GET_COMP(X: out COMPLEX);
end;
```

and which alternately puts together a complex number from calls of PUT_RL and PUT_IM and then delivers the result on a call of GET_COMP.

2 Write the body of a task whose specification is

```
task CHAR_TO_LINE is
    entry (PUT(C: in CHARACTER);
    entry GET(L: out LINE);
end;
```

where

```
type LINE is array (1 .. 80) of CHARACTER;
```

The task acts as a buffer which alternately builds up a line by accepting successive calls of PUT and then delivers a complete line on a call of GET.

14.3 Timing and scheduling

As we have seen an Ada program may contain several tasks. Conceptually it is best to think of these tasks as each having its own personal processor so that provided a task is not waiting for something to happen it will actually be executing.

In practice, of course, most implementations will not be able to allocate a unique processor to each task and indeed, in many cases, there will be only one physical processor. It will then be necessary to allocate the processor(s) to the tasks that are logically able to execute by some scheduling algorithm. This can be done in many ways.

One of the simplest mechanisms is to use time slicing. This means giving the processor to each task in turn for some fixed time interval such as 10 milliseconds. Of course, if a task cannot use its turn (perhaps because it is held up awaiting a partner in a rendezvous), then a sensible scheduler would allocate its turn to the next task. Similarly if a task cannot use all of its turn then the remaining time could be allocated to another task.

Time slicing is somewhat rudimentary since it treats all tasks equally. It is often the case that some tasks are more urgent than others and in the face of a shortage of processing power this equality is a bit wasteful. The idea of a task having a priority is therefore introduced. A simple scheduling system would be one where each task had a distinct priority and the processor would then be given to the highest priority task which could actually run. Combinations of time slicing and priority scheduling are also possible. A system might permit several tasks to have the same priority and time slice between them.

Ada allows various scheduling strategies to be used. If an implementation has the concept of priority, then the priority of a task can be indicated by a pragma appearing somewhere in the task specification as for example

```
task BUFFERING is
    pragma PRIORITY(7);
    entry PUT ...
    ...
end;
```

In the case of the main program, which, as we have seen, is also considered to be a task, the pragma goes in its outermost declarative part.

The priority must be a static expression of the subtype PRIORITY of the type INTEGER but the actual range of the subtype PRIORITY depends upon the implementation. Note that the priority of a task is static and therefore cannot be changed during the course of execution of the program. A larger priority indicates a higher degree of urgency. Several tasks can have the same priority but on the other hand a task need not have an explicit priority at all.

The effect of priorities on the scheduling of Ada tasks is given by the following rule taken from the LRM

> If two tasks with different priorities are both eligible for execution and could sensibly be executed using the same processing resources, then it cannot be the case that the task with the lower priority is executing while the task with the higher priority is not.

This rule says nothing about tasks whose priorities are not defined nor does it say anything about tasks with the same priority. The implementation is therefore free to do whatever seems appropriate in these cases. Moreover, nothing prevents an implementation from having PRIORITY'FIRST = PRIORITY'LAST in which case all tasks could be time sliced equally and the concept of priority disappears. The rule also contains the phrase 'could sensibly be executed using the same processing resources'; this is directed towards distributed systems where it may not be at all sensible for a processor in one part of the system to be used to execute a task in a different part of the system.

In the case of a rendezvous, a complication arises because two tasks are involved. If both tasks have explicit priorities, the rendezvous is executed with the higher priority. If only one task has an explicit priority then the rendezvous is executed with at least that priority. If neither task has a defined priority then the priority of the rendezvous is not defined. Of course, if the accept statement contains a further entry call or accept statement then the rules are applied once more.

The rendezvous rules ensure that a high priority task is not held up just because it is engaged in a rendezvous with a low priority task. On the other hand, the order of accepting the tasks in an entry queue is always first in first out and is not affected by priorities. If a high priority task wishes to guard against being held up because of lower priority tasks in the same entry queue, it can always use timed out or conditional calls as we shall see in the next section.

The use of priorities needs care. They are intended as a means of adjusting relative degrees of urgency and should not be used for synchronisation. It should not be assumed that just because task A has a higher priority than task B that the execution of task A precludes the execution of task B. There might be several processors or later program maintenance might result in a change of priorities because of different real time requirements. Synchronisation should be done with the rendezvous and priorities should be avoided except for fine tuning of responsiveness.

A task may be held up for various reasons; it might be waiting for a partner in a rendezvous or for a dependent task to terminate. It can also be held up by executing a delay statement such as

```
delay 3.0;
```

This suspends the task (or main program) executing the statement for at least three seconds. (We have to say 'at least' because after the expiry of the interval there might not be a processor immediately available to execute the task.) The expression after the reserved word **delay** is of a predefined fixed point type DURATION and gives the period in seconds.

The type DURATION is a fixed point type so that the addition of durations can be done without systematic loss of accuracy. If we add together two fixed point model numbers we always get another model number; this does not apply to floating point. On the other hand we need to express fractions of a second in a convenient way and so the use of a real type rather than an integer type is much more satisfactory.

Delays can be more easily expressed by using suitable number declarations, thus

```
SECONDS: constant:=1.0;
MINUTES: constant:=60.0;
HOURS: constant:=3600.0;
```

We can then write for example

```
delay 2*HOURS+40*MINUTES:
```

in which the expression is of type universal real and automatically converted to DURATION.

A delay statement with a zero or negative argument has no effect.

Although the type DURATION is implementation defined we are guaranteed that it will allow durations (both positive and negative) of up to at least one day (86 400) seconds. Delays of more than a day (which are unusual) would have to be programmed with a loop. A point to watch is that there is no guaranteed maximum delta; a crude implementation of type DURATION using 16 bits could well have an actual delta of 3 seconds.

More sophisticated timing operations can be performed by using the predefined package CALENDAR whose specification is

```
package CALENDAR is
    type TIME is
        record
            YEAR: INTEGER range 1901 .. 2099;
            MONTH: INTEGER range 1 .. 12;
            DAY: INTEGER range 1 .. 31;
            SECOND: DURATION;
        end record;
    function CLOCK return TIME;
```

```
    function "+"(A: TIME; B: DURATION) return TIME;
    function "+"(A: DURATION; B: TIME) return TIME;
    function "-"(A: TIME; B: DURATION) return TIME;
    function "-"(A: TIME; B: TIME) return DURATION;

end CALENDAR;
```

A value of the type TIME is a combined time and date with the component SECOND giving the DURATION since midnight of the day concerned. The range of YEAR is constrained so that the leap year calculation is simplified. A careful distinction must be made between TIME and DURATION. TIME is absolute but DURATION is relative.

The current TIME is returned by a call of the function CLOCK. The result is, of course, returned in an indivisible way and there is no risk of getting the time of day and the date inconsistent around midnight as there would be if there were separate functions delivering the individual components of the current time and date.

The various overloadings of "+" and "−" allow us to add and subtract times and durations as appropriate.

As an example of the use of the package CALENDAR suppose we wish a task to call a procedure ACTION at regular intervals, every 5 minutes perhaps. Our first attempt might be to write

```
loop
    delay 5*MINUTES;
    ACTION;
end loop;
```

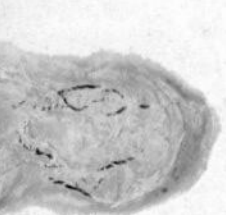

However this is unsatisfactory for two reasons. Firstly we have not taken account of the time of execution of the procedure ACTION and the overhead of the loop itself, and secondly we have seen that a delay statement sets a minimum delay only. So we will inevitably get a cumulative timing drift. This can be overcome by writing for example

```
declare
    use CALENDAR;
    INTERVAL: constant DURATION:=5*MINUTES;
    NEXT_TIME: TIME:=FIRST_TIME;
begin
    loop
        delay NEXT_TIME-CLOCK();
        ACTION;
        NEXT_TIME:=NEXT_TIME+INTERVAL;
    end loop;
end;
```

In this formulation NEXT_TIME contains the time when ACTION is next to be called; its initial value is in FIRST_TIME and it is updated exactly on each iteration by adding INTERVAL. The delay statement is then used to delay by the difference between NEXT_TIME and the current time obtained by calling

CLOCK. This solution will have no cumulative drift provided the mean duration of ACTION plus the overheads of the loop and updating NEXT_TIME and so on do not exceed INTERVAL. Of course, there may be a local drift if a particular call of ACTION takes a long time or other tasks temporarily use the processors. There is one other condition that must be satisfied for the required timing to be obtained: the interval has to be a model number.

Exercise 14.3

1 Write a generic procedure to call a procedure regularly. The generic parameters should be the procedure to be called, the time of the first call, the interval and the number of calls. If the time of the first call passed as parameter is in the past use the current time as the first time.

14.4 Select statements

The select statement allows a task to select from one of several possible rendezvous.

Consider the problem of protecting a variable V from uncontrolled access. We might consider using a package and two procedures READ and WRITE.

```
package PROTECTED_VARIABLE is
   procedure READ(X: out ITEM);
   procedure WRITE(X: in ITEM);
end;

package body PROTECTED_VARIABLE is
   V: ITEM;

   procedure READ(X: out ITEM) is
   begin
      X:=V;
   end;

   procedure WRITE(X: in ITEM) is
   begin
      V:=X;
   end;
begin
   V:=initial value;
end PROTECTED VARIABLE;
```

However this is generally unsatisfactory. For one thing, the initial value is set in a rather arbitrary way. It would be better if somehow we could ensure that a call of WRITE had to be done first. We could, of course, have an internal state marker and raise an exception if READ is called first but this complicates the interface. The major problem, however, is that nothing prevents different tasks in our system from calling READ and WRITE simultaneously and thereby causing interference. As a more specific example suppose that the type ITEM is a record giving the coordinates of an aircraft or ship.

```
type ITEM is
    record
        X_COORD: REAL;
        Y_COORD: REAL;
    end record;
```

Suppose that a task A acquires pairs of values and uses a call of WRITE to store them into V and that another task B calls READ whenever it needs the latest position. Now assume that A is half way through executing WRITE when it is interrupted by task B which promptly calls READ. It is clear that B could get a value consisting of the new *x*-coordinate and the old *y*-coordinate which would no doubt represent a location where the vessel had never been. The use of such inconsistent data for calculating the heading of the vessel from regularly read pairs of readings would obviously lead to inaccuracies.

The reader may wonder how the task A could be interrupted by task B anyway. In a single processor system with time slicing it may merely have been that B's turn came at an unfortunate moment. Alternatively B might have a higher priority than A; if B had been waiting for time to elapse before taking the next reading by obeying a delay statement, then A might be allowed to execute and B's delay might expire just at the wrong moment. In practical real time situations things are always happening at the wrong moment!

The proper solution is to use a task rather than a package, and entry calls rather than procedure calls. Consider now

```
task PROTECTED_VARIABLE is
    entry READ(X: out ITEM);
    entry WRITE(X: in ITEM);
end;

task body PROTECTED_VARIABLE is
    V: ITEM;
begin
    accept WRITE(X: in ITEM) do
        V:=X;
    end;
    loop
        select
            accept READ(X: out ITEM) do
                X:=V;
            end;
        or
            accept WRITE(X: in ITEM) do
                V:=X;
            end;
        end select;
    end loop;
end PROTECTED_VARIABLE;
```

The body of the task starts with an accept statement for the entry WRITE; this ensures that the first call accepted is for WRITE so that there is no risk of the variable being read before it is assigned a value. Of course, a task could call READ before any task had called WRITE but the calls of READ will be queued until a call of WRITE has been accepted.

Having accepted a call of WRITE, the task enters an endless loop containing a single select statement. A select statement starts with the reserved word **select** and finishes with **end select**; it contains two or more alternatives separated by **or**. In this example each alternative consists of an accept statement – one for READ and one for WRITE.

When we encounter the select statement various possibilities have to be considered according to whether calls of READ or WRITE or both or neither have been made. We consider these in turn.

- If neither READ nor WRITE has been called then the task is suspended until one or the other is called and then the corresponding accept statement is obeyed.
- If one or more calls of READ are queued but there are no queued calls of WRITE then the first call of READ is accepted and vice versa with the roles of READ and WRITE reversed.
- If calls of both READ and WRITE are queued then an arbitrary choice is made.

Thus each execution of the select statement results in one of its branches being obeyed and one call of READ or WRITE being dealt with. We can think of the task as corresponding to a person serving two queues of customers waiting for two different services. If only one queue has customers then the server deals with it; if there are no customers then the server waits for the first irrespective of the service required; if both queues exist, the server rather capriciously serves either and makes an arbitrary choice each time.

So each time round the loop the task PROTECTED_VARIABLE will accept a call of READ or WRITE according to the demands upon it. It thus prevents multiple access to the variable V since it can only deal with one call at a time but does not impose any order upon the calls. Compare this with the task BUFFERING in Section 14.2 where an order was imposed upon the calls of PUT and GET.

Another point to notice is that this example illustrates a case where we have two accept statements for one entry. It so happens that the bodies are identical but they need not be.

The reader may wonder what the phrase 'arbitrary choice' means when deciding which alternative to choose. The intent is that there is no rule and the implementor is free to choose some efficient mechanism that nevertheless introduces an adequate degree of non-determinism so that the various queues are treated fairly and none gets starved. A random choice with equal probability would be acceptable but hard to implement efficiently. The most important point is that a program must not rely on the selection algorithm used; if it does, it is erroneous.

A more complex form of select statement is illustrated by the classic problem of the bounded buffer. This is similar to the problem in Section 14.2 except that up to N items can be buffered. A solution is

```
task BUFFERING is
    entry PUT(X: in ITEM);
    entry GET(X: out ITEM);
end;
```

```
task body BUFFERING is
    N: constant:=8;                          -- for instance
    A: array (1 .. N) of ITEM;
    I, J: INTEGER range 1 .. N:=1;
    COUNT: INTEGER range 0 .. N:=0;
begin
    loop
        select
            when COUNT < N =>
            accept PUT(X: in ITEM) do
                A(I):=X;
            end;
            I:=I mod N+1; COUNT:=COUNT+1;
        or
            when COUNT > 0 =>
            accept GET(X: out ITEM) do
                X:=A(J);
            end;
            J:=J mod N+1; COUNT:=COUNT-1;
        end select;
    end loop;
end BUFFERING;
```

The buffer is the array A of length N which is a number set to 8 in this example. The variables I and J index the next free and last used locations of the buffer respectively and COUNT is the number of locations of the buffer which are full. Not only is it convenient to have COUNT but it is also necessary in order to distinguish between a completely full and completely empty buffer which both have I = J. The buffer is used cyclically so I need not be greater than J. The situation in Fig. 14.1 shows a partly filled buffer with COUNT = 5, I = 3 and J = 6. The portion of the buffer in use is shaded. The variables I and J are both initialised to 1 and COUNT is initialised to 0 so that the buffer is initially empty.

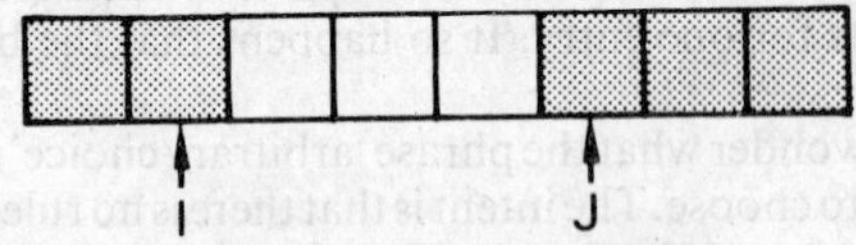

Fig. 14.1 The bounded buffer

The objective of the task is to allow items to be added to and removed from the buffer in a first in first out manner but to prevent the buffer from being overfilled or under emptied. This is done with a more general form of select statement which includes the use of guarding conditions.

Each branch of the select statement commences with

```
when condition =>
```

and is then followed by an accept statement and then some further statements. Each time the select statement is encountered all the guarding conditions are evaluated. The behaviour is then as for a select statement without guards but containing only those branches for which the conditions were true. So a branch will be taken and the corresponding rendezvous performed. After the accept statement a branch may contain further statements. These are executed by the server task as part of the select statement but outside the rendezvous.

So the guarding conditions are conditions which have to be true before a service can be offered. The accept statement represents the rendezvous with the customer and the giving of the service. The statements after the accept statement represent bookkeeping actions performed as a consequence of giving the service and which can be done after the customer has left but, of course, need to be done before the next customer is served.

In our example the condition for being able to accept a call of PUT is simply that the buffer must not be full; this is the condition COUNT < N. Similarly we can accept a call of GET provided that the buffer is not empty; this is the condition COUNT > 0. The statements in the bodies of the accept statements copy the item to or from the buffer. After the rendezvous is completed, the index I or J as appropriate and COUNT are updated to reflect the change of state. Note the use of **mod** to update I and J in a cyclic manner.

Thus we see that the first time the select statement is executed, the condition COUNT < N is true but COUNT > 0 is false. Hence only a call of PUT can be accepted. This puts the first item in the buffer. The next time both conditions will be true so either PUT or GET can be accepted, adding a further item or removing the one item. And so it goes on; allowing items to be added or removed with one of the guarding conditions becoming false in the extreme situations and thereby preventing overfilling or under emptying.

A few points need emphasis. The guards are reevaluated at the beginning of each execution of the select statement (but their order of evaluation is not defined). An absent guard is taken as true. If all guards turn out to be false then the exception SELECT_ERROR is raised. It should be realised that a guard need not still be true when the corresponding rendezvous is performed because it might use global variables and therefore be changed by another task. Later we will discuss an example where guards could change unexpectedly. In the example here, of course, nothing can go wrong. One guard is always true, so SELECT_ERROR can never be raised and they both only involve the local variable COUNT and so cannot be changed between their evaluation and the rendezvous.

For our next example consider again the task PROTECTED_VARIABLE. This allowed either read or write access but only one at a time. This is somewhat severe; the usual classical problem is to allow only one writer of course, but to allow several readers together. A simple solution is shown below. It takes the form of a package containing a local task.

```
package READER_WRITER is
    procedure READ(X: out ITEM);
    procedure WRITE(X: in ITEM);
end;

package body READER_WRITER is
    V: ITEM;

    task CONTROL is
        entry START;
```

```
        entry STOP;
        entry WRITE(X: in ITEM);
    end;

    task body CONTROL is
        READERS: INTEGER:=0;
    begin
        accept WRITE(X: in ITEM) do
            V:=X;
        end;
        loop
            select
                accept START;
                READERS:=READERS+1;
            or
                accept STOP;
                READERS:=READERS-1;
            or
                when READERS = 0 =>
                accept WRITE(X: in ITEM) do
                    V:=X;
                end;
            end select
        end loop;
    end CONTROL;

    procedure READ(X: out ITEM) is
    begin
        CONTROL.START;
        X:=V;
        CONTROL.STOP;
    end READ;

    procedure WRITE(X: in ITEM) is
    begin
        CONTROL.WRITE(X);
    end WRITE;

end READER_WRITER;
```

The task CONTROL has three entries, WRITE to do the writing and START and STOP associated with reading. A call of START indicates a wish to start reading and a call of STOP indicates that reading has finished. The task is wrapped up in a package because we wish to provide multiple reading access. This can be done by providing a procedure READ which can then be called reentrantly; it also enforces the protocol of calling START and then STOP.

So the whole thing is a package containing the variable V, the task CONTROL and the access procedures READ and WRITE. As stated, READ enforces the desired calls of START and STOP around the statement X:=V; the procedure WRITE merely calls the entry WRITE.

The task CONTROL declares a variable READERS which indicates how many readers are present. As before it begins with an accept statement for WRITE to ensure that the variable is initialised and then enters a loop containing a select statement. This has three branches, one for each entry. On a call of START or STOP the count of number of readers is incremented or decremented. A call of WRITE can only be accepted if the condition READERS= 0 is true. Hence writing when readers are present is forbidden. Of course, since the task CONTROL actually does the writing, multiple writing is prevented and, moreover, it cannot at the same time accept calls of START and so reading is not possible when writing is in progress. However multiple reading is allowed as we have seen.

Although the above solution does fulfil the general conditions it is not really satisfactory. A steady stream of readers will completely block out a writer. Since writing is probably rather important, this is not acceptable. An obvious improvement would be to disallow further reading if one or more writers are waiting. We can do this by using the attribute WRITE'COUNT in a guard so that the select statement now becomes

```
select
    when WRITE'COUNT = 0 =>
    accept START;
    READERS:=READERS+1;
or
    accept STOP;
    READERS:=READERS-1;
or
    when READERS = 0 =>
    accept WRITE(X: in ITEM) do
        V:=X;
    end;
end select;
```

The attribute WRITE'COUNT is the number of tasks currently on the queue for the entry WRITE. The use of the count attribute in guards needs care. It gives the value when the guard is evaluated and can well change before a rendezvous is accepted. It could increase because another task joins the queue – that would not matter in this example. But, as we shall see later, it could also decrease unexpectedly and this would indeed give problems. We will return to this example in a moment.

There are also various other forms of select statement. It is possible for one or more of the branches to start with a delay statement rather than an accept statement. Consider

```
select
    accept READ(. . .) do
    . . .
    end;
or
    accept WRITE(. . .) do
    . . .
    end;
```

```
        delay 10*MINUTES;
        -- time out statements
    end select;
```

If neither a call of READ nor WRITE is received within 10 minutes then the third branch is taken and the statements following the delay are executed. The task might decide that since its services are no longer apparently required it can do something else or maybe it can be interpreted as an emergency. In a process control system we might be awaiting an acknowledgement from the operator that some action has been taken and after a suitable interval take our own emergency action

```
    OPERATOR.CALL("PUT OUT FIRE");
    select
        accept ACKNOWLEDGE;
    or
        delay 1*MINUTE;
        FIRE_BRIGADE.CALL;
    end select;
```

A delay alternative can be guarded and indeed there could be several in a select statement although clearly only the shortest one with a true guard can be taken. It should be realised that if one of the accept statements is obeyed then any delay is cancelled – we can think of a delay alternative as waiting for a rendezvous with the clock. A delay is of course set from the start of the select statement and reset each time the select statement is encountered. Finally note that it is the start of the rendezvous that matters rather than its completion as far as the time out is concerned.

Another form of select statement is one with an else part. Consider

```
    select
        accept READ(...) do
        ...
        end;
    or
        accept WRITE(...) do
        ...
        end;
    else
        --alternative statements
    end select;
```

In this case the final branch is preceded by **else** rather than **or** and consists of just a sequence of statements. The else branch is taken at once if none of the other branches can be immediately accepted. A select statement with an else part is rather like one with a branch starting **delay** 0.0; it times out at once if there are no customers to be dealt with. A select statement cannot have both an else part and delay alternatives.

There is a subtle distinction between an accept statement starting a branch of a select and an accept statement anywhere else. In the first case the accept statement is bound up with the workings of the select statement and is to some extent conditional. In the second case, once encountered, it will be obeyed come what may. The same distinction applies to a delay statement starting a branch of an accept statement and one elsewhere. Thus if we change the **or** to **else** in our emergency action to give

```
select
    accept ACKNOWLEDGE;
else
    delay 1*MINUTE;
    FIRE_BRIGADE.CALL;
end select;
```

then the status of the delay is quite different. It just happens to be one of a sequence of statements and will be obeyed in the usual way. So if we cannot accept a call of ACKNOWLEDGE at once, we immediately take the else part. The fact that the first statement is a delay is fortuitous – we immediately delay for one minute and then call the fire brigade. There is no time out.

If a select statement has an else part then SELECT_ERROR can never be raised. The else part cannot be guarded and so will always be taken if all branches have guards and they all turn out to be false.

There are two other forms of select statement which are rather different; they concern a single entry call rather than one or more accept statements. The timed out entry call allows a sequence of statements to be taken as an alternative to an entry call if it is not accepted within the specified duration. Thus

```
select
    OPERATOR.CALL("PUT OUT FIRE");
or
    delay 1*MINUTE;
    FIRE_BRIGADE.CALL;
end select;
```

will call the fire brigade if the operator does not accept the call within one minute. Again, it is the start of the rendezvous that matters rather than its completion. Finally there is the conditional entry call. Thus

```
select
    OPERATOR.CALL("PUT OUT FIRE"):
else
    FIRE_BRIGADE.CALL;
end select;
```

will call the fire brigade if the operator cannot immediately accept the call.

The timed out and conditional entry calls are quite different to the general select statement. They concern only a single unguarded call and so these select statements always have exactly two branches – one with the entry call and the other with the alternative sequence of statements.

Timed out and conditional calls are useful if a task does not want to be unduly delayed when a server task is busy. They correspond to a customer in a shop giving up and leaving the queue after waiting for a time or, in the conditional case, a highly impatient customer leaving at once if not immediately served.

Timed out calls, however, need some care particularly if the COUNT attribute is used. A decision based on the value of that attribute may be invalidated because of a timed out call unexpectedly removing a task from an entry queue. Consider for example the package READER_WRITER. As it stands the entry calls cannot be timed out because they are encapsulated in the procedures READ and WRITE. However, we might decide to provide further overloadings of these procedures in order to provide timed out facilities. We might add, for example

```
procedure WRITE(X: in ITEM; T: DURATION; OK: out BOOLEAN) is
begin
    select
        CONTROL.WRITE(X);
        OK:=TRUE;
    or
        delay T;
        OK:=FALSE;
    end select;
end WRITE;
```

Unfortunately this is invalid. Suppose that one writer is waiting (so that WRITE'COUNT = 1) but the call is timed out between the evaluation of the guards and the execution of an accept statement. There are two cases to consider according to the value of READERS. If READERS = 0, then no task can call STOP since there are no current readers; a call of START cannot be accepted because its guard was false and the expected call of WRITE will not occur because it has been timed out; the result is that all new readers will be unnecessarily blocked until a new writer arrives. On the other hand, if READERS > 0, then although further calls of WRITE correctly cannot be accepted, nevertheless further calls of START are unnecessarily delayed until an existing reader calls STOP despite there being no waiting writers. We therefore seek an alternative solution.

The original reason for using WRITE'COUNT was to prevent readers from overtaking waiting writers. One possibility in cases of this sort is to make all the customers call a common entry to start with. This ensures that they are dealt with in order. This entry call can be parameterised to indicate the service required and the callers can then be placed on a secondary queue if necessary. This technique is illustrated by the solution which now follows. The package specification is as before.

```
package body READER_WRITER is
    V: ITEM;
    type SERVICE is (READ, WRITE);

    task CONTROL is
        entry START(S: SERVICE);
        entry STOP_READ;
```

```
        entry WRITE;
        entry STOP_WRITE;
    end CONTROL;

    task body CONTROL is
        READERS: INTEGER:=0;
        WRITERS: INTEGER:=0;
    begin
        loop
            select
                when WRITERS = 0 =>
                accept START(S: SERVICE) do
                    case S is
                        when READ => READERS:=READERS+1;
                        when WRITE => WRITERS:=1;
                    end case;
                end START;
            or
                accept STOP_READ;
                READERS:=READERS-1;
            or
                when READERS = 0 =>
                accept WRITE;
            or
                accept STOP_WRITE;
                WRITERS:=0;
            end select;
        end loop;
    end CONTROL;

    procedure READ(X: out ITEM) is
    begin
        CONTROL.START(READ);
        X:=V;
        CONTROL.STOP(READ);
    end READ;

    procedure WRITE(X: in ITEM) is
    begin
        CONTROL.START(WRITE);
        CONTROL.WRITE;
        V:=X;
        CONTROL.STOP_WRITE;
    end WRITE;

end READER_WRITER;
```

We have introduced a variable WRITERS to indicate how many writers are in the system; it can only take values of 0 and 1. All requests initially call the common entry START but have to wait until there are no writers. The count of readers or writers is then updated as appropriate. In the case of a reader it can then go ahead as before and finishes by calling STOP_READ. A writer, on the other hand, must wait until there are no readers; it does this by calling WRITE and then finally calls STOP_WRITE in order that the control task can set WRITERS back to zero. Separating STOP_WRITE from WRITE enables us to cope with time outs as we shall see; we also take the opportunity to place the actual writing statement in the procedure WRITE so that it is similar to the read case.

In this solution, the variable WRITERS performs the function of WRITE'COUNT in the previous but incorrect solution. By counting for ourselves we can keep the situation under control. The calls of START and WRITE can now be timed out provided that we always call STOP once a call of START has been accepted. The details of suitable overloadings of READ and WRITE to provide timed out calls are left as an exercise.

Finally note that the above solution has ignored the problem of ensuring that the first call is a write. This can be catered for in various ways, by using a special initial entry, for instance, or by placing the readers on a second auxiliary queue so that they are forced to wait for the first writer.

Exercise 14.4

1 Rewrite the body of the task BUILD_COMPLEX of Exercise 14.2(**1**) so that the calls of PUT_RL and PUT_IM are accepted in any order.

2 Write additional procedures READ and WRITE for the package READER_WRITER in order to provide timed out calls. Take care with the procedure WRITE so that the calls of the entries START and WRITE are both timed out appropriately.

14.5 Task types

It is sometimes useful to have several similar but distinct tasks. Moreover, it is often not possible to predict the number of such tasks required. For example we might wish to create distinct tasks to follow each aircraft within the zone of control of an air traffic control system. Clearly such tasks need to be created and disposed of in a dynamic way not related to the static structure of the program.

A template for similar tasks is provided by a task type declaration. This is identical to the simple task declarations we have seen so far except that the reserved word **type** follows **task** in the specification. Thus we may write

```
task type T is
    entry E(...);
end T;

task body T is
    ...
end T;
```

The task body follows the same rules as before.

To create an actual task we use the normal form of object declaration. So we can write

```
X: T;
```

and this declares a task X of type T. In fact the simple form of task declaration we have been using so far such as

```
task SIMPLE is
    ...
end SIMPLE;
```

is exactly equivalent to writing

```
task type anon is
    ...
end anon;
```

followed by

```
SIMPLE: anon;
```

Task objects can be used in structures in the usual way. Thus we can declare arrays of tasks

```
AT: array (1 .. 10) of T;
```

records containing tasks

```
type REC is
    record
        CT: T;
        ...
    end record;
R: REC;
```

and so on.

The entries of such tasks are called using the task object name; thus we write

```
X.E( ... );
AT(I).E( ... );
R.CT.E( ... );
```

A most important consideration is that task objects are not variables but behave as constants. A task object declaration creates a task which is permanently bound to the object. Hence assignment is not allowed for task types and nor are the comparisons for equality and inequality. A task type is therefore a limited private type and so could be used as the actual type corresponding to a formal generic parameter specified as limited private and as the actual type in a private part corresponding to a limited private type. Although task objects behave as constants, they cannot be declared as such since a constant declaration needs an explicit initial value. Subprogram parameters may be of task types; they are always passed by reference and never copied and so the formal and actual parameters always refer to the same task.

In Section 14.1 we briefly introduced the idea of dependency. Each task is dependent on some unit and there is a general rule that a unit cannot be left until all tasks dependent upon it have terminated.

A task declared as a task object (or using the abbreviated simple form) is dependent upon the enclosing block, subprogram or task body in which it is declared. Inner packages do not count in this rule – this is because a package is merely a passive scope wall and has no dynamic life. If a task is declared in a package (or nested packages) then the task is dependent upon the block, subprogram or task body in which the package or packages are themselves declared.

We saw earlier that a task becomes active when the declaring unit reaches the **begin** following the declaration. The activation of a task can be thought of as a two stage process. First the declarations of the task body are elaborated but while this is being done the parent unit is not allowed to proceed. It is only when the elaboration of the declarations is complete that the new task is set off in parallel with the declaring task.

The reason for treating the elaboration of the declarations in this way concerns exceptions. The reader may recall that exceptions raised during the elaboration of declarations are not handled at that level but immediately propagated. So any exceptions raised in the declarations could not be handled by the new task at all, yet clearly we need to provide a capability to handle them somewhere. Hence they are propagated to the unit declaring the task and behave as if raised immediately after the **begin**. It would clearly make life rather difficult if an exception were propagated from the new task to the declaring task after the declaring task had moved on in parallel. So the declaring task is held up until all the new tasks are activated. If several tasks are declared in the same unit then the order of their activation is not defined.

Task objects can be declared in a package and although not dependent on the package are nevertheless set active at the **begin** of the package body. If the package body has no initialisation statements and therefore no **begin**, then a null initialisation statement is assumed. Worse, if a package has no body, then a body with just a null initialisation statement is assumed. So the task CONTROL in the package READER_WRITER of the previous section is set active at the end of the declaration of the package body.

Tasks can also be created through access types. We can write

```
type REF_T is access T;
```

and then we can create a task using an allocator in the usual way

```
RX: REF_T:=new T;
```

The type REF_T is a normal access type and so assignment and equality comparisons of objects of the type are allowed. The entry E of the task accessed by RX can be called as expected by

```
RX.E( . . . );
```

Tasks created through access types obey slightly different rules for activation and dependency. They are made active immediately upon evaluation of the allocator whether it occurs in a sequence of statements or in an initial value – we do not wait until the ensuing **begin**. Furthermore, such tasks are not dependent upon the unit where they are created but are dependent upon the block, subprogram body or task body containing the declaration of the access type itself.

If a task is a component of an object then the activation and dependency rules are just as if the task was the whole object. This applies both in the case of a directly declared object and an object created through an access type.

Note that the entries in a task can be called as soon as it is declared and even before it is made active – the call will just be queued. This is necessary so that tasks that call each other can be declared without problems.

A common use of task types is for the creation of agents. An agent is a task that does something on behalf of another task. As an example suppose a task SERVER provides some service that is asked for by calling an entry REQUEST. Suppose also that it may take SERVER some time to provide the service so that it is reasonable for the calling task USER to go away and do something else while waiting for the answer to be prepared. There are various ways in which the USER could expect to collect his answer. He could call another entry ENQUIRE; the SERVER task would need some means of recognising the caller – he could do this by issuing a key on the call of REQUEST and insisting that it be presented again when calling ENQUIRE. This corresponds to taking something to be repaired, being given a ticket and then having to exchange it when the repaired item is collected later. An alternative approach which avoids the issue of keys, is to create an agent. This corresponds to leaving your address and having the repaired item posted back to you. We will now illustrate this approach.

First of all we declare a task type as follows

```
task type MAILBOX is
     entry DEPOSIT(X: in ITEM);
     entry COLLECT(X: out ITEM);
end;
task body MAILBOX is
     LOCAL: ITEM;
begin
     accept DEPOSIT(X: in ITEM) do
          LOCAL:=X;
     end;
     accept COLLECT(X: out ITEM) do
          X:=LOCAL;
     end;
end MAILBOX;
```

A task of this type acts as a simple mailbox. An item can be deposited and collected later. What we are going to do is to give the identity of the mailbox to the server so that the server can deposit the item in the mailbox from which the user can collect it later. We need an access type

```
type ADDRESS is access MAILBOX;
```

The tasks SERVER and USER now take the following form

```
task SERVER is
    entry REQUEST(A: ADDRESS; X: ITEM);
end;

task body SERVER is
    REPLY: ADDRESS;
    JOB: ITEM;
begin
    loop
        accept REQUEST(A: ADDRESS; X: ITEM) do
                REPLY:=A;
                JOB:=X;
        end:

                -- work on job

        REPLY.DEPOSIT(JOB);
    end loop;
end SERVER;

task USER;

task body USER is
    MY_BOX: ADDRESS:=new MAILBOX;
    MY_ITEM: ITEM;
begin
    SERVER.REQUEST(MY_BOX, MY_ITEM);
    -- do something while waiting
    MY_BOX.COLLECT(MY_ITEM);
end USER;
```

In practice the user might poll the mailbox from time to time to see if the item is ready. This is easily done using a conditional entry call.

```
select
    MY_BOX.COLLECT(MY_ITEM);
    -- item collected successfully
else
    -- not ready yet
end select;
```

It is important to realise that the agent serves several purposes. It enables the deposit and collect to be decoupled so that the server can get on with the next job. But perhaps more important, it means that the server need know nothing about the user; to call the user directly would mean that the user would have to be of a particular task type and this would be most unreasonable. The agent enables us to factor off the only property required of the user, namely the existence of the entry DEPOSIT.

If the decoupling property were not required then the body of the agent could be written as

```
task body MAILBOX is
begin
    accept DEPOSIT(X: in ITEM) do
        accept COLLECT(X: out ITEM) do
            COLLECT.X:=DEPOSIT.X;
        end;
    end;
end MAILBOX;
```

The agent does not need a local variable in this case since it only exists to aid closely coupled communication. Note also the use of the dotted notation in the nested accept statements in order to distinguish the two uses of X; we could equally have written X:=DEPOSIT.X; but the use of COLLECT is more symmetric.

14.6 Termination and exceptions

A task can terminate in various ways as well as running into its final end. It will have been noticed that in many of our earlier examples, the body of a task was an endless loop and clearly never terminated. This means that it would never be possible to leave the unit on which the task was dependent. Suppose for example that we needed to have several protected variables in our program. We could declare a task type

```
task type PROTECTED_VARIABLE is
    entry READ(X: out ITEM);
    entry WRITE(X: in ITEM);
end;
```

so that we can just declare variables such as

```
PV: PROTECTED_VARIABLE;
```

and access them by

```
PV.READ(...);
PV.WRITE(...);
```

However, we could not leave the scope of PV without terminating the task in some way. We could, of course, add a special entry STOP and call it just before leaving the scope but this would be inconvenient. Instead it is possible to make a task automatically terminate itself when it is of no further use by a special form of select alternative.

The body of the task can be written as

```
task body PROTECTED_VARIABLE is
    V: ITEM;
begin
    accept WRITE(X: in ITEM) do
        V:=X;
    end;
```

```
        loop
            select
                accept READ(X: out ITEM) do
                    X:=V;
                end;
            or
                accept WRITE(X: in ITEM) do
                    V:=X;
                end;
            or
                terminate;
            end select;
        end loop;
    end PROTECTED_VARIABLE;
```

The terminate alternative is taken if the unit on which the task depends has reached its end and all sibling tasks and dependent tasks are terminated or are similarly able to select a terminate alternative. In such circumstances the whole set of tasks are of no use since they are the only tasks that could call their entries and they are all dormant. Thus the whole set automatically terminates.

In practice, this merely means that all service tasks should have a terminate alternative and will then quietly terminate themselves without more ado.

Strictly speaking, the initial WRITE should also be in a select statement with a terminate alternative otherwise we are still stuck if the task is never called at all.

A terminate alternative may be guarded. However, it cannot appear in a select statement with a delay alternative or an else part.

Selection of a terminate alternative is classified as normal termination – the task is under control of the situation and terminates voluntarily.

At the other extreme the abort statement unconditionally and immediately terminates one or more tasks. It consists of the reserved word **abort** followed by a list of task names as for example

```
    abort X, AT(3), RX.all;
```

If a task is aborted then all tasks dependent upon it or a subprogram or block currently called by it are also aborted. Abortion is immediate; any delay is cancelled; if the task is on an entry queue, it is removed. If the task is engaged in a rendezvous when it is aborted, then we also have to consider the effect on the partner. This depends on the situation. If the caller is aborted, then the called task is not affected and the rendezvous (with a ghost!) carries on to completion. On the other hand if the called task is aborted, then the calling task receives the exception TASKING_ERROR. The rationale is simple; if a task asks for a service and the server dies so that it cannot be provided then the customer should be told. On the other hand, if the customer dies, too bad – but we must avoid upsetting the server who might have the database in a critical state.

The abort statement is very disruptive and should only be used in extreme situations. It might be appropriate for a command task to abort a complete subsystem in response to an operator command.

A slightly less severe possibility is to raise the special exception FAILURE which is an attribute of every task. To raise this exception we write

```
raise T'FAILURE;
```

This exception behaves as other exceptions but takes precedence over them. Thus if T was in the process of looking for a handler for some other exception, that other exception is forgotten. The FAILURE exception can be handled in the usual way by **others** or by a handler such as

```
when T'FAILURE =>
```

but such a handler can only appear in the task body itself.

If the failure exception is raised when the task is delayed or suspended on a select or accept statement then the delay or suspension is cancelled so that the exception can be handled immediately. Similarly the task is removed from an entry queue if it is on one. If the task is actually engaged in a rendezvous as the calling partner, then it waits until the rendezvous is completed before searching for a handler. If the task is the called partner then the calling partner receives TASKING_ERROR. Of course, if the accept statement handles the exception itself then that is the end of the matter anyway.

An important difference between being aborted and having an exception is that in the latter case, dependent tasks are not affected. An exception is not propagated out of a unit until all dependent tasks have terminated – this applies to all exceptions and not just to FAILURE.

If an exception other than failure is raised during a rendezvous (that is, as a consequence of an action by the called task) and is not handled by the accept statement, then it is propagated into both tasks as the same exception. Remember that FAILURE is propagated as TASKING_ERROR to the caller but stays as FAILURE in the called task.

Finally, if any exception is not handled by a task at all then, like the main program, the task is abandoned and the exception is lost; it is not propagated to the parent unit because it would be too disruptive to do so. However, we might expect the run time environment to provide a diagnostic message.

The purpose of the failure exception is to allow a task to be informed that it is in a mess so that it can tidy up and terminate in an orderly manner or perhaps start afresh if that is possible. A structure such as the following could be imagined.

```
task body T is
     OK: BOOLEAN;
begin
   loop
      begin
         ...
         ...
      exception
         when T'FAILURE =>
            -- tidy up if possible
         if OK then
               accept RESTART;
```

```
                else
                    exit;
                end if;
            end;
        end loop;
    end T;
```

If the task considers that it is OK to start again then it waits for a call of RESTART to confirm that it can do so. Otherwise it terminates gracefully.

The command task might contain a sequence such as

```
    raise T'FAILURE;
    select
        T.RESTART;
    else
        delay 60*SECONDS;
        abort T;
    end select;
```

If the task does not acknowledge its ability to restart by accepting the entry call within a minute of having failure raised, then it is ruthlessly aborted.

There is an attribute TERMINATED which can be interrogated to see if a task has terminated. But of course it must be remembered that between discovering that a task has not terminated and taking some action based on that information, the task could become terminated. However, the reverse is not possible since a task cannot be restarted and so it is quite safe to take an action based on the information that a task has terminated. Note that aborting a task which is already terminated has no effect.

Raising failure in another task should not be taken lightly; it is not quite so severe as aborting a task but it is an asynchronous interference and difficult to cope with. As an illustration of the impact of abnormal termination and how it can be coped with, we will reconsider the task CONTROL in the package READER_WRITER in Section 14.4 and its final form

```
    task body CONTROL is
        READERS: INTEGER:=0;
        WRITERS: INTEGER:=0;
    begin
        loop
            select
                when WRITERS = 0 =>
                accept START(S: SERVICE) do
                    case S is
                        when READ => READERS:=READERS+1;
                        when WRITE => WRITERS:=1;
                    end case;
                end START;
            or
                accept STOP_READ;
                READERS:=READERS-1;
            or
```

```
            when READERS = 0 =>
               accept WRITE;
         or
               accept STOP_WRITE;
               WRITERS:=0;
         end select;
      end loop;
   end CONTROL;
```

Suppose that a reading task has called START and is then aborted before it can call STOP_READ. The variable READERS will then be inconsistent and can never be zero again. All writers will therefore be locked out for ever. Similarly if a writing task has called START and is then aborted before it can call STOP_WRITE then all other users will be locked out for ever. A similar analysis applies if the calling tasks are disrupted by receiving the FAILURE exception.

The difficulty we have run into is that our task CONTROL assumes certain behaviour on the part of the calling tasks and this behaviour is not guaranteed. (We had a similar difficulty with our elementary solution to this example in Section 14.4 regarding the COUNT attribute and timed out entry calls.) We can overcome our new difficulty by the use of intermediate agent tasks which we can guarantee cannot be aborted.

The following shows the use of agents for the readers; a similar technique can be applied to the writers. The package body now becomes

```
   package body READER_WRITER is
      V: ITEM;
      type SERVICE is (READ,WRITE);

      task type READ_AGENT is
         entry READ(X: out ITEM);
      end;

      type RRA is access READ_AGENT;

      task CONTROL is
         entry START(S: SERVICE);
         entry STOP_READ;
         entry WRITE;
         entry STOP_WRITE;
      end;

      task body CONTROL is
            -- as before
      end CONTROL;

      task body READ_AGENT is
      begin
         select
            accept READ(X: out ITEM) do
               CONTROL.START(READ);
               X:=V;
               CONTROL.STOP_READ;
            end;
```

```
         or
             terminate;
         end select;
     end READ_AGENT;

     procedure READ(X: out ITEM) is
         A: RRA:=new READ_AGENT;
     begin
         A.READ(X);
     end READ;
     procedure WRITE(X: in ITEM) is
     begin
         ...
     end WRITE;

 end READER_WRITER;
```

If we now abort or raise FAILURE in the task calling the procedure READ then either the rendezvous with its agent will be in progress, in which case it will be completed, or the rendezvous will not be in progress, in which case there will be no interference. The agent therefore either does its job completely or not at all. Note that if we made the agent a direct task object (rather than an access to a task object) then aborting the task calling the procedure READ would also immediately abort the agent because it would be a dependent task. Using an access type makes the agent dependent on the unit in which the READER_WRITER is declared and so it can live on. On the other hand if we only want to guard against failure but not abort then a direct agent can be used; the failing task will wait for the agent to terminate normally.

The agent contains a select statement with a terminate alternative. This ensures that if the user task is aborted between creating the agent and calling the agent then nevertheless the agent can quietly die when the unit on which it depends is left.

It is worth summarising why the above solution works

- the agent is invisible and so cannot be aborted or failed;
- if the calling task in a rendezvous is abnormally terminated, the called task (the agent) is not affected;
- the agent is an access task and is not dependent on the caller.

The moral is not to use abort or failure without due care; or, as in life, if you cannot trust the calling tasks, use indestructible secret agents.

Finally it should be mentioned that an attempt to call an entry of a terminated task also raises TASKING_ERROR in the caller. Furthermore, however a task terminates, all tasks queued on its entries again receive TASKING_ERROR.

Exercise 14.6

1 Rewrite the task BUFFERING of Section 14.4 so that it has the following specification

```
task BUFFERING is
    entry PUT(X: in ITEM);
    entry FINISH;
    entry GET(X: out ITEM);
end;
```

The writing task calls PUT as before and finally calls FINISH. The reading task calls GET as before; a call of GET when there are no further items raises the global exception DONE.

14.7 Resource scheduling

When designing tasks in Ada it is important to remember that the only queues over which we have any control are entry queues and that such queues are handled on a strictly first in first out basis. This might be thought to be a problem in situations where requests are of different priorities or where later requests can be serviced even though earlier ones have to wait.

Requests with priorities can be handled by a family of entries. A family is rather like a one dimensional array. Suppose we have three levels of priority given by

```
type PRIORITY is (URGENT, NORMAL, LOW);
```

and that we have a task CONTROLLER providing access to some action on a type DATA but with requests for the action on three queues according to their priority. We could do this with three distinct entries but it is neater to use a family of entries. Consider

```
task CONTROLLER is
    entry REQUEST(PRIORITY) (D: DATA);
end;

task body CONTROLLER is
begin
    loop
        select
            accept REQUEST(URGENT) (D: DATA) do
                ACTION(D);
            end;
        or
            when REQUEST(URGENT)'COUNT = 0 =>
            accept REQUEST(NORMAL) (D: DATA) do
                ACTION(D);
            end;
        or
            when REQUEST(URGENT)'COUNT = 0 and
                    REQUEST(NORMAL)'COUNT = 0 =>
            accept REQUEST(LOW) (D: DATA) do
                ACTION(D);
            end;
        end select;
    end loop;
end CONTROLLER;
```

REQUEST is a family of entries, indexed by a discrete rate which in this case is the type PRIORITY. Clearly this approach is only feasible if the number of priority values is small. If it is large, a more sophisticated technique is necessary. We could try checking each queue in turn thus

```
task body CONTROLLER is
begin
    loop
        for P in PRIORITY loop
            select
                accept REQUEST(P) (D: DATA) do
                    ACTION(D);
                end;
                exit;
            else
                null;
            end select;
        end loop;
    end loop;
end CONTROLLER;
```

Unfortunately this is not satisfactory since it results in the task CONTROLLER continuously polling when all the queues are empty. We need a mechanism whereby the task can wait for the first of any request. This can be done by a two stage process; the calling task must first sign in by calling a common entry and then call the appropriate entry of the family. The details are left as an exercise for the reader.

We now illustrate a quite general technique which effectively allows the requests in a single entry queue to be handled in an arbitrary order. Consider the problem of allocating a group of resources from a set. We do not wish to hold up a later request that can be satisfied just because an earlier request must wait for the release of some of the resources it wants. We suppose that the resources are represented by a discrete type RESOURCE. We can conveniently use the generic package SET_OF from Section 13.2.

```
package RESOURCE_SETS is new SET_OF(RESOURCE);
use RESOURCE_SETS;
```

and then

```
package RESOURCE_ALLOCATOR is
    procedure RESERVE(L: LIST);
    procedure RELEASE(L: LIST);
end;

package body RESOURCE_ALLOCATOR is

    task CONTROL is
        entry FIRST(L: LIST; OK: out BOOLEAN);
        entry AGAIN(L: LIST; OK: out BOOLEAN);
        entry RELEASE(L: LIST);
    end;
```

```
task body CONTROL is
    FREE: LIST:=FULL;

    procedure TRY(L: LIST; OK: out BOOLEAN) is
    begin
        if L <= FREE then
            FREE:=FREE-L;
            OK:=TRUE;            -- allocation successful
        else
            OK:=FALSE;           -- no good, try later
        end if;
    end TRY;
begin
    loop
        select
            accept FIRST(L: LIST; OK: out BOOLEAN) do
                TRY(L, OK);
            end;
        or
            accept RELEASE(L: LIST) do
                FREE:=FREE+L;
            end;
            for I in 1 ..AGAIN'COUNT loop
                select
                    accept AGAIN(L: LIST, OK: out BOOLEAN)do
                        TRY(L, OK);
                    end;
                else
                    exit;
                end select;
            end loop;
        end select;
    end loop;
end CONTROL;

procedure RESERVE(L: LIST) do
    ALLOCATED: BOOLEAN;
begin
    CONTROL.FIRST(L, ALLOCATED);
    while not ALLOCATED loop
        CONTROL.AGAIN(L, ALLOCATED);
    end loop;
end RESERVE;

procedure RELEASE(L: LIST) do
begin
    CONTROL.RELEASE(L);
end RELEASE;

end RESOURCE_ALLOCATOR;
```

This is another example of a package containing a control task; the overall structure is similar to that of the package READER_WRITER introduced in Section 14.4. The package RESOURCE_ALLOCATOR contains two procedures RESERVE and RELEASE which have as parameter the list L of resources to be acquired or returned; the type LIST is from the instantiation of SET_OF. These procedures call the entries of the task CONTROL as appropriate.

The task CONTROL has three entries, FIRST, AGAIN and RELEASE. The entries FIRST and AGAIN are similar; as well as the parameter L giving the list of resources required, they also have an out parameter OK which indicates whether the attempt to acquire the resources was successful or not. The accept statements for FIRST and AGAIN are identical and call a common procedure TRY. This checks the list L against the list FREE of available resources using the inclusion operator "<=" from (the instantiation of) SET_OF. If all the resources are available, FREE is altered correspondingly using the symmetric difference operator "−" from SET_OF and OK is set TRUE; if they are not all available, OK is set FALSE. The entry RELEASE returns the resources passed as the parameter L by updating FREE using the union operator "+" from SET_OF . Note that the declaration of FREE gives it the initial value FULL which is also from SET_OF.

The entries FIRST and AGAIN are called by the procedure RESERVE. It makes an immediate attempt to acquire the resources by a call of FIRST; if they are not all available, the Boolean ALLOCATED is set FALSE and the request is queued by calling AGAIN. This call is then repeated until successful. The entry RELEASE is merely called by the procedure RELEASE.

The body of CONTROL is the inevitable select statement in a loop. It has two branches one for FIRST and one for RELEASE. Thus a call of RELEASE is always acceptable and a call of FIRST is also accepted promptly except when the task is dealing with the consequences of RELEASE. After a call of RELEASE, the requests which could not be satisfied on their call of FIRST and were consequently placed on the AGAIN queue are reconsidered since the resources made available by the call of RELEASE may be able to satisfy one or more requests at arbitrary points in the queue. The queue is scanned by doing a rendezvous with each call; a user which cannot be satisfied places itself back on the queue by a further call of AGAIN in the procedure RESERVE. In order that each user should only have one retry the scan is done by a loop controlled by AGAIN'COUNT which is, of course, evaluated just once at the start of the loop. The accept statement is placed inside a select statement with an else part containing an exit statement; this ensures that the system does not deadlock if a waiting task is aborted.

Exercise 14.7

1 Rewrite the task CONTROLLER as a package containing a task in a way which avoids continuous polling. The package specification should be

```
package CONTROLLER is
    procedure REQUEST(P: PRIORITY; D: DATA);
end;
```

14.8 Comparison with packages

Tasks and packages have a superficial lexical similarity – they both have specifications and bodies. However, there are many differences

- A task is an active construction whereas a package is passive.
- A task can only have entries in its specification. A package can have anything except entries. A task cannot have a private part.
- A package can be generic but a task cannot. The general effect of a parameterless generic task can be obtained by a task type. Alternatively the task can be encapsulated by a generic package.
- A package can appear in a use clause but a task cannot.
- A package can be a library unit but a task cannot. However, a task body can be a subunit.

The overall distinction is that the package should be considered to be the main tool for structuring purposes whereas the task is intended for synchronisation. Thus typical subsystems will consist of a (possibly generic) package containing one or more tasks. This general structure has as we have seen the merit of giving complete control over the facilities provided; internal tasks cannot be unwillingly aborted and entry calls cannot be unwillingly timed out if they are not visible.

Finally we illustrate the use of task types as private types by the following generic package which provides a general type BUFFER.

```
generic
   N: NATURAL;
   type ITEM is private;
package BUFFERS is
   type BUFFER is limited private;
   procedure PUT(B: in out BUFFER; X; in ITEM);
   procedure GET(B: in out BUFFER; X: out ITEM);
private
   task type CONTROL is
      entry PUT(X: in ITEM);
      entry GET(X: out ITEM);
   end;
   type BUFFER is
      record
         MONITOR: CONTROL;
      end record;
end;
package body BUFFERS is
   task body CONTROL is
      A: array (1 .. N) of ITEM;
      I, J: INTEGER range 1 .. N:=1;
      COUNT: INTEGER range 0 .. N:=0;
   begin
      loop
         select
            when COUNT < N = >
            accept PUT(X: in ITEM) do
               A(I):=X;
            end;
```

```
                    I:=I mod N+1; COUNT:=COUNT+1;
                or
                    when COUNT > 0 =>
                    accept GET(X: out ITEM) do
                        X:=A(I);
                    end;
                    J:=J mod N+I; COUNT:=COUNT−1;
                or
                    terminate;
                end select;
            end loop;
        end CONTROL;
        procedure PUT(B: in out BUFFER; in ITEM) is
        begin
            B.MONITOR.PUT(X);
        end PUT;

        procedure GET(B: in out BUFFER; X: out ITEM) is
        begin
            B.MONITOR.GET(X);
        end GET;
    end BUFFERS;
```

The buffer is implemented as a task object of the task type CONTROL so that when we declare an object of the type BUFFER a new task is created which in turn declares the storage for the actual buffer. Calls of the procedure PUT and GET access the buffer by calling the corresponding entries of the appropriate task. Note that the select statement contains a terminate alternative so that the task object automatically disappears when we leave the scope of its declaration. Moreover, the system is robust even if the calling task is aborted or failed.

Exercise 14.8

1 A boot repair shop has one man taking orders and three others actually repairing the boots. The shop has storage for 100 boots awaiting repair. The person taking the orders notes the address of the owner and this is attached to the boots; he then puts the boots in the store. Each repairman takes boots from the store when he is free, repairs them and then posts them.

Write a package COBBLERS whose specification is

```
package COBBLERS is
    procedure MEND(A: ADDRESS; B: BOOTS);
end;
```

The package body should contain four tasks representing the various men. Use an instantiation of the package BUFFERS to provide a store for the boots and agent tasks as mailboxes to deliver them.

Checklist 14

A task is active whereas a package is passive.

A task specification can contain only entries.

A task cannot be generic.

A task name cannot appear in a use clause.

Entries may be overloaded and renamed as procedures.

The COUNT attribute can only be used inside the task owning the entry.

An accept statement must not appear in a subprogram.

Do not attempt to use priorities for synchronisation.

A delay sets a minimum only.

The order of evaluation of guards is not defined.

A select statement can have just one of an else part, a single terminate alternative, one or more delay alternatives.

A terminate or delay alternative can be guarded.

Several alternatives can refer to the same entry.

A terminate alternative may not appear in an inner block that declares task objects or access types referring to task objects.

Beware of the COUNT attribute in guards.

Task types are limited private.

A task declared as an object is dependent on a block, subprogram or task body but not a package.

A task created by an allocator is dependent on the block, subprogram or task body containing the access type definition.

A task declared as an object is made active at the following (possibly notional) **begin**.

A task created by an allocator is made active at once.

Do not use **abort** or raise FAILURE without good reason.

Unhandled FAILURE in a rendezvous becomes TASKING_ERROR in the caller.

External Interfaces

In this chapter we consider various aspects of how an Ada program interfaces to the outside world. This includes obvious areas such as input-output, interrupt handling and so on but we will also consider the mapping of our abstract Ada program onto an implementation. However, the discussion in this chapter cannot be exhaustive because many details of this area will depend upon the implementation. The intent, therefore, is to give the reader a general overview of the facilities available.

15.1 Input and output

Unlike many other languages, Ada does not have any intrinsic features for input-output. Instead, existing general features such as subprogram overloading and generic instantiation are used. This has the merit of enabling different input-output packages to be developed for different application areas without affecting the language itself. On the other hand this approach can lead to a consequential risk of anarchy in this area; the reader may recall that this was one of the reasons for the downfall of Algol 60. In order to prevent such anarchy the LRM proposes two standard packages for input-output. We discuss the general principles of these packages in this and the next section. For further fine detail the reader should consult the LRM. Furthermore, the reader is warned that these packages may be changed in the light of experience.

Two categories of input-output are recognised and we can refer to these as binary and text respectively. As an example consider

```
I: INTEGER:=75;
```

We can output the binary image of I onto file F by

```
WRITE(F, I);
```

and the pattern transmitted might be (on a 16 bit machine)

```
0000 0000 0100 1011
```

In fact the file can be thought of as essentially an array of the type

```
array (FILE_INDEX range <>) of INTEGER
```

On the other hand we can output the text form of I by

```
PUT(F, I);
```

and the pattern transmitted might then be

0010 1111 0010 1101

which is the representation of the characters '7' and '5' without parity bits. In this case the file can be thought of as an array of the type

```
array (FILE_INDEX range <>) of CHARACTER
```

There are two packages with identifiers INPUT_OUTPUT and TEXT_IO for these two categories of input-output. The package TEXT_IO itself uses the more general package INPUT_OUTPUT which we will now consider in more detail. We will return to TEXT_IO in the next section.

The specification of the package INPUT_OUTPUT has the following form

```
generic
   type ELEMENT_TYPE is limited private;
package INPUT_OUTPUT is
   type IN_FILE is limited private;
   type OUT_FILE is limited private;
   type INOUT_FILE is limited private;
   type FILE_INDEX is range 0 .. implementation_defined;

   -- overloaded operations on files such as

   procedure CREATE(FILE: in out OUT_FILE; NAME: STRING);
   procedure OPEN(FILE: in out IN_FILE; NAME: STRING);
   procedure CLOSE(FILE: in out IN_FILE);
   function IS_OPEN(FILE: in out IN_FILE) return BOOLEAN;
   function NAME(FILE: IN_FILE) return STRING;
   procedure DELETE(NAME: STRING);
   function SIZE(FILE: IN_FILE) return FILE_INDEX;
   function LAST(FILE: IN_FILE) return FILE_INDEX;
   procedure TRUNCATE(FILE: OUT_FILE; TO: FILE_INDEX);

   -- overloaded input-output operations such as

   procedure READ(FILE: IN_FILE; ITEM: out ELEMENT_TYPE);
   function NEXT_READ(FILE: IN_FILE) return FILE_INDEX;
   procedure SET_READ(FILE: IN_FILE; TO: FILE_INDEX);
   procedure RESET_READ(FILE: IN_FILE);
   procedure WRITE(FILE: OUT_FILE; ITEM: ELEMENT_TYPE);
   function NEXT_WRITE(FILE: OUT_FILE) return FILE_INDEX;
   procedure SET_WRITE(FILE: OUT_FILE; TO: FILE_INDEX);
   procedure RESET_WRITE(FILE: OUT_FILE);

   function END_OF_FILE(FILE: IN_FILE) return BOOLEAN;

   -- Various exceptions

   NAME_ERROR:   exception;
   USE_ERROR:    exception;
   STATUS_ERROR: exception;
   DATA_ERROR:   exception;
   DEVICE_ERROR: exception;
   END_ERROR:    exception;
```

```
private
    ...
end INPUT_OUTPUT;
```

The package has a single generic parameter giving the type of element to be manipulated.

Externally a file has a name which is a string but internally we refer to a file by using objects of type IN_FILE, OUT_FILE and INOUT_FILE according to whether read-only, write-only or read-write access is required. Manipulation of files is done using various subprograms which are overloaded according to file type (IN_FILE, OUT_FILE, INOUT_FILE) as appropriate. (Only one overloading of each is shown above.)

Suppose we have a file containing measurements of various populations and that we wish to compute the sum of these measurements. The populations are recorded as values of type INTEGER and the name of the file is "CENSUS 47". (The form of the external file name is dependent upon the implementation.) The computed sum is to be written onto a new file to be called "TOTAL 47". This could be done bv the following program.

```
with INPUT_OUTPUT;
procedure COMPUTE_TOTAL_POPULATION is
    package INTEGER_IO is new INPUT_OUTPUT(INTEGER);
    use INTEGER_IO;
    DATA_FILE: IN_FILE;
    RESULT_FILE: OUT_FILE;
    VALUE: INTEGER;
    TOTAL: INTEGER:=0
begin
    OPEN(DATA_FILE, "CENSUS 47");
    while not END_OF_FILE(DATA_FILE) loop
        READ(DATA_FILE, VALUE);
        TOTAL:=TOTAL+VALUE;
    end loop;
    CLOSE(DATA_FILE);

    -- now write the result

    CREATE(RESULT_FILE,"TOTAL 47");
    WRITE(RESULT_FILE,TOTAL);
    CLOSE(RESULT_FILE);
end COMPUTE_TOTAL_POPULATION;
```

The first thing we do is instantiate the generic package INPUT_OUTPUT with the actual parameter INTEGER. The use clause enables us to refer to the entities in the created package directly.

The file with the data to be read is referred to via the object DATA_FILE of type IN_FILE and the output file is referred to via the object RESULT_FILE of type OUT_FILE. Note that these types are limited private; this enables the implementation to use techniques similar to those described in Section 9.3 where we discussed the example of the key manager.

The call of OPEN establishes the object DATA_FILE as referring to the external file "CENSUS 47". (If it was already referring to a file then STATUS_ERROR would be raised.) The external file is then opened for reading and positioned at the beginning.

We then obey the loop statement until the function END_OF_FILE indicates that the end of the file has been reached. On each iteration the call of READ copies the item into VALUE and positions the file at the next item. TOTAL is then updated. When all the values on the file have been read, it is closed by a call of CLOSE.

The call of CREATE creates a new external file with name "TOTAL 47" and establishes RESULT_FILE as referring to it. We then write our total onto the file and then close it.

As mentioned earlier a file can be considered as a one dimensional array. The elements in the file are ordered and each has an associated positive index of type FILE_INDEX. This index ranges from 1 to an upper value which can change – elements can be added to the end of the file or the file can be truncated. It is possible that not all elements in the current index range are defined – that is, the file may have holes in it. The function LAST returns the current maximum index and SIZE returns the number of defined elements; these will be the same unless the file has holes.

Associated with a file is a current read position or a current write position or both according to its type. When a file is opened or created, the current write position is set to 1 and the current read position is set to the index of the first defined element (usually 1), or to 1 if no element is defined.

Calls of READ and WRITE automatically increase the current read or write position as appropriate. On reading, undefined elements are skipped. Various other subprograms enable specific manipulation of these read and write positions. Thus a call of NEXT_READ returns the current read position; SET_READ sets the position to the given value and RESET_READ sets it back to the beginning as for OPEN. Similar subprograms apply to writing.

As an illustration of the manipulation of these positions we can alter our example to write the total population onto the end of an existing file called "TOTALS". The last few statements then become

```
    -- now write the result
    OPEN(RESULT_FILE, "TOTALS");
    SET_WRITE(RESULT_FILE, LAST(RESULT_FILE)+1);
    WRITE(RESULT_FILE, TOTAL);
    CLOSE(RESULT_FILE);
end COMPUTE_TOTAL_POPULATION;
```

Exercise 15.1

1 Write a generic library procedure to copy a file onto another file but with the elements in reverse order. Pass the external names as parameters.

15.2 Text input-output

Text input-output, which we first met in Chapter 2, is the more familiar form and provides two overloaded procedures PUT and GET to transmit values as streams of characters as well as various other subprograms such as NEW_LINE for layout control. In addition the concept of current default files is introduced so that every call of the various subprograms need not tiresomely repeat the file name. Thus if F is the current default output file, we can write

```
PUT("MESSAGE");
```

rather than

```
PUT(F,"MESSAGE");
```

There are two current default files, one of type TEXT_IO.OUT_FILE (or OUT_FILE for short) for output, and one of type TEXT_IO.IN_FILE for input. There is no type INOUT_FILE in the package TEXT_IO.

When we enter our program these two files are set to standard default files which are automatically open; we can assume that these are attached to convenient external files such as an interactive terminal or (in olden days) a card reader and line printer. If we wish to use other files and want to avoid repeating the file names in the calls of PUT and GET then we can change the default files to refer to our other files. We can also set them back to their original values. This is done with subprograms

```
function STANDARD_OUTPUT return OUT_FILE;
function CURRENT_OUTPUT return OUT_FILE;
procedure SET_OUTPUT(FILE: OUT_FILE);
```

with similar subprograms for input. The function STANDARD_OUTPUT returns the initial default output file, CURRENT_OUTPUT returns the current default output file and the procedure SET_OUTPUT enables us to change the current default output file to the file passed as parameter – this file must be open otherwise STATUS_ERROR will be raised.

Thus we could bracket a fragment of program with

```
F: OUT_FILE;
...
OPEN(F, ...);
SET_OUTPUT(F);
-- use PUT
SET_OUTPUT(STANDARD_OUTPUT());
```

so that having used the file F, we can reset the default file to its standard value.

The more general case is where we wish to reset the default file to its previous value which may, of course, not be the standard value. The reader may recall that the types IN_FILE and OUT_FILE are limited private and therefore values cannot be assigned; at first sight, therefore, it might not seem possible to make a copy of the original current value. However, with suitable contortion it can be done by using the parameter mechanism. We could write

```
procedure JOB(OLD_FILE, NEW_FILE: OUT_FILE) is
begin
     SET_OUTPUT(NEW_FILE);
     ACTION;
     SET_OUTPUT(OLD_FILE);
end;
```

and then

```
JOB(CURRENT_OUTPUT(), F);
```

When we call JOB, the present current value is preserved in the parameter OLD_FILE from whence it can be retrieved for the restoring call of SET_OUTPUT. However, although this works, it does feel a bit like standing on one's head!

The full specification of TEXT_IO is rather long and so only the general form is reproduced here.

```
package TEXT_IO is
   package CHARACTER_IO is
   new INPUT_OUTPUT (CHARACTER);
   type IN_FILE is new CHARACTER_IO.IN_FILE;
   type OUT_FILE is new CHARACTER_IO.OUT_FILE;

   -- Character Input-Output
   procedure GET(FILE: IN_FILE; ITEM: out CHARACTER);
   procedure GET(ITEM: out CHARACTER);
   procedure PUT(FILE: OUT_FILE; ITEM: CHARACTER);
   procedure PUT(ITEM: CHARACTER);

   -- String Input-Output
   procedure GET(ITEM: out STRING);
   procedure PUT(ITEM: STRING);
   function GET_STRING return STRING;
   function GET_LINE return STRING;
   procedure PUT_LINE(ITEM: STRING);

   -- Generic package for Integer Input-Output
   generic
      type NUM is range <>;
      ...
   package INTEGER_IO is
      procedure GET(ITEM: out NUM);
      procedure PUT(ITEM: NUM;
                    WIDTH: INTEGER:=0;
                    BASE: INTEGER range 2..16:=10);
      ...
   end INTEGER_IO;

   -- Generic package for Floating Point Input-Output
   generic
      type NUM is digits <>;
      ...
   package FLOAT_IO is
      procedure GET(ITEM: out NUM);
      procedure PUT(ITEM: NUM;
                    WIDTH: INTEGER:=0;
                    MANTISSA: INTEGER:=NUM'DIGITS;
                    EXPONENT: INTEGER:=2)
      ...
   end FLOAT_IO;
```

```
    -- Similar generic package for Fixed Point

    -- Boolean Input-Output

    procedure GET(ITEM: out BOOLEAN);
    procedure PUT(ITEM: BOOLEAN;
                  WIDTH: INTEGER:=0;
                  LOWER_CASE: BOOLEAN:=FALSE);
    ...

    -- Generic package for Enumeration Types

    generic
        type ENUM is (<>);
        ...
    package ENUMERATION_IO is
        procedure GET(ITEM: out ENUM);
        procedure PUT(ITEM: ENUM;
                      WIDTH: INTEGER:=0;
                      LOWER_CASE: BOOLEAN:=FALSE);
        ...
    end ENUMERATION_IO;

    -- Layout control such as

    function LINE(FILE: OUT_FILE) return NATURAL;
    function COL(FILE: OUT_FILE) return NATURAL;
    procedure SET_COL(FILE: OUT_FILE; TO: NATURAL);
    procedure NEW_LINE(FILE: OUT_FILE; N: NATURAL:=1);
    procedure SKIP_LINE(FILE: IN_FILE; N: NATURAL:=1);
    function END_OF_LINE(FILE: IN_FILE) return BOOLEAN;
    procedure SET_LINE_LENGTH(FILE: OUT_FILE; N: INTEGER);
    function LINE_LENGTH(FILE: OUT_FILE) return INTEGER;
    ...

    -- Default input and output manipulation

    function STANDARD_OUTPUT return OUT_FILE;
    function CURRENT_OUTPUT return OUT_FILE;
    procedure SET_OUTPUT(FILE: OUT_FILE);
    ...

    -- Various exceptions

    NAME_ERROR: exception
        renames CHARACTER_IO.NAME_ERROR;
    ...
    END_ERROR: exception
        renames CHARACTER_IO.END_ERROR;
    LAYOUT_ERROR: exception;

end TEXT_IO;
```

The package TEXT_IO contains an instantiation of the generic package

INPUT_OUTPUT with the type CHARACTER as parameter. Thus text files may be opened and closed by calls such as

```
TEXT_IO.CHARACTER_IO.OPEN(F,. . .);
```

although with appropriate use clauses this reduces to just OPEN(F,. . .) as we assumed in our example above. The types IN_FILE and OUT_FILE are derived from the corresponding types in CHARACTER_IO and the various exceptions are also renamed.

Procedures PUT and GET occur in two forms for each type, one with the file and one without; both are shown only for type CHARACTER.

In the case of type CHARACTER, a call of PUT just outputs that character; for type STRING a call of PUT outputs the characters of the string.

A problem arises in the case of numeric and enumeration types since there is not a fixed number of such types. This is overcome by the use of internal generic packages for each category. Thus for integer input-output we instantiate the package INTEGER_IO with the appropriate type thus

```
package MY_INTEGER_IO is new INTEGER_IO(MY_INTEGER);
use MY_INTEGER_IO;
```

For integer output, PUT has format parameters WIDTH and BASE which have default values of 0 and 10 respectively. The integer is output as an integer literal without underscores and leading zeros but with a preceding minus sign if negative. It is padded with leading spaces to fill the field width specified; if the field width is too small, it is expanded as necessary. Thus the default width of 0 results in the field being the minimum to contain the literal. If base 10 is specified, explicitly or by default, the value is output using the syntax of decimal number; if the base is not 10, the syntax of based number is used.

A similar technique is used for floating point. The value is output as a decimal number without underscores and leading zeros but with a preceding minus sign if negative. The format parameters give the field width, the total number of digits in the mantissa (the decimal point occurs after the first digit which is non zero except for 0.0) and the minimum number of digits in the signed exponent after the letter E (leading zeros are supplied if necessary). Base 10 is always used and the value is rounded to the mantissa size specified.

Boolean values are output as TRUE or FALSE. Again a default field of zero is used. If the field has to be padded then the extra spaces go after the value and not before as with the numeric types. Upper case is normally used, but lower case may be specified.

Other enumeration types again use the generic technique and the format is the same as for the Boolean type. A value of a character type which is a character literal is output in single quotes.

Note the subtle distinction between PUT defined directly for the type CHARACTER and for enumeration values.

```
TEXT_IO.PUT('X');
```

outputs the single character X, whereas

```
package CHAR_IO is
    new TEXT_IO.ENUMERATION_IO(CHARACTER);
    CHAR_IO. PUT('X');
```

outputs the character X between single quotes.

Input using GET works in an analagous way. In the case of the type CHARACTER the next character is read. In the case of the type STRING, the procedure GET reads the exact number of characters as determined by the actual parameter, whereas GET_STRING skips leading spaces and newlines and reads up to but not including the next space or newline. In the other cases, leading spaces and newlines before the data item are skipped. If the data item is not of the correct form, DATA_ERROR is raised.

A text file is considered as a sequence of lines. The characters in a line have a column position starting at 1. The line length can be fixed or variable. A fixed line length is appropriate for the output of tables, a variable line length for dialogue. The line length can be changed within a single file. It is initially not fixed.

On output a call of PUT will result in all the characters going on the current line starting at the current position in the line. If, however, the line length is fixed and the characters cannot fit in the remainder of the line, a new line is started and all the characters are placed on that line starting at the beginning. If they still will not fit, LAYOUT_ERROR is raised. If the line length is not fixed, the characters always go on the end of the current line.

The layout may be controlled by various subprograms. In most cases there are overloadings for both input and output files; in these cases if the file is omitted then it is taken to apply to the output case and the default output file is assumed. In a few cases, a subprogram only applies to one direction and then omitting the file naturally gives the default in that direction.

The function COL returns the current position in the line and the procedure SET_COL sets the position to the given value.

The procedure NEW_LINE (output only) outputs the given number of newlines (default 1) and resets the current column to 1. Spare positions at the end of a line are filled with spaces. The procedure SKIP_LINE (input only) similarly moves on the given number of lines (default 1) and resets the current column. The function END_OF_LINE (input only) returns TRUE if the line length is not set or we have reached the end of a fixed line. The function LINE returns the current line number from the start of the file.

The function LINE_LENGTH returns the current line length if it is fixed and zero if it is not. The procedure SET_LINE sets the line length fixed to the given value; a value of zero indicates that it is not to be fixed.

The subprograms PUT_LINE and GET_LINE are particularly appropriate for fixed length lines. A call of the procedure PUT_LINE outputs the string and moves to the next line; a call of function GET_LINE returns the characters up to the end of the line and moves to the next line. Successive calls of PUT_LINE and GET_LINE therefore manipulate whole lines.

The package TEXT_IO may seem somewhat elaborate but for simple output all we need is PUT and NEW_LINE and these are quite straightforward as we have seen.

Exercise 15.2

1 What do the following calls output?

```
a) PUT("FRED")          d) PUT(120,8,8);
b) PUT(120);            e) PUT(-38.0);
c) PUT(120,8);          f) PUT(0.07,12,3,1);
```

Assume that the real values are of a type with **digits** = 6.

15.3 Interrupts

An interrupt is another form of input. In Ada this is achieved through the rendezvous mechanism. From within the program, an interrupt appears as an entry call performed by an external task whose priority is higher than that of any task in the program. The interrupt handler is then naturally represented in the program by a task with accept statements for the corresponding entry. The entry is identified as an interrupt by what is known as a representation specification giving the relevant hardware address.

As an example suppose a program wishes to act upon an interrupt arising from the closing of an electrical contact and the interrupt is associated with the address 8# 72#. We could write

```
task CONTACT_HANDLER is
    entry CONTACT;
    for CONTACT use at 8# 72#;
end;

task body CONTACT_HANDLER is
begin
    loop
        accept CONTACT do
            ...
        end;
    end loop;
end CONTACT_HANDLER;
```

The body of the accept statement corresponds to the direct response to the interrupt. The rule that the external mythical task has a priority higher than that of any software task ensures that the response takes precedence over ordinary tasks.

An interrupt entry will usually have no parameters but it can have **in** parameters through which control information is passed. An accept statement for an interrupt entry can also occur in a select statement.

The detailed behaviour of interrupt entry calls is somewhat dependent upon the implementation. They could for example appear as conditional entry calls and therefore be lost if the response task is not ready to execute the corresponding accept statement. The exact interpretation of the address in the representation specification is also dependent on the implementation.

15.4 Representation specifications

In the last section we introduced the representation specification as a means of informing the compiler of additional information about the interrupt entry. Representation specifications take various forms and apply to various entities.

Their general purpose is to provide the compiler with directions regarding how the entity is to be implemented.

An address specification is of the form used for the entry. It can be used to assign an explicit address to an object, to indicate the start address of the code body of a subprogram, package or task, or as we have seen, to specify an interrupt to which an entry is to be linked.

A length specification allows us to specify the amount of storage to be allocated for objects of a type, for the collection of an access type and for the working storage of a task. This is done by indicating the value of certain attributes. Thus

```
type BYTE is range 0..255;
for BYTE'SIZE use 8;
```

ensures that objects of the type BYTE occupy only 8 bits.

The space for access collections and tasks is indicated using the attribute STORAGE_SIZE. In these cases the unit is not bits but storage units. The number of bits in a storage unit is implementation dependent and is given by SYSTEM. STORAGE_UNIT in the package STANDARD. Thus if we wanted to ensure that the access collection for

```
type LIST is access CELL;
```

will accommodate 500 cells then we write

```
for LIST'STORAGE_SIZE use
    500*(CELL'SIZE/SYSTEM.STORAGE_UNIT);
```

Similarly the data space for a task (or each task of a task type) can be indicated by

```
for MAIL_BOX'STORAGE_SIZE use 128;
```

The actual delta of a fixed point type can also be indicated by a length specification.

An enumeration type representation can be used to specify, as an aggregate, the internal integer codes for the literals of an enumeration type. We might have a status value transmitted into our program as single bit settings, thus

```
type STATUS is (OFF, READY, ON);
for STATUS use (OFF => 1, READY => 2, ON => 4);
```

There is a constraint that the ordering of the values must be the same as the logical ordering of the literals. However despite the holes, the functions SUCC, PRED, POS always work in logical terms.

The final form of representation specification is used to indicate the layout of a record type. Thus if we have

```
type REGISTER is range 0 .. 15;
type OPCODE is (. . .);
type RR is
    record
        CODE: OPCODE;
        R1   : REGISTER;
        R2   : REGISTER;
    end record;
```

which represents a machine instruction of the RR format in the IBM system 370, then we can specify the exact mapping by

```
for RR use
    record at mod 2;
        CODE at 0 range 0 .. 7;
        R1   at 1 range 0 .. 3;
        R2   at 1 range 4 .. 7;
    end record;
```

The optional alignment clause

```
at mod 2;
```

indicates that the record is to be aligned on a double byte boundary; the alignment is given in terms of the number of storage units and in the case of the 370 a storage unit would naturally be one 8-bit byte.

The position and size of the individual components are given relative to the start of the record. The value after **at** gives a storage unit and the range is in terms of bits. The bit number can extend outside the storage unit; we could equally have written

```
R1 at 0 range 8 .. 11;
```

If we do not specify the location of every component, the compiler is free to juggle the rest as best it can. However, we must allow enough space for those we do specify and they must not overlap unless they are in different alternatives of a variant.

Finally it should be noted that a representation specification must occur in the same declaration list as the declaration of the entity it refers to. Representation specifications occur after declarations and use clauses but before program components.

15.5 Implementation considerations

It is hard to be specific in this area since so much depends upon the implementation. However, there is a package SYSTEM inside the package STANDARD which gives the values of various machine constants. These include the size of a storage unit, the memory size in storage units and the smallest and largest integer values supported by the implementation.

Various pragmas enable us to set certain parameters of the implementation, and attributes enable us to read the value of certain parameters. The predefined pragmas and attributes are listed in Appendix 1 although an implementation is free to add others.

Some pragmas enable us to guide the compiler regarding the balance of the implementation between integrity and efficiency and also between space and time.

The pragma SUPPRESS can be used to indicate that the run time checks associated with detecting conditions which could give rise to exceptions can be omitted if to do so would lead to a more efficient program. However, it should be remembered that a pragma is merely a recommendation and so there is no guarantee that the exception will not be raised. Indeed it could be propagated from another unit compiled with checks.

The checks corresponding to the exception CONSTRAINT_ERROR are ACCESS_CHECK (checking that an access value is not null when attempting to access a component), DISCRIMINANT_CHECK (checking that a discriminant value is consistent with the component being accessed or a constraint), INDEX_CHECK (checking that an index is in range), LENGTH_CHECK (checking that the number of components of an array match) and RANGE_CHECK (checking that various constraints are satisfied).

The checks corresponding to NUMERIC_ERROR are DIVISION_CHECK (checking the second operand of /, **rem** and **mod**) and OVERFLOW_CHECK (checking for numeric overflow).

The check corresponding to STORAGE_ERROR is STORAGE_CHECK (checking that space for an access collection or task has not been exceeded).

The pragma takes the form

```
pragma SUPPRESS(RANGE_CHECK);
```

in which case it applies to all operations in the unit concerned or it can list the types and objects to which it is to be applied. Thus

```
pragma SUPPRESS(ACCESS_CHECK, LIST);
```

indicates that no checks are to be applied when accessing objects of the access type LIST.

The other pragmas in this category apply to the balance between speed and time. They are CONTROLLED, INLINE, OPTIMIZE and PACK; they are described in Appendix 1.

Finally there are various machine dependent attributes defined for real types. For example there is the attribute MACHINE_ROUNDS which indicates whether rounding is performed for the type concerned. Another is the attribute MACHINE_OVERFLOWS which indicates whether NUMERIC_ERROR is raised for computations which exceed the range of the type. If a program uses these attributes then care is required if portability is to be ensured.

15.6 Unchecked programming

Sometimes the strict integrity of a fully typed language is a nuisance. This particularly applies to system programs where, in different parts of a program, an object is thought of in different terms. This difficulty can be overcome by the use of a generic function called UNCHECKED_CONVERSION. Its specification is

```
generic
    type SOURCE is limited private;
    type TARGET is limited private;
function UNCHECKED_CONVERSION(S: SOURCE)
                                        return TARGET;
```

As an example, values of the type STATUS of Section 15.4 might arrive in our program as values of type BYTE. In order to perform the conversion we first instantiate the generic function thus

```
function BYTE_TO_STATUS is
    new UNCHECKED_CONVERSION(BYTE, STATUS);
```

and we can then write

```
B: BYTE:= ...
S: STATUS;
...
S:=BYTE_TO_STATUS(B);
```

The effect of the unchecked conversion is nothing; the bit pattern of the source type is merely passed on unchanged and reinterpreted as the bit pattern of the target type. Clearly certain conditions must be satisfied for this to be possible; an obvious one which may be imposed by the implementation is that the number of bits in the representations of the two types must be the same. We cannot get a quart into a pint pot.

Another area where the programmer can be given extra freedom is in the deallocation of access types. As mentioned in Section 11.3 there may or may not be a garbage collector. In any event we may prefer to do our own garbage collection perhaps on the grounds that this gives us better timing control in a real time program. We can do this with a generic procedure called UNCHECKED_DEALLOCATION. Its specification is

```
generic
    type OBJECT is limited private;
    type NAME is access OBJECT;
procedure UNCHECKED_DEALLOCATION(X: in out NAME);
```

If we take our old friend

```
type LIST is access CELL;
```

then we can write

```
procedure FREE is
    new UNCHECKED_DEALLOCATION(CELL, LIST);
```

and then

```
L: LIST;
...
FREE(L);
```

After calling FREE, the value of L will be **null** and the cell will have been returned to free storage. Of course, if we mistakenly still had another variable referring to the cell then we would be in a mess; the program would be erroneous. If we use unchecked deallocation then the onus is on us to get it right. We should also insert

```
pragma CONTROLLED(LIST);
```

to tell the compiler that we are looking after ourselves and that any garbage collector should not be used for this access type.

The use of both these forms of unchecked programming needs care and it would be sensible to restrict the use of these generic subprograms to privileged parts of the program.

15.7 Other languages

Another possible form of communication between an Ada program and the outside world is via other languages. These could be machine languages or other other high level languages such as FORTRAN. The LRM prescribes general methods but the actual details will obviously depend so much upon the implementation that an outline description seems pointless and the reader is therefore referred to specific documentation for the implementation concerned.

Finale

This final chapter covers various overall aspects of Ada. The first three sections summarise topics which have of necessity been introduced in stages throughout the book in order to reveal their overall coherence and underlying relationships. There is then a section on the important issue of portability. Finally we discuss the general topic of program design as it relates to Ada.

16.1 Names and expressions

The idea of a name should be carefully distinguished from that of an identifier. An identifier is a syntactic form such as FRED which is used for various purposes including introducing entities when they are declared. A name, on the other hand, may be more complex and is the form used to denote entities in general.

Syntactically, a name starts with an identifier such as FRED or an operator symbol such as "+" and can then be followed by one or more of the following in an arbitrary order

- one or more index expressions in brackets; this denotes an element of an array,
- a discrete range in brackets; this denotes a slice of an array,
- a dot followed by an identifier, operator or **all**; this denotes a record component, an access value or an entity in a package, task, subprogram, block or loop,
- a prime and then an identifier, possibly indexed; this denotes an attribute,
- an actual parameter list in brackets; this denotes a function call.

A function call in a name must deliver an array, record or access value and must be followed by indexing, slicing, attribution or component selection. This is not to say that a function call must always be followed by one of these things; it could deliver a value as part of an expression, but as part of a name it must be so followed. This point is clarified by considering the assignment statement. The left hand side must be a name whereas the right hand side is an expression. Hence, as we saw in Section 11.5, we can write

```
SPOUSE(P).BIRTH:=NEWDATE;
```

but not

```
SPOUSE(P):=Q;
```

although

```
Q:=SPOUSE(P);
```

is of course perfectly legal. (Ada is somewhat less consistent than Algol 68 in this respect.)

Names are just one of the primary components of an expression. The others are literals (numeric literals, enumeration literals, strings and **null**), aggregates, allocators, function calls (not considered as names), type conversions and qualified expressions as well as expressions in brackets. Expressions involving scalar operators were summarised in Section 4.9. For convenience all the operators and their predefined uses are shown in Fig. 16.1. Remember that an expression may also involve the short circuit forms **and then** and **or else** and the membership tests **in** and **not in** although these are not technically classed as operators.

Operator	*Operand(s)*		*Result*
and or xor	BOOLEAN		same
	one dim BOOLEAN array		same
= /=	any, not limited private		BOOLEAN
< <= > >=	scalar		BOOLEAN
	one dim discrete array		BOOLEAN
+ − (binary)	numeric		same
&	one dim array		same
+ − (unary)	numeric		same
not	BOOLEAN		same
	one dim BOOLEAN array		same
*	integer	integer	same
	fixed	integer	same fixed
	integer	fixed	same fixed
	fixed	fixed	univ fixed
	floating	floating	same
/	integer	integer	same
	fixed	integer	same fixed
	fixed	fixed	univ fixed
	floating	floating	same
mod rem	integer	integer	same
**	integer	non neg integer	same integer
	floating	integer	same floating

Fig. 16.1 Predefined operators

The observant reader will notice that the syntax in Appendix 4 uses the syntactic form 'simple_expression' in some cases where 'expression' might have been expected. One reason for this is to avoid a potential ambiguity regarding the use of **in** as a membership test with ranges.

From time to time we have referred to the need for certain expressions to be static. As explained in Chapter 2 this means that they can be evaluated at compilation time. An expression is static if all its constituents are one of the following

- a literal or literal expression,
- an aggregate with static choices and components,
- a constant initialised by a static expression,
- a predefined operator, the predefined function ABS, a membership test or a short circuit control form,
- a static attribute or a functional attribute with static parameters,
- a qualified or converted static expression provided that any constraint involved is static,
- a selected component of a record constant initialised by a static expression,
- an indexed component of an array constant initialised by a static expression, provided the index expressions are static.

It is important to distinguish between static expressions and literal expressions. A literal expression is also evaluated at compilation time but the result is one of the universal numeric types and the possible constituents are more restricted than for static expressions. Literal expressions were described in Chapter 12.

The final point we wish to make about expressions concerns array bounds. If an expresssion delivers an array value then it will have bounds for each dimension. Such an expression can be used in various contexts which can be divided into categories according to the rules regarding the matching of the bounds.

The first category includes assignment and initialisation in an object declaration. In these cases the bounds of the expression do not have to match the bounds of the object; all that matters is that the number of components in each dimension is the same. Thus as we saw in Section 6.2 we can write

```
V: VECTOR(1..5);
W: VECTOR(0..4);

...
V:=W;
```

The same matching rules apply in the case of the predefined equality and relational operators.

The second category of contexts includes those where an array is used as an actual parameter, as a function result, as an initial value in an allocator or in a qualified expression. In all of these cases an array type or subtype is involved but it may or may not be constrained. If it is constrained then the bounds must exactly match; if it is not constrained then the 'result' takes the bounds of the expression. Thus if we had a function

```
function F return VECTOR(1 .. 5) is
   V: VECTOR(1 .. 5);
   W: VECTOR(0 .. 4);
begin
   ...
```

then we could write **return** V but not **return** W. If, however, the specification had been

```
function F return VECTOR
```

then we could write either **return** V or **return** W.

There are complications with array aggregates. In the case of a named aggregate without **others** the bounds are evident; such an aggregate can be used in any of the above contexts. In the case of a positional aggregate without **others** the bounds are not evident although the number of components is; such an aggregate can also be used in any of the above contexts – in the case of the second category with a constrained type the bounds are taken to be those required by the constraint – in all the cases of the first category and those of the second category with an unconstrained type the lower bound is given by S'FIRST where S is the index subtype. Finally, if an aggregate (positional or named) contains **others**, then neither the bounds nor the number of components is evident; such an aggregate can only be used in a situation of the second category with a constrained type.

Similar rules apply to nested aggregates; the context of the whole aggregate is applied transitively to its components.

Somewhat surprisingly, array type conversion described in Section 6.2 does not fit neatly into either of the above two categories. If the type is constrained, then the matching rules of assignment are used; if the type is unconstrained, then the result takes the bounds of the operand as for qualification.

Exercise 16.1

1 Given

```
L: INTEGER:=6;
M: constant INTEGER:=7;
N: constant:=8;
A: constant array (1 .. L) of INTEGER:=(1 .. L => 0);
B: constant array (1 .. M) of INTEGER:=(1 .. M => 0);
C: constant array (1 .. N) of INTEGER:=(1 .. N =>0);
```

then classify the following as literal, static or dynamic expressions and give their type.

a) L+1	d) A(L)
b) M+1	e) B(M)
c) N+1	f) C(N)

16.2 Type equivalence

It is perhaps worth emphasising the rules for type equivalence. The basic rule is that every type definition introduces a new type. Remember the difference between a type definition and a type declaration. A type definition introduces a type whereas a type declaration also introduces an identifier referring to it. Thus

```
type T is (A,B,C);
```

is a type declaration whereas

```
(A,B,C)
```

is a type definition.

Most types have names but in a few cases a type may be anonymous. The obvious cases occur with the declarations of arrays and tasks. Thus

```
A: array (I range L..R) of C;
```

is short for

```
type anon is array (I range <>) of C;
A: anon(L..R);
```

and

```
task T is ...
```

is short for

```
task type anon is ...
T: anon;
```

More subtle cases occur where an apparent type declaration is actually only a subtype declaration. This occurs with array types, derived types and numeric types

```
type T is array (I range L..R) of C;
```

is short for

```
type anon is array (I range <>) of C;
subtype T is anon(L..R);
```

and

```
type S is new T constraint;
```

is short for

```
type anon is new T;
subtype S is anon constraint;
```

and finally

```
type T is range L..R;
```

is short for

```
type anon is new integer_type;
subtype T is anon range L..R;
```

where integer_type is one of the predefined integer types.

As an interesting example of the rules of this and the previous section we will briefly analyse the statement

```
R.A:=P.A & (P.N+1..R.N => 0);
```

which occurs in the notes in the answer to Exercise 11.1(6). This also gives us the opportunity to present a more formal definition of the operator '&'.

For any type of the form

```
type T is array (I range <>) of C;
```

the definition of & is given by

```
function'&'(X,Y: T) return T is
    R: T(I'FIRST..I'VAL(I'POS(I'FIRST)+X'LENGTH+Y'LENGTH-1));
begin
    R(R'FIRST..I'VAL(I'POS(I'FIRST)+X'LENGTH-1)):=X;
    R(I'VAL(I'POS(I'FIRST)+X'LENGTH)..R'LAST):=Y;
    return R;
end;
```

with additional overloadings for the special cases where one operand is a scalar.

Now consider the type POLYNOMIAL in section 11.1

```
type POLYNOMIAL(N: INTEGER range 0..MAX:=0) is
    record
        A: array (0..N) of INTEGER;
    end record;
```

The component A in this discriminated record is of anonymous type

```
type anon is (INTEGER range <>) of INTEGER;
```

and the individual components R.A of all records R of the type POLYNOMIAL are, of course, all of the same anonymous type which, for convenience, we will refer to as T. The predefined operator '&' will apply to the type T.

So in our example

```
R.A:=P.A & (P.N+1..R.N => 0);
```

P.A is an array of type T with bounds 0 and P.N. The named aggregate is also of type T and has bounds of P.N+1 and R.N. Since R.A is also of type T the call of '&' can be identified as legal.

When '&' is called the formal parameters X and Y take the bounds of the actual parameters. The lower bound of the local variable R is therefore INTEGER'FIRST and the upper bound is

```
INTEGER'VAL(INTEGER'POS(INTEGER'FIRST)+P.N+1+
                                    R.N-P.N-1)
```

which reduces to

```
INTEGER'FIRST+R.N
```

The bounds of the result are therefore also INTEGER'FIRST and INTEGER'FIRST+R.N. The result can then be assigned to R.A (whose bounds are 0 and R.N) because although the bounds are not identical nevertheless the number of components is the same. The statement is therefore legal.

Finally, when interpreting the rule that each type definition introduces a new type, remember that generic instantiation is equivalent to text substitution in this respect. Thus each instantiation of a package with a type definition in its specification introduces a distinct type. It will be remembered that a similar rule applies to the identification of different exceptions. Each textually distinct exception declaration introduces a new exception; an exception in a recursive procedure is the same for each incarnation but generic instantiation introduces different exceptions.

16.3 Structure summary

Ada has four structural units in which declarations can occur; these are blocks, subprograms, packages and tasks. They can be classified in various ways. First of all packages and tasks have separate specifications and bodies; for subprograms this separation is optional; for blocks it is not possible or relevant since a block has no specification. We can also consider separate compilation: packages, tasks and subprogram bodies can all be subunits but only packages and subprograms can be library units. Note also that only packages and subprograms can be generic. Finally, tasks, subprograms and blocks can have dependent tasks but packages cannot since they are only passive scope control units. These various properties of units are summarised in Fig. 16.2.

Property	*Blocks*	*Subprograms*	*Packages*	*Tasks*
separation	no	optional	yes	yes
subunits	no	yes	yes	yes
library units	no	yes	yes	no
generic units	no	yes	yes	no
dependent units	yes	yes	no	yes

Fig. 16.2 Properties of units

We can also consider the scope and nesting of these four structural units. (Note that a block is a statement whereas the others are declarations.) Each unit can appear inside any of the other units and this lexical nesting can in principle go on indefinitely although in practical programs a depth of three will not often be exceeded. The only restrictions to this nesting are that a block, being a statement, cannot appear in a package specification but only in its body (and directly only in the initialisation sequence) and of course none of these units can appear in a task specification but again only in its body. In practice, however, some of the combinations will arise rarely. Blocks will usually occur inside subprograms and task bodies and occasionally other blocks. Subprograms will occur as library units and inside packages and less frequently inside tasks and other subprograms. Packages will usually be library units or inside other packages. Tasks will probably nearly always be inside packages and occasionally inside other tasks or subprograms.

The Language Reference Manual is a little vague about the concept of an Ada program. This is perhaps to be expected since Ada is about software components, and undue concern regarding what constitutes a complete program is probably out of place particularly bearing in mind the growing concern with distributed and parallel systems. However, for simple systems we can regard a program as composed out of the library units in a particular program library. The LRM does not prescribe how the program is to be started but as discussed in Sections 2.2 and 8.2 we can imagine that one of the library units which is a subprogram is called by some magic outside the language itself. Moreover, we must imagine that this originating flow of control is associated with an anonymous task. The priority of this task can be set by the pragma PRIORITY in the outermost declarative part of this main subprogram.

The main program will almost inevitably use dependent library units such as TEXT_IO. These have to be elaborated before the main program is entered and again we can imagine that this is done by our anonymous task. The order of these elaborations is not precisely specified but it must be consistent with the dependencies between the units. If no consistent order exists then the program is illegal; if there are several possible orders and the behaviour of the program depends on the particular order then it is erroneous.

A further point is that the LRM does not prescribe whether a main program can have parameters or not or whether there are restrictions on their types and modes. Again this is in line with the view that Ada is about the open world of components rather than the closed world of complete programs. It may indeed be very convenient for a main program to have parameters, and for the calling and parameter passing to be performed by the magic associated with the interpretation of a statement in some non-Ada command language.

The final point we wish to make in this section concerns the mathematical library. The LRM does not prescribe the existence of such a library in the way that it does prescribe packages for input and output. However, we have rather assumed its existence in Section 4.9 and also in Exercise 2.2(1). One of the problems that the mathematical library has to overcome concerns the derived nature of user defined floating point types. The rules for derived types are such that any library for a predefined type such as FLOAT will not automatically become inherited by a derived type such as REAL. Instead the mathematical library is best constructed as a generic package

```
generic
    type F is digits <>;
package MATHS_LIB is
    function SQRT(X: F) return F;
    function LOG(X: F) return F;
    ...
end MATHS_LIB;
```

We can then use the mathematical library with a type such as REAL by writing

```
package REAL_MATHS_LIB is new MATHS_LIB(REAL);
use REAL_MATHS_LIB;
```

16.4 Portability

An Ada program may or may not be portable. In many cases a program will be intimately concerned with the particular hardware on which it is running; this is particularly true of embedded applications. Such a program cannot be transferred to another machine without significant alteration. On the other hand it is highly desirable to write portable program libraries so that they can be reused in different applications. In some cases a library component will be totally portable; more often it will make certain demands on the implementation or be parameterised so that it can be tailored to its environment in a straightforward manner. This section contains general guidelines on the writing of portable Ada programs.

One thing to avoid is erroneous programs. They can be insidious. A program may work quite satisfactorily on one implementation and may seem superficially to be portable. However, if it happens to depend upon some undefined feature then it will be erroneous and its behaviour on another implementation cannot be guaranteed. A common example in most programming languages occurs with variables which accidentally are not initialised. It is often the case that the intended value is zero and furthermore many operating systems clear the program area before loading the program. Under such circumstances the program will behave correctly but may give surprising results when transferred to a different implementation. So the concept of erroneous programs is not confined to Ada. In the previous chapters we have mentioned various causes of erroneous programs. For convenience we summarise them here.

An important group of situations concerns the order of evaluation of expressions. Since an expression can include a function call and a function call can have side effects, it follows that different orders of evaluation can sometimes produce different results. The order of evaluation of the following is not defined

- the operands of a binary operator,
- the destination and value in an assignment,
- the components in an aggregate,
- the parameters in a subprogram or entry call,
- the index expressions in a multidimensional name,
- the expressions in a range,
- the guards in a select statement.

There are two situations where a junk value can arise

- reading an uninitialised variable before assigning to it,
- returning from a function without a result by running into the final end.

There are two situations where the language mechanism is not defined

- the passing of array, record and private parameters,
- the algorithm for choosing a branch of a select statement.

There are also situations where the programmer is given extra freedom to overcome the astringency of the type model; abuse of this freedom can lead to erroneous programs. Examples are

- suppressing exceptions,
- unchecked deallocation,
- unchecked conversion.

Finally we recall from the last section that the order of elaboration of library units is not defined.

Numeric types are another important source of portability problems. The reason is, of course, the compromise necessary between achieving absolutely uniform behaviour on all machines and maximising efficiency. Ada uses the concept of model numbers as the formalisation of this compromise. In principle, if we rely only on the properties of the model numbers then our programs will be portable. In practice this is not easy to do; the reader will recall the problems of overflow in intermediate expressions discussed in Section 12.1.

There are various attributes which, if used correctly, can make our programs more portable. Thus we can use BASE to find out what is really going on and MACHINE_OVERFLOWS to see whether NUMERIC_ERROR will occur or not. But the misuse of these attributes can lead to very non-portable programs.

There is however one simple rule that can be followed. We should always declare our own real types and not directly use the predefined types such as FLOAT. Ideally, a similar approach should be taken with integer types, but the language does encourage us to assume that the predefined type INTEGER has a sensible range.

Another area to consider is tasking. Any program that uses tasking is likely to suffer from portability problems because instruction execution times vary from machine to machine. This will affect the relative execution times of tasks as well as their individual execution times. In some cases a program may not be capable of running at all on a particular machine because it does not have adequate processing power. Hard guidelines are almost impossible to give but the following points should be kept in mind.

Take care that the type DURATION has a small enough delta for the application. Remember that regular loops cannot easily be achieved if the interval required is not a model number.

Avoid the unsynchronised use of shared variables as far as possible. Sometimes, timing considerations demand quick and dirty techniques; consult your friendly real time specialist if tempted.

The use of the abort statement and failure exception will also give portability problems because of their asynchronous nature.

Avoid also the overuse of priorities. If you need to use priorities to obtain adequate responsiveness then the program is probably stretching the resources of the machine.

The finite speed of the machine leads to our final topic in this section – the finite space available. It is clear that different machines have different sizes and so a program that runs satisfactorily on one machine might raise STORAGE_ERROR on another. Moreover, different implementations may use different storage allocation strategies for access types and task data. We have seen how representation specifications can be used to give control of storage allocation and thereby reduce portability problems. However, the unconsidered use of recursion and access types is best avoided.

Exercise 16.4

1 The global variable I is of type INTEGER and the function F is

```
function F return INTEGER is
begin
    I:=I+1;
    return I;
end F;
```

Explain why the following fragments of program are erroneous. Assume in each case that I is reset to 1.

a) I:=I+F();
b) A(I):=F();
c) AA(I,F()):=0;

16.5 Program design

This final section considers the question of designing Ada programs. At the time of writing there are no serious Ada compilers in existence and consequently no body of accumulated experience in the actual use of Ada. Hence the guidelines in this section must be treated with some caution although there seems little reason to doubt their general validity. Note also that we are only addressing the question of designing programs in Ada. It is assumed that the reader has some knowledge of the general principles of program design.

There are various low level and stylistic issues which are perhaps obvious. Identifiers should be meaningful. The program should be laid out neatly – the style used in this book is based on that recommended from the syntax in the LRM. Useful comments should be added. The block structure should be used to localise declarations to their use. Whenever possible a piece of information should only be written once; thus number and constant declarations should be used rather than explicit literals. And so on.

Programming is really all about abstraction and the mapping of the problem onto constructions in the programming language. We recall from Section 1.2 that the development of programming languages has been concerned with the introduction of various levels of abstraction and that Ada in particular introduces a degree of data abstraction not present in other practically used languages.

An important concept in design and the use of abstractions is information hiding. Information should only be accessible to those parts of a program that need to know. The use of packages and private data types to hide unnecessary detail is the cornerstone of good Ada programming. Indeed as we have stated before Ada is a language which aims to encourage the development of reusable software components; the package is the key component.

Designing an Ada program is therefore largely concerned with designing a group of packages and the interfaces between them. Often we will hope to use one or more existing packages. For this to be possible it is clear that they must have been designed with consistent, clean and sufficiently general interfaces. The difficulties are perhaps in deciding what items are sufficiently related or fundamental to belong together in a package and also how general to make the package. If a package is too general it might be clumsy and inefficient; if not general enough it will not be as useful as it might.

The interface to a package is provided by its specification; at least that provides the syntax of how to use the interface, the semantics must also be defined and that can only be provided by a natural language commentary. Thus consider the package STACK of Section 8.1; its specification guarantees that it will provide subprograms PUSH and POP with certain parameter and result types. However the specification does not, of itself, guarantee that a call of POP will in fact remove and deliver the top item from the stack. From the point of view of the language it would be quite acceptable for the package body to be

```
package body STACK is
    procedure PUSH(X: INTEGER) is
    begin
        null;
    end;

    function POP return INTEGER is
    begin
        return 0;
    end;
end STACK;
```

However, in our imagined future world of the software components industry anyone selling such package bodies would soon go out of business.

We will now discuss some categories of related items that might make up useful packages.

A very simple form of package is one which merely consists of a group of related types and constants and has no body. The packages SYSTEM and ASCII inside STANDARD are in this category. A further example in Section 8.1 is the package DIURNAL; this does not seem a good example – if it has an array TOMORROW then surely it should also have YESTERDAY. Better examples might be packages of related mathematical constants, conversion constants (metric to imperial say), tables of physical and chemical constants and so on. The last could be

```
package ELEMENTS is
    type ELEMENT is (H, He, Li, ...);
        -- beware of Indium – In is reserved!
    ATOMIC_WEIGHT: array (ELEMENT) of REAL
                      := (1.008, 4.003, 6.940, ...);
    ...
end ELEMENTS;
```

Another case is where the package contains functions related by application area. An obvious example is the mathematical library mentioned in Section 16.3. The individual functions in such a case are really independent although for efficiency SIN and COS for example are likely to share a common procedure. The package body enables us to hide such a procedure from the user because its existence is merely an implementation detail.

Sometimes a package is needed in order to hide a benevolent side effect – an obvious example is the package RANDOM in Exercise 8.1(**1**).

Packages such as INPUT_OUTPUT encapsulate a great deal of hidden information and provide a number of related services. A problem here is deciding whether to provide additional subprograms for convenience or to stick to only those absolutely necessary. The package TEXT_IO contains many convenience subprograms.

Many packages can be classified as means of providing controlled access to some form of data base. The data base may consist of just one item as in the package RANDOM or it could be the symbol tables of a compiler or a grand commercial style data base and so on. The package BANK in Section 9.3 is another example.

An important use of packages is to provide new data types and associated operations. Obvious examples are the packages COMPLEX_NUMBERS (Section 9.1), RATIONAL_NUMBERS (Exercise 9.1(**2**)) and QUEUES (Exercise 11.4(**3**)). In such cases the use of private types enables us to separate the representation of the type from the operations upon it. In a way the new types can be seen as natural extensions to the language.

Packages of this sort raise the question of whether we should use operators rather than functions. Ada is not so flexible as some other languages; new operator forms cannot be introduced and the precedence levels are fixed. This ensures that over-enthusiastic use of operators cannot lead to programs that do not even look like Ada programs as can happen with languages such as POP–2. Even so Ada provides opportunities for surprises. We could write

```
function "-"(X,Y: INTEGER) return INTEGER is
begin
    return STANDARD."+"(X,Y);
end "-";
```

but it would obviously be very foolish to do so. Hence a good general guideline is to minimise surprises.

Operators should be considered for functions with a natural mathematical flavour. As a general rule the normal algebraic properties of the operators should be preserved if this is possible. Thus "+" and "*" should be commutative. Mixed type arithmetic is best avoided but there are situations where it is necessary.

The definitions of the operators in the package COMPLEX_NUMBERS have the expected properties and do not allow mixed working. Perhaps we should also have added unary "+" and "−" for completeness as we did for the package RATIONAL_NUMBERS. It would be nice if type conversion could be done by overloading the type name so that we could write COMPLEX(2.0) rather than CONS(2.0, 0.0). However Ada does not allow this. Type conversion of this form is restricted to the predefined and derived numeric types.

On the other hand, consider the operators in the package CALENDAR in Section 14.3. Here the very essence of the problem requires mixed type addition but commutativity is preserved by providing two overloadings of "+".

When introducing mathematical types such as COMPLEX and RATIONAL_NUMBERS it is always best to use private types. We will then need to provide constructor and selector functions as well as the natural operations themselves. It will usually be the case that construction and selection are best done with functional notation whereas the natural operations can be done with the operators. However, in the case of rational numbers the division operator "/" provides a natural notation for construction.

There is a general and difficult question of how much to provide in a package for a mathematical type. The bare minimum may be rather spartan and incur all users in unnecessary creation of additional subprograms. To be generous might make the package too cumbersome. For instance should we provide a relational operator and if so should we provide all four? Should input-output be included? We leave such questions for the reader to answer from his or her own experience according to the needs of the application.

Another important issue is storage allocation. This is well illustrated by a type such as POLYNOMIAL introduced in Section 11.1. If this is implemented using a discrimated record thus

```
type POLYNOMIAL(N: INTEGER range 0 .. MAX:=0) is
    record
        A: array (0 .. N) of INTEGER;
    end record;
```

then in the case of unconstrained polynomials the compiler will allocate the maximum space that could be required. Hence it is important that the range of the discriminant has a sensible upper bound. If we had written

```
type POLYNOMIAL(N: INTEGER:=0) is ...
```

then each unconstrained polynomial would have had the space for an array of length INTEGER'LAST and we would presumably soon run out of storage.

If all the polynomials are to be fairly small then using a discriminated record is probably satisfactory. On the other hand if they are likely to be of greatly varying size then it is probably better to use access types. Indeed a mixed strategy could be used – a fixed array for the first few terms and then the use of an access type for the remainder. In order that such alternative implementation strategies can be properly organised and hidden from the user it is clear that the polynomial should be a private type. The design of a suitable package is left as an informal exercise for the reader.

In designing packages there is the question of what to do when something goes wrong. This bring us to exceptions. Although not new to programming languages they are nevertheless not widely used except in PL/I and the experience with PL/I has not been satisfactory. However, exceptions in Ada are different to those in PL/I in one most important aspect. In Ada one cannot go back to the point where the exception was raised but is forced to consider a proper alternative to the part of the program that went wrong.

Having said that, exceptions nevertheless need care. In Chapter 10 we warned against the unnecessary use of exceptions and in particular the casual raising of the predefined exceptions since we have no guarantee, when handling such an exception, that it was raised for the reason we had in mind.

The first goal should always be to have clean and complete interfaces. As an example consider again the factorial function and the action to be taken when the parameter is illegal. We could consider

- printing a message,
- returning a default value,
- returning a status via a Boolean parameter,
- calling an error procedure,
- raising an exception.

Printing a message is highly unsatisfactory because it raises a host of detailed problems such as the identity of the file, the format of the message and so on. Moreover, it gives the calling program no control over the action it would like to take and some file is cluttered with messages. Furthermore there is still the question of what to do after having printed the message.

Another possibility is to return a default value such as -1 as in Exercise 10.1(**2**). This is not satisfactory since there is no guarantee that the user will check for this default value upon return. If we could rely upon the user doing so then we could equally rely upon the user checking the parameter of the function before calling it in the first place.

If we wish to return an auxiliary status value via another parameter then, as we saw when discussing PUSH and POP in Section 10.2, we can no longer use a function anyway and would have to use a procedure instead. We also have to rely upon the caller again as in the case of the default value.

We could call a global procedure to be supplied by the user. This means agreeing on a standard name which is unsatisfactory. We cannot pass the error procedure as a parameter and to resort to the generic mechanism really is using a steam hammer to crack a nut. In any case we still have the problem, as with printing a message, of what to do afterwards and how to return finally from the function. It is highly naive to suppose that the program can just stop. The manager of the steelworks would not wish the control part of the program to stop just because of a minor error in some other part; there must be a way of carrying on.

There are only two ways out of a subprogram in Ada; back to the point of call or by a propagated exception (the global goto and label parameters of other languages are effectively replaced by the exception). We seem to have eliminated the possibility of returning to the point of call as not reliable and so have to come to the conclusion that the raising of an exception is the appropriate solution.

Another criterion we should consider when deciding whether to use exceptions is whether we expect the condition to arise in the normal course of events or not. If we do then an exception is probably wrong. As an example the end of file condition in the package INPUT_OUTPUT is tested for by a Boolean function and not an exception. We naturally expect to come to the end of the file and so must test for it – see the answer to Exercise 15.1(**1**).

On the other hand if we are using the package STACK in say an interpreter for mathematical expressions, then, provided that the interpreter is written correctly, we know that the stack cannot underflow. An exception for this unexpected condition is acceptable. Note also that when using INPUT_OUTPUT, if we accidentally attempt to read after the end of the file then an exception (END_ERROR) is raised.

The raising of exceptions is, however, not a panacea. We cannot sweep the problem under the carpet in this way. The exception must be handled somewhere otherwise the program will terminate. In fact this is one of their advantages – if the user does nothing then the program will terminate safely, whereas if we return status values and the user does nothing then the program will probably ramble on in a fruitless way.

The indiscriminate use of **others** in an exception handler should be avoided. If we write **others** we are really admitting that anything could have gone wrong and we should take appropriate action; we should not use **others** as shorthand for the exceptions we anticipate.

Another major design area concerns the use of tasks. It is usually fairly clear that a problem needs a solution involving tasks but it is not always clear how the various activities should be allocated to individual tasks.

There are perhaps two major problems to be solved regarding the interactions between tasks. One concerns the transmission of messages between tasks, the other the controlling of access to common data by several tasks.

The rendezvous provides a natural mechanism for the closely coupled transmission of a message; examples are provided by the interaction between mother and the other members of her family in the procedure SHOPPING in Section 14.2 and by the interaction between the server and the customer in the package COBBLERS of Exercise 14.8(**1**). If the transmission needs to be decoupled so that the sender can carry on before the message is received then some intermediary task is required. Examples are the task BUFFERING in Section 14.4 and the task type MAILBOX in Section 14.5.

Controlled access to common data is, in Ada, also done by an intermediary task whereas in other languages it may use passive constructions such as monitors or low level primitives such as semaphores. The Ada approach usually provides a clearer and safer solution to the problem. An example is the task PROTECTED_VARIABLE in Section 14.4. Quite often the task is encapsulated in a package in order to enforce the required protocol; examples are the package READER_WRITER of Section 14.4 and the package RESOURCE_ALLOCATOR of Section 14.7.

Sometimes the distinction between message passing and controlling data access is blurred; the task BUFFERING at the macro level is passing messages whereas at the micro level it is controlling access to the buffer.

Another categorisation of tasks is between users and servers. A pure server task is one with entries but which calls no other tasks whereas a pure user has no entries but calls other tasks. The distinction is emphasised by the asymmetry of the naming in the rendezvous. The server does not know the names of user tasks whereas the user tasks must know the names of the server tasks in order to call their entries. Sometimes a task is part server and part user; an example is the task type READ_AGENT in Section 14.6.

One problem when designing a set of interacting tasks is deciding which way round the entries are to go. Our intuitive model of servers and users should help. The entries belong in the servers. Another criterion is provided by the consideration of alternatives; if a task is to have a choice of rendezvous via a select statement then it must own the entries and therefore be a server. A select statement can be used to accept one of several entry calls but cannot be used to call one of several entries.

It cannot be emphasised too much that raising failure in or aborting tasks must not be done casually. These statements are for extreme situations only. One possible use is in a supervisory task where it may be desirable to close down a complete subsystem in response to a command from a human operator.

The reason for wishing to avoid abort and failure is that they make it very difficult to provide reliable services as we saw with the package READER_WRITER in Section 14.6. If we know that the users cannot be abnormally terminated then the fancy use of secret agents is not necessary; indeed that example should be considered as illustrating what can be done rather than what should be done.

A multitasking Ada program will often be seen as a set of cooperating tasks designed together. In such circumstances we can rely on the calling tasks to obey the necessary protocols and the design of the servers is then simplified.

The use of timed out entry calls also needs some care but is a very natural and common requirement in real time systems. Services should where possible be able to cope with timed out calls.

Finally there are generics and the whole question of parameterisation. Should we write specific packages or very general ones? This is a familiar problem with subprograms and generics merely add a new dimension. As stated at the beginning of this section there is as yet little experience of the use of Ada and so it seems somewhat premature to give advice in this area. Indeed, in the imagined future market for software components it is likely that packages of all sorts of generalities and performance will be available. We can conclude by imagining a future conversation in our local software shop

Customer: Could I have a look at the reader writer package you have in the window?

Server: Certainly sir. Would you be interested in this robust version – proof against abort and failure? Or we have this slick version for trusty callers. Just arrived this week.

Customer: Well – it's for a cooperating system so the new one sounds good. How much is it?

Server: It's 250 Eurodollars but as it's new there is a special offer with it – a free copy of this random number generator and 10% off your next certification.

Customer: Great. Is it validated?

Server: All our products conform to the highest standards sir. The parameter mechanism conforms to ES98263 and it has the usual international multitasking certificate.

Customer: OK, I'll take it.

Server: Will you take it as it is or shall I instantiate it for you?

Customer: As it is please. I prefer to do my own instantiation.

. . .

On this fantasy note we come to the end of this book. It is hoped that the reader will have gained some general understanding of the principles of Ada as well as a lot of the detail. Further understanding will come with use and the author hopes that he has in some small way prepared the reader for the future.

Appendix 1 Reserved Words, Attributes and Pragmas

This appendix lists the reserved words and predefined attributes and pragmas. An implementation may define additional attributes and pragmas but not additional reserved words.

The lists of attributes and pragmas are taken from Appendices A and B of the LRM. The references have been altered to correspond to appropriate sections of this book.

A1.1 Reserved words

The following words are reserved; their use is described in the sections indicated.

abort	14.6
accept	14.2
access	11.3
all	11.3
and	4.7, 4.9
array	6.1
at	15.4
begin	4.2, 7.1, 8.1, 14.1
body	8.1, 14.1
case	5.2, 11.2
constant	4.1
declare	4.2
delay	14.3
delta	12.4, 13.2
digits	12.3, 13.2
do	14.2
else	4.9, 5.1, 14.4
elsif	5.1
end	4.2, 7.1, 8.1, 14.1, 14.2
entry	14.2
exception	10.1
exit	5.3
for	5.3, 15.4
function	7.1

generic	13.1
goto	5.4
if	5.1
in	4.9, 5.3, 7.3
is	4.3, 5.2, 7.1, 8.1, 11.2, 14.1
limited	9.2, 13.2
loop	5.3
mod	4.5, 15.4
new	11.3, 11.6, 13.1
not	4.7, 4.9
null	5.2, 6.5, 11.2, 11.3
of	6.1
or	4.7, 4.9, 14.4
others	5.2, 6.2, 10.1
out	7.3
package	8.1
pragma	2.5
private	9.1, 13.1
procedure	7.3
raise	10.2
range	4.4, 6.2, 13.2, 15.4
record	6.5
rem	4.5
renames	8.5
return	7.1, 7.3, 14.2
reverse	5.3
select	14.4
separate	8.3
subtype	4.4
task	14.1
terminate	14.6
then	4.9, 5.1
type	4.3
use	8.1, 15.4
when	5.2, 5.3, 10.1, 11.2, 14.4
while	5.3
with	8.2, 13.3
xor	4.7

The reserved words **delta**, **digits** and **range** are also used as attributes.

A1.2 Predefined attributes

The following attributes are predefined in the language.

Attribute of any object or subprogram X

ADDRESS A number corresponding to the first storage unit occupied by X (see 15.4). Overloaded on all predefined integer types.

Attribute of any type or subtype T *(except a task type)*

BASE Applied to a subtype, yields the base type; applied to a type, yields the type itself. This attribute may be used only to obtain further attributes of a type, e.g. T'BASE'FIRST (see 12.1).

Attribute of any type or subtype (except a task type), or object thereof

SIZE The maximum number of bits required to hold an object of that type (see 15.4). Of type INTEGER.

Attributes of any scalar type or subtype T

FIRST The minimum value of T (see 4.8).

LAST The maximum value of T (see 4.8).

IMAGE If X is a value of type T, T'IMAGE(X) is a string representing the value in a standard display form.

For an enumeration type, the values are represented, in minimum width, as either the corresponding enumeration literal, in upper case, or as the corresponding character literal, within quotes.

For an integer type, the values are represented as decimal numbers of minimum width. For a fixed point type, the values are represented as decimal fractions of minimum width, with sufficient decimal places just to accommodate the declared accuracy. For a floating point type, the values are represented in exponential notation with one significant characteristic digit, sufficient mantissa digits just to accommodate the declared accuracy, and a signed three-digit exponent. The exponent letter is in upper case. For all numeric types, negative values are prefixed with a minus sign and positive values have no prefix.

VALUE If S is a string, T'VALUE(S) is the value in T that can be represented in display form by the string S. If the string does not denote any possible value, the exception DATA_ERROR is raised; if the value lies outside the range of T, the exception CONSTRAINT_ERROR is raised. All legal lexical forms are legal display forms (see 3.3 and 3.4).

Attributes of any discrete type or subtype

POS If X is a value of type T, T'POS(X) is the integer position of X in the ordered sequence of values T'FIRST . . T'LAST, the position of T'FIRST being itself for integer types and zero for enumeration types (see 4.8).

VAL If J is an integer, T'VAL(J) is the value of enumeration type T whose

POS is J. If no such value exists, the exception CONSTRAINT_ERROR is raised (see 4.8).

PRED If X is a value of type T, T'PRED(X) is the preceding value. The exception CONSTRAINT_ERROR is raised if X=T'FIRST (see 4.8).

SUCC If X is a value of type T, T'SUCC(X) is the succeeding value. The exception CONSTRAINT_ERROR is raised if X=T'LAST (see 4.8).

Attributes of any fixed point type or subtype T

DELTA The delta specified in the declaration of T (see 12.4). Of type universal real.

ACTUAL_DELTA The delta of the model numbers used to represent T (see 12.4). Of type universal real.

BITS The number of bits required to represent the model numbers of T (see 12.4). Of type universal integer.

LARGE The largest model number of T (see 12.4). Of type universal real.

MACHINE_ROUNDS True if the machine performs true rounding (to nearest even) when computing values of type T (see 15.5). Of type BOOLEAN.

Attributes of any floating point type or subtype T

DIGITS The number of digits specified in the declaration of T (see 12.3). Of type universal integer.

MANTISSA The number of bits in the mantissa of the representation of model numbers of T (see 12.3). Of type universal integer.

EMAX The largest exponent value of the representation of model numbers of T (see 12.3). The smallest exponent value is minus EMAX. Of type universal integer.

SMALL The smallest positive model number of T (see 12.3). Of type universal real.

LARGE The largest model number of T (see 12.3). Of type universal real.

EPSILON The difference between unity and the smallest model number of T greater than unity (see 12.3). Both unity and T'EPSILON are model numbers of T. Of type universal real.

MACHINE_RADIX The radix of the exponent of the underlying machine representation of T (see 15.5). Of type universal integer.

MACHINE_MANTISSA The number of bits in the mantissa of the underlying machine representation of T (see 15.5). Of type universal integer.

MACHINE_EMAX The largest exponent value of the underlying machine representation of T (see 15.5). Of type universal integer.

MACHINE_EMIN The smallest exponent value of the underlying machine representation of T (see 15.5). Of type universal integer.

MACHINE_ROUNDS True if the machine performs true rounding (to nearest even) when computing values of type T (see 15.5). Of type BOOLEAN.

MACHINE_OVERFLOWS True if, when a computed value is too large to be represented correctly by the underlying machine representation of T, the exception NUMERIC_ERROR is raised (see 15.5). Of type BOOLEAN.

Attributes of any array type or subtype, or object thereof

FIRST If A is a constrained array type or subtype, or an array object, A'FIRST is the lower bound of the first index (see 6.1).

FIRST(J) Similarly, the lower bound of the J'th index, where J must be a static integer expression (see 6.1).

LAST If A is a constrained array type or subtype, or an array object, A'LAST is the upper bound of the first index (see 6.1).

LAST(J) Similarly, the upper bound of the J'th index, where J must be a static integer expression (see 6.1).

LENGTH If A is a constrained array type or subtype, or an array object, A'LENGTH is the number of elements in the first dimension of A (see 6.1).

LENGTH(J) Similarly, the number of elements in the J'th dimension, where J must be a static expression (see 6.1).

RANGE If A is a constrained array type or subtype, or an array object, A'RANGE is the range A'FIRST .. A'LAST (see 6.1).

RANGE(J) Similarly, the range A'FIRST(J) .. A'LAST(J), where J must be a static integer expression (see 6.1).

Attribute of any record type with discriminants

CONSTRAINED If R is an object of any record type with discriminants, or of any subtype thereof, R'CONSTRAINED is true if and only if the discriminant values of R cannot be modified (see 11.1). Of type BOOLEAN.

Attributes of any record component C

POSITION The offset within the record, in storage units, of the first unit of storage occupied by C (see 15.5). Of type INTEGER.

FIRST_BIT The offset, from the start of C'POSITION, of the first bit used to hold the value of C (see 15.5). Of type INTEGER.

LAST_BIT The offset, from the start of C'POSITION, of the last bit used to hold the value of C. C'LAST_BIT need not lie within the same storage unit as C'FIRST_BIT (see 15.5). Of type INTEGER.

Attribute of any access type P

STORAGE_SIZE The total number of storage units reserved for allocation for all objects of type P (see 15.4). Overloaded on all predefined integer types.

Attributes of any task, or object of a task type, T

TERMINATED True when T is terminated (see 14.6). Of type BOOLEAN.

PRIORITY The (static) priority of T (see 14.3). Of type universal integer.

FAILURE The exception that, if raised, causes FAILURE within T (see 14.6).

STORAGE_SIZE The number of storage units allocated for the execution of T (see 15.4). Overloaded on all predefined integer types.

Attribute of any entry E

COUNT Momentarily, the number of calling tasks waiting on E (see 14.4). Of type INTEGER.

A1.3 Predefined pragmas

The following pragmas are predefined in the language.

CONTROLLED Takes an access type name as argument. It must appear in the same declarative part as the access type definition. It specifies that automatic storage reclamation should not be performed for objects of the access type except upon leaving the scope of the access type definition (see 11.3).

INLINE Takes a list of subprogram names as arguments. It must appear in the same declarative part as the named subprograms. It specifies that the subprogram bodies should be expanded inline at each call (see 15.5).

INTERFACE Takes a language name and subprogam name as arguments. It must appear after the subprogram specification in the same declarative part or in the same package specification. It specifies that the body of the subprogram is written in the given other language, whose calling conventions are to be observed (see 15.7).

LIST Takes ON or OFF as argument. This pragma can appear anywhere. It specifies that listing of the program unit is to be continued or suspended until a LIST pragma is given with the opposite argument.

MEMORY_SIZE Takes an integer number as argument. This pragma can only appear before a library unit. It establishes the available number of storage units in memory (see 15.5).

OPTIMIZE Takes TIME or SPACE as argument. This pragma can only appear in a declarative part and it applies to the block or body enclosing the declarative part. It specifies whether time or space is the primary optimisation criterion.

PACK Takes a record or array type name as argument. The position of the pragma is governed by the same rules as for a representation specification. It specifies that storage minimisation should be the main criterion when selecting the representation of the given type (see 15.5).

PRIORITY Takes a static expression as argument. It must appear in a task (type) specification or the outermost declarative part of a main program. It specifies the priority of the task (or tasks of the task type) or the main program (see 14.3).

STORAGE_UNIT Takes an integer number as argument. This pragma can only appear before a library unit. It establishes the number of bits per storage unit (see 15.5).

SUPPRESS Takes a check name and optionally also either an object name or a type name as arguments. It must appear in the declarative part of a unit (block or body). It specifies that the designated check is to be suppressed in the unit. In the absence of the optional name, the pragma applies to all operations within the unit. Otherwise its effect is restricted to operations on the named object or to operations on objects of the named type (see 15.5).

SYSTEM Takes a name as argument. This pragma can only appear before a library unit. It establishes the name of the object machine (see 15.5).

Appendix 2 Predefined Language Environment

As mentioned earlier, certain entities are predefined through their declaration in a special package STANDARD. It should not be thought that this package necessarily actually exists; it is just that the compiler behaves as if it does. Indeed, as we shall see, some entities notionally declared in STANDARD cannot be truly declared in Ada at all. The general effect of STANDARD is indicated by the following outline specification which is taken from Appendix C of the LRM.

```
package STANDARD is
    type BOOLEAN is (FALSE,TRUE);

    function "not"(X: BOOLEAN) return BOOLEAN;

    function "and"(X,Y: BOOLEAN) return BOOLEAN;
    function "or"(X,Y: BOOLEAN) return BOOLEAN;
    function "xor"(X,Y: BOOLEAN) return BOOLEAN;

    type INTEGER is implementation defined;

    function "+"(X: INTEGER) return INTEGER;
    function "-"(X: INTEGER) return INTEGER;
    function ABS(X: INTEGER) return INTEGER;
    function "+"(X,Y: INTEGER) return INTEGER;
    function "-"(X,Y: INTEGER) return INTEGER;
    function "*"(X,Y: INTEGER) return INTEGER;
    function "/"(X,Y: INTEGER) return INTEGER;
    function "rem"(X,Y: INTEGER) return INTEGER;
    function "mod"(X,Y: INTEGER) return INTEGER;
    function "**"(X: INTEGER; Y: INTEGER range 0 .. INTEGER'LAST)
                                                    return INTEGER;
    -- Similarly for SHORT_INTEGER and LONG_INTEGER if implemented

    type FLOAT is implementation defined;

    function "+"(X: FLOAT) return FLOAT;
    function "-"(X: FLOAT) return FLOAT;
    function ABS(X: FLOAT) return FLOAT;

    function "+"(X,Y: FLOAT) return FLOAT;
    function "-"(X,Y: FLOAT) return FLOAT;
    function "*"(X,Y: FLOAT) return FLOAT;
    function "/"(X,Y: FLOAT) return FLOAT;
    function "**"(X: FLOAT; Y: INTEGER) return FLOAT;
```

```
-- Similarly for SHORT_FLOAT and LONG_FLOAT if implemented

-- The following characters comprise the standard ASCII character set
-- Character literals corresponding to control characters are not iden-
   tifiers. They are indicated in italics in this definition

type CHARACTER is

    (nul,  soh,  stx,  etx,         eot, enq,  ack,  bel,
     bs,   ht,   lf,   vt,          ff,  cr,   so,   si,
     dle,  dc1,  dc2,  dc3,         dc4, nak,  syn,  etb,
     can,  em,   sub,  esc,         fs,  gs,   rs,   us,
     ' ',  '!',  '"',  '#',         '$', '%',  '&',  ''',
     '(',  ')',  '*',  '+',         ',', '-',  '.',  '/',
     '0',  '1',  '2',  '3',         '4', '5',  '6',  '7',
     '8',  '9',  ':',  ';',         '<', '=',  '>',  '?',

     '@',  'A'   'B',  'C',         'D', 'E',  'F',  'G',
     'H',  'I',  'J',  'K',         'L', 'M',  'N',  'O',
     'P',  'Q',  'R',  'S',         'T', 'U',  'V',  'W',
     'X',  'Y',  'Z',  '[',         '@', ']',  '^',  '_',
     '`',  'a',  'b',  'c',         'd', 'e',  'f',  'g',
     'h',  'i',  'j',  'k',         'l', 'm',  'n',  'o',
     'p',  'q',  'r',  's',         't', 'u',  'v',  'w',
     'x',  'y',  'z',  '{',         '|', '}',  '~',  del);

package ASCII is

    -- Control characters:

    NUL: constant CHARACTER:=nul;
    SOH: constant CHARACTER:=soh;
    STX: constant CHARACTER:=stx;
    ETX: constant CHARACTER:=etx;
    EOT: constant CHARACTER:=eot;
    ENQ: constant CHARACTER:=enq;
    ACK: constant CHARACTER:=ack;
    BEL: constant CHARACTER:=bel;
    BS:  constant CHARACTER:=bs;
    HT:  constant CHARACTER:=ht;
    LF:  constant CHARACTER:=lf;
    VT:  constant CHARACTER:=vt;
    FF:  constant CHARACTER:=ff;
    CR:  constant CHARACTER:=cr;
    SO:  constant CHARACTER:=so;
    SI:  constant CHARACTER:=si;
    DLE: constant CHARACTER:=dle;
    DC1: constant CHARACTER:=dc1;
    DC2: constant CHARACTER:=dc2;
    DC3: constant CHARACTER:=dc3;
    DC4: constant CHARACTER:=dc4;
```

```
        NAK: constant CHARACTER:=nak;
        SYN: constant CHARACTER:=syn;
        ETB: constant CHARACTER:=etb;
        CAN: constant CHARACTER:=can;
        EM:  constant CHARACTER:=em;
        SUB: constant CHARACTER:=sub;
        ESC: constant CHARACTER:=esc;
        FS:  constant CHARACTER:=fs;
        GS:  constant CHARACTER:=gs;
        RS:  constant CHARACTER:=rs;
        US:  constant CHARACTER:=us;
        DEL: constant CHARACTER:=del;

        -- Other characters

        EXCLAM       : constant CHARACTER:='!';
        SHARP        : constant CHARACTER:='#';
        DOLLAR       : constant CHARACTER:='$';
        QUERY        : constant CHARACTER:='?';
        AT_SIGN      : constant CHARACTER:='@';
        L_BRACKET    : constant CHARACTER:='[';
        BACK_SLASH   : constant CHARACTER:=' ';
        R_BRACKET    : constant CHARACTER:=']';
        CIRCUMFLEX   : constant CHARACTER:='^';
        GRAVE        : constant CHARACTER:='`';
        L_BRACE      : constant CHARACTER:='{';
        BAR          : constant CHARACTER:='|';
        R_BRACE      : constant CHARACTER:='}';
        TILDE        : constant CHARACTER:='~';

        -- Lower case letters

        LC_A: constant CHARACTER:='a';
        ...
        LC_Z: constant CHARACTER:='z';

    end ASCII;

    -- Predefined types and subtypes

    subtype NATURAL is INTEGER range 1 .. INTEGER'LAST;
    subtype PRIORITY is INTEGER range implementation_defined;

    type STRING is array (NATURAL range <>) of character;

    type DURATION is delta implementation_defined range
                           implementation_defined;

    -- The predefined exceptions

    CONSTRAINT_ERROR: exception;
    NUMERIC_ERROR   : exception;
    SELECT_ERROR    : exception;
    STORAGE_ERROR   : exception;
    TASKING_ERROR   : exception;
```

```
-- The machine dependent machine SYSTEM

package SYSTEM is
    type SYSTEM_NAME is
                        implementation_defined_enumeration_type;

    NAME: constant SYSTEM_NAME:=implementation_defined;
    STORAGE      : constant       :=implementation_defined;
    MEMORY_SIZE: constant         :=implementation_defined;
    MIN_INT      : constant       :=implementation_defined;
    MAX_INT      : constant       :=implementation_defined;
    ...
end SYSTEM;

for CHARACTER use  -- 128 ASCII character set without holes
    (0,1,2,3,4,5,...,125,126,127);

pragma PACK(STRING);

end STANDARD;
```

The above specification is not complete. There are, of course, also various overloadings of =, /=, <, <=, > and >=. Moreover, each further type definition introduces new overloadings of some operators. All types, except limited private types, introduce new overloadings of = and /=. All scalar types and discrete one dimensional array types introduce new overloadings of & and those with BOOLEAN components also introduce new overloadings of **and**, **or**, **xor** and **not**. Finally, all fixed point types introduce new overloadings of +, −, *, / and ABS.

In addition there are also certain other predefined library units such as CALENDAR (see Section 14.3), INPUT_OUTPUT (see Section 15.1) and TEXT_IO (see Section 15.2).

Appendix 3 Glossary

The following glossary is reproduced from Appendix D of the LRM:

Access type: An access type is a type whose objects are created by execution of an allocator. An access value designates such an object.

Aggregate: An aggregate is a written form denoting a composite value. An array aggregate denotes a value of an array type; a record aggregate denotes a value of a record type. The components of an aggregate may be specified using either positional or named association.

Allocator: An allocator creates a new object of an access type, and returns an access value designating the created object.

Attribute: An attribute is a predefined characteristic of a named entity.

Body: A body is a program unit defining the execution of a subprogram, package, or task. A body stub is a replacement for a body that is compiled separately.

Collection: A collection is the entire set of allocated objects of an access type.

Compilation unit: A compilation unit is a program unit presented for compilation as an independent text. It is preceded by a context specification, naming the other compilation units on which it depends. A compilation unit may be the specification or body of a subprogram or package.

Component: A component denotes a part of a composite object. An indexed component is a name containing expressions denoting indices, and names a component in an array or an entry in an entry family. A selected component is the identifier of the component, prefixed by the name of the entity of which it is a component.

Composite type: An object of a composite type comprises several components. An array type is a composite type, all of whose components are of the same type and subtype; the individual components are selected by their indices. A record type is a composite type whose components may be of different types; the individual components are selected by their identifiers.

Constraint: A constraint is a restriction on the set of possible values of a type. A range constraint specifies lower and upper bounds of the values of a scalar type. An accuracy constraint specifies the relative or absolute error bound of values of a real type. An index constraint specifies lower and upper bounds of an array index. A discriminant constraint specifies particular values of the discriminants of a record or private type.

Context specification: A context specification, prefixed to a compilation unit, defines the other compilation units upon which it depends.

Declarative part: A declarative part is a sequence of declarations and related information such as subprogram bodies and representation specifications that apply over a region of a program text.

Derived type: A derived type is a type whose operations and values are taken from those of an existing type.

Discrete type: A discrete type has an ordered set of distinct values. The discrete types are the enumeration and integer types. Discrete types may be used for indexing and iteration, and for choices in case statements and record variants.

Discriminant: A discriminant is a syntactically distinguished component of a record. The presence of some record components (other than discriminants) may depend on the value of a discriminant.

Elaboration: Elaboration is the process by which a declaration achieves its effect. For example it can associate a name with a program entity or initialise a newly declared variable.

Entity: An entity is anything that can be named or denoted in a program. Objects, types, values, program units, are all entities.

Entry: An entry is used for communication between tasks. Externally an entry is called just as a subprogram is called; its internal behaviour is specified by one or more accept statements specifying the actions to be performed when the entry is called.

Enumeration type: An enumeration type is a discrete type whose values are given explicitly in the type declaration. These values may be either identifiers or character literals.

Exception: An exception is an event that causes suspension of normal program execution. Bringing an exception to attention is called raising the exception. An exception handler is a piece of program text specifying a response to the exception. Execution of such a program text is called handling the exception.

Expression: An expression is a part of a program that computes a value.

Generic program unit: A generic program unit is a subprogram or package specified with a generic clause. A generic clause contains the declaration of generic parameters. A generic program unit may be thought of as a possibly parameterised model of program units. Instances (that is, filled-in copies) of the model can be obtained be generic instantiation. Such instantiated program units define subprograms and packages that can be used directly in a program.

Introduce: An identifier is introduced by its declaration at the point of its first occurrence.

Lexical unit: A lexical unit is one of the basic syntactic elements making up a program. A lexical unit is an identifier, a number, a character literal, a string, a delimiter, or a comment.

Literal: A literal denotes an explicit value of a given type, for example a number, an enumeration value, a character, or a string.

Model number: A model number is an exactly representable value of a real numeric type. Operations of a real type are defined in terms of operations on the model numbers of the type. The properties of the model numbers and of the operations are the minimal properties preserved by all implementations of the real type.

Object: An object is a variable or a constant. An object can denote any kind of data element, whether a scalar value, a composite value, or a value in an access type.

Overloading: Overloading is the property of literals, identifiers, and operators that can have several alternative meanings within the same scope. For example an overloaded enumeration literal is a literal appearing in two or more enumeration types; an overloaded subprogram is a subprogram whose designator can denote one of several subprograms, depending upon the kind of its parameters and returned value.

Package: A package is a program unit specifying a collection of related entities such as constants, variables, types and subprograms. The visible part of a package contains the entities that may be used from ouside the package. The private part of a package contains structural details that are irrelevant to the user of the package but that complete the specification of the visible entities. The body of a package contains implementations of subprograms or tasks (possibly other packages) specified in the visible part.

Parameter: A parameter is one of the named entities associated with a subprogram, entry, or generic program unit. A formal parameter is an identifier used to denote the named entity in the unit body. An actual parameter is the particular entity associated with the corresponding formal parameter in a subprogram call, entry call, or generic instantiation. A parameter mode specifies whether the parameter is used for input, output or input-output of data. A positional parameter is an actual parameter passed in positional order. A named parameter is an actual parameter passed by naming the corresponding formal parameter.

Pragma: A pragma is an instruction to the compiler, and may be language defined or implementation defined.

Private type: A private type is a type whose structure and set of values are clearly defined, but not known to the user of the type. A private type is known only by its discriminants and by the set of operations defined for it. A private type and its applicable operations are defined in the visible part of a package. Assignment and comparison for equality or inequality are also defined for private types, unless the private type is marked as limited.

Qualified expression: A qualified expression is an expression qualified by the name of a type or subtype. It can be used to state the type or subtype of an expression, for example for an overloaded literal.

Range: A range is a contiguous set of values of a scalar type. A range is specified by giving the lower and upper bounds for the values.

Rendezvous: A rendezvous is the interaction that occurs between two parallel tasks when one task has called an entry of the other task, and a corresponding accept statement is being executed by the other task on behalf of the calling task.

Representation specification: Representation specifications specify the mapping between data types and features of the underlying machine that execute a program. In some cases, they completely specify the mapping, in other cases they provide criteria for choosing a mapping.

Scalar types: A scalar type is a type whose values have no components. Scalar types comprise discrete types (that is, enumeration and integer types) and real types.

Scope: The scope of a declaration is the region of text over which the declaration has an effect.

Static expression: A static expression is one whose value does not depend on any dynamically computed values of variables.

Subprograms: A subprogram is an executable program unit, possibly with parameters for communication between the subprogram and its point of call. A subprogram declaration specifies the name of the subprogram and its parameters; a subprogram body specifies its execution. A subprogram may be a procedure, which performs an action, or a function, which returns a result.

Subtype: A subtype of a type is obtained from the type by constraining the set of possible values of the type. The operations over a subtype are the same as those of the type from which the subtype is obtained.

Task: A task is a program unit that may operate in parallel with other program units. A task specification establishes the name of the task and the names and parameters of its entries; a task body defines its execution. A task type is a specification that permits the subsequent declaration of any number of similar tasks.

Type: A type characterises a set of values and a set of operations applicable to those values. A type definition is a language construct introducing a type. A type declaration associates a name with a type introduced by a type definition.

Use clause: A use clause opens the visibility to declarations given in the visible part of a package.

Variant: A variant part of a record specifies alternative record components, depending on a discriminant of the record. Each value of the discriminant establishes a particular alternative of the variant part.

Visibility: At a given point in a program text, the declaration of an entity with a certain identifier is said to be visible if the entity is an acceptable meaning for an occurrence at that point of the identifier.

Appendix 4 Syntax

The following syntax rules are taken from Appendix E of the LRM. The rules have been rearranged to correspond to the order of introduction of the topics in this book but individual rules have not been changed.

It should be noted that the rules for the construction of lexical units, which are under the subheading of Chapter 3, have a slightly different status to the other rules since spaces and newlines may be freely inserted between lexical units but not within lexical units.

A rule for 'character literal' has been added and the rule for 'selected component' has been amended to include the case 'character literal'

The rules have been sequentially numbered for ease of reference; an index to them will be found in Section A4.2.

A4.1 Syntax rules

Chapter 2

1 pragma ::= **pragma** identifier [(argument {,argument})];

2 argument ::= [identifier =>] name
  | [identifier =>] *static*_expression

Chapter 3

3 identifier ::= letter { [underscore] letter_or_digit}

4 letter_or_digit ::= letter | digit

5 letter ::= upper_case_letter | lower_case_letter

6 numeric_literal ::= decimal_number | based_number

7 decimal_number ::= integer [. integer] [exponent]

8 integer ::= digit {[underscore] digit}

9 exponent ::= E [+] integer | E – integer

10 based_number ::= base # based_integer [. based_integer] # [exponent]

11 base ::= integer

12 based_integer ::= extended_digit {[underscore] extended_digit}

13 extended_digit ::= digit | letter

14 character_literal ::= 'character'

15 character_string ::= "{character}"

Chapter 4

16 declaration ::= object_declaration | number_declaration
| type_declaration | subtype_declaration
| subprogram_declaration | package declaration
| task_declaration | exception_declaration
| renaming_declaration

17 object_declaration ::=
identifier_list : [**constant**] subtype_indication [:= expression];
| identifier_list : [**constant**] array_type_definition [:= expression];

18 number_declaration ::=
identifier_list : **constant** := *literal*_expression;

19 identifier_list ::= identifier {, identifier}

20 assignment_statement ::= *variable*_name := expression;

21 block ::=
[*block*_identifier:]
[**declare**
declarative_part]
begin
sequence_of_statements
[**exception**
{exception_handler}]
end [*block*_identifier];

22 type_declaration ::=
type identifier [discriminant_part] **is** type_definition;
| incomplete_type_declaration

23 type_definition ::=
enumeration_type_definition | integer_type_definition
| real_type_definition | array_type_definition
| record_type_definition | access_type_definition
| derived_type_definition | private_type_definition

24 subtype_declaration ::=
subtype identifier **is** subtype_indication;

25 subtype_indication ::= type_mark [constraint]

26 type_mark ::= *type*_name | *subtype*_name

27 constraint ::= range_constraint | accuracy_constraint
| index_constraint | discriminant_constraint

28 range_constraint ::= **range** range

29 range ::= simple_expression .. simple_expression

30 enumeration_type_definition ::=
(enumeration_literal{, enumeration_literal})

31 enumeration_literal ::= identifier | character_literal

32 name ::= identifier | indexed_component | slice
| selected_component | attribute | function_call
| operator_symbol

33 attribute ::= name'identifier

34 literal ::= numeric_literal | enumeration_literal
| character_string | **null**

35 expression ::= relation { **and** relation}
| relation { **or** relation}
| relation { **xor** relation}
| relation { **and then** relation}
| relation { **or else** relation}

36 relation ::=
simple_expression [relational_operator simple_expression]
| simple_expression [**not**] **in** range
| simple_expression [**not**] **in** subtype_indication

37 simple_expression ::=
[unary_operator] term {adding_operator term}

38 term ::= factor {multiplying_operator factor}

39 factor ::= primary [** primary]

40 primary ::= literal | aggregate | name | allocator
| function_call | type_conversion | qualified_expression
| (expression)

41 logical_operator ::= **and** | **or** | **xor**

42 relational_operator ::= = | /= | < | <= | > | >=

43 adding_operator ::= + | – | &

44 unary_operator ::= + | – | **not**

45 multiplying_operator ::= * | / | **mod** | **rem**

46 exponentiating_operator ::= **

47 type_conversion = type_mark (expression)

48 qualified_expression ::=
type_mark'(expression) | type_mark'aggregate

Chapter 5

49 sequence_of_statements ::= statement {statement}

50 statement ::=
{label} simple_statement | {label} compound_statement

51 simple_statement ::= null_statement
| assignment_statement | exit_statement
| return_statement | goto_statement
| procedure_call | entry_call
| delay_statement | abort_statement
| raise_statement | code_statement

52 compound_statement ::= if_statement | case_statement
| loop_statement | block
| accept_statement | select_statement

53 label ::= <<identifier>>

54 null_statement ::= **null**

55 if_statement ::= **if** condition **then**
sequence_of_statements
{**elsif** condition **then**
sequence_of_statements}
[**else**
sequence_of_statements]
end if;

56 condition ::= *boolean*_expression

57 case_statement ::=
case expression **is**
{**when** choice {| choice} => sequence_of_statements}
end case;

58 choice ::= simple_expression | discrete_range | **others**

59 discrete_range ::= type_mark [range_constraint] | range

60 loop_statement ::=
[*loop*_identifier:] [iteration_clause] basic_loop [*loop*_identifier];

61 basic_loop ::= **loop**
sequence_of_statements
end loop

62 iteration_clause ::=
for loop_parameter **in** [**reverse**] discrete_range
| **while** condition

63 loop_parameter ::= identifier

64 exit_statement ::= **exit** [*loop*_name] [**when** condition];

65 goto_statement ::= **goto** *label*_name;

Chapter 6

66 array_type_definition ::=
array (index {, index}) **of** *component*_subtype_indication
| **array** index_constraint **of** *component*_subtype_indication

67 index ::= type_mark **range** <>

68 index_constraint ::= (discrete_range {, discrete_range})

69 indexed_component ::= name(expression {, expression})

70 slice ::= name (discrete_range)

71 aggregate ::= (component_association {, component_association})

72 component_association ::= [choice {| choice}=>] expression

73 record_type_definition ::= **record**
component_list
end record

74 component_list ::= {component_declaration} [variant_part] | **null**;

75 component_declaration ::=
identifier_list : subtype_indication [:= expression];
| identifier_list : array_type_definition [:= expression];

76 selected_component ::=
name.identifier | name.**all** | name.operator_symbol
| name.character_literal

Chapter 7

77 subprogram_declaration ::= subprogram_specification;
| generic_subprogram_declaration
| generic_subprogram_instantiation

78 subprogram_specification ::=
procedure identifier [formal_part]
| **function** designator [formal_part] **return** subtype_indication

79 designator ::= identifier | operator_symbol

80 operator_symbol ::= character_string

81 formal_part ::= (parameter_declaration {; parameter_declaration})

82 parameter_declaration ::=
identifier_list : mode subtype_indication [:= expression]

83 mode := [**in**] | **out** | **in out**

84 subprogram_body ::= subprogram_specification **is**
declarative_part
begin
sequence_of_statements
[**exception**
{exception_handler}]
end [designator];

85 procedure_call ::= *procedure*_name [actual_parameter_part];

86 function_call ::= *function*_name actual_parameter_part
| *function*_name ()

87 actual_parameter_part ::=
(parameter_association {, parameter_association})

88 parameter_association ::=
[formal_parameter =>] actual_parameter

89 formal_parameter ::= identifier

90 actual_parameter ::= expression

91 return_statement ::= **return** [expression];

Chapter 8

92 package_declaration ::= package_specification;
| generic_package_declaration
| generic_package_instantiation

93 package_specification ::= **package** identifier **is**
{declarative_item}
[**private**
{declarative_item}
{representation_specification}]
end [identifier]

94 package_body ::= **package body** identifier **is**
declarative_part
[**begin**
sequence_of_statements
[**exception**
{exception_handler}]]
end [identifier];

95 declarative_part ::=
{declarative_item}{representation_specification}{program_component}

96 declarative_item ::= body | use_clause

97 program_component ::= body | package_declaration | task_declaration
| body_stub

98 body ::= subprogram_body | package_body | task_body

99 use_clause ::= **use** *package*_name {, *package*_name} ;

100 compilation ::= compilation_unit

101 compilation_unit ::= context_specification subprogram_declaration
| context_specification subprogram_body
| context_specification package_declaration
| context_specification package_body
| context_specification subunit

102 context_specification ::= {with_clause [use_clause]}

103 with_clause ::= **with** *unit*_name {, *unit*_name} ;

104 subunit ::= **separate** (*unit*_name) body;

105 body_stub ::= subprogram_specification **is separate**;
| **package body** identifier **is separate**;
| **task body** identifier **is separate**;

106 renaming_declaration ::= identifier : type_mark **renames** name;
| identifier : **exception renames** name;
| **package** identifier **renames** name;
| subprogram_specification **renames** name;

Chapter 9

107 private_type_definition ::= [**limited**] **private**

Chapter 10

108 exception_handler ::=
  when exception_choice {| exception_choice} =>
    sequence_of_statements

109 exception_choice ::= *exception*_name | **others**

110 exception_declaration ::= identifier_list : **exception**;

111 raise_statement ::= **raise** [*exception*_name];

Chapter 11

112 discriminant_part ::=
  (discriminant_declaration {; discriminant_declaration})

113 discriminant_declaration ::=
  identifier_list : subtype_indication [:= expression]

114 discriminant_constraint ::=
  (discriminant_specification {, discriminant_specification})

115 discriminant_specification ::=
  [*discriminant*_name {| *discriminant*_name} =>] expression

116 variant_part ::= **case** *discriminant*_name **is**
    {**when** choice {| choice} => component_list}
  end case;

117 access_type_definition ::= **access** subtype_indication

118 incomplete_type_declaration ::= **type** identifier [discriminant_part];

119 allocator ::= **new** type_mark [(expression)]
  | **new** type_mark aggregate
  | **new** type_mark discriminant_constraint
  | **new** type_mark index_constraint

120 derived_type_definition ::= **new** subtype_indication

Chapter 12

121 integer_type_definition ::= range_constraint

122 real_type_definition ::= accuracy_constraint

123 accuracy_constraint ::=
  floating_point_constraint | fixed_point_constraint

124 floating_point_constraint ::=
  digits *static*_simple_expression [range_constraint]

125 fixed_point_constraint ::=
  delta *static*_simple_expression [range_constraint]

Chapter 13

126 generic_subprogram_declaration ::=
  generic_part subprogram_specification;

127 generic_package_declaration ::=
generic_part package_specification;

128 generic_part ::= **generic** {generic_formal_parameter}

129 generic_formal_parameter ::=
parameter_declaration;
| **type** identifier [discriminant_part] **is** generic_type_definition;
| **with** subprogram_specification [**is** name];
| **with** subprogram_specification **is** <>;

130 generic_type_definition ::=
(<>) | **range** <> | **delta** <> | **digits** <>
| array_type_definition | access_type_definition
| private_type_definition

131 generic_subprogram_instantiation ::=
procedure identifier **is** generic_instantiation;
| **function** designator **is** generic_instantiation;

132 generic_package_instantiation ::=
package identifier **is** generic_instantiation;

133 generic_instantiation ::=
new name [(generic_association {, generic_association})]

134 generic_association ::=
[formal_parameter =>] generic_actual_parameter

135 generic_actual_parameter ::= expression | *subprogram*_name
| subtype_indication

Chapter 14

136 task_declaration ::= task_specification

137 task_specification ::= **task** [**type**] identifier [**is**
{entry_declaration}
{representation_specification}
end [identifier]];

138 task_body ::= **task body** identifier is
declarative_part
begin
sequence_of_statements
[**exception**
{exception_handler}]
end [identifier];

139 entry_declaration ::=
entry identifier [(discrete_range)] [formal_part];

140 entry_call ::= *entry*_name [actual_parameter_part];

141 accept_statement ::= **accept** *entry*_name [formal_part] [**do**
sequence_of_statements
end [identifier]];

142 delay_statement ::= **delay** simple_expression;

143 select_statement ::= selective_wait | conditional_entry_call
| timed_entry_call

144 selective_wait ::= **select**
[**when** condition =>]
select_alternative
or [**when** condition =>]
select_alternative]
[**else**
sequence_of_statements
end select;

145 select_alternative ::= accept_statement [sequence_of_statements]
| delay_statement [sequence_of_statements]
| **terminate**;

146 conditional_entry_call ::= **select**
entry_call [sequence_of_statements]
else
sequence_of_statements
end select;

147 timed_entry_call ::= **select**
entry_call [sequence_of_statements]
or
delay_statement [sequence_of_statements]
end select;

148 abort_statement ::= **abort** *task*_name {, *task*_name};

Chapter 15

149 representation_specification ::=
length_specification | enumeration_type_representation
record_type_representation | address_specification

150 length_specification ::= **for** attribute **use** expression;

151 enumeration_type_representation ::= **for** *type*_name **use** aggregate;

152 record_type_representation ::= **for** *type*_name **use**
record [alignment_clause;]
{*component*_name location;}
end record;

153 location ::= **at** *static*_simple_expression **range** range

154 alignment_clause ::= **at mod** *static*_simple_expression

155 address_specification ::= **for** name **use at** *static*_simple_expression;

156 code_statement ::= qualified_expression;

A4.2 Syntax index

This index lists the syntactic categories in alphabetical order and gives the number of their definition in the previous section.

Category	Definition number
abort_statement	148
accept_statement	141
access_type_definition	117
accuracy_constraint	123
actual_parameter	90
actual_parameter_part	87
adding_operator	43
address_specification	155
aggregate	71
alignment_clause	154
allocator	119
argument	2
array_type_definition	66
assignment_statement	20
attribute	33
base	11
based_integer	12
based_number	10
basic_loop	61
block	21
body	98
body_stub	105
case_statement	57
character_literal	14
character_string	15
choice	58
code_statement	156
compilation	100
compilation_unit	101
component_association	72
component_declaration	75
component_list	74
compound_statement	52
condition	56
conditional_entry_call	146
constraint	27
context_specification	102
decimal_number	7
declaration	16
declarative_item	96
declarative_part	95
delay_statement	142

Category	Definition number
derived_type_definition	120
designator	79
discrete_range	59
discriminate_constraint	114
discriminant_declaration	113
discriminant_part	112
discriminant_specification	115
entry_call	140
entry_declaration	139
enumeration_literal	31
enumeration_type_definition	30
enumeration_type_representation	151
exception_choice	109
exception_declaration	110
exception_handler	108
exit_statement	64
exponent	9
exponentiating_operator	46
expression	35
extended_digit	13
factor	39
fixed_point_constraint	125
floating_point_constraint	124
formal_parameter	89
formal_part	81
function_call	86
generic_actual_parameter	135
generic_association	134
generic_formal_parameter	129
generic_instantiation	133
generic_package_declaration	127
generic_package_instantiation	132
generic_part	128
generic_subprogram_declaration	126
generic_subprogram_instantiation	131
generic_type_definition	130
goto_statement	65
identifier	3
identifier_list	19
if_statement	55
incomplete_type_declaration	118
index	67
index_constraint	68
indexed_component	69
integer	8
integer_type_definition	121
iteration_clause	62

Category	Definition number
label	53
length_specification	150
letter	5
letter_or_digit	4
literal	34
location	153
logical_operator	41
loop_parameter	63
loop_statement	60
mode	83
multiplying_operator	45
name	32
null_statement	54
number_declaration	18
numeric_literal	6
object_declaration	17
operator_symbol	80
package_body	94
package_declaration	92
package_specification	93
parameter_association	88
parameter_declaration	82
pragma	1
primary	40
private_type_definition	107
procedure_call	85
program_component	97
qualified_expression	48
raise_statement	111
range	29
range_constraint	28
real_type_definition	122
record_type_definition	73
record_type_representation	152
relation	36
relational_operator	42
renaming_declaration	106
representation_specification	149
return_statement	91
select_alternative	145
select_statement	143
selected_component	76
selective_wait	144
sequence_of_statements	49
simple_expression	37
simple_statement	51
slice	70

Category	Definition number
statement	50
subprogram_body	84
subprogram_declaration	77
subprogram_specification	78
subtype_declaration	24
subtype_indication	25
subunit	104
task_body	138
task_declaration	136
task_specification	137
term	38
timed_entry_call	147
type_conversion	47
type_declaration	22
type_definition	23
type_mark	26
unary_operator	44
use_clause	99
variant_part	116
with_clause	103

Answers to Exercises

Specimen answers are given to all the exercises. In some cases they do not necessarily represent the best technique for solving a problem but merely one which uses the material introduced at that point in the discussion.

Answers 2

Exercise 2.2

1
```
package SIMPLE_MATHS is
    function SQRT(F: FLOAT) return FLOAT;
    function LOG(F: FLOAT) return FLOAT;
    function EXP(F: FLOAT) return FLOAT;
    function SIN(F: FLOAT) return FLOAT;
    function COS(F: FLOAT) return FLOAT;
end SIMPLE_MATHS;
```

The first few lines of our program PRINT_ROOTS could now become

```
with SIMPLE_MATHS, SIMPLE_IO;
procedure PRINT_ROOTS is
    use SIMPLE_MATHS, SIMPLE_IO;
    . . .
```

Answers 3

Exercise 3.3

1 The following are not legal identifiers
- b) contains &
- c) contains hyphens and not underscores
- e) adjacent underscores
- f) does not start with a letter
- g) trailing underscore
- h) this is two legal identifiers
- i) this is legal – but it is a reserved word

Exercise 3.4

1
- a) legal – real
- b) illegal – no digit before point
- c) legal – integer
- d) illegal – integer with negative exponent
- e) illegal – closing # missing
- f) legal – real
- g) illegal – C not a digit of base 12
- h) illegal – no number before exponent
- i) legal – integer – case of letter immaterial
- j) legal – integer
- k) illegal – underscore at start of exponent
- l) illegal – integer with negative exponent

2
- a) $224 = 14 \times 16$
- b) $6144 = 3 \times 2^{11}$
- c) 4095.0
- d) 4095.0

3 a) 32 ways

```
41, 2#101001#, 3#1112#, ...
    10#41#, ... 16#29#
41E0, 2#101001#E0, ... 16#29#E0
```

b) 40 ways. As for example (a) plus, since 150 is not prime but $2 \times 3 \times 5^2 = 150$ also

```
 2#1001011#E1
 3#1212#E1
 5#110#E1
 5#11#E2
 6#41#E1
10#15#E1
15#A#E1
```

and of course

```
15E1
```

Exercise 3.5

1 a) 7   c) 1
b) 1   d) 12

2 a) This has 3 units
the identifier delay
the number 2.0
the single symbol ;

b) This has 4 units
the identifier delay2
the single symbol .
the number 0
the single symbol ;

Case (a) is a legal delay statement, (b) is just a mess.

Answers 4

Exercise 4.1

1 `R: REAL:=1.0;`

2 ```
ZERO: constant REAL:=0.0;
ONE: constant REAL:=1.0;
```

but better to write number declarations

```
ZERO: constant:=0.0;
ONE: constant:=1.0;
```

3 a) **var** is illegal – this is Ada not Pascal
b) terminating semicolon is missing
c) a constant declaration must have an initial value
d) no multiple assignment – this is Ada not Algol
e) nothing – assuming M and N are of integer type
f) 2PI is not a legal identifier

Exercise 4.2

1 There are four errors
1 semicolon missing after declaration of J, K
2 K used before a value has been assigned to it
3 = instead of := in declaration of P
4 Q not declared and initialised

Exercise 4.5

1 a) –105   e) –3
b) –3   f) 19683
c) 0   g) –1
d) –3   h) 2
```

2 All variables are real.
a) B**2 – 4.0*A*C
b) (4.0/3.0)*PI*R**3
c) (P*PI*A**4)/(8.0*L*ETA)

Exercise 4.6

1 a) SAT c) 2
b) SAT

2 a) **type** RAINBOW **is** (RED,ORANGE,YELLOW,GREEN,BLUE,INDIGO,VIOLET);
b) **type** FRUIT **is** (APPLE,BANANA,ORANGE,PEAR);

3 GROOM'VAL ((N–1) **mod** 8)

or perhaps better

GROOM'VAL((N–1) **mod** (GROOM'POS(GROOM'LAST)+1))

4 D:=DAY'VAL((DAY'POS(D)+N–1) **mod** 7);

5 If X and Y are both overloaded literals then X < Y will be ambiguous. We would have to use qualification such as T'(X) < T'(Y).

Exercise 4.7

1 T: **constant** BOOLEAN:=TRUE;
F: **constant** BOOLEAN:=FALSE;

2 The values are TRUE or FALSE, not T or F which are the names of constants.

a) FALSE d) TRUE
b) TRUE e) FALSE
c) TRUE

3 The expression is always TRUE. The predefined operators **xor** and /= operating on Boolean values are the same.

Exercise 4.9

1 All variables are real except for N in example (c) which is integer.

a) 2.0*PI*SQRT(L/G)
b) M_0/SQRT(1.0 – (V/C)**2)
c) SQRT(2.0*PI*REAL(N))*REAL(N)/E)**N

2 SQRT(2.0*PI*X)*EXP(X*LN(X)–X)

Answers 5

Exercise 5.1

1
```
declare
    END_OF_MONTH: INTEGER;
begin
    if MONTH = SEP or MONTH = APR or MONTH = JUN or
                                        MONTH = NOV then
        END_OF_MONTH:=30;
    elsif MONTH = FEB then
        if YEAR mod 4 = 0 then
            END_OF_MONTH:=29;
        else
            END_OF_MONTH:=28;
        end if;
```

```
        else
            END_OF_MONTH:=31;
        end if;

        if DAY /= END_OF_MONTH then
            DAY:=DAY+1;
        else
            DAY:=1;
            if MONTH /= DEC then
                MONTH:=MONTH_NAME'SUCC(MONTH);
            else
                MONTH:=JAN;
                YEAR:=YEAR+1;
            end if;
        end if;
    end;
```

If today is 31 DEC 2099 then CONSTRAINT_ERROR will be raised on attempting to assign 2100 to YEAR. Note that the range 1901 .. 2099 simplifies the leap year calculation.

2
```
    if X < Y then
        declare
            T: REAL:=X;
            begin
            X:=Y;    Y:=T;
        end;
    end if;
```

Exercise 5.2

1
```
    declare
        END_OF_MONTH: INTEGER;
    begin
        case MONTH is
            when SEP | APR | JUN | NOV =>
                END_OF_MONTH:=30;
            when FEB =>
                if YEAR mod 4 = 0 then
                    END_OF_MONTH:=29;
                else
                    END_OF_MONTH:=28;
                end if;
            when others =>
                END_OF_MONTH:=31;
        end case;
        -- then as before
        ...
    end;
```

2
```
    subtype WINTER is MONTH_NAME range JAN .. MAR;
    subtype SPRING is MONTH_NAME range APR .. JUN;
    subtype SUMMER is MONTH_NAME range JUL .. SEP;
    subtype AUTUMN is MONTH_NAME range OCT .. DEC;
    ...
    case M is
        when WINTER => DIG;
        when SPRING => SOW;
        when SUMMER => TEND;
        when AUTUMN => HARVEST;
    end case;
```

Note that if we wished to consider winter as December to February then we could not declare a suitable subtype.

3
```
case D is
    when 1..10 => GORGE;
    when 11..20 => SUBSIST;
    when others => STARVE;
end case;
```

We cannot write 21 .. END_OF_MONTH because it is not a static range. In fact **others** covers all values of type INTEGER because although D is constrained, nevertheless the constraints are not static.

Exercise 5.3

1
```
declare
    SUM: INTEGER:=0;
    I: INTEGER;
begin
    loop
        GET(I);
        exit when I<0;
        SUM:=SUM+I;
    end loop;
end;
```

2
```
declare
    COPY: INTEGER:=N;
    COUNT: INTEGER:=0;
begin
    while COPY mod 2 = 0 loop
        COPY:=COPY/2;
        COUNT:=COUNT+1;
    end loop;
    ...
end;
```

3
```
declare
    G: REAL:=-LN(REAL(N));
begin
    for P in 1..N loop
        G:=G+1.0/REAL(P);
    end loop;
    ...
end;
```

Exercise 5.4

1
```
for I in 1..N loop
    for J in 1..M loop
        if condition_O_K then
            I_VALUE:=I;
            J_VALUE:=J;
            goto SEARCH;
        end if;
    end loop;
end loop;

<<SEARCH>>
```

This is not such a good solution because we have no guarantee that there may not be other places in the program from where a goto statement leads to the label.

Answers 6

Exercise 6.1

1
```
declare
    F: array (0 .. N) of INTEGER;
begin
    F(0):=0; F(1):=1;
    for I in 2 .. F'LAST loop
        F(I):=F(I-1)+F(I-2);
    end loop;
    ...
end;
```

2
```
declare
    MAXI, MAXJ: INTEGER:=1;
    MAX: REAL:=A(1, 1);
begin
    for I in 1 .. N loop
        for J in 1 .. M loop
            if A(I, J) > MAX then
                MAX:=A(I, J);
                MAXI:=I;
                MAXJ:=J;
            end if;
        end loop;
    end loop;
    -- MAXI, MAXJ now contain the result
end;
```

3
```
declare
    DAYS_IN_MONTH: array (MONTH_NAME) of INTEGER
        :=(31, 28, 31, 30, 31, 30, 31, 31, 30, 31, 30, 31);
    END_OF_MONTH: INTEGER;
begin
    if YEAR mod 4 = 0 then
        DAYS_IN_MONTH(FEB):=29;
    end if;
    END_OF_MONTH:=DAYS_IN_MONTH(MONTH);

    -- then as Exercise 5.1 (1)
end;
```

4
```
YESTERDAY: constant array (DAY) of DAY
    :=(SUN, MON, TUE, WED, THU, FRI, SAT);
```

5
```
BOR: constant array (BOOLEAN, BOOLEAN) of BOOLEAN
    :=((FALSE, TRUE), (TRUE, TRUE));
```

6
```
UNIT: constant array (1 .. 3, 1 .. 3, ) of REAL
    :=((1.0, 0.0, 0.0),
       (0.0, 1.0, 0.0),
       (0.0, 0.0, 1.0));
```

Exercise 6.2

1
```
DAYS_IN_MONTH: array (MONTH_NAME) of INTEGER
    :=MONTH_NAME'(SEP|APR|JUN|NOV => 30,
                  FEB => 28, others => 31);
```

2
```
ZERO: constant MATRIX:=(1 .. N => (1 .. N => 0.0));
```

3 This cannot be done with the material at our disposal at the moment. See Exercise 7.1(**6**).

4 **type** BBB **is array** (BOOLEAN, BOOLEAN) **of** BOOLEAN;

Exercise 6.3

1
```
ROMAN_TO_INTEGER: constant array (ROMAN_DIGIT) of INTEGER
            :=(1,5,10,50,100,500,1000);
```

2
```
declare
    V: INTEGER:=0;
begin
    for I in R'RANGE loop
        if I /= R'LAST and then
            ROMAN_TO_INTEGER(R(I))<ROMAN_TO_INTEGER(R(I+1)) then
            V:=V-ROMAN_TO_INTEGER(R(I));
        else
            V:=V+ROMAN_TO_INTEGER(R(I));
        end if;
    end loop;
    ...
end;
```

Note the use of **and then** to avoid attempting to access R(I+1) when I = R'LAST.

Exercise 6.4

1 WHITE,BLUE,YELLOW,GREEN,RED,PURPLE,ORANGE,BLACK

2 a) BLACK c) RED
b) GREEN

3
```
not (TRUE xorTRUE)=TRUE
not (TRUE xor FALSE)=FALSE
```

the result follows.

4 An aggregate of length one must be named.

5
```
if R'LAST >= 2 and then R(R'LAST-1..R'LAST)="IV" then
    R(R''LAST-1..R'LAST):="VI";
end if;
```

6 The lower bound of the result of & is the lower bound of the subtype which is NATURAL'FIRST.

Exercise 6.5

1
```
declare
    DAYS_IN_MONTH: array (MONTH_NAME) of INTEGER
        :=MONTH_NAME'(SEP|APR|JUN|NOV =>30, FEB => 28, others => 31);
    END_OF_MONTH: INTEGER;

begin
    if D.YEAR mod 4 = 0 then
        DAYS_IN_MONTH(FEB):=29;
    end if;
    END_OF_MONTH:=DAYS_IN_MONTH(D.MONTH);
    if D.DAY /= END_OF_MONTH then
        D.DAY:=D.DAY+1;
```

```
    else
        D.DAY:=1;
        if D.MONTH /= DEC then
            D.MONTH:=MONTH_NAME'SUCC(D.MONTH);
        else
            D.MONTH:=JAN;
            D.YEAR:=D.YEAR+1;
        end if;
    end if;
end;
```

2 C1, C2, C3: COMPLEX;

a) C3:=(C1.RL+C2.RL, C1.IM+C2, IM);
b) C3:=(C1.RL*C2.RL−C1.IM*C2.IM, C1.RL*C2.IM+C1.IM*C2.RL);

3
```
declare
    INDEX: INTEGER;
begin
    for I in PEOPLE'RANGE loop
        if PEOPLE(I).BIRTH.YEAR >= 1950 then
            INDEX:=I;
            exit;
        end if;
    end loop;
    -- we assume that there is such a person
end;
```

Answers 7

Exercise 7.1

1
```
function ABS(X: INTEGER) return INTEGER is
begin
    if X >= 0 then
        return X;
    else
        return -X;
    end if;
end ABS;
```

2
```
function FACTORIAL(N: INTEGER range 0. .INTEGER''LAST) return NATURAL is
begin
    if N=0 then
        return 1;
    else
        return N*FACTORIAL(N-1);
    end if;
end FACTORIAL;
```

3
```
function OUTER(A, B: VECTOR) return MATRIX is
    C: MATRIX(A''RANGE, B'RANGE);
begin
    for I in A'RANGE loop
        for J in B'RANGE loop
            C(I,J):=A(I)*B(J);
        end loop;
    end loop;
```

4
```
type PRIMARY_ARRAY is array (INTEGER range <>) of PRIMARY;
function MAKE_COLOUR(P: PRIMARY_ARRAY) return COLOUR is
    C: COLOUR:=(F, F, F);
begin
    for I in P'RANGE loop
        C(P(I)):=T;
    end loop;
    return C;
end MAKE_COLOUR;
```

Note that multiple values are allowed so that

MAKE_COLOUR((R, R, R)) = RED.

5
```
function VALUE(R: ROMAN_NUMBER) return INTEGER is
    V: INTEGER:=0;
begin
for I in R'RANGE loop
        if I /= R'LAST and then
            ROMAN_TO_INTEGER(R(I)) < ROMAN_TO_INTEGER(R(I+1)) then
            V:=V-ROMAN_TO_INTEGER(R(I));
        else
            V:=V+ROMAN_TO_INTEGER(R(I));
        end if;
    end loop;
    return V;
end VALUE;
```

6
```
function MAKE_UNIT(N: INTEGER range 0 .. INTEGER'LAST)
                                        return MATRIX is
    M: MATRIX(1 .. N, 1 .. N);
begin
    for I in 1 .. N loop
        for J in 1 .. N loop
            if I = J then
                M(I, J):=1.0;
            else
                M(I, J):=0.0;
            end if;
        end loop;
    end loop;
    return M;
end MAKE_UNIT;
```

We can then declare

UNIT: **constant** MATRIX:=MAKE_UNIT(N);

7
```
function GCD(X, Y: INTEGER range 0 .. INTEGER'LAST)
                return INTEGER range 0 .. INTEGER'LAST is
begin
    if Y = 0 then
        return X;
    else
        return GCD(Y, X mod Y);
    end if;
end GCD;
```

or

```
function GCD(X, Y: INTEGER range 0 .. INTEGER'LAST)
            return INTEGER range 0 .. INTEGER'LAST is
    XX:INTEGER:=X;
    YY:INTEGER:=Y;
    ZZ:INTEGER;
begin
    while YY /= 0 loop
        ZZ:=XX mod YY;
        XX:=YY;
        YY:=ZZ;
    end loop;
    return XX;
end GCD;
```

Note that X and Y have to be copied because formal parameters behave as constants.

Exercise 7.2

1
```
function "<"(X, Y: ROMAN_NUMBER) return BOOLEAN is
begin
    return VALUE(X) < VALUE(Y);
end "<";
```

2
```
function "+"(X, Y: COMPLEX) return COMPLEX is
begin
    return (X.RL+Y.RL, X.IM+Y.IM);
end "+";

function "*"(X, Y: COMPLEX) return COMPLEX is
begin
    return (X.RL*Y.RL-X.IM*Y.IM, X.RL*Y.IM+IM*Y.RL);
end "*";
```

3
```
function "<"(P: PRIMARY; C' COLOUR) return BOOLEAN is
begin
    return C(P);
end "<";
```

4
```
function "<="(X, Y: COLOUR) return BOOLEAN is
begin
    return (X and Y) = X;
end "<=";
```

Exercise 7.3

1
```
procedure SWAP(X, Y: in out REAL) is
    T: REAL;
begin
    T:=X;  X:=Y;  Y:=T;
end SWAP;
```

2
```
procedure REVERSE(X: in out VECTOR) is
    R: VECTOR(X'RANGE);
begin
    for I in X'RANGE loop
        R(I):=X(X'FIRST+X'LAST-I);
    end loop;
    X:=R;
end REVERSE;
```

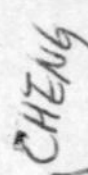

or maybe

```
procedure REVERSE(X: in out VECTOR) is
begin
   for I in X'FIRST..X'FIRST+X'LENGTH/2-1 loop
      SWAP(X(I), X(X'FIRST+LAST-I));
   end loop;
end REVERSE;
```

This procedure can be applied to an array R or type ROW by

```
REVERSE(VECTOR(R));
```

3 The fragment is erroneous because the outcome depends upon whether the parameter is passed by copy or by reference. If it is copied then A(1) ends up as 2.0; if it is passed by reference then A(1) ends up as 4.0.

Exercise 7.4

1
```
function ADD(X: INTEGER; Y:INTEGER:=1) return INTEGER is
begin
   return X+Y;
end ADD;
```

The following 6 calls are equivalent

```
ADD(N)                      ADD(X => N)
ADD(N,1)                    ADD(N,Y => 1)
ADD(X => N,Y => 1)          ADD(Y => 1,X => N)
```

Exercise 7.5

1 The named form of call

```
SELL(C => JERSEY);
```

is unambiguous since the formal parameter names are different.

Answers 8

Exercise 8.1

1
```
package RANDOM is
   MODULUS: constant:=2**13;
   subtype SMALL is INTEGER range 0..MODULUS;
   procedure INIT(SEED: SMALL);
   function NEXT return SMALL;
end;

package body RANDOM is
   MULTIPLIER: constant:=5**5;
   X: SMALL;

   procedure INIT(SEED: SMALL) is
   begin
      X:=SEED;
   end INIT;
   function NEXT return SMALL is
   begin
      X:=X*MULTIPLIER mod MODULUS;
      return X;
   end NEXT;
end RANDOM;
```

2
```
package COMPLEX_NUMBERS is
    type COMPLEX is
        record
            RL, IM: REAL:=0.0;
        end record;

    I: constant COMPLEX:=(0.0, 1.0);

    function "+"(X, Y: COMPLEX) return COMPLEX;
    function "-"(X, Y: COMPLEX) return COMPLEX;
    function "*"(X, Y: COMPLEX) return COMPLEX;
    function "/"(X, Y: COMPLEX) return COMPLEX;
end;
package body COMPLEX_NUMBERS is

    function "+"(X, Y: COMPLEX) return COMPLEX is
    begin
        return (X.RL+Y.RL, X.IM+Y.IM);
end,"+";

    function "-"(X, Y: COMPLEX) return COMPLEX is
    begin
        return (X.RL-Y.RL, X.IM-Y.IM);
    end "-";

    function "*"(X, Y: COMPLEX) return COMPLEX is
    begin
        return (X.RL*Y.RL-X.IM*Y.IM, X.RL*Y.IM+X.IM*Y.RL);
    end "*";

    function "/"(X, Y: COMPLEX) return COMPLEX is
        D: REAL:=Y.RL**2+Y.IM**2;
    begin
        return ((X.RL*Y.RL+X.IM*Y.IM)/D, (X.IM*Y.RL-X.RL*Y.IM) /D);
    end "/";

end COMPLEX_NUMBERS;
```

Exercise 8.2

1

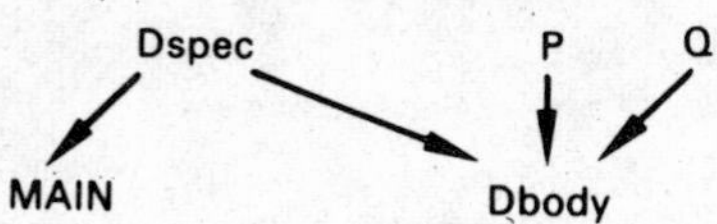

There are 18 different possible orders of compilation.

Exercise 8.3

1

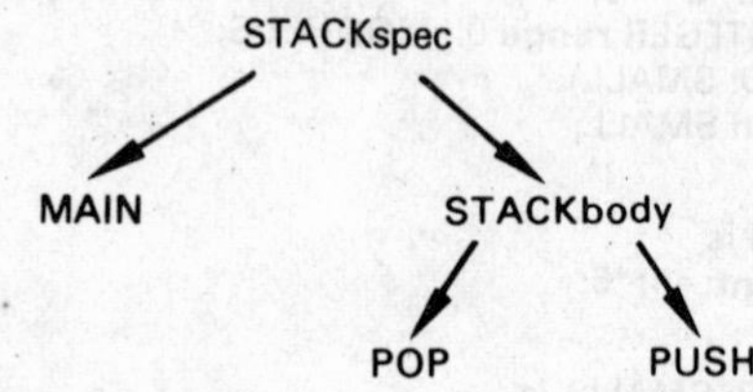

Answers 9

Exercise 9.1

1 Inside the package body we could write

```
function "*"(X: REAL; Y: COMPLEX) return COMPLEX is
begin
    return (X*Y.RL, X*Y.IM);
end "*";
```

but outside we could only write

```
function "*"(X: REAL; Y: COMPLEX) return COMPLEX is
    use COMPLEX_NUMBERS;
begin
    return CONS(X, 0.0)*Y;
end "*";
```

and similarly with the operands interchanged.

2
```
package RATIONAL_NUMBERS is
    type RATIONAL is private;

    function "+"(X: RATIONAL) return RATIONAL;          -- unary +
    function "-"(X: RATIONAL) return RATIONAL;          -- unary -

    function "+"(X, Y: RATIONAL) return RATIONAL;
    function "-"(X, Y: RATIONAL) return RATIONAL;
    function "*"(X, Y:RATIONAL) return RATIONAL;
    function "/"(X, Y: RATIONAL) return RATIONAL;

    function "/"(X: INTEGER; Y: NATURAL) return RATIONAL;
    function NUMERATOR(R: RATIONAL) return INTEGER;
    function DENOMINATOR(R: RATIONAL) return NATURAL;
private
    type RATIONAL is
        record
            NUM: INTEGER;      --numerator
            DEN; NATURAL;      --denominator
        end record;
end;

package body RATIONAL_NUMBERS is

    function NORMAL(R: RATIONAL) return RATIONAL is
        --cancel common factors
            G: NATURAL:=GCD(ABS(R.NUM), R.DEN));
    begin
        return (R.NUM/G, R.DEN/G);
    end NORMAL;
    function "+"(X: RATIONAL) return RATIONAL is
    begin
        return X;
    end "+";

    function "-"(X: RATIONAL) return RATIONAL is
    begin
        return (-X.NUM, X.DEN);
    end "-";

    function "+" (X, Y: RATIONAL) return RATIONAL is
    begin
        return NORMAL((X.NUM*Y.DEN+Y.NUM*X.DEN, X.DEN*Y.DEN));
    end "+",

    function "-"(X, Y: RATIONAL) return RATIONAL is
    begin
        return NORMAL((X.NUM*Y.DEN-Y.NUM*X.DEN, X.DEN*Y.DEN));
    end "-";

    function "*"(X, Y: RATIONAL) return RATIONAL is
    begin
        return NORMAL((X.NUM*Y.NUM, X.DEN*Y.DEN));
    end "*";
```

```
function "/"(X, Y: RATIONAL) return RATIONAL is
begin
    return NORMAL((X.NUM*Y.DEN, X.DEN*Y.NUM));
end "/";

function "/"(X: INTEGER, Y: NATURAL) return RATIONAL is
begin
    return NORMAL((X, Y));
end "/";

function NUMERATOR(R: RATIONAL) return INTEGER is
begin
    return R.NUM;
end NUMERATOR;

function DENOMINATOR(R: RATIONAL) return NATURAL is
begin
    return R.DEN;
end DENOMINATOR;

end RATIONAL_NUMBERS;
```

3 Although the parameter base types are both INTEGER and therefore the same as for predefined integer division, nevertheless the result types are different. The result types are considered in the overload resolution of functions. See Section 7.5.

Exercise 9.2

1
```
package STACKS is
    type STACK is limited private;
    EMPTY: constant STACK;
    ...
private
    ...
    EMPTY: constant STACK:=((EMPTY.S'RANGE => 0), 0);
end;
```

Note that EMPTY has to be initialised because it is a **constant** despite the fact that TOP which is the only component whose value is of interest is automatically initialised anyway.

2
```
function EMPTY(S: STACK) return BOOLEAN is
begin
    return S.TOP = 0;
end EMPTY;
function FULL(S: STACK) return BOOLEAN is

begin
    return S.TOP = MAX;
end FULL;
```

3
```
function "="(A, B: STACK_ARRAY) return BOOLEAN is
begin
    if A'LENGTH /= B'LENGTH then
        return FALSE;
    end if;
    for I in A'RANGE loop;
        if A(I) /= B(I+B'FIRST-A'FIRST) then
            return FALSE;
        end if;
    end loop;
    return TRUE;
end "=";
```

Note that this uses the redefined = (via /=) applying to the type STACK. This pattern of definition of array equality clearly applies to any type.

4
```
procedure ASSIGN(S: in STACK; T: out STACK) is
begin
    T.TOP:=S.TOP;
    for I in 1 .. S.TOP loop
        T.S(I):= S.S(I);
    end loop;
end;
```

5
```
package STACKS is
    type STACK is private;
    procedure PUSH(S: in out STACK; X: in INTEGER);
    procedure POP(S: in out STACK; X: out INTEGER);
private
    MAX: constant:=100;
    DUMMY: constant:=0;
    type STACK is
        record
            S: array (1 .. MAX) of INTEGER:=(1 .. MAX => DUMMY);
            TOP: INTEGER range 0 .. MAX:=0;
        end record;
end;
package body STACKS is
    procedure PUSH(S: in out STACK; X: in INTEGER) is
    begin
        S.TOP:=STOP+1;
        S.S(TOP):=X;
    end;

    procedure POP(S: in out STACK; X: out INTEGER) is
    begin
        X:=S.S(TOP);
        S.S(TOP):=DUMMY;
        S.TOP:=S.TOP-1;
    end;
end STACKS;
```

Note the use of DUMMY as default value for unused components of the stack.

Exercise 9.3

1
```
private
    MAX: constant:=1000;        -- no of accounts
    subtype KEY_CODE is INTEGER range 0 .. MAX;
    type KEY is
        record
            CODE: KEY_CODE:=0;
        end record;
end;
package body BANK is
    BALANCE: array (KEY_CODE range 1 .. KEY_CODE'LAST) of MONEY
        :=(BALANCE'RANGE => 0);
    FREE: array (KEY_CODE range 1 .. KEY_CODE'LAST) of BOOLEAN
        :=(FREE'RANGE => TRUE);

    function VALID(K: KEY) return BOOLEAN is
    begin
        return K.CODE /= 0;
    end VALID;

    procedure OPEN_ACCOUNT(K: in out KEY; M: in MONEY) is
    begin
        if K.CODE = 0 then
```

```
            for I in FREE'RANGE loop
                if FREE(I) then
                    FREE(I):=FALSE;
                    BALANCE(I):=M;
                    K.CODE:=I;
                    return;
                end if;
            end loop;
        end if;
    end OPEN_ACCOUNT;

    procedure CLOSE_ACCOUNT(K: in out KEY; M: out MONEY) is
    begin
        if VALID(K) then
            M:=BALANCE(K.CODE);
            FREE(K.CODE):=TRUE;
            K.CODE:=0;
        end if;
    end CLOSE_ACCOUNT;

    procedure DEPOSIT(K: in KEY; M: in MONEY) is
    begin
        if VALID(K) then
            BALANCE(K.CODE):=BALANCE(K.CODE)+M;
        end if;
    end DEPOSIT;

    procedure WITHDRAW(K: in out KEY; M: in out MONEY) is
    begin
        if VALID(K) then
            if M > BALANCE(K.CODE) then
                CLOSE_ACCOUNT(K, M);
            else
                BALANCE(K.CODE):=BALANCE(K.CODE)-M;
            end if;
        end if;
    end WITHDRAW;
    function STATEMENT(K: KEY) return MONEY is
    begin
        if VALID(K) then
            return BALANCE(K.CODE);
        end if;
    end STATEMENT;
end BANK;
```

Various alternative formulations are possible. It might be neater to declare a record type representing an account containing the two components FREE and BALANCE.
Note that the function STATEMENT does not return a defined result if the key is not valid. This is not good programming style but is not actually erroneous unless the calling program makes use of the undefined result.

2 An alternative formulation which represents the home savings box could be that where the limited private type is given by

```
type BOX is
    record
        CODE: BOX_CODE:=0;
        BALANCE: MONEY;
    end record;
```

In this case the money is kept in the variable declared by the user. The bank only knows which boxes have been issued but does not know how much is in a particular box. The details are left to the reader.

3 Since the parameter is of a private type, it is not defined whether the parameter is passed by copy or by reference. If it is passed by copy then the call of ACTION will succeed whereas if it is passed by reference it will not. The program is therefore erroneous. However this does not seem a very satisfactory answer and might be considered a loophole in the design of Ada.

Answers 10

Exercise 10.1

1
```
procedure QUADRATIC(A, B, C: in REAL;
                    ROOT_1, ROOT_2: out REAL; OK: out BOOLEAN) is
    D: constant REAL:=B**2-4.0*A*C;
begin
    ROOT_1:=(-B+SQRT(D))/(2.0*A);
    ROOT_2:=(-B-SQRT(D))/(2.0*A);
    OK:=TRUE;
exception
    when NUMERIC_ERROR =>
        OK:=FALSE;
end QUADRATIC;
```

2
```
function FACTORIAL(N: INTEGER) return INTEGER is
    function SLAVE(N: INTEGER range 0..INTEGER'LAST) return NATURAL is
    begin
        if N = 0 then
            return 1;
        else
            return N*SLAVE(N-1);
        end if;
    end SLAVE;
    begin
    return SLAVE(N);
exception
    when CONSTRAINT_ERROR|STORAGE_ERROR|NUMERIC_ERROR =>
        return -1;
end FACTORIAL;
```

Exercise 10.2

1
```
package RANDOM is
    BAD: exception;
    MODULUS: constant:=2**13;
    subtype SMALL is INTEGER range 0..MODULUS;
    procedure INIT(SEED:SMALL);
    function NEXT return SMALL;
end;

package body RANDOM is
    MULTIPLIER: constant:=5**5;
    X: SMALL;

    procedure INIT(SEED: SMALL) is
    begin
        if SEED mod 2 = 0 then
            raise BAD;
        end if;
        X:=SEED;
    end INIT;

    function NEXT return SMALL is
```

```
      begin
         X:=X*MULTIPLIER mod MODULUS;
         return X:
      end NEXT;
   end RANDOM;
```

2
```
   function FACTORIAL(N: INTEGER) return INTEGER is
      function SLAVE(N: INTEGER range 0..INTEGER'LAST) return NATURAL is
      begin
         if N = 0 then
            return 1;
         else
            return N*SLAVE(N-1);
         end if;
      end SLAVE;
   begin
      return SLAVE(N);
   exception
      when CONSTRAINT_ERROR|STORAGE ERROR =>
         raise NUMERIC_ERROR;
   end FACTORIAL;
```

Exercise 10.3

1
```
   package BANK is
      ALARM: exception;
      subtype MONEY is INTEGER range 0..INTEGER'LAST;
      type KEY is limited private;
      -- as before
   private;
      -- as before
   end;

   package body BANK is
      BALANCE: array (KEY_CODE range 1..KEY.CODE'LAST) of MONEY
         :=(BALANCE'RANGE => 0);
      FREE: array (KEY_CODE range 1..KEY_CODE'LAST) of BOOLEAN
         :=(FREE'RANGE=> TRUE);
      function VALID(K: KEY) return BOOLEAN is
      begin
         return K.CODE /= 0;
      end VALID;

      procedure VALIDATE(K: KEY) is
      begin
         if not VALID(K) then
            raise ALARM;
         end if;
      end VALIDATE;

      procedure OPEN_ACCOUNT(K: in out KEY; M; in MONEY) is
      begin
         if K.CODE = 0 then
            for I in FREE'RANGE loop
               if FREE(I) then
                  FREE(I):=FALSE;
                  BALANCE(I):=M;
                  K.CODE:=I;
                  return;
               end if;
            end loop;
```

```
        else
            raise ALARM;
        end if;
    end OPEN_ACCOUNT;

    procedure CLOSE_ACCOUNT(K: in out KEY; M: out MONEY) is
    begin
        VALIDATE(K);
        M:=BALANCE(K.CODE);
        FREE(K.CODE):=TRUE;
        K.CODE:=0;
    end CLOSE_ACCOUNT;

    procedure DEPOSIT(K: in KEY; M: in MONEY) is
    begin
        VALIDATE(K);
        BALANCE(K.CODE):=BALANCE(K.CODE)+M;
    end DEPOSIT;

    procedure WITHDRAW(K: in out KEY; M: in out MONEY) is
    begin
        VALIDATE(K);
        if M > BALANCE(K.CODE) then
            raise ALARM;
        else
            BALANCE(K.CODE):=BALANCE(K.CODE)-M;
        end if;
    end WITHDRAW;

    function STATEMENT(K: KEY) return MONEY is
    begin
        VALIDATE(K);
        return BALANCE(K.CODE);
    end STATEMENT;
end BANK;
```

For convenience we have declared a procedure VALIDATE which raises the alarm in most cases. The ALARM is also explicitly raised if we attempt to overdraw but as remarked in the text we cannot also close the account. An attempt to open an account with a key which is in use also causes ALARM to be raised. We do not however raise the ALARM if the bank runs out of accounts but have left it to the user to check with a call of VALID that he was issued a genuine key; the rationale is that it is not the user's fault if the bank runs out of keys.

Answers 11

Exercise 11.1

1 TRACE((M'LENGTH, M))

If the two dimensions of M were not equal then CONSTRAINT_ERROR would be raised. Note that the lower bounds of M do not have to be 1; all that matters is that the number of components in each dimension is the same.

2
```
package STACKS is
    type STACK(MAX: INTEGER range 0 .. INTEGER''LAST) is limited private;
    EMPTY: constant STACK(0);
    ...
private
    type STACK(MAX: INTEGER range 0 .. INTEGER'LAST) is
    record
            S: array (1 .. MAX) of INTEGER;
            TOP: INTEGER:=0;
        end record;
    EMPTY: constant STACK(0):=(0, (EMPTY.S'RANGE => 0), 0);
end;
```

We have naturally chosen to make EMPTY a stack whose value of MAX is zero. Note that the function "=" only compares the parts of the stacks which are in use. Thus we can write S = EMPTY to test whether a stack S is empty irrespective of its value of MAX.

3
```
function FULL(S: STACK) return BOOLEAN is
begin
    return S.TOP = S.MAX;
end FULL;
```

4
```
Z: POLYNOMIAL:=(0, (0 => 0));
```

The named notation has to be used because the array has only one component.

5
```
function "*"(P, Q: POLYNOMIAL) return POLYNOMIAL is
    R: POLYNOMIAL(P.N+Q.N):=(R.N, (R.A'RANGE => 0));
begin
    for I in P.A'RANGE loop
        for J in Q.A'RANGE loop
            R.A(I+J):=R.A(I+J)+P.A(I)*Q.A(J);
        end loop;
    end loop;
    return R;
end "*";
```

It is largely a matter of taste whether we write P.A'RANGE rather than 0 .. P.N.

6
```
function "-"(P, Q: POLYNOMIAL) return POLYNOMIAL is
    SIZE: INTEGER;
begin
    if P.N > Q.N then
        SIZE:=P.N;
    else
        SIZE:=Q.N;
    end if;
    declare
        R: POLYNOMIAL(SIZE);
    begin
        for I in 0 .. P.N loop
            R.A(I):=P.A(I);
        end loop;
        for I in P.N+1 .. R.N loop
            R.A(I):=0;
        end loop;
        for I in 0 .. Q.N loop
            R.A(I):=R.A(I)-Q.A(I);
        end loop;
        return NORMAL(R);
    end;
end "-";
```

There are various alternative ways of writing this function. We could initialise R.A by using slice assignments

```
R.A(0 .. P.N):=P.A;
R.A(P.N+1 .. R.N):=(P.N+1 .. R.N => 0);
```

or even more succinctly by

```
R.A:=P.A & (P.N+1 .. R.N => 0);
```

7
```
procedure TRUNCATE(P: in out POLYNOMIAL) is
begin
    if P'CONSTRAINED then
        raise TRUNCATE_ERROR;
```

```
    else
        P:=(P.N-1, P.A(0..P.N-1));
    end if;
end TRUNCATE;
```

Exercise 11.2

1
```
procedure SHAVE(P: in out PERSON) is
begin
    if P.SEX=FEMALE then
        raise SHAVING_ERROR;
    else
        P.BEARDED:=FALSE;
    end if;
end SHAVE;
```

2
```
procedure STERILISE(M: in out MUTANT) is
begin
    if M'CONSTRAINED and M.SEX /= NEUTER then
        raise STERILISE_ERROR;
    else
        M:=(NEUTER, M.BIRTH);
    end if;
end STERILISE;
```

3
```
type FIGURE is (CIRCLE, SQUARE, RECTANGLE);
type OBJECT(SHAPE: FIGURE) is
    record
        case SHAPE is
                when CIRCLE =>
                 RADIUS: REAL;
            when SQUARE =>
                 SIDE: REAL;
            when RECTANGLE =>
                 LENGTH, BREADTH: REAL;
        end case;
    end record;
```

4
```
function AREA(X: OBJECT) return REAL is
begin
    case X.SHAPE is
        when CIRCLE =>
            return PI*X.RADIUS**2;
        when SQUARE =>
          return X.SIDE**2;
        when RECTANGLE =>
            return X.LENGTH*X.BREADTH;
    end case;
end AREA;
```

Note the similarity between the case statement in the function AREA and the variant part of the type OBJECT.

Exercise 11.3

1
```
procedure APPEND(FIRST: in out LINK; SECOND: in LINK) is
    L: LINK:=FIRST;
begin
    if FIRST = null then
        FIRST:=SECOND;
    else
        while L.NEXT /= null loop
            L:=L.NEXT;
```

```
        end loop;
        L.NEXT:= SECOND;
    end if;
end APPEND;
```

2
```
function SIZE(T: TREE) return INTEGER is
begin
    if T = null then
        return 0;
    else
        return SIZE(T.LEFT)+SIZE(T.RIGHT)+1;
    end if;
end SIZE;
```

3
```
function COPY(T: TREE) return TREE is
begin
    if T = null then
        return null;
    else
        return new NODE(T.VALUE, COPY(T.LEFT), COPY(T.RIGHT));
    end if;
end COPY;
```

Exercise 11.4

1
```
procedure PUSH(S: in out STACK; X: in INTEGER) is
begin
    S:=new CELL(X, S);

exception
    when STORAGE_ERROR =>
        raise ERROR;
end;

procedure POP(S: in out STACK; X: out INTEGER) is
begin
    if S = null then
        raise ERROR;
    else
        X:=S.VALUE;
        S:=S.NEXT;
    end if;
end;
```

2
```
procedure PUSH(S: in out STACK; X: in INTEGER) is
begin
    S.LIST:=new CELL(X, S.LIST);
end;

procedure POP(S: in out STACK; X: out INTEGER) is
begin
    X:=S.LIST.VALUE;
    S.LIST:=S.LIST.NEXT;
end;

function "="(S, T: STACK) return BOOLEAN is
    SL: LINK:=S.LIST;
    TL: LINK:=T.LIST;
begin
    while SL /= null and TL /= null loop
        SL:=SL.NEXT;
        TL:=TL.NEXT;
```

```
        if SL.VALUE /= TL.VALUE then
            return FALSE;
        end if;
    end loop;
    return SL = TL;
end "=";
```

3
```
package QUEUES is
    EMPTY: exception;
    type QUEUE is limited private;
    procedure JOIN(Q: in out QUEUE; X: in ITEM);
    procedure REMOVE(Q: in out QUEUE; X: out ITEM);
    function LENGTH(Q: QUEUE) return INTEGER;
private
    type CELL;
    type LINK is access CELL;
    type CELL is
        record
            DATA: ITEM;
            NEXT: LINK;
        end record;
    type QUEUE is
        record
            COUNT: INTEGER:=0;
            FIRST, LAST: LINK;
        end record;
end;

package body QUEUES is
    procedure JOIN(Q: in out QUEUE; X: in ITEM) is
        L: LINK;
    begin
        L:=new CELL(DATA => X, NEXT => null);
        Q.LAST.NEXT:=L;
        Q.LAST:=L;
        Q.COUNT:=Q.COUNT+1;
    end JOIN;

    procedure REMOVE(Q: in out QUEUE; X: out ITEM) is
    begin
        if Q.COUNT = 0 then
            raise EMPTY;
        end if;
        X:=Q.FIRST.DATA;
        Q.FIRST:=Q.FIRST.NEXT;
        Q.COUNT:=Q.COUNT-1;
    end REMOVE;

    function LENGTH:(Q: QUEUE) return INTEGER is
    begin
      return Q.COUNT;
    end LENGTH;

end QUEUES;
```

Exercise 11.5

1
```
function HEIR(P: PERSON_NAME) return PERSON_NAME is
    MOTHER: WOMANS_NAME;
begin
    if P.SEX = MALE then
        MOTHER:=P.WIFE;
```

```
   else
      MOTHER:=P;
   end if;
   if MOTHER = null or else MOTHER.FIRST_CHILD = null then
      return null;
   end if;
   declare
      CHILD: PERSON_NAME:=MOTHER.FIRST_CHILD;
   begin
      while CHILD.SEX = FEMALE loop
         if CHILD.NEXT_SIBLING = null then
            return MOTHER.FIRST_CHILD;
         end if;
         CHILD:=CHILD.NEXT_SIBLING;
      end loop;
      return CHILD;
   end;
end HEIR;
```

2
```
procedure DIVORCE(W: WOMANS_NAME) is
begin
   if W = null or else (W.HUSBAND = null or  W.FIRST_CHILD /= null then
      return;          -- divorce not possible
   end if;
   W.HUSBAND.WIFE:=null;
   W.HUSBAND:=null;
end DIVORCE;
```

Exercise 11.6

1
```
package P is
   type LENGTH is new REAL;
   type AREA is new REAL;
   function "*"(X,Y: LENGTH) return LENGTH;
   function "*"(X,Y: LENGTH) return AREA;
   function "*"(X,Y: AREA) return AREA;
end;

package body P is
   function "*"(X,Y: LENGTH) return LENGTH is
   begin
      raise NUMERIC_ERROR;
   end;

   function "*"(X,Y: LENGTH) return AREA is
   begin
      return AREA(REAL(X)*REAL(Y));
   end;
   function "*"(X,Y: AREA) return AREA is
   begin
      raise NUMERIC_ERROR;
   end;

end P;
```

Answers 12

Exercise 12.1

1 P: on A: INTEGER, on B: SHORT_INTEGER
Q: on A: LONG_INTEGER, on B: INTEGER
R: on A: cannot be implemented, on B: LONG_INTEGER

2 No, the only critical case is type Q on machine A. Changing to ones complement changes the range of INTEGER to

−32767 .. +32767

and so only INTEGER'FIRST is altered.

3
a) INTEGER
b) illegal – type conversion must be explicit
c) MY_INTEGER'BASE
d) INTEGER
e) universal integer
f) MY_INTEGER'BASE

4 **type** LONGEST_INTEGER **is range** SYSTEM.MIN_INT..SYSTEM.MAX_INT;

Exercise 12.2

1
a) illegal
b) INTEGER
c) universal real
d) INTEGER
e) universal real
f) universal integer

2 R: **constant**:=N*1.0;

Exercise 12.3

1 1/8

2 REAL has B=17, FLOAT has B=24
The values of the variables P and Q are model numbers. The result P/Q is the model interval

$\frac{2}{3}(1-2^{-24}), \frac{2}{3}(1+2^{-25})$

The result (P/Q*Q) is the model interval

$2(1-2^{-24}), 2(1+2^{-23})$.

On assignment to R this is widened to the model interval
$2(1-2^{-17}), 2(1+2^{-16})$

Note that this result is independent of the precision of FLOAT.

3 In this case P and Q are numbers of type universal real and the computation is performed exactly at compilation. The result is that R is assigned the model number 2.0.

4 529 = 8 (= possible mantissae)
×33 (= possible exponents)
×2 (= possible signs)
+1 (= zero)

5
```
function HYPOTENUSE(X,Y: REAL) return REAL is
     TINY: constant REAL:=2.0**(-2*REAL'MANTISSA);
begin
     if ABS(X) < TINY and ABS(Y) < TINY then
        return SQRT((X/TINY)**2+(Y/TINY)**2)*TINY:
     else
        return SQRT(X**2+Y**2);
     end if;
end HYPOTENUSE;
```

Note that 2.0**(−2*REAL'MANTISSA) is a literal expression of type universal real.

Exercise 12.4

1 $\frac{1}{10}(1-2^{-12}), \frac{1}{10}(1+2^{-14})$

Answers 13

Exercise 13.1

1
```
generic
    type ITEM is private
package STACKS is
    type STACK(MAX: INTEGER range 0..INTEGER'LAST) is limited private;
    procedure PUSH(S: in out STACK; X: in ITEM);
    procedure POP(S: in out STACK; X: out ITEM);
    function "="(S,T: STACK) return BOOLEAN;
private
    type STACK(MAX: INTEGER range 0..INTEGER'LAST) is
        record
            S: array (1..MAX) of ITEM;
            TOP: INTEGER:=0;
        end record;
end;
```

The body is much as before. To declare a stack we must first instantiate the package.

```
package BOOLEAN_STACKS is new package STACKS(ITEM => BOOLEAN);
use BOOLEAN_STACKS;
S: STACK(MAX => 30);
```

2
```
generic
    type THING is private;
package P is
    procedure SWAP(A,B: in out THING);
    procedure CAB(A,B,C: in out THING);
end P;

package body P is
    procedure SWAP(A,B: in out THING) is
        T: THING;
    begin
        T:=A; A:=B; B:=T;
    end;

    procedure CAB(A,B,C: in out THING) is
    begin
        SWAP(A,B);
        SWAP(A,C);
    end;
end P;
```

Exercise 13.2

1
```
function "not" is new NEXT(BOOLEAN);

generic
    type BASE is range <>;
package RATIONAL_NUMBERS is
    type RATIONAL is private;
    function "+"(X: RATIONAL) return RATIONAL;
    function "-"(X: RATIONAL) return RATIONAL;
    function "+"(X,Y: RATIONAL) return RATIONAL;
    function "-"(X,Y: RATIONAL) return RATIONAL;
    function "*"(X,Y: RATIONAL) return RATIONAL;
    function "/"(X,Y: RATIONAL) return RATIONAL;

    subtype NAT_BASE is BASE range 0..BASE'LAST;
```

```
    function "/"(X: BASE; Y: NAT_BASE) return RATIONAL;
    function NUMERATOR(R: RATIONAL) return BASE;
    function DENOMINATOR(R: RATIONAL) return NAT_BASE;
private
    type RATIONAL is
        record
            NUM: BASE;
            DEN: NAT_BASE;
        end record;
end;
```

3
```
generic
    type INDEX is (<>);
    type FLOATING is digits <>;
    type VEC is array (INDEX range <>) of FLOATING;
    type MAT is array (INDEX range <>, INDEX range <>) of FLOATING;
function OUTER(A,B: VEC) return MAT;

function OUTER(A,B: VEC) return MAT is
    C: MAT(A'RANGE,B'RANGE);
begin
    for I in A'RANGE loop
        for J in B'RANGE loop
            C(I, J):=A(I)*B(J);
        end loop;
    end loop;
    return C;
end OUTER;
function OUTER_VECTOR is new OUTER(INTEGER,REAL,VECTOR,MATRIX);
```

4
```
package body SET_OF is
    function MAKE_SET(X: LIST) return SET is
        S: SET:=EMPTY;
    begin
        for I in X'RANGE loop
            S(X(I)):=TRUE;
        end loop;
        return S;
    end MAKE_SET;
    function MAKE_SET(X: BASE) return SET is
    begin
        return (X => TRUE others => FALSE);
    end MAKE_SET;

    function DECOMPOSE(X: SET) return LIST is
        L: LIST(1 .. SIZE(X));
        I: NATURAL:=1;
    begin
        for E in SET'RANGE loop
            if X(E) then
                L(I):=E;
                I:=I+1;
            end if;
        end loop;
        return L;
    end DECOMPOSE;

    function "+"(XY: SET) return SET is
    begin
```

```
        return X or Y;
    end "+";

    function "*"(X,Y: SET) return SET is
    begin
        return X and Y;
    end "*";

    function "-"(X,Y: SET) return SET is
    begin
        return X xor Y;
    end "-";

    function "<"(X: BASE; Y: SET) return BOOLEAN is
    begin
        return Y(X);
    end "<";

    function "<="(X,Y: SET) return BOOLEAN is
    begin
        return (X and Y) = X;
    end "<=";

    function SIZE(X: SET) return INTEGER is
        N: INTEGER:=0;
    begin
        for E in SET'RANGE loop
            if X(E) then
                N:=N+1;
            end if;
        end loop;
        return N;
    end SIZE;

end SET_OF;
```

Exercise 13.3

1

```
function G(X: REAL) return REAL is
begin
    return EXP(X)+X-7.0;
end;
...
function SOLVE_G is new SOLVE(G);
...
ANSWER: REAL:=SOLVE_G();
```

2 Assuming

```
type BOOL_ARRAY is array (INTEGER range <>) of BOOLEAN;
```

we have

```
function AND_ALL is new APPLY(INTEGER,BOOLEAN,BOOL_ARRAY,"and")
```

3 A further generic parameter is required to supply a value for zero.

```
generic
    type INDEX is (<>);
    type ITEM is private;
    ZERO: in ITEM;
    type VEC is array (INDEX range <>) of ITEM;
    with function "+"(X,Y: ITEM) return ITEM;
function APPLY(A: VEC) return ITEM;

function APPLY(A: VEC) return ITEM is
    RESULT: ITEM:=ZERO;
```

```
begin
    for I in A'RANGE loop
        RESULT:=RESULT+A(I);
    end loop;
    return RESULT;
end APPLY;
```

and then

```
function AND_ALL is new APPLY(INTEGER, BOOLEAN, TRUE, BOOL_ARRAY, "and");
```

4
```
generic
    type ITEM is limited private;
    type VECTOR is array (INTEGER range <>) of ITEM;
    with function "="(X, Y: ITEM) return BOOLEAN is <>;
function EQUALS(A, B: VECTOR) return BOOLEAN;

function EQUALS(A, B: VECTOR) return BOOLEAN is
begin
    -- body exactly as for Exercise 9.2(3)
end EQUALS;
```

We can instantiate by

```
function "=" is new EQUALS(STACK, STACK_ARRAY, "=");
```

or simply by

```
function "=" is new EQUALS(STACK, STACK_ARRAY);
```

in which case the default parameter is used.

5 The generic specification could be

```
generic
    type ITEM is private;
    type INDEX is (<>);
    type VECTOR is array (INDEX range <>) of ITEM;
    with function "<"(X, Y: ITEM) return BOOLEAN·
procedure SORT(A: in out VECTOR);
```

The generic body corresponds closely to the procedure SORT in Section 11.3. The types NODE and TREE are declared inside SORT because they depend on the generic type ITEM. The incrementing of I cannot be done with "+" since the index type may not be an integer and so we have to use INDEX'SUCC. Care is needed not to cause CONSTRAINT_ERROR if the array embraces the full range of values of INDEX.

Answers 14

Exercise 14.1

1
```
procedure SHOPPING is

    task GET_SALAD;

    task body GET_SALAD is
    begin
        BUY_SALAD;
    end GET_SALAD;

    task GET_WINE;

    task body GET_WINE is
    begin
        BUY_WINE;
    end GET_WINE;

    task body GET_MEAT is
    begin
        BUY_MEAT;
    end GET_MEAT;
```

```
begin
   null;
end SHOPPING;
```

Exercise 14.2

1
```
task body BUILD_COMPLEX is
   C: COMPLEX;
begin
   loop
      accept PUT_RL(X: REAL) is
         C.RL:=X;
      end;
      accept PUT_IM(X: REAL) is
         C.IM:=X;
      end;
      accept GET_COMP(X: out COMPLEX) is
         X:=C;
      end;
   end loop;
end BUILD_COMPLEX;
```

2
```
task body CHAR_TO_LINE is
   BUFFER: LINE;
begin
   loop
      for I in BUFFER'RANGE loop
         accept PUT(C: in CHARACTER) do
            BUFFER(I):=C;
         end;
      end loop;
      accept GET(L: out LINE) do
         L:=BUFFER;
      end;
   end loop;
end CHAR_TO_LINE;
```

Exercise 14.3

1
```
generic
   FIRST_TIME: CALENDAR.TIME;
   INTERVAL: DURATION;
   NUMBER: INTEGER;
   with procedure P;
procedure CALL;

procedure CALL is
   use CALENDAR;
   NEXT_TIME: TIME:=FIRST_TIME;
begin
   if NEXT_TIME < CLOCK() then
      NEXT_TIME:=CLOCK();
   end if;
   for I in 1 .. NUMBER loop
      delay NEXT_TIME-CLOCK();
      P;
      NEXT_TIME:=NEXT_TIME+INTERVAL;
   end loop;
end CALL;
```

Exercise 14.4

1
```
task body BUILD_COMPLEX is
   C: COMPLEX;
   GOT_RL, GOT_IM: BOOLEAN:=FALSE;
```

```
begin
    loop
        select
            when not GOT_RL =>
            accept PUT_RL(X: REAL) is
                C.RL:=X;
            end;
            GOT_RL:=TRUE;
    or
        when not GOT_IM =>
        accept PUT_IM(X: REAL) is
            C.IM:=X=X;
        end;
        GOT_IM:=TRUE;
    or
            when GOT_RL and GOT_IM =>
            accept GET_COMP(X: out COMPLEX) is
                X:=C;
            end;
            GOT_RL:=FALSE;
            GOT_IM:=FALSE;
        end select;
    end loop;
end BUILD_COMPLEX;
```

An alternative solution is

```
task body BUILD_COMPLEX is
    C: COMPLEX;
begin
    loop
        select
            accept PUT_RL(X: REAL) is
                C.RL:=X;
            end;
            accept PUT_IM(X: REAL) is
                C.IM:=X;
            end;
        or
            accept PUT_IM(X: REAL) is
                C.IM:=X;
            end;
            accept PUT_RL(X: REAL) is
                C.RL:=X;
            end;
        end select;
        accept GET_COMP(X: out COMPLEX) is
            X:=C;
        end;
    end loop;
end BUILD_COMPLEX;
```

At first sight this might seem simpler but the technique does not extrapolate easily when a moderate number of components are involved because of the combinatorial explosion.

2

```
procedure READ(X: out ITEM; T: DURATION; OK: out BOOLEAN) is
begin
    select
        CONTROL.START(READ);
    or
        delay T;
        OK:=FALSE;
        return;
```

```
        end select;
        X:=V;
        CONTROL.STOP_READ;
        OK:=TRUE;
    end READ;

    procedure WRITE(X: in ITEM; T: DURATION; OK: out BOOLEAN) is
        use CALENDAR;
        START_TIME: TIME:=CLOCK();
    begin
        select
            CONTROL.START(WRITE);
        or
            delay T;
            OK:=FALSE;
            return;
        end select;
        select
            CONTROL.WRITE;
        or
            delay T-(CLOCK()-START_TIME);
            CONTROL.STOP_WRITE;
            OK:=FALSE;
            return;
        end select;
        V:=X;
        CONTROL.STOP WRITE;
        OK:=TRUE;
    end WRITE;
```

Note how a shorter time out is imposed on the call of WRITE.

Exercise 14.6

1
```
task BUFFERING is
    entry PUT(X: in ITEM),
    entry FINISH,
    entry GET(X: out ITEM),
end,

task body BUFFERING is
    N: constant:=8,
    A: array (1..N) of ITEM,
    I,J: INTEGER range 1..N:=1,
    COUNT: INTEGER range 0..N:=0,
    FINISHED: BOOLEAN:=FALSE,
begin loop
        select
            when COUNT < N =>
            accept PUT(X: in ITEM) do
                A(I):=X,
            end;
            I:=I mod N+1; COUNT:=COUNT+1;
        or
            accept FINISH;
            FINISHED:=TRUE;
        or
            when COUNT > 0 =>
            accept GET(X: out ITEM) do
                X:=A(J);
            end;
            J:=J mod N+1; COUNT:=COUNT-1;
        or
```

```
            when COUNT = 0 and FINISHED =>
            accept GET(X: out ITEM) do
                raise DONE;
            end;
        end select;
    end loop;
exception
    when DONE =>
        null;
end BUFFERING;
```

This example illustrates that there may be several accept statements for the same entry in the one select statement. The exception DONE is propagated to the caller and also terminates the loop in BUFFERING before being quietly handled. Of course the exception need not be handled by BUFFERING because exceptions propagated out of tasks are lost, but it is cleaner to do so.

Exercise 14.7

1
```
package CONTROLLER is
    procedure REQUEST(P: PRIORITY; D: DATA);
end;

package body CONTROLLER is

    task CONTROL is
        entry SIGN_IN(P: PRIORITY);
        entry REQUEST(PRIORITY) (D: DATA);
    end;

    task body CONTROL is
        TOTAL: INTEGER:=0;
        PENDING: array (PRIORITY) of INTEGER:=(PRIORITY => 0);
    begin
        loop
            if TOTAL = 0 then
                accept SIGN_IN(P: PRIORITY) do
                    PENDING(P):=PENDING(P)+1;
                    TOTAL:=1;
                end;
            end if;
            loop
                select
                    accept SIGN_IN(P: PRIORITY) do
                        PENDING(P):=PENDING(P)+1;
                        TOTAL:=TOTAL+1;
                    end;
                else
                    exit;
                end select;
            end loop;
            for P in PRIORITY loop
                if PENDING(P) > 0 then
                    accept REQUEST(P) (D: DATA) do
                        ACTION(D);
                    end;
                    PENDING(P):=PENDING(P)-1;
                    TOTAL:=TOTAL-1;
                    exit;
                end if;
            end loop;
        end loop;
    end CONTROL;

    procedure REQUEST(P: PRIORITY; D: DATA) is
```

```
    begin
        CONTROL.SIGN_IN(P)
        CONTROL.REQUEST(P) (D)
    end REQUEST
end CONTROLLER;
```

The variable TOTAL records the total number of requests outstanding and the array PENDING records the number at each priority. Each time round the outer loop, the task waits for a call of SIGN_IN if no requests are in the system, it then services any outstanding calls of SIGN_IN and finally deals with a request of the highest priority. We could dispense with the array PENDING and scan the queues as before but there is a slight risk of polling if a user has called SIGN_IN but not yet called REQUEST.

Finally note that the solution will not work if a called task is aborted; this could be overcome by the use of agents.

Exercise 14.8

1

```
package COBBLERS is
    procedure MEND(A: ADDRESS; B: JOB);
end;

package body COBBLERS is
    type JOB is
        record
            REPLY: ADDRESS;
            ITEM: BOOTS;
        end record;
    package P is new BUFFERS(100, JOB);
    use P;
    BOOT_STORE: BUFFER;

    task SERVER is
        entry REQUEST(A: ADDRESS; B: BOOTS);
    end;

    task type REPAIRMAN;
    TOM, DICK, HARRY: REPAIRMAN;

    task body SERVER is
        NEXT_JOB: JOB;
    begin
        loop
            accept REQUEST(A: ADDRESS; B: BOOTS) do
                NEXT_JOB:=(A, B);
            end;
            PUT(BOOT_STORE, NEXT_JOB);
        end loop;
    end SERVER;

    task body REPAIRMAN is
        MY_JOB: JOB;
    begin
        loop
            GET(BOOT_STORE, MY_JOB);
            REPAIR(MY_JOB.ITEM);
            MY_JOB.REPLY.DEPOSIT(MY_JOB.ITEM);
        end loop;
    end REPAIRMAN;

    procedure MEND(A: ADDRESS; B: BOOTS) is
    begin
        SERVER.REQUEST(A, B);
    end;
end COBBLERS;
```

We have assumed that the type ADDRESS is an access to a mailbox for handling boots. Note one anomaly; the stupid server accepts boots from the customer before checking the store – if it turns out to be full, he is left holding them. In all, the shop can hold 104 pairs of boots – 100 in store, 1 with the server and 1 with each repairman.

Answers 15

Exercise 15.1

1
```
with INPUT_OUTPUT;
generic
    type ELEMENT is private;
procedure REVERSE(FROM, TO: STRING);
procedure REVERSE(FROM, TO: STRING) is
    package IO is new INPUT_OUTPUT(ELEMENT);
    use IO;
    INPUT: IN_FILE;
    OUTPUT: OUT_FILE;
    X: ELEMENT;
begin
    OPEN(INPUT, FROM);
    OPEN(OUTPUT, TO);
    SET_WRITE(OUTPUT, SIZE(INPUT));
    while not END_OF_FILE(INPUT) loop
        READ(INPUT, X);
        WRITE(OUTPUT, X);
        SET_WRITE(OUTPUT, NEXT_WRITE(OUTPUT)-2);
    end loop;
     CLOSE(INPUT);
      CLOSE(OUTPUT);
  end REVERSE;
```

Exercise 15.2

1 The output is shown in string quotes in order to reveal the layout. Spaces are indicated by s. In reality of course, there are no quotes and spaces are spaces.

a) "FRED"
b) "120"
c) "sssss120"
d) "ss8#170#
e) "−3.80000E+01"
f) "sssss7.00E−2"

Answers 16

Exercise 16.1

1 a) dynamic INTEGER
b) static INTEGER
c) literal universal integer
d) dynamic INTEGER
e) static INTEGER
f) dynamic INTEGER

Exercise 16.4

1 a) The order of evaluation of the operands I and F() of "+" is not defined. As a result the effect could be
```
   I:=1+2;      -- I first
or I:=2+2;      -- F() first
```
b) The order of evaluation of the destination A(I) and the value F() is not defined. The effect could be
```
   A(1):=2;      I first
or A(2):=2;      -- F() first
```
c) The order of evaluation of the two indexes is not defined. The effect could be
```
   AA(1,2):=0;    -- I first
or AA(2,2):=0;    -- F() first
```

Index

abort statement, 228
ABS, 31, 187
accept statement, 203
access types, 154
  generic parameters, 196
  tasks, 224
ACTUAL_DELTA, 187
Ada, Countess of Lovelace, 2
Ada Programming Support Environment
  (APSE), 3, 10
addition, 30
agents, 225, 231
aggregates, 66, 156
  array, 66, 72, 76, 258
  bounds of, 69
  mixed, 72, 83, 148
  named, 70, 83, 115
  positional, 66, 69, 72, 76, 83
  record, 83, 144, 151
  with **others**, 71, 83, 98, 169, 258
all, 157, 159
allocator, 155, 160
and, 38, 43, 77, 93
and then, 43, 50, 94
anonymous types, 67, 174, 179, 185, 223, 259
array, 63
  access types, 168
  aggregates, 66, 72, 76, 258
  assignment, 67, 72, 81
  bounds and constraints, 68, 89, 97, 168, 195, 259
  generic parameters, 195
  one dimensional operators, 77
  parameters, 89, 97
  slice, 81, 148
  types, 67, 259
ASCII, 75, 112, 281
assignment, 22, 45
  array, 67, 72, 81
  private, 120, 123
  record, 83, 146, 151
at, 249, 251
attributes, 18, 30, 64, 275

BASE, 177, 185
base type, 28, 41
based number, 19
begin, 24, 87, 107, 202
BITS, 187
block, 24, 104, 132
block structure, 4
body, 107, 201
body stub, 113
BOOLEAN, 37

CALENDAR, 209
case, 51, 150
cases of alphabet, 9, 16, 74, 76, 94
case statement, 51, 58
catenation, 80
CHARACTER, 75, 281
character literals, 74, 104
character set, 16
character strings, 76, 93
character types, 74
choice, 52, 152
CLOCK, 209
collection, 160, 169
comments, 20
compilation unit, 110
component, 63, 82, 143
composite types, 63, 143
concatenation, 80
conditional entry call, 219
constant, 23
constant declarations, 23, 69, 120, 157
CONSTRAINED, 148
CONSTRAINT_ERROR, 33, 36, 41, 45, 63, 88, 89, 99, 131, 145, 161, 162, 166, 179, 252
constraints, 28
  access types, 160, 164
  discriminent, 144, 148, 152, 164, 192
  index of array, 68, 89, 97, 168, 195, 259
  on parameters, 97, 103, 148, 200
  range, 28, 35, 174, 177
control characters, 74, 80

CONTROLLED, 254
control structures, 47
COUNT, 205, 217, 220

data abstraction, 4, 7, 265
declarations, 9, 22, 102, 109
declare, 24
default discriminants, 146, 148
default files, 244
default initial values, 83, 128, 146, 148, 155, 165
default parameters, 100, 103, 117, 123, 199
delay statement, 209
delay alternative, 217
DELTA, 18, 187
delta, 18, 186, 193
dependency of compilation units, 111, 113, 122
dependency of tasks, 202, 224
dereferencing, 157, 169
derived types, 169, 177, 259
DIGITS, 18, 185
digits, 18, 182, 193
discrete range, 52
discrete types, 41
discriminant constraints, 144, 148, 152, 164, 192
discriminated records, 143, 164, 193
division, 30
division by zero, 45
do, 203
DURATION, 209
dynamic, 13

elaboration, 24
else, 43, 48, 218
elsif, 49
EMAX, 185
embedded systems, 1
end, 24, 87, 107, 202, 203
entry, 203
entry family, 233
entry queue, 205
enumeration literals, 34
enumeration types, 34, 74
EPSILON, 185
erroneous programs, 13, 22, 45, 88, 97, 105, 160, 213, 254, 262, 263
errors, 12
exception, 131
exception declaration, 135
exception handler, 131
exception propagation, 133, 139, 224, 229
exceptions, 7, 10, 13, 60, 131, 224, 229, 252, 261, 269
execution, 24
exit, 56
exit statement, 56, 59, 105, 133
exponentiation, 31, 33
expression, 23, 42, 255

FAILURE, 229
FALSE, 37
file, 242
FIRST, 30, 35, 41, 64, 74, 185
fixed point types, 5, 180, 186
FLOAT, 9, 182, 264
floating point types, 180, 182
for, 57, 249
for statement, 57
function, 87
function result, 97, 133, 145, 147, 166

garbage collection, 160, 253
generic, 189
generic instantiation, 190, 261
generic parameters, 190
generic units, 7, 189, 271
goto, 60
goto statement, 60, 105, 133
guards, 215

identifiers, 9, 17
if statement, 47
in, 43, 94, 95, 100, 192
initial values, 22, 72
- access types, 156, 160
- arrays, 66, 69, 72
- private types, 120, 123
- records, 83, 144

initialisation of packages, 107, 109, 133
in out, 95, 99, 141, 192
INPUT_OUTPUT, 241
input-output, 5, 13, 240
INTEGER, 29, 59, 64, 176, 264
integer literals, 18, 178
interrupts, 249
is, 27, 51, 87, 107, 150, 199, 201

label, 60, 61, 105
Language Reference Manual, 3, 5, 6
LARGE, 181, 185, 187
LAST, 30, 35, 41, 64, 74, 185
LENGTH, 64, 74

lexical unit, 16
library unit, 8, 110, 262
linear elaboration, 25
line length, 17
limited, 123, 193
limited private, 123, 163
literal expression, 178, 180, 257
LONG_FLOAT, 182
LONG_INTEGER, 176
loop statement, 55
loop parameter, 57, 104

MACHINE_OVERFLOWS, 252
MACHINE_ROUNDS, 252
main program, 8, 111, 133, 202, 262
MANTISSA, 185
MAX_INT, 179
MIN_INT, 179
mixed notation, 72, 83, 100, 148, 200
mod, 31, 93, 251
model numbers, 181, 182
modes, 95, 192
multiplication, 30

named aggregates, 70, 83, 115
named block, 104, 105
named discriminants, 144, 148
named loop, 59, 105
named parameters, 99, 115, 190
names, 255
new, 155, 169, 190
not, 38, 43, 77, 93
not in, 43, 94
null, 51, 84, 152, 155
null aggregate, 71, 76
null array, 69, 71
null range, 35, 69
null record, 84, 154
null slice, 81
null statement, 51
null string, 76, 79
number declaration, 23, 178
numbers, 18, 178, 180
NUMERIC_ERROR, 10, 45, 89, 131, 179, 252
numeric literals, 18
numeric types, 29, 176, 259

objects, 22
of, 63
one component aggregates, 72, 76
one dimensional array operators, 77
operators, 42, 45, 93, 100, 104, 112, 113, 256, 267
or, 38, 43, 77, 93, 213
or else, 43, 94
others, 52, 71, 83, 98, 100, 132, 152, 169, 258
out, 95, 99, 141, 192
overloading, 10, 26, 75, 112, 113, 115
  entries, 206
  enumeration literals, 35, 58
  operators, 93
  subprograms, 102, 173, 190
package, 107
package, 107, 114, 266
package initialisation, 107, 109, 133
parameterless calls, 92, 200
parameters, 95, 190
  constraints, 97, 103, 148, 200
  mechanism, 97, 126, 141, 148, 158, 174, 192, 223
  mixed, 100, 200
  named, 99, 115, 190
  positional, 99, 190
portability, 263
  POS, 36, 41
positional aggregates, 66, 69, 72, 76, 83
positional discriminants, 144, 148
positional parameters, 99, 190
pragma, 13, 278
precedence, 33, 38
PRED, 36, 41
PRIORITY, 208, 262
private, 120, 193
private types, 119, 145, 161, 173, 237
procedure, 95
program components, 109
programming in the large, 7

qualification, 35, 41, 71, 75, 102, 174

raise statement, 135
RANGE, 18, 65, 72, 74
range, 18, 29, 35, 68, 174, 177, 193, 251
readability, 7
REAL, 29, 182
real literals, 18, 180
real types, 41, 180
record, 82
  aggregates, 83, 144, 151
  assignment, 83, 146, 151
  components, 115, 128
  discriminants, 143, 164, 193
  variants, 150

recursion, 89, 94, 102, 110, 140, 159, 163, 193
renames, 116
renaming, 116, 139, 153, 192, 206
rendezvous, 203, 270
rem, 31, 93
remainder, 31
representation specifications, 249
reserved words, 9, 17, 273
resource management, 126, 136, 234
return, 87, 88
return statement, 88, 98, 105, 133, 206
reverse, 57

scalar types, 22, 41
scheduling, 207, 233
scope, 25, 103, 114, 138, 160
SELECT_ERROR, 131, 215
select statement, 212
semicolons, 9, 48, 87
separate, 113
separate compilation, 110
sets, 78, 196, 234
shared variables, 211, 264
SHORT_FLOAT, 182
SHORT_INTEGER, 176
short circuit conditions, 43
side effects, 105, 267
SIZE, 250
slice, 81, 148
SMALL, 185
software components, 4, 265
STANDARD, 12, 112, 116, 280
statements, 9, 47, 61
static, 13
static expression, 53, 178, 182, 186, 192, 257
static subtype, 53
Steelman, 2, 6
Stoneman, 3, 6
STORAGE_ERROR, 89, 131, 162, 252
STORAGE_SIZE, 250
STORAGE_UNIT, 250
STRING, 75
string, 76, 80
strong typing, 7, 27, 253, 259
structure, 261
stub, 113
subprogram, 87
  body, 102, 108
  call, 92, 110
  declaration, 102
  generic parameters, 197, 206
  parameters, 95
  specification, 102, 108
subtraction, 30
subtype, 28
subtypes, 28, 35, 68, 118, 148, 168, 174, 177, 185, 259
subunits, 110, 114
SUCC, 36, 41
SUPPRESS, 252
syntax, 15, 52, 288
SYSTEM, 179, 251, 283

task, 201
TASKING_ERROR, 131, 228, 229, 232
tasks, 7, 201, 270
  activation, 202, 224
  dependency, 202, 224
  objects, 221
  parameters, 223
  termination, 202, 227
  types, 221
terminate, 228
TERMINATED, 230
terminology, 13
TEXT_IO, 245
then, 43, 47
TIME, 209
timed entry call, 219
timing, 207
TRUE, 37
type, 27, 221
  anonymous, 67, 174, 179, 185, 223, 259
  classification, 40
  conversion, 31, 41, 73, 98, 171, 177, 258, 268
  declaration, 27, 68, 259
  definition, 27, 68, 259
  equivalence, 28, 68, 78, 89, 259
  generic parameters, 193
  qualification, 35, 41, 71, 75, 102, 174
  task, 221

UNCHECKED_CONVERSION, 253
UNCHECKED_DEALLOCATION, 253
unconstrained array type, 68, 89, 97, 168, 195, 259
unconstrained discriminant, 147, 192
underscore, 9, 17, 18
universal fixed, 187
universal integer, 178
universal real, 180
use, 109, 249
use clause, 109, 112, 115, 203

variables, 22

variant parts, 150
VAL, 36, 41
visibility, 4, 25, 103, 106, 114

when, 51, 56, 131, 152, 214
while statement, 56
with, 111, 198
with clause, 111, 114

xor, 38, 77, 93

+ , 30, 93, 187
– , 30, 93, 187
* , 30, 93, 187
/ , 30, 93, 187
** , 31, 33, 93
= , 31, 37, 73, 84, 94, 120, 123, 163
/= , 31, 37, 73, 84, 94, 120, 123, 163
> , 31, 37, 79, 93
<= , 31, 37, 79, 93
> , 31, 37, 79, 93
>= , 31, 37, 79, 93
<> , 68, 193, 199
& , 80, 93, 260

人世悲劇之起源之一在於人的感情也是隨時間而流动的，——無常之一种.

故而追求"不朽的感情"本身已註定為一悲劇.

160

"MURDER AT HOGANS CORNER, WASHINGTON"

-AN AMERICAN DESTINY-

by

WALLACE LOUIS EXUM

 For information write The Chart House, P. O. Box 342, Ocean Shores, Washington, 98569

Author's Published Works:

"BATTLESHIP, PEARL HARBOR, 1941"
Only One Got Underway
ISBN: 0-89865-093-3 (5 editions)
Library of Congress Catalog
Number 80-22891

"MURDER AT HOGANS CORNER, WASHINGTON"
An American Destiny
ISBN: 0-9634866-0-8
Library of Congress Cataloging
in Publication Data

Printed in U.S.A. by Snohomish Publishing Co.
Snohomish, Washington 98290

SECOND EDITION

MRS. VIRGINIA IRENE BARSIC, 1941-1991

C O N T E N T S

ILLUSTRATIONS

III Virginia Barsic
IX The Apartment Building
X Apartment Floor Plan
XI Hogans Corner
XII Grays Harbor, Mason, and Thurston, Counties
XIII Letter From Booth Gardner, Governor of Washington State
109 One of Ginny's Poems

CHAPTERS

Part 1

"Oh God! Not here, in our Little Town!"

1. MURDER.................. 1
2. DISCOVERY, AND FLIGHT...30
3. INVESTIGATION...........47
4. APPREHENSION............62
5. THE NEWS BREAKS........ 90

Part 2

"In all my 15 years of Judicial Public Service, This is the most Brutal and Senseless Murder-"

6. GRAYS HARBOR COUNTY COURTHOUSE.............109
7. 1ST TRIAL; JURY DELIBERATES; RESULT....126
8. 2ND TRIAL; JURY DELIBERATES; RESULT....166
9. SENTENCING.............200
10. "MURDER IS EVERYBODY'S BUSINESS"..208

ADDENDUM..............219

In kindest memory of Virginia Barsic, and to the surviving members of her family.

Mrs. Barsic was a generous, vibrant, and life-loving lady. Ginny, as she was known to all her friends (she had no enemies that I could determine), was also an accomplished and published poet, having won several awards for her poems, including 'The Golden Poet' award from the State of Washington. She of course, like the rest of us, had her faults, which along with her good points, should not have, but may have, contributed to the loss of her life. Ginny would surely hope for Justice but she would also wish for healing and recovery to all those involved, especially the children. And that some real sense might come from it all.

I wish to express my deepest appreciation to Judge Michael Spencer and Judge David Foscue; Grays Harbor County Prosecutor Steward Menefee and Chief Prosecutor Gerald Fuller; Defense Attorneys Jim Heard and John Farra; Sheriff's Detectives William Stocks and D.A. Smythe. And to all other members of the law enforcement and judicial system in Grays Harbor County and the State of Washington. All whose trust, time, and efforts made this book possible. A very special thanks to my good friends here on the Beach, Mr. Bob Focht and his fine Staff at the "North Coast News"; Mr. Stan Christerson at "Chris-by-the Sea"; Mr. Gordy Buchanan, Quartermaster of V.F.W. Post, Hogans Corner. And to my good friends and shipmates, Retired Admiral Herb Bridge and Retired Maritime Editor for the Seattle Times, Mr. Glen Carter, both of Seattle, who took an interest in this case as I did.

Mrs. Barsics' photograph, courtesy of; Mr. Greg Barsic; Kits Cameras, South Shore Mall; and Wheeler Photography, Loma Linda, Calif.

Most particularly and lovingly
to my dear wife,
JOYCE
Her hard work on the word-processor, and feminine insights and judgements, were all invaluable to this book.

And to our dear daughter,
MARILYN
Who saw the importance of it all for her generation and carefully contributed to the final edit of this book.

Authors Note:

This murder trial is only the second such trial that I have attended in my 65 years of life, and in which I stayed with from beginning to end. The earlier case and trial which attracted my attention about 12 years ago also had some U.S. Navy background. And that murder took place in a slightly similar setting, a small community known as Monks Corner; an historic horse and saber-clattering American Revolutionary area about 30 miles inland from Charleston, South Carolina. Two young enlisted U.S. Sailors were brutally murdered near there during the summer of 1980 for a small amount in the cash box while they were 'moon-lighting'; working late hours at a gas station-mini-mart establishment to supplement their family incomes instead of having to go on food stamps.

I was still serving on active duty at the time and between duty assignments, leaving behind a Minesweeper in Charleston Harbor and about to go on to three years instructor duty at the U.S. Naval Officers Candidate School, Newport, Rhode Island. During that 5-day trial, in which the defendants were ultimately found guilty, the courtroom was always packed with observing spectators. Joyce and I, living nearby, were barely able to find seats during that trial, and sometimes had to stand in the back of the courtroom if we wanted to stay and listen.

In this case and trial concerning Mrs. Virginia Barsic, the courtroom at Montasano, Grays Harbor County Courthouse was most always just sparsely filled with spectators. Were it not for the fact that Mrs. Barsic had two sons on active duty with the U.S. Navy, I would have, in all probability, followed the case and trial only through the local news media.

It was during the pre-trial motions that Joyce and I had a necessary occasion to be in the courthouse at Montesano one afternoon, to up-date our U. S. Passports commensurate with an up-coming trip to England we were committed to, that I got my first glimpse of two of the defendants accused in the killing of Mrs. Barsic. Because of the extraordinary brutality of her death, and learning that the motions were underway while we were there, I quietly stepped in and took a seat in the nearly empty courtroom spectators section. Almost automatically, I found some scraps of paper in my coat pockets and began taking notes.

However, it was not until some two weeks after the trials and sentencing had ended that I decided, with much encouragement from friends and acquaintances, that I might attempt this book. There is one other reason for my direct interest in the case: Some months prior to her death, I had the pleasant experience of becoming acquainted with Mrs. Barsic face to face. My brief meeting with her took place when I stopped into a local motel office inquiring about a friend and his wife I had not seen around Ocean Shores in several weeks and who had worked as office managers at that motel. Mrs. Barsic in her buoyant, and delightfully courteous manner, let me know my friend and his wife had left town because of his wife's ill health; (my friend's wife had cancer, as I later learned). Mrs. Barsic was simply a very nice lady to talk with, and she asked to be remembered to my wife Joyce.

Joyce, at the time (and still does) worked the desk and phones at a local motel-condo-house rental agency, filling reservations for out-of-town people wanting to get away to the beach, mostly from the Seattle area, for weekends. Mrs. Barsic sometimes answered the phone at the motel she was working for. She was also a cleaning lady, for motel rooms, and had numerous nice friends in and around Ocean Shores. Joyce and I were just two of her friends.

Finally, as with all such murder cases; investigations, trials, examinations and cross examinations, and the search for human truth, there are always left some doubts and unanswered questions, and that age-old element called mystery. This murder case is no exception. Moreover, there are broad social and moral implications in this case that are currently National in scope and all of us, in one way or another, are affected by them.

W. L. E.

The Tri-Plex Apartment

W.L.E.

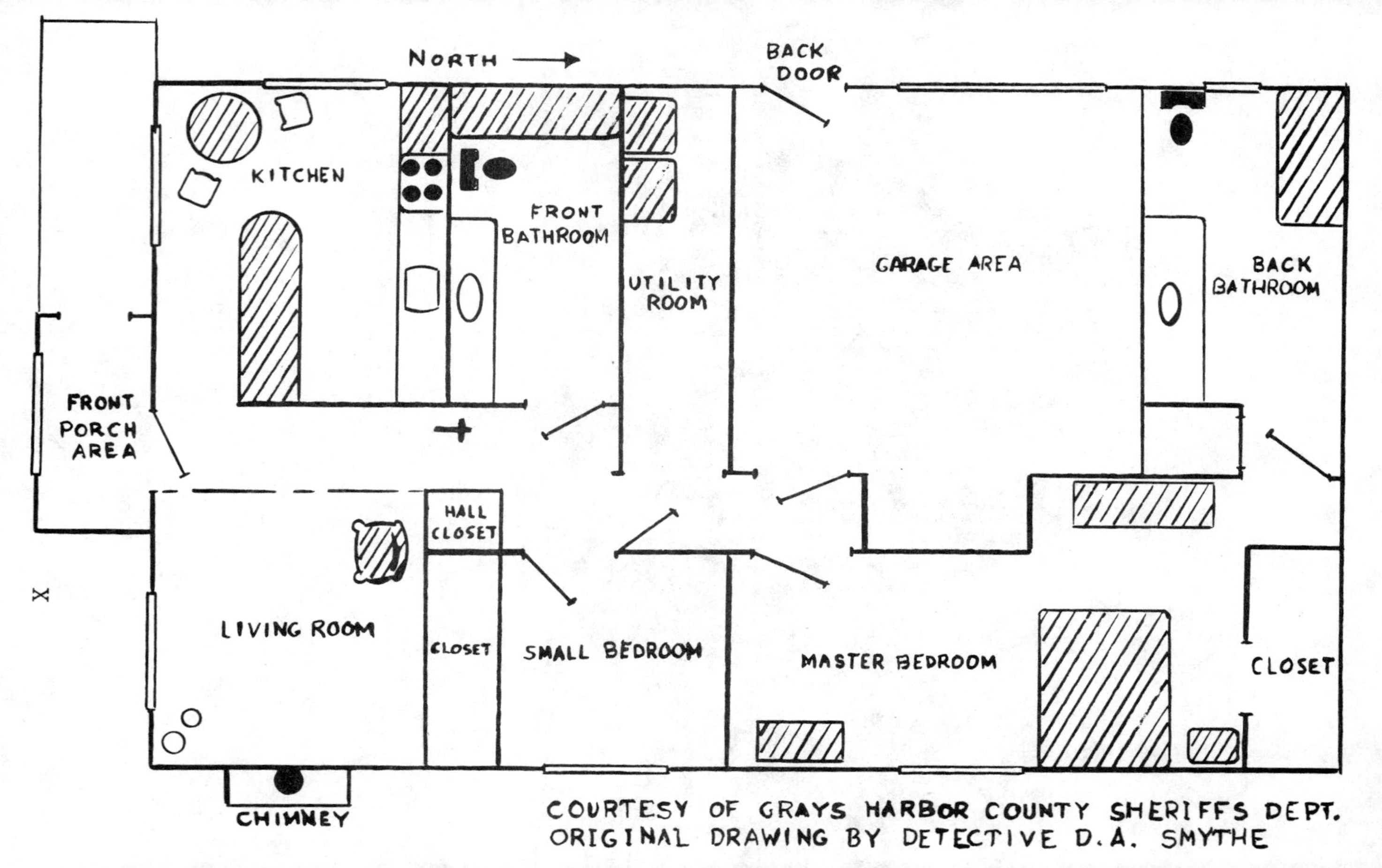

COURTESY OF GRAYS HARBOR COUNTY SHERIFFS DEPT.
ORIGINAL DRAWING BY DETECTIVE D.A. SMYTHE

X

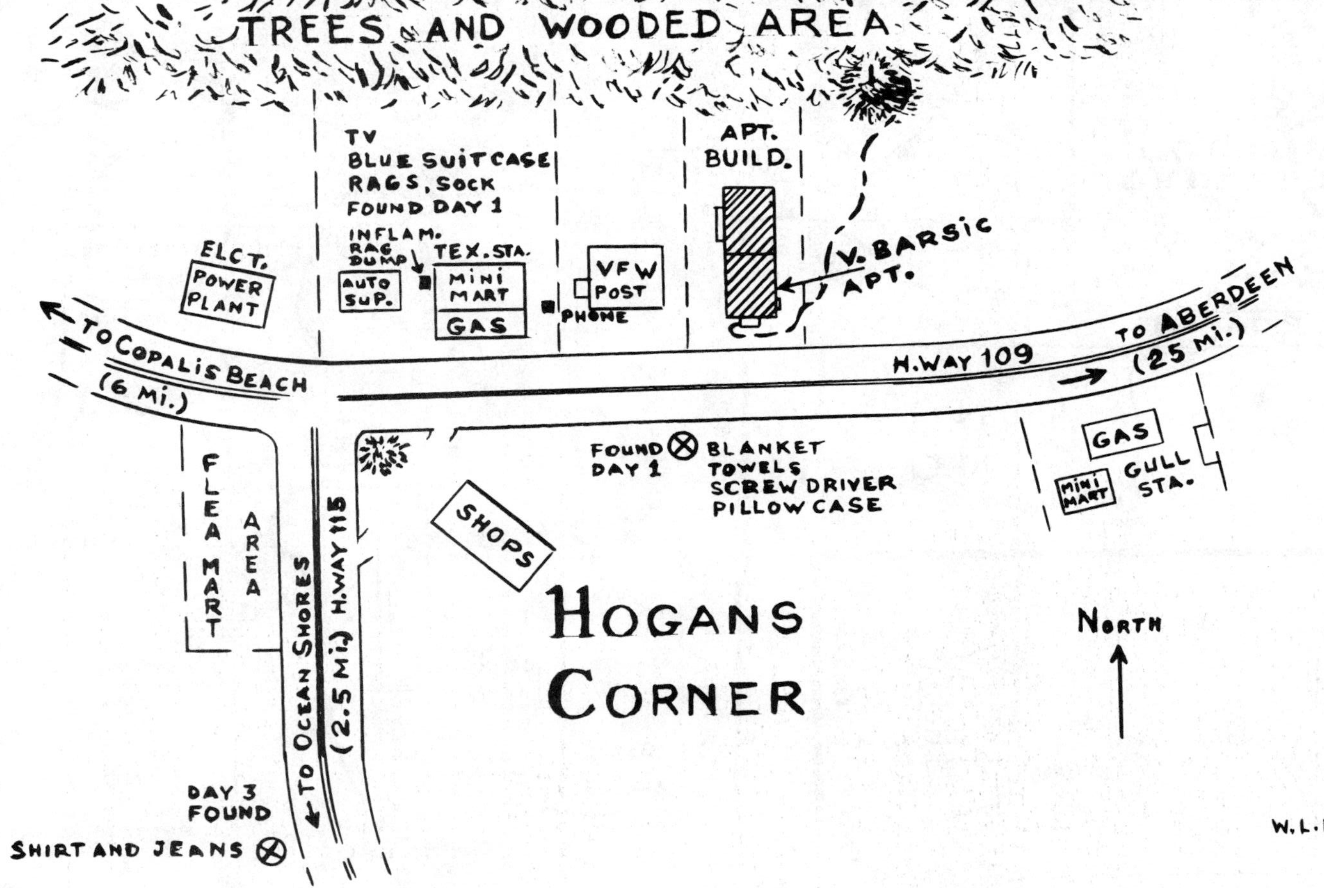

TREES AND WOODED AREA
TV
BLUE SUITCASE
RAGS, SOCK
FOUND DAY 1
INFLAM. RAG DUMP
TEX. STA.
MINI MART
GAS
AUTO SUP.
APT. BUILD.
V. BARSIC APT.
VFW POST
PHONE
ELCT. POWER PLANT
TO COPALIS BEACH
(6 MI.)
H. WAY 109
TO ABERDEEN
(25 MI.)
GAS
MINI MART
GULL STA.
FOUND DAY 1
BLANKET
TOWELS
SCREW DRIVER
PILLOW CASE
FLEA MART AREA
TO OCEAN SHORES
(2.5 MI.) H. WAY 115
SHOPS
HOGANS CORNER
NORTH
DAY 3 FOUND
SHIRT AND JEANS
W.L.E.

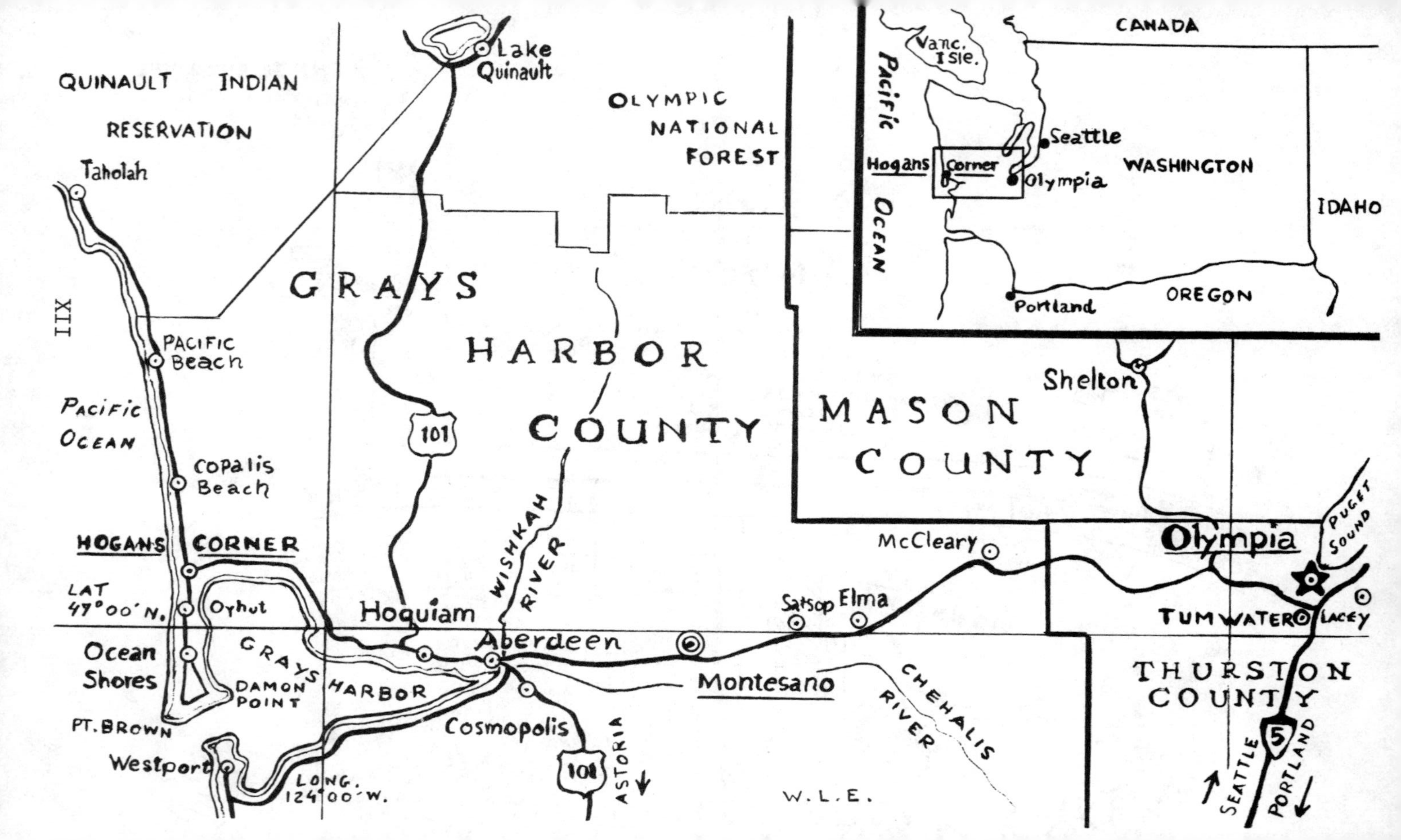
QUINAULT INDIAN
RESERVATION
Taholah
Lake Quinault
OLYMPIC
NATIONAL
FOREST
GRAYS
HARBOR
COUNTY
MASON
COUNTY
101
PACIFIC Beach
Pacific
Ocean
Copalis Beach
HOGANS CORNER
LAT 47°00′N.
Oyhut
Ocean Shores
DAMON POINT
GRAYS HARBOR
PT. BROWN
Westport
LONG. 124°00′W.
Hoquiam
Aberdeen
WISHKAH RIVER
Cosmopolis
ASTORIA
Montesano
CHEHALIS RIVER
W.L.E.
Satsop
Elma
McCleary
Shelton
Olympia
PUGET SOUND
TUMWATER
LACEY
THURSTON
COUNTY
5
SEATTLE
PORTLAND
CANADA
Vanc. Isle.
Pacific
Ocean
Hogans
Corner
Seattle
Olympia
WASHINGTON
IDAHO
Portland
OREGON

State of
Washington
Office of the
Governor

December 2, 1991

Wallace L. Exum, CWO-4
U. S. Navy (Retired)
Post Office Box 342
Ocean Shores, Washington 98569

Dear Mr. Exum:

Thank you for the information you sent me about Mrs. Virginia Barsic. The circumstances surrounding her death were very tragic, and must have been a great shock to her family and to her community.

I appreciated your taking the time to share your perspective about this unfortunate news with me and others in your community. I trust that in the event you have had an opportunity to have contact with members of her family, you have extended to them heartfelt sympathy on behalf of all of us. Mrs. Barsic sought to uphold high standards and show young people there is a better path. She leaves us a legacy to be valued and remembered.

Sincerely,

Booth Gardner

Booth Gardner
Governor

This is a true story. With the exception of Mrs. Virginia Barsic and the names listed on the Dedication Page, all other names in this Book connected to the Barsic case have been changed or entirely omitted, to protect families, children, and individuals however slight or directly involved. Chief references were police and sheriffs reports, courtroom trial transcripts, and official statements from witnesses. And personal notes, observations, and conversations which I experienced during the course of events as they developed. I take full responsibility for the narration as I have tried to be as accurate as possible. W.L.E.

PART ONE

"OH GOD! NOT HERE, IN OUR LITTLE TOWN!"

CHAPTER ONE: MURDER

Her eerie screams and feeble resistance finally came to an end. It was shortly before 5 a.m., Monday the 26th of August, 1991. Ginny had put up a good fight during the previous 40 minutes, but after the last 10 minutes of diminishing frenzied struggle, she had to give up her life.

Ginny was only 5 feet 3 inches in height, and she was out-numbered by strong youngsters less than half her age. But she left numerous scratch and bite marks on two of them which they could not hide. Even as she lay still in that small hallway, with three of them standing over her, there was yet some doubt as to whether she was still alive. If she did have some small pulse left it would not last long, with her life blood pouring out from some 30 stab wounds, and both her eyes nearly gouged out. There was no '911' for her.

Outside in the cool early-morning damp night air it was still dark. A steady 10 knots breeze came in from the Pacific Ocean. And if you stood perfectly still you could clearly hear the pounding surf on the beach about a 1,000 yards directly west, and you could hear the crickets and frogs croaking down around the marshy bottom between Ginny's apartment and the beach. A three-quarter moon was approaching the south-western horizon, and except for some scudding clouds building from the northwest there were, like glimmering sequins on a party dress, countless twinkling stars on an otherwise black velvet sky. It was still school vacation for most youngsters and they could sleep in, but for a number of parents and working people in the Hogans Corner and Ocean Shores middle class neighborhoods, alarm clocks would be going off near them, stirring those people out of bed to begin a new week of work and tourist activity. It would be a good hour before the first rays of dawn would come across the eastern sky, and still another half hour to sunrise. The summer temperatures would predictably climb to about 70 degrees by noon.

But now, back inside Ginny's ground floor apartment, an additional bloody ritual of sorts had just taken place, and the three young people were breathing hard and thinking fast what to do next. Beer cans, bottles, and half eaten or empty bags of corn chips were scattered in most every room. All the lights in the apartment were burning brightly. Their clothes, hands and faces, in bloody grotesque disarray reflected the fight Ginny had put up for her life. The older of the three, a 20 year old, tall and slender young woman, could have easily passed, in an earlier moment in time, as a sister of Brook Shields. The two young men, both 18 years each, still had their boyish good looks and good builds, at about 150 and 160 pounds. One, the blond-headed youth with only slightly longer hair than normal, was sucking the little finger on his right hand, and would later claim at his trial he was, "-in shock." The other youngster, clad only in a dark pair of sweat pants and a couple inches shorter in height than his friend and with neatly cut black hair, was painted in blood, from his face to his waist. He would later make no denials at his trial about his part in the killing of Ginny, who had just turned 50 four months earlier.

To be precise, there were a total of six young people staying at Ginny's apartment that weekend, and two of them, a boy of 17 and his girlfriend of 14, had fled the apartment only minutes before Ginny's final struggle for her life. The sixth young person was another 14 year old girl, dark complected and heavy set, who had passed out from alcohol; they had all been drinking heavily during that weekend at Ginny's apartment, and this young girl was still curled up on the floor in a corner of the living room, sleeping it off, having barely come awake a few times because of the noise around her.

It seemed there were knife marks, and human blood splattered every where; the walls,the floors, the bathrooms, even some on the ceilings, and the sight and smell of it all nauseated Tammy Muller, the attractive 20 year old. She was slightly shaking all over when Marvin Garba, the dark haired youth stated in matter-of-fact tones, "We got to start cleaning this crap up and get the hell out'a here. It'll be daylight pretty soon." Tammy answered, with a shuddering voice, "You look awful, and you ought to take a shower!"

"What about Ginny! What are we going to do with her!" more of a statement than a question, Craig Borman, the blond haired boy, of lesser weight, said in earnest. Then Tammy stepped away, came back with a cream colored blanket and tossed it next to Ginny's body.

Marv had left the small hallway for the bathroom and was already in the process of taking a quick shower. Tammy began having an argument with Craig. "-I won't do it! I didn't make this goddam mess. I'll wipe the walls down, but I won't clean up the blood clots. I won't do it!"

"Alright, alright! I'll get the floors, but you get started on the walls.", and added, "We've got to move it!" They both had towels and rags at this time.

Marv wasn't long with his shower, and in a few minutes, came back out drying himself with one of Ginny's bath towels and went directly to an overnite bag in the living room corner, and began getting dressed with some fresh clothes. After tying on his jogging shoes he picked back up his damp towel and began cleaning up the blood clots with Craig. There was so much of it, and they were losing time. Both boys stopped almost together and began concentrating on Ginny's body.

"We've got to move her!" said Marv. "You know that pile of dirt in the back?"

"I know it!" answered Craig. Then they both began wrapping Ginny up in the cream colored blanket.

With help from Craig, Marv got Ginny in the blanket and hoisted her up over his right shoulder. But after only a few steps toward the front door, Ginny slipped out of the bloody blanket and back down onto the floor, with a shuddering thump-bump.

Tammy stopped wiping down one of the inboard walls, and cried, "My god, what are you guys doing now?"

"It ain't gonna work!" Marv said, ignoring Tammy. "She's dead weight and too slippery. We could cut her up and take the pieces out easier."

"Hell no!" answered Craig. "Lets just put her back on the blanket and pull her out there!"

"Alright, lets try it."

But it didn't work that way either. With Ginny now rolled back on the blanket, the two young men began tugging at their corner-ends. They only made a few steps closer to the front door when the blanket ripped apart between the ends they were tugging.

"The hell with it!" one of them said. There was now only one way left. Craig and Marv each took one of Ginny's ankles, and this time they easily dragged her, on her back, across the floor to the front door. A quick look around outside; all seemed clear, and they began tugging and dragging Ginny's body again, still dressed in her light grey leotard bottoms and dark poncho style pull-over shirt. This time they were successful.

Out the front door, over and around the concrete thresh- hold, across the gravel front yard, and into the next property and empty lot directly east. It still wasn't all that easy for them. They had to practically make their own path in the dark. Up and down gullies, over rocks and brush. Seldom in a straight line, and mostly up hill. The sound of frogs echoed around them, and the moonlight and shimmering stars gave them just enough light to see where they were going. It is likely they stopped a couple times on their way, to catch their breath before going on and because of the severe pain Craig was experiencing from Ginny's deep bites on his right hand, especially his right little finger.

Altogether it took them about 5 minutes to get to the dirt pile up near the edge of the trees. A bulldozer had scraped up a pile of brush and dirt there some weeks earlier. They didn't spend anytime digging a grave. They just pulled Ginny over to the far side of the dirt pile, took a few moments breather, and with their hands began scooping and pulling the red dirt over her. Thinking they had her pretty well covered, they took a few more moments breather, while looking down on the shallow grave. Then, one of them, knowing that Ginny's upper poncho had slipped off during the dragging, ran back along their path, found it, came back and dropped it down near the top of the pile then they spread a little dirt over it too.

Turning with a glance for the short run back down, all seemed clear. One of the teenagers feet touched something hard and long. He reached down to pick it up. It was a 2 x 2 inch wooden pole about 6 feet in length. He started to chuck it away, but had a better idea. It would make a good marker, in case they had to come back. And no one would notice it but them. So he stepped back to about where Ginny was, and muscled it down in the dirt about a foot. The pole went down between Ginny's covered out-stretched right arm and her chest.

The lights were all still on in the apartment below and they quickly made their way back there, and to Tammy, who was still doing a little cleaning up. She was glad they were back as it was getting spooky being all alone in that apartment, except for Sonja Cortell, who was still 'crashed' in the far corner of the living room.

Back up on the rude dirt mound, that stark pole in the moonlight would be the only grave monument Ginny would ever have on this earth. After state and county medical examiners and pathologists completed their findings, Ginny's body, what there was left of it, would be carefully and religiously cremated before the week was out.

After a few more moments of wiping down walls and floors, one of the boys said, "I don't know why we should clean this place up. We ought'a trash it!"

"Yea!" answered the other youth. "Make it look like Ginny went out, and came back with a boyfriend-."

"And her husband came in and caught'em, and they had a big fight."

"That's it! It makes sense!"

With their clever new plan now established, they began putting the bloody rags and towels in a pile. Tammy, going along with this better idea, stepped over to one of the Indian bowls on a stand near the fireplace, and pulled it over. The bowl crashed to the floor, and out scattered a dozen or so shells Ginny had lovingly collected from the beach during the past few months.

Now all three began preparing to leave Ginny's apartment for good; an intention at least for the moment. Craig took his pants off for a cleaner pair, and slipped on a fresh pullover shirt from Marv's overnight bag. Marv told Tammy to get rid of the blanket, pillow case, and after wiping it off, the small orange and black phillips-head screwdriver they had used on Ginny earlier. "Stash this stuff outside somewhere," he said.

Tammy took the items in hand, went out the front door, and in the dark crossed straight over to the other side of the highway and simply tossed them beyond the gully's soft shoulder, into the brush. On her return she found Craig and Marv had a few more rags and towels in their hands. Tammy went over to Sonja, now laying stretched out in her corner of the livingroom, and shook her. Sonja came awake enough to hear Tammy urge her, "-get up! Get up! We're leaving now. Come on and get up."

Taking a last look around the front section of the apartment, one of the boys walked over to the kitchen table and, finding a pencil and piece of scratch paper, wrote a two-word vulgar note, and placed it in the center of the table.

Tammy had several pieces of inexpensive jewelry tucked away in her jean pockets and a couple of stiff bracelets on her left wrist which she had picked up earlier from Ginny's blond dresser in the back bedroom. Then she quickly packed up her blue-grained suitcase, and she was ready to leave. The boys had a few souvenirs of their own in their pockets. Then, with Craig carrying Ginny's small TV and Marv with the last of the bloody rags and towels in one hand, and Sonja's two overnight bags in the other, they all departed into the night air.

The four of them; Sonja was still groggy from her awakened deep sleep, quietly walked in front of the VFW building directly west, and continued on past the front of the all night Texaco mini-mart. No one noticed them in the slightest. Marv and Craig detoured over and around to the far side of the gasoline island to the west side of the mini-mart building, and found a flammable rag-dumping container there. After lifting the metal lid, Marv dropped the rags and towels in the dark container. Then Craig took a few steps beyond the container and heaved the TV set into the brush. Tammy, following the boys over, stepped in the brush and placed her blue suitcase and Sonja's tote-bags near the TV set. They were just too heavy to carry. It was done. Now all they had to do was get back into Ocean Shores, and Dan's place.

The distance from Hogans Corner to the impressive flag-stone monument entrance of the resort community of Ocean Shores, is two and a half miles. And another mile to Dan's apartment building, nestled in along one of the evergreen tree lane drives between the harbor side and beach side of the picturesque community.

The first light blue shades of dawn were developing across the Monday morning sky as the small group crossed the intersection of Hogans Corner and began their walking trek, on the right side of highway 115. The boys set a leisurely pace and occasionally conversed in low tones, while the girls, a few steps behind, also conversed in hushed tones.

Robert Noonan, the 17 year old, and his 14 year old girlfriend, Tina Murphy, were at that moment hidden in the grass and behind the short trees up on the southeast corner of Hogans Corner. They had been observing their young companions and their actions around Ginny's apartment building during the previous 20 minutes.

Earlier, at about 4:45 a.m., and after Bob and Tina could no longer stand the madness of what was going on inside Ginny's apartment, they just knew they had to get out of there. They stood in the shadows of the VFW building on the other side of the cyclone fence, wild-eyed, crying and arguing together what they should do. Then they heard the side door of Ginny's apartment open, looked over and saw Tammy step outside, and lean on the apartment building west wall a moment. Then she started walking toward the front of the apartment building.

Bob, in anguished tones, trying not to get too loud about it, shouted over to her, "Tammy! Come on with us! Get away from there!"

Tina, in the same low but deliberate voice, called to Tammy, "Bob's right! Come on with us! You got to get away from there!"

Tammy faintly saw them in the darkness, but didn't answer right away. The front door of the apartment opened and Marv stood silhouetted in the door way. Tammy knew he was there, then glanced back to Bob and Tina, who were still saying, "-come on! Come on!"

"I can't!" she said. "I'm going to stay with the guys. Anyway, Sonja's still crapped out in the corner. I'm staying. You go on!"

Bob tried one last time, "You're gonna get 15 years for this if you stay. I know what I'm talk'n about! Come on!" But it was no use. Tammy didn't answer back. She just turned and stepped back into the apartment the way she came. Bob Noonan could hardly talk anymore; in fact he didn't speak in full sentences for several hours. At this moment he just sat on the ground in front of the VFW building and began crying. Tina Murphy, who had been his friend and lover for several months, sat down beside him and tried to comfort him in her arms.

Between sobs, Bob managed to say, "-got to get away from here!" and "-wish I had a cigarette." With Tina's help, he was able to get up off the ground, and they started walking toward the lights of the Texaco mini-mart, next to the VFW building. He just couldn't talk anymore. They carefully managed to get inside the brightly lit interior of the mini-mart. The steady hum of the refrigeration units, keeping the milk, pop, and beer cold, greeted them as they stepped over to the main counter.

A middle-aged woman seated behind the counter heard the door chimes ring and stopped her inventory list checking, and looked up at the two young people in front of her. She could tell at a glance the teenagers were distraught, and thought they had just been informed that one of the boy's parents had just died, or something. The young girl asked if they could purchase a pack of cigarettes.

The duty mini-mart manager was in no habit of selling cigarettes, beer or the like to teenagers, and almost said no. But out of sympathy to the distraught youngsters, she asked what brand he would like. Bob still couldn't talk, and had to write down on a slip of paper his selected brand. She even thought the boy might be deaf. After the transaction was complete, the duty night manager gave them one more look of curious sympathy, then went back to her inventory checking. She would remember them alright. They were both about the same height, at about five and a half feet, and about the same length of hair; Bob's was dark brown and curly; lots of it. And Tina's, a little lighter and straighter. He being a quite skinny 130 pounds, Tina probably weighed 10 pounds more than Bob.

Back out in the night air, they both made the decision to hurry away from there, and walk to Ocean Shores. Maybe get a bite to eat and catch the early morning bus from there back to the Aberdeen-Hoquiam area. So they crossed over the all quiet intersection to the southeast corner. But Tina was curious to find out what the others were going to do next around Ginny's apartment. So she led Bob up the high embankment, and they lay down in the grass behind the short trees and waited. Bob fell asleep almost immediately.

It wasn't long before Tina dimly observed Marv and Craig step out of the apartment, look around, and began dragging something behind them. Out the front door, around to the east side, and into the next lot over. She lost sight of them, but they returned empty handed in a few minutes, and went back into the lighted apartment. In another ten minutes or so, Tina then saw all four of them leave the apartment with bundles and bags in their hands. They were certainly leaving for good, she thought.

After observing them deposit or throw away most of the items they were carrying, around the west side of the Texaco mini-mart, she nudged Bob awake. Bob raised up, and from their hiding place they saw the four young people cross the intersection and walk directly in front of them on the other side of highway, going toward Ocean Shores. The first crack of dawn had come and they could see Craig step away from the group.

"Look at'em!" Bob quietly said, "He's freaking out again!"

"No!" Tina answered. "He just threw something away." Then they saw Craig quickly rejoin his friends.

Bob and Tina watched them a few more moments, then relaxed back on the damp grass. On his back and with his eyes closed, Bob moaned, "They're crazy! They're all crazy!" Then he fell asleep again. Tina occasionally lifted herself up on one elbow, and finally saw Marv, Craig, Tammy, and Sonja walk out of sight, down the road to Ocean Shores. Looking back down at Bob, she was trying to think.

In that early dawn and heavy stillness, even the frogs had quieted down, welcome new sounds now came to Tina's ears. It was the sounds of civilization and reality. First she heard, then caught sight of a car, coming up from Ocean Shores. The driver came to the stop sign at Hogans Corner, made a right turn and headed off in the direction of Aberdeen. The driver of this car would later make a statement to the police that he had passed four young people, two girls, one a tall blonde, and two boys, walking south along Highway 115 at about 5:45 a.m., while traveling north on his way to work.

Then some minutes later, Tina heard the distant machine noise of an approaching road vehicle, coming from the east. She attempted to shove Bob awake again. It was the early morning bus, a bright yellow Grays Harbor County bus coming out from Aberdeen. At this moment the bus was passing the Gull Station on its left and slowing down for the intersection. It would make its rounds on the North Beach and would eventually make its way back to the Aberdeen-Hoquiam area by 7:15 a.m. But first, the driver would make a scheduled stop here, at Hogans Corner, before going on to Ocean Shores.

Tina shoved and pushed Bob fully awake, and pulled him up to his feet. They had to make that bus. They ran out of their hiding place, down the embankment, darted back across the intersection and crossed in front of the bus just as it came to a complete stop. The whoosh of the front door opened, they immediately climbed in, and Tina paid their fare. The driver moved the bus away from the Texaco mini-mart and made a hard turn left as the two youngsters struggled to get a seat on the right side, halfway down the aisle of the almost empty bus. It was 6 a.m.

Now on the straightaway, along Highway 115, the driver settled his bus down to a steady 40 miles an hour. Bob and Tina were glad to be moving. They knew they would be passing their four companions pretty soon. They also knew the bus made only scheduled stops, and no chance the driver would pick them up half way down the highway.

Sure enough, Tina could see up ahead in the distance their friends of the past weekend, walking along on the same side of the highway as the bus. The driver steered a little to the left and over the center of the highway, allowing a safe distance from the walking group. Tina and Bob hunkered down a little and gave no attention out the bus window as they went by.

Another mile or so and the driver began slowing down for the sharp curve ahead, and into the small village of Oyhut, situated just outside the gates of Ocean Shores. On the right side, the newly built North Beach High School went by, and on the left, the post office and one of the community's drive-in banks. They were now at the flag-stone monument entrance. The driver slowed the bus to a crawl, made a sharp left turn, and drove the bus between the two monuments. They were inside Ocean Shores.

As the bus moved along on Point Brown Avenue, passing the small tourist shops and eating establishments along the way, not yet opened, Bob and Tina were beginning to feel more heart broken and frightened than ever. They knew they were irretrievably separated from the normal crowds of people who would soon be enjoying what appeared to be a pretty good day coming up. If only they had not joined up with those other four young people there at the major bus stop in Aberdeen some 60 hours earlier. The nightmare of the past three days was beginning to crush in on them, especially Bob. If only it was just a nightmare; if only.

The bus continued on to the center of town, made a left turn around the traffic island, and came to a complete stop in front of Ocean Shore's only real super market in town. Another few moments, and it was on its way again, threading through the evergreen tree-covered residential areas of the narrow Washington coast peninsula. Now going south on Dolphin Avenue, the bus passed close to Dan's two-story apartment building.

Another few turns and jogs and they were on Olympus Street headed for the Ocean Shores Marina.

On his way the driver of the bus had to slow down, or move over and make room for an occasional car now on the road, or a vehicle backing out of its driveway to take the driver to work.

Leaving the tree-lined drives behind, the bus broke into the wide clearing with the marina in full view. The sky over Grays Harbor was clearing to the east, and it was almost sunrise. Seagulls were screeching and fluttering around the back entrance of the large restaurant which commanded the whole area of the marina. Halyards on the few sailboats that were still moored in the sheltered cove were clattering against their masts, all encouraging their master-mariners they were ready to continue their summer sailing, in Grays Harbor or out on the challenging Pacific Ocean.

Again the driver of the bus made only a momentary stop, took on a few more passengers, and he was on his way again, this time on a northwest run back into town, to the Ocean Shores Inn. This six-mile leg took its passengers along a decidedly different picturesque terrain, a winding road with gently moving high dune grass on either side of the bus. Then the passengers, particularly on the left side of the bus, had a good view of the Pacific sand dunes, and the occasional luxurious homes that comfortably rested high on the beach, in full view of this part of the massive Pacific Ocean. This part of the community of Ocean Shores is not unlike the rugged sea and wind-swept landscape of Cornwall and the Dartmouth Moors, located on the other side of the world, at the southwestern tip of England. But for two of the passengers on this bus ride, they were anxious to make time and get away from it all.

Pulling into the beach entrance at the Ocean Shores Inn; the oldest, sprawling, and most well-known establishment in Ocean Shores, the driver announced over his shoulder, there would be a "-10 minute stop," before proceeding back to Hoquiam. The time was about 6:20 a.m. when the driver angle-parked his bus in front of the Inn, and set his safety hand brakes.

Reluctant at first, Bob and Tina were the last passengers to climb out, and into the salt air. The sandy beach and gently rolling surf were just a kite-string distance on their left side. The warm full morning sun was now rising over the whole community. It would be nice to get a cup of coffee and have a cigarette before going on the 25 mile ride back to Hoquiam. And they weren't worried too much about seeing their four friends, who they stopped regarding as friends hours ago. They would only be walking through the entrance gate about that time anyway; a good mile from the Inn.

Most of the occupants in the coffee-shop section of the restaurant were seated at the counter, and conversations ranged from the tourist activity of the past weekend to the victorious soldiers of Desert Storm who would soon be coming home from Iraq. The town was quite proud of having a number of young men and women serving in uniform, during the Persian Gulf campaign. Bob and Tina, trying to keep their distance from other people, especially from inquiring friendly eyes, found a table on the far side of the room next to a window.

They checked over what little money they had, and decided they needed to conserve it. They had no real appetite anyway. So when the smiling waitress came over, they knew they wanted only coffee. And Tina asked the waitress if just coffee would be alright, since they were at a table.

As a matter of fact, the attractive waitress

standing in front of Tina and Bob was a good friend of Virginia Barsic. Ginny had often enjoyed breakfast or lunch at the Inn over the past few years, and was on pleasant greeting terms with a number of people at the counter that morning. And Ginny loved talking about her two sons who were serving on active duty in the Navy.

"Sure!" the waitress answered, "Com'n right up!"

Bob was almost finished with his first cigarette and lit the second one with the butt-end of the first one. His eyes were blood shot and both youngsters appeared as if they had just come off the beach after having spent the night out there, with their rumpled clothes on. And they smelled bad. Tina knew he was fighting hard from going into a crying jag. And she truly sympathized with him. She too was needing sympathy, and he was not unaware of that. He squeezed her hands together in his. He also knew she was not as involved in the past weekend nightmare as he was. And he was glad for that.

Ten minutes can go by awfully fast. They downed two cups of coffee each, and Bob finished three cigarettes before they saw the bus driver over at the counter get up and start for the cash register. The driver turned and waved at one of the occupants still at the counter, then headed out for his bus. Bob and Tina got up with their coffee ticket, paid their bill and followed him out.

There were already a half dozen people waiting alongside the bus, ready to board. And, following the driver in, including a few new passengers who had been enjoying their morning coffee with the driver back at the counter, Bob and Tina found their same seat on the right side of the bus. They settled in for the 45-minute ride to Hoquiam. The driver started up the diesel engine, and began backing around, then headed east, across Ocean Shores Boulevard, made his turn at the traffic island onto Point Brown Avenue, and headed north.

No question about it. There they were, the four of them; Tammy, Sonja, Craig, and Marv all standing just outside of the BP gas and mini-mart, on the east side of Point Brown Avenue. Marv had just walked out with two packs of cigarettes he had purchased from inside. For a split second all four of them were right below Tina and Bob's window, as the bus went by.

Tammy and Sonja both got a glimpse of them peering out from the moving bus, as Marv was sharing one of the packs of cigarettes with Craig.

With the shock of knowing they were all so near again, even though Bob knew there was a good chance of seeing them on the road again, he turned with flowing tears to Tina and, trying to keep his anguished voice down, said, "The freaks! They're crazy! They're all crazy!" Then he buried his face in his own hands. Tina reached over with her right arm and tried to comfort him.

A middle aged, nicely dressed woman, seated a few rows behind, couldn't help noticing the two youngsters up ahead of her. It was 6:35 a.m. They were observed as being in tearful despair, with the teenage girl doing her best to comfort her boyfriend. The woman, a frequent rider of the weekday morning bus, would later call in her own observations to the police of the touching young people. They became indelible in her mind by the time they reached the Hoquiam bus depot.

For a few moments Tammy stared at the back of the yellow bus as it continued north on up Point Brown Avenue. It made a right turn at the monuments and went out of sight. Then she turned and began following her three companions, walking on toward the center of town. They still had a little under a mile to hike it to Dan's place.

Earlier, on their 2 mile walk from Hogans Corner, the trip had been mostly uneventful. Shortly after they started out, Craig had rolled up his other shirt and jeans with blood on them, and flung them over onto the west side of the highway embankment. Bringing up the rear with Sonja, who wanted to know, "-what's going on?", Tammy informed her that Ginny was dead, but left out the details as to how she died.

A few paces ahead, Marv talked to Craig about the real "-Power!" he felt. He said he could jump ten feet in the air if he really wanted to. Craig, on the other hand, and feeling more down to earth, talked about how he hoped the recent past events wouldn't interfere with his plans to go into college that Fall. He gritted his teeth about it, and almost felt like crying. Marv consoled him saying, "-don't worry about it, man! We're blood brothers now, ya know? We made our pact back there, remember?" Craig felt a little chill with that remark and Tammy, seeing him shiver, stepped up and gave him her black and pink jacket.

A car came over the hill in front of them, and passed them going in the opposite direction. In a few moments the car made a U turn behind them, came back, and passed them again, now traveling in their same direction. All four of the youngsters followed the car as it went by. After about ten minutes the same car returned, now going in the original direction as when they first saw it. A lone driver was in the car. Marv and Craig both thought they were being 'shadowed'. The thought crossed Marv's mind that maybe Bob and Tina had got to the cops, and squealed on them. "I'll kill um, if I catch um!", he said. And from his pants, he withdrew a black handled long knife, which had come from Ginny's kitchen. He tossed it from hand to hand, and referred to it as his new "-baby!"

Craig got even more concerned and agitated, still thinking over his chances to get into college, as he had been planning and saving for the past several months.

The driver of the car, who had just passed them three times, was in no way 'shadowing' them. In his haste to get out of his house and going on his way to work that morning, he simply realized before reaching Hogan's Corner, he had forgot his eye glasses, turned around, went back home, got them off the kitchen table, and was now properly on his way to work in Aberdeen, though now running a little late.

The group finally got to the monuments guarding Ocean Shores. Now walking on the east side of Point Brown Avenue, and ten minutes later, they arrived in front of the BP mini-mart, another all-night establishment. The sun was up, and another new day was beginning. Since they were out of cigarettes Marv stepped in and came back out with two packs, just as the bright yellow Grays Harbor County bus went by them.

Now all they had to do was to cover a little less than a mile to Dan's apartment. For Craig it meant a shower and clean clothes; clothes that he had stashed there for some time. He had been living in and out of Dan's since school vacation had started in June. And since Dan was a school teacher in the area, and an acquaintance of his mom's, who was also a school teacher up in the Lake Quinault district, Craig's parents thought it was a fine arrangement for their son during the summer months.

After reaching the traffic island in the middle of town they crossed over that intersection and walked east, keeping the Shop Rite super market on their right side. Now they were just a few blocks away. They cut some corners and got on Sunset Drive. Another ten minute walk and they were there. Dog tired, foot sore, they were now at the lower glass double doors of Dan's two story apartment. It was almost 7 a.m. Craig stepped up and tried to slide the drape covered glass door on over, another tug and it slid open. The two girls, who had momentarily, sat on the edge of the natural wood porch, got back up and followed Craig and Marv on in.

On the other side, in the darkened living room, a middle aged woman; a drop-by, drop-in kind of friend of Dan's, who had been sharing the evening with him had fallen asleep on the couch after their watching a couple of old movies on late night TV. Now the disturbance at the glass door brought the woman awake, and out from under the warm blanket she had over her on the couch. Almost in the dark she got up and moved to the door. With the drapes pulled aside, she recognized Craig Borman right away. He was the young boy who she had met a few times and who she knew had been staying with Dan off and on during the past several weeks. Dan had told her the night before that Craig was out "Partying" and wouldn't be back that night. Now here he was, with his friends coming in right behind him. "We're really tired," Craig said, "and need to get some sleep."

The woman gave way, turned back, and began folding up the blanket on the couch. With all these youngsters coming in she decided to let Dan know about it. She next climbed the stairs, knocked on the bedroom door at the top of the landing. On hearing Dan rustling in his bed on the other side, she opened the door, stepped in, and began letting him know Craig had just returned and with a number of his friends. They were all downstairs. At that moment Craig, who had followed her upstairs a few seconds later, stuck his head in and announced to Dan he was back, and with his friends. They were going to stay downstairs and get some needed sleep, while Craig would occupy the spare bedroom.

The woman remained in Dan's bedroom awhile longer, talking to him about her plans of the day, then went back downstairs. She glanced around at the young people who were already curled up in various places and positions around the living room floor and on the couch. She got her shoes on, picked up her personal belongings and departed. Dan, back up in his bedroom rolled over and went back for a few more hours of sleep.

Almost at the same moment that Dan was positioning his pillow more comfortably under his head, the Grays Harbor County bus was pulling into the Hoquiam bus depot.

Every passenger on the bus departed, and the woman who had been observing Bob and Tina from a few rows behind, lost them in the crowd out on the depot platform. Most people transferred to another bus for the short ride into Aberdeen.

Tina promised Bob she would meet him again, after she went home to clean up, and pack a few things for the trip to Olympia which they had decided on during their ride in from Ocean Shores. Tina's mother's home was not far from the Hoquiam bus depot. They would meet again at that bus platform around noon. Bob was also going to his mom's home to clean up. She lived in a single story small bungalow on the edge of Elma, a small community situated just off the Aberdeen-Olmpia freeway, and about four miles east of the Satsop nuclear power plant which the people of the State of Washington had been debating over the past several years.

On the bus platform, Tina and Bob hugged and kissed good-by, then she began making her way home. Bob turned and boarded a different county bus for the ride to his home. In a few minutes the bus was passing through Aberdeen, and after Montesano, got up to 50 MPH while traveling east. The temperature was climbing, and it was warm and comfortable in the bus. Bob fell back asleep almost immediately. He was so deep in sleep that he missed getting off in Elma, but came awake in time to get off at McCleary, the next little town six miles further east.

Bob hitched a ride back to Elma, and got to his mom's place. He wasted little time in getting some fresh clothes on, and found some more money. As soon as he could he got back to the freeway turn-in and caught the next bus back to Aberdeen. He was feeling a little better now anyway; hungry too.

He arrived back in Aberdeen about ten a.m., and got off at the main Aberdeen bus station; a landmark public structure the people of the county had raised money to restore to its original picturesque shape and look, only a few years earlier.

Bob knew he was a couple hours early and would just stick around there until the next bus to Hoquiam. It was here that the whole thing really began. It was here at the Aberdeen bus station he and Tina met and hooked up with Craig, Marv, Tammy and Sonja. They were all just going to 'party' that weekend and have a good time. There would be a state-wide police alarm out for all six of them before this time the next day. But right now, Bob was beginning to feel a little sick again, just thinking about it all. Then he saw a familiar face, in the crowd around the bus station. It was his old buddy Pete Nicholson, a 19 year old from high school days.

They talked awhile, and, without mentioning anything about the past weekend, Bob stated he and Tina were going to Olympia that afternoon. Pete too was out of school and enjoying the summer vacation, and said he would like to go along, maybe spend one night with Bob and Tina in Olympia. The 11:30 a.m. bus for Hoquiam came along, and they both got on, and in a few minutes they were back at the bus platform where Bob and Tina parted about three and a half hours earlier.

The two boys walked the few blocks to Tina's home. She was about ready, and slipping a few more clothes and other personal items into her blue and black duffel bag. She looked a lot fresher than when Bob last saw her. While in her mom's home, Bob took advantage of the opportunity to take a quick shower. He also made himself a sandwich from the frige. Tina's mother, a few weeks earlier, had remarked that she liked Bob.

In a short while Bob and Tina were back on the bus, and with their new companion. It was a little after 2 p.m. when the bus passed through Aberdeen. Pete clearly saw they had something on their minds. They would tell him a little about it before they all got to Olympia, some 50 miles east.

Meanwhile, at 2 p.m. back in Ocean Shores, rain clouds from the north were beginning to move southward, threatening the otherwise warm afternoon, vacationing tourist, and residence alike. There is a quaint old proverb in the State of Washington that says, 'If it isn't raining around here now, it's about to!'

In his apartment, over on Sunset Drive, Dan had climbed out of bed about 9:30 that morning. After his shower, he went downstairs to start the coffee and get the kitchen in order. Marv was still sleeping on the couch while Sonja was spread out on the floor, each with a sleeping bag belonging to Dan. After his wake-up cup of coffee, and checking the refrigerator supply, he decided to take a walk to the Shop Rite super market and came back with enough breakfast groceries for all. Dan was a tall, fleshy built man of about a 190 pounds, light complected and in his early fortys. Just before he made his walk to the store another teenaged girl dropped in, a Patty Dyke. Patty was acquainted with Craig so Dan left Patty to talk with Craig if he came down while Dan was gone.

He got back about 10:30 and started right in making breakfast. Craig came downstairs with Tammy following him. He was wearing a pair of bright, flower-print shorts. They all talked awhile, as Dan finished up at the stove. Craig said they had all been drinking over at Ginny's and he had no idea what occurred during the night. He went on to say they left early because Ginny's husband was due in at anytime, from his fishing job up around Alaska. He was "-a big guy", and they all wanted to be out before he arrived. They cleaned up the apartment before they left, though.

Marv, hearing Craig and Dan talking in the kitchen, got up off the couch, and came in to confirm what Craig was saying. Dan and Patty noticed the scratch marks on Marv's face, and they asked him about it. Marv mumbled something about his getting scratched up while going through some high brush or something. The subject was changed and they began talking about current sports, baseball in particular. Patty left the apartment about then.

Craig told Dan they would all be going to Olympia today. They had a ride with some friends who would be coming by later on. After breakfast, Dan stated he had some work to do away from the apartment, and would be gone most of the afternoon. Craig asked if Dan would give him a lift over to Marcie's place. She would be working at one of the gift shops near the Inn across from the beach. Craig brought out some recent polaroid snap shots, and showed them to Dan, saying he wanted to show them to Marcie, one of his girlfriends in town, before they all left for Olympia.

There were five photos in all, indicating they had had a good time over at Ginny's. There were two shots of Craig and Tammy; one of Craig, Marv, and Bob; one showing Craig sitting on Bob's shoulders; and one of Craig and Ginny. The photos did indeed indicate that a good time had been had by all. Ginny may have even taken some of the photos herself. She had on the same clothes they buried her in.

Dan said he had a little work he wanted to do

out back of his apartment first, and also had to make a visit to a friend in the neighborhood, then he would take Craig over to see Marcie. With that, the boys helped clean up the kitchen, then they started looking around for their clothes to put on. Craig decided he would put on a different pair of shoes than the ones he wore the night before.

The two girls were up now, and they too began freshening up. After awhile Sonja came in to the kitchen to get something to eat. Tammy seldom ate breakfast so she only nibbled a little at the food on the table. The boys turned on the TV set, and skipped around channels looking for a show worth watching.

Craig left the TV and went back into the kitchen. From there he made a number of phones calls, all to his friends. Some in the Ocean Shores area, including Marcie, and some as far away as Lacey, a community bordering on Olympia. After completing his calls he came back in the living room and announced that his friends from Olympia were on their way and would pick them up in a couple hours. Then Craig motioned to Marv, and the two boys went out for a little stroll in the back yard together, leaving the girls alone with the TV.

At about 1 p.m. Craig had a phone call from Marcie. She was looking for him to drop by the Gift Shop before leaving town. Shortly after Craig hung up Dan drove up at the back of his apartment. Craig, on seeing Dan, asked if he would be able to drive him over to Marcie's pretty soon. Dan had a few gardening tools he was putting in the back of his pickup truck, and gloves he wanted, and would be ready in a minute or so.

Craig climbed in the truck, with Marv next to the window. Marv wanted to go too. They had some words, then with Dan behind the wheel they were all set. It didn't take five minutes to get to the beach, a quick right turn on to Ocean Shores Boulevard, a short drive north, and they were there. Marv climbed out, went behind the truck, and headed across the boulevard to the sand and beach. He would wait for Craig there. Craig climbed out of the truck, and stepped into the Gift Shop just as two smiling customers were leaving. Then Craig jumped back out again, flagging down Dan. He had forgotten his pictures resting on the seat of the truck. With them now in hand he went back in to see his friend Marcie.

Out on the sand, where Marv had found himself a driftwood log to rest on, he could see the activity on the beach was really busy that day, either way he looked. People were really enjoying themselves. Kites of all colors and shapes were fluttering aloft with the offshore winds. There was one in shape of a dragon, and another, even larger, shaped like Dumbo the baby elephant. The most fun and active kites appeared to be those that were hooked together, soaring up and down and flashing every color of the rainbow. Other, more down to earth activity, were the noisy little mo-peds darting along the hard sand next to the surf. And there were at least two roped off areas in the soft sand renting out horses for people to ride, all the way down to the Jetty at Point Brown and back, if they wished. Cars were also allowed and running on the beach at that time, although a number of residents of the town were still complaining about them, driving too fast along the surf and clam beds. What Marv didn't see was many people actually in the surf. The Alaska Gulf Stream coming down along the West Coast of the United States kept these waters just too cold even for occasional waders.

It was almost 2 p.m. when Marv heard, then saw Craig approach him. He had left Marcie and her Gift Shop and had just crossed over the Boulevard and onto the sand near where Marv had been resting on the log. They both walked south toward the Inn, staying in the sand. There was no argument between them as they walked on together.

Part of their conversation was about maybe leaving the country, maybe get to Australia or some place like that. And they thought that a great idea. Big cargo ships were pulling out of Grays Harbor every day, steaming across the Pacific and making for ports all over the world. But Marv would like to see his mom down in Oregon before they took off. Other thoughts and ideas popped in and out of their conversation. None would be firmly settled on, except Marv felt he should go back down to Oregon for awhile. Maybe send some new crack up to Craig.

Nice as their plans may have sounded, Craig was getting more and more concerned about losing his chance to go to college. Marv was feeling sympathetic towards his 'Blood brother', even to the point of saying he would cover for him if things got really tight. After all, one of them should go to college if he could make it. Marv then pulled his knife out and without further words he gripped the handle of the knife, which he had affectionately referred to as his "baby", and threw it into the surf, as far out as he could.

In another moment they left the sand and walked back across the boulevard, and headed for Dan's apartment. They didn't want to miss their ride out of town, and especially Craig's ride to Olympia. It is unlikely that Marv gave any thought to it, as he followed his 'Blood brother', but on turning his back to the beach and all its activity he had enjoyed observing only moments earlier, he was likely never to see and enjoy the beach and the ocean again in his lifetime.

They were over half way to Dan's when Craig found that he had left his photographs back on Marcia's glass case at the Gift Shop. He would call her as soon as he got back to Dan's place, and tell her to "-burn them!"

No sooner had Marv and Craig walked up the wood steps to Dan's apartment and the sliding glass front entrance, than a dusty brown four-door Maverick drove up and parked in the front driveway. Two young girls, 18 and 19 years old, got out and came toward Craig and Marv, and greeted them with "Hi Craig, are you ready to go? We've got to be back in 'Oly' by 5 O'clock!"

"We're ready, we're all ready! Can you drop my friends off at Aberdeen on the way?"

"No problem!" the heavy set girl answered, "But just let's get going!"

The two girls followed Craig and Marv into the apartment. Tammy and Sonja got up from watching TV and turned their attention to the new girls, as Craig introduced everyone all around. Tammy and Sonja were packed and ready. Craig said he had one quick phone call to make before leaving. It was to Marcie. It was 2:20 p.m.

Dan was off doing yard work for his friend, so the six young people left the apartment empty of life as the Maverick drove away, and on out of Ocean Shores.

Cindy and Maxine sat up front as the four companions of the past 68 hours occupied the rear seat. Marv, at the left rear window, then Sonja and Tammy, and Craig at the right rear window.

Going back up Highway 115, which the four in the back seat had taken over an hour to hike earlier that morning, the Maverick slowed to make the stop sign at Hogans Corner. Without fully stopping, Cindy turned her car right, and they were on their way toward Aberdeen. Tammy was the only one who leaned over to get a glimpse of Ginny's apartment as they went by. All the lights were still on in the apartment. Craig reached over with his right hand, onto Tammy's face, and pulled her back, saying "Don't look!" The time was about 2:35 p.m. Back at the Gift Shop young Marcie Swanson was agonizing over Craig's visit and their talk just about 30 minutes earlier, and especially over his last phone call to her.

In less than an hour a sharp thinking Ocean Shores police officer would be professionally curious about Craig Borman and his friends, and would notify the Gray's Harbor County Sheriffs Office in Montesano over his findings and suspicions.

Eighteen year old Marcie Swanson, an attractive five foot five inches with light brown wavy hair and weighing about a hundred and eighteen pounds, was no ordinary young woman. Though she would have been happy just being one. She had graduated from North Beach High School with honors. She was the youngest of five children in her family. Her older sister, a practicing nurse, had graduated from the same high school some years earlier and had left behind a swimming record at school that was still unbroken. Her two older brothers were on active duty, one in the U. S. Air Force and the other in the medical department of the U. S. Navy. Her next older brother worked at one of the better restaurants in town.

Not that her parents had had it all that easy. They were certainly not rich, economically. But they were steady. The parents loved their children, and the children respected their parents. Her 59 year old father had been working for the City of Ocean Shores for years, at the waste disposal plant at the edge of town. Her mother, a tall, almost blonde woman of 54, had a rather no-nonsense stately bearing about her whenever it came down to crisis or business. Mr. and Mrs. Swanson were the kind of people you knew you could count on if you were right, and you could expect to get straightened out if you were wrong. And Marcie knew right from wrong. Now that Mrs. Swanson's children were mostly on their own, she could take a job of her own. She was a part-time motel manager, ironically, at the same motel Ginny worked for.

What lifted Marcie out of the ordinary was in herself. Through the years she had painfully observed the hardships and heart breaks of so many of her young school friends who had lost their families because of separation and divorce. She felt their broken hearts right along with them. Another thing that made Marcie a little different from her friends, was her love of poetry and writing which she thought she might like to pursue someday. And with Ginny, the accomplished poet, writer, and romantic thinker, whom she had met through her mother, well "-they just hit it off right from the start!" Marcie truly liked Ginny.

But now she was going to have to mature, even more painfully and faster them she ever dreamed. And she would need all the love, help, and guidance her parents could provide. Craig had just dropped a number of pieces of an already exploded 'bomb' right in her lap. She still couldn't believe it and didn't want to. But there it was.

After Craig's last phone call and instructions to "burn them.", and his announcement that he and his friends were leaving town, Marcie glanced over at the photos again. Could it all really be true, or could it be just silly teenage pranks and mischief? Marcie phoned her steady boyfriend, a young man who had a job at a hamburger stand in town. He wasn't working at that moment, and since Marcie sounded very worried he would drive right over. He brought a teenage buddy with him who knew Marcie and who had been visiting with him when Marcie called.

The two boys arrived at the Gift Shop in minutes, and immediately began mulling over Craig's remarks that Marcie related to them. One of them suggested, "-let's call your mother and find out if Ginny has come to work today or not."

"Good idea!" the other boy said, as he fingered over the photos on the glass top counter.

Marcie's mother answered the phone at the motel, only about five minutes walk south from the Gift Shop. "No, she hasn't shown up, and I need her!"

Marcie then tried to explain to her mother that Ginny may be dead. Marcie's tone of voice told her mother that her daughter could be telling the truth. She wouldn't lie about a thing like that. Mrs. Swanson, after only a moments thought, directed Marcie to close the Gift Shop immediately, bring the pictures and come right to the motel, which she did. She brought her two friends with her. Marcie's mother wanted to hear it all straight from her daughter before calling the police.

After looking over the photos Mrs. Swanson checked Ginny's number at Hogans Corner. There was no answer. Without putting the phone back on the cradle, she dialed the Ocean Shores Police Department. Mrs. Swanson wanted to talk to an officer who she and her husband had known as a friend over the years. The dispatcher told her that the officer she mentioned was currently out on another job. "Was there someone else who could help you?"

"I am Mrs Swanson at the Ocean Shores Motel. Could you please send over someone. I have my daughter with me, and I think we have a kettle of worms here. Oh, and could the officer please be a person of some compassion. My daughter is very distraught and only 18 years old."

At the other end of the line, the dispatcher asked Mrs. Swanson if she could be a little more specific as to the nature of her calling the police.

"An employee of ours may have been murdered!"

CHAPTER TWO: DISCOVERY, AND FLIGHT

It was at 3:20 p.m. when Officer Mark Wade got the assignment to check out a possible homicide. In uniform, Wade left the nearly new police station, which the City of Ocean Shores voters had granted their Police Department only a year before. He climbed in the white Rover van for the short drive to the motel. Wade had been with this force only a matter of months, having left a similar law enforcement position behind in a small town in central California for what he felt would be a better area to work and live in with his beautiful wife of only five years. Wade, of average height and build, in his middle thirties, short dark brown hair, was a lot of fun when away from the job but completely serious when in uniform and on the job. Wade drove into the car port area of the motel, shut off the engine, and walked into the motel lobby. Mr. Swanson, having come from his work to be with his daughter, greeted the officer and took him back to see Marcie in the conference room behind the main desk. Mrs. Swanson stayed out front as she was still on duty there. Wade put Marcie at ease as best he could and asked her to go ahead and relate her story in her own words.

The officer listened intently while occasionally looking at the photos. At the end of Marcie's vivid related experience with Craig, Wade asked Mr. Swanson if he could use his phone. With the affirmative he called his supervisor, repeated some of the details, and strongly suggested a call be put into Montesano for the aide of a County Sheriffs detective concerning a possible homicide at Hogans Corner. Turning back to Marcie, Wade asked if she would please return to the station with him, and repeat her story there, in writing, in front of a Grays Harbor County officer who was on his way.

With Mrs. Swanson still on duty at the desk, Mr. Swanson readily agreed to accompany his daughter and remain with her during her statement and through any further questioning the police might have. At the Station, they didn't have long to wait when a sheriff's car drove up and Detective Gary Parfitt came in, introduced himself around, then gave his full concentration to Marcie. With the kind of gentleness years of experience had taught him to use in such cases, Parfitt walked into the interview room and sat down near Marcie. Marcie's boyfriends who came along to the Police Station in support of her stayed in the background during most of the questioning. They would be called upon to help at a later time.

At the table Marcie was given a pen and a long yellow pad with lined paper and asked to repeat her story in her own hand. With encouragement from her father she picked up the pen and began writing. She produced a seven page statement, and never once looked up from her writing. Often though, toward the end, she had to wipe the tears from her eyes. On one occasion Wade went out of the room and came back with a styrofoam cup of water. Marcie stopped a moment, took a couple sips, then went back to writing. Her ordeal took no more than 15 minutes. She relaxed back and said, "That's it!" Parfitt asked if she was sure there was nothing else she would like to add. Marcie thought a moment, picked back up the pen and wrote one more paragraph. The following is her account:

"8-26-91 I called Craig at 1 p.m. He said, hi how are you. I really miss you. Lets get together. I need to talk to you. But first I have to wait for a call from my friend in Olympia. Craig said he would call me back, so I waited for about half hour and called him back. Craig said his friend hadn't called him yet. I said I don't care, you better be here in 10 minutes. Craig said OK, and in 5 minutes Craig was at my shop. Craig came in and said, Oh, I forgot my pictures, so he went out and flagged down his ride and got the pictures. (He) came back in and show(ed) me 4 pictures. The first was him and his girlfriend, (and the) second was him and his girlfriend. Third (was) Craig and Bob. Fourth (was) Craig, Bob and Marv. And then we small talked for a moment, and then Craig popped off and said, do you know the lady that lives downstairs from Kim? I said yes, you mean Ginny? Craig said ya, we killed her. I kind of grinned thinking he was kidding. But all he could say is, you don't believe me do you. I said yes, but how could you do something like this. Craig said, I don't know. Ginny just started freaking out and the next thing I know she was dead. I said where is Ginny? Craig said she's still in Hogan's Corner. I said where did this happen, at her house? He said yes. I said, what and why would make you do this (thing)? Craig didn't say anything. Craig said, should I kill myself? I said no. If you kill yourself, then Marv will kill himself. And how could I live with myself knowing all this. Craig said, I need some help. I told him to go to the police. He said no, I can't go to jail and sit in a cell and think about what I did. So I got out the phone book and told (him) to call the crisis line. Craig (said) no, they'll trace it. I said, no they won't they can't do that. So I pick up the phone and tried to call the crisis line, but I hung up. I said to Craig, they won't believe me. So I asked him to go to his parents. He said no, I can't look my parents in the eye and tell them I killed someone. Then I asked him how did you kill Ginny? He said, with a knife they stabbed her to death. I said, how do you think your not go(ing to) get caught when there's blood every where, on the carpet and things. Craig said it was in the hallway on the monolium. There's no evidence. I said, who did it? Craig said, Marv did most of it. And I said, what did you do, hold her down while Marv stabbed her, and he said yes. I said did you have the knife? He said, for a few minutes. And what about Bob? Craig said, no he just held her. I said, didn't she try to fight? Craig said, yes, for a moment. And then I was almost in tears, so was Craig. I said, how does Marv feel? Craig said, he feels bad. We were out in the woods crying all morning, think how we could do this. He told me he had to go away I said, who could live with yourself knowing that her family is looking for her. Then he was about to say after it was all over she was lying there and then he stopped. Two customers came into my shop. I gave him a cigarette, to go smoke. By that time I was so shocked that I didn't know what to do. So he went outside and smoked a few minutes and peaked his head in and said he had to go and to have a nice day, with a sad look on his face. I saw him walk away and never saw him again. The(n) about 15 min later, he call me. But before the call I picked up the pictures and there were five this time, the last picture was of him and Ginny, and I started to get scared. The phone rang, it was Craig. He said, I forgot the pictures. Will you burn them for me. I said yes. He said, I have to go but I will call you and let you know where I am. I hate to say good-bye but I have to. I'll miss you & I love you. And he hung up. I called him back and said, come say good bye before you leave. And Craig said, you get off at 4:00, I'll be there. I said, does your girlfriends know? And he said, yes they were there, and mine helped me. I have to go, Bye Marcie. I didn't see or here from him again."

(Signed) Marcie Swanson

Co-signed) Wm. Gary Parfitt, 08/26/91

(ADDENDUM) page 7 of 7

"Craig said, I don't know why I killed her. I loved that old lady. I think Marv's crazy. I said, Craig, were you guys drunk? He said no."

(signed) Marcie Swanson.

(co-signed) Wm. Gary Parfitt, 08/26/91

While they were still not certain that what she had related in her statement was entirely true, everyone in the interview room were struck by her obvious sincerity, composure, and open willingness to cooperate in any further way she could. She had, probably without knowing it, set the pace and attitude for one of the most cooperative, meticulous and successful criminal investigative efforts in Washington State's history. Not only reaching over city and county lines but into other U.S. States as well. Her Dad was very proud of her.

After a brief huddle with the other officers Parfitt, a former U. S. Marine, got on the phone and called his immediate superior and requested further assistance and backup from Montesano. Detectives Doug Smythe, Lane Youmans, and S. C.

Larson, would shortly be on their way to Ocean Shores and Hogans Corner. Over 50 Police and Sheriff Officers throughout the State would find themselves intensely involved in case number 91-6965, especially over the next 72 hours. Some officers would find little or no time to sleep until all six youths were found and in custody. The man assigned to take immediate overall charge of the case was Detective Bill Stocks, a ten year veteran with the Grays Harbor County Sheriffs Office. Stocks was, at that moment, following up on a routine forgery case up in Taholah, a mostly Indian community some 35 miles directly north of Ocean Shores. He received his new assignment after his police radio told him to call in at the nearest phone. Parfitt had faxed in Marcie's statement to Montesano, and his chief of detectives filled Stocks in on what he could possibly expect to find when he got down to Hogans Corner. Stocks was ordered to investigate and report back, and was also informed that support officers were enroute to the scene, and to use them as needed. It was about 5 p.m.

It had been raining for several minutes in Taholah when Stocks got back into his unmarked 4 door light blue Chevy Caprice, and headed south on the Coast Highway 109. Actually the 'unmarked' car was quite apparent to any trained eye; two radio antennas and black walled tires. Otherwise it was a good, fast 'company' car and Stocks liked it.

Driving at a good clip along the Coast, Stocks had time to think during the half-hour drive. Washington's highways, especially off the freeways, can be beautiful and the scenery breathtaking. But they can also be deadly, with hair-pin turns and sudden darkness that may swallow you up because of miles of tall evergreens that block out the sun, if the sun is shinning. Stocks always drove with his lights on, day or night. There was still plenty of daylight left, with the sun setting at about 8 p.m. So while driving on he thought some more. Occasionally Stocks caught glimpses of the long rolling Pacific surf pounding the beach beyond out his right window. He had had many cases involving juveniles over the years, and he was well acquainted with many of them living in the County. He was no different then most other officers of law enforcement, in that he considered himself a better officer if he could steer a kid away from jail than to have to go out and catch one to put him in jail. No question about it though, there were some wild youngsters out there. But most of those were just guilty of say hacking off the hood ornament of a fancy car, or experimenting with pot, something like that. He hoped he wasn't investigating a real murder. He hoped it was only some kids out to shake up the cops or something.

Stocks decided he would go through Hogans Corner, straight to the police station in Ocean Shores. And see for himself this young lady named Marcie. After all it would be only a five minute drive back to Hogans Corner if she registered true with him. Anyway he had beaten the oncoming rain clouds down. They were still moving south and would catch up to him later that day.

On reaching Hogans Corner Stocks took a quick look around for any police activity, saw none, then made the right turn onto 115. He thought again, either the support hadn't arrived yet, or the whole thing was a false alarm. But he hadn't received any such cancellation reports on the police radio. It was 5:32 p.m. when he parked his blue Chevy in front of the Ocean Shores Police Station. Marcie was still there with her father. Inside, Stocks greeted all those present, especially his friend and fellow detective Gary Parfitt. Parfitt was one of those humans who most always seemed to be wearing a cheerful grin. He wasn't wearing a grin this time. Parfitt informed Stocks that another development had occurred that might be related to this affair. People at the Texaco mini-mart had called in earlier in the day to report they had found some rags and other articles mixed in their diesel container located on the west side of their building. The rags appeared to have blood on them. One of the articles was a single white 'tube' sock that also appeared to be saturated with blood. Then Parfitt introduced Stocks to Marcie.

Stocks had only a few words with her, after he scanned her original statement. She assured Stocks she was no more certain that a serious crime had actually taken place than he was. Marcie was only certain of what Craig had told her. That was enough for Stocks. Following Marcie's described location of Ginny's apartment again, Stocks announced he was on his way to check it all out. Before departing Detective Stocks directed that Parfitt check again for any further pertinent information that Marcie may have forgotten, and get statements from her two boyfriends which might later prove helpful. On his drive back out of Ocean Shores, he decided Marcie was telling the truth, as far as she knew it to be. With that, a dull ache began in the pit of his stomach, relevant to what he might discover out there at Hogans Corner.

About half way to the Corner Stocks made radio contact with Deputy Sheriff S. C. Larson who, drivving west from Aberdeen, was also nearing the Corner, and they agreed to meet there. They arrived almost at the same time, and both parked along the east side of the cyclone fence next to the VFW hall. It was 6:15 p.m.

Being that it was still quite warm for that time of day Detective Stocks left his sport jacket inside the Chevy. He stepped over to Larson, who was in uniform, shook hands, and then proceeded with their first investigation around the apartment building, particularly Ginny's lower forward section of the building. They walked to the front porch area first.

Even before getting to the front door they both noticed streaks of brown marks leading from the door, across the cement threshold, and around the covered porch area, and onto the gravel and grass front yard. The drag marks continued on into the rugged empty lot immediately East of the apartment building. They both stooped down to examine more closely those reddish brown drag marks.

Larson rose up, followed by Stocks, and they each took a window and peered through the thin lace curtains into the brightly lit apartment. Larson first noticed, through the west window, there was decorative fish netting on one of the living room walls and a number of small Japanese glass floats hanging from the netting. On further glancing around the apartment's interior he observed more reddish brown splatters, especially a large one on the white linoleum floor of the kitchen. On the kitchen table below him he saw a single sheet of paper with the words "Fuck You" scrawled on it.

Stocks noticed through his window empty beer bottles, cans and crumbled corn chip wrappers scattered around the interior. They both observed a single white tube sock laying on the carpeted living room floor. And Stocks immediately recalled Parfitt's remarks about the diesel rag container and the report of another 'tube' sock. That part of the living room also had other scattered material on it but could not clearly be made out. Then Stocks too noticed what appeared to be more blood and drag markings, which led to the front door of the apartment.

Stepping away from the window Stocks went around to the side rear door and routinely knocked. He knew there would be no answer but he did it anyway. Then, stepping away from the building he told Larson to continue on and follow the drag marks and see where they led. He was going over to the phone booth next to the Texaco station and put a call into Montesano. He had seen enough to at least partly confirm Marcie's statement.

He talked first with Chief Criminal Investigator Mike Whelan and then to his friend and fellow detective Doug Smythe. As he was describing the details of his discovery to Smythe, Larson hurried up to the phone booth to tell Stocks he had just found a body. It was 6:24 p.m.

Stocks told Smythe to hang on and he would get right back to him. He wanted to see for himself. Leaving the receiver dangling he followed Larson back over across the VFW property, in front of the apartment building, and on into the lot directly east. As he walked on through the brush it began to sprinkle at first, then the rain began coming down heavy. The dark clouds back up in Taholah had drifted down and finally caught up with him again at Hogans Corner.

It was just as Larson had described on the careful walk to the mound. The body was lying face up, just beneath the surface of the dirt. And apparently a female. Her small right hand, outstretched and protruding from the dirt had red finger nails. So did the nails on her toes, also protruding up. At her visible ankles she appeared to be wearing what once was white or gray leotards. From there a thin layer of dirt covered her up to the nose. Her eye sockets were visible and traumatized. She had dark brown, rather auburn hair. The small body was lying stretched out in an east-west direction, the feet being west. A wooden pole reaching about five feet in the air stuck straight up from the upper right side of the body. All this was observed in a matter of seconds.

The rain was coming down pretty heavy as the two men again carefully, began coming down off the mound. They were moving fast, and each knew what they must do. Keep the area intact as much as possible for the medical examiners, and other officials who would later be on the scene.

As Stocks headed for the phone booth, Larson went to his car and brought back to the mound a plastic tarp to cover the body and the immediate area around it. Back on the phone Stocks confirmed there was a victim and that he and Larson would immediately seal off the whole area as much as practical. He also told Smythe he would FAX in a rough sketch of the scene; the location of the body, legal address of the apartment, and a copy of Marcie's statement. A search warrant was needed immediately. Smythe answered that he would wait for the FAX material, obtain the search warrant, and be out with it as soon as possible. Stocks wanted to see again these photos that Marcie had back at the Ocean Shores police station.

Bob and Tina, with their new companion Pete, arrived in downtown Olympia, about 4 p.m. They got off the bus at the main bus terminal, located only a few blocks from the State Capitol. They deposited their luggage into a bus locker there and began walking around town together. They mingled with the multitude of people out on the streets and sidewalks who had just gotten off work and who were on their way home to their families and friends for another summer's Monday evening.

Pete had already heard some of their secret experiences, while riding on the bus toward the Capitol city. Now as they drifted around the public area near the Olympia marina, located on the north central edge of the city. Pete wanted to know more. "Just what happened out at Ocean Shores? Tell me!"

They couldn't hold their terrible secret any longer and they were glad to have someone to talk with, especially a friend around their own age. So they gave Pete every detail they could remember, including Ginny's "-bloody murder screams." Bob told Pete how he himself had "-freaked out", and that he grabbed Tina and got out of there. And he told how he warned Tammy if she didn't come with them she "-would be sorry when she was in jail for fifteen years."

The three young people had a bite to eat at one of the nearby fast food restaurants, and then found themselves strolling around the marina area again. Gazing down from the sea wall they watched couples and some whole families spending the summer evening working on their little sail or motor boats which were neatly tied up to the wooden floats. Snappy names were visible on some of the rigs like "Gung Ho", "Windfree", and "Adventure".

Turning away from the happy scene they continued on walking along the waterfront. It seemed they walked around and talked for hours until they got really tired and decided they should get some sleep. So they spent the night in one of the public restrooms near the marina docks.

Back in Aberdeen, Marv, Tammy, and Sonja too had been just walking around town. Earlier, at about the same time Bob, Tina, and Pete were coming into Olympia, Craig and his girlfriends from Lacey drove into Aberdeen. They gassed up at a cut rate station, then headed up Market street. Craig directed the girls to stop at a branch bank which Craig had his college savings in. He came out of the bank with about 250 dollars in cash, after closing out his account. On the sidewalk, he gave Marv about 100 dollars of it, then turned and hugged and kissed Tammy and Sonja. Before climbing back in the Maverick, Craig told Sonja he would give her a call later that evening from Lacey, after he got settled in.

Joining the two girls up front, the Maverick pulled away from the curb and moved on through Aberdeen. They rumbled across the Wishkah River Bridge, continued on up a couple hundred yards, then pulled into a MacDonalds on the right hand side for a quick lunch. Across the highway and back down about a 100 yards was the Town Motel.

Marv and the two girls walked the couple blocks over to the familiar Aberdeen bus station. The area was crowded with visitors, people coming and going on the large colorful buses. They just missed the bus they wanted, and would have to wait another forty minutes for the next cross-town bus over to South Shore Mall. To kill a little time Marv took the girls across the street to one of his favorite places in town, the Book Store. While they had numerous books and magazines for sale in the front of the store, they also had a wide variety of video games in the back and upstairs.

Inside, Marv bought three more packs of cigarettes, three cans of pop and changed a ten dollar bill into quarters, then found some real fun video games to play for the next half hour. The little bells were ringing, buzzers sounding, and psychedelic lights flashing when Sonja reminded Marv it was time to go, if they wanted to catch that bus. Marv didn't want to leave the Book Store just yet. He told the girls to go on and he would catch the next bus over to the Mall. He agreed to stick around inside the Mall and wait there until the girls got done with their business over at Sonja's foster parents house, located a couple blocks from the mall.

With that agreement Sonja and Tammy made the ten minute ride over to the South Shore Mall. They got off the bus at the Mall stop, crossed over the highway and walked the two blocks south to Sonja's foster home. The girls stepped through the picket fence, climbed the porch steps, walked in and found the foster mother in the kitchen preparing the evening dinner. Tammy sat down on the couch in the living room and started playing with a little gray kitten. Sonja began telling the kindly woman she was going away with Tammy, to live with Tammy and her mother who had a nice home over in Carson, way up along the Columbia River,on the Washington State side. While continuing with the food preparations the woman said, "Is that really what you want to do, Sonja?"

Sonja answered, in an edgy and uncertain manner "Yes Maam. I think I should."

In the living room, Tammy called out, "Sonja, let's get going, Mom's waiting at the mall." Sonja, taking a bite to eat from the table said she didn't want to leave on any bad terms, but felt this is what she should do. She reached over and hugged her foster mother, saying she would eat with Tammy and her mother later on. It was a warm evening, so she left her coat behind as she and Tammy walked to the front door. Before the girls got outside her foster mother called out and said she had had a call from Craig just a few minutes before the girls walked in. He said he would call back later. It looked like it might rain in awhile, giving some relief to the heat.

Back at the mall, while walking around inside, Marv had found a 'dealer' and purchased a few grams of pot from him. Then on catching sight of the two girls walking toward him, near one of the designer teen stores, Marv came up and quietly let them know he had just picked up a couple of pipe fulls of pot, and, "-lets go out behind this place and blow a snoot full!"

And that's what they did, only Tammy didn't take any. Just Sonja and Marv. Marv said there was a good movie playing back in the mall that he wanted to see. And he would treat the girls if they wanted to see it too. But first they would have to eat something. They were really getting hungry. Back inside, there were several fast food counters at one end of the mall with a dozen or more small tables and chairs conveniently placed nearby. Sonja and Tammy got hamburgers and shakes at one counter. Marv, being a vegetarian, selected a big salad at another counter.

After dinner they made their way to another section of the mall, purchased their ticket, and went into see "Blind Date". Their ticket stub registered 7:10 p.m., 26 Aug. 1991.

After seeing the movie clear through, Marv and the girls went outside. It was now dark. They caught the next bus and road it back to the familiar bus station. They were getting tired and sleepy by this time and they needed to find a motel or something right away before the tourists got all the available rooms in town.

Sonja got a suggestion from one of the girls she knew hanging around the bus station.The Town Motel, was just a short walk from there, over the bridge, and on down a ways on their left. During their walk to the motel they decided to use the fictitious names they had selected for each other earlier. Marv would be "Marcus Wittem", Tammy would be "Shelley Maran" (she first thought 'Maranda', but that sounded too much like Miranda Rights). They hadn't fully decided on Sonja's new name.

Before turning into the motel area, they decided on a plan. Only the girls would approach the desk, it would look better that way. Tammy would do all the talking. They would just be two girls abandoned by their boyfriends, and with only a few dollars between them. But they could come up with some jewelry for collateral if they needed to. And after getting their room for the night they would give the high sign to Marv, who would be hanging around outside somewhere. And they would leave the room door open for him.

It all worked just as they thought it might. The lady at the desk was very sympathetic. She didn't want the collateral, as she could plainly see it was only costume jewelry anyway. But the desk manager played it their way, took the jewelry and let the "stranded" girls have the 30 dollar room, number 17, for half price. It was going on

10 p.m. The desk night manager would remember them alright; the tall attractive blonde, the shorter heavy set dark young girl, and especially the Indian or Hawaiian youth who left with the girls the next morning. They certainly stood out together.

Meanwhile, over in the Olympia area, Craig also was getting settled in for the night. And as Bob and Tina, he too just had to talk with someone about that past terrible weekend. But the way he would put it it would be a little different story, and different than what he told Marcie earlier in the day.

After their lunch at MacDonalds the three young people got underway again and headed out of town, and on to the freeway going toward Olympia. Nineteen year old Cindy drove a little over the speed limit not wanting to be late for her evening shift at Denny's Restaurant, located in Lacey. Maxine, age 18, had the day off from her studies and practice at the Lacey beauty college. It was Maxine who first met Craig, three or four months earlier. He had impressed Maxine with his plans to start into college this coming fall. He was going to enroll in pre-med classes in Olympia and eventually get a practicing medical license. And he was looking around for someone he could room with and share expenses with. He would get a part time job in the Olympia area and things would all work out fine for his new planned future.

On the forty-five minute drive, moving on toward Olympia, Craig was on the quiet side and said very little. He seemed to be in deep thought. The girls knew he had something on his mind but didn't press him. They just talked mostly between themselves. They talked about the nice crew of young people working at Denny's, and about Maxine's friends at the beauty college. And they talked about the new house they were moving into around Tumwater, a community a little south of Olympia. They were really fixing the place up. Several working young people were going to live there together and would share all expenses. Craig would be an ideal addition to their group.

They got to Denny's at about 4:45 p.m. giving

Cindy time to get ready for work. The girls found a table in the smoking section while Craig made a couple phone calls. They had coffee waiting on his return. Cindy told Maxine she could take the Maverick and drive Craig over to see the new house in Tumwater, and see what he thought of it. Cindy then excused herself from the table. She had to get ready and go to work.

Getting back in the Maverick, Craig asked Maxine if she would take him over to the Capitol Mall as he needed to get a few new clothes. Then they would go over to see the new place. Craig said he also wanted to talk to her about a serious problem he had. Maxine surely liked Craig, and told him that would be fine with her.

The Capitol Mall was only a little out of the way and Craig wasn't long in making his selection of a new shirt, pants, and a new pair of shoes. Back in the Maverick they were on their way again, through the heavy evening traffic. Staying mostly off the freeways and on the main arteries going south. Maxine finally got to the address, an ideal location on Old Highway 99.

Inside Craig showed an interest in what the girls had been fixing up for the past several days. New painting had been completed on the walls, and they even had some good second hand furniture in place around the rooms.

"Now what's this serious problem you have Craig? You got a girl pregnant or something?"

It was just getting dark outside when Maxine asked Craig her sympathetic question, and told him to sit down, as she turned on the lights before joining him.

"No" he answered, "It's worse than that!", then Craig went on to tell Maxine about the awful past weekend he had just experienced. And about the nice old lady they had got acquainted with, and how she invited them into have a party in her house back in the Ocean Shores area.

Craig said everything was going along fine until "-these three other guys came by and just moved into our party. They were on a killing spree. They just went wild, and stabbed the old lady to death for no reason. Me and Marv, we couldn't handle it and got the girls out of there. We walked around the property and later we went back, to see if we could do anything. The other guys who killed her were gone. There was blood every where. So me and Marv started trying to clean the place up. It was a mess."

"Are you kidding me! Who were those guys?"

Craig went on to say he "didn't know them, and didn't hang out with guys like that."

"What happened to the old lady?"

"She got carried off into the woods!"

Maxine just sat there in front of Craig awhile, and could hardly believe what she had just heard. Craig could see she was shocked and dumbfounded about what he had told her, and said in a sad voice "you don't believe me, do you!"

Craig went on to say he was thinking about leaving the country, going to Mexico or someplace. He started crying. She couldn't tell if he was crying for the old lady, or crying for himself. Maxine, in exasperation, said, "These things happen in New York or Chicago. They don't happen in Olympia or Grays Harbor. Come on!"

They went over the story again together, with not much difference in it from Craig. Maxine felt he might be holding something back, as he seemed a little vague about it all. He struck her as being in shock or something. Craig talked about how this really changes his nice plans to go to college, and was sorry he got her involved in this terrible thing. Minutes turned into a few hours.

They were getting a little hungry, so Maxine said they should get going back to Denny's, and have some dinner there. They would talk more about it later on. Cindy would expect them to be at Denny's when she got off work at 11 p.m.

Cindy spotted Maxine and Craig at one of the tables in the smoking section at about 10:30. She had been working the no smoking section. The clock rolled onto 11 p.m. She got out of her uniform and came over to join her two friends at the table, and brought over a cup of coffee with her. Cindy was too tired to have any dinner with them, and just wanted to call it a day.

On their way back to the new place on Old Highway 99 there was very little said, except Cindy talked about some of the interesting people she had waited on during the evening. And the tips had been good. By the time they all got home it was almost midnight. Except for a few friendly words nothing more was talked about. The girls fixed up a place in one of the bedrooms for Craig, then they too curled up in their room and went to sleep. Maxine, without mentioning anything to her girlfriend about Craig's startling news, finally got to sleep a little after Cindy. They were all pretty exhausted. Within 24 hours Maxine would be voluntarily repeating her conversation with Craig to the Olympia police, as much as she could remember, and Cindy would be with her, with her own similar supporting statement of conversation with Craig.

Back at Hogans Corner, all the lights in Ginny's apartment were still on. No less then a dozen officers and other trained technical personnel were busy gathering all the evidence and information they could obtain. A good deal had been discovered and a lot of action had taken place in the area of Hogans Corner since 6:30 p.m. Most of the Officers would work on throughout the night.

CHAPTER THREE: INVESTIGATION

Detective Doug Smythe had a little while to wait, after Stocks' phone call to him earlier about 6:30 p.m. that Monday evening. But he put his time to good use. He prepared all the necessary papers, then got on the phone and located the nearest available district court judge. He also changed from his gray slacks into a pair of jeans. Then slipped on his field shoes. Stocks had told him on the phone to, "-get on your grubbies, Doug! It's raining, and it's a muddy mess around here."

Shortly after Stocks phone call, Chief Deputy Whelan had a meeting with Grays Harbor County Sheriff Dennis Morrisette, and informed him of all that had been discovered at Hogans Corner to that point, including the general confirmation of Marcie's statement. The two men agreed, since there was a good chance of apprehending all the young suspects before they scattered too far, they should immediately put all available manpower on the case. They would alert the Aberdeen, Hoquiam, and Olympia police departments as soon as they had more practical information to work with. Meanwhile Morrisette would take Chief Deputy Neal Darrow with him. They would make the drive to Hogans Corner and overview the investigation's progress, leaving a skeleton crew behind. Smythe would wait for the FAX material, and get the search warrants ready.

When the FAX material finally came in Smythe was ready. With the material in one hand and his black and red DARE cup filled with coffee in the other, Smythe departed the Sheriff's office in Montesano. He got into his black Ford sedan, drove through town, and got on the eastbound side of the freeway. He arrived at Judge Stephen Brown's tree-lined private residence in Elma in little more than 10 minutes. It was about 9:20 p.m.

The Judge invited Smythe into his study, carefully looked over Stocks faxed-in material, and then signed into law active search warrants into Ginny's apartment and around the immediate area, including the adjoining lot directly east of the triplex apartment building. And to confiscate and photograph what ever evidence they could discover. With this authorization in hand Smythe paid his respects to Judge Brown and got back on the freeway heading west. He didn't stop again until he got to Hogans Corner.

Smythe was just about the same height and build of his friend, Detective William A. Stocks, at about 175 pounds, and a little over 6 feet. And while on duty they wore similar clothes; sport coat, slacks, shirt and tie, as did the other detectives associated with the Grays Harbor County Sheriffs Office. Stocks and Smythe even had similar, medium size mustaches. And they were both about the same age, at 40. They were dedicated professionals. Beyond all that, their similarity stopped. While Stocks, dark haired, and always seemed on the verge of a smile and ready to listen to anyone who might have something interesting or humorous to say, his friend Smythe, on the other hand was more serious in nature. He could smile and laugh when he wanted, but more often he would have a fixed searching gaze on you until he felt you earned a smile from him. Smythe was prematurely gray. Both men were keenly committed to law enforcement, and each had their own effective approach to police detection. They were in truth, a good balance to each other, and they knew it.

When Smythe finally arrived on the scene, at about 11:30 p.m., the area all around Ginny's apartment was a bee hive of activity, and brightly lit up between the Gull Station and the Texaco Station. He found a clear spot in the VFW lot, got out and made his first contact with detective Lane Youmans, who had arrived earlier and was placed in charge of the scene in Stocks absence. Stocks had rejoined Parfitt over in Ocean Shores. Youmans quickly filled in Smythe on developments to the moment: Deputy Allan Gallanger was assigned to canvas the immediate neighborhood for more evidence, and to look for persons having any knowledge of the death of Mrs. Barsic, while Larson continued to contain the area, and laying additional plastic coverings over the drag trail in the east lot. It was still raining at Hogans Corner. The Ocean

Shores Police Department had provided additional assistance in sending out officers to take photos and video tapes of the area.

While carefully widening his area of search, Gallanger discovered a large blue suitcase and two tote bags in the brush just west of the Texaco mini mart. The small TV set was also found. They were photographed. Gallanger sent several other officers to extend the search onto the south side of Highway 109. From almost directly across from the apartment, Gallanger was notified that items of bedding were discovered over the highway ditch; a cream colored blanket, a brown stained pillow case with towels in it. These items were also photographed, while another officer placed a bright orange marking tape around the area of discovery.

While this additional evidence was being flagged, a sharp eyed female officer spotted something under the brush near the blanket, Micki Treat pressed back the brush to expose a small phillips-head screwdriver with a black and orange plastic handle. Gallanger escorted Smythe around to observe all that had been discovered so far. Detective Youmans was checking more closely the open garage area next to Ginny's apartment. He and Gallanger had also made contact with the people living upstairs.

Earlier, back in Ocean Shores, Stocks and Parfitt had been making considerable headway in identifying, at least by name and physical description, the young people who had been staying at Ginny's apartment that weekend. Especially Parfitt who, with the aid of other teenagers who had learned of Ginny's death and had come forward to help in the evening's investigation, had correctly determined there were a total of six young people staying at Ginny's that weekend. And had even discovered their names. Marvin Garba was already known to the Ocean Shores Police as Marvin Whitefox. Robert Noonan was known to have been living in the Aberdeen-Hoquiam area with his girlfriend Tina whose last name had not yet been determined. Marvin's girlfriend was determined to be Sonja Cortell, and there was an active Warrant out for her arrest at that moment. Craig Borman had been living and working in Ocean Shores for the past two months. He had a job in a fast-food restaurant on Point Brown Avenue. His girlfriend of the weekend was named Tammy. Her last name, also had not been determined.

Stocks made several photo copies of the polaroid shots, supplied by Marcie while determining the phone number and address of Dan's apartment there in town. With the photo prints and the names of the young people on the prints, Stocks, Parfitt and two Ocean Shores Police Officers drove over to Dan's apartment.

Except for Patty Dyke, who had had some words with Craig shortly before he and his friends left for Olympia earlier that day, no one was home. Satisfying the Officers curiosity over her being alone in Dan's apartment, she explained that Dan often left his doors unlocked for friends and students of his who may wish to drop in and use his apartment while he was out. On learning that the officers were at this moment conducting a serious investigation, Patty readily identified Crag Borman and Marvin Garba in the photos, and gave first names of most of the others in the prints. Patty then repeated the earlier conversation she had with Craig. Craig had told her they were, "-partying at the woman's house in Hogans Corner all weekend. And her husband was coming home, so they had to leave. This lady told Craig that they had to leave before her husband arrived or else he would beat her."

Before the officers departed one of the Ocean Shores officers stated it was urgent that they should make contact with Dan as soon as possible. Stocks noticed a pair of boy's shoes lying on the wooden steps.

Stocks returned to Hogans Corner and joined Smythe who had the search warrants. They decided, since the rain had made the area extremely muddy and wishing to disturb the actual crime scene as little as possible, they would wait until daylight or until the rain stopped before entering the apartment. Meanwhile they would continue to gather evidence and make contact with as many of the immediate neighbors in the area as possible. Then Stocks departed for Aberdeen.

A good radio contact system had been established between the officers at Ocean Shores and those at Hogans Corner. At about 11:50 p.m. the Ocean Shores police informed the working officers at Hogans Corner that Dan and Patty had just arrived at the station and wanted to give all the information they had to the investigation. They both had statements to make. Detective Smythe and Chief Investigator Darrow got in the car and drove to the station, to cover the interview and take their statements.

A new day was arriving, Tuesday, 27 August. And up on the mound, Ginny's body still lay covered. The coroner and medical people would also conduct their investigation when it became daylight. Meanwhile throughout the night, and while the other officers continued gathering additional evidence and information, Deputy Larson maintained a security vigil over the drag-path and the grave mound itself. Almost, he thought, "-like an honor guard." He would maintain his vigil until relieved at about 5 a.m. by Deputy Wright.

At the Ocean Shores Police Station Smythe and Darrow both interviewed Dan and Patty separately, Dan first: Dan began with how Craig had been living in his apartment for the past two months. Craig had not paid anything to date but would start by paying 400 dollars on September 1st. Then Dan went on to describe the events of the past weekend as he remembered them. Craig and Marv, Marv had been working at the Shop Right market for awhile, went to Aberdeen early Friday morning. At about 10 p.m. Craig called and asked for a ride back to Ocean Shores. And said Craig would meet him at the Aberdeen Bus Station. After finishing up a few chores Dan drove to Aberdeen. He didn't find them right away, but on driving around he spotted Marv and his girlfriend, and following near by was Craig, with two other girls and a guy. Marv and Craig introduced the other four youngsters to Dan. The tall blonde really stood out.

They said they wanted a motel room in Ocean Shores. To Dan, Craig didn't seem to be completely alert, not drunk but maybe on pot. And Craig gave the impression that if Dan didn't take them all to Ocean Shores Craig would stay in Aberdeen. So he got them settled into his pickup truck, with a number of their tote bags. Before leaving Aberdeen the boys directed Dan to pick up a case of beer they had stashed under a dumpster next to the bus station.

Arriving in Ocean Shores they all drove around looking for a motel room. They did not find one, at least in the price range they wanted. They drove around for about an hour or so.

Dan didn't want all these people staying in his apartment, they might trash it. Anyway he had another friend staying with him that night. So, he drove out to Hogans Corner and to the upper apartment where Marv had been occasionally staying during the past few weeks. Marv and Dan went up the stairs on the west side of the triplex apartment building and checked with the people living there. They didn't want six young people crashing into their apartment either.

Going back downstairs with Marv, Dan found that two of the girls were already inside Ginny's apartment. Ginny had invited them in saying they could all stay the night. (Ginny had a severe toothache at this time) Dan had never met Ginny so he went in, sat down with her and then had a beer on this warm summer evening. After the young people got all their luggage inside, and he was satisfied they were settled in for the night Dan departed and drove back to his apartment at Ocean Shores. He arrived at his own home about 3 a.m., Saturday morning.

Saturday afternoon Dan drove back over to see how things were. Everything seemed alright. However, Craig had obviously been drinking. Dan didn't stay long but came back again Saturday night, at about 11 p.m. He had a few beers with them. Dan saw that Craig was very drunk, but also saw that he went to sleep. Dan left the apartment around 2 a.m. Sunday morning. Dan drove back over to the apartment again, Sunday afternoon. It was about 2:30 p.m. when he arrived. He had another beer with them, then left for the last time. He had to go and fill his propane tank. That Sunday night Dan watched late movies with his middle-aged lady friend until about midnight. Then he went upstairs to bed leaving his friend on the couch down in the living room.

Dan didn't see Craig and his friends again until they walked into his apartment, and up to his bedroom at about 7 a.m. Monday morning. His lady friend down on the couch let them in, then she left sometime afterwards. Patty Dyke came by around 9 a.m. or so. They had some pleasant words together then Patty left his apartment sometime between 9:15 and 9:30. Dan told how the four young people stayed at his apartment, waiting for Craig's ride to Olympia. Dan then related the rest of his day to the Detectives, including his driving Craig over to see Marcie.

Detective Smythe and Chief Darrow then interviewed Patty Dyke. Patty's statement coincided with Dan's, then she added some fresh information. Patty's boyfriend, being Craig's best friend, had been fixing up his 20 year old Firebird and wanted to show it off to Craig and his friends who he knew were all staying out at Ginny's. At about 7:30 p.m. Sunday evening her boyfriend arrived at Ginny's and took Craig and some of his friends for a drive down Highway 115 into Ocean Shores and back. Craig's friend Marvin showed her boyfriend a large Rambo type knife with its tip broken off and asked if her boyfriend could fix it. Patty's boyfriend said he could and placed it in the glove compartment of his car.

Later, after dropping off Craig and his friends back at Ginny's, her boyfriend finally arrived at Patty's for their Sunday evening date. It was about 9 p.m. Sometime after midnight, Monday morning, Patty and her boyfriend got in his car and headed out for a drive to Aberdeen. Shortly after making the right hand turn at Hogans Corner, Patty saw Craig, Marv and some other people walking into the parking lot of the Gull Station. Then while driving on to Aberdeen Patty's boyfriend reached into the glove compartment and brought out Marv's Rambo knife to show Patty. They stayed out all night, and her boyfriend got her home before dawn. He had to hurry and get back to Quinault, and get ready to go to work there that Monday morning.

Patty had touched base with Dan at his place around 11 p.m. He had been out all evening, having enjoyed dinner and a few beers at a local Pub. Finally hearing the rumor that Ginny had been murdered the night before, which Dan could hardly believe, they both decided they should go to the Ocean Shores police station and tell all they know. They both remembered those large scratch marks on Marv's face.

It was about 3:30 a.m. Tuesday morning when Dan and Patty finished and signed their statements in front of Smythe and Darrow. Smythe then asked Dan about any items or clothing that may have been left behind in his apartment by Craig and his friends who had gone to the Olympia area. Dan answered that it was entirely possible they had, and that the officers were welcome to drive over and see for themselves.

At Dan's apartment detectives Smythe and Parfitt placed several items of clothing including shoes in to plastic bags. The items were all found in the downstairs area of the apartment and Dan stated they were items that did not belong to him. Then Smythe and Parfitt headed back to Hogans Corner. While Smythe began checking out the open garage area leading into Ginny's apartment, Parfitt climbed the stairs to the upper apartment and began questioning again those persons living there. Mrs. Knox, the woman of the upstairs apartment, in her late thirties was cooperative in her statement to Parfitt. She knew Ginny pretty well and was on good speaking terms with her since she and her daughter Kim had moved into the upper back apartment a month earlier. Ginny had been living in the lower forward downstairs apartment about a month before she and her daughter moved in. As she understood it, Ginny's previous home, had been a log house nestled in a wooded section of Ocean Shores, which she and her husband Greg had shared the previous year. This was the fishing season and Greg, a commercial fisherman, was off on his job on a fishing vessel off the Coast of Alaska.

Ginny, living alone in the log cabin, became frightened over what she thought were the sounds of prowlers around her log home in Ocean Shores. She began looking around for a suitable house or apartment with neighbors she could see and talk with everyday. The triplex apartment building at Hogans Corner seemed ideal for her and Greg for when he returned. Ginny's apartment was also large enough for other members of her family who might come and visit someday. She was a real nice lady, and only about 5 feet 3 inches tall, maybe about a hundred and thirty five pounds. She kept a nice clean home.

Marvin Garba was also pretty well known to Mrs. Knox. Marv and her son had become friends while they were working together down in Newberg, Oregon earlier in the year.

Mrs. Knox's son, on figuring he could get a better job in Ocean Shores now that the tourist season was coming on, wanted to be nearer his mom and sister, he decided he would leave Newberg and try his luck in Ocean Shores. His friend Marv didn't seem to have any other friends in Newberg so he brought Marv with him. Mrs. Knox allowed Marv to stay in her apartment with her son until they found a job and got a place of their own. Mrs. Knox's son quickly obtained a job at one of the upper class motels in town and moved in with another friend closer in. Mrs. Knox had to tell Marv to move out too, which he did but left some of his clothes with Mrs. Knox. Marv had found a job, and was working in the super market.

On the past weekend in question, Mrs Knox knew that Marv, and Craig who she had met earlier, were staying at Ginny's along with some of their friends. There was loud rock and roll noise going on in Ginny's apartment but since it was down and forward of her own apartment it wasn't too disturbing. Mrs. Knox was terribly disturbed by Ginny's death, and said her daughter Kim would also make a statement.

Stocks had pulled into the VFW parking lot some minutes after Smythe and Parfitt drove up. Stocks had just returned from the Aberdeen area where he had been running down leads, supplied to him by Ocean Shores Officers, and teenagers who wanted to help. The two different names he had, putting aside Craig Borman and Marvin Garba for the moment, were Robert Noonan, Sonja Cortell and their last known addresses in Aberdeen.

There was no response at the address he had for Noonan. But he had better luck at the address he had for Cortell. Even at that late hour Sonja's foster family was more then willing to help and assist in locating Sonja. At this South Aberdeen single story home, near South Shore Mall, the foster mother, a little haggard and in her late 30's, related how Sonja and her new girlfriend Tammy had dropped in and stayed only a short while before leaving again, about 5 p.m. the previous day. She also stated Sonja said she might not return. And had left a jacket she had been wearing. The foster mother and her husband willingly gave up the jacket to Stocks, and they remembered that Craig had called for Sonja and Tammy again after the girls left, but left no return phone number. Stocks thanked them for their assistance, and with Sonja's discarded jacket, he stepped off the porch, walked through the picket fence gate and got back in his blue Chevy for the dark wet ride back to Hogans Corner. The rain had let up, and by the time he returned to the Corner it had stopped altogether.

Considering the dryer weather it was decided to enter Ginny's apartment. Actually the garage door was open and that part of the apartment had already been carefully investigated. The door leading into the apartment from the garage was also unlocked. The detectives all placed plastic coverings over their shoes and got into plastic gloves. It was about 5 a.m. Tuesday morning.

Each Officer was prepared, and they carefully began their internal investigation of Ginny's apartment. They photographed every unusual aspect they found. Swab samples of blood were taken from the floors and walls. Finger prints were made from all items which appeared to have been recently handled. They found several breaks and holes in the sheet rock walls which some appeared to be surrounded with more blood, all with the appearance of having been made with recent violent force.

In the master bedroom on the night stand next to the bed, a number of pills were visible near an almost empty bottle of Vicks NyQuil. Some green residue was still in the plastic cup next to the NyQuil bottle. The bed itself was in disarray, with some blood smears on the bedding. On top the blond dresser across the room and near the sewing machine there was a scattering of feminine items that appeared to have come from an emptied out purse. The top of the sewing machine also had a clutter of small change and a number of overturned family photographs.

There were blood stains and markings in both bathrooms. And what appeared to be knife stabs in the walls and casings in the hallway area. Smythe also began taking measurements of each room and utility space, achieving a working diagram of the whole apartment.

Not only were numerous finger prints taken, there were also obvious red stained foot and shoe prints on the linoleum floors of the hallway and kitchen areas, to be impressed, photographed, and cataloged. While they did not speak of it during their careful examination and investigation, the smell and feeling of recent horror and violence was all around them. The actual place of death, down on the floor of the small hallway, was established from the pattern of scattered blood spots that ran up and along the hallway walls.

The officers, feeling they had completed most of their investigation in Ginny's apartment, took a coffee break over at the Texaco Mini Mart, while leaving behind a uniformed officer guarding over Ginny's apartment.

Detective Gallanger came over with his report and statement he had recently obtained from Kim Knox, Mrs. Knox's daughter. Kim stated she had become nicely acquainted with Ginny during the month she and her mother had occupied the upstairs apartment. They would visit together at least three times a week, and would speak to each other every day. This weekend, on Sunday evening when Kim got off work, she parked and went up to Ginny's front door to pick up her dog. Marv came out and said "-Hi, how are you doing!" Kim asked what was going on and he answered "We're partying!" Kim left the front entrance and walked around to the kitchen window. Inside she saw a mess of beer cans and bottles. A dark haired skinny kid stuck his head at the window, and Marv introduced him as Bob. Bob's chubby girlfriend came up behind and hugged him. Marv asked Kim to come in and "party" with them. Kim looked around for Ginny but didn't see her, and thought that unusual. Kim took her dog and went upstairs. Twenty minutes later, about 6:30 p.m., Kim came back out calling for her dog again. He did not answer so she went down to Ginny's apartment and peered through the kitchen window again. In the living room Marv had a dark haired girl sitting on his lap. Kim asked Marv if he had seen her dog. Marv said no. Again Kim didn't see anything of Ginny. After some more calling Kim's dog came up to her. Fifteen minutes later the dog took off again and Kim went back downstairs to the kitchen window again and asked the occupants in the living room about her dog. The dark haired girl said he wasn't there.

About this time a silver-primed car came squealing into the apartment driveway. Marv got out from the passenger side holding Kim's dog. Marv said he was sorry he did that. Marv introduced Kim to the driver, who said he was from the Quinault area. The teenage owner of the car took Kim for a short drive to show off his car. When they got back to the apartment the driver asked to come up to Kim's apartment. Kim said no. She went upstairs and the driver went into Ginny's apartment.

Upstairs Kim found her mother cooking spaghetti and Kim's boyfriend was there. Marv came up and said he and Craig were going to buy a car and make a trip to Oregon. Marv appeared to be really drunk. Kim went into her mother's bedroom to talk to her mom. When they came back out everyone was gone. Kim went into the bathroom and took a shower for the date she had planned with her boyfriend later that evening. When she came out of the bathroom there was Marv and Craig standing in the hallway. All Marv had on was a long tee shirt, all Craig had on was a pair of red shorts. Craig said he was sorry, and Marv said "I'm too drunk to be embarrassed." Kim's mother came in the hall and told the boys to get some clothes on. She got them some clothes from those that were left in her apartment by Marv. Then Kim's mother fixed them each a plate of Spaghetti so they might sober up. Two of the girls from downstairs came up and they had some spaghetti too. Kim asked about Ginny. The blonde girl said Ginny was, "-weird!" Craig said something about Ginny drinking NyQuil and some other things. And Craig said something like we over-dosed her and she could be dead. We might have killed her.

Kim packed up dinner for her boyfriend, got her dog and left the apartment, and did not return until 10:30 a.m. Monday morning.

After their coffee, Stocks, Smythe, Youmans, and Parfitt, concluded that with day light nearing and the rain stopped they could expect the coroner and other medical people to be on the scene at any moment. They needed to get one last look at the body before it was taken away. As they were walking over toward the empty lot a police car and a mortuary van drove up and parked in the VFW lot. It was the coroner and his staff, and people from Colman's Chapel in Hoquiam. The officers escorted the new arrivals up to the mound.

After the coroner had the body uncovered and made his detailed findings, he then turned the rest of the task of removal over to the hands of the people from Colman's. During all this careful procedure the detectives standing nearby observed there were numerous stab wounds around the neck, breast, and chest area. And on turning the body over there clearly appeared to be numerous stab wounds in the back. A body bag was provided, and Ginny's body was gently placed inside. With the small bag resting in the rear of the mortuary van, the van then departed the area. It was about 6:30

a.m. The sun was rising over Hogans Corner for a new day.

At the close of WWII, battle hardened troops were stunned, often brought to tears, on witnessing the barely living and the dead during the liberation of concentration camps in the Philippines and in central Europe. Detective Smythe's father, a Chief Warrant Officer, was one of those who stayed on in Europe, attached to the U.S. Army's Counter Intelligence Service. Detective Stocks' father also served in the Army during the war.

A helpful unexpected phone call rang in Ginny's apartment. It was from Mrs. Barny Parker stating she was an aunt of Virginia Barsic and could help with notifying next of kin. Sergeant Larry Shelton of the Grays Harbor County Sheriffs Department, and a distant relative of the Parkers, was assigned to assist in that part of the on going gathering of information.

By this time a state-wide search was underway for the six young people who had stayed at Ginny's apartment that past weekend. Their physical descriptions and the first names and last names too were known, except for Tammy's and Tina's. The police were also checking for any past criminal records on file on any of the full names that were known. Especially alerted were the Olympia Police Department, the Aberdeen and Hoquiam Police, and Police in Newberg, Oregon.

The sheriff's officers on the scene took breakfast breaks in shifts at the Homeport Restaurant back in Ocean Shores, and then returned to the crime scene for more investigative and interrogative work. It was now full daylight, Tuesday morning, but more rain clouds were coming in over the Ocean's horizon.

Over at number 17 at the Town Motel in Aberdeen, Marv, Tammy, and Sonja were just getting out of bed, and taking turns getting into the shower. Before going to sleep the night before Marv had checked around news channels to see if any word was coming in regarding Hogans Corner. And this morning, after his shower, he was checking news channels again.

With no reports coming over the TV the youngsters turned the knob around to a children's animated cartoon, then began getting more fully dressed. Even though they departed from the other side of the main entrance to the motel the manager noticed the three people leave. Tammy waved and said she would be back to pay the rest of the room rate later on. At that moment they were getting hungry again, so they made it across the highway and went into MacDonalds, the same MacDonalds that Craig and his friends enjoyed their lunch the previous afternoon.

After breakfast the three young people journeyed back across the Wishkah River Bridge and headed for the Book Store where Marv enjoyed playing video games. Getting bored with the machines Marv had something else working on his mind. He had an idea that may give him and the girls more breathing time, and would confuse the cops when they finally came looking around Ginny's apartment.

Back out on Wishkah street, walking west, Marv began explaining his plan to the girls. He would go back to Hogans Corner, dig up Ginny's body, carry it back inside her apartment, then burn the whole place down. He would also go around the Texaco mini mart, find Tammy's suitcase and Sonja's tote bags and bring them back to Aberdeen for the girls. The girls argued with Marv a little, whether or not it was a good idea to go back there. Marv remained determined with his new idea, as they continued walking west along the south side of Wishkah Street. They covered five blocks of walking and now had the Red Lion Motel parking lot on their left side. It was just past 11:05 a.m. And it had started raining again.

Being a one way street in a westerly direction, a blue and white Aberdeen Police car came along and drove close by the leisurely walking young people. The officer inside glanced over at them, then slowly pulled up and parked next to the curb and waited for them to walk up to his patrol car.

CHAPTER FOUR: APPREHENSION

Just as the three young people came abeam to his patrol car Sergeant John Delia of the Aberdeen Police Department opened his left front door, stepped out onto the curb and confronted them. He spoke to the tall blonde female first.

"Just a routine stop, Miss. Please let me see your identification!"

Tammy looked at her two companions then back to the officer, and said, "I'm sorry but I don't have any."

"What is your name please?"

"Shelly!"

"Are you new to this area?"

"Oh, we've been around a few days."

Marv smiling, confirmed Tammy, "Ya, just a few days." Sonja, standing next to Marv, said nothing.

"Well, where have you been staying?"

"At the Town Motel!", Tammy answered with a smile, glancing back down the street, and back to the officer again.

Delia then turned his attention to Marv, and asked, "What is your name sir?"

"Oh! My name's Marcus, Marcus Wittem!"

"When were you born, Mr. Wittem?"

"June first, Nineteen Seventy. Anything wrong?"

Delia had been studying Marv closely. The numerous scratch marks around his face, though lightly scabbed over, appeared to have been made within the last day or two. Some of the marks had deep half-moon shapes to them, like maybe from fingernails. He then gave his attention to Sonja.

"And you, Miss. What is your name please?"

"Sonja!" she answered .

"Sonja Cortell?"

"Yes!"

All this took less then a minute. Delia knew from his working list Sonja was wanted on a Juvenile Warrant. He then stated he needed to talk to all three of them in more detail and since it was raining would they please have a seat in the rear of his patrol car. Delia opened the left back door. A flash of light, followed by a crack of thunder accompanied the summer shower.

Without hesitation the three companions moved in out of the rain, with Tammy first, then Marv and Sonja. But they made a small complaint, about there being only two seats in the rear of the patrol car and making it a little cramped for them. Delia announced that he would take them to the Station where there was more room, and then mentioned he had knowledge that people from another agency wanted to talk to them also.

"That'll be OK!, That'll be fine", they answered. With Delia up front, and buckled in, and the engine still running he moved away from the curb. With an opening in the traffic Delia, at moderate speed, wheeled his patrol car across Wishkah Street and got on Michigan Street. Another few moments then he headed up Market Street for the seven blocks drive back to the Aberdeen Police Station.

Earlier this Tuesday morning Sergeant John Delia, six feet, ruddy complected, solid built, and also in his early forties, reported in for duty at 5 a.m. Among his fellow officers he was known as 'lucky John', having been on the scene at the right place and at the right time on a number of critical cases which had developed in the Aberdeen area over the years. His closer friends would tell you he is simply a very alert and sharp police officer.

Shortly after his early morning arrival he was notified there had been a homicide discovered out in the Ocean Shores area and that the sheriffs people were looking for six suspects. A teletype had been issued state-wide listing the names and descriptions of all six, but without the last names of two of them.

Delia, the morning shift supervisor, studied the teletype message then made copies of it and passed them out to the other patrol officers on his shift. Also mentioned in the teletype was that some of the suspects had been seen in the Aberdeen area on the previous day. The duty patrol officers all departed the station, some in response to a number of assignments that had been issued out early that morning. After investigating and clearing a few assignments himself Sergeant Delia had begun cruising west on Wishkah Street, and then about 11:10 a.m. he spotted three young people walking together near the Red Lion motel. One was a tall blonde female. Now with the three young people in the rear of his patrol car Delia pulled in and parked under the wide over-hang of the Aberdeen Police Station. Delia escorted the three detainees through the double doors, on around the main desk, and back to his office. He invited them to sit down while he logged them in back at the main desk. Leaving them alone a few moments Delia then got on the phone to let the sheriff's people in Montesano know that he had what he believed to be three of the suspects they were looking for on the teletype. Then Delia went back to another section of the station, found Detective Sergeant Bob Johnson and informed him of his pick up of the three youngsters he found walking in town, and of his conclusions.

The detective was already aware of the homicide out at Hogans Corner, having reviewed the state-wide teletype shortly after his own arrival to the station at 8 a.m. Detective Johnson followed Delia back to his office, glanced in at the young people, studied them a moment, and agreed they were likely three of the people in the messages. He half smiled at Delia and told him to go back in and keep them company. Johnson would ensure that the Sheriff's people were informed and were on their way. Delia then stepped back in, sat down and joined them in small conversation.

'Marcus Wittem' informed Delia that he had an address in Portland, Oregon. 'Shelly Maran' said she had another first name and it was Tammy. And that she had come out from Carson to visit her Dad, Paul Muller, who lives in Cosmopolis, and gave his phone number.

Turning to Sonja, Delia said he was sorry but that since there was an existing Warrant out for her from the Grays Harbor County Juvenile Department he was placing her under arrest. Delia then pressed a button on his desk and asked for a juvenile officer to come to his office. Sonja was then escorted to another part of the Station. Turning back to Tammy and Marv, Tammy asked Johnson what they were being held for, what did the police want to talk to them about. Delia answered her by saying it was a matter that the sheriff's officers were engaging in and that he didn't have adequate information on the subject to discus it with her but that they would be along in a few minutes. Tammy became a little nervous, and said she had some luggage which she had left out near a service station at Hogans Corner.

Tammy let it out that she and her two companions, along with some other friends, had spent Saturday and Sunday night with a lady named Ginny at Hogans Corner, but that Ginny got mad and made them all leave about midnight. Tammy added that Sonja had left some of her luggage around the service station too. Then they all walked to another friend's house in Ocean Shores. It took about an hour and a half to walk it, then they ended up at the Town Motel.

Back at Hogans Corner, while still processing evidence at the scene, Stocks got word at 11:30 a.m. from Montesano that the Aberdeen police had picked up what looked like three of the six suspects, and they were being detained at the Aberdeen Police Station. Stocks immediately got in touch with Detective Sergeant Bob Johnson for confirmation. Johnson described the three young people, and concluded they were in fact Marvin Garba, Tammy Muller, and Sonja Cortell. Johnson mentioned Sonja's active Warrant and that she was now in formal custody. Also that the three had apparently spent the last night at the Town Motel.

Stocks requested that Johnson send one of his men over to the Town Motel, and if confirmed, to seal off the room. Johnson was ahead of Stocks on that point and stated that a detective was already on his way to the Town Motel. Stocks thanked his counterpart at the Aberdeen police force and announced he was on his way. Then leaving behind Smythe and Youmans to continue with their investigative work, Parfitt joined Stocks for the rainy ride to Aberdeen. They arrived at the Station about 12:05 p.m.

After the two sheriff's officers shook hands with Johnson and congratulated his force for their apparent success Johnson briefed Stocks and Parfitt on developments up to the moment. The three suspects had indeed spent the night at the Town Motel. Detective Clarkson, of the Aberdeen Police, had obtained a copy of the registration, the collateral jewelry, and had found a movie ticket stub from the South Shore Mall theater. Room number 17 had been sealed for later further investigation.

Johnson also stated that none of the three had admitted to any crime, only that they had spent a couple nights with a lady out at Hogans Corner. And that they had voluntarily come to the station with Delia. While the officers were in conversation the two suspects, not under arrest, were outside on the walkway of the station having a smoke under the watchful eye of Sergeant Delia. Johnson asked the two young people to come back in, and they were then introduced to Stocks and Parfitt.

From the past 17 straight hours of intensive investigation Stocks and Parfitt knew they were now looking at Tammy and Marv. Stocks decided that he and Parfitt would interview Tammy first. They utilized an empty back office with three chairs and a table for that purpose, while Delia kept further company with Marv in his office. Making no mention of a specific crime, other than what they had found and believed that an assault of some kind had taken place at Hogans Corner over the weekend, Stocks started off by asking Tammy if she would tell them about where and what she had been doing over the past few days.

Tammy immediately began explaining that she and five of her friends had met and "partyed" almost the whole weekend with a lady out at Hogans Corner. Then after the lady "freaked out and started bitching at them" they left and stayed with Craig at his residence, then they traveled to Aberdeen by bus and stayed overnight in a motel. She admitted she had lied to the officers about her name, and that her real name was Tammy Muller.

Stocks and Parfitt made it clear that she was being questioned as to her being a possible witness to a felony assault, an investigation they were currently conducting. Tammy, at this point, was very friendly and talkative. She laughingly projected a carefree attitude during the early part of the interview. Tammy, referring to the lady by name, said Ginny was bitching at them to clean up the house, which they did. She and her friends had been drinking beer and wine coolers, and Ginny had been drinking "NyQuil".

With Stocks and Parfitt encouraging her to give as much detail as she could remember, Tammy went on to say that none of the six were over twenty one, and that Ginny had purchased some of the booze for them. But after Ginny started bitching at them, they left. Tammy said they all left Ginny's about 4 a.m. Sunday morning. And left the apartment clean "not extremely clean, but neat and tidy". But 'Marcus' and Craig ran back. She stated she did not know what happened back in the apartment during that forty five minutes. Then Tammy said that Ginny had left earlier saying she wanted them to be gone by the time she got back. Tammy said she did not know why 'Marcus' and Craig went back.

At this point Stocks advised Tammy that the officers were aware that Marvin's name was not Marcus. Tammy was surprised that the officer knew this. Then she went on to tell about Dan first trying to get them situated with the people upstairs from Ginny. Tammy also admitted that all six had paired off and had sex while at Ginny's, and further admitted that Tina and Sonja were probably only 14 or 15.

Parfitt, carefully but firmly informed Tammy that they didn't believe she was telling them all the truth of what happened, especially Sunday night. Tammy got a little agitated, and said she couldn't remember everything. With Stocks and Parfitt staring at her, waiting for more details, Tammy became animated with her hands and rolled her eyes back, her face was flushed.

Stocks then said they had obtained a search warrant and had gone into Ginny's apartment and found much evidence of a terrible struggle. There were foot, hand and fingerprints, and much evidence of blood around the floors and walls. Tammy then became extremely agitated and had the appearance of becoming physically ill. She said she thought she might be pregnant again. Then she declared she didn't understand this conversation, especially saying things about blood.

Changing the subject Stocks asked Tammy about the jewelry she used as collateral at the Town Motel. Tammy said the jewelry was her own. Parfitt said there was evidence back at the apartment that some of Ginny's jewelry was missing. Tammy began to cry and her hands were shaking, then she became loud and angry at the officers. First, all they wanted was to know about where she was and what she was doing over the weekend. Now they were talking about blood, and stuff like that. Then Tammy asked the officers to please tell her more about what they had found in the apartment. Stocks replied that at this point in time he would have to cease questing her as a witness, and would read her Rights to her. They told her it appeared she was not telling all the truth, and that she was probably involved in the homicide at Hogans Corner. Stocks then began reading her rights from a form.

Tammy held her hands over her face and began crying again. She stood up from her chair, then sat back down again. As Stocks continued reading her rights, Tammy said, "the same thing is going to happen to me if I say anything". Stocks continued reading her rights point by point. Then Tammy began uttering "They killed her, they killed her". She went on to say "Marv did it. Craig and Bob held her down, and Craig stabbed Ginny too". She only wiped down one wall. And now she wanted to tell the whole truth. In her own hand she completed a nine page statement to detective Parfitt. The time was about 1 p.m.

Back over in the sergeants' office, Delia and Johnson had been taking turns sitting with Marv. At one point Delia went out and brought back coffee for Marv, and for himself also. In light conversation Marv found that he and Delia shared a common interest: Karate.

Marv revealed to Delia how he had obtained a "Brown belt" level in the martial arts while living in Riverside, California a few years earlier. Marv played in tournaments, wanted to pursue it further but could not obtain a sponsor. Delia told Marv he too had studied Karate, fought in tournaments, and had reached "Black belt" level. Then together they began describing various moves and techniques.

At one point, while demonstrating hand maneuvers, Delia's focus fell on a recent large cut on Marv's right hand. Marv stated, "Never hit anybody with an open jaw!"

"What do you mean?"

Marv explained he had to hit a friend of his the other night because his friend came out of a sleep and struck his girlfriend. Marv didn't like that, so he had to hit his friend and the blow landed on his friend's teeth. That's how he got the cut. Marv then changed the subject, and revealed another physical form he had excelled in; Marv was a skateboard champion down in California, but again he couldn't find a sponsor. Then their subject went back to karate, and Marv told Delia how he could break bricks with his head.

At this point Johnson came in and relieved Delia for lunch, and brought in lunch for Marv. Then Johnson began keeping Marv company for awhile. A short time earlier Detective Johnson had met with Grays Harbor County Prosecutor Steward Menefee and his Chief Criminal Deputy Prosecutor Gerald Fuller, who had been keeping track of the events in progress. They were delighted that an early contact had been made with at least half the suspects, and were satisfied the case was progressing well.

During the company-keeping with his young suspects Johnson learned that Marv's heritage was "Apache Indian". Marv displayed a tattoo on his left arm he had received when he was younger that was in relation to being an Apache Indian. Marv asked Johnson specifically what Stocks and Parfitt wanted to talk to him about. Johnson answered that he simply wasn't able to discuss the case with Marv, but that the County detectives would be with him soon.

Stocks, on leaving Parfitt with Tammy, informed Johnson by intercom phone he now had enough information to proceed with Marv. Tammy had confessed to having been involved in Ginny's death, and had implicated Marvin Garba.

Marv was then brought into a different interview room, and in the presence of Delia, following behind, Stocks told Marv that he was placing him under arrest for murder in the death of Virginia Barsic. And then began reading him his Miranda Rights and warnings. Marv then stated he wanted to have an attorney represent him. At the conclusion of listening to his rights Marv said he wanted to ask some questions.

"I might not be able to answer all the questions you want to ask", answered Stocks. With no further words from Marv, Stocks turned to Delia and asked that Marvin Garba be formally booked.

Marv was then taken back to the detention area and turned over to another officer. His clothes were taken from him and he was directed to get into the standard prisoner coveralls. He was then mugged and fingerprinted. Delia in observance, called Stocks in the booking room and stated he saw numerous scratch marks on Marv's chest, sides and back areas, and injuries on his hands and knuckles. A camera was loaded and Stocks took pictures of all Marv's injuries. Johnson then came in and over-saw the remaining procedure for felony suspect booking, as Stocks and Delia returned to the desk area to complete the paper work.

After a few minutes Johnson joined them in the hallway and stated that Marv wanted to make a statement, but not to Stocks. He wanted to make a statement to Johnson and Delia; Delia because he knew all the right Karate "-moves". Stocks said if Marv was initiating the contact then the Aberdeen officers were free to take his statement, but that in any case he could not participate. Johnson and Delia then re-advised Marv on his rights, to which Marv did not invoke and said he now wanted to make a statement to them, he wanted to tell them what happened and to get it off his shoulders. He said he didn't want an attorney anymore. Johnson reminded Marv that he and Delia were police officers and would do their jobs. Marv said he understood that. Marv then signed the Waiver of Rights form, which was then signed by both officers. Then Johnson told Marv to start at the beginning, when all six first got together. Delia remained in the room the entire period.

The time was 1:40 p.m. when Marv began his 10 page written statement with how they all met at the main Aberdeen bus station. Then he proceeded with Dan taking them all to Ocean Shores. Marv told how the people upstairs from Ginny's was getting ready for bed and didn't want them but Ginny was willing to take them in. The next day, Saturday, he went and picked up his final check at the Super Market. They used a local cab to get around, to the liquor store. Back at Ginny's "they all began partying again". Then he and Craig discussed plans to go to Oregon in a day or so to get "blotter acid", bring it back and sell it for a profit. He and Craig also discussed robbing the Ocean Shores Bank, for later in the week. Shortly after Sunday midnight, Bob Noonan began running off at the mouth and told everybody in the apartment about his and Craig's plans to make a dope run to Oregon. This really upset Ginny, who was already upset because of the messy apartment. "Ginny really flipped out and said she was going to tell the cops about the drug run. She also started telling everyone to get out." Marv and Craig talked and decided they couldn't let her live, she knew too much. They used sign language indicating the cutting of Ginny's throat. Tammy was also mad at her because Ginny was "ragging" at her over Tammy giving up her child. Marv then continued on how he, Craig and Bob had a hand in killing Ginny. Marv admitted he did most of the stabbing. Then Marv, in his own hand, with paper and pencil rough sketched the floor plan of the apartment and diagramed where Ginny was killed, and where everyone was at the time. Then he added "Boy, did she want to live. That woman really wanted to live." When we thought she was dead, she would sit up again. She said, "why are you doing this, I didn't do anything to you guys."

While Parfitt was finishing up with Tammy's statement in the other interview room, Stocks made contact with Sonja in the juvenile part of the Station. Stocks informed her that he was engaged in investigation of a homicide. She was aware that she was being held on an unrelated juvenile warrant. Before any questions, Stocks read her juvenile rights under Washington State laws. Sonja acknowledge her rights and wished to wave them as she wanted to make a statement. Stocks asked her to please put it in writing, which she did. She made a two page statement, and asked Stocks, if he would help her finish the last part, which he did. Sonja indicated she was asleep during the early morning hours of Monday. However, it was her recollection that Tammy and Tina occupied the back master bedroom some of the time. In a neat left handed scroll she went on to say that it was a "stupid" weekend, they paired off and had "sex orgies". Sonja stated that she walked in on the guys in the bathroom and observed them in the act of cutting their hands with a knife to be blood brothers. And they were talking about stealing a car which she thought they were just joking. Ginny bitched about everything, also she said Ginny called the boat her husband was on and she was told he may be home on Monday. Sonja slept most all of Sunday night and through early Monday morning. When they left she was told that Tina and Bob had "freaked out" and they left early. And that Ginny had got mad, "freaked out", and left the house and they had to leave before she got back. Later they told her Ginny got hit in the head and it broke her neck. And she was told that Ginny was buried way under a big pile of dirt. Tammy told her that Marv and Craig even talked about killing her too, because she was a "narc". But they decided I could live, Tammy said.

Sonja told Stocks she would be willing to talk to him again if he needed to. Leaving Sonja behind in the juvenile section of the station, Stocks rejoined Parfitt. They were going over Tammy's statement in another interview room when Delia stepped in and told them Marv had just made a 10 page statement confessing his part in the killing of Ginny, and that he was very cooperative. The two Sheriffs Officers suggested that Delia might go back to Marv and see if he would be willing to return to Hogans Corner and assist the investigating team there in further clarifying the crime scene and locating any other evidence.

Delia returned to Stocks and Parfitt and stated that Marv's response was "no problem", but that he wanted Delia to be with him at all times, as he enjoyed talking to Delia. It was then a little before 4 p.m., and preparations were made to transport Marv back to Hogans Corner. Deputy Sheriff Shumate would accompany them.

Meanwhile, County Prosecutor Menefee and his Chief Criminal Prosecutor Fuller had returned to Montesano and were assembling all the officer's reports and follow-up reports which were coming in, and which they were receiving copies of. Menefee and Fuller decided to pull into the picture three detectives from their County Drug Task Force, to help in apprehending the suspects; Craig Borman, Robert Noonan, and Tina Murphy, who were still at large. Detectives Patrick, Haymon, and McGowen were assigned the task of reviewing all officer reports and statements from witnesses that were available to them at the moment.

In reading through again Patty Dyke's statement particularly at the end of her statement on the last page, it appeared to Detective Patrick that Patty may have a mutual friend who was acquainted with one of the two girls who came to Ocean Shores to pick up Borman, driving him to the Olympia area Monday afternoon. Patty had listed her name as Debby Raft, living with her parents just outside the monuments of Ocean Shores. And also listed her phone number. The time was about 3 p.m.

Patrick gave the name and number to Detective Haymon, to try it out and see where it led. Haymon dialed the number and he reached Debby's mother. Mrs. Raft did indeed have a daughter who was acquainted with Craig Borman. Mrs. Raft took a call from Craig herself on Monday afternoon asking for Maxine's phone number in Olympia. Mrs. Raft said Craig was in a hurry. She found the number and gave it to him.

And she was even able to give Haymon Maxine's address in Olympia. Haymon thanked Debby's mother, then made his next call to the Olympia Police Department. He reached Detective Trevor Seal, who wanted to know who was in charge of the case. He was informed it was Detective Bill Stocks.

Earlier this Tuesday morning, after Craig, Maxine and Cindy had gotten up in the new house which the two girls were fixing up out on Old Highway 99 in Tumwater, the three young people climbed back in Cindy's Maverick and drove over to Lacey. Maxine needed to check into the beauty college there. Nearby was a Winchell's Doughnut place and they had a little breakfast.

Maxine had still not told her girlfriend Cindy about the startling conversation she had had with Craig the night before. Maxine was not only a little frightened over Craig's story, she was getting a little angry about the whole thing. Maxine got up from the table and said she was going to walk over to the beauty college, and would meet Cindy and Craig there at Winchell's later that afternoon.

Cindy had an exercise class she was scheduled for, also nearby, and she drove with Craig over to that place. Craig stayed in the car. In about an hour Cindy returned to her car and found Craig sleeping in the back seat. Cindy felt there was something going on she didn't know about. After waking him up Craig joined her in the front seat, and then she invited Craig to tell her what was bothering him.

Craig began talking about his college plans again, and that his plans may be in doubt now. He then got around to telling Cindy about his terrible past weekend. He was with his friend Marv and his girlfriend Tammy and along comes these "three other guys". He then proceeded to tell Cindy exactly the same story he told Maxine the night before. Craig ended his story by saying he "-didn't feel it was morally right.", and that he "-knows he should have done something, but didn't know how to do it or what to do." He "-was just too scared."

At about 3:30 p.m. Detective Seal, at the Olympia Police Station, who had read the state-wide teletype message that morning, and was just briefed by Detective Haymon of the Grays Harbor County Sheriff's Office on the unfolding events in the Hogans Corner case to that moment, asked for their assistance. Seal then held a conference with Detective Russ Geis. Seal and Geis quickly decided to drive to the address of Maxine's parents home, out on South East 8th Street and arrest Borman there on a probable cause homicide Warrant, if he showed up.

On arrival the two officers got out and, with Seal taking a quick look around the house a moment, Geis went up and rang the bell. Maxine's father answered the door, and on observing their identification invited them inside. Maxine's younger brother was with their dad. Maxine's father, very cooperative, informed Geis that he had met Craig on a previous occasion but didn't know where either Craig or his daughter Maxine was at that moment. Seal briefly gave Maxine's father the reason why they were there. Maxine's father said he would take his young son for a short walk outside, leaving the officers in his house alone for awhile.

Within five minutes the phone rang, and Geis answered it. A female voice on the other end identified herself as Maxine, and she wished to speak with her father. She also wanted to know who she was speaking with. Geis informed her he was a friend of her father's, that he had just stepped out on an errand but would return in a few minutes. Over the phone Maxine began to cry, and wanted to know what was going on. She also said she wanted her dad to come and pick her up. Geis asked where she was and who she was with. Maxine answered that she, Cindy and Craig were at Winchell's Doughnut shop. Geis warmly said he would pass that on to her father as soon as he returned. And they hung up.

Only moments later the father and son returned.

Seal informed him of his daughter's call, while Geis was out on the police radio talking to Central Dispatch. With his message and instructions completed, and leaving the volume up on the police radio Geis returned to the house. Both officers thanked Maxine's father for his cooperation and assistance. As they were walking back to the car the news came over the police radio that Craig Borman had been arrested without incident and that the girls who were with him at the Doughnut shop were unharmed. The time was about 4:15 p.m.

At about 4:15 p.m., back in the Aberdeen Police station, preparations were being made to escort and transport Marv back to Hogans Corner. In his police marked orange coveralls, handcuffed and ankle chained, Marv was led outside. A County Sheriff's car was made ready and Marv was placed in the rear seat with Sergeant Delia seated next to him. Deputy Steve Shumate at the wheel.

During the forty-minute drive Marv and Delia made only small talk, mostly about karate tournaments. All officers still working at the crime scene were made aware that Marv was on his way. The brown and white sheriffs car arrived in the apartment's driveway about 5:30 p.m. All the officers working outside stopped to gaze at the car as it pulled in.

Detective Smythe stepped over to the car and, with Delia, assisted Marv out and onto the driveway. The deep scratch marks on Marv's face and exposed upper chest area were so noticeable that Smythe couldn't help but ask Marv how he got them. Without hesitation Marv answered, in a matter of fact tone. "Oh, I got them from Ginny, when I was killing her."

"Will you show us how you did it?" asked Smythe, as the officer gestured toward the open garage area.

Again without hesitation, Marv hobble-walked behind Smythe and Delia. Deputy Dan Kolilis joined Detective Lane Youmans bringing up the rear. The five people entered the apartment from the garage area. The four officers let Marv walk around the apartment freely, allowing him to describe in his own words and actions what took place during his last minutes of Ginny's life, with only occasional clarifying questions from Smythe. Smythe asked Marv if he would re-enact, the murder.

"Sure!" answered Marv. He began by saying Ginny was in the hallway bathroom, upset, and she called for him to come and talk with her. Marv moved toward the bathroom and Ginny came out. Marv raised his arms toward her sympathically, to calm her down. From the bathroom door Ginny stepped toward Marv with her arms toward him, in relief that everything was going to be all right. Only when Marv got close enough he threw a quick arm lock on her head and flipped her over his shoulder. She landed in the hallway on her back.

He instantly covered her. He was handed a pillow and he first tried to smother her. Craig was standing at her feet. Bob was standing near her left arm. Smothering her was not working, so Marv threw off the pillow and with his left index and middle finger made a deep thrust into her right eye socket, past his second knuckle. Then he tried a three-finger karate choke hold. Thinking he may have succeeded in her death at that time, Marv got up from her and -for the continuing re-enactment for the officers- got off the floor and walked toward the utility room. Craig called to him and said she was still alive. Marv quickly turned around and pounced on her again, this time trying a chin and throat Karate move and a head twist that should have broken her neck. He tried violently to twist her head from her neck two or three times, he said, in continuing re-enactment. Marv was getting exhausted, rose up at his knees while over Ginny, looked around on the floor and caught sight of a screw driver. The same screw driver that they had used earlier to work on the bathroom door knob. He said it was there, he just grabbed it, turned, and thrust it into her eye, clear to the handle and twisted it. He didn't remember if he stabbed her in the chest with it or not. What happened then, asked Smythe. Marv said he got up again and started walking toward the rear of the apartment, and someone called to him and said she was still alive. Marv turned and said, get me a knife. He knew then he had to finish the job, or Ginny would go to the police telling them they tried to murder her. He had to finish it. He said he didn't remember who gave him the knife but when he got it he jumped back on Ginny and freaked out. He stabbed her repeatedly in the front, then he couldn't stand to look at her bloody face anymore so he rolled her over and began stabbing her in the back, five or six times. Leaving the knife in her back, Craig grabbed it and he stabbed her several times more. Marv then took the knife away from Craig and stabbed Ginny some more in her back. Smythe asked Marv who assisted him in holding Ginny down. Marv answered Craig and Bob, but Bob didn't do any of the stabbing. Bob only held her arm down part of the the time. Then Bob freaked out, that's how the holes in the walls got there. Bob kicked the walls.

Marv then told the officers he took a shower in the hall bathroom, then came out and tried to take Ginny out on the blanket but it didn't work so he and Craig drug her outside and around the building up to the dirt mound. Smythe asked Marv about the shirt the officers found buried near the body up on the mound. He said Craig must have done that. Marv confirmed that the cream colored blanket, screwdriver, and blood wiping items were taken over and thrown in brush across the highway. While in the apartment Marv had also shown the officers some clothing he had stuffed in the tank behind the toilet bowl. Asked about the knife markings in the door casings Marv replied most of them were put there by himself while they rolled Ginny's body over.

The officers were at times struck by Marvin's matter of fact cooperative tone, but observed that he would get a little excited and carried away while down on the hallway floor, re-enacting the murder.

Marv was led back out through the garage door into the early evening air. He was then placed back in the sheriff's car with Delia. Then with Shumate behind the wheel again, the car cleared the area of Hogans Corner at about 6:30 p.m. Smythe turned to his friends Kolilis and Youmans. They had some words together, then Smythe departed the area about 7 p.m. After the Sheriffs' car transporting Marv got to Aberdeen, Sergeant Delia was dropped off at his station, then Deputy Shumate continued on to Montesano and to the Grays Harbor County jail, located behind the Courthouse.

Back in Olympia, Detectives Geis and Seal, after leaving Maxine's parents home, arrived in the police station shortly after Craig was brought in. The two detectives made contact with him, and Seal read the Miranda rights to the blond headed youth. Craig said he understood them, then said he did not want to talk about the case and wanted a lawyer. No statement of any kind was obtained from Craig, at this time. Craig was advised to disrobe and he was given the customary orange coveralls to put on. His street clothes were then placed in a brown paper sack.

With the Grays Harbor County Sheriffs office notified of Craig Borman's arrest, Detectives Haymon and Patrick were assigned to drive to Olympia and transport Craig back to Montesano. At about 8:30 p.m. Patrick and Haymon took custody of Craig. They also took custody of Craig's street clothing plus three sealed brown bags and a gray back-pack that had been brought into the station by Cindy after his arrest. The officers then escorted Craig, in handcuffs, out to the patrol car and placed him inside for the trip back to Montesano.

Early on the drive back, and on the Olympia to Aberdeen freeway, Craig asked Haymon seated next to him, "Who is in charge of the case?"

Haymon responded, "Detective Stocks is in charge of the investigation".

Craig said he would like to talk to the person in charge about what happened. Haymon stated that he and Patrick were assigned only to this portion of the investigation but that Craig could probably talk to Stocks if he wanted. Then Haymon reminded Craig that in Olympia he had refused to talk under his Miranda rights, and that he had declared he wanted an attorney. He was entitled to have an attorney present while he talked to Stocks.

Craig answered that he just decided he didn't need an attorney, and would like to talk, "-about what happened to Ginny, you know, I didn't kill her". Haymon cautioned and advised Craig it would be better to wait until they got to the Grays Harbor County Jail. For the remainder of the trip Craig asked only occasional questions, about living conditions in the jail, and if Bob and Tina had been picked up yet. Haymon told Craig they were still at large.

At 9:50 p.m. Craig was brought into one of the interview rooms at the county jail. Before the actual interview took place Haymon read again all of Craig's Constitutional rights from the advice-and-rights form, which Craig signed including the waiver form. During the interview Haymon listened with occasional questions, while Patrick wrote then typed Craig's statement. When completed, each page was thoroughly read over by Craig. He made some corrections then he signed each page.

Craig began, as Tammy, Marv, and Sonja had, with their meeting and coming together at the Aberdeen Bus station. And about Dan taking them all out to Ocean Shores, and eventually taking them to Hogans Corner. When Craig in his statement got to early Monday morning he said he remembered "Ginny was laying on the floor with Marv on top of her. There was blood all over the place. Marv had blood all over himself. Bob was crying. I feel Marv killed Ginny. Ginny had blood all over her chest, her eyes was gouged and there was blood on her face. After this I didn't see Ginny move, I think she was dead." During the interview, on two separate occasions, Craig asked if he could take a cigarette break. On one of these breaks Craig informed Haymon that he had created a story for his girlfriends, Maxine and Cindy, that other people had killed Ginny because he didn't want those girls to be scared of him.

On clarifying questions which Haymon asked, Craig had several lapses of memory, especially during the time Ginny was killed. After the interview and statement signing Craig was taken back to the prisoner receiving area and booked on second degree murder charges. Craig's statement was not tape recorded.

About 10:30 p.m., Maxine and Cindy walked into the Olympia Police Station wishing to speak with Detective Geis. They came in because they wanted to make a statement as to their involvement in bringing Craig out from Ocean Shores to Olympia, and their experience and conversations which they had with him over the past evening and day. Geis was called in, and he selected a room with a tape recorder. Geis interviewed Maxine first. The time the taping began was approximately 11 p.m. She spoke to Geis and to the recorder about her late night conversation she had with Craig who was worried about the events of his past weekend that ended with a woman being killed out near Ocean Shores. And about the "three bad guys" who came along and did the killing. Maxine stated she told Cindy she was done with Craig. And then later said "I'm gonna tell'em where you are. If you come with me there might be some hope. Tell the truth and nothing but the truth, Craig, and all you can expect is what comes to ya." Maxine further stated, "The main reason I'm coming to you guys now and everything, is because I didn't come to you last night when I just found out". She went on to say, "-I just felt rotten, I felt betrayed, and I felt used."

Detective Geis turned off the tape at about 11:15 p.m. With Maxine escorted out to the waiting area, Geis turned his attention to Cindy, who was waiting to make her statement. Back in the same interview room, now with Cindy, Geis turned his tape back on. It was 11:25 p.m.

As with Maxine, Cindy began her statement with her full name, address, age, and employment. Her story agreed with Maxines' except she didn't hear about Craig's terrible experience until early that morning. Craig also told her about the "-three other guys", and, "He couldn't believe his friends had done that, but obviously they're not true friends if they could do that and leave him being responsible for it." Close to the end, Cindy stated

"I'm a friend of his. I'll always be a friend and I love him no matter what." and finally, "I tell all my friends I love him." With the last interview concluded, Geis turned off the tape at about 11:37 p.m.

Across town, and almost in the shadow of the State Capitol building, Tina Murphy and Bob Noonan were still in company with Bob's friend, Pete Nicholson. They had spent an uncomfortable night in one of the wash rooms, next to the yacht basin piers close to downtown Olympia. During this day, Tuesday, 27 August, Bob and Tina talked some more with Pete about the bad past weekend, as they rested in Sylvester Park. Tina said she was forced to stay in Ginny's back bedroom during the killing. She heard her screams.

Bob thought it would be a good idea to walk over to the library, check over the state's daily papers and see if there was any news reported on the incident out at Hogans Corner. They had no idea their other four companions of the past weekend had been picked up and arrested, and were presently in the Grays Harbor County Jail. There was no news yet about Ginny in the daily papers.

By the end of the day, after he had called around, Pete finally was able to secure a one night's stay at a friend's home in South Olympia for him and his two companions. They still had one more day and a night to go before they were discovered.

On the following morning, Wednesday, 28 August, Stocks was busy attempting to obtain any past criminal records on Marv, Craig, Tammy, and Sonja. Concerning Marv, Stocks was in touch with the police department at Newberg, Oregon. Marv's last known residence before coming to Ocean Shores. Stocks was also still coordinating further evidence gathering out at the crime scene. Early that morning Tammy, being held in the county jail, asked to speak again to Detective Parfitt. She had some corrections and additional information to give him. Tammy informed Parfitt that she remembered Craig had thrown some of his wrapped up clothes over along the right side of the highway as they were walking to Dan's place that Monday morning. Parfitt informed Smythe of Tammy's further disclosures.

Smythe reached Hogans Corner about 10 a.m., and joined Deputy Gallanger who was collecting and brown-bagging all discovered movable evidence. With Tammy's remarks about Craig discarding items of clothing along Highway 115 while they were walking to Ocean Shores, Smythe and Gallanger proceeded to walk south along 115 to see what they could find. Keeping to the right side, Gallanger up on the brush area, Smythe walked the soft shoulder.

About a quarter mile south of Hogans Corner Smythe spotted a small cloth bundle in front of him about three feet to the right of the asphalt pavement. On close examination the two officers found it to be a pair of blue jeans, with a pink and brown cotton long sleeve shirt wadded up in the jeans. The items, especially the shirt, appeared to be the same clothing which appeared on Craig in the polaroid photos that Marcie gave to the police. Both items appeared to have blood stains on them. The items and the area which they were found were photographed. The items of clothing were brought back to Hogans Corner. These latest items were bagged and labeled, and placed with the other brown bags ready to take to Montesano.

At about 12:30 p.m. Stocks had Craig brought out from the jail, and into a selected interview room. With Haymon present, Craig was asked if he still wanted to talk, to help the police clear up the murder of Mrs. Barsic. Craig said yes, he would like to help. Craig again was read his full Miranda Rights, to which he willingly signed and waived.

Stocks began right with the knife used to kill Ginny, which, in Craigs previous statement with Haymon and Patrick, he stated he never saw. But now he stated, after thinking about it, he did recall seeing a knife with a long black handle. But again he stated he never saw it used on Ginny. Stocks asked Craig about the contact he made with Marcie just before leaving Ocean Shores. Craig said he told Marcie he was thinking of suicide and asked her advice. She told him he ought to go to the police, and he told her he would think about it. Craig made no mention of the photos he left with her. Only after Stocks said they were being held in evidence did he admit he told Marcie she should burn them.

Craig stated that he cried with Marcie about the killing, and after he left her he ran along the beach before returning to Dan's apartment. Stocks brought Craig back to the murder. He remembered Bob freaking out during the incident. Craig remembered Marv talking about the power he took from Ginny after he killed her. Craig said the only time he came in contact with Ginny was when he helped Marv drag the body out to the dirt mound. He recalled nothing about a shirt found partly buried near the body, or about a marker pole. Craig said Marv must have placed the marker there because he only threw a couple of scoops of dirt on Ginny then ran back to the apartment. After leaving the apartment he remembered the girls had some luggage. When asked about the TV set Craig said he thought it belonged to one of the girls.

Stocks asked Craig if he received any injuries from Ginny. Craig answered, no. Stocks pointed to his little finger on his right hand, which was black and blue. Craig said it was nothing. He had hurt the finger in a work accident. How? Craig stated that a roll of felt had fallen on his hand which was resting on a bundle of shakes.

At this point Stocks told Craig he believed Craig was lying about his involvement in the killing. Craig was then informed that Marv and Tammy both said Craig assisted in the homicide. Craig denied it, and said at no time did he stab or hold her down. The interview concluded shortly there after.

At about 1 p.m. Smythe returned to Montesano and the Sheriff's office, with the brown paper bags of evidence. After lunch Smythe touched base with Stocks, and it was decided that Smythe should conduct another interview with Marv, if he was still willing to talk to them. The time was about 2:30 p.m.

Marv was still willing. He said he would like

to talk about it some more. Marv had been brought in from the jail area, handcuffed, and in his orange coveralls. Smythe asked him if he would like a cup of coffee before proceeding, which Marv indicated he would. Then, with Haymon in attendance again, Marv was read his full rights again, which he signed and waived. Marv stated that he and Craig decided to kill Ginny because Bob had blabbed off about their plan to go to Oregon and bring back micro-dot acid. Smythe wanted to know what happened to the knife he used on Ginny. Marv said he didn't know what happened to it. Smythe then showed Marv a collection of knives he had brought from Ginny's kitchen. Marv said none of them looked like the one he used. Smythe then showed him the orange and black screwdriver that was found across from Ginny's apartment. Marv stated it did indeed look like the one. The screwdriver and knives were then removed from the interview room.

Coming back to the actions of the murder, Marv stated that he still couldn't recall who handed him the pillow. He remembered Ginny saying, from under the pillow, "you're killing me, you're killing me!" And Marv answered back, "Yeah, you're right!" Marv also recalled Ginny saying, "I didn't do anything to you guys!"

Marv went on to say he tried to cut her throat, and that Craig had bit her on the neck. Smythe asked Marv to explain that. Marv answered that when Craig put his hand over Ginny's mouth to stop her screams she bit his finger, so Craig got mad and bit her on the neck. Smythe asked which finger. Marv answered it was Craigs little finger. Marv said Craig didn't stab her in the front, only in the back. Smythe asked how did Craig get the knife, and Marv answered that he may have given it to him, or it was still sticking out of her back when Craig pulled it out and started stabbing her.

Haymon asked if Bob Noonan stabbed Ginny. Marv answered no. He just held her for a few moments then Bob freaked out.

During this interview Smythe stated to Marv that killing someone just because she found out you were going to make a drug deal sounds weak. Marv admitted it was, but that he and Craig talked about killing someone before, and they wanted to see what it was really like.

Marv continued with more about the same he had stated in his interviews with Johnson and Delia the previous day. This interview concluded about 4 p.m., and then Marv was led back to his cell.

With the public's right and need to know, Grays Harbor County Sheriff Dennis Morrisette made a press release this Wednesday. After all, with the almost constant traffic of Sheriffs' and police cars going and coming from Hogans Corner, passing through Hoquiam and Aberdeen, to say nothing of the several parked and flashing cars around the triplex apartment at the Corner, something almost unheard of must have happened in the public's midst.

The press release stated there had been a murder commited in the Hogans Corner area over the past weekend and apparently six young people were involved. Four of the six had been apprehended and a diligent search was underway to locate the other two. Robert Noonan's name was mentioned, along with an un-named female, as being sought. The release also stated the investigation and search for evidence was continuing. An autopsy of the victim was conducted that morning by State medical examiners and the County Coroner. Morrisette made it clear at the end of his release that he and his Sheriff's Department were in great appreciation for the help and assistance received by the Ocean Shores police, Aberdeen and Hoquiam police, and the Olympia and Lacey police departments.

In Olympia, Pete Nicholson was able to secure only a one night's stay at his friend's home, for him self, Tina Murphy and Bob Noonan. They would have only one more night together, then they would have to face the authorities who they guessed must be out looking for them by now.

This Wednesday morning the three made their way back to downtown Olympia, and to the Greyhound bus station located almost in sight of the Capitol dome. Pete, by this time, while still not knowing everything that had occurred out at the beach, was strongly committed in trying to help his friends and staying with them. Bob and Tina, each at various times, told him, "-the less you know, the better for you."

Inside the crowded bus station Bob opened his rented locker and drew out Tina's blue and black bag and his own brown army duffel bag, for a change of clothing and clean up. He also took out enough money to see them through dinner. They didn't like to carry excess money around because of bums who might take it away from them. After changing in the rest rooms and replacing their other clothes in the bags, and securing the locker, they walked back through town and back down to the marina area. They didn't relish sleeping in the washrooms again but the shower stalls were great. They would enjoy another shower there.

From the washrooms they walked over to look down again at the beautiful little boats still gently bobbing in the water and tied up to the slip piers of the marina. They tried to be light hearted during the rest of the afternoon but it was not all that easy, knowing the police must be out looking all over for them. Tina thought about trying to reach her foster mother. So did Bob, with his own mother. He did try to reach her just before he and Tina met up with those four other characters at the Aberdeen Bus Station that last Friday night. She wasn't home when he called.

Now, after walking around the marina area most of the afternoon and evening, they decided they should start figuring out a new place to stay, their last night. Not far from the docks they found a hideaway that might work out. It was a boxcar, resting on a railroad track spur, located behind a cut-rate market called "The Yard Birds". The boxcar, painted green and white, the colors and logo of the Great Northern Pacific, was a gift to the local Lions Club. It was used by the general public as a drop-off for old magazines and newspapers. Once a month members of the Lions Club would empty out the car of old newspapers, which often included just plain trash and garbage, and it would be hauled away and eventually turned back into paper pulp.

All resulting in a small income for the Lions Club.

The three youngsters walked up the steps of the wooden platform, peered in through the open boxcar doors they saw the possibilities; at least the boys did. Tina thought it was awful dirty and dank inside, and didn't smell good at all.

Walking around inside the unlighted car, Pete and Bob assured Tina they could clear away a space at the south end of the car and clean it up a bit. They could stack up the damp rotting bundles, make a kind of barrier and path to their cleared space, and they could have a real hideout. No one could find them. And they would have a kind of fort, and a party of their own.

Back out in the warm evening air they found a steady drizzle coming down from the gray low overcast. Tina was still not sure it was all a good idea but she soon decided, with a smile, to join in with Bob's and Pete's new adventure. She would help them. But first they would have to stock up on some food and stuff from the nearest market. They remembered passing a Seven-Eleven store a block or two away and went straight for it. They came back to the boxcar with two sacks; hotdog weenies, buns, mustard, cheese, corn chips, bread, milk, soft drinks, and a few other light items to have their own kind of party. Before mounting the wooden platform again the three young people, Tina, 14; Bob, 17; and Pete, 18; took a quick glance around to see if anyone was watching them, then they re-entered the boxcar for the night.

During the next morning, Thursday, 29 August, and at different intervals, two vehicles, a car, then a pickup truck drove up to the Lions Club boxcar. The drivers got out, climbed the platform, stepped in and deposited their bundles of old papers on to the wooden deck of the boxcar, then departed the area.

At about 11:30 a.m. an anonymous call came over 911 about the boxcar. The receiver referred the call to the Olympia Police Department for their possible action. Then, about 11:50 a.m., a patrolling officer out on duty and cruising in the marina area was dispatched to check on a report that possible vagrants may be living in the Lions Club boxcar. Within minutes Officer Batch drove up next to the boxcar, got out and climbed the steps and went in. With his flash light he caught a little movement over the bundles of paper, then heard the low voices of a male and female. Batch then ordered everyone out. Three people emerged. Batch confronted Tina first. She readily gave her correct full name and age. Turning to the older male, Pete gave his name to the officer as " Peter Lions". Then Bob gave his name as "Billy Munoy". Batch, not believing their answers, called for a backup then returned his attention back to his three detainees.

On further questioning Bob admitted his real name was Robert Noonan. Batch, remembering the name, checked his list of felony Warrants outstanding, then verbally placed Bob and Tina under arrest. The officer made another call into his dispatcher. Shortly another police car was on its way, carrying detectives Geis and Seal.

The second officer to arrive was directed to transport Tina to the Olympia Police Station. As Batch was attempting to place handcuffs on Bob, Bob reached in his left front pocket, pulled out the locker key and tried to hand it to Pete. Batch intercepted the movement and confiscated the key. On finishing handcuffing the youth, Batch then placed Bob in the rear of his patrol car. Geis and Seal arrived at that moment, and then took charge of Pete. All were transported to the police station. Montesano was called, and informed that the last two suspects in the Hogans Corner murder case were now in custody.

A cheer and sigh of relief was heard and made through- out the Sheriff's offices, attached to the northeast corner of the Grays Harbor County Courthouse in Montesano. Detectives Parfitt and Smythe were assigned to go to Olympia and transport them back.

CHAPTER FIVE: THE NEWS BREAKS

While Detectives Smythe and Parfitt were enroute to Olympia, Lieutenant Clark Taylor, Homicide Division of the Olympia Police Department, interviewed Pete Nicholson. Taylor informed Pete that his purpose for talking with him was to determine what his association was with the other two people who were just arrested on homicide Warrants.

After a few moments Pete told the officer all he knew since joining Bob and Tina, about noon Monday. Pete's overriding conclusion was that Bob and Tina were witnesses to a murder but did not themselves participate. They just wanted to get away from the other four people, and get away from the area. Bob had admitted to Pete that he saw them killing Ginny, that Tina was forced to stay in the back bedroom. And that Bob, on seeing Marv go crazy with the screwdriver, freaked out. Pete stated that when they got to Olympia they checked all their baggage into locker number 761 at the Greyhound Bus Station. Pete stated that most of the items, still in the locker, were Bob's and Tina's, but that a few items there were his, like a pair of Union Bay pants. Except for half eaten food stuff nothing was left in the boxcar.

Taylor concluded the interview at about the same time that Parfitt and Smythe arrived at the Olympia Police Station; 2 p.m. Taylor gave Smythe and Parfitt a copy of his interview he just had with Pete, and all the information he had on the other two arrested youngsters.

The two Grays Harbor sheriffs officers made a preliminary interview with the three young people, then leaving them to remain in custody at the station, obtained search warrants for the Grayhound locker and for the Lions Club boxcar. Then, with two Olympia police officers in company, they drove the few blocks over to the boxcar to examine it first. The boxcar was being guarded by a cadet police officer who greeted them as they drove up and parked by the wooded platform.

Climbing up and stepping inside, the officers found the east end of the car was just as Pete had discribed. Nothing but food items; some items still in a brown Seven-Eleven bag, other such items half eaten and soda pop cans half empty. Leaving behind the pathetic scene at the boxcar, the officers then drove over to the Greyhound bus station. There at locker number 716 they took possession of Tina's 'turquoise' and black nylon bag and Bob's army duffle bag. Also in the locker was a plastic blue bag. with the words "Woman's World" displayed on it. And a brown cotton zippered bag containing numerous inexpensive jewelry items; bracelets, earrings and rings.

Carefully tagging and counting all bulk items, to be internally itemized later, the officers carried the confiscated baggage out to the sheriff's car and then drove back to the Olympia Police Station. The time was almost 3:30 p.m. Parfitt and Smythe would interview Tina first. With long years of experience the officers knew that the earlier the interview or interrogation the better. The more likely for truth and accurancy. That is if one wants to remember and tell the truth.

Tina was brought into the interview room, still in her same clothes. Her manner was a cross between fright and hostility. Parfitt conducted most of the interview, with Smythe only an occasional interjection. Parfitt put Tina at ease as best he could. He began by telling her she was being considered only as a material witness to the homicide case. Under the law, Parfitt would still have to read her Miranda rights and particularly those that applied to juveniles. After the reading of her rights, Tina stated she understood them and did want to talk to the officers.

Tina wanted to know about Marv and Craig. Parfitt answered they were both safe in jail. Tina stated she was afraid of both of them, particularly after what they had done. With Parfitt's reassurance that she had nothing to fear Tina began her story. And, just as her previous companions had, who were now in jail, she described their getting together at the Aberdeen bus stop. Bob and Craig were both old acquaintances from school days. Craig had a large amount of money on him and he and Marv wanted to buy some beer and pot. They paid a bum to get them a case of beer. Craig found a dealer and purchased some pot. They hung around the bus station and drank beer and smoked pot. Tina and Bob only drank a little of their beer. Bob went with Craig and Marv down an alley and smoked some pot with them. The reason Bob and Tina were at the bus station was that she and Bob, having just missed their bus, were waiting for another bus to take them out to Bob's mother's place. She said Bob's mother liked her and they were going to visit her.

Now with their beer and pot Marv and Craig wanted to find some girls and have a party. The bus from Olympia came in and two girls got off. It was Tammy and Sonja. Tina recognized her friend Sonja, but was not acquainted with Tammy. Marv paired up with Sonja and Craig with Tammy. Marv wanted everyone to go to Ocean Shores, the girls wanted to stay in town. They had a discussion. Craig called his friend Dan who would come pick them up and carry them all to Ocean Shores. Tina and Bob were afraid they might get stranded out there but Marv assured them he would bring them back to Aberdeen in a car he would get. Craig and Marv got another case of beer and hid it under a dumpster. Pretty soon Craig's friend Dan showed up with his pickup truck. Marv and Craig loaded Tammy's and Sonja's baggage in the rear of the truck and, with the case of beer, they all headed out for Ocean Shores. It was right about sunset as they drove out of Aberdeen, and it was dark when they got to the beach.

Dan didn't want them all staying at his place so he drove them around trying to find a motel. It was the tourist season and the rooms were mostly taken. They did find one motel with a vacancy but the price was over a hundred dollars. Dan eventually took them out to Hogans Corner, and to the apartment upstairs where Marv once stayed. He had some of his things still there. While Dan and Marv were upstairs a lady called to them from her downstairs window. She asked Tina, still in the truck, if Tina wanted to see her "snake pit". Tina was reluctant to go inside a strange woman's place, especially with the woman talking about snake pits.

Tina eventually asked, how do you get in there, and the woman motioned her around to the front entrance. The woman took Tina by the hand and showed her all through the apartment. Tina was relieved there were no snake pits. The woman's apartment was neat and clean. What she had was numerous decorative beach items. Driftwood and shells. There was a carved Indian statue, and two large clay pots by the fire place which had other beach items in them. Since the people upstairs did not want her friends the woman said they could all spend the night at her place. She got them each a blanket and said they could all stay in the living room. Her name was Ginny.

While Tina continued with her account of the weekend to Parfitt, Smythe left the room a few moments to make a phone call to Montesano. He returned as she was getting to Monday morning. Tina mentioned that Marv and Craig were in the bathroom and saw them cutting their hands together in some kind of blood brotherhood. And they wanted Bob to join in with them.

At about 1 a.m. Monday morning she and Tammy went to the Gull station to get some things. On the way back they saw someone lurking in the bushes. They were frightened, but it turned out to be only Marv. Marv wanted to rip off the station and he asked the girls how much money they saw in the till. The girls told him there was only a few dollars in it, that it wasn't worth it. And they talked him into going back to the apartment.

A couple hours later while they were all setting in the livingroom drinking beer, all of a sudden Craig and Marv got up and forced Tammy and Tina into the back bedroom, slammed the door and told them not to come out. Tina said she tried to open the door but Craig held the knob from the other side and wouldn't let her out. Tammy took her in the back bathroom where Ginny's jewelry was and told her to take what she wanted. Tammy told her the boys were only going to scare her. Tina went back to the door leading into the hall. She opened it and saw Marv on top of Ginny who was screaming. Craig was at Ginny's feet. Bob ran back to Tina in the back bedroom, came in and started freaking out. Bob hit and kicked the walls with his fist and foot. Bob said they're killing Ginny out there. Then she and Bob ran out of the bedroom, down the hall, past Ginny on the floor, and into the living room. Bob grabbed Tina's hand and they ran out the front door and over in front of the VFW. Bob was shaking and couldn't talk. Tina said she had on Tammy's shoes so she ran back in, got her own shoes on, and ran back out. Bob was freaking out again in front of the VFW.

Parfitt continued taking Tina's statement to its conclusion. She signed it and was then escorted back to the juvenile section of the station. Smythe and Parfitt left the station for some refreshment. They talked the situation over, then mentally prepared themselves to go back and take Bob's statement.

Back in the same interview room Bob was brought in and seated at the same table Tina had occupied earlier. It was about 7 p.m. Again, Parfitt would conduct most of the interviewing. The officer explained that Bob was not being examined as a material witness as Tina but because some of the others had implicated him in having taken part in the homicide he was being interviewed as a possible accomplice in the crime.

Bob, without handcuffs and in his same street clothes, stated that once before he had cooperated with the police over a previous criminal investigation and in the end it had gone hard on him. Both officers assured Bob that they would do their duty in this case but at this point what they wanted was his side of the story. Bob then agreed to talk, and he began by saying he had no part in the killing of Ginny. Before allowing him to go further Parfitt read Bob's Rights to him, which he said he understood, and signed as such. Bob was quite nervous.

Bob's five page statement generally agreed with all the others about how they all met at the bus station, and eventually got out at Ocean Shores. In the end he drew lines and X's on a floor plan of Ginny's apartment and described the death scene, which was very similar to Marv's. But he had some additional details that neither Marv nor any of the others talked on. He related how Ginny had first invited Tina into her apartment. On following her in he found Ginny taking her by the hand and showing her around. They were laughing together and in good spirits. Ginny invited all six of them to spend the night. She got warm blankets and pillows out for each of them. They could all sleep in the living room. Bob went on to say that Ginny was a real nice lady and didn't deserve what happened to her. Saturday after breakfast Ginny got out her polaroid camera and they took pictures of themselves in the living room. Then Bob went on to say that in secret Craig and Marv talked a lot about robbing the Shop Rite super market, and stealing a car. And they talked about making a run to Oregon on a drug deal. Bob showed a slice mark on his hand to Smythe and Parfitt saying that he joined Craig and Marv on a blood brotherhood act in the bathroom. But he said he told them he would have no part in any robberies. Marv told him that he, Bob, would be the driver and might have to pull the trigger during the robbery. Craig said we're all going to be rich here pretty soon. Bob said Craig would come up with the ideas and Marv would act on them. Marv would go around talking macho stuff, and would use his karate to knock Bob to the floor, and with his foot down on him would say how easy Marv could kill Bob. Ginny caught Craig and Tammy having sex in the hall bathroom and got mad at them. She said they would all have to clean up her place and get out.

At this point Bob could not go on. He became extremely agitated, nervous, and shook all over. Smythe and Parfitt stopped the interview for about 10 minutes. They got him a drink of water then encouraged him to proceed.

Bob continued to say that Ginny got mad at Tammy because Tammy told her she gave up her baby and Ginny couldn't understand how any woman could give up her baby.

Then all of a sudden, while Ginny was in the hall bathroom, they took Tina to the back bedroom. Bob went back to get his girlfriend, and Ginny came out of the hall bathroom. Then arms and hands were flying around all over the place. Bob got hit in the face with a pillow. He turned and continued going back to get Tina. As he and Tina were coming back toward the front of the apartment he saw Marv on top of Ginny with a pillow, and Ginny kept screaming and fighting back and turning her head away from under the pillow. Bob said he saw Craig holding her feet and Craig said, "Get her. Get her". Marv was laughing and had a screwdriver, then Marv said, "Where's my knife, where's my knife." Once it looked like Marv got up and kicked Ginny in the head.

It was at this point Bob said he took Tina and they both ran out the front door, and went over to the front of the VFW building. Bob described how Tammy came out from the side of the apartment and Bob and Tina encouraged her to come with them. But she wouldn't do it. Parfitt helped him finish his statement. Then with the interview concluded Bob nervously looked over each page and, with Parfitt and Smythe, they signed each page. The time was 8:45 p.m.

Leaving Parfitt gathering up the interview material at the table, Smythe got up, opened the door and stepped into the hallway. An Olympia police officer walked up and gave Smythe some information he might like to be aware of. Down in the lobby and out on the steps leading into the station, reporters and TV crews had gathered. They were waiting for a statement and maybe some film footage of the last boy and girl who had been sought in the Grays Harbor homicide case. The news had reached the public. Six teenagers were involved in a grisly murder of a fifty year old woman out at Hogans Corner over the past weekend. Four of these had been picked up earlier in the week and now the last two had been captured and were being held in the Olympia police station, soon to be transported back to Montesano.

Smythe called Parfitt out to the hallway to discuss the matter there. Rejoining Bob, still sitting at the table, forlornly staring at the floor, the two officers informed him of the circumstances down at the front of the station. The officers had a quick plan, if Bob would like to cooperate with it. Bob agreed to it immediately. The Olympia police also approved.

With Bob between them and each holding onto one of Bob's thin arms the Grays Harbor officers walked him to the back elevator, down and out to the rear police parking area. There, Smythe brought his unmarked Ford up to the back steps and, in seconds, all three were on there way to Montesano. Tina would be transported to the Juvenile Department of Grays Harbor County the following day. Pete Nicholson, Bob and Tina's friend, was released as having no real connection to the case.

With all six youngsters now in custody, four of them; Marv, Craig, Bob, and Tammy, being held in the Grays Harbor County Jail, located in a newer building attachment at the northeast corner of the Grays Harbor County Courthouse and the two 14 year olds, Sonja and Tina, being held and quartered in the Juvenile Detention Center, situated near the Chehalis River and about halfway between downtown Aberdeen and Montesano, the legal judicial system concerning the six had taken control. The investigation was, however, still on-going. The Sheriffs Department and offices were conveniently located on the bottom floor of the jail.

On Friday morning 30 August, and after a good night's sleep, Stocks was going through his stack of returns on their past criminal records, starting with Marv's, from the Newberg, Oregon Police Department. Marv had been arrested on numerous charges, ranging from simple run away from home to shoplifting, burglary, assault, alcohol and drug substance abuse. He had also been charged with supplying alcohol to other minors. Marv had been arrested for illegal driving, no insurance, no valid license, no headlights. The Newberg Police had broken up drug and alcohol 'partys' which Marv initiated in various motel rooms around Newberg. Marv stated to responding officers at his 'party' that he was bored and just wanted to have a good time. This party took place at the Town and Country Motel in

Newberg, Oregon on the 24th of June, exactly two months prior to his 'party' at Ginny's. Early in 1991 Marv was taken to the Newberg Community Hospital for possible drug overdose. He survived.

Craig's past record was not so long. Craig, as a juvenile had been arrested for burglary and forced entry in to a warehouse off Lake Quinault, and released to his father. Craig was suspected in a burglary of a private residence where two guns were stolen. He was also charged on drug abuse in 1986. In 1988 Craig was questioned involving an assault case up in the Lake Quinault area.

Bob also had a police record dating back to 1988. Burglary, theft, littering, residential burglary.

Tammy's record up in the Carson area dated back to 1985, with malicious mischief, theft of property, jewelry scam, loud party, family fight, and several ambulance calls. Tammy's file described her as 5 feet 10 inches, light brown hair, green eyes, 120 pounds.

Marv and Craig were formally arraigned and brought before the bench, charged with murder. Court appointed attorney Jim Heard was given the task of defending Marv, on an insanity plea. Attorney John Farra was appointed to represent Craig, who pleaded not guilty. Tammy was arraigned and charged with first degree criminal assistance. In plea bargaining, with her attorney, she eventually entered a plea of guilty to first degree criminal assistance. Bob, at first charged with murder was eventually accepted as a material witness for the State of Washington, as were Tina and Sonja.

Because of the existing teeth marks on Ginny's body and on Craig's hand and little finger, prosecutor Stew Menefee and his Assistant Prosecutor Jerry Fuller requested and obtained a court order to make casts of Craig's teeth and that his hand injuries were to be examined, all by a retained local dentist. A cast of Marv's teeth were also ordered. A cast mold of Ginny's teeth had already been obtained, coinciding with the state's pathology report on Ginny's body. Blood and saliva samples were ordered and taken from Marv and Craig.

Their foot and hand prints were also made in evidence. There was talk that Marv and Craig might plead self defense from Ginny's biting and scratching as she tried to save her life. This course of defense did not develop.

The Sheriffs Department and other police in the Grays Harbor area were beginning to receive a number of calls from people young and old alike, who thought they may have important information that might be of help in the investigation. Among them, the man who had started out on Monday morning without his glasses, had to return home for them then completed his trip to work. He passed these four young people three times, who were walking along the highway toward Ocean Shores. The man made his report to the Ocean Shores police. Then there was the woman who rode the bus from Ocean Shores to Hoquiam, and couldn't help noticing the distraught young couple seated just ahead of her. They made a lasting impression on her. She called and made her report to Stocks himself.

There were still a number of unanswered questions about the case which they were not yet satisfied with, so Stocks and Smythe made another trip out to Hogans Corner, pulled into the Gull Station mini-mart, and made contact with the evening desk manager, Mrs. Churchill.

On observing the officers identification Churchill stated she would be quite willing to give any help she could. She was acquainted with Ginny and was so sorry to learn of her death. During the two months Ginny lived in the apartment across the street she would often visit the Texaco or Gull station mini-marts. She had no car, so, either friends would pick her up to go into town and to work or she would take the bus.

Churchill stated that on that Sunday evening, at about 5 or 6 p.m., Ginny came in with a tall nice looking blonde young woman. They bought some beer and a few other items. Ginny paid cash and as Churchill was handing back the change to Ginny, the tall blonde put her hand out to receive the change. With Churchill hesitating, Ginny dropped her hand and said, "Oh, that's OK. She's my daughter." On another incident later in the evening, maybe two hours later, Churchill went on to say, the tall attractive blonde returned to the Gull mini-mart. This time she came in with a girlfriend, about 14 or 15 years old; darker blonde hair, short and stocky built. They went over to the medicine shelves, discussing NyQuil. They brought to the counter a green box containing a bottle of NyQuil. The "tall pretty blonde" asked Churchill. "Will this really put you to sleep?" Mrs. Churchill took the box, and read the label-claims, that says it relaxes one enough so they can go to sleep. "That's just what I want." She paid for it in cash, then both girls left. Mrs. Churchill did not see Ginny, nor any of the young people again.

Smythe and Stocks went back to the medicine shelves and compared the price labeling on the NyQuil boxes in front of them to a copy of the box and label found in Ginny's apartment bedroom. They were the same. The officer thanked Mrs. Churchill for her statement and departed the mini-mart.

While at Hogans Corner Stocks and Smythe took the short drive over to the triplex apartment. The apartment managers, Mr. and Mrs. Brown, who normally lived in the apartment directly North of Ginny's apartment, were back from their holiday trip to California. They had gotten only as far as Oregon, staying over night with friends when Mr. Brown had a hunch and thought he should give Ginny a call, Tuesday morning, to see if everything was OK. Mr. Brown then learned of Ginny's death. Mr. and Mrs. Brown called their holiday off and headed back to Hogans Corner.

Mr. and Mrs. Brown welcomed Stocks and Smythe in to their back apartment and after seating them they expressed to the officers their honest grief. Ginny had moved into the front apartment two months ago because she was afraid she had "burglar problems" on Ensign road over in Ocean Shores. Mr. and Mrs. Brown had her in for dinner on occasions. "She was a caring, creative person". Mrs. Brown went on to say, "I saw her trying to help some people who had car trouble out on the road in front of the apartment one day." Thursday evening she came by "for her usual dinner and drop in. She was anxious for her husband to get home." She said she "-was in considerable tooth and back pain and was told she needed surgery". On that Friday morning, just before the Browns left on the holiday, they saw Ginny again. "She seemed to be feeling fine. And she read me some of her poems. She wrote about her twins, and youngest son, and of her childhood. She was hanging out her kitchen window waving good-by on Friday the 23rd. She had the cat's food and dishes in the garage. She would always be at her kitchen window to see who was coming and going, keeping an eye on things. There was no reason for anyone to want to kill Ginny." Stocks had been writing their statement as they talked. The Browns looked over the written statement, signed it, then the officers departed.

Smythe and Stocks had very little to say during their return drive to Montesano.

Time slows down for no one. Other criminal cases of various severity, including murder, were ongoing in Grays Harbor County, one of the largest counties in the State of Washington. And these cases too demanded the attention of the Sheriff's officers and the judicial system. But the very character of the Barsic case would continue to hold a kind of special interest to all legal and law enforcement personal in the County for months to come.

Time and opportunity permitting, Detective Stocks and his friend Detective Smythe and now Deputy Prosecutor Fuller, would render as much assistance as they could in helping the Barsic family, who were then gathering in the area, to cope with the tragedy.

Gregory Barsic was approached with the news of his wife's death while on duty in the wheelhouse of his fishing boat off the coast of Southern Alaska. The skipper of the boat had Greg relieved at his station then, in private, informed him of the radio message. Greg, with the skipper's assistance, made his way to Dutch Harbor and a flight down to Seattle, then out to Ocean Shores. Greg had been commercially fishing since the 29th of May.

Greg and Ginny had been married about five years. Her previous husband had died of natural causes some years earlier. Ginny had five children from that marriage, two girls and three boys. The girls were living in the San Diego area. Two of her sons were serving on active duty in the Navy. The other son had been with Greg, commercially fishing from the same boat. Matt had departed two weeks early. He stopped off and visited with his mother for a day or two before going on to his home in Montana. Matt was planning to get married. Greg was planning to come home to Ginny in another ten days or so. He wanted to come back with as much money as he could. Greg was no 'big guy'. About five foot nine inches tall; a hundred fifty five pounds, light brown hair, and near the same age as Ginny. Greg Barsic also had served in the Navy, for sixteen years. He left the Navy as a First Class Petty Officer, having served mostly on aircraft carriers. After their marriage in San Diego Ginny, who could hardly stand being alone, and, considering long carrier cruises, she and Greg decided to give civilian life a try. They would try to put it together up in Grays Harbor, where Ginny had a couple of distant relatives living in that area. It was hard finding the kind of work Greg wanted to do. So he went back to sea, this time fishing with not so long absences. In the Navy, absences could be a year or more. Greg would later say that he and Ginny had experienced only two arguments between them, their five years of marriage. One had to do with a playful argument over bed covers they shared. The other was private. Ginny was lonely and a little angry at Greg for not coming home sooner. Greg wished that he had come home sooner.

Stocks first met Greg at the triplex apartment. Later he brought Greg back to his desk at the Sheriffs Office and they talked awhile. Greg stated that he would like to have Ginny's tablet of poetry and a number of old photos she had placed in a tupper-ware canister. Greg identified the small TV set which was picked up in the brush as his and

Ginny's.

Members of the grief stricken family gathered for memorial services at Colman's Mortuary Chapel in Hoquiam. Besides a dozen or so of the immediate family, numerous friends and acquaintances had driven to Hoquiam from Ocean Shores for the Services. A portion of Ginny's obituary, which appeared 11 September, in the North Coast News, a weekly paper serving the beach area, read as follows: "Virginia Irene Barsic, 50, a three year resident of the North Coast died August 26 of injuries inflicted during a conflict with young people she had befriended. She was a published poet who had won the Golden Poet award several times. She was born April 2, 1941 in Bremerton, Washington. She was raised attending schools in Ketchikan, Alaska. She graduated from high school in 1960. While living in San Diego she met and married Gregory Barsic early 1987. During the time she lived on the North Coast she was employed as a clerk at the Ocean Shores Motel".

The obituary went on to list all members of the family including her two sons on active duty with the U.S. Navy. Ginny had a brother living in Texas, and another in Australia. The long column ended with, "Memorial Services were held last week."

That afternoon following the services, and under a warm sunny sky, the family drove their cars back the twenty miles to Ocean Shores. They continued through town, and on out to the marina area. The procession left the paved road of Point Brown Avenue and got on the gravel road leading out to Damon Point.

Halfway down the road they parked their cars and walked the rest of the way, crunching gravel as they went. The grim faced family, mostly short in stature like Ginny, but giant in heart, only occasionally talked among themselves as they approached the Point. Damon Point, a beautiful weather-worn rock and sandy beach jutting out on the bay side at the south eastern tip of the Ocean Shores peninsula, was a perfect picture setting. There, on a small rocky perch overlooking the calm sea water gently lapping the shore line, where generations of children have gathered up glistening agates, sea shells, and lovely shaped driftwood, Ginny's ashes were scattered.

The first media coverage, 28 August, appeared across the bottom half of page one of the afternoon edition of the Aberdeen news. In bold half inch letters the paper stated, "Four of six murder suspects in custody". A two by four inch photo showed Kolilis, Smythe, and Youmans at the front entrance of Ginny's apartment, "considering the evidence". The accompanying article, mostly quoting Chief Deputy Darrow, stated that the victim, a 50 year old woman of Hogans Corner was apparently stabbed to death Monday morning. The victim's name could not be released until all the next of kin were notified. "All the pieces have yet to be put together and the investigation is still proceeding". The article went on to list the ages of the suspects at 17 to 20. Still at large, a young male and female. The report also stated that an Aberdeen police sergeant was credited with apprehending the first three, and quick police work in Lacey resulted in the fourth arrest.

Most every day for the next several weeks daily or weekly community papers in the Grays Harbor area, would carry page-one news of '-the murder in the apartment located next to the VFW hall at Hogans Corner'. Occasionally, Seattle evening TV news would make announcements of the progress on the sensational murder case out at Hogans Corner, near Ocean Shores.

For a wider understanding of Virginia Barsic, a short history of Ginny's hometown and the people of Ocean Shores would seem most appropriate at this point: Before the advent of the white man, American Indians of various tribes, Quinaults in particular, made good use of the 6,000 acre peninsula as a trading and feasting ground. During his circumnavigation of the world, 1578 thru 1580, the first successfully completed by a ship's Commander, Sir Francis Drake altered his epic westerly voyage and explored north along the coasts of what we know as

South and North America. Drake, staying in sight of land, sailed close by the Ocean Shores Peninsula in June of 1579. Reaching a recorded latitude of about 51 degrees North, near the great island now known as Vancouver Island, Drake and his Golden Hinde reversed their course and sailed south, passing the Peninsula again before continuing west.

Some two hundred years later English Navigators, Captain James Cook, followed by Captain George Vancouver, sailed by the Peninsula in their search for the 'North West Passage'. Then, shortly after the American Revolutionary War, Yankee Captain Robert Gray, U.S. Navy, under orders, sailing in the Lady Washington from Rhode Island, rounded the Horn then up the West Coast of the New World to lay claim to the vast Pacific Northwest for the new United States. After discovering and exploring part of the Columbia River, Gray in his sloop rigged Lady Washington, then sailed further North. On 7 May, 1792, Gray sailed in and dropped anchor in what is now known as Grays Harbor.

With growing white settlements and land exploration came the Gold Rushes of Canada and Alaska in the 1890's. Together with the abundant wealth of fishing and timber, flourishing settlements in Grays Harbor now became towns and cities. Grays Harbor, the largest deep water port on the Washington Coast currently accommodates world ocean going freighters year round.

In early 1960 a group of Seattle attorneys and developers, seeing the possibilities, got together and purchased the entire Ocean Shores Peninsula from the Damon and Minard families who had owned the land and who were making use of it as cattle grazing land. Among the investing developers was popular actress and singer Ginny Simms. Ginny, of WWII entertainment fame, and her husband envisioned what Ocean Shores could become; a resort and retirement community, and a golfing tournament area that could rival Bing Crosby's Pebble Beach, California golfing destination fun spot. It could happen.

To help make it happen, Ginny got together with her good friend and equally popular singer of the sixty's, Pat Boone. Together they contacted and successfully rounded up some of the most well known personalities of the Golden Age of Entertainment; Alice Fay, Phil Harris, Fred MacMurray, Clint Eastwood, Bill Bixby, 'Broadway' Joe Namath, Milton Berle, Forest Tucker, Denise Darcell, David Janssen, Hoagy Carmichael, and even some of the offspring of Bing Crosby. Singers and band leaders of the era also joined in from Hollywood to lend a hand. And some of the best names in professional golfing appeared. They all came up to Ocean Shores and had fun participating in the first "Pat Boone Golf Classic". That was in the summer of 1968.

But the big developing 'Boom' didn't take place quite as fast as was hoped. Ocean Shores developed, and is developing, at its own pace. The streets are now mostly paved, with nautical names like 'Sea Horse', 'Polaris', 'Taurus', 'Sand Dune', and 'Butter Clam'. The telephone lines are all up. An air strip is in place on the east central part of the Peninsula, and sportsman and sportswomen still enjoy the 18-hole golf course. Maybe 15 percent of the lots have finished homes on them, while most of the balance of the plotted lots are owned by people hoping to build their dream homes on some day. A fine convention center is in place, paid for by the people of the community, which hosts various activities and business conventions year round. Four huge motels are spread out on or close to the beach near the center of town. They fill up on most weekends and major holidays. The sumptuous condominiums of Ocean Shores are mostly located down near the rugged weather beaten jetty of Point Brown.

It is a beautiful little town really, and nice people abound with energy everywhere. And around every political November the town takes on its humorous nick name 'Open Sores', instead of Ocean Shores.

Ginny Simms' dream for Ocean Shores did not entirely take place but it certainly had a good start. And, at its own pace, is still growing. It is unlikely that Ginny Simms ever had contact with Ginny Barsic. However, it is equally likely they would have been friends had they met. Both were outgoing, creative, hard working, and enjoyed life and people.

§ § § § § § § § § §

It was almost 3 p.m. on the afternoon of Wednesday the twenty eighth of August, two days after the death of Virginia Barsic, that I reached in and drew out the day's mail from our rented box. The Post Office, a neat one-storied gray structure with flag pole and adjoining parking lot is located on the south side of 115 just up from the monuments that lead back into Ocean Shores.

Back in my red Olds I headed back into town. Driving between the monuments, I decided not to stop in to visit with Joyce as I usually do after my daily trips to the Post Office and before making the four mile drive back down Ocean Shores Boulevard, to our beach home. The reason for my nearly not stopping in was because of my less than good mood resulting from an irritating experience I had had with a new neighbor who recently moved in down the street from us.

But I changed my mind at the last second, shook off my irritation, turned in and parked at the side of the Ocean Front Beach Rental Offices. These offices are on the ground floor, North end of the first building you pass on the right after coming through the monuments. The offices are shared with the Chamber of Commerce people who occupy the front section as you walk in. After entering I usually chat a moment or two with the nice Chamber people, but no one was there. Continuing on through, balancing with my cane as I went, I spotted Joyce standing among some of her co-workers and Chamber friends in the middle of the large reservation room. They were all talking in hushed tones. Normally you would find this group cheerfully going about their business, answering phones, mailing out, or handing out colorful brochures about the town to pleasant walk-in visitors. And I usually don't stay long, these people being just too busy. Not this time, and the phones were all on hold.

Joyce, stepping away from the group, came over and said, "Oh honey! Have you heard about poor Ginny!"

No, I had not, and I wasn't able to place the woman, at least not right then. Joyce went on to tell me about Ginny being murdered in her own apartment out at Hogans Corner over the weekend, and, from what was reported in the afternoon papers, by six teenagers. "That's terrible!" I answered, still not being able to place her, or even adjusting my mind to the news. I had other things on my mind.

The truth and seriousness of it all began to sink in a little deeper when one of Joyce's lady friends walked over to show me the afternoon Aberdeen news. There, across the bottom half of the front page, in bold print, "Four of six murder suspects in custody."

More to herself rather than to me, Joyce's friend somberly sighed and said, "Oh God! Not here, in our little town!" I thought she was going to cry.

GYPSY WIND

SOMETIMES MY MIND WILL WANDER LIKE THE GYPSY WIND;

CARESSING THE LEAVES IN THE TREES, EVER SO SOFTLY

TOUCHING THE WINGS OF THE BUTTERFLY, OR MAYBE

YOUR LIPS IN ITS PASSING - SO GENTLE, YET PROMISING

YOU, YOUR WILDEST DREAM.

by Virginia Barsic

One of Ginny's poems, graciously lent from Mr. Greg Barsic to the author of this book.

PART TWO

**"-In all my 15 years
of Judicial Public Service
This is the most
Brutal and Senseless Murder-"**

CHAPTER SIX: GRAYS HARBOR COUNTY COURTHOUSE

Over the years I have found that the human mind just doesn't want to accept some things, especially crazy things, such as six teenagers killing a middle aged woman down the street. There are other things to think about. Like perhaps thinking about my new neighbor who irritated me the previous day over his political argument which he pressed. I didn't want to get into a political argument with him, my new neighbor. As a matter of fact, in the beginning I rather liked this man, who was about my same age.

Many years earlier I had discovered that priceless rule that says; if you want to make friends and keep them, stay away from such potentially explosive subjects as opinions on politics or religion. Especially since neither subject can be pinned down to any absolutes. It's like trying to nail up a hand full of jello to the wall. Let the other man, or woman, have their faith-ins, and you enjoy yours, if you have any. Now a good game of chess, that's another thing. But my new neighbor, he pressed on and on.

Over in Seattle, during the Gulf War, a good deal of the evening news focused on flag burners. My neighbor found an opportunity to discuss the subject with me. Never having felt myself a super patriot, still, I thought the subject rather ridiculous. But my neighbor pressed, "Which would you rather burn, the American Flag or the Constitution?" I could not keep him from it, and he pressed on, "Come on now, which would you really rather burn the flag or the-"

"Neither one, you idiot!" and that was the end of our beautiful friendship that might have been.

Here in beautiful Ocean Shores, almost in seclusion, Joyce and I have enjoyed being in touch with one of nature's truly awesome spectacles; the Pacific Ocean, almost right out our front door. While no longer on the fast track, still, we are very much aware of the violent world that exists around us; drive-by-shooter's, serial killers, and a couple dozen bloody civil and border wars going on all around the world. To watch the news, on any given evening, one would think the whole world is in violent conflict with its self, if not outright Armageddon. But since we are retired, at least I am, we enjoy life and each other on a very simple day to day scale. And, like the few friends we do have who believe, if the world wants to blow its head off, well there's not much we can do about it. So, as Bogart would say, 'go ahead and do it'.

Simple enough? It was simple enough for me until the death of Ginny Barsic, and, reportedly, how she died. And as my father would say, 'that got me out of my chair', so to speak. Being a member of the Veterans of Foreign Wars, one of the few organizations I do belong, I was quite familiar with the area around Hogans Corner, having made irregular once-a-month meetings there.

Keeping up with developments on the Barsic case in the daily news out of Aberdeen, it seemed each time Hogans Corner was mentioned the VFW next to the victim's apartment was also mentioned. Thinking kindly of my good friend Gordy Buchanan, Quartermaster of the VFW Post in the North Beach area, who was in fact more like a shepherd always looking out after his flock of old warriors, I couldn't help but think he was probably taking it all pretty badly. During the days when he is not out checking on his member's well being you would most likely find him at the VFW hall. And his own health wasn't all that good either. I decided to stop in to see him the next time I had a trip going out of town. And I did have one coming up. Joyce and I needed to drive over to Montesano, to Grays Harbor County Courthouse, and check on our passports that needed up dating. We were scheduled to be in London in early December.

It was Monday, the 2nd of September, one week after the death of Virginia Barsic. Joyce had a couple days off so, after securing the house and with our old passports in a manila envelope we headed out of Ocean Shores. Since we were going to the Courthouse I should put on a tie. Joyce, looking fresh as a red rose in one of her nice dresses said we ought to pick-up our mail before driving past the Post Office. In the nearly twenty five years of marriage never have I observed Joyce in a pair of jeans. Slacks of all colors, blouses, sweaters in the fall, dresses, coats, jackets. But never a pair of jeans. Even her shoes were always nice to look at; high heels, low heels, and occasionally a pair of low cut tennis shoes. Whenever she would clean the house, which was at least once a week, she would be in an older pair of slacks. It was always fun going on a drive out of town with her. As long as we were going to Montesano she wanted to stop into Sprouse Reitz there, to look for some more yarn she needed to finish up an afghan or something she was working on.

The very moment after making the right turn at Hogans Corner the fluttering out American flag from its pole over in front of the VFW hall caught my eye. And I remembered that I should stop in there. And there was Gordy's white compact car parked on the side of the Hall. Safely getting through the traffic I pulled in and parked next to his car. Not expecting to be very long I left Joyce in the red coupe Olds, going through our mail.

Inside I found Gordy seated at the end of one of the long combination bench tables working over an article which he was preparing for print, in the North Coast News, concerning recognition of school children in the area who had met his standards for Citizen Achievement Awards. He was always doing things like that.

His hair was almost as white as mine, and in his no nonsense gravel voice he told me I was just in time for a fresh cup of coffee. And he was glad I stopped in. Yes he was concerned over the shocking events that had occurred in the apartment across the way.

"Damn!" he said, " Wish I'd have been around to help Ginny, when she needed someone. Damn!"

"Gordy, did you know that women? Tell me what she looked like. I think I might have met her once."

"She was a real nice lady. Spunky too. She had two sons on active duty in the United States Navy".

"What did she look like?"

"Well, she was just a little woman. Auburn haired, always bright and cheerful. If she saw my car she would come over and visit. I'd stop whatever I was doing and we'd talk awhile. I think she was a little lonely though and maybe felt a little abandoned."

"What else, Gordy?"

"Well, I'll tell you this", he said, after pouring out two coffees, and pointing over to his walls that had a number of old photos and newspaper clippings taped up describing the attack on Pearl Harbor, "she had brains, and she was interested in us. I took her all over the building and she asked questions about all the history on the walls around here. That's when she told me about her two sons. She was real proud of all her children. She sure liked kids."

"Where'd she work?"

"She worked at one of the motels in town, and at another one up the beach, Moclips I think." Gordy then smiled, and added, "She said she was the best cleaning lady they ever had."

"Just a cleaning maid?"

"Ya, that's all. Except she was also a poet. She brought over some of her poems one afternoon while my misses was here. I'm not a poet but they sure sounded pretty good to me. And my wife liked her too. I think she would recite her poems to anyone, if they would listen."

I asked Gordy if anyone had come around the VFW asking about her, and he answered, "No, but I've had a few phones calls from people saying how sorry they were to hear about her. I had one dumb call from a woman who said, maybe she asked for it."

"What?"

"That woman made me so mad!"

With Joyce waiting out in the car, and wanting to let Gordy get back to what he was doing, I downed the rest of my coffee, got up and moved toward the door. I asked if he would come out and say hello to Joyce before we pulled away. Joyce liked Gordy. "A real American Hero!"

Steadying with my cane, I put my hand on Gordy's shoulder. Not wanting to leave him in a depressed mood I smiled and said, "You remember when we were kids, we would help old ladies across the street. We sure wouldn't molest them".

"I remember. And sometimes I think it's a whole different world."

"Gordy, If you ever run across one of Mrs. Barsic's poems will you please get it over to me?"

"Sure will!" he answered, as he bent down to the open car window. Joyce took his hand in warm greeting as I glanced up at 'Old Glory' noisily snapping at attention above his building. In another few moments Joyce and I were on our way.

The forty-five minute drive to Montesano was mostly spent in just light talk. Joyce read me a nice letter from among the mail. It was from our friend Retired Admiral Herb Bridge over in Seattle, congratulating us and our Marilyn for her recent graduation from the airline academy and who was now working for American Airlines down in central California. While driving along I was trying to remember what we were doing over the previous week-end. Then I remembered: That Sunday night we watched, on our VCR, the 1958 film classic, "The Brothers Karamazov", with Yul Brynner in the principal role of Dmitri. Long before it was made into a film the internationally famous book by Russian author Fyodor Dostoevski was, as I recalled, required reading where I attended high school.

Joyce and I arrived in Montesano about 2:20 p.m. that afternoon. We found a vacant spot close to the front of the courthouse, parked, locked the car, then walked up the first few steps leading to the entrance. It took some thirty paces on the concrete walk to reach the bronze door. The architecture of the massive building has an almost greek gothic look about it, with its four huge sand stone columns centrally grouped together in pairs, and two smaller marble columns stationed on either side of the bronze door. I had no idea that I would be spending long hours in this impressive building over the next several months. More over, this was the first time I had ever approached the building, or had any need to. It is well worth a few more descriptive words of its exterior and immediate grounds before entering: On either side of the walkway are trimmed three foot hedges which guard the almost park-like front lawns. There is a convenient drinking fountain on the narrow walk leading over to the new additional office building on the right. On the left side, directly across the circular drive, is what may have been the judge's home in post Victorian times, with an obvious carriage house in the rear.

Looking up from the main walkway it is clear there are three prominent floors of activity going on in both wings. Further looking up one would be impressed with the central dome commanding the whole structure, and a Roman numeral clock looking out on the city of Montesano below it. A small cupola at the very top of the dome probably housed a bell or horn at one time.

Now, walking up the last three granite steps to the bronze door, and passing between a few court house characters out having a smoke, which they obviously cannot enjoy inside, I pulled the heavy door and we walked in. Directly at our feet, in marble tiles, the words "Grays Harbor County Courthouse, 1910" greeted us on our entering.

Joyce and I continued over near the main interior marble steps, and asked a tall neatly dressed young man coming down the steps where we should go to check on passport information. The man smiled back and said, "Up the steps, and on your left, to the County Clerks Office". This gentleman, Mr. James Hagarty of the Prosecutors Office, as I would later learn, would be most helpful and considerate to Joyce and myself during the next five months.

Climbing the steps at a slower pace we were passed by by a number of younger people briskly going up and coming down the same steps, and continuing on about their business. Standing at the counter inside the County Clerk's office an attractive young woman came up and offered to help us. Joyce had our old passports out of the manila envelope and began explaining our needs. At my left elbow there were two stacks of eight and a half by eleven inch stapled white sheets. As Joyce continued speaking to the clerk there were people, who looked like they might be attorneys or attorneys' assistants, who would come in, reach over and take a packet from the stacks, and then depart the Clerk's office.

Glancing down at the stacks I noticed one stack was headed 'civil' and the other 'criminal'. On closer inspection of the 'criminal' stack, and with my glasses on, I noticed down one of the columns the names Marvin Garba, and Craig Borman. Beside their names were the statement '3.5 Hearing'. The figures did not signify a passing grade to me.

In a brief gesture, I stopped the next person who took a packet from the criminal stack and asked her what the '3.5 hearing' meant. She immediately stated, with a certain authority, "Oh, that's a legal term meaning, a hearing to verify that a person's rights have not been violated while they were being interrogated."

"Thank you, maam!" And I thoughtfully reminded myself that every profession has its own jargon. Example; '3.5'.

I probably shouldn't have but I took one of the 'criminal' packets, and with Joyce we turned and left the room. Out in the busy hallway Joyce had two pink forms in her hands which she explained that we had to take home, fill them out, and return then with new passport pictures of us to the Clerks office. And should return them soon if we wanted to have our new passports in our hands in time for our flight to London. Joyce then said she was going to find the ladies room and would meet me down in the lobby in a few minutes.

Standing alone I stopped another young person who looked like he might be an attorney. It wasn't all that hard to distinguish them; suits and ties, while many of the other people passing around me wore open collared shirts and jeans, some with just 'T' shirts and jeans. I was told that a 3.5 hearing was underway in Judge Foscue's Chambers at that moment. And Judge Foscue's Chambers were where? "Third floor, west-wing!"

Looking up the marble steps and figuring Joyce would be at least another five minutes, I shifted a little on my cane and began climbing up the steps to the third deck. On reaching the top step I found a number of people there in various street attire, speaking in quiet conversations. Little knots of people and what looked like attorneys in the middle of these small groups also conversing in low conversations. And most of the conversing activity was near the east-wing, just outside Superior Courtroom Number One. I stepped over and peered through the large windows of the closed door leading into Courtroom Number Two. There didn't seem to be much activity inside, then another 'attorney' looking type carrying a stack of written material asked my pardon. I was in his way. He then opened the glass windowed door with his free hand and stepped in. I followed him in, and quietly sat down at the nearest long oak seat.

That seat, I thought, surely was one of the hardest seats that I ever sat on in my life. Those seats would surely discourage any courtroom groupie, from enjoying an afternoon 'soap opera', I was certain. Trying to be as inconspicuous as possible, still I made a quick glance around the room. There was seating for at least two hundred people, I guessed. Yet there were little more than a dozen people in the church-like room, including myself and the judge. The court, while not at trial, was in session. The judge, a light or prematurely gray haired bespeckled young man, everyone looks young to me these days, and with his black robes on was thoughtfully listening to testimony from a uniformed officer who occupied the witness chair. The officer was being questioned by a medium height, rather thin, man in a light gray sports jacket and dark gray slacks. His light brown hair was close cropped and he had on a pair of brown and white tennis shoes. His words were not clearly audible from where I was sitting, so I just continued to observe around the room. The room faced north, and just behind the judge two vividly colored mural paintings dominated the entire back wall. I did not study the paintings at this time.

To the left and behind me were four or five other men, at least two of these were also in uniform. The others were in sport coats and ties, two of which were seated together. Both had moustaches; one dark haired, the other prematurely gray. At the defendants table, just inside the gate and to the left in the arena, a medium size man in a dark brown suit was also thoughtfully listening to the testimony. The most striking thing about this man was his head; rather large. An FDR kind of head. At the prosecutor's table were two men, the one who had just preceded me into the courtroom, and the other, seated at his left. All I could see were their backs directly in front of me. The jury box, located a little ahead and to the right of the prosecutor's table was empty.

At the far side of the room, near the west windows, a female officer, in the uniform of a Deputy Sheriff, stood looking down at the two young men in bright orange police coveralls, who were seated in the front row behind the defendants table. The female officer, tall, dark long hair and good figure was very attractive. In another outfit and in another period of time, she could have passed as a female singer in front of Harry James' orchestra. But that was in another time, and this female officer was now sternly looking down at her charges. It is entirely possible, being a 35 mile driving distance between Ocean Shores and Montesano I might have ended my first hand observing interest then and there, except for the following incident: The two young men, still in their teens, one dark haired and the other with a little longer then normal blond hair, were, like a couple of naughty boys, softly giggling together over their own private joke. And during class as the teacher is trying to give the day's lesson. The female officer firmly stepped over to them, reached down and un-handcuffed them, then separated them. She moved the dark haired youth closer to the far end of the seat, and moved the blond youth down the seat, about six feet closer in my direction.

If one is interested, you learn the player's names in any scene: Judge David Foscue, at the judge's chair; Sergeant Delia at the stand; being questioned by defense attorney Jim Heard; at the defense table was also defense attorney John Farra; at the prosecutors table was County Prosecutor Steward Menefee and Chief Criminal Prosecutor Gerald Fuller; the two moustached plain clothes men were Detectives Bill Stocks and Doug Smythe; the female Sheriffs Officer, Ruth Perdue. The two young men in orange coveralls were defendants Marvin Garba and Craig Borman.

Joyce would probably be down around the entrance to the courthouse by then, and looking around for me. So I departed the courtroom as quietly as I came in. Joyce was looking for me.

Over at the little shopping center of Montesano I found a good place to park, in front of Sprouse Reitz. I walked around outside while Joyce went in looking for her yarn. In fifteen minutes we were on our way again. On the drive back home, after Joyce brought out the yarn to tell me it was exactly what she was looking for, I attempted to tell her about the experience that I had just had up in Courtroom Number Two. Glancing over at her while driving I could see her eye-brows narrowed when I told her about the two defendants in the courtroom. She had not gotten over the death of Mrs. Barsic any more than I had. She suggested that maybe we ought to attend the trial. I had learned, before leaving the courthouse, that the first trial, concerning Marvin Garba, was scheduled to take place sometime in late October, maybe early November. Dates of trials, as I also learned, are often moved to later dates due to preparation readiness. We would check again when we brought our completed passport forms back next Monday. If there was any more pre-trial courtroom activity concerning those two young boys Joyce wanted to see some of it as I had. I told her about the hard seats. She said she could bear it if I could.

On reflex, I had made a few mental notes to myself on some scraps of papers I found in my coat pockets while seated in the courtroom. Now I was anxious to get home and look over that 'criminal' packet I had taken from the counter back in the clerk's office. I felt guilty about it and hoped I didn't leave anyone short of their copy. It would tell me the names of the attorneys; defense and prosecution, and would give advancing dates of 'discovery' actions coming up. And, driving through Aberdeen, while stopping at Denny's for a cup of coffee, I picked up a copy of the Aberdeen news. The paper was running articles about the Barsic case in most every daily edition at that time.

The week rolled by pretty fast, then another day off for Joyce came up, Monday the 9th of September. With our pink forms filled out, and new photos we had obtained from Durney Travel Agency pasted in the proper box, we were on our way back to Montesano again. I wanted to know something about Ginny's two boys who were serving on active duty with the Navy. Were they in town? How were they making it? Joyce was concerned about Ginny's husband and her other children. Were we getting interested in something that maybe we should stay out of? There is such a thing as 'mind your own business'. And we certainly had other business of our own, which was crowding our schedule coming up that fall. Never mind, we could work around it. And I did want to know how those boys were doing. Could I be of any help to them? Being retired from the Navy, maybe I could be of some assistance. We will stop all interest this day if we find there is no need for us.

Back in the courthouse, at about 2 p.m., we climbed the marble steps to the 2nd floor. Again the bustling traffic of people were about the same as the previous Monday. If anything, maybe more people running around. Joyce gave our pink forms to the same young women in the clerks office the last time we were in. All was in order, then Joyce paid out cash to process our passports, at about thirty five dollars each. After thanking the young woman, a smiling Miss Janice, we were about to turn away when I asked Janice if I could take one of the copies from the two stacks of packets resting on the left side of the counter. The young women, glancing to my left then to my right, nodded in approval.

Out in the hallway I adjusted my glasses and scanned down the columns, over to the 2nd page, and found the lines, State of Washington VS Garba and Borman. This time, with a little more knowledge of the jargon, and the players, I pointed out to Joyce that the two defendants were being given a discovery hearing that afternoon in Superior Court Number One: Judge Michael Spencer presiding. We climbed the marble steps to the third floor.

Making our way between the little groups of people and just before stepping into Superior Courtroom Number One, a uniformed male officer motioned Joyce and myself back from entering the room. Another officer was coming along, and leading a line of eight or ten orange clothed handcuffed men into the courtroom. The two young men at the end of the line were Marvin and Craig. Another uniformed officer followed them all in, and led them all over to the far side, front row of courtroom seats. Then the spectators, and probably some witnesses, were allowed in. Joyce and I found space about four rows back from the front row. The court had been on a ten minute recess while the judge pondered a point of law, or so Joyce leaned over and told me from what she had learned from the woman seated next to her. There were no people in the jury box, and the judge had been rendering decisions and handing down various sentences all that day. There were probably forty to sixty people in the courtroom at that moment.

Architecturally, this room in the east-wing was identical to the west-wing courtroom, and both facing north. The only difference was in the arena; the area of attorney battle and debate. That being, the prosecutor's table was on the left side, and the defense table on the right. And the jury box, still inboard, now on the left side. Behind the judge's bench, as in the west-wing courtroom, two striking mural paintings seemed to cry out for attention from the entire back wall. Dividing the two paintings, and above the judge's bench, lettered in gold, the words, "Justice: The hope of all who are just. The dread of all who are wrong".

"All rise! The court is now in session, Judge Spencer presiding!"

The black robed judge, stepping in from a panel door at the far end of the room, took his seat and began addressing the two attorneys standing before him. Again, the judge looked quite young to me, maybe in his early forties, and also light complected. While the judge in the West wing courtroom had a sort of young boyish Paul Newman look about him, this one, looking more like he would be at home coaching a little league baseball team, had a kind of young Gene Hackman type of appearance. Both judges however, were absolutely professional. Spencer, perhaps a little less formal in his vocabulary.

One by one cases were called out and people with their attorneys would come to stand before the judge for his rendered sentencing, or extension of date for sentencing or trial date. Some people were called straight from the spectators section around us, as well as from the line of handcuffed persons. By 4 p.m. that afternoon, after swiftly dealing with burglars, child or wife molesters, non-payment support, shoplifters, drunk drivers, and the like, the courtroom thinned out. Only Joyce and I were left seated in the spectators section, and I felt uncomfortably conspicuous. Of the line of handcuffed prisoners, over in the far right section of the courtroom, only two remained.

Marvin and Craig, who were easily recognizable from earlier newspaper photos, were again quietly enjoying their private joke together. Craig, seated on the far side this time, leaned over and said something to his friend, and then his eyes locked on mine. He quietly said something more to his friend, then Marv turned to his left and both boys starred back at me. They were smiling, but their eyes on me were firm and set. It was not a chilling feeling, as I recalled. It was more like an introduction of some kind. I let them win the staring contest and joined Joyce observing the four attorneys in conversation with the judge. The two boys were then motioned by a uniformed guard to get up. I was rather wishing Joyce was not beside me as both boys were led out of the courtroom. Still smiling, but firmly starring at me, they were led in front of us by only a few feet.

Feeling it was time for us to leave I began looking around for my cane. From the group of four attorneys still conversing, standing over by the judge, one of then came around the bench, and walked over to me. In a slight smile, he asked if I could take a message to Mr. Greg Barsic. I answered that I would sure try. He gave me his card with a phone number on it.

"My name is Jerry Fuller, please ask him to call me at his convenience."

"Yes sir!" I answered, and we shook hands.

Back on the road for Ocean Shores and home, Joyce and I had a good talk. She thought it awful that those boys didn't seem the least remorseful over Ginny's death. "Hell, did Saddam Hussein look the least remorseful over all those dead Kuwaites he had killed, or even the death of his own troops?" And I added, "It seems nobody wants to be remorseful over any bad thing they do anymore". Then I got to thinking about all those detectives, police officers, and attorneys back there that have to deal with that kind of thing everyday. Joyce then said, "Did you notice we were the only ones left in the spectator section who were interested in Ginny's case?"

"Well, I think other people are interested too. It's just that we were there today. Anyway, before we left I learned that the first trial is scheduled to start on Tuesday the nineteenth of November. We'll be back from Pearl by then."

"We're going back?"

"Let's stick with it a while longer. That young attorney from the prosecutor's office gave me a little job to do. And I'm going to do it. Except I don't know where to start looking for Ginny's husband."

"I'll tell you a good place to start. One of the girls at the office told me there was a big jar on the cash counter in the dinning room of the Ocean Shores Inn. People have been putting money in it for Greg to help take care of some of the funeral expenses. That big jar is half full already. Some people care."

After driving through the monuments I dropped Joyce off at her office. Then I drove over to the Inn. Sure enough, there was a jar; a big fruit or mayonnaise jar with a taped sign on it that said "for Greg Barsic and Ginny's Funeral Expense." One of the waitress talking in a group near the cash register told me she could get a message to Mr. Barsic if I wanted to leave it with her. She looked right to me so I gave her the card and told her to have Mr. Barsic call that number. I started to leave my name but didn't. I did put a few dollars in the jar before departing the Inn.

Nine days later, 18 September, Joyce with a few days off drove with me over to the small community of Chehalis, for the purpose of undergoing a cataract operation on my right eye which had given completely out a year or so earlier. The Pacific Cataract Institute at Chehalis is one fine organization of well trained professional people, and I was in and out on the same day. Stereo and real technicolor came back, giving me better vision.

On the following 10th of October Joyce and I boarded a Northwest 747 at Sea-Tac Airport for a week's working visit in Pearl Harbor. We paid the regular retired officer's rate and stayed at the Admiral Lockwood BOQ during the week. It rained a good deal of the time. The Barsic family was seldom from our thoughts and private conversations. It was almost like taking Ginny with us. She would have enjoyed that trip.

On our return home, checking the mail first, I found that our new passports had arrived, I also found there was little talk on the Barsic case in the papers or among our few friends in town. However, during one afternoon while waiting at one of the check-out lines in the super market in town I couldn't help over-hearing two men in front of me talking. One said, "-I heard the woman out at Hogans Corner was running some kind of drug operation, and that's why she got killed and the papers won't print it." Before I could challenge the remark the man had paid his bill and was walking out of the store. And I was ashamed of myself for not thinking fast enough; or was it strong enough, to make a reaction. Summer had turned to fall. It was November, a chill in the air, and the day of the first trial finally came around. Marv and Craig would be tried separately; Marv first.

I missed the first day and a half of the trial because of calls I was receiving from London; actually they were calls from an RAF base just outside of London jointly operated by American airmen, wishing to confirm my arrival and schedule time in early December. However, I had not missed much of the real trial. What was accomplished on Tuesday was the final selection and seating of the jury; seven women and five men, with two alternates. Judge Spencer had made his initial comments to the jury, the prosecution made its opening remarks and outlined the state's first degree murder case against Marv, then the defense rose and stated its position in defending Marv on the grounds of insanity. The judge then ordered the prosecutor to call its first witness. Deputy Sheriff Steve Larson related how he had first found the body of Mrs. Barsic.

On Wednesday the 20th of September, I drove alone to Montesano. Joyce had to work that day. It had been raining and I was glad she had fixed me a thermos of coffee for the drive. I arrived at the courthouse at about 1:05 p.m. So far, all I had really known was what I had read in the papers, what my friend Gordy Buchanan had told me, and what I had observed to be two young un-remorseful defendants.

The jury heard the pathologist describe the knife wounds, bites, and other injuries found on the body. Then Dan took the stand and he testified on the circumstances of how he had picked up and brought the six young people from Aberdeen out to Ocean Shores, and eventually dropping them off at the triplex apartment building at Hogans Corner.

Following Dan, the next witness would be Robert Noonan.

CHAPTER SEVEN: 1ST TRIAL; JURY DELIBERATES; RESULT

On entering the courthouse, and reaching the courtroom third floor level, I felt sure it would be difficult to find a good seat, maybe no seat at all. Not so. There were only about twenty people in the entire room, excluding jurors. The afternoon session had not begun as yet. Moving down the third row I settled on a space a few feet from a nicely dressed small woman, in her early fifties, who occupied the end space of the long bench seat next to the center aisle. Most of the people seated around me, I guessed, were either civilian or police witnesses.

Marvin Garba, seated at the defense table in the arena was dressed in dark slacks and a black, blue, and white woven sweater. He sat on the far side of his attorney, Jim Heard. At the prosecutor's table, over the rows of sparsely filled seats, and across the short wooden fence guarding the arena sat Prosecutor Menefee, and his chief assistant Gerald Fuller.

"All rise! The Court is now in session. The State of Washington Versus Marvin Garba. Judge Spencer presiding." The judge came out, took his seat, then asked both sides in the arena if they were ready. With their affirmative he then ordered the Jury brought in. After they entered, took their seats and appeared settled, the judge then directed the prosecutor to call its previous witness. The time was about 1:20 p.m.

Dan, still under oath, returned to the witness chair, answered a few last questions, then was dismissed. The judge then directed the prosecution to call its next witness. Fuller, on his feet, stated in easy tones, "The prosecution calls Robert Noonan!"

Bob walked in from the outer lobby, stepped up beside the witness chair, was duly sworn, and then took the chair which had a small microphone attached to it at face level. Fuller, in dark slacks and grey tweed sport coat walked over closer to Bob and began his questioning. The time was 1:30 p.m.

Q: Sir, would you state your name for us?

A: Robert Noonan.

Q: Can you slide your chair up a little bit so we can hear you in the microphone?

A:(witness complied) Robert Noonan.

Bob was quite neat looking, a little undernourished maybe. His dark curly hair, far from any crew-cut was however, neatly combed. He wore a dark blue sweater over a white shirt and tie. He didn't look as though he weighed more then 135 pounds. He was somewhat nervous but deliberate in his tone of voice.

Q: Mr. Noonan, how old are you?

A: Eighteen.

Q: Do you know the defendant?

A: Yes, I do.

Q: Do you recall where you met the defendant?

A: Yes, I do.

Q: Where?

A: At the Aberdeen bus terminal.

Q: Do you remember what day it was?

A: Friday.

Q: What were you doing at the bus depot?

A: Attempting to get a hold of my mother.

Q: Who were you with?

A: My girlfriend, Tina.

Q: And about what time was this?

A: Anywhere between 6 and 8 PM.

Q: Now, prior to that time did you know the defendant?

Bob glanced to his left, over at Marv sitting at the defense table, then back at Fuller, and answered, No I didn't.

Q: How did you meet him?

A: Through a semi-acquaintance, Craig Borman.

Q: Where was Craig?

A: He was with Marvin Garba.

Bob went on to describe how the six of them got together. He said he was in a phone booth in the bus terminal area and was on his third try to reach his mother when Craig, recognized him, came up and they just started talking together. Fuller asked what prompted them to get together. Bob's answer was, "boredom". Fuller went on to ask Bob what they did at the bus depot. Bob answered, "smoked some marijuana, conversation, and planned partying." And that they almost decided to find a motel room in Aberdeen and stay there for the night. But then Craig's friend Dan came along in his truck, they all piled in and went out to Ocean Shores, taking a case of beer with them.

Dan drove them all around Ocean Shores looking for a motel and found none, except one, and they wanted, "135 dollars a night." That was too steep for them, so Dan drove them to one last place, out at Hogans Corner and to a place where Marv had some friends who lived upstairs in an apartment building there. While Marv was upstairs, finding out they were not wanted there, the woman downstairs, from her kitchen window, invited them all in to spend the night.

Fuller asked what kind of things they did on Saturday. Bob answered that they did more "-drinking and listening to music." They took a cab ride, Marv got his last pay check from the super market and bought more alcohol.

Fuller touched lightly on Sunday, then went directly to early Monday morning.

Q: Do you recall the early morning hours of Monday at the apartment?

A: Actually not. I was passed out until minutes before the happening.

Q: Do you recall what first drew your attention?

A: Yes, I do.

Q: What was that?

A: My girlfriend being forcefully made toward the back bedroom.

Q: Where were you?

A: I was siting in the chair by the front door.

Fuller then stepped over to a large framed cork board with a blown up diagram of the floor plan of Ginny's apartment. The juror's attention were also drawn to it. Fuller continued questioning Bob.

Q: This is diagram marked number 16. Can you see it from there?

A: Yes I can.

Q: What is it?

A: It's Mrs. Barsic's apartment.

Q: Where were you?

A: Just to the right as you enter the front door.

Q: Now what was it you heard?

A: "Come on Tina!" and "Get her back there."

Q: Who was saying it.

A: Marv.

Q: The defendant?

A: And Tammy, yes.

Q: What?

A: Marv was telling Tammy and Tammy was doing it.

Q: What did you do when you heard that?

A: I got up

Q: Where did you go?

A: Toward Marv, Tammy, and my girlfriend.

Q: What did you see?

A: I seen Tammy go into the back bedroom. Tina was already there. Craig pulled the door shut and was holding the door shut. I could tell someone was trying to pull it open because it was opening about three inches and then he would pull it shut again.

Q: What were you trying to do?

A: Get passed Marv to get in the bedroom to find out why they were shoving my girlfriend in there.

Q: Did Craig say anything to the people in there?

A: "Tammy, keep her in there."

Q: What did you do when you went down the hall?

A: Like I said, I tried to go past Marv. Marv got really physical and slammed me up against the wall.

Fuller, standing by the taped up drawing of the floor plan, and pointing to it, established from Bob the commotion going on in the hallway leading to the back bedroom of the apartment. Ginny, at this point, stepped out of the hall bathroom to see what was going on. She ordered "Everybody stay away from my bedroom", and she cut between Bob and Marv.

Q: What happened then.

A: All of a sudden a pillow materialized. I don't know if Craig handed it to him or he picked it up from around the corner, but Marv had a pillow. She was slammed into me. He pushed her up against me. And I didn't know if he was going after her with the pillow or if he planned on hitting me with it.

Bob went on to testify that for a moment the pillow covered his face. Fighting to get it off, the next thing he saw was Ginny on the floor with Marv on top of her, almost in front of the bathroom door.

Q: In this area?

A: Right there, yes. "Can everyone see?", Fuller asked the jury, then continuing with Bob.

Q: On her side, on her back?

A: It wasn't like she was sitting still. It was a squabble.

Q: What was the defendant doing?

A: He was straddling her, and was attempting to put the pillow over her face.

Q: On his knees! What was Mrs. Barsic doing?

A: Winning! She was fighting back and doing a very good job if it.

Q: How was she fighting back?

A: She was punching and scratching and kicking, winning.

There was a pause in Fuller's questioning. Not a sound in the whole courtroom. In another moment, with his pointer stick in hand, Fuller picked up the questioning.

Q: What were you saying?

A: I was yelling, "What's going on? Hey, stop it, break it up", you know.

Q: Where was Craig?

A: He was standing right about where I was.

Q: Was he saying anything?

A: "Get her. Get her." And I-.

Q: What did you do?

A: I stood there. Like an idiot, I froze.

Q: Then what?

A: Marv said, "Help me get her. Grab her feet."

Q: Who did he direct that to?

A: Craig. And Craig did just that. She was beating her heels on the linoleum and making quite a bit of noise.

Q: So what did Craig do?

A: Craig eventually was able to secure her feet. It took him awhile but he secured her feet.

Q: What did you do then?

A: I'm not exactly sure what to call it. I freaked out. I didn't- I had- I don't know. It was weird. I just wanted to leave all of a sudden, just tweaked out. I wanted to leave. I ran back and I got my girlfriend.

Under further questioning, Bob went on to say that when he got in the back bedroom he was screaming, and Tammy pushed him on the bed and told him to "calm down!" Still screaming, Bob got off the bed and kicked a hole in the bedroom wall, then grabbing Tina, he said, "We're leaving." Hurrying back down the hall Bob said he saw Ginny alone, laying on the floor. She was moving and making noise. He did not recall where Craig was at this time but did recall seeing Marv around the kitchen area. Bob was standing and waiting for Tina to hurry up and find her things so they could get out of there. She was over near the carved Indian. Fuller asked Bob if, besides the pillow, did he observe any other weapon in the hands of Marvin Garba. Bob said he heard Marv calling, "Where's my knife. Where's my knife." And that Marv passed Bob with a screw driver in hand. It was at this time Bob and Tina were on their way to the front door.

Fuller then took Bob over his recollection of experiences after leaving the apartment. His plea for Tammy to join him and Tina out in front of the VFW, to their bus ride into Ocean Shores, and continuing bus ride to Hoquiam. Fuller's final question to Bob was. "Mr Noonan, did you have anything to do with the killing of Virginia Barsic?" He answered, "No I did not." Fuller, looking at the judge, then stated, "That's all I have with the witness, your honor."

Still on the stand Bob was reminded that he was still under oath, and now faced cross examination, from attorney Jim Heard. Heard would give his client, Marvin Garba, the best defense he could through-out the trial. Heard took Bob over the same ground Fuller had covered the previous two hours; where and how they all got together, beginning with Bob trying to reach his mother by phone. Heard brought out how Marv and Craig got a "Bum" to buy them a case of beer, and that the three boys, had been drinking and smoking pot, and almost stayed in a motel in Aberdeen. But Craig's friend Dan came along with his truck and they all left for Ocean Shores. Heard asked Bob how long he had lived in the Grays Harbor area. "All my life", was his answer. Bob also said he had not visited Ocean Shores many times in his life.

Heard got the same answers that Fuller had drawn from Bob as to how they all ended up at Ginny's apartment. Bob said Tina was the first one in the apartment, and he could hear Ginny and Tina, "They were giggling and laughing, sounded like they were getting along great". In a little while Ginny said, "Come on in", we could crash the night. That Saturday, "-someone brought out a camera. We took pictures of everybody laughing, and acting silly". Heard established that they all drank heavily throughout Saturday. Then the defense attorney touched on their scheme to go to Oregon.

Bob related that he heard bits and pieces all that weekend about stealing a car, going to Oregon and making money. And that Marv had pressured Bob in a plan to rob the Shop Rite super market. And Marv was going to give Bob a shotgun to help in the robbery. Bob told Tina about it, and said Marv was crazy. And Marv practiced karate, sometimes on Bob. Bob was "leery" about Marv.

Heard attempted to establish that Bob was more of a willing participant than just a standby frozen observer. After all, Bob had joined in the blood brotherhood thing. Going on into Monday morning, Heard drew out of Bob the same story he had related to Fuller. Some moments before he and Tina left the apartment, Bob recalled catching a glimpse of Marv twisting Ginny's head in what might have been an attempt in breaking her neck. Bob was pretty sure Ginny was still alive when he and his girlfriend went out the front door.

At this moment the judge called for an afternoon break. The time was almost 3 p.m. The jury retired from the room first, then Marv was led from the defense table out of the room. Then the rest of the people in the courtroom took their recess. At 3:20 everyone was back in place, including the ten or so spectators. Bob was reminded he was still under oath. Heard then picked up his cross examination where he left off. Continuing to probe Bob's credibility. At one point Bob told of Ginny's developing anger over Craig and Tammy having sex in her hall bathroom. Heard challenged Bob on a number of his remarks he had made on the five-page statement that Detective Parfitt and Smythe recorded shortly after his arrest in Olympia, but Bob held firm. Then Heard got to the heart of his thrust.

Q: Since you didn't know whether Mrs. Barsic was dead or alive; you know she was still alive when you left there, would you please tell this jury why, during all those ensuing hours, why didn't you call the police. Why didn't you tell someone to see if this woman was alive and maybe needed help? Why didn't you do that, Mr. Noonan?

Bob shrunk even deeper in the witness chair, his color drained and his hands fidgeted. He must have known someone was going to ask him that question sooner or later. He caught his breath, and in his boyish voice,

A: Check my criminal record and you will see why I do not care too much for any dealing that I have with the police, good or bad, relating to me or not. I do not talk to the police unless they are arresting me. That is not an excuse for not trying to find out whether or not she was okay. Maybe I didn't want to know. We didn't call. That's the only answer I can give.

Heard stayed with this line of questioning another fifteen minutes, then, "That's all I have, your honor". The court adjourned at 4:36 p.m. It would re-convene at 9 a.m. the following morning, Thursday, November 21. Tammy would be the morning witness, followed by Tina in the afternoon. Then on Friday morning Marv would take the stand, and it would all be in the hands of the jury by that afternoon.

That Thursday morning found me in about the same

seat which I occupied during, Bob's testimony, and, as before, several spaces between me and the nicely dressed middle aged woman on my right. She had arrived before I did, which was about five minutes to nine. Settling in I glanced around and counted only eight people in the spectators section. It would remain that count throughout the day. In the quiet of the courtroom, which felt almost like being in church, I studied the two large wall murals facing me from either side of the judge's seating area. Both of the vividly painted murals were Biblical in message, and had probably been in place at the time of the grand opening of the courthouse in 1910. The painting on the right depicted two seated figures being instructed by an angel representing 'Justice' holding up the balancing scales. The equally large mural on the left of the judge's seating area depicted 'Cain' after he had slew his brother 'Able'. Cain was being driven out of Paradise by two floating angels, to the East of Eden in to the land of Nod.

"All rise! The court is now in session. Judge Spencer presiding. The State of Washington versus Marvin Garba." Before the Deputy Clerk Adrienne Abrahamson had finished her command and announcement, the judge had stepped in and was seated. Looking to his left, then his right, seeing that everyone was in place, including the court reporter, Diane Stanley, he then directed the jury to be brought in and for the prosecution to continue its case.

"The State calls Tammy Muller to the stand." From the outer lobby, Tammy walked in and was sworn-in. As before, Gerald Fuller, on his feet, approached the witness chair. Tammy was dressed simply; low heel black slippers, dark slacks, and white blouse with sleeves. Tall, blondish hair, and even at my distance, some twenty feet from her, her eyes shown clear and green. She was, without doubt, a very attractive young woman. Her initial manner was one of nervous cooperation. In his same low-key manner the light brown haired Deputy Prosecutor began,

Q: Would you state your name for us please?

A: Tammy Muller.

Q: Ms. Muller, how old are you?

A: Twenty.

Fuller then established that Tammy had left her mother's home in Carson, caught the bus to visit her dad who was living in Cosmopolis. Traveling in the bus from Olympia to Aberdeen she met, for the first time, another girl, Sonja Cortell who was on her way to her foster home in the Aberdeen area. Arriving at the Aberdeen bus station Tammy's new friend Sonja recognized in the crowd her friend Tina, who was with her boyfriend Bob. Bob was also with his friend Craig, who was with his friend Marv. Tammy had no acquaintance with any of them prior to that Friday.

Tammy's story was near identical to Bob's testimony; how the six of them got together, almost staying at a motel in Aberdeen, Craig's friend Dan coming with his truck and taking them all to Ocean Shores. Tammy also testified; after not being able to find a motel they almost had decided to spend the night on the beach in the sand. As with Bob's testimony it was Tina who first entered the lower apartment, at Ginny's invitation. The following morning Tammy states she made breakfast, then they all began drinking again. Ginny had brought out her polaroid camera and a number of pictures were taken. On Sunday, she remembered Craig's friend came by with his car. On Sunday evening she remembered Marv talking about how many people he had killed. Marv bragged about having killed 15 people. Craig bragged about having "popped off" one with a gun at 200 yards.

Q: When did you realize something was wrong?

A: When Marv looked at Craig and drew his finger across his throat and pointed toward Ginny, who was in the hall bathroom. He said, "It's time."

Q: Where were you at this time?

A: I was sitting in Craig's lap.

Fuller, using his pointer at the apartment floor plan, clarified from Tammy for the jury that she and Craig were in one of the living room chairs at that moment. Marv was sitting before them, Indian style, in front of her and Craig. Sonja was lying in one of the corners in the living room.

Q: How did you know Ginny was in the bathroom?

A: Because you could hear her. I think she was cleaning or something.

Tammy stated that Tina called and asked Tammy to come to the back bedroom. In the back bedroom Tina told Tammy she was getting scared with all the talk about killing people. Then Craig came to the back bedroom door.

Q: What happened when Craig Borman came to the door?

A: He said, "You girls are going to have to stay in here." I asked him why. He said, "Because she's going to call the cops." then Marv came up behind Craig and said, "Get in the bedroom" or "Get in the bathroom." So we went into the back bathroom and shut the door.

Q: What happened when you got in the bathroom?

A: We heard a loud thump on the walls and then a scream, and that's when we ran out of the bathroom.

Tammy went on to say that when she and Tina came out of the bathroom they ran into Bob. Bob was freaking out. It was like a head on collision. Bob began kicking the wall, with his feet, his hands, and his head. He said, "They're killing her. They' re killing her." Tammy said she opened the door and looked down the hall, to see for herself.

Q: Describe what you saw.

A: Her eyes were black all the way from halfway through her forehead all the way down past her nose and there was blood coming out of her eyes. Tammy went on to say Marv had a screw driver. Fuller asked Tammy to come off the stand, take the pointer and show where every one was at that moment. Tammy did so. Then the court reporter broke in, saying, "I can't hear." Fuller motioned to Tammy to retake the stand, and describe the positions from there.

Q: What did you think was going on?

A: They sure as hell weren't knocking her out.

Q: Pardon me?

A: They were killing her. I said, "Oh, my God, you're killing her". Marv just smiled and said, "What a rush." And he talked about the power he had.

Tammy then said she went back to the bathroom and got sick. When she came out Bob and Tina were leaving. Fuller asked her what she saw next.

A: I saw Craig stabbing her in the back.

Q: Where was Marv?

A: He was doing something gross by her neck. He was on one knee, one knee up.

Q: What did you do when you saw this?

A: I think that's when I went to the garage door. Tammy said she wanted to go with Bob and Tina.

Q: Did you see where the knife came from?

A: Yes, I did.

Q: How did you see that?

A: I saw Craig through the window when I was outside. Tammy went on to say she saw Craig walk all the way to the end of the kitchen counter, opened a drawer, pulled out a knife, walked back and handed it to Marv.

Q: What made you come back inside?

A: Marv.

Tammy went on to say that Marv ordered her in to the back bedroom again. She went to the back bedroom, stayed a few moments then came back out and saw Craig stabbing Ginny. Then Craig ordered her to get back in the bedroom. He said, "Just get the fuck out of here".

Q: Did you come out of the bedroom one final time?

A: Yes. Marv was standing over her body, saying some kind of chant. Wiping blood on himself. He was only wearing pants. He was barefoot, no shirt.

Tammy's voice began trailing off into soft spoken responses. She was staring down at the floor in front of her and her fingers continued crumbling a damp handkerchief in her hands. Fuller interrupted her and said, "Can everyone hear?" One juror answered, "No". Tammy looked up and said, "I'm sorry".

Under further questioning she went on to say that Craig said, "Tammy, you're going to have to clean this up". She said her response was, "No, I'm not going to clean it up. There's blood clots all over.", and he said, "You're going to have to clean it up or Marv's going to kill you."

Q: Did you see what happened to Ginny Barsic, what happened to her body?

A: They drug her out side and that's the last time I saw her.

Fuller's further questioning brought out that she had indeed helped in the wiping down the walls. "They gave stuff to me, dropping it on the floor in front of me, and said, clean it up." She said Marv had timed it all and that it took about 40 minutes from the time they started on Ginny until she died. She was sure they left the house at about 5:50 a.m. Tammy admitted when she left with them she had taken some of Ginny's jewelry with her. Why did they trash the house, and take the TV set, Fuller asked. To make it look like a robbery, she answered. And she further admitted to dumping over a container of shells.

She admitted to taking bloody items across the street and throwing them over in the brush. Then, with Sonja now up, they all went out and over to the other side of the Texaco mini-mart and deposited most of what they were carrying in that area. And then they all walked to Dan's place. Fuller then put the same kind of question to Tammy as Heard had to Bob.

Q: Why didn't you just leave? Why didn't you just run out the door and leave?

A: Because, I mean, you think these are people you can trust and everything. I mean, yeah, you may not know them long but you don't think they're going to kill somebody. Every time you leave you got Marv Garba saying, "Go back in the bedroom." You're going to push your luck after he just got done killing somebody? There's blood all over his body, all over the house, and there's a dead body laying there. I don't know anybody that's going to say, excuse me Marv, I'm leaving.

With further questioning Tammy said that after Marv slit her throat and was drinking her blood, Craig kept saying, "She bit me, She bit me. I can't believe she bit me." Then when Tammy asked Marv why her eyes looked like that, he said, "Because the bitch scratched me." Then Tammy went on to tell everything she could remember, from Dan's apartment, to when she, Sonja, and Marv were finally picked up around noon the next day in front of the Red Lion Motel. Fuller, after a few more detailed questioning, then asked,

Q: Tammy, you pled guilty to your part in this incident, didn't you?

A: Yes, I did.

Q: In fact you pled guilty to the crime called Rendering Criminal Assistance in the First Degree, did you not?

A: Yes, I did.

Q: Beyond that, have I asked you to do anything more here today than to tell the truth as you recall it?

A: You haven't.

With a few more such questions Fuller then said, "Nothing further." He stepped away, took his seat at the prosecution table, leaving Tammy to face the defense.

Heard, got up, walked, around his table and approached Tammy, and began his cross examination. Heard's first questions was, "Ms. Muller, would you tell us, please, why you entered a guilty plea to rendering criminal assistance?"

A: Because we couldn't prove duress.

Q: Couldn't prove duress?

A: Uh-huh.

Q: You did this, according to you, well I guess, the rendering of criminal assistance was cleaning up the blood?

A: Uh-huh.

Q: Is that right?

A: Yes, Sir.

Q: You did it only because Craig said, "If you don't clean it up. Marv's going to kill you", is that right?

A: That's one of the reasons.

Q: I'm sorry?

A: That's one of the reasons.

Q: Well, tell us about the other reasons.

A: Because Marv himself said he would kill me if I didn't.

Heard brought Tammy's attention to a copy of her

first statement she had made to Detectives Stocks and Parfitt shortly after being taken in for questioning in Aberdeen. The defense attorney questioned her extensively over the gaps in her original statement to the testimony she had just given with the prosecuting attorney. Tammy said she hadn't recalled everything right away but did provide the detectives with additional information as she remembered it. Again, she admitted taking some of Ginny's jewelry. She stated again at the time of the killing Marv told her to go in the bathroom, and Craig said she and Tina were to stay there. Heard, going over his notes he had taken during her direct examination, asked about Craig's announcement that, "Marv was going to knock Ginny out because she was going to call the cops." Tammy said, "We asked why knock her out. Why not just leave. Craig, she said, said "No, No, we can't just leave. It's too late." Heard brought up Tammy's visit to the Gull Station mini-mart for NyQuil.

Q: And you went over there specifically to look for some sort of medication that would do what?

A: That would get rid of Ginny's toothache long enough so she could go to sleep because she was crying, because it hurt so bad and she couldn't go to sleep."

Heard attempted to establish that Tammy had planned to give Ginny the NyQuil and get her to sleep so as to more easily steal her jewelry. Tammy denied it, saying it was not her that gave the NyQuil to her but that it was Craig, and that Ginny had taken over half the bottle of medicine. Tammy stated that Ginny said, "Can I have some more?" Tammy said, "No because you're not suppose to take that much", but she liked Craig and said she considered him like her son.

Q: But she still didn't go to sleep?

A: She was off and on. She'd lay down for a little while and then somebody would hear her crying, so somebody would walk in and she'd ask for more.

Desperate for any kind of relief from the pain of her throbbing toothache, Ginny may have wanted to try some of their marijuana.

Heard, while attempting to ascertain where everyone was just prior to the assault drew from Tammy that Tina was in the back bedroom putting vaseline on her lips because they were chapped. At that point the judge called for a morning break. The time was 10:30 and they would re-convene at 10:45 a.m.

After the fifteen minute recess, and everyone was in place again, Heard resumed his questioning. Getting to the time of the assault the attorney asked Tammy,

Q: What did you do in the back bathroom the minute you heard this thump and muffled scream?

A: We plugged our ears.

Q: What?

A: We plugged our ears.

Q: You plugged your ears?

A: Yes Sir.

Q: What made you and Tina decide to unplug your ears?

Tammy answered by saying she thought they had knocked her out but they heard someone in the bedroom, they opened the door, and there was Bob. Heard, staying in the bathroom, asked, "You are saying that you and Tina stood in the bathroom and literally put your fingers in your ears?" No, she answered, "We sat down on the floor and covered our ears." Incredulous, Heard asked where in any of her previous statements does this appear. No where, she admitted.

From here on Tammy's responses were a repeat of her earlier statements, and nearly identical with Bob's. At one point Tammy stated that while she was watching Craig stabbing Ginny he looked up and said, "I'm sorry you had to see this." Later she remembered Bob and Tina over by the VFW warning her she might get fifteen years in prison if she stay-ed. She said she looked toward Marv, back to Bob and Tina, and said "I can't."

Heard was able to establish that Tammy had lied in her early statement to Stocks and Parfitt, con-cerning how much cleaning up she actually did. Now she said she had cleaned and wiped down walls and floors. Toward the end of the cross examination Heard and Fuller exchanged objections over how many times Tammy should admit her lying about the wall and floor cleaning. Then Heard declared, "That's all I have, your honor." On redirect, Fuller clarified with Tammy that she had talked with the police a second time to make corrections and give additional information for the record. Heard objected to the 'leading' way in which Fuller was establishing this fact. The judge sustained the objection. Fuller went on to establish that the jewelry Tammy had taken from Ginny's apartment was of little real value. Tammy readily identified the rolled up pants and shirt which she saw Craig toss on the right side of the road on their walk to Dan's place. There was no objection to the items being admitted into evidence.

The judge called for another morning recess and the trial to continue at 11:20 a.m., which it was. However, without the presence of the jury, a number of motions were made and all were accepted. Among them; Heard withdrew the 'insanity' part of the defense.

The jury was led in and Tina Murphy took the stand. Direct examination from the prosecution would be conducted this time by Steward Menefee, the County Prosecutor. Menefee, a Vietnam war veteran, somewhat shorter man than Fuller, was well dressed in a gray suit. In his middle 40's and with a slightly balding forehead. He rose from the table and, staying well back from the witness chair, began his examination with a similar easy voice as Fuller. Tina, in the witness chair, blondish, plump, and in a dark blouse and dark, very short skirt, was ready. The time was 11:26 a.m.

Q: Would you state your full name please?
A: Tina Ann Murphy.
Q: Tina, how old are you?
A: Fifteen.
Q: You just turned 15?.
A: Yes
Q: Would you have been 14 in August?
A: Yes.
Q: Do you know Bob Noonan?

A: Yes.

Q: How long have you known Bob?

A: Probably about 3 years.

Q: What is your relationship with him?

A: He's my boyfriend.

Menefee was establishing how it was that she and Bob were at the Aberdeen bus station when the judge politely broke in, and said, "Excuse me. Can everyone hear?" Without waiting for a response he added, "Let me make an observation. If you don't keep your voice up, she's not going to keep her voice up."

"I'll move over here, your honor." Menefee moved in closer to the witness chair, then continued his questioning.

Tina had never met Marv, Craig, or Tammy before that evening at the bus stop. She had been acquainted with Sonja during the past two years. Her boyfriend Bob was acquainted with Craig from school days.

Menefee carefully took her over the same ground covered by Fuller with Bob and Tammy; Friday night, Saturday, Sunday. Until Monday night, Tina's testimony was no different. Menefee, bringing Tina's attention to the large cork board holding the blown up diagram of Ginny's apartment floor plan, continued his probing with,

Q: What bedroom was Ginny in?

A: In the master bedroom.

Q: Is that this bedroom right here?

A: Yeah. Tina remembered Ginny got up, came in the living room, and talked to all of them. Then Ginny went in to the hall bathroom.

Q: Why did you go in to the master bedroom?

A: To put vaseline on my lips.

Q: Who went with you?

A: Tammy.

At this point it is interesting to note that Tina's responsive manner seemed mistrustful of the judicial system. Perhaps even contempt.

Q: Did Tammy go with you for the same reason or why was she going in there?

A: I have no idea. I think just to go to the bathroom.

Q: What happened when you tried to open the

door?

A: It wouldn't open, but that was earlier.

Q: That was earlier?

A: That was before. Right before we went to the bathroom, I think.

Q: Let me take you back, then before you went in the bathroom-

A: Yeah.

Q: Where was Marv and Craig at that time?

A: Outside the door.

Q: And did they say anything to you as you went back into the bedroom?

A: Yeah.

Q: They said don't come out?

A: Yeah.

Q: You tried to open it?

A: Yeah.

Q: Was it locked or was someone holding it?

A: Well, I don't think there was a lock on the door, so someone was holding it.

On answering the questioning Tina went on to say that she and Tammy went in the back bathroom. While there she heard a scream, then kicking and thumping noise. Turning to Tammy she asked, what's going on.

Q: What did she tell you?

A: "They're going to kill her."

Q: Did she say anything else?

A: Oh, she goes, "Well, not really. They wouldn't kill her, not really. They just want to scare us." Tina went on to say she began hearing other screaming when coming out of the bathroom.

Q: Do you recall being told to cover your ears?

A: Yeah.

At this point Heard objected to the leading nature of the questioning. The judge sustained the objection. Menefee reworded his line of questioning and brought out from Tina that Tammy had told her to cover her ears. He then carefully brought testimony from Tina that she went to the bedroom door leading into the hallway, opened it, and saw Marv on top of Ginny with a pillow over her face. Menefee had Tina come off the stand, take the pointer, and indicate the area in the hall where Ginny was lying and in what direction she lay. Returning to the witness chair Tina further testified she saw Craig at Ginny's feet. She started walking towards Ginny then Marv told her to get back in the bedroom. She saw Bob sitting in a chair in the livingroom, shaking.

Q: What did you say?

A: I told him, "Come on, lets go." Then Tina returned to the bedroom. Bob soon came back to the bedroom and kicked the wall. Tammy was packing her suit case.

Q: Did you leave the master bedroom?

A: Yeah.

Q: Where did you go?

The judge broke in and said, "Why don't we stop there." Menefee agreed, then the judge turned to Tina, and said, "You may step down." Glancing over at the circular clock high on the east wall, which read 12 noon, the judge stated he would like to resume the trial at about 1:15 p.m. The trial resumed at 1:20 p.m. The judge reminded Tina she was still under oath.

Menefee began by saying, "Tina, before we left for lunch, I was asking you about what had taken place when you and Bob Noonan had gone back down the hall to the master bedroom." Tina related that after gathering up her things she and Bob hurried back through the hall, heading for the front door.

Q: When you left the Barsic apartment, was Virginia Barsic still alive?

A: I had thought so at the time.

Q: What made you think that?

A: She had moved.

Heard broke in, "I'm sorry. I can't hear that answer." Not waiting for instruction, Tina spoke up, "She was moving, or she had moved."

Tina, under continued questioning, related how she and Bob ran out the door and stood by the fence next to the VFW. Soon she saw Tammy emerge from the apartment and she and Bob urged Tammy to come with them. Tammy declined. A moment later Tina, leaving Bob at the fence next to the VFW, dashed back into the apartment to locate her shoes, found them in the front livingroom then ran back out to

Bob. Menefee tried to get her to recall what she saw on returning to the inside of the apartment. She related she had only a quick glance of Marv near Ginny, no more. She was trying to keep from looking. She grabbed her shoes and ran back out.

Menefee could get no more clear visual sighting of the on-going murder of Ginny from Tina. He was able to track Tina and Bob on the bus to Ocean Shores, and that Tina and Bob got a brief glimpse of the four of them standing in front of the mini-mart while she and Bob were on the bus going out of Ocean Shores. In his last few questions before relinquishing to the defense Menefee took Tina back to the apartment and established that Sonja Cortell slept through the entire assault curled up by the carved Indian in the livingroom; that during the assault against Ginny, Marv had nothing on except a pair of sweat pants, at least as she remembered. And that "No", she had no idea that Ginny was going to be murdered prior to the attack. Then from Menefee, "Nothing further your honor."

As before, Heard took over the cross examination. The attorney brought the questioning back to when Tina and Tammy were in the back bathroom. In his questioning Heard, as other attorneys, detectives and police officers before him, got mixed up on Tammy's and Tina's first names, being similar in sound. However, Heard corrected and went on.

Tina stated, while in the bathroom, Tammy told her they were going to kill Ginny, then Tammy qualified it all by saying, "-They wouldn't really do that. They're just trying to scare us." Heard, as with Bob and Tammy, brought up the subject of her first statement with the police, shortly after she and Bob were picked up in Olympia. At one point during Heard's questioning, Tina became almost defiant:

Q: You did tell the police in your statement that you started helping her pack her clothes, right?

A: Well, I stood by her a couple seconds, momentarily, yes.

Q: That's not what your statement says, is it Ms. Murphy?

A: Don't change my words.

Q: I'm sorry?

A: Don't change my words.

Heard left the bath room activity, and reconstructed her's and Bob's experience of leaving the apartment, observing them all from a secluded grassy place, catching the bus to Ocean Shores, and briefly observing them again in front of the mini-mart from the bus going out of town heading for Hoquiam. Then Heard got to the question that seemed to cry for an answer.

Q: Why didn't you go to the police, Ms. Murphy, and tell them that, I think there's something very bad going on at Hogans Corner; a lady is being assaulted. I don't know whether she's dead or alive?

A: Because it didn't seem like it really happened.

Q: What was going on inside that apartment didn't bother you in the least, then, did it?

A: Yes it did.

Q: Did it bother you enough to try to alert the authorities?

A: No, that thought did not even cross my mind.

Q: Well, when did it cross your mind?

A: When I was sitting in juvenile hall.

From this point on Tina's responses to Heard's questions were mostly vague or defiant: "I don't remember; I wasn't looking; I have no idea; Possiibly; Probably; I don't know; Maybe". Heard's last question to Tina before retiring from his cross examination, in reference to one of Tina's earlier responses,

Q: And you saw a small smudge of blood on Marv's chest?

A: Yes.

Heard then declared, "I have nothing further." From the judge, "Any redirect?" From Prosecutor Menefee, "No, your honor." The court then recessed at 2:36 p.m. It re-convened at 2:56 p.m.

Following the court's re-convening, Aberdeen and County officers, Robert Johnson, Lane Youmans, Douglas Smythe, Michael Haymon, each in that order, were sworn in and took their turns at the stand. Each related his part and experience in the investigation and apprehension of Marvin Garba, and Marv's admitting to his part in the death of Mrs. Virginia Barsic. Menefee then declared "The State rests, your honor." The judge then excused the jury. At 4:12 p.m., the court was adjourned and directed to continue the following morning, at 9 a.m. Marvin Garba would then take the stand in his own defense.

At 9:04 a.m., with everyone in place, the judge indicated to Mr. Heard to proceed. The attorney began with, "May it please the court your honor, we'll call Marvin Garba."

Marv, without ankle or handcuffs, strolled up to the witness chair, turned, raised his right hand, and took the oath. All members of the jury, eyes fixed on Marv, followed his every movement.

Q: For the record, please state your full name and spell your last name.

A: My name is Marvin Grant Garba. G-a-r-b-a.

Q: How old are you, Marv?

A: I'm eighteen.

Q: Where were you born, Marv?

A: Arizona.

Q: What's your folk's name?

Heard, taking Marv through his childhood and family life, established that he had no real family life. He had never known his real father. His mother had several husbands and lovers. At five years old, his earliest memories were of excessive alcohol and sex. He would be left alone to fend for himself. And with his younger sister, he experienced heavy drinking in the family, what family there was.

Fuller spoke up with an objection: Since the insanity part of Marv's defense had been withdrawn then the trial should proceed relative to the events that had taken place at Hogans Corner. Heard responded that he felt the jury had a right to know of Marv's background. The judge agreed with Heard and directed him to continue.

Under Heard's continued line of questioning Marv related how, on one occasion, his step father stuffed him in a mattress, placed him behind the refrigerator and pushed the refrigerator against him.

Q: For what reason?

A: Because I'd run out of the house and go play with the other kids and he didn't want me to.

Marv went on to remember he was moved in and out of unstable households, and eventually sent to an orphanage. In time his mother took him from the orphanage. She now had a new husband and would try family life again. After a couple pretty good years his new stepdad began using a barber's type razor strap on Marv. His mother and stepdad both would use this razor strap on him. He observed his stepfather abusing Marv's sister. Marv declared that alcohol and drugs were in constant use in the house. His stepfather and mother finally separated while living in Michigan, then he, his mother and sister, moved to Oregon. He had an aunt and uncle living there. Marv had problems with his cousins. They were all into drugs and alcohol. He started using crack at age 13. Marv was stealing pot from his mom about this time. They would argue all the time. Marv's first jobs were working for farmers and nurseries. He saved his money in a jar in his room but his mother, who was always on welfare, would take it for her bar visits. They never had a house that eventually they would be evicted from. Marv continued describing beatings from his mom. His running away from home. His being locked in his room. He had been in physical fights with his mom, and on one occasion she struck him with a telephone because Marv was going to tell on her, to a boyfriend of her's, that she had found a new boyfriend. She also took a knife to him. He separated from his mother the previous year. The only time he remembered his mother being sober was when she didn't have the money to buy alcohol.

Marv worked at various restaurants in Newberg, often staying at shelters there. He had a hard time making any real friends there. Then he made friends with a young man near his age who would share drugs with him. The kind of drugs they were on were the kind that would make you taste light, hear color, and feel sound. These new drugs were so good, and so available, they were thinking about buying and selling them. His new friend had a mother and sister living near a place called Ocean Shores, Washington. They could "Fry" and "Grill" up there.

They quit their jobs in Newberg, took the bus to Ocean Shores, stayed with his friend's mother and sister at Hogans Corner for awhile, and found jobs in Ocean Shores almost right away. Marv then made friends with a new acquaintance named Craig Borman. He stayed with Craig for a few days who had a room with a friend named Dan.

Marv's first job in Ocean Shores was bussing tables at a nice restaurant called The Galley. But after a few days he was fired because he came in late, following a rock concert he had attended the night before. Then he got a job at the super market. After a month or so at this job Marv quit because he was thinking about going back to Oregon. But he had been having a good time in Ocean Shores, especially with his new friend Craig. They would 'party' nearly every night, with drugs and alcohol, which, according to Marv, were easily had if you knew the right people.

Heard, following his careful and skillful handling of Marv's early and growing-up life, bringing it all out for the jury's consideration, then brought Marv directly to the week-end that ended in horror. It all began with a not so innocent bus ride to Aberdeen. And they had money in their pockets.

Q: What were you and Craig doing, if anything, on Friday, August 23rd of this year?

A: Going to town looking for women.

Q: What time did you go into town.?

A: We took the 12:40 p.m. bus out of Ocean Shores.

Marv stated that neither of them had been drinking, and only started drinking at about 5 p.m., sometime after arriving in Aberdeen. They had got a bum to purchase a case of beer for them. Then they met up with one of Craig's friends, Bob Noonan, and his girlfriend. According to Marv they all drank some beer and smoked some pot; the pot having been purchased about the time they acquired the case of beer. Then they met two girls who had just got off the bus coming in from Olympia. They had some baggage with them. Bob's girlfriend had recognized one of them. Then they all kind of paired off; Marv and Sonja, Craig and Tammy, Bob and his girlfriend Tina.

Marv's story as to how they all got out to Ocean Shores with Craig's friend Dan; looking around for a motel there, and ending up at the apartment building at Hogans Corner agreed perfectly with all the other testimony. He included that if they couldn't stay at the apartment they would build a fire in the sand and stay the night on the beach. But at the apartment they were in luck. After being told upstairs that they were not wanted, then on going back downstairs Marv noticed everyone going into the apartment below. Marv and Craig both had met Ginny before, Marv having roomed upstairs for a few days before moving in with Craig in town. Ginny was, "-a nice lady."

Again, Marv's recollection of Friday night, Saturday, and Sunday all agreed with previous testimony. Around 1 p.m. Sunday he and Craig, Marv remembered, were standing out in front of Ginny's apartment looking over at the Texaco mini-mart and discussing stealing a car, any car, and drive down to Portland. But they ruled it out because there was only one road out of the town. They were sure to get caught. Later that evening, Marv, by himself, was thinking about robbing the Gull mini-mart across the street. Then he and Craig talked about stealing the van from the people upstairs. They were pretty drunk at that time, and running around in their underwear. Heard asked if there was a plan to rob the super market. Yes, they had a plan to take the night deposit by force, by waiting behind the car belonging to the store manager who would be taking it to the bank. They would jump out at the right moment, take the manager to the jetty, drop him off there, drive back to Hogans Corner, leave the manager's car there, steal the van and drive down to Oregon. Then there was a plan to rob Ginny. Marv said he didn't like the plan at first because he liked Ginny. She was a nice lady. But nothing was coming together and Marv wanted to get down to Oregon. They thought having the NyQuil would put her to sleep. And it did for awhile. Marv stated that Bob and Tina had no knowledge of their plans to rob Ginny.

Ginny had gotten up and out of her back bedroom, came in and started telling them all they had made a mess of her house and would have to leave. Her house was a disaster. And they should clean it up. Ginny went to the hall bathroom, very agitated. Marv stated he had taken a "hit" of LSD just before approaching Ginny, who came out of the hall bathroom. Marv stated that he just wanted to calm her down. Heard stated that there was previous testimony about a pillow, and could Marv explain that. Marv answered that he remembered the pillow, and that somebody, he couldn't remember who, had handed it to him. There was a blur of arms everywhere. Heard went on with his questioning.

Q: Marv, I want you to tell the jury, please, when you went toward that bathroom, did you have any intention of killing or even assaulting Virginia Barsic.

A: No, I didn't. I had no intention. Why? She was a nice lady. There would be no reason for it, Okay? Let's put it this way, what kind of lady would take six kids, four of which she had no idea who they were, in to her house, let us stay there, feed us. There's no reason to even be angry with her.

As to Bob's, Tammy's, and Tina's testimony on the stand, which he observed the last two days, he said some of it was true while other of their testimony was not. Marv went on to say, at Dan's he agreed to take the whole rap if they were caught. Then he said he especially didn't want Craig to loose his chance to go to college. Marv said Craig cared a great deal about that. It scared him.

Q: And yet you told the police that Craig stabbed her a few times in the back. Is that correct?

A: He didn't do that till after she was dead.

Q: I beg your pardon?

A: He didn't do that until after she was dead.

Q: Tina Murphy testified she said, "You can't be killing this lady. You can't do this." Did that in fact happen?

A: It's possible.

Marv went on to relate, responding to Heard's questioning, how he had tried to smother her with the pillow, but Ginny had fought back, clawing and screaming. He wanted to stop her clawing. He stabbed her in the eyes with the screwdriver, then with his fingers. He tried breaking her neck. He would get up, someone would tell him she was moving and still alive. He would turn, and there she was again, trying to sit up. Marv would jump on her again and try to finish it. After the screwdriver, he asked for a knife. He thinks Craig got it for him. Ginny was becoming like a "zombie". Marv said, "I killed you. You're dead." But she would sit up again. "I was trying to get her to stop moving." Now on her side, and with the knife, he continued to stab her until she stopped moving.

Q: Why did you drink the blood?

A: First kill. For strength.

For protection, Marv used Ginny's blood to paint, "-a tree and the earth on my chest."

Q: Why did you need that protection, Marv, if she was already dead?

A: Because I didn't want her to get up again.

Heard referred back to the pathologist's testimony that, despite all of the stab wounds and other injuries to the body none had severed a major artery. And that no one wound would have been sufficient to cause immediate death.

And instead of Marv's claim that he hip-threw her six feet, considering the size of the hall,

Q: "More like three feet?"

A: "More like four feet."

Heard presented a color photo of the body as it was found by the police, indicating it was only partly covered with dirt. Marv insisted that he and Craig left the body on the mound completely covered.

Appealing to Marv to look in to his "heart of hearts", did he plan to kill Ginny? His answer was, "No". Marv stated that he was sorry. "I can not apologize enough for that. It happened".

Q: You realize that you will have to pay for what you did?

A: Yes, I do.

Q: And you accept that punishment?

A: Yes I do, I have no choice but to accept it. Heard, then turned to the judge, saying, "That's all I have." The judge, scanning the room, and stopping at the jury, said, "Ladies and Gentlemen, we're going to take a break at this time before we start cross examination. We'll recess until about five minutes to eleven." The time was 10:40 a.m.

The trial actually resumed at 10:52. With Menefee in support and remaining at the prosecutors table, Fuller rose and approached Marv, now having returned to the witness chair.

It is interesting to note; throughout Heard's examination of Marv, the young defendant's manner was relaxed, cooperative, and even helpful. Marv would often look over at the jury, to clarify an expression of drug jargon he had just used, or to help the jury to understand a physical move he may have made while in the process of assaulting Ginny.

There was no hostility in Marv's face as the young assistant prosecutor began his cross examination.

Q: After your arrest, did you tell any of the law enforcement officers that you had taken LSD at any time during that week-end?

A: No, I did not.

Q: So, you intentionally lied or withheld that information from them?

Heard broke in, "Objection! That's argumentative!" The judge overruled, and indicated Fuller to proceed. Fuller repeated his question, and Marv answered, " Yes."

Q: You also didn't tell your friends that you had it, did you?

A: That is not correct.

Q: Who beside you knew that you had this LSD?

A: Craig knew, and Sonja saw me tripping out while walking down the road.

Fuller got Marv to admit that none of his other companions knew that he had LSD. Fuller was attempting to establish that Marv had no LSD at all that weekend. Marv declared he had taken "two hits" that weekend. Fuller asked Marv if anyone had seen him take LSD. Marv admitted no one saw him take any. Fuller asked Marv when did he take these two hits. Marv stated that he took one just before his plan to rob the Gull Station. Fuller stayed with Marv's robbery plans; to rob the Gull Station; to steal a car at the Texaco Station; to steal a van from the people upstairs from Ginny; to rob the super market; and to rob Ginny. Why were all these robberies planned? To make a run to Oregon, Marv said.

Q: You were desperate to get to Oregon?

A: Yes.

Q: To get to your LSD source?

A: One of the reasons, yes.

Marv implicated Craig as being part of all robbery plans. He and Craig went upstairs to locate the keys to the van. The family upstairs interrupted them, so they had spaghetti instead. Shortly, according to Marv, they came back down to Ginny's apartment. He and Craig discussed how Ginny was getting angry, about the mess in the apartment and finding out about their drug run to Oregon. Referring to Marv's earlier statement he made in the Aberdeen Police Station,

Q: You told Sergeant Johnson that you turned to Craig and said "It's time."

A: Yes, I did.

Q: "It's time", meaning it's time to kill Ginny Barsic?"

A: Yes, I did.

At this point Fuller was trying to establish if in fact Marv was the only one who actually killed Ginny.

Q: You said Craig stabbed Mrs. Barsic, didn't you?

A: Yea.

Q: If you were trying to protect Craig, why didn't you just say--

A: Because I also forgot to mention the woman was dead when he did this.

Q: But if you're trying to protect Craig, why didn't you say, Hey, everybody left and ran out the door and I stayed?

A: Because Tammy had caught Craig stabbing her after she was dead. If the cops would have asked her, she would have said that, and then it would--

Q: so Tammy was telling the truth then, when she said that she saw Craig--

A: Stab her, yes.

After the assault, and over at Dan's, Fuller brought out that he and Craig had talked over some plan of explanation that would put the blame mostly on himself. Now, back in the apartment during the assault,

Q: You took this three-fingered hold?

A: Two to one, yeah.

Q: Two fingers?

A: Two to one.

Marv then demonstrated with his fingers to Fuller and to the jury.

Q: And that didn't work?

A: Eventually worked.

Marv went on to demonstrate his choking and eye gouging techniques he used.

Q: All right, you started to stand up and someone said, "She's not dead, She's still alive".

A: Yes.

Q: And you turned around and found the screwdriver?

A: Yes.

Marv explained he spotted the screwdriver in the corner less than two feet from him, reached over, grabbed it, then looking down at Ginny, began stabbing her eyes with it. And he may have stabbed her in other places with it. But this method wasn't killing her. Someone said, "She's still alive." Still in a sitting position over her, he said, "Get me a knife. Get me a knife." He wanted to finish it. Marv admitted, after being handed the knife he stabbed her in the chest, in the eyes, and tried to cut her throat. Marv, no longer able to stand looking at her face, turned her over and began stabbing her in the back.

Q: And when you finally decided she was dead you did this "first kill" business, drink her blood and painted your chest with her blood?

A: Yes.

With more questioning from Fuller, Marv rememb-ered being asked to take a shower, which he did. He suggested cutting up Ginny's body but that wasn't necessary, they would bury her. On dragging her body out to the mound Marv remembered seeing stars. He didn't have a flashlight but thought he and Craig had covered her completely. On Fuller's suggesting that he and Craig might not have done a good job of burying her, Marv answered, "That's a possibility." Marv also said, "We stepped back and we couldn't see her. So we decided that was alright." On his last question to Marv, Fuller asked, "You're telling us the truth today?" Marv answered, "Yes." Fuller then looked over to the judge and said, "Nothing further."

On re-direct examination Heard asked Marv about his plan to steal the van from the people upstairs, go down to Oregon, buy acid and come back up to sell it in the Ocean Shores area. Marv answered, "No, I was not going to come back up and sell it. I was going to give it to Craig and he was going to come back because he was going to college here." Heard then brought from Marv that he had no premed-itation of killing Ginny on his first approach to her as she came out of the hall bathroom.

Q: Marv, you seem adamant about the fact that she was dead when you started to get up the first time. Even today, in your mind, was she alive or dead at that point?

A: I'm not sure. At that time I believed that she was dead and trying to get up to attack me. Heard then stated, "Thank you. That's all I have."

On re-cross examination, with Marv still in the witness chair, Fuller asked, "All right, and you and Craig, when in Portland, were going to buy some LSD?" Marv answered, "I was going to buy some for him and he could come back up." There were no further questions put to Marv. And no exceptions made, from either the defense or the prosecution.

Marvin returned to his table, the judge instr-ucted the Jury, then directed that closing summat-ions were next in order. Fuller was first. There was no question of murder having taken place. The argument was, was it premeditated; murder in the first degree? Or was it an act that took place during a violent argument, with no thought of murder in the beginning; murder in the second degree? Fuller argued passionately that from the witnesses testimony, including some of Marv's own words, that premeditation was in the defendant's mind, moment to moment, all during the struggle, right up to the death of Ginny. Fuller's closing arguments lasted a little more than half an hour. He asked justice for Ginny, and justice for the people of the State of Washington.

Heard began his summation on Marv's miserable and abused background which preceded his drug habits. Habits that gave him an escape from his tormented life. Drugs where he could feel sound, hear color, and taste light. He was no longer in full control of his senses. He didn't wish to hurt Ginny, to calm her down perhaps , but not to hurt her. It all got out of hand. Heard was equally passionate in his hopes that the jury would take pity on Marv, and bring in a verdict of second degree murder.

With the judge's announcement that the trial was complete he then directed the jury to retire from the courtroom and deliberate upon their verdict. The time was 2:10 p.m., Friday, November 22nd, 1991; Exactly 13 weeks from the time the six young people were coming together at the bus station in Aberdeen.

On this final day of Marv's trial Joyce was with me. We stayed to ourselves, in a row of seats behind the prosecutors table. There were no more than six people occupying seats around us. The nicely dressed attentive woman, always a few seats to my right, got up and departed the courtroom. Out in the third floor lobby she was joined by a casually dressed neat young man in his early twenties. I noticed earlier he always sat in a row by himself, well back in the courtroom. Leaning forward, arms resting on the top row in front of him, his head resting on his arms, he would be intently studying the drama of the trial in front of him.

Walking down the marble stairs to the ground floor, Joyce made a stop at the ladies room. She would meet me outside near the courthouse steps. Then we would stay around and see if the jury would return with an early verdict.

For years I had been attempting to quit smoking, not because of all the anti smoking news in the media, but simply because I should. I had turned to chewing gum but still occasionally carried a pack of cigarettes in one of my pockets. I shook one out, and lit it. On descending the steps just outside the courthouse, I couldn't help noticing the woman with the young man off to my right. They were standing over near the flag pole, in what appeared to be in deep conversation.

Not wishing to disturb their privacy I waited a few moments until their conversation had ended. They were just forlornly standing there. I felt they must be related to Ginny in some way. Cane in hand, and putting my cigarette out, I walked up to them. If I had had a hat on I would have removed it. My six foot one inch frame seemed to tower over them. I asked if I could be of any assistance.

Firmly staring up at me, she asked, "Are you a reporter or something?"

"No maam!", I answered. Without giving her a chance to respond, and truly wanting to put her at ease, I continued, "I'm just an American citizen, Maam. And I am interested in Mrs. Barsic's two sons who I understand are in the Navy."

Still not quite sure, she gave me a partial smile, and said, "This is one of them right here." Turning to the young man, just a bit taller then she, I smiled, held out my hand, and he took it.

I soon learned their names; Mrs. Martha Duncan, and Seaman Allen Duncan. Mrs. Duncan was a distant cousin to Ginny. Her home was over in Kirkland, near Seattle. Allen was on humanitarian leave from his ship down in San Diego. Allen referred to the woman as his "Aunt Martha." They were both staying in a motel in Ocean Shores. I was glad to see Joyce coming down the steps, and walk over to us.

Following polite introductions, Allen put his hands in his pockets and with a partial smile said he needed to take a walk around the block. Martha let him go, then turning to Joyce and me, she said. "Isn't this a terrible thing?" She shuddered and said, "Where is everyone? Don't they care?"

"I think so, Maam.", I answered. "They're probably all just working right now." Joyce added, "Everyone's keeping up with it, I think." Joyce went on to say she thought one of the spectators in the courtroom was a reporter for the Aberdeen news. I knew the woman was holding back tears.

"Can we sit down somewhere?", Joyce asked, looking around. And the three of us walked over and sat on the seat just off the walkway leading to the far side of the courthouse. On asking about the other children, Martha stated that the other son in the Navy was going through shock and was in counseling aboard his ship which was back in Norfolk, Virginia. Ginny's other son, following the funeral services, was over in Montana staying with relatives there. Ginny's two daughters, also in their early twenties, were down in the San Diego area, having nightmares and trying to hold down their jobs. One was working in a Target store in a shopping mall just out of San Diego. Allen was hyper and extremely restless, she said. Every night he could barely sleep. Martha, on the phone each evening, was trying to keep the family around the country informed.

At one point she asked, "What are you doing here? Sometimes I think everyone ought to be here, and then other times I think no one should be here, it's all so horrible."

Clumsily I tried to answer, "Well Maam, we're retired, at least I am. And we don't live so far away." Helplessly trying to find some better words, I added, "You're a darn sight better man then I am, carrying that kind of load on you." She said she was glad we were there, and then her tears burst, and flowed. Between sobs, and catching her breath, she said, "Ginny was a good girl. Whatever her faults, she didn't deserve that stuff."

Leaving the two women to talk some more I got up in time to see Allen coming back from his walk. I tried to find out what he did in the Navy. He was in no mood to talk about that, so we just walked around together. At one point I left him with the two women and went down the street and brought back some coffee for the four of us.

At a little after 5 p.m. one of the men with the prosecutor's office came over to us and said the court was being re-convened. We thought the jury was coming back having reached their verdict. But it was not to be, at least for the moment. Up in the courtroom, with everyone in place again, the jury foreman stood up and declared they had not reached a verdict as yet and requested adjournment for the weekend. The judge, after checking with both counsels, agreed. He warned the jury not to discuss the case with anyone, then he granted the adjournment until Monday morning at 9 a.m.

Back out on the courthouse steps, Martha said she would drive Allen back to the motel in Ocean Shores, pick up her things, then drive home to Kirkland. She would be back at the courthouse on Monday morning. Meanwhile, Allen would stay at the motel. He was acquainted with the motel manager there. Also he wanted to get together with Greg Barsic that evening and on Saturday.

Joyce and I offered, if we could be of any assistance to please let us know. We gave our phone number to Allen and Martha both.

Joyce did not have to work that Saturday so we slept in until around nine. We woke up to a heavy rain and wild wind outside. After our showers I fixed a fire in the fireplace while she made the breakfast. We occasionally talked about what must be going through that whole family right then. Then the phone rang. It was Allen. He was with Mr. Barsic at Allens' motel apartment. And would I be available to take them out to Damon Point. They had no car between them. They wanted to pay a short visit to the place where his mother's ashes were scattered. It was about 10:30 a.m. They had already had breakfast.

I asked Allen to give me 15 minutes and I would be right over, then we hung up. Joyce was observing the miserable weather outside, and after my telling her of the phone conversation, she said, "After their visit with Ginny bring them back here if you can. I'll keep the fire going, straighten up the house, and have some hot lunch waiting for them."

"I think they'll need it.", I said, after coming around the glass breakfast table for one more cup of coffee. Glancing outside at the worsening weather, I then went to the living room closet and pulled out my old wool-lined Navy jacket.

Driving up Ocean Shores Boulevard, the windshield wipers clearing my vision ahead, I thought about Greg Barsic. Why he had not been at the trial. But I was to discover he was a very tender-hearted man. He tried the first day but could not stand it thereafter. He was counting on Allen to keep him posted. But Allen was just as tender-hearted as Greg. However, Allen simply felt he had to be there.

They were both ready and standing in the rain as I drove up. Reaching over I opened the door for them. Greg, who I had never met, climbed in the rear, put his hand forward and we shook hands. With Allen up front with me I drove off and drove around the first opening I came to, then we were on our way back down Ocean Shores Boulevard.

There was not much talk on the drive. From the back seat, Greg said he had heard from Allen about Joyce and my sincere interest in the whole affair and that he was truly grateful. I answered that Joyce and myself would be available for any assistance they might need.

After driving past Point Brown then heading east, we came to the clearing at the Marina. Because of the rain I almost missed the right turn. I stopped, backed up, then got on the gravel road leading out to Damon Point. Driving out as far as I safely could, I put the Olds in park, turned off the engine, then we all got out. The rain was really coming down hard, and I felt bad for not bringing foul weather coats for them. I stayed several paces behind as they walked up to the jagged perch from where Ginny's ashes had been scattered there almost three months earlier.

The salt water churned in noisy confusion below them. Out across the bay whitecaps danced off irregular swells coming in on the tide. A freighter was heading out to sea, pushing up white water at her bow. Despite the nasty weather a patch of blue was showing up behind the rain cloud's northward movement.

The two men turned away, then we got back in the Olds. They were soaked to the skin. I was probably much dryer then they were. And I think they fully expected to be driven right back to their motel. Going up Ocean Shores Boulevard, I made the left turn at Butter Clam Road, and another left turn onto Sand Dune Way, and we were home.

Once inside, you could smell and hear the nice crackling fire Joyce had kept going in the fireplace. Coming up the inside passage to our top floor livingroom the pleasant aroma of fresh coffee and clam chowder was enough to warm anybody up. And it did. Joyce also had hot tuna sandwiches for us. Our livingroom view of the Pacific Ocean and the weather outside indicated that patch of blue had widened. The wind was still strong but the gray clouds had given way to a chilly sunny afternoon. Both men warmed up by the fire.

Our conversations stayed light. While Joyce talked with Greg I went over and turned on our large TV screen to see what was happening with the 'Apple Cup'. The Washington Huskies were playing the Washington Cougars. The game ended with a final score; Huskies 56 to the Cougars' 21. Allen sat with me for awhile. He seemed to get interested, then became restless. He walked out on the weather deck. Paced around a bit then came back in to the game. The game was over and I turned the TV off. We warmly talked awhile longer, then both men decided it was time for them to go. They truly thanked us for the hospitality. And on Monday morning would Joyce and I pick up Allen at the motel? We assured them we would do exactly that. With that, Joyce wished them both well and kissed each one on the cheek. Then I drove them back to the motel.

On Sunday morning, as I also later learned, a church congregation in Ocean Shores was being urged by its Pastor to pray for a just verdict for Ginny, and prayers for Ginny's family.

Monday morning, at about 8 a.m. we spotted Allen standing in front of the motel with his sea bag at his side waiting for us. Joyce had three thermoses of coffee for the 45 minute trip back to Montesano. We talked very little during the drive. Mrs. Martha Duncan was already waiting at the courthouse steps as I drove up. I let Joyce and Allen out then found a place to park.

Joining the three of them at the bottom of the steps I found there was no word from the jury as yet. Bringing the thermos bottles with me, we all had some coffee together. Allen and Martha spoke of the many phone calls they had made and received from family members around the country. Allen had been in touch with his uncle in Australia over the weekend. His uncle had invited Allen to come and visit with him for awhile. Allen was strongly considering it.

Attorney Jim Heard was out on the top step leading into the courthouse. He was alone having a smoke, and very much in a sad faced attitude. Leaving Joyce with Martha and Allen I walked up and joined him with a smoke of my own. Heard was aware of my presence throughout the trial. We shook hands. Our conversation continued on the extreme difficulty some young people have growing up in todays society. Heard was a liberal minded attorney, and had handled many cases involving civil rights violations. He was appointed to take the Garba case. Heard felt the jury would probably bring in a verdict of murder in the first degree. He also felt that Garba was truly dangerous, to himself as well as to others. And that he probably hated all women. I found Heard a very warm-hearted man, a man who would do the best job he could under the Constitution and with any client he was appointed to defend. I also found him intellectually interesting. He read deep literature and enjoyed classical music.

The morning wore on and around 11:30 we learned that the jury was still out, and was then having lunch. Which of course meant that Martha, Allen, Joyce and I might find time for a quick lunch ourselves. We went to a nice old-fashioned european style restaurant about a block down from the courthouse, and had soup and sandwiches.

On our walk back up to the courthouse we met Mr. Menefee and Mr. Fuller. They were most kind and courteous to Martha and Allen, and even to Joyce and myself. They were confident of the jury reaching a proper verdict, and soon. Soon was the word. We were all notified about 12:30 p.m. that the jury had indeed reached its verdict and would shortly be entering the jury box.

Being a little slower then the rest *, I followed behind and arrived in the courtroom just as the bailiff announced "All rise!" Then, after everyone was seated, I walked in. Joyce was next to Martha who was in the same seat she had occupied throughout the trial. Allen was at his back row, looking like he might wish to be left alone. Also present was a bearded young man with a small note pad, who I took to be a reporter for the Aberdeen news. I sat down next to Joyce.

All the attorneys were in place before the judge. Marv, handcuffed, was seated beside his attorney. "Ladies and gentleman of the jury, have you reached a verdict?" The foreman rose and announced, "We have, your honor." "What is your verdict?" "We find the defendant, Marvin Garba, guilty of murder in the first degree."

* *On 17 Feb. 1945, at Iwo Jima, the author received gunshot injuries to his left hip.*

CHAPTER EIGHT: 2ND TRIAL; JURY DELIBERATES; RESULTS

"On behalf of Grays Harbor County, indeed all the people of the State of Washington, I wish to congratulate you in reaching your decision." Speaking to the jury, seated at his right, Judge Spencer continued. "This was an horrendous case of great tragic and violent proportions. We are living in a day and age where many people in our land are feeling that our justice system is breaking down. You, ladies and gentleman, have proved otherwise. Again I want to thank you. You are dismissed." Turning to the prosecution and defense counsels, the judge announced that sentencing will be conducted at a later date. And to the courtroom in general, "This trial is concluded."

The bearded reporter, in his late twenties, approached Allen as he walked out of the courtroom. Allen of course was relieved over the verdict. The reporter quoted him as saying, "I'm just happy it worked out this way. It's been a hell'ova a week."

Down on the courthouse steps Joyce and I stood back from Allen as he embraced his Aunt Martha. They had some words together, then they walked over to us. Martha said she needed to make some calls, and would not be going back to Kirkland until late that evening. Allen had decided to leave for Australia, and would catch the next bus out of Aberdeen, heading toward Sea-Tac Airport.

On splitting up, Allen said he would not make the Borman trial. Martha said she hoped we might sit with her through that trial. It was scheduled to commence some time in early January. Joyce said that we would try. With Martha having departed, Allen asked if we could get him and his sea bag to the Montesano bus station, which we did.

It was some time before the bus departed, so that gave us a chance to talk a while. Allen was still very much in grief over the loss of his mother, and the way it happened. But he was not a vindictive young man and, I sensed that before his mother's death he had been quite liberal in his views. He now felt the other three ought to receive some kind of punishment too. Including Garba, Borman and Tammy, they were all guilty of something, if only just negligence. He was, however, sure they hadn't participated as strongly as Garba and Borman, considering all the testimony. And Tammy; she at least pleaded guilty. Tammy had approached him during one of the recesses from the trial to express her shame and sorrow. And Allen accepted it as best he could under the circumstances. At one point during our conversation, he looked up at the bright blue sky, free from rain clouds, and said, "The sun came out for my mom today." Joyce then told him that our home was always open to him. And that she was sure that the people of Grays Harbor County were terribly saddened over his mothers death, and that everyone was surely wishing him well.

Allen was now without any living parents. Joyce and I were old enough to be his grandparents, and being a young man, I thought I should also try to make a worthwhile point or two for him: Grieve of course, but his mom would surely want him to find happiness and move on with his life, which she was so proud of. Joyce and I expressed our warm agreement over his decision to visit his uncle in Australia. The bus came and he left with it.

The Craig Borman trial would take place in about forty days. We had a full schedule ourselves for the rest of the year and time would go by fast. That evening, after the Garba trial, I stopped off for a short visit with Greg Barsic at the small trailer he was temporally staying in, in Ocean Shores. He was of course relieved on hearing the news of the conviction. I asked Greg if he had a recent picture of Ginny. From his wallet he drew out a bent and ragged edged color photo of his wife. One look and I immediately recognized her as the same lady who assisted me many months earlier.

We had only a few days to get ready for London. Just before our departure, I took a chance and sent a letter off to Governor Booth Gardner, with a copy of Ginny's Obituary and an accompanying article from the North Coast News. While I assured him of my awareness that many such tragic cases had been reported on in various areas around the State, indeed around the nation, during the past year, I was hoping he might respond in some way to Ginny's family and her community on what appeared to have been simply a middle aged woman who had befriended six young people to spend the night at her apartment when they had no other place to stay, and then lost her life doing it.

From Sea-Tac, Joyce and I arrived at London's Heathroe Airport on a cold December 3rd evening. We were met by a young American naval officer who assured us all accommodations and schedule was set and waiting. After about an hour's drive we passed through the guarded gate of Upper Heyford RAF Base. Our apartment for our entire two weeks stay was at the BOQ on that famous airbase; famous for its part in the air defense of southern England during the Nazi Blitz of 1940.

There are unique times that come along in anyone's life that simply do not lend themselves to words. This was surely one of them. Can the reader understand: We took Ginny with us. She needed some fun and a brake from that terrible trial as we did. And she was with us most every moment.

The purpose for our being in England resulted from invitations from there for us to come and sign copies of a book I had authored some years earlier. It having to do with the only battleship that got underway during the attack on Pearl Harbor. The Allied Nations were recognizing the 50th anniversary of the attack, which of course brought the United States into World War Two. The book had been in print almost continuously since it was first published in 1974. The book was no longer available in regular book stores but was continuing to do very well in military exchanges around the world. Part of the proceeds from the book's sales were being given to the American Navy and Marine Corps Relief Society. Joyce and I had always payed our own way and paid our living and room expenses while on such invited adventures. It was always a lot of fun, and it gave me a chance to get next to the younger people now involved in our military.

With Joyce always at my side, I signed copies at two RAF bases. Then on the 6th and 7th of December I signed copies at the military exchange at the American Embassy at Grosvenor Square. Then, with all available copies nearly sold out, the following week found us completely on our own. The Brit-Rail passes, which Joyce had purchased earlier, allowed us to board trains and travel through the country side; down to South Hampton, up to Oxford, and over to York. While visiting Warwick Castle we climbed through Guy's and Ceasar's towers. Then on our way up through Scotland we passed near Lockerby, where the downing of the 747 took place the previous year. Every train station had Christmas carolers singing for the throngs of bustling people traveling through or waiting at these stations. Perhaps the high point of our adventure took place near Saint Paul's in London Town. A Chief Security Inspector, Mr. John Whitehead, who we accidentally met in London, gave us a grand tour of Old Baily Courthouse where countless famous, or infamous, trials had taken place over the past 200 years. Hogans Corner and Montesano were seldom from my mind.

We had a marvelous time and met so many truly kind people while in Merry Ole England. Probably the nicest experience we had was on our walk around Berkley Square. The weather was bitter cold, no one else around, as we carefully observed the little romantic messages carved on park benches, left by lovers probably long since gone, about their own appreciation for that beautiful park. For us it became time to leave England and go back home. As we were boarding the plane for Sea-Tac we learned that the IRA had set off terrorist bombs in several rail stations around England. Anyway I had a book signing scheduled for the weekend before Christmas, at McChord Air Force Base near Tacoma, Washington. Then our Marilyn would be home for Christmas. We would take flowers to Damon Point.

The second week of January, 1992, came and that found Joyce and myself giving thoughts to the Craig Borman trial. It was, from a learning call to the clerks office, firmly scheduled to commence, with jury selection on 7 January. With the new year and people trying to pay off Christmas bills we guessed there probably would be even less people in the spectators section of the courtroom than during the Garba trial. Mrs. Martha Duncan would be there, and likely alone if we didn't attend with her. Anyway, we had something very special for her. Immediately on our return to Ocean Shores from England, and picking up our mail from the post office, we pleasantly discovered a most kind letter from Governor Gardner. And we were anxious to get it in to Martha's hands. It certainly wouldn't take the place of Ginny, but it might help with the pain the whole family must still be suffering from. Greg Barsic was very appreciative of the Governor's kind words. Greg talked to me of his wish to some day publish all of Ginny's poems. Above all, Joyce and I figured, since we had come this far with the court case we should see it through to its end.

It was a cold gray morning, Tuesday, January 7th, when I backed the Olds out of the garage to begin our trip to Montesano. Not many visitors come to Ocean Shores this time of year so Joyce was able to get most of the week off. Down at her office her co-worker and best friend in town, Helen Christerson, would handle what few calls might come in for beach rentals. After closing the garage door Joyce climbed in beside me with her two thermos bottles of hot coffee. She also brought along a small wicker basket containing several freshly baked muffins wrapped in a warm hand towel. Joyce was always doing little things like that. It had rained most of the night before so the roads were still wet, and you could feel and hear the wheels dashing thorough the many puddles along the way. The Olds was warm inside and Joyce pushed in an old Nat Cole tape she had found the last time we shopped at Fort Lewis Exchange.

Arriving at the courthouse it seemed there were fewer parking spaces available near the front than as before. Circling the courthouse block I came to a car that was obviously pulling out, so I waited a moment, then backed in to that empty space. Out on the courthouse steps we threaded our way through a number of people who were gathered there in small groups talking about their cases while out having their smoke.

At the now familiar third deck courtroom level Judge Spencer's east-wing was busy with maybe forty to fifty people inside as the judge heard and ruled on the many calender cases before him. Judge David Foscue's west-wing courtroom was not so busseling. Maybe a half dozen people in the spectators section there as the judge listened to the selection of prospective jurors. It was in this courtroom, with Judge Foscue presiding that the final legal testimony and conclusions would be heard and played out concerning the murder of Virginia Barsic.

Seated near the center aisle in the first row, and in the same firm alert manner was Mrs. Martha Duncan. Joyce quietly moved in and sat down beside her. And I followed in, sitting next to Joyce. The two women exchanged some quite words of greetings then we gave our attention to the legal proceedings underway in front of us.

Attorney John Farra was in the process of interrogating a prospective juror as to her ability and willingness to be fair with his client, the defendant Craig Borman, if she were selected to sit on the jury. She assured the defense attorney she could and would. "Despite all the adverse publicity Mr. Borman has received in the news media these past several months?" "Yes, certainly!" she answered. Farra, in his polite and strong voice, leaned forward on his table and continued his questioning of the woman: Had she ever sat on a murder trial before? Was she personally acquainted with any member of law enforcement people of Grays Harbor County? The woman answered no to each of his questions. The jury selection and questioning continued on through the morning, and with prosecuting attorney Gerald Fuller doing his best to obtain a strong jury who would fairly listen to the State's case against Craig Borman.

At around 11:40 a.m. Judge Foscue called for a

noon break. Martha, Joyce and myself had a light lunch at the Cook House restaurant near the main intersection of Montesano. Martha was most happy that we would be joining her during this second trial. She felt uneasy about it with so many weeks having lapsed between the two trials. We tried to assure her that the system would work to its just ends. Martha stated that Allen was now in Australia staying with his uncle there, and Ginny's two daughters down in the San Diego area were still in a bad way, still trying to cope with the loss of their mother. Martha would be spending her evenings at an Aberdeen motel for the duration of the trial.

Following the noon break the court went back into session. By 3:45 p.m. a jury had been selected from some forty candidates. Seven women and five men, with two female alternates. The Judge then gave the new paneled jury instructions and procedures as to periodic breaks during the trial, and briefly how a trial is expected to be conducted. Then, turning to the prosecution side of the arena, asked if the State was ready with its opening remarks. "We are, your honor!", declared Fuller. Leaving Detective Stocks at the table, who would assist him through-out the trial in keeping the agenda of witnesses and items of evidence in proper order, the 44 year old prosecuting attorney adjusted his glasses and walked over to address the jury.

With no dramatics of any kind but with conviction and sincerity Fuller outlined the murder case they must deal with for the next several days. He would bring to then some sixteen witnesses, and about seventy items of evidence for their careful consideration. Then Fuller described the events that led up to the murder of Virginia Barsic, the murder itself, and some of its aftermath. And he described how Craig Borman had a role in all of it, and shared with Marvin Garba the killing of Virginia Barsic. Fuller then told the jury that after they had considered all the testimony and evidence, he was confident they would bring in a verdict of murder in the First Degree, which was what the State of Washington was asking for. Fuller then thanked the jury for their attention then returned to his table. The time was 4:27 p.m. The judge then adjourned the court, to reconvene at 9 a.m. the following morning, Wednesday, 8 January 1992.

Even if there had been no heavy overcast it still would have been near dark outside with the sun having gone down at about 4:15 p.m. Out on the lighted courthouse walkway, with a dampness and chill in the air, Martha and Joyce shared some words of encouragement. We walked Martha to her car parked just across the street, said our goodnights and promised to see her again in the morning.

We were about five minutes early on this Wednesday morning. As Joyce and I came around, holding on to the third floor banister, we saw a number of people in various conversations who were standing in groups or sitting on chairs and benches just outside both courtrooms. Again a uniformed guard was escorting a line of mostly dark blue coveralled prisoners into courtroom number one; two were in orange colored coveralls. All were handcuffed together. Some of those in the prisoner line were females. Turning to our right into Judge Foscues courtroom, we found our same places over next to Martha. She had been even earlier then we. "All rise!"

With everyone in place and re-seated, the judge then directed Mr. Farra to make his opening statement for the defense. With Craig seated at his left, Farra got up, and like Fuller before him, walked over to face the jury. He then gave the defense's position. Farra freely stated that a terrible murder had indeed taken place. And that he and his client, "Mr. Borman", were deeply sorry for that. Farra, like Fuller, then proceeded to take the jury through events of how the young people met at the bus station in Aberdeen. He also admitted that everyone of them had been drinking and smoking marijuana. They were all having their kind of 'party'. And that they all had sex in Ginny's apartment. But that they, especially his client, were not being charged with that kind of misconduct. "Mr. Borman" was being charged with murder, of which he had nothing to do with. In fact, Farra went on, his client had a love for Ginny. Craig was living away from his parents during the summer months, when the crime took place, working in Ocean Shores and saving money preparing to go into coll-ege that fall. Farra warned the jury that the pro-secution would bring witnesses before them and pre-sent evidence which were all nothing more then cir-cumstantial at best. His client was not guilty, and he was confident that the jury would be fair and open, and would return Craig to his parents. Farra spoke to the jury for 37 minutes.

With Farra now back at his table, and with Craig seated on his left, the judge then addressed the jury. He advised them they were permitted to take notes if they so desired. Note pads and pencils were provided for all members of the jury.

There was no doubt about it; seated at the de-fense table some twenty feet over, to my left, Craig Borman had visibly made a remarkable change in himself. His manner and appearance were decid-edly different. He was no longer the cocky 'fun-and-games' young man I had observed four months earlier. Craig had a neat, college kind of appear-ance about him now. His blond hair was almost crew-cut, and he wore a light brown sweater over an open collard white shirt. His manner was completely bus-iness like and alert. Craig had neither the look of guilt nor innocence; he had the look of determin-ation on his boyish face. Joyce found it hard to believe this was the same young man she had observ-ved during the pre-trial hearings. Craig, I thou-ght, had a good attorney.

Directly behind the defense table and over the small wooden fence that separated the arena from the spectators section sat members of Craig's fam-ily, at least that's who they appeared to be. In this front row was his mother, sitting across the aisle from Martha, and who I took to be his father, another man, then another woman, and a girl of fourteen or fifteen. Then another woman of near age to Craig's mother. There were also a few people sitting just behind them in the second row. Sitting behind the prosecution's section; "Ginny's secti-on", we called it, was only Martha, Joyce and myself.

"The State calls Deputy Sheriff Steve Larson!", as its first witness. Larson, coming from the back of the courtroom, stepped up to the witness chair, which was identical to the one in the east-wing, and was sworn in. With Fuller taking him through the details again of how he had discovered Ginny's body, the prosecutor then stepped back to his table and returned with a number of eight-by-ten color photos of the body and the surrounding mound area, of which were admitted in evidence. Fuller's next witness was Detective Stocks. Stocks, leaving the prosecutors table for the witness chair, described again his part in being assigned in charge of the case and his discovery of various related items and circumstances at the crime scene. Then he returned to the prosecutors table. Additional items were admitted in evidence, including some of Ginny's clothing she wore at the time of her death. Blood stains, old mud and numerous knife holes were still visible for the jury to consider.

The State then called Sheriff's Officer Jeff Meyers, the officer who, with the aid of the Texaco mini-mart people, discovered bloody items that had been placed in the diesel rag container located just west of the Texaco station. The next witness called was Detective Youmans who described the violent condition which he found in the apartment. At the end of Youmans' testimony the judge called for a twenty minute break in the trial. It was 10:30 a.m.

Leaving Joyce and Martha to converse and go to the ladies room, I ventured down and stepped out onto the courthouse steps to have a smoke during the recess. Early on I found that if one really wants to catch some additional color and drama around courthouses they ought not to neglect the courthouse steps. On one occasion, during a recess, I overheard a group of five men talking about how they, or someone, had been caught and accused of stealing a generator. It was a huge industrial type generator which took several men to load it in the back of a pickup truck. When stopped by the police in Aberdeen none of the five young men knew how it got in the back of their truck. Some-one else must have put it there. These five young men had gone into a bar for a beer or two and when they came out the police were looking at the big generator in the back of their truck. Someone else must have put it there while they were in having their beer.

During another recess occasion, and while out on the steps, a young man asked me for a light which I obliged. He then told me how the cops just wouldn't lay off him and his "-blowing pot!". I suggested maybe it would be a good idea to give up blowing pot. He immediately answered, "I might as well give up rock and roll!" To that I gave him another suggestion, "Why not give up on rock and roll?" With a frown he replied, "I might as well give up on pot!" Still frowning, and obviously wanting to keep our conversation going, he stated, "You don't like rock music, do ya!" Without hesitation, I answered, "Yes I do. I particularly like Rachmaninov's Concerto Number Two in C minor, and Rachmaninov's Concerto Number One in F sharp minor." "Who are those guys?", he asked. Realizing I had probably been unfair, I went over to his rock music, and said, "I saw on CNN yesterday there's a new postage stamp coming out on Elvis Presley. Which do you like the old Elvis or the new Elvis?" Right away my friend answered with a smile, "The old Elvis, of course! Which do you like?" "Well," I answered, "I'm still thinking about it."

Now on this recess occasion, just after stepping outside, I came onto an argument of sorts taking place between a startling looking couple in their middle thirties. They were of medium height and both dressed all in black leather, with shiny chrome rings in place of buttons on their jackets. The man, with straggly long dark brown hair was a dead ringer for Charles Manson. And, coincidentally, the women was addressing him, "-you tell'um Charlie! They can't do that to us! You just tell'um so!"

'Charlie' was now looking more at me than at his female companion, and angerly he said, "Take my kid away from me, will he! I'm going back up there and kick Judge Spencer's ass, that's what I'm gona' do!"

"No Charlie!", the woman broke in, while holding his arm, "There's too many of 'um. Anyway, he might kick ass back."

Now I couldn't tell whether 'Charlie' was looking for encouragement or discouragement from me but he was sure looking at me strongly. I ventured an answer to him. "She just might have a point there Charlie. If I were you I'd listen to her."

With that, 'Charlie' continued looking at me pretty hard for a moment. Then, while turning back to his companion, he said "Come on! Let's get the hell out'a here!" He made one last remark that I could hear as they walked down the courthouse walkway. "It's still a free country, ain't it?"

Back up in Judge Foscue's courtroom the trial had re-convened. Detective Smythe was on the stand. And there were several more items which were being admitted in as evidence. Among them were included the long sleeved tan and wavy striped shirt rolled up inside the acid-washed blue jeans which Craig allegedly had tossed on to the right side of Highway 115 as he, Marv, Tammy, and Sonja had been walking to Ocean Shores. There were nine items in all, and each was carefully drawn from brown paper bags and held up to the jury for their consideration. At one point the bag containing the blood stained blanket split apart. And the blanket fell on the table.

Noon break was called for at 11:40 a.m. The judge stated the trial would re-convene at 1 p.m. Martha, Joyce and myself had our lunch again at the Cook House. The booth and tables there were comfortable and the food was good. Martha told us she had a small business of her own over in Kirkland; a nice house cleaning business that was doing pretty well considering so many couples having to work out of their homes together to make ends meet.

The trial became more interesting and heightened that afternoon. The next witness up for the State was Mr. Charles Soloman, a forensic crime lab technician who introduced almost a dozen items of matching blood samples, and types pertaining to

Ginny, Craig and his other companions of that weekend. Soloman was followed by Officer Mark Wade of the Ocean Shores Police. Wade being the first member of law enforcement to be called on to investigate a possible homicide which may had taken place out at Hogans Corner. He described his meeting with Marcie Swanson, and the polaroid photos she brought to the station with her. And his statement she had made concerning her afternoon meeting with Craig at the Gift Shop. With Wade now off the stand Fuller's next witness was Marcie herself. She had been waiting on a bench out in the lobby area between the two courtrooms for her name to be called.

Marcie, looking quite nervous and somewhat frightened, took the stand and began answering questions put to her by Fuller. There is of course no way that an attorney on either side of the arena can put questions to a young witness, or key witness, especially one who formerly was a close friend of the defendant, and make that witness feel completely at ease with his questions. But Fuller tried, and he had a murder trial to proceed with. Occasionally Marcie would look over at Craig who was leaning forward at his table intently listening to her answers. Fuller drew from her, not her entire statement she had made that previous summer evening, but key words and phrases of her statement she had signed her name to. At times Marcie was near tears and entirely inaudible. She described Craig's and Marv's plan to go down to Portland, and the last phone call she had had with Craig telling her to burn the photos. Marcie was finally excused from the stand, and before reaching the doors out of the courtroom she burst in to tears.

The very next witness brought to the stand, and who also had been waiting out in the lobby for his name to be called, was Dan. On the stand, Dan, tieless and simply dressed in a white shirt and dark pants, described himself as being a teacher from the Lake Quinault school district. Then, in response to Fuller's questions, described his part in bringing the six young people out to Ocean Shores and eventually dropping them off at Ginny's apartment. Dan was on the stand most of the afternoon, including after the afternoon recess. One of his last statements was that in his opinion Ginny, "-just liked having kids around her." She had no hostility towards any of the six youngsters.

Late in the afternoon Dan was followed by Robert Noonan to the stand. Bob, neatly dressed as during the Garba trial, was just as nervous as before. And at times would take a deep breath in an effort to compose himself. Though he had no sport coat or jacket on, his combed hair, clean shaven face, dark sweater over a white shirt and tie certainly gave him a better appearance than any member of the jury. They were all loosely attired. Of the men on the jury, not one had a tie or coat on, they were mostly in jeans and three of them had beards. Of the females on the jury, not one of them wore a dress. They were all in jeans or slacks. These were, however, obviously hard working people. From their ranks, here on the Olympic Peninsula, came such notable achievers as Elton Bennett of Hoquiam; certainly one of the finest silk screen artists the country has ever had. Originals and signed prints of his sensitive works are deeply appreciated and highly valued through out the Northwest. Another Olympic Peninsula man, hardly out of his teens, won the Congressional Medal of Honor for almost single handedly and successfully defending a critical base area during the war in Vietnam. Like Bennett, he no longer lives but his name lives on: USS Marvin Shields. Marvin was from Port Townsend, Washington.

Fuller brought Bob from the time he and his girlfriend Tina got together with Craig and his friends at the bus station, to Ginny's apartment. Coming right to the early morning of the murder. Bob recounted the same story he had given in the Garba trial. Bob testified he heard Craig call out "-get her, get her" as Ginny was fighting to pull away from Marv. Bob then testified that he saw Craig move to Ginny's feet and knelt down to hold her legs down at her ankles. Fuller asked Bob to come off the stand and demonstrate to the jury the position he remembered Craig being in as he held Ginny down at her ankles. Bob hesitated a moment, then got off the stand and knelt down. With one knee on the floor his other knee up Bob thrust his two hands out near the floor and held them there. He looked up at Fuller who said he could then return to the witness chair.

After quickly conferring with Craig at the defense table Farra got up and walked over to Bob. Bob did not change his story. After a few minutes Farra asked Bob about the 'blood brotherhood' ritual he, Craig and Marv had sworn together earlier that weekend. Bob admitted that it had occurred and that he did join Marv and Craig in that ritual. With no more questions from either the defense or prosecution, Judge Foscue adjourned the trial. The time was 4:30 p.m.

At 9:02 a.m. on Thursday, another grey cold morning, the State's next witness was Tammy Muller. She also was neatly dressed; in white blouse, dark slacks and low heeled shoes. Her blonde hair was combed out in large waves around her head. She went through the same story as in the Garba trial. Most every point Fuller brought out from her she gestured with her arms and hands. On several occasions her chin would crinkle up and quiver as if in a cross from being angry or on the verge of tears. In her left hand she held a wadded up handkerchief. Coming to that early Monday morning, she remembered again her sitting in Craigs lap as Marv who was seated on the floor in front of them, drew his finger across his throat and said "It's time!". Ginny had just left them in the living room after giving them a stern talking to and had gone into the hall bathroom. She needed to clear them all out of her apartment so she could get ready to go to her Monday morning motel work. While she was cleaning up her bathroom Marv made his finger gesture to Craig and Tammy and said, "It's time! She's going to call the cops."

From Fuller's questioning, Tammy went on to say she saw Craig get the knife from the kitchen and after Marv stabbed her she saw Craig stab her. Tammy admitted taking some of Ginny's jewelry. She also admitted to helping clean up the blood from the walls and floors. And that she had pleaded guilty to rendering criminal assistance in the first degree. Tammy had also recalled that Ginny had a mother-child relationship with all of them. And that she took NyQuil for her toothache.

With Fuller's direct questioning concluded the judge then directed the court into morning recess. The time was 10:28.

Martha and Joyce later told me that while on this recess, and in the ladies room, they heard Tammy say out loud to herself, "He's not going to get a free ride on me!" After the recess, and back on the stand, Farra now cross examined Tammy. Farra was not able to get Tammy to change her story. He questioned her about any deals she may have made with the police, and about her pleading guilty to criminal assistance. With Farra's cross examination concluded, Tammy left the stand in tears. On leaving the stand she walked over and sat down two or three spaces to my right on the same row for a few moments then departed from the courtroom. While I did not look directly at her I did glance over to her hands. They were shaking and moving her damp wadded handkerchief among her fingers. She had no fingernails. Farra, Fuller and the judge exchanged a few words in quiet conference then the judge announced the court would now take its noon break. It was 11:47.

The court re-convened at 1:19 p.m. Detective Smythe, still under oath, was recalled to testify again about his having found Craig's pants and shirt on the side of 115. The items were placed in a plastic bag which in turn went into a paper sack. Smythe was then replaced at the stand by Detective Youmans. Youmans then testified that he had later conducted a detailed study and search of Craig's discarded garments back at the crime lab of the Sheriffs' department. From the pants pockets Youmans had removed two items of jewelry which were said to be earrings belonging to Ginny. Fuller held up the earrings to the court and they too were accepted as evidence. Fuller then called to the stand Sonja Cortell.

Sonja, with shoulder length dark hair and dark complexion, rather lounged in the witness chair than sat up. She wore a dark jacket over a dark colored blouse. Her jeans were tight over very thick thighs. Despite her over weight, her facial features were very attractive. With cool casualness Sonja testified how she and Tammy met on the bus from Olympia to Aberdeen. And that the only one she had prior acquaintance with was Tina Murphy. The others were all new to her.

All she could remember about that early Monday morning was when Tammy woke her from her all night sleep she was having in the corner of Ginny's livingroom. She remembered someone telling her that Ginny had left and was no longer in her apartment. She heard no struggle during her sleep. On leaving the apartment she remembered the others wanted to leave things looking like a burglary had taken place. On the walk to Dan's place Tammy had told her that Ginny was in fact dead. On reaching Dan's place she went back to sleep.

The next witness called was Tina Murphy. Tina, wearing the same outfit she wore at the Garba trial, took the stand and gave the same story she had testified to two months earlier. The only real difference was in her manner. She had not softened in her abrupt responses, but her voice was almost inaudible. On several occasions she was urged to speak up and into the microphone. One juror stated she could not hear the witness. As a matter of fact, Bob, Tammy, and Sonja before her, were all asked to speak up and speak into the mike at one time or another during their testimony. The court reporter also had asked for repeats. Tina spoke again about the NyQuil for Ginny's toothache, and about Tammy telling her in the back bedroom, They-'re going to kill her!" Tina then reverted back to her non-committal responses: "Maybe so; I don't remember; Ya, they could have."

The court was recessed at 2:50 p.m. During this recess, and without the presence of the jury, Marvin Garba was brought into the courtroom as a possible witness for the State. Marv was accompanied by his attorney, Jim Heard, and two uniformed sheriff's officers. He was in the same civilian clothes he had worn during his own trial. He looked as though he had put on five to ten pounds more since I had last observed him. He was rather smiling and displayed no serious expression on his dark face the entire time he was in the courtroom. Marv and Craig exchanged glances. I thought of the monkey-and-the-organ-grinder. But which was which?

Before the judge's bench Farra was strongly objecting to Marv testifying in Craig's trial. Fuller strongly urged the judge to allow Marv's testimony to be heard in court. Judge Foscue stated he would listen to the two attorney's more formal arguments on the subject later in the day and would make a decision on the following morning. Marv was then led out of the courtroom.

The court re-convened at 3:05 p.m. The State's next witness was University of Washington Pathologist Susan Kae Schnell. Ms. Schnell's appearance was almost out of a modern mystery movie. At about thirty-five and weighing about 130 pounds, she wore a dark blue one piece dress with a white collar at the top. Her hair was jet black in a page-boy style. Her skin was a flawless pale white. Her cheek bones were high and her eyes were dark and alert. She wore a small amount of deep red lipstick. All in all she was quite attractive and not one might guess as being an expert in pathology. But she was.

It was deepening gray outside and were it not for the lighting in the courtroom the large room would have been engulfed in almost total darkness. Schnell began her testimony in a un-emotional strong, clear voice while referring to a small stack of notes and photographs at her side. The deceased female body which Schnell had been assigned to make a pathological study on, and which was identified as that of Virginia Barsic's, had some thirty stab wounds in the front, back, head and face areas. There were slash cuts and what appeared to be bites at the neck and throat. The eyes had received serious injuries. The knife wounds had been four to six inches deep, and had L shapes to them. Different weapons were probably used. The body's liver and lungs had been punctured.

At this time Mrs. Martha Duncan got up and left

the courtroom. In a moment Joyce followed her out.

Schnell continued to state that in her opinion not one of the wounds were, by itself, sufficient to cause immediate death. In all probability she bled to death. Schnell went on to say the body had a large amount of mud and some vegetation growth on it at the time the forensic pathological study began. Color photos of the body were offered in evidence. Farra objected to them being passed to the jury. The judge over-ruled the objections.

The State's next witness was Doctor Paul Pritchard, a local dentist who's practice was in the Grays Harbor area. Prichard, a stout man in his late fifties wore a sport coat, tie, and slacks. He had a firm expression on his face and clear audible voice throughout his testimony. Pritchard also had a stack of notes and a few small boxes. The contents of which he referred to.

Pritchard had taken casts of Ginny's teeth, and that of Craig's and Marv's. He was absolutely emphatic in his report. Craig had indeed been bitten by Ginny as the two wounds on Craig's right hand and small finger had indicated. Also as indicated Craig's teeth cast matched the bite marks at Ginnys neck. The teeth casts and his report was accepted in as evidence. A moment after Pritchard left the stand the judge then adjourned the trial to the following morning. It was 4:27 p.m. Before leaving the bench, and after the jurors had departed, Judge Foscue stated to both counsels that he would listen to further arguments at 8 a.m. as to whether to admit Marv's testimony into the trial.

Shortly before 10 a.m. Friday morning, the judge announced his decision; Marvin Garba would not be allowed to testify. In fact, Marv had invoked his Fifth Amendment Rights and refused to testify against Craig; his blood brother. Then, except for some clarifying remarks from Detectives Lane Youmans and William Stocks, the prosecution rested its case. Stocks' remarks were a repeat of Craig's statement to him that Craig had injured his right hand during a lumber accident. A twenty minute recess was called then the trial resumed, mainly from the defense side of the arena. Mrs. Martha Duncan was not present in the courtroom this morning. Only Joyce and myself were on the prosecution side of the room.

John Farra's first words were to call for a mistrial. After a few moments of listening to his cause, Judge Foscue denied Farra's motion and ordered the trial to proceed. With the jury back in place and both sides ready Farra called his first witness; Craig's mother. Mrs. Borman stepped from the front row, moved to the center aisle and walked to the witness stand. She was sworn in, then sat forward on the witness chair; her hands folded in her lap and legs crossed beneath the seat. In her middle thirties Mrs. Borman was a handsome woman. She had medium length brown hair and wore a light blue knit sweater and snug fitting jeans over a good figure. While obviously worried she was trying hard to remain composed in her plea for her son. The outstanding feature of Craig's mother was her puffy lower eyelids. She had quite obviously been experiencing tears for sometime. She glanced over at the jury then back to Farra. She was ready for his questioning. She would not be on the stand long.

Mrs. Borman stated she was a school teacher up in the Lake Quinault district. Married, with two children, a younger teenage daughter and Craig. She and Mr. Borman, a forestry employee, were acquainted with Dan and approved of their son spending the summer months at his place in Ocean Shores while Craig worked there, saving money to go into college that fall. She admitted she had lost some control over Craig but firmly believed her son could not possibly be guilty of the crime of which he stands accused. She gave the jury one last longing look, then returned to her seat in the front row.

With her jeans and casual attire I got the distinct impression she was conveying to the jury she was really one of them.

Farra's next witness was a young man who had taken leave from the Navy to be a character witness for Craig from his school days. But since this young sailor had not had any recent experience with Craig, certainly not that weekend, the judge ruled against his testifying. He was not relevant to the case.

The defenses' next witness was allowed to testify. It was Craig's best friend who had come by Ginny's apartment that Sunday afternoon to show off his new car which was ready to be painted. Craig's friend came into Ginny's apartment that afternoon with a new rock and roll tape with a new sound he wanted everyone to hear. Before he could get it in the tape recorder Ginny, "Freaked out". She had grabbed the tape and threw it on the floor. Ginny said she was tired of having to listen to rock and roll and that her house was a mess because of all of them. Craig's best friend said he, "was shocked over Ginny freaking out like that."

At about 11:30 a.m. Craig Borman took the stand in his own defense, with Farra as his defense attorney. From the very start Craig had complete control of himself. He had the look of determination and self assurance. Craig followed all his other companions of how they met at the Aberdeen bus station, and how they arrived out at Hogans Corner, and into Ginny's apartment. Yes, they had all been drinking pretty heavy that weekend, and yes he had had sex with Tammy several times through the weekend.

Right at twelve noon the judge called for a lunch break. The court re-convened at 1:17 p.m., and Craig resumed the witness chair and continued with his testimony. Farra took him to the early hours of Monday morning. Craig stated that he had been drinking so heavy he didn't remember all that happened. He did remember there was an altercation between Marv and Ginny but it was hazy. "I was in shock! I couldn't believe what was happening. I was shocked!" Then he stated. "Ginny was my friend!" He tried to "formulate it" all in his mind but just hasn't "been able to do it".

Farra asked Craig to explain his remarks to Marcie. Craig chuckled over that. He said Marcie was also his friend, and hoped she still was. He was just talking privately with her, never believing it would ever be repeated. It was a private conversation and didn't mean all that much. At

Winchell's Doughnut place he wanted to give himself up. Farra, with firmness coupled with compassion, asked Craig if he was truly sorry for Ginny's death. Craig hesitated a moment, then putting his hands close together declared, "She was my friend. I am sorry for her death." Then he put one hand to his forehead and appeared to be in tears. At 2:10 p.m. Farra indicated he had concluded with Craig's direct testimony. Judge Foscue glanced over to the west wall clock and called for a 20 minute recess. Craig returned to the defense table, sat down then blew air from his puffed up cheeks. He then turned and smiled at his family and friends.

Martha Duncan had returned to the courthouse and joined Joyce and myself walking back into the courtroom. The recess was over and Martha returned to the seat she had occupied earlier in the week. The time was 2:35 p.m.

With the court back in session Craig was directed to return to the stand. He had removed his light brown sweater and was now in slacks and open collared white long sleeve shirt. The shirt had light tan pin stripes and its pressed creases indicated it was straight from its cellophane wrapper. Craig's features were set and firm. He was ready for Fuller.

"Now, Mr. Borman. Please tell this court again about what happened during the time Marvin Garba was attacking Mrs. Barsic; Where and what were you doing at that time?"

"I told you, Mr. Fuller, I can't remember it all very clearly. I was in shock from it all."

"You were at her feet. And from earlier testimony, you saw Mrs. Barsic struggling to get free from Marvin. And you said, 'Get her! Get her!'. Isn't that right, Mr. Borman?"

"No, Mr. Fuller, you got that wrong. I didn't say that. I said, 'Get off of her. Get off of her!"

"And the pillow, Mr. Borman. You didn't try to help smother Mrs. Barsic?"

Continuing in his strong tones, Craig answered, "No, Mr. Fuller. I did not!"

"How did it happen that you came to receive bite wounds on your right hand from Mrs. Barsic?"

"I was trying to get the pillow off of her face. And she bit me while I was pulling at the pillow. I couldn't believe she would bite me."

"She was fighting for her life, Mr. Borman. Couldn't you believe that?"

"As I said before, the whole thing seemed like a nightmare. I couldn't believe it was happening. I just stood there. I was in shock from it all. I saw my good friend Ginny being killed before my eyes." Craig stopped and took a drink of water from a cup near the stand. Then he turned back to face Fuller.

Fuller asked Craig about Marv pulling his finger across his throat and saying it was 'time'. Craig did not remember seeing Marv do that. Then Fuller asked him about going to the back bedroom and holding the door to keep the girls from coming out. Craig answered he did nothing of the kind. Fuller then asked how Craig got Ginny's blood on his pants. He replied that it must of happened while he helped Marv drag Ginny's body out to the pile of dirt in back of the apartment. Craig said he slipped and fell on her.

Fuller attempted to demonstrate. "Just how could you fall on her while dragging her by the leg?" Craig responded by saying "I don't know, Mr. Fuller, but that's what happened. I fell on her!"

The prosecuting attorney then asked what his relationship was with Marv. Craig answered that he had only known Marv for a few months. He was kind of crazy at times. "But I found him interesting." Fuller asked him about telling Marcie to 'Burn' the polaroid photos. Craig shrugged his shoulders and said, "I have no recollection of that." Fuller then asked him about taking Ginny's TV set when they left the apartment. "I thought it belonged to one of the girls," he answered. Fuller then brought Craig to his signed statement that he had made to Detective Haymon, and to his remarks he had made to Detective Stocks. Craig's response was that he knew Stocks was trying to make a liar out of him. Fuller kept the pressure on Craig awhile longer, then he turned to the judge and said, "I have no further questions of this witness, your honor."

The judge then stated Craig could return to the defense table.

Farra had only one more witness. He called Maxine to the stand. Maxine; one of the two girls who gave Craig and his friends a lift to Aberdeen, then took Craig to the Olympia area with the thought of maybe having Craig share their new fixed-over house while Craig attended his medical classes that Fall. Maxine was on the stand only a few minutes with her story, which included her being with Craig at the time of his arrest.

The judge granted a short recess while Farra conferred with Craig at their table. The time was 3:45.

With the recess over and every one in place as before, the judge then directed Farra to proceed. Farra stood up from his table and announced, "The defense rests, your honor."

For the State, Fuller had one rebuttal witness in Detective Michael Haymon. With Haymon on the stand Fuller tried to get all of Craig's signed statement read into the record he had made with the detective shortly after Craig's arrest. Farra successfully argued since it was not tape recorded there could be too many errors in it.

Since it was Friday evening Judge Foscue instructed the jury that they were not to discuss the case with anyone over the weekend. And that they should return on Monday morning, and be ready to hear the closing arguments. Then the judge adjourned the court. It was 4:05 p.m. Two uniformed officers, who were always standing off to one side of the courtroom, walked over to the defense table to escort Craig back to his county jail cell. Before leaving the courtroom Craig turned and smiling waved to his family and friends.

Down on the courthouse steps and continuing on the long walk-way Joyce and myself offered to take Martha to dinner at our now favorite place there in Montesano; 'The Cook House'. It was only two blocks away but being damp and dark out I decided we should get in the Olds and drive over. A convenient spot was open right in front of the restaurant, so after parking we walked in and found a nice secluded table in the rear. Starting with hot coffee Martha began with saying she had a funny feeling about the way the trial was going. Little things such as, the large cork board holding the apartment floor plan that had been shifted from Judge Spencer's courtroom over to Judge Foscue's court. Many references were made to it but now it was pushed to one side of the arena and partially blocked the view from the jury and us. Not compl-etely but enough where to the jury had only a clear view of Craig's family and friends pulling for him. Martha had a glimpse of what she thought was one or two jurors dozing off during the trial. There were some seventy items of evidence the prosecution had presented. Was the jury really considering them all?

Craig had certainly handled himself well on the stand. Too well, Martha thought. What a clever boy. Would the jury see through his glibness? Did they even want to? Fuller had no doubt carried the prosecution's case forcefully and professionally. But would it be enough? Coming back to Craig; he had a certain kind of courage alright. He almost debated with Fuller. And he argued back with Fuller. He appeared to have learned how to argue early in his young life. And he sure looked like 'joe college'. All of this seemed to be pulling away from Ginny, she felt. Ginny was the one murdered. Ginny didn't kill anybody. Or even try to kill anyone.

Martha ate only about half her dinner. She again stated how glad she was that we were there with her. And couldn't possibly have sat alone much longer. After a last cup of coffee I picked up the bill, which she tried to pay her share. We got back in the Olds and took her to her own car parked near the courthouse. She stated she was going back to Kirkland that night and would not be returning on Monday. Her work at home was piling up on her. But the real reason, I guessed, the strain of the trial was piling up on her.

Joyce said she had been spending too many days away from her own work and would probably not be able to return either. I promised that I would see it through. And we would keep Martha informed of all developments by phone. She hugged and kissed us good-by, then she drove off into the darkness. She would surely cry on the way home.

The sun was out. Joyce had left for work early that morning. I didn't get out of bed until about 8:30 a.m. After a quick shower I found that Joyce had made the coffee, and a warm pot of cream-of-wheat was waiting on the stove for me. She had left a note at my place at the breakfast table. "Honey. Call me at work as soon as the verdict comes in. Good luck for Ginny!"

The drive to Montesano was clear, the air crisp and cold. On the tape deck I listened to Rimsky-Korsakov's 'Scheherazade', played by the London Symphony Orchestra, conducted by Pierre Monteux, while occasionally taking a sip of hot coffee from the thermos. I arrived at the courthouse at 10:20 a.m., so said the clock up near the top of the old courthouse. I hoped I had not missed any of the proceedings. I hadn't.

Again I made my way through the throngs of busy people coming and going through the courthouse. Mr. Hagarty coming down the steps, gave me a courteous greeting as I was reaching the top step of the third level. Stepping into the west courtroom I moved over to the far end seat of the front row next to the center aisle. No one occupied any of the seats around or behind me. Directly over the wooden fence Mr. Fuller and Detective Stocks were standing next to their table in conference. On the table were their papers and a small open box which contained Ginny's teeth impressions. Across the center aisle, behind the defense table, Craig's family and friends were in conference with Mr. Farra. Craig was sitting at his table and was firmly staring at me. "Not this time", I thought. "This time I'll stare you down". We remained fixed in our staring down contest at least a half minute when Farra stepped over to him to ask a question or make a statement. Craig turned and gave his attention to Farra. I considered it a draw.

It was warm inside, the sun was coming in nicely

through the south windows so I took off my old navy flight jacket, leaving my tan sweater over my light blue shirt and red and black striped tie. I was placing my cane on the rug floor just as the judge came in. Nadine Raubuck commanded, "All rise!"

With the State and Defense both having rested and after giving the jurors instructions on the difference between first and second degree murder charges, he then directed the closing arguments to proceed. The prosecution was first up. Fuller spoke for 52 minutes. He attempted to bring into focus for the jury that entire weekend which ended in horror. He spoke of the deliberate planned murder of Virginia Barsic. Even if it had only been planned a few minutes before the act, it was still planned. And there was no evidence that anyone in that apartment made any physical attempt to stop it. Indeed there was evidence and testimony that Craig had actually participated in the crime of murder. Fuller ended his eloquent closing arguments pleading that a civilized society can not turn its back on deliberate murder. He asked the jury to bring in a conviction of murder in the first degree. I glanced over at Craig's family. They all appeared to be in deep thought. Craig's mother was staring down at the space in front of her. It was just past noon. The judge then called for a twenty minute recess.

Farra began his closing arguments at 12:23 p.m. He spoke for 67 minutes. A child, out in the lobby between the two courtrooms, was screaming for its mother as Farra rose to deliver his statements. Farra did not give near the tempo of passion in his address to the jury as Fuller had. He told the jury to go ahead and look at those seventy items of evidence. They were weak and all circumstantial at best. He reminded the jury that Tammy had pleaded guilty to criminal assistance in the first degree and that she probably wanted Craig to suffer some punishment too. Farra carried a paper cup of water with him as he walked back and forth in front of the jury, and occasionally took a sip. His theme on the case was that it was weak and could not be considered very strong in the light of real scrutiny. He asked the jury to return a verdict of not guilty, and return Craig to his family and allow him to go on with his plans to enter college.

After Farra returned to his table and sat down, Fuller took another ten minutes in his rebuttal to Farra's closing arguments. He was not as powerful as in his address an hour and a half earlier, but made a number of thoughtful points he hoped the jurors would consider. Again he asked for a conviction in the first degree.

Glancing over at the jury it appeared to me that some of them were either in deep thought or had nodded off to sleep. The judge declared that the trial had ended and it was now in their hands. He sent them out to begin their deliberation at 1:43 p.m. Looking over at Craig's defending section it appeared there were six to seven people in the front row with about five or six teenage youngsters occupying the second row. They all stood up gathering sympathetic support among themselves. Just as I was about to depart the courtroom with cane in hand, Mr. Fuller and Detective Stocks approached me from across the wooden rail. Fuller held out his hand and stated, he was glad the jury saw someone in the courtroom who cares for Ginny. Detective Stocks also held out his hand and thanked me for being there. In turn, I thanked them. And stated that I felt they had done a good job. With my jacket back on I departed the courthouse.

I walked over and had a good lunch at the Cook House. Some members of the jury were also having their lunch there. They finished before I did, then I went back to await the news of their verdict.

It was almost 3:p.m. when I walked through the heavy doors. An event took place at 3:10 which I shall return to later on.

In my walk around inside the old courthouse I almost began thinking of it as a kind of friend. There were other people leisurely walking around from floor to floor as I was. And they certainly had more to lose or gain then I did; they were members of Craig's family and friends, and I did have empathy for them.

While waiting, I began studying the old building in more detail. On the first floor upon entering, and on the left side, a two foot bronze plaque was in place in memorial with the names of 37 service members from Grays Harbor who had lost their lives in WWI. On the right side taking up an entire wall was a mural painting depicting Governor Stevens signing a treaty with the Indians in 1855. Directly opposite that wall, on the left side, another large mural featured Captain Robert Gray meeting with the Indians after his coming ashore on May 7th, 1792. Another nearby mural illustrated the developing fishing and lumber industry of Grays Harbor. Deeper in on the first floor another plaque commemorated two Sheriffs Officers; Colin McKenzie and A.V. Elmer who lost their lives while tracking down the notorious murderer John Tornow in 1912. On the second floor, and opposite the County Clerks office, was a fine law library where many a student of law had spent long hours searching out notable decisions and precedence through the years. Marble tile and inlaid mosaics seemed to be every place I walked. The banisters were all carved from fine wood. Old brass lamps were carefully appointed throughout the building. On the third floor, and directly beneath the main dome area one could observe the Fresco art that looked like it could match any quality of art in Saint Peter's Basilica, with angelic figures and noble words of Justice and Truth. On wandering back in to Courtroom Number Two. I studied more carefully the murals at either side of Judge Foscue's bench. The one on the right featured a mother and her child. The mother, in ancient attire, held the child on her left knee while holding a tablet containing the Ten Commandments on her right knee. The mural was simply titled "Instruction". The mural on the left side illustrated a black winged angel holding a lighted torch over a woman wearing a cape who seemed to be contemplating good over evil. This mural was titled "Transgression".

Back out in the lobby between the two courtrooms I took a seat at the center bench. Mr. John Farra, Craig's attorney, happened to be passing and he sat down with me for a few minutes of conversation. He seemed not so cold nor so sure of himself. We shook hands. I explained my interest in the case, which began with my learning of Ginny's two sons on active duty with the Navy. In a moment of relaxed frankness he stated that this would be the last such case he would take. He had worked diligently on it over the past five months and it had been hard on him. He also stated he had a friend who was interested in taking in a murder trial but that this one was so brutal that his friend came only one day and decided against returning. John Farra had noticed my quiet interest in the trial, and he added that he was truly sorry over Ginny's death and the way she died. Farra asked about Ginny's husband and I said that he had attended only once or twice and could not return. Farra answered that he could understand that, of course. "Nice talking with you!", and that ended our conversation. He had a tired look on his face.

At about 6:15 p.m., and still no verdict, I had a smoke out on the courthouse steps, and another interesting conversation. This time it was with one of the youngsters from the second row behind Craig's parents. This young man needed a cigarette and I gave him one. He stated he was a good friend of Craig's, and that he was living in Ocean Shores with his parents. "That's good!" I answered. He said his parents had just started to live together again. "What?", I asked. Then he explained; they had been divorced for sometime. One of his parents had remarried but that didn't work out. They got a divorce and now his parents were trying it out again. I told him, "That's a beautiful story. But they are going to need all the help they can get from you. After all, they probably got back together for you, son." "Yep. They probably did", he answered. "You won't get any medals for it down here", I said, "but you'll probably get some up there if you give them a hand and give them some slack." "That's a good way to put it!", he said. We shook hands, and that was the end of that conversation.

Members of the jury came out and went to supper,

over at the Cook House again. I followed at a good distance behind them, and found a table of my own there. After dinner I called Joyce to let her know the jury was still out but I would keep sticking around for their result. She would have a light snack ready when I got home. It was 10 p.m.

Back up on the third floor level I was resting on the bench between the two courtrooms. Various members of Craig's family were walking around me near by, and I had the distinct feeling some of them wanted to talk to me. But I was not in a talking mood, especially with Craig's mother. Judge Foscue came out of his office area and said he would check with the jury and if it didn't look like they were close to a verdict he would send them home for the night. Every one thanked him and I stayed at the bench. A very dramatic incident then occurred. Mrs. Borman sat down at a chair directly in front of me, and with a member of her family, which could have been her husband, in a chair beside her. Mrs. Borman broke into the most gosh-awful sobs and tears, and my heart really went out to her. Her sobs and tears were getting worse. Her face was buried in the man's arms. I got up and stepped over and said to the man, "Please accept my best wishes for you and your family." With that I started to turn back to my seat at the bench and Mrs. Borman got up and tearfully stated to me that she was so sorry for what happened to Ginny. Her tears were real.

A different member of the family, a ruddy, well built man, took her from my arms and he too stated they were all deeply sorry for what happened to Ginny, and thanked me for trying to comfort his wife.

Judge Foscue came out from his office area and kindly stated he was sending the jury home for the night, and that they would go back into deliberation the following morning. Joyce had hot chocolate and a slice of dutch apple pie waiting when I got home, shortly before midnight. Martha Duncan, and one of Ginny's daughters from San Diego had called for any news of the verdict. Joyce called them back to let them know the jury had retired for the night and that I would return to Montesano the following morning to wait it out.

The following morning, Tuesday, 14 January, I arrived at the courthouse at 9:50 a.m.. The jury would reach its verdict this date. The Borman family and Craig's friends had arrived at the courthouse before me. I wasn't there long before Craig's father came up wishing to share a few words with me. Borman carefully chose his words: He sincerely wished me to convey to all members of Ginny's family the Borman family's heart-felt regrets for all the pain and suffering they must be going through. I promised I would give them his words.

With the morning wearing on and trying to keep to myself, wondering from floor to floor and exploring areas of the courthouse I had not observed before, I would occasionally pass members of Craig's family and friends doing much the same. Craig's aunt and uncle had driven over from the Seattle area to give their visible support during the trial. They seemed to be truly a nice couple; tall, in their late thirties, and both school teachers. Craig's grandmother was there; medium height, nicely dressed, very pleasant face. She looked very much like Dame May Whitty who played fine character parts in movies of the thirties and forties. Craig's grandmother was up from Oregon to lend her support to her family.

During one of my visits out on the courthouse steps one of Craig's female friends of about seventeen was there. We shared a brief conversation of some human values, I thought. She had no home of her own but with a girl or boyfriend whose parents might allow her in for the night. She was certain that Craig was not guilty of such a crime. I asked her about her mother and father. "Oh, they kicked me out a long time ago.", she said. "They disowned me! They even told my older sister who's married and got a home of her own, if she ever lets me in they will disown her too."

"I'm sorry to hear that. What did you do to deserve that?"

She shrugged her shoulders and said, " I didn't do anything that bad. But I wish I had a home of my own." Then she went on to say, "There are millions of kids like me around. I run into them all the time."

This young women, only a girl really, was intelligent. Short blonde hair, about five foot five inches tall. Large brown eyes. She wore a thin, light wind-breaker type jacket. Looking up at me, she said, "Why does everyone seem to be worrying about bugs, bees, birds, whales, and owls? And they all seem to be worrying about starving Ethiopians or other such people. Why don't people get concerned about us? People like me?"

I was about ready to ask her if she would like to walk over and have some lunch with me but another young teenage friend came out on the steps, they had some pleasant words together, then both went back inside the courthouse, arm in arm.

Later that afternoon I ran into Mr. Fuller coming down the steps from the second floor. He had a frown on his face, and more to himself than to me, he said, "The jury just sent word out, they want to know if Bob Noonan suffers from dyslexia. Dyslexia? He doesn't have dyslexia! Anyway, what the hell does that have to do with the case?" Fuller then went into his office.

I had one last encounter with Craig's mother. It was after dinner, and about 7 p.m. I had been trying to keep a respectful distance from Craig's family. I was sitting on a bench in an alcove on the second floor. Mrs. Borman walked over and standing before me she said again how sorry she was for everything. Then she said, "I just don't know what I'm going to do if they take my son away from me. I just don't know what I'm going to do." Minutes later we were informed that the jury had reached its verdict. At 7:12 p.m. a half smiling Craig was brought up from the jail below. He was escorted out of the elevator, handcuffed and legcuffed, and with a uniformed officer on either side, was further escorted directly into the courtroom. At 7:13, following behind all Craig's family and friends, I entered the courtroom and occupied the same seat I had been using throughout the trial. It was now 7:15 p.m.

Across the aisle, in the first two rows of seats, everyone was hugging and kissing each other for luck. At 7:20 Fuller came in alone and sat down at the prosecution table in front of me. Judge Foscue then entered his courtroom. While standing he asked that all those present to please hold all displays of emotion in respect of the jury. Then he sat down. I glanced around and counted a total of twelve people, including myself, in the courtroom spectators section. Eleven of them were across the aisle behind the defense table. Farra had joined Craig there. Craig turned around and gave his mother one last gesture of encouragement. Seated near his mother was the short dark haired man from the Aberdeen news. The jury filed in and quickly occupied their seats in the jury box. It was 7:22. The jury foreman, a dark haired bearded man in his shirt sleeves, handed the slip of paper to the bailiff, who in turn handed it to the judge. Opening it up and looking at it, Judge Foscue's head made a slight but distinct backward movement. He then handed the open slip to the bailiff standing at his right.

The bailiff, in an authoritative voice, read from it: " On the charge of first degree murder, the jury finds, not guilty. On the charge of second degree murder, the jury finds, not guilty."

CHAPTER NINE: SENTENCING

If the 'Yankee Clipper', Joe DiMaggio, had stepped up to plate and sent one out of the ball park at Yankee Stadium, the crowds would be roaring even before he had hit the ball. On the other hand, had one of the team's star pitchers stepped up to the same plate, same game, and same crowd, and sent one out in the same way as Joe had, that crowd would have been momentarily stunned. They would have been hushed for a split second, and then they would have roared. It would be expected of Joe; it would not be expected of the pitcher.

For a split second the eleven people on the other side of the aisle, including Craig Borman at the defense table, were all stunned. Then their sounds of joy erupted. Cheers, screams, and tears sprang up, and probably echoing through out the old courthouse building.

Judge Foscue dismissed the jury then he got up and departed back into his chambers. Mr. Fuller got up, and with out a word he too departed the courtroom. I remained seated and could not help feeling some gladness for Craig's family and friends. I did not, however, think this euphoria would last long with them. A night or two maybe, if that long, then some other reality would set in, I thought. A few more moments then I too got up to leave. Craig's father, uncle, and then Craig's aunt were the first to reach me before I got through the door leading out of the courtroom. Again they expressed their sorrow for Ginny and her surviving family. And they certainly seemed genuine about it. I could not help stating, "Craig's had a lucky break I think. A real lucky break, and now he has a chance to make some kind of turnaround for himself, if he can." The three adults agreed that he should. Then some of Craig's friends came over to me, and I wished them all well. Other than that single moment of observing Craig immediately after the verdict was read, I did not see him, or his mother again. However I was to hear from her later on. Before leaving the courthouse I did see Mr. Farra for a few moments and congratulated him on his succes.

When I arrived home that night Joyce told me, over a fresh cup of coffee, of the several phone calls that had come from Martha and other members of Ginny's family. I almost chickened out, wanting to leave Joyce to break the news to them, but, taking a deep breath, decided I should follow through myself. They were, as expected, first incredulous, then sorry, then angry, then filled with sorrow again, in that order.

Next day, on the front page lower right hand corner of the Aberdeen news, 15 January 1992, there appeared an almost incredible statement about the jury's verdict. In bold print the words read, "Youth found innocent in North Beach Murder." The article beneath the bold print went on to say that the jury found, "-Craig Borman innocent-". Innocent? The jury didn't find him "Innocent"; they found Craig Borman "Not Guilty" of the level of crime for which he stood trial for. There is a wide difference, I thought.

Five days later, Monday January 20th, and at about 10:45 p.m. as Joyce and myself were having one last cup of hot chocolate before retiring, the phone rang. Joyce took the call and it turned out to be Craig's mother on the other end, wishing to talk to me. Mrs. Borman again stated how sorry she was for all the pain and heartache she knew Ginny's family must be suffering. Mrs. Borman also stated she and her family were grateful for what kindness she felt that I had given to them. She went on to describe how she and all members of her family were able to play various musical instruments together. Craig's younger sister, an honor student, plays the flute for the Quinault High School band. Craig himself plays the drums.

Mrs. Borman's call lasted some twenty five minutes. In her sincerest terms she gave me the impression she was in deepest sorrow over all the horrible circumstances. I expressed to her my assurances that I was certain that Craig's whole family, at least those whom I had come in contact with, were fine people. She then wished to know if I had passed onto members of Ginny's family the

Borman family's sympathy and condolences to them, to which I assured her that I had. Mrs. Borman's last words to me were her belief that Craig was really a good boy at heart and that I would come to realize that too if I got to know him. Craig had just spent over four months in jail with hardened criminals. Had he not paid his dues? Her son would have to live with it for the rest of his life, she was sure. I offered that if Craig's father would like to bring him by I would be interested in talking with him, not about the murder but about his future life. She said she would talk to them about that. She thanked me again, then we hung up.

On the following morning, Tuesday the 21st of January, Joyce and I got up at 5 a.m. Like Ginny, Joyce had been suffering from a severe tooth problem which had also been affecting her left ear. At Madigan Army Hospital she was scheduled for an operation to take place at 10 a.m. but she needed to be there at 8 a.m. to complete additional tests and check-in procedures. This was also the day that Judge Spencer was scheduled to sentence Marvin Garba. The sentencing would probably take place late in the morning, as Joyce had learned from a call to the Clerk's office the previous afternoon. Shortly after arriving at Madigan Joyce and her doctor assured me that it would not be a critical operation, but a necessary one for her health. Joyce urged me to drive back to Montesano, take notes, and come back and tell her everything that had happened in Judge Spencer's courtroom.

I arrived back at Montesano about 9:35 a.m. For a middle of January day the weather was unusually warm, the sun was out and the streets were dry. I had seen a lot of snow around this area during this time in past years. Up in the lobby area between the two courtrooms the usual number of groups of people were walking around and talking to each other. Among then I saw Mr. Greg Barsic. Catching sight of me he turned back to a couple of young women standing with him, then he brought them over to me. They turned out to be two of Ginny's children. They had caught a plane and flown up from San

Diego early that morning and had arrived just before I got to the courthouse. Their faces were drawn and firm. They were here to see justice in action. They were both attractive looking, slight of build and about 5 foot three or four inches tall. Peggy, at twenty three, was just slightly more distraught then her sister Ammie. They both had the look of 'are people around here really going to do their job for our mother or not'.

They were quite angry and concerned over Craig "-getting off like he did." I tried to be reassuring that Craig, remembering Mrs. Borman's words, would have to live with what happened for the rest of his life. The girls were not so reassured about that. Ginny's friend, Joanne, who had been standing to one side stepped over and tried to console the girls.

Another large train of prisoners were brought in to Courtroom Number One. Most in dark blue coveralls, some in orange coveralls. Three or four were women. Then at 10:25 Marv, handcuffed and in orange coveralls was escorted in the courtroom. He was followed in by his attorney Jim Heard. State's Attorney Fuller was already in the courtroom. I brought up the rear, coming in behind Greg, Joanne, and Ginny's children.

The familiar "All Rise!" was sounded, Judge Spencer entered then quickly occupied his place. The first business he would address would be the Garba case. He was ready to pronounce sentence on him, but would listen to both prosecution and defense attorneys first.

Fuller and Heard stood before the judge with Garba standing to one side. Heard asked for a week's postponement. A heated argument took place between the three men. The judge was ready, and Fuller argued that he was ready and mentioned that members of Ginny's family had just flown up from California, and were now in the courtroom. Heard's voice was not clearly audible but it sounded as though he was waiting for one last psychology evaluation on Marv that was due with in a few days. Judge Spencer finally agreed to the postponement and announced, he would hand down his sentence on

Marv on the following Monday morning. All parties will be ready at that time.

Ginny's daughters, with Joanne, left the courtroom in tears, especially Peggy. Greg remained in the courtroom long enough to observe Marv being escorted from the room, then he too departed. Out on the courthouse steps Ammie was shaking all over. Her sister Peggy was in near convulsive tears. "Where's the Justice", she kept repeating. "Where's the Justice!"

That afternoon following the judge's postponement, I got back to Madigan, and from her bed, while unable to speak, Joyce gestured me to relate from my notes the happenings at the courthouse. She was truly sorry for Ginny's daughters. They took a plane back to San Diego the next day.

Justice did come to Marv on the following Monday, the 27th of January. During that week, Joyce spent two nights in bed at the Army Hospital. I brought her home Thursday afternoon. On the morning of Marv's sentencing Joyce had recovered enough to go with me to the courthouse. She still couldn't speak distinctly which was why her other good friend at the office, Mrs. Norma Holmberg, let her have a few more days off from answering phones. Joyce wanted to be in the spectators section behind the prosecution table and help represent Ginny from there.

The drive to Montesano took the usual 45 to 50 minutes. It would be appropriate at this time to cover the sentence that was handed down from Judge Foscue to Tammy Muller: On the afternoon of Monday the 13th of January, about an hour and a half after Judge David Foscue had sent Craig's jury out to begin their deliberation on his trial, the court was called back into session. It was 3:10 p.m. In company with her attorney Mr. Tom Copland, Tammy was called and she came and stood before the judge. Gerald Fuller stood at her right side. The judge, after reviewing her past criminal record and reviewing her plea of guilty to rendering criminal assistance in the first degree, allowed the two attorneys to make statements. Fuller called for sentencing and recommended that she be placed in the Grays Harbor County jail for six months. Fuller stated that his recommendation would have been much stronger had Tammy not pleaded guilty. He went on to say that Tammy had, soon after her arrest, fully cooperated with the law enforcement and judicial systems in the Virginia Barsic murder case. Mr. Copland then made his plea that Tammy was truly sorry for her actions and involvement in Ginny's death. He strongly asked the judge to render the minimum sentence on her. The maximum sentence the judge could have handed down was five years imprisonment and 10,000 dollars fine. The judge then let Tammy speak for herself.

At all times, as Tammy stood before the judge, she was visibly quivering all over. Her hands in front of her were constantly twisting her handkerchief. Her face was wet with tears. She cried over how sorry she truly was. Without doubt Judge Foscue was touched by the young woman's regretful manner and appearance in front of him.

Judge Foscue clinched his jaws, then looking around the courtroom asked if any member of Ginny's family or friends were present. Fuller turned completely around and pointing over to me, said to the judge, "This gentleman was a friend of Mrs. Barsic, and is a friend to her family and has been observing the case almost from the beginning. He is the only one in the room, your honor." The judge firmly looked over to me and asked, "Do you have anything to say at this time?" Tammy turned her wet face toward me as I answered, "No Sir."

With Tammy back facing the judge he then handed down his sentence of 7 months in the County jail, with one month taken off having already been served. He also ordered Tammy to eventually pay $2,500 in court appointed attorney costs, and to render 240 hours of community service upon her release. As I later learned, her jail term would not commence until after Marv's sentencing.

Passing directly in front of me, with her mother and older brother following behind, Tammy reached down and put her arms around me and stated again how sorry she was for everything. Like a grandfather might, I patted her on her back and said,

"Mind your mother now, and best wishes to you all." Tammy's mother took my hand for a moment, then so did her brother.

Joyce and I arrived at the courthouse at about 10:45 a.m. Judge Spencer had been handing down rulings on a number of cases since 9 a.m. At 10:45 he called for a 20 minute recess. Then at 11:04, "All Rise!" Judge Spencer entered the courtroom to the sounds of a loud crying baby. The judge glanced at his bailiff who in turn walked over to the left side of the spectators section and quietly but firmly told the woman she would have to take her baby out of the courtroom, which she did. Glancing around the spectators section I saw only a handful of people. The few I did see appeared to be office workers on their lunch break. I also caught a glimpse of the Aberdeen news reporter with his note pad.

The judge then took up a few lesser cases and motions, then, "The State of Washington versus Marvin Garba!" Simultaneously Fuller, from the prosecutors table, and Heard from the defense table walked up to stand before the judge. Marv, handcuffed and orange clad, was escorted by a uniformed Sheriffs officer to a position directly in front of the judge and standing between Fuller and Heard. Heard stated, "We're ready, your honor." Fuller, with the case file in his arms, spoke next. "The State asks for exceptional sentencing in the case of Mr.Marvin Garba, your honor." Heard countered with, "The defense claims prejudice against Mr. Garba, your honor, in the State's introduction and presentation to the jury such brutally graphic photos for the jury's visible consumption." Fuller returned with, "We felt the necessity of showing to the jury the brutality of the crime, Your Honor."

Fuller then compared Marvin to "Charles Manson", a thrill-kill type murderer. Fuller asked the court for the exceptional sentencing in Marvin's case; 53 years and 4 months behind bars. Heard then argued for a lesser sentence, and wished the court to consider Marvin's horrible childhood background: The abuse he received from an unfit mother and cruel stepfathers. And that Marv was drunk and not in his right mind at the time of the Barsic killing. Fuller then quoted Marvin's own words, "My first kill"; he wanted to see how it felt to kill. Fuller also said that Marvin should be kept apart from other prisoners while serving his time.

Judge Spencer denied the defenses motion for prejudice, then turning directly to Marv, "Do you have any comments, Mr. Garba, before I pass sentence on you?" Marv had been looking downward during the arguments going on around him. He shifted his weight from one leg to the other, and with very little emotion softly replied "I am very sorry that I killed someone I knew. "The judge then made his own remarks

"Many good citizens and productive people have come from bad environments, Mr. Garba, and I sympathize with that." Looking squarely and firmly into Marvin's eyes, the judge continued, "But you still had better choices you could have made. There is testimony from State psychiatrist that you have abused and tortured animals prior to your first human kill. You show no real remorse or real sorrow for what you have done. Mr. Fuller says this is the most brutal murder case he has ever had to try, and I can tell you I have been trying murder cases longer then he has. In all my 15 years of judicial public service, this is the most brutal and senseless murder I have ever had to try. You freely tortured Mrs. Barsic, looked in her eyes and saw fear there, as you first used a screwdriver then a knife, to gouge out her eyes. You have completely disregarded all moral conduct in a civilized society, and are a clear danger to others. I am convinced you would kill again, given the opportunity. I agree with Mr. Fuller, and recommend that you not come in contact with other people while serving your sentence. Further more, if I could I would impose a life sentence on you. The pain and suffering you have caused so meny people should also be taken into account. I realize the State Board which automatically reviews exceptional sentencing could reduce my sentencing on you, but in all conscience, I can not impose a lesser sentence myself. I sentence you to 640 months in prison!"

CHAPTER TEN: "Murder is Everybody's Business"

Since the dawn of the recorded human experience, millenniums ago, when people first gathered at the waters edge trying to put together a civilization; fisherman and hunters trading their catches, to people who could build places to live in, who in turn would trade their results to people who could farm, thereby meeting the basic needs of clothing shelter and food, there soon developed among them the need for fair and honest rules. Peaceful rules so they could develop their talents and raise their families in some kind of collective safety. In a short time when it was discovered that living among them would be a person or persons who, because of envy, greed, and jealousy would disturb this new fragile civilized society and divide them from their peace and day to day happiness, these new civilized people would be forced to drive those kind of people out and away, back to the jungle if that was the way they chose to live. And still later, when it was found those people couldn't or wouldn't be driven out, the rules then had to become laws, if they were to survive.

All of the above may very will be an over simplification but it is not far from the truth, as most professional historians or social science instructors might tell you. Too often these days it is the simplest truths which seem buried. Nevertheless, with more rules and more laws, and changes in the rules and laws to meet the developing and growing societies and civilizations the new laws become debatable and argued over. Except one: Murder.

Oliver Wendell Holmes; 1841-1935, one of civilization's most prominent justices, stated, during one of his lectures to budding law students at Harvard College, "Murder is everybody's business!" Holms became an Associate Justice of the U. S. Supreme Court, and also served as Chief Justice of the Massachusetts Supreme Court. He lectured on both consitutional and common law. During that lecture which he delivered in 1882, he went on to say, "Murder is the one act of lawlessness that is most feared and must be dealt with if civilization is to survive."

Murder of course can and does occur in single isolated events, such as young Robert Franks who was, in 1924, murdered in a Chicago suburb by two college youths named Leopold and Loeb. Murder can and has occurred on massive scales such as six million people being shoved into ovens during the reign of Nazism, and by the Samurai reign that saw about 300,000 old men, women and children slaughtered in the single Chinese city of Nanking in 1937. Both of these events were systematic and sanctioned by their governments. The civilized world became appalled and reacted; World War Two.

At the other end of this extreme 'Right Wing' scale is the extreme 'Left Wing' scale which seems constantly trying to bring down any form of government to the abyss of Anarchy. In Edward Crankshaw's fine book, "The Fall of the House of Hapsburg", Crankshaw quotes Greek philosophy which states, "Every society carries within it the seeds of it's own decay." Of the two extremes, anarchy may be the most violent of all. Witness the Los Angeles Riots of 1992. Although the French may celebrate 'Bastille Day', they would quickly tell you an elected government is surely better than no government. All this may seem to be getting away from the murder of Ginny Barsic. It is not.

In my own life time our country, and the world, has doubled in its population. It will likely triple in the reader's lifetime. Putting that together with the startling figures of violent crime which have increased over a thousand percent since the death of John Kennedy our country shows unmistakable signs of severe social problems now and ahead that this current and coming generations will have to deal with if it is to survive. Rays of hope do shine through; a black man standing over an injured white man, trying to protect the man from further injury or even death during the Los Angeles riots of 1992.

Judge David Foscue will tell you, should you meet him, there are clearly multi-levels of social implications surrounding the murder of Mrs. Virginia Barsic: Children trying to grow up safely and with real meaning in their lives in today's violent society. Parents trying to keep their families together in what appears to be a morale and ethically negative changing world around them.

A National Geographic article which appeared in a 1990 issue gave a graphic illustration; considering the multiplying population growth and the steady increase of crime across our country, unless some positive changes occur soon in our own behavior our current and future generations will surely see chaotic life as the norm, if it hasn't happened already. Any respect for human life will have long departed. Even now, in today's greed oriented society, John Kennedy's nobel remark; 'Ask not what your country', etc, etc, seems to carry no more nobility than yesterday's tuna fish sandwich.

But there is hope. I saw it and read about it; a sixteen year old boy ran into a burning home over in Seattle last winter and pulled out a couple of old people who would have surely burned to death were it not for his built-in courage and quick action. And then hope takes a beating when we learn about a group of young boys over in the Bellevue District who tied a donkey to a tree and beat him to death. The donkey's only value to himself and to children was that children liked to ride around on his back, and the donkey liked it too. Stay with me now.

In a totalitarian society we would be stuck with who or what ever was in power. Winston Churchill once stated that he didn't altogether like American Democracy but he quickly added that it was the best hope for human beings in this world. Thomas Jefferson, while contemplating future American generations holding this new Democracy, wondered would there come along a generation which could not handle it. "People will get no better government than they deserve.", Kennedy once said.

George Orwell's prediction that our Government would one day become 'Big brother' doesn't seem to have hit the mark as much as Walt Kelly's comic strip character 'Pogo' who stated, "We have met the enemy and he is us". It would surely seem that if any institution has become our 'Big brother' or

'Big sister', it would be the American television media. If Americans so wish to vote George Bush out of office including his party and entire administration they are free to do so; not so with Dan Rather, or any of the other major networks and news organizations. And certainly not any news organization on CNN. Americans have always been able to take bad news when it comes along, but maybe it's in the way bad news is reported in the media today that people find so irritating. Rights? All over the media, everyone seems to be clamoring for their Rights. At twelve years of age, I recall my father telling me, when the subject of Rights came up, and firmly looking down at me, he said, "The best Right you really have is to be the best human being you can be, and in this country that's a whole lot." Then with a smile, he added, "You may have fun figuring that all out some day". Maybe his remark has little meaning in today's world but it did for me then and though I have failed from time to time, it still holds value for me now.

To observe the TV news media in action on any given day; National in particular, one would surely think that the entire country was in one huge argument with its self. Leaderless and with no possible solutions on the horizon. Deep into controversy and getting deeper. Sensible thinking for our children? With the media's help it seems fashionable to believe; Lee Harvey Oswald didn't kill Kennedy, it was the CIA; it wasn't the fault of the Soviets who shot down the 007 flight over Sakhlin, it was somehow the Republicans fault; it wasn't the fault of the Japanese who bombed Pearl Harbor, it was somehow the Democrats fault; and Elvis Presley is alive and well and secretly living over in the next county. But just let someone come along with a practical thought or what seems to be a worthwhile idea, the media will supply a counter person who will debunk and devour that first person faster than a lizard's sticky tongue on a sitting butterfly.

Example: About eight or ten months before the L.A. riots a Black gentleman appeared on CNN's 'Cross Fire'. Quite naturally the Black gentleman expressed his concerns over the huge rate of unemployment among Black males around the country who seem to be loosing their families. And with no other area of opportunity open to them they are turning to drugs, drug dealing and violence, and ultimately getting killed or going into prisons. Now this gentleman offers up his practical thought; "What with all the government jobs being created and new government sponsored jobs for minorities that came along why can't Black men have a fair share of them instead of all of those jobs being pounced on by flocks of women who are given every preference, and -" "What?", says Michael Kensley and Bob Novak, "All you want to do is send them all back to the kitchen, don't you!" Now this Black gentleman tried to defend himself by stating that he wasn't against women, he was simply trying to reason for a fair share of those jobs for Black men. He was immediately debunked, and the conversation went over to another topic. The very next day while on a business trip to Seattle I observed a female out on I-5 running a steam roller. And I couldn't help thinking about the Black gentleman on 'Cross Fire'. What does this all have to do with Ginny? All the children involved, except perhaps Craig, came from broken homes.

Thousands upon thousands of essentially male jobs have been lost because of the declining timber industries in the Northwest and in other areas of the country, to say nothing of the hundreds of thousands related construction jobs lost. Lost because of power struggles going on between environmentalists and the timber industries, neither of which could give much more than a hoot for the spotted owl. Other similar issues have had shattering impacts on family life across our country in recent years. With the help of Ted Turner's CNN, environmentalists have been frightening people for years over such catch phrases as 'Acid Rain', 'Global Warming', and the 'Ozone' threat. Spokespersons representing MIT; Massachusetts Institute of Technology, recently joined other responsible organizations who clearly state there are no appreciable dangers in any of those areas of environmental topics. Despite TV, and all its talk shows, most people, male and female, black and white, do want to get along in fair peace with each other, and work at it everyday.

During the Korean war the official goal adopted by North Korean commanders of camps holding American Prisoners of War was to plant the seeds of confusion in those prisoners; compromise trust in their elected and appointed leaders. And debunk all heroic figures in American history. In short; no role models. Just one day's view of the American TV media might lead one to think the news and other commercial programs are being run by North Korean minded POW camp commanders. No role models. Not one of those six youngsters at Hogans Corner had the simple courage to call 911. At the time they had no respect for property, the very basic rules of decency, or law enforcement. How could they, after years of Dukes-of-Hazard type shows; dumb cops ramming their police cars against other dumb cops, while the happy teenager makes his get away. And lastly, and most obvious of all, with the possible exception of Bob Noonan, none had any real regard or respect for human life. Not even pity. Mostly just indifference. A study of this single case might leave us to believe we have ceased any forward civilized progress and are now rapidly marching backwards, away from any human progress.

This of course is not so. There are countless examples every day, of youngsters as young as four years of age who call 911, or call the next door neighbor if there is a life threatening situation. He may go in to a little shock later, but he calls 911 first.

We may very well be at the cross roads of our destiny. Senator Warren Rudman, the highly regarded and respected Representative from the State of New Hampshire, and virtually assured of reelection, announced during an interview on C-Span, his decision not to run again for public office. His dissatisfaction over a slow moving if not grid-locked Congress and Senate was one reason. But clearly his other reason was because of people themselves. They have consistently voted in one party to the White

House and sent the other party into the control of Congress. This is not checks and balances, he says, but grid-lock and confusion. And the people want to blame all their ills on the government, and want more assistance from the government. Four trillion dollars in debt would certainly indicate the government's willingness to assist in the country's problems, declares Rudman. And only about 60% of eligible voters will actually vote when November comes around. Surely, civic responsibilities is the twin pillar to civil freedoms.

The law enforcement and judicial systems may work very well but ultimately a case will go to the people, the jury, to do their part. It took a number of juries in New York for one of them to finally put John Gotti behind bars. A case involving the Ku Klux Klan in some areas of the country may take several juries but one will finally get to a just verdict. Still, in another case, a jury may want to feel that the victim of a violent crime is somehow as guilty as the criminal.

In Rio de Janerio and Buenos Aires, two of the largest cities in South America, home owners and shop keepers have turned to hiring 'Security Guards', death squads in reality, to eliminate roving gangs of killer children as a means of controlling daily and nightly violence from their streets and neighborhoods. That is in South America.

In Grays Harbor County, and with Ocean Shores in focus, every church, civic, and business organization in town contributes action, time, and money, to the betterment, recognition, and just plain help to its young people in this area. Scholarships and awards of every kind, including job opportunities, are generously made available to them. The VFW, the Elks, Lions, and Kiwanas. Both small town newspapers; the North Coast News and the Beacon. Every restaurant in town; the Home Port, the Ocean Shores Inn. Doug's Pharmacy, and every hotel and motel, are all actively involved in caring for their community's children. Including my good friend, a thoroughly tough ex U.S. Marine, Mr. Dick Morris, owner of the only super market in town, who seems constantly on the look out for ways in which to assist young people. And this includes the fire and police departments of Ocean Shores who have been doing their part. And I've seen it in fine teachers in the area. One in particular comes to mind: A forty or so year old woman at Grays Harbor College whose very life is devoted to sending her young people out in the world with knowledge, and the ability to deal with the world, not with force but with honest self discipline and simple kindness. Ms. Vaughan surely reminds me of a teacher I once had as a child; she too truly loved her job and her students But all these efforts together can not do it all.

The parents of this community's young people, by and large, are doing what they can to help their children get a good start in life. Frankly, and it may be a revelation to some, there is nothing in the marriage vows that says any thing about children, but those vows do say a lot about commitment and responsibility. Even in the Ten Commandments, the only mention of children is in the Fifth Commandment; "Honor thy father and thy mother." Our children need and should believe in their country and its laws. And they will, when they can first believe in their parents, even before they can believe in themselves. Their role models begin with their parents. Parents who remain steadfast, loyal, and true to each other. Parents who salute the flag and don't run red lights. A father who will be truly devoted to a child's mother, and help with the dishes. A mother who can make a good peanut butter sandwich on one hand, and get out dad's slippers on the other. Now that's civilization.

Most people in our society, around the world for that matter, are still kind, generous, and decent human beings, and have the Good Samaritan spirit in their hearts. There should be no doubt however, about a deadly growing segment of people with in our civilized society who, instead of going off to the 'land of Nod', would, out of jealousy and envy, the oldest of sins, rather stick around and divide us all: Women against men, father against mother, parents from children, neighbor against neighbor, and so on until any form of civilized home or elected government becomes impossible. Which returns us to Dostoevski's nineteenth century masterpiece story of murder and anarchy; "The Brothers Karamazov". It is a classic study of the choices within each of us between good and evil, which seems as valid today as it must have been then. Perhaps high school teachers will once again make it required reading of their students. Perhaps not. And perhaps the media will turn away from being a dividing force, and once again be a service to people. Perhaps not.

As to "the-monkey-and-the-organ-grinder." The answer to that riddle seems a lot clearer now. What is even more clear, having viewed both trials, either Craig lied on the witness stand or his companions of the weekend, who were in a position to witness the murder of Virginia Barsic, lied on the witness stand: Those who saw or did not see Craig stabbing Ginny; Bob who saw or did not see Craig holding Ginny's legs down. And, "-get her, get her!" phonetically speaking, has a decidedly different sound then, "get off of her, get off of her", or even "get off her, get off her." No matter how you say it, the number of syllables and pitch emphasis are unmistakenly different to the ear. Someone lied. And what of the dentist's testimony concerning Craig?

Curiously, Craig stands out from the other five in a number of incidences: He appears to be the only one who might have had a chance at college. The others seem to have had no chance or interest there. Craig stands out as being the only one of the six who was photographed in all five of Ginny's polaroid pictures. And the only one of the six who was not in company with one or more of the others when he was arrested. And, excluding Sonja who was asleep during the final minutes of Ginny's life, all testimony from the other four children were generally the same, contrasting Craig's. All that may have no bearing, only that it remains curious.

The following is a message sent from Craig, in his own neat hand, to Tammy before she testified against him at his trial: "Tammy, I don't know if this is against the law, but I am writing this letter to you anyway. I hardly know where to start, but I'd like to start by saying you've been on my mind nearly everyday for the past couple of months. We shared some special moments together, and some not so great moments, but through this, I'd still like to be your friend. I've been talking to______ and he told me you're doing OK. I am really glad to hear that. He also tells me what you two have talked about. I was really relieved to hear what he said you had to say about what happened out at the beach. He told me not long ago that he hasn't talked with you for a while now. Is everything OK? My lawyer told me this morning you took the plea agreement. I was worried about it for awhile that Fuller had you where he wanted you. I know he's offered you only six months in jail if you testify against me. But, if what ____ told me was true, I should not have that much to worry about. I have a feeling we're all going to come out of this thing OK. I am really kicking myself for not grabbing you and getting out of there like Tina did with Bob. But, what's done is done. I only hope we can still be friends through this thing. There's so much I have to talk to you about, but I'd like to wait to get a response from you first. Tammy, I know we can beat this thing if we stick together. It looks like my trial date will be moved to January. That should give you the holidays home with your family. It's going to be hard being in here over Christmas, but I'll survive. I'm glad this postponement will give you a few more months of freedom. I want you to know that I said a lot of things that weren't true that weekend we met. I think you got the wrong impression of the kind of person I really am. I think hanging around with Marvin can do that to a person. When this is over and done with, I'd like to have another chance to get to know you if you'll have me. I wish we had gotten to know each other a little differently to begin with. But like human beings, all we can do is try until we get it right. I still feel for you and I miss you very much. Please write back. Love Craig."

It would be only natural to wonder what might have happened if Marv and Craig had been tried together instead of separately: No time difference, and with the same jury. In other States, they very well may have been tried together. However, as I now understand, it was a possible violation of the 6th Amendment to their Constitutional Rights which in this case allowed them to be tried separately. Other states judicial systems may also have reached similar conclusions to try them separately if the case was identically presented to court.

While waiting for the jury's verdict to come in on Craigs trial, Craig's father seated on a bench next to me, said, "There are things we may never know what happened out there." True enough. But we do know that Ginny didn't stab herself thirty times, and she didn't kill any of those six children. Try picturing Ginny biting Craig as he is "pulling" the pillow "off" her head; not one bite but two bites. Is it possible that Craig told the truth on the witness stand? Yes it is. And is it probable?

Destiny. "Oh God, not here, in our little town." But it did happen. And to a small fifty year old women, who didn't have an enemy in the world. She loved children, and by and large children loved her. Murder, truly is, everybody's business if civilization is to survive.

ADDENDUM:

During and since the writing of this book a number of events and circumstances have occurred which would seem of further interest to the reader:

Bob Noonan and Tina Murphy; are no longer experiencing the close relation they once had, though they see each other from time to time. According to Tina, who Joyce and I recently, and by chance, ran into between aisles at a cut-rate variety store in Aberdeen, stated that she is now studying for her GED high school exam and is living with her mother. Tina, in a very pleasant and warm way, said Bob still seems to be getting himself in and out of trouble. She hopes he can get his life together and in a better direction some day.

Sonja Cortell; I haven't been able to track as to how she is doing. I drove slowly by her foster mother's house one afternoon, but didn't stop. The yard needed mowing and the roof looked as though it could use some attention, other wise it appeared that children were living there, and happily it is hoped.

Tammy Muller; is near to being released from the Grays Harbor County jail. She has become more then just the old saying, a 'model prisoner'. She has become friends with all the guards and most of the prisoners there. She is the hope of all of them, that she will make it in her new world out there. Her mother and brother have given Tammy every support they can. Being a few hundred miles distance between Carson and Montesano they haven't been able to visit with Tammy as often as they would have liked but they do keep in touch by phone and mail. Tammy's grandmother needs her in her antique gift shop which is located in a little town near Carson. Nice customers drop in there from time to time, especially during the tourist season. During her confinement I have visited Tammy three times and never once asked her about the murder itself. Only to join all the guards and her chaplain in encouraging her with her new life that is waiting for her. Tears break through some times, between her anticipation of getting back with her mother and brother, and with her grandmother who has a job waiting for her. She refers to Ginny as, "That nice lady!" and refers to me as her "Grandpa!" She hopes to meet Joyce some day. Joyce has been sending her pocket money for feminine things she may need.

Marvin Garba; just before his being transferred from Montesano to the correctional center at Shelton to begin serving his sentencing, there appeared in the North Coast News an item revealing Marv's apparent suicide attempt. He had climbed a table and tied one end of a towel to an air vent and the other end around his neck and jumped from the table. It didn't work, but he was placed on suicide watch from then on. During early April of 1992, the Washington State Court of Appeals met to review Marv's trial and Judge Spencer's Exceptional Sentencing. That court found that Marv had indeed received a fair trial and upheld Judge Spencer's sentencing by refusing a formal review. A further curious note on Marv: At the time of being picked up in front of the Red Lion Motel in Aberdeen he gave one of his alias names to the detaining officer as "Marcus Whittem". The name 'Whittem' has no significance but the name 'Marcus Whitman' does. Dr. Marcus Whitman, an early pioneer of the Great Northwest, had offered his services to the U.S. Government and became a medical missionary. In 1835 he and his party were the first whites to cross the Rockys in a covered wagon. He established a mission for the Indians near Fort Walla Walla. During the fall of 1847 Marcus Whitman, his wife, and twelve others associated with the mission were murdered. Some mystery still surrounds that incident.

On the evening of 3 February, 1992, I spoke with Craig's mother on one last occasion. It was quite a different conversation from the first one which I shared with her, shortly after Craig's trial. She was disappointed that I had not come across the aisle to join the Borman family in support of Craig. Also, she was now feeling that Craig, at Hogans Corner, was just, "at the wrong place at the wrong time." She went on to say that Craig was now back living at home but had an "unreal and unfair" experience. He wanted to go back to his old high school and perhaps teach some youngsters there how to play the drums. Only, according to Mrs. Borman, a controversy developed among the school officials there over his being allowed to come in contact with the students at the school. She was somewhat perturbed over that. At one point she said she could understand how Craig and other children could feel bored at Lake Quinault. She took that back, and then said Craig was really only out, "feeling his oats." "Feeling his oats, Maam?" I asked. I wished them all well, and then we hung up.

Marcie Swanson; is still living with her parents in Ocean Shores. Instead of working in the Gift Shop she is now an Administrative Assistant with one of the local newspaper offices in town where she will no doubt have a better opportunity to develop her writing talents.

Detective Bill Stocks; has since advanced to Sergeant. He is back in uniform and is driving on the night shift. He likes the hours because it gives him more time to be with his beautiful wife Dianne, who works at the Safeway Store in Aberdeen, and gives him more time to spend with their son, Ryan.

Detective Doug Smythe; is still doing day work out of the Grays Harbor County Sheriffs Office. And he misses his 'buddy', Bill Stocks. Doug Smythe has a remarkable avocation. He is a fine artist in his own right, and that ability has come in handy on numerous Sheriffs department cases. He does however diligently pursue that added talent in his spare time and produces remarkable color works on animals in the wild. Numbered prints of his work grace numerous homes in the Grays Harbor area. He also is blessed with a beautiful wife, Lorri, who gives dancing instructions, mostly to children.

Detective Lane Youmans; was honored as the Outstanding Officer of the Year during 1990. He has two teenage sons and his lovely wife, Terri, works parttime at a bank in Aberdeen.

Detective Gary Parfitt; a recent rookie on the force, and an ex marine, was named this year's Outstanding Officer for 1991.

Attorneys John Farra and Jim Heard share offices in a law firm in Aberdeen and continue defending clients who's wealth may not be great but their problems are.

County Prosecutor Steward Menefee; has held his elected position for four years and may seek the judgeship opening which will be available in July of this year.

Chief Criminal Prosecutor Gerald Fuller; has had numerous hard cases to deal with since the Barsic case, and travels each working day from his home in Elma and leaves behind his two sons in the capable hands of their full time mother, Sandra, also a lovely woman.

Judge David Foscue, a deep reader of world history and evening volunteer and consultant in local stage presentations in Aberdeen, still occupies his bench in Superior Court Room Number Two and continues to deal with tough human cases that come before him.

Judge Michael Spencer; while still occupying the bench in Superior Court Number One, and handing down decisions on all kinds of difficult cases and problems that come before him in Grays Harbor County, has made it known that he intends to step down in July and join a local law firm in Aberdeen, putting him back into the arena where he can work closer with the people.

Ginny's children have not and will never get completely over their mother's death and how she died. However, they did have a reunion together on this past Mother's Day, in Spokane, Washington. They have all found a closer relationship with each other, and have become able to smile and even laugh over little loving tricks she would play on them, keeping their good sense of humor alive. Greg Barsic has gone back to fishing up in Alaska again. And he wants to some day get all of Ginny's poems published. I have read some of them, and they are more than worthy of publication. Ginny's favorite poet was Shelley, her favorite movies were, 'The Sound of Music', 'Doctor Zhivago', and 'Casablanca' Her favorite songs were, 'As Time goes by' and 'Love is a many Splendered Thing'.

A few words on the development of this book: Before I found myself caught up in the tragic death of Virginia Barsic, as I believe anyone would have given a similar perspective, I had been getting ready to try a fact based novel about China, focusing on a time soon after World War Two. The Chinese Communists had gained momentum and were about to cross the Yangtze River into Southern China. Being in Shanghai at that moment of unfolding history, and thinking it would be fun to put together a real adventure story based upon my own experiences there, I was almost ready to begin it when I learned of Mrs. Barsic's terrible fate at Hogans Corner. While admittedly thinking about it before the second trial had run its course, it wasn't until after my last phone conversation with Mrs. Borman, and a long walk on the beach in front of our home, that I concluded that someone should try to put it all together. It seemed to me more than an American tragedy, but part of an American destiny that this and future generations may be faced with. And the thought of it all became clearly much bigger and more important than me and my generation.

Prior to Ginny's murder the triplex apartment building at Hogans Corner held no interest for me and was hardly noticed during my occasional travels between Ocean Shores and Aberdeen over the years since my retirement. Except for periodic visits to the VFW hall and occasional fill-ups for gas at the mini-mart stations near the apartment I would seldom stop. Like most other people, I suppose, I would just make the traffic light then drive on.But after the first reports of the crime that building certainly did hold my attention, and still does.

During the time of the investigations and trials I never failed to glance over at it while driving by. At the end of August and early September there were most always one or two police cars parked near the apartment, which had strips of orange tape around the garage and front door area. It never occurred to me to stop and get a closer look until after the second trial. And even then I was not feeling all that comfortable about stopping. However, one afternoon in late February, after I decided to attempt the manuscript, and realizing that a few inclusive illustrations would be necessary, I did stop. On the soft shoulder directly across the highway from it. With my sketch pad in hand I began some preliminary drawings of the apartment and the surrounding areas. There were no longer police cars on the scene, only a van and a young man in coveralls who appeared to be moving household items in or out of Ginny's apartment. Placing my sketch pad back inside the Olds I waited for a clearing in the traffic then drove over and parked in the VFW lot, then walked over to the young man.

Courteously, I introduced myself and stated that I was in the process of trying to put a book together on the events of the previous August, and if it wouldn't be too inconvient might I be allowed to walk through the apartment. After a long moment of studying me he said it would be alright with him but he would have to check with his misses first. They were in fact moving out and his wife was inside boxing things together for their move. I waited outside near his van which was parked near Ginny's kitchen window. After about two minutes both of them came out, she walking ahead of him. She was dressed in dark slacks and short sleeve blouse, the color I don't remember. What I do vividly remember was her dignity; a pleasant five foot two or three inches, long jet-black straight hair parted in the middle that came down to her waist. She looked to be about thirty, half or full Indian, and quite pretty despite her firm hostel facial expression on me. I expected her to say I was not welcome, for which I was prepared to apologize for my intrusion and depart.

"Are you on Ginny's side?". she asked.

Without hesitation, I replied, "I'm on the side of justice, I think, Maam!"

"Well, that's good enough for me." And she added, "If you are on the side of justice then that puts you on the side of Ginny. You can come in."

I thanked her, and followed them in through the front door. Her husband continued taking boxes out to the van as she escorted me through every room. I was immediately struck by the size of the interior, being smaller than I expected. The living room ceiling was open-beamed and a large brass fan in place there. Over in the kitchen-dinning room area a number of packed boxes and dishes were stacked on the long counter waiting to be taken to the van. Looking to my right, the fireplace was covered over by a sheet of plywood or something. Before proceeding through the hallway the woman turned to me and pointed down to the floor and said, "This is where it happened. Right here."

She went on to point out what looked like knife marks, clearly visible on the lower hall corner post, and what appeared to be fresh white paint and patches of spread-on white plaster on the walls in the small hallway area. The feeling of violence was all around me and I had the urge to turn around and leave, but instead I followed her down the hall. There were a couple children playing in the small bedroom to my right, then I glanced into the center bathroom to my left. Staying behind her we entered the main bedroom. She immediately drew my attention to a hole in the east wall over near the window, a few inches up from the floor, and I remembered the testimony of Bob Noonan having kicked a hole in the wall in Ginny's bedroom. Then I followed the woman into the back bathroom.

"Do you smell it?", she asked, and repeated, "Do you smell it? It's Ginny's perfume!" She went on to say, "I'd know that smell anywhere. She was my best friend. And did you know, she was the same size as me?"

Frankly, I couldn't smell anything, except it smelled like a clean bathroom. But I did not contradict her.

"That's one reason we got to get out of here. I just can't stand smelling it any longer." Then she added, with almost a sob in her voice, "Ginny was a good girl, and I miss her."

Back outside in the sunshine, I thanked them both for letting me go through the apartment. I have no idea how long after Ginny's death they were allowed to move in, as I did not ask. But I had the impression it wasn't long. I shook hands with them both, and wished them well and added that I thought it was a good idea that they had found another place to call home. They were both nice people, and they wished me well with my book. I did not continue any more sketching that day. Before departing Hogans Corner I learned that the lot directly east of the apartment would be leveled and a mini-storage building would be erected there soon.

During the first editing of this book, Joyce and I received a letter from the Honorable Paul H. Conner, Washington State Senator representing the 24th District, which takes in Ocean Shores and half of Grays Harbor County. Conner, who has been a personal friend to Joyce and myself for over 20 years, stated at the end of his letter, "We must stop young criminals from offending, and impress upon them that what they are doing is wrong, and we must do it while they are still young enough to learn and change their ways." Dan was seldom from my thoughts, whom I shall leave to the judgement of the reader.

As to Ginny herself, she had a right to live out her life like the rest of us, and chances are she would have, except for a number of fateful circumstances which worked against her, that Friday evening at the bus stop in Aberdeen, and later in Ocean Shores. But that's all gone now and her ashes lie at Damon Point. All the world loved Will Rogers, and he died in a firey plane crash near Point Barrow, Alaska, while on a fishing trip there in 1935. And the whole country cried. Little Judy Garland died a lonely death in 1969, and the whole country cried. But Will Rogers' grand humor still lives today, and Judy's wonderful performance in the Wizard of Oz can still send children and adults over the rainbow. Which only proves its how you live, not so much how one dies that counts. These past four months of writing about Ginny has given me a certain tender insight about her and her character. Just talking to her friends and acquaintances was enough. She always kept her home neat and clean, gave and responded to simple human kindness, and knew the value of hard work. I am sure she would have been somewhat overwhelmed and embarrassed from all the attention, tears, and hard work that was rendered in her behalf in Grays Harbor and Thurston Counties. And if there is a receiving line up there she's going to want to thank them everyone. Death came to Ginny in a pickup truck, but I'll always remember her looking up at me with those beautiful vulnerable eyes of hers, and cheerfully saying, "Have a nice day, and tell Joyce I said hello?"

3 p.m., Memorial Day, 1992, W.L.E., Ocean Shores, Washington